ADVANCED PROGRAMMING AND PROBLEM SOLVING WITH PASCAL

SECOND EDITION

G. MICHAEL SCHNEIDER

MACALESTER COLLEGE
ST. PAUL, MINNESOTA

STEVEN C. BRUELL

UNIVERSITY OF IOWA
IOWA CITY, IOWA

JOHN WILEY & SONS
NEW YORK CHICHESTER BRISBANE TORONTO SINGAPORE

Copyright © 1981, 1987 by John Wiley & Sons, Inc.

All rights reserved. Published simultaneously in Canada.

Reproduction or translation of any part of
this work beyond that permitted by Sections
107 and 108 of the 1976 United States Copyright
Act without the permission of the copyright
owner is unlawful. Requests for permission
or further information should be addressed to
the Permissions Department, John Wiley & Sons.

Library of Congress Cataloging in Publication Data:

Schneider, G. Michael.
    Advanced programming and problem solving with PASCAL.

    Includes index.
    1. PASCAL (Computer program language)   2. Structured
programming.   I. Bruell, Steven C.   II. Title.

QA76.73.P2S35   1987   005.13'3   86-24609
ISBN 0-471-83744-X

Printed in the United States of America

10 9 8 7 6 5 4 3 2 1

PREFACE

A great deal has happened to the course CS2 since its original description in the ACM Curriculum '78, in March 1979, and since the appearance of the first edition of this text in January 1981. The ACM established a curriculum committee task force to study and, if necessary, revise and update the description of the course to reflect the growth and maturity of computer science in the preceding six years. Their conclusion, published in the *Communications of the ACM* in August 1985, was that CS2 has two distinct components, each of which is a fundamentally important part of the overall course. These two components are (1) advanced data structures, including abstract data types, methods for implementing these abstractions, and algorithms for sorting and searching, and (2) the principles of software development as they relate to the specification, design, implementation, and verification of programs in an orderly and disciplined fashion.

Our second edition has been significantly restructed and reorganized to reflect the changes and suggestions made by that CS2 task force. The text is now divided into three parts that cover the two major components of the second programming course mentioned above. Part One discusses advanced topics in the area of data structures, whereas Parts Two and Three together address the issue of programming methodology and software engineering.

Part One, Chapters 2 to 8, is a treatment of the topics of data structures, data abstraction, and algorithms for sorting and searching. Chapters 2 and 3, which begin their treatment of data structures where the student left off in CS1, introduce the standard linear structures—stacks, queues, dequeues, and lists. They present both an array and record implementation (Chapter 2) and a linked list implementation (Chapter 3) of the representations. Once the student has seen a single data structure (e.g., a queue) implemented in two very different ways, he or she is ready to be introduced to one of the most important ideas in the entire course, data abstraction, which is the topic of Chapter 4. The student will learn what an abstract data type is and how to formally specify one, and will see how this specification can be separate from and independent of its underlying implementation. This is a critically important topic. If CS1 is viewed as emphasizing procedural abstraction, then the course CS2 should be considered as concentrating on the issue of data abstraction.

Chapter 5 discusses the topic of recursion. The idea is first treated separately and within its own chapter but is then utilized repeatedly throughout the text, especially in the algorithms for trees introduced in Chapter 6 and for sorting and searching presented in Chapter 7. This latter chapter uses a new taxonomy for sorting and searching that should help the student to organize and understand the large number of algorithms and techniques that we present. This classification scheme was first described in the *Communications of the ACM* in March 1985 by Professor Susan Merritt, and we are indebted to her for the use of this idea.

The last chapters in this part of the text present two additional classes of data structure, trees (Chapter 6) and files (Chapter 8), which some may wish to introduce in CS2 rather than postpone until a later course. The instructor may include some or all of this material into a discussion of advanced data types.

Altogether, Part One is a thorough treatment of those advanced topics in data structures that have been recommended for inclusion in the course CS2 by the ACM Curriculum Committee Task Force. It contains a significant amount of new material not included in the first edition. This reflects the increasing concern in the second programming course on concepts related to data structures and abstract data types.

Parts Two and Three cover the areas of software engineering and program development. These chapters have been structured and sequenced to parallel the milestones that occur in the software life cycle—specification (Chapter 10), design (Chapters 11 and 12), coding and style (Chapters 13 and 14), testing and verification (Chapter 16), efficiency (Chapter 17), and documentation and maintenance (Chapter 18).

Part Two, Chapters 9 to 15, covers those phases of the software development process that are carried out *prior* to the implementation phase. This part of the text introduces the student to the important operations that must be successfully completed before coding can ever begin, including the feasibility study, problem specification, high-level design, and detailed design. It introduces concepts that are important to the successful completion of large software projects, such as modularity, abstraction, information hiding, module cohesion, module independence, and programming teams. Part Two concludes with a large case study that demonstrates the theoretical ideas from the preceding five chapters being put into actual practice. Chapter 15 contains the complete specification, design, and implementation of a discrete event simulation program to model the behavior of a student terminal room. The program is approximately 700 lines in length and includes 24 separate programming modules. By textbook standards it is an enormous program, but, more than any theoretical discussion, it demonstrates the importance of the principles of software engineering in developing correct, efficient, and elegant software.

Part Three, Chapters 16 to 18, treats that part of the software life cycle that *follows* the implementation phase. This includes debugging, empirical testing, formal verification, algorithm efficiency, coding efficiency, documentation, and program maintenance.

A significant amount of new material has been added to the two parts of the text dealing with software development. There is new material on formal methods for problem specification in Chapter 10, new material on formal methods for high-level program design in Chapter 11, an enlarged treatment of modularity and information hiding in Chapter 12, more information on verification, assertions, and correctness in Chapter 16, and a new discussion on programming environments and support tools in Chapter 18. In addition, the chapters on programming style from the first edition have been moved to this section. Now this important material appears in a more appropriate context—within the implementation section of the overall life cycle.

The instructor using this text can choose the emphasis that he or she wishes to give to the course. Those who feel that the topics of data abstraction and advanced data types are central to CS2 can spend more time on Chapters 2 through 8 and less time on Chapters 9 through 18. Those who feel that the central focus of a second course should be program development and software engineering would simply reverse this emphasis. In either case, we have included sufficient material so that there is an adequate treatment of both of these critically important topics.

We would like to thank a number of people who helped us during the preparation of this second edition and who helped bring the project to a most successful conclusion. Thanks go to Mr. Tim Barry of the University of Minnesota who helped in the development and testing of the abstract data type programming examples, Ms. Kathy Grundhoefer of Macalester College for typing the manuscript, and Mr. Gene Davenport of John Wiley & Sons for being so supportive of the entire project. A very special thanks to Professor Murray Allan and the faculty of the Computer Science Department of the University of New South Wales, Sydney, Australia, who hosted one of the authors during the writing of this book. They were very gracious hosts and made our writing project more a joy than a task. Finally, our deepest thanks to Professor Tony Gerber of the University of Sydney, who is both a valued colleague and a very special friend.

G. Michael Schneider
Steven C. Bruell

CONTENTS

PART ONE
DATA STRUCTURES, ABSTRACT DATA TYPES, AND RECURSION

ix

PART TWO
PROGRAM DEVELOPMENT

9   An Overview of the Program Design Process   227

10   The Problem Specification Phase   243

11   Program Design Techniques   269

PART THREE
PROGRAM IMPLEMENTATION CONCERNS

APPENDICES

CHAPTER 1

INTRODUCTION

1.1
Introduction

This is a text on advanced programming concepts. In it we introduce and discuss the full range of operations that are part of the complex task called computer programming.

We begin from the premise that the reader has already had an introductory programming course (or something equivalent) and knows how to code in the high-level programming language called Pascal. Because of the limited time typically available, these first courses must, of necessity, spend the majority of their time introducing the concept of an algorithm, the syntax of Pascal, and the correct translation of some well-known algorithms into Pascal. In a sense they can be viewed as classes that teach the student how to *code* well. We now want to expand those ideas and teach the student how to *program* well.

It is important to distinguish the terms coding and programming. *Computer programming* is the entire series of steps involved with solving a problem on a computer. While this, of course, includes *coding*—the process of writing syntactically and semantically correct statements in some programming language—it also involves many other important and intellectually demanding operations:

- Problem specification.
- Program design and decomposition.
- Data structure specification and implementation.
- Algorithm selection and analysis.
- Coding.
- Debugging.

1

- Testing and formal verification of correctness.
- Documentation.
- Maintenance.

As this list clearly shows, a great deal of important preparatory work must be done before we ever arrive at the coding stage.

We must first develop a clear and unambiguous specification of the problem, so that the problem we ultimately do solve is the right one! Then, as with any large task, whether it is a program, term paper, or architectural design, we must decompose it into smaller and simpler subtasks, each of which can be worked on independently, in order to make the original problem intellectually manageable. This technique, called *divide and conquer,* is a common problem-solving strategy and one that is widely used in programming. Finally, we take each of the subtasks that we created in the previous step and select the best data representations and algorithms for solving that task. These representations and algorithms are selected independent of the language being used or the computer system on which it will run. We merely concern ourselves with choosing the most efficient and most easily understood methods and representations.

Only after all this preparatory work has been done, and done well, are we ready to begin the coding phase—to select a programming language and implement and execute our algorithms. Coding, which for so many students occupies ''center stage'' in the design of a computer program, is, in reality, a somewhat low-level and mechanical operation that is initiated relatively late in the overall software life cycle.

Even after the solution is coded, much work is still left to do. We must locate and remove all errors, test and verify the program for correctness, and finish writing and polishing whatever documentation is necessary to ensure that the program can be easily understood, used, and, if necessary, changed.

Even when all of these previous operations have been completed, the overall job of programming is still not finished! Software products are expensive, and they represent sophisticated pieces of technical development. Because of the time and money invested in their design and implementation, they tend to be used for long periods. Therefore, programmers will typically have a continuing responsibility to maintain programs (i.e., fix, update, or modify them) 5, 10, or even 15 years after they were initially constructed.

The point of this discussion has been to make you realize that there is much more to programming than learning the syntactic rules of a specific language and having the ability to successfully code the small programs usually assigned in a first course. Although these skills are important, programming requires an understanding of a number of additional and very important concepts such as problem-solving paradigms, data and procedural abstraction, recursion, program decomposition, the analysis of algorithms, and program verification, to name just a few. It also requires excellent written and oral communications skills for interaction with users and other technical specialists, and for the preparation of well-written, high-quality documentation.

In the remainder of this text we will be introducing you to a number of these important concepts. The material in this book is divided into three major sections, each of which addresses an important area of advanced programming work:

Part One: Data Structures, Abstract Data Types, and Recursion
Part Two: Program Development
Part Three: Program Implementation Concerns

In this chapter we will give a brief overview of the ideas and concepts presented in the three major sections of the book.

1.2
Overview of the Text

1.2.1   Part One: Data Structures, Abstract Data Types, and Recursion

One of the most powerful ideas in problem solving is the idea of *abstraction*—the ability to treat a subject as a broad general concept while temporarily neglecting the enormous amount of underlying detail associated with that subject. Without abstraction, we would not be able to manage or even understand any large, complex system. (Imagine the president of General Motors not being able to view the company in terms of major divisions, but only in terms of every worker, every assembly line, every engine!)

We have already been introduced in the first programming course to one extremely powerful aspect of this concept, called *procedural abstraction*. Using the Pascal procedure and function mechanisms, we can develop modules, get them working, and then place them in a programming library. For example, a quicksort procedure:

```
procedure qsort(list, N);     { Use quicksort to sort an integer array called
                                list of length N, N ≥ 2, into ascending order. }
```

From now on we treat this module, and all others in our library, as if they were part of the language. We utilize them without regard for the enormous amount of detail associated with how they work, as in the following code fragment:

```
for i := 1 to 100 do
    read (Exam_Score[i]);     { Input 100 exam scores }
qsort (Exam_Score, 100);      { and sort them }
```

The above code makes perfectly good sense even if we are totally unfamiliar with the details and workings of the quicksort sorting algorithm. This ability to hide the underlying detail of the implementation of an algorithm is why the procedure mechanism is considered one of the most conceptually important parts of Pascal or, indeed, any high-level programming language.

In Part One (Chapters 2–8) we extend the ideas and capabilities of abstraction to

FIGURE 1.1 The Hierarchy of Data Types.

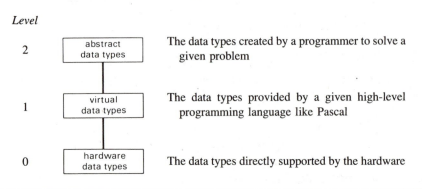

Level

2 | abstract data types | The data types created by a programmer to solve a given problem

1 | virtual data types | The data types provided by a given high-level programming language like Pascal

0 | hardware data types | The data types directly supported by the hardware

include data structuring, and we develop the *abstract data type*. To explain this idea, let's first introduce the concept of a data type hierarchy, as shown in Figure 1.1.

The hardware, itself, provides the programmer with very few interesting data types and data structures. (The study of what data types are actually supported directly in hardware and how it is done is part of the computer science course called Principles of Computer Organization.) Typically, the only data types directly implemented in hardware are signed and unsigned integers, reals, and characters.

The wealth of interesting data types that are part of Pascal—subranges, user-defined scalars, boolean, arrays, records, sets, pointers—do not actually "exist" in the sense of being represented and manipulated by the underlying hardware. The language (actually the compiler) creates these *virtual data types* out of the available hardware facilities. For example, the Pascal compiler may implement the data type *boolean* by mapping the logical values true and false into the integer values −1 and +1. It appears to the programmer as if these virtual data types actually do exist as primitives of the machine, and the language lets you use them and create with them directly in your programs. It is the compiler's responsibility, rather than the programmer's, to worry about the "messy details" of translating these virtual types into actual hardware instructions and data types. As programmers and problem solvers, we are freed from being limited to only what the hardware has to offer. Instead, we are able to use whatever data structures the language designer chooses to provide us, which, in the case of Pascal, is quite extensive.

We now want to carry that idea one step further. Why should we feel constrained to use only those data types provided by the language? What if we wish to create a program that needs a data representation which is not supported in Pascal? Why can we not use the same strategy mentioned above. Why can we not think, design, and create using whatever data representation we want and worry later about the messy details involved with translating those ideas into a virtual data type supported by the underlying programming language. That is exactly what we do, and these programmer-created data representations are called *abstract data types*. They free us from the limits imposed by a given programming language, regardless of how interesting or how powerful that language might be. In addition, data abstraction enforces a separation between the high-level view of a data type and its underlying implementation. One need not know how it is being implemented internally in order to use it properly.

For example, we may be developing a program to manage a large railroad switching yard. Rather than think of this facility in terms of an array or record structure, it might be more natural to simply view it using an abstract data type called "train" made up of abstract objects called "engines" and "boxcars." A train will be any ordered sequence of one or more engines followed by zero or more boxcars.

var
    T, T1, T2: train;
    E1, E2:   engine;
    B1, B2:   boxcar;

In addition we will also want to describe the operations that can be carried out on these data objects. For example,

```
create(T)            { create a new train T of length 1 }
add_engine(E1, T1)   { put engine E1 at the head of train T1 }
add_boxcar(B1, T1)   { add boxcar B1 to the end of train T1 }
compare(T1, T2)      { is true if trains T1 and T2 have the exact same number
                       of engines and boxcars, otherwise it is false }
length(T)            { returns the total number of engines and boxcars in
                       train T }
```

We can sketch out a solution to the train yard problem using our abstract data types "train," "engine," and "boxcar," and the operations defined for these types. Later on, after this part of the problem is finished, we can select an underlying implementation for these abstract types. We may choose, for example, to implement type "train" as a one-dimensional array or, possibly, we may use a singly linked list. However, the key point is that the programmer does not need to know and it should not matter. The programmer has designed and created in terms of "trains," *not* in terms of Pascal arrays or linked lists, and the solution should be totally unaffected by whatever technique is ultimately used to implement these abstract objects. This is identical to the situation that exists when we declare an integer variable in Pascal:

var x: integer;

We think only in terms of the virtual data type *integer,* and we are totally unaware of (and unconcerned) whether the hardware represents integers using a 16-bit sign/magnitude notation or a 32-bit, one's complement scheme.

Together with procedural abstraction, data abstraction is one of the most powerful problem-solving tools available. It lets you create powerful data representations and manipulate them with a set of complex operations, all the while hiding the welter of underlying detail necessary to support these abstractions. The programs that result are much more closely related to the high-level problem being solved than to the lower-level issues of hardware or programming language. For example,

```
var
    T: train;
    E: engine;
    B: boxcar;

begin
    create(T);              { create a new train with 1 engine, no boxcars }
    add_engine(E, T);       { attach a second engine }
    repeat
        add_boxcar(B, T)    { keep adding boxcars }
    until length(T) = 100   { until there are 100 cars connected }
```

Part One of the text will introduce you to the concept of abstract data types, including how to create, implement, and use them.

Some languages directly support this feature by providing program units, variously called *packages* or *modules,* which contain all aspects of the abstract data type definition. (Languages that offer this feature include Ada and Modula-2.) Pascal does not include these extended language capabilities, and not all aspects of data abstraction can be directly translated into Pascal. However, this does not in any way prevent the Pascal programmer from making full use of this important tool during the program specification and design stages, regardless of whether all of these ideas will or will not end up being completely translated into the programming language.

In addition to introducing the principles of data abstraction, Part One will also introduce the student to a number of other important concepts in the area of data structures:

- Introduction to the linear data structures called stacks and queues and their underlying implementations.
- Introduction to some interesting linked data structures, including singly and doubly linked lists and generalized and binary trees.
- An overview of the problem-solving paradigm called recursion.
- An overview of algorithms for sorting and searching various data structures.
- A review of the Pascal file type.

1.2.2 Parts Two and Three: The Overall Software Life Cycle

As we mentioned at the very beginning of the chapter, one of the most important principles introduced in this text is the fact that there is so much more to programming than merely coding. Looking back at the list on pages 1 and 2, we see that a number of important steps must be successfully completed before one reaches the coding stage, and a number of operations must follow its completion.

Frequently, however, students are not introduced to these other important steps in the programming process as part of their first course in computer programming. For example, most students are given, as the starting point for a class project, a complete and unambiguous specification document describing the exact problem to be solved. (They call it a homework assignment!) They are generally unaware that most problems start out in a much less well-defined state and must go through a great deal of clarification, disambiguation, and revision before they can form the basis for a workable problem. They do not realize that their instructor has carried out the specification and definition phase for them.

Similarly, many students skip over the crucially important program design and decomposition phase because of the small size of their problems. The length of most programs in a first course is about 50 to 250 lines, and they usually contain between 1 and 10 separate program units. In theory, any program benefits from time spent on planning, design, and modularization; however, programs of this small size can usually be coded directly from the specification documents, and students often do skip over the design phase. Even when a student successfully carries out a good program design, they do not always see the immediate benefit or need for it, since the problem was so small and simple. (From the student's point of view it would be like outlining a one-paragraph memo!) However, by skipping over both the specification and design stages, it is possible to create and reinforce the incorrect idea that the proper way to solve a problem is to leap immediately into writing Pascal statements..

Similarly, students are frequently not introduced to some of the important operations that follow coding. Students rarely produce extensive written documentation, except for some in-line comments in the source code. Continuing program maintenance is also generally not addressed since, once finished, student programs are rarely used again.

To rectify these omissions, Parts Two and Three (Chapters 9–18) describe the entire *life cycle* of a software product, from initial development of the requirements to the creation of the finished documentation and ongoing program maintenance. Part Two, Chapters 9 to 15, covers the precoding development process, including problem specification, design techniques, and design evaluation. Part Three, Chapters 16 to 18, covers implementation issues such as debugging, testing, formal verification, documentation, and maintenance.

Many of the reasons for using the techniques introduced in this portion of the text become apparent only when applied to large, complex problems. Therefore, we have included, in Chapter 15, the step-by-step development of a large case study project—a program to simulate the behavior of a student terminal room. The finished program contains about 600 lines, 21 separate program units, and numerous interesting data structures and abstract data types. Although quite small by "real-world" standards, it should be large enough to motivate the importance of and need for extensive planning and design in the development of correct software. It is doubtful whether most beginning students would be able to get a program of this size and complexity working correctly without following the ideas and principles laid down in Parts Two and Three of the text.

A second important principle we introduce is the *formal representation* of a problem specification and design. Although natural language (i.e., English) is, and probably will remain, the most popular notation for specifying problem statements, it suffers from a number of serious flaws, the most severe one being its lack of precision. For example, the following problem statement is highly ambiguous.

> Given a list of integers $A_1, \ldots, A_n$ and a single key value x, find the location i in the list such that $A_i = x$. If x does not occur in the list, find the location i of the value A_i that is closest to x.

What value should we return if x occurs two or more times in the list? For example, given the following values:

$$A = 5, 8, 13, 7, 8, 11 \qquad x = 8$$

Do we return $i = 2$ or $i = 5$? Similarly, what does the English word "closest" mean? It could mean numerically closest. It could also mean lexically closest—the greatest number of similar digits in the same position—so that "899" would be considered closer to "999" (two out of three digits the same) than would "1000" (no digits the same). (There are a number of other problems with this statement that are not discussed here, such as what to do if $n \leq 0$.) The point is that natural language does not always provide the precision needed to create clear and unambiguous problem statements that can form the basis for developing correct programs.

For this reason we introduce some well-known formal representation techniques that can be helpful in creating and expressing more accurate problem specifications. These techniques include the following:

- Decision tables.
- Finite state machines.
- Structure charts.
- Predicate calculus.

The use of formal representation techniques stresses the fundamental importance of accuracy and exactness in the development of computer programs. For example, the previous problem statement could have been more accurately expressed in the first-order predicate calculus as follows:

Input: $n > 0$

$A_1, \ldots, A_n, x$ all of which are integers

Output: determine a value i, such that

$$[(A_i = x) \wedge \forall_{j<i}(A_j \neq x)] \vee$$
$$[\forall j(A_j \neq x) \wedge \min_{\forall i}(|x - A_i|)]$$

which formally states the following:

1. If the value occurs more than once in the list, we return the location of the *first* occurrence of that value.

2. If the value does not occur anywhere in the list, we return the location of the value that is numerically closest to x in absolute value. If more than one value is equidistant from x in absolute value, we may return the location of *any* of these equidistant values.

In addition to the use of case studies and the introduction of formal representations in program specification and design, a number of other fundamental concepts are discussed in the portion of the text on software development.

- Structured coding.
- Programming style.
- Empirical testing methods.
- Formal verification and program proving.
- Computational complexity and the analysis of algorithms.
- Documentation standards and guidelines.
- Programming tools and support environments.

1.3
Conclusion

Unlike an introductory programming course, which usually has a very specific and well-defined focus (algorithms, the Pascal language), the topic of advanced programming is rather an eclectic one. It draws together a great many different ideas from different parts of the discipline of computer science. It is concerned with introducing the student to new ideas in data structures, data abstraction, and algorithms for ordering, searching, and modifying data structures. It presents the problem-solving paradigm called recursion and shows how it can be a powerful alternative to iteration. It introduces formalized models for the specification, design, and verification of programs. It also discusses the overall development of large, complex, real-world software, from initial specification through final documentation.

However, regardless of how many different and varied topics may be covered, the overall goals are still the same: teaching the fundamental principles of programming and problem solving and learning how to design and implement correct, high-quality software.

PART ONE

DATA STRUCTURES, ABSTRACT DATA TYPES, AND RECURSION

CHAPTER 2

LINEAR DATA STRUCTURES AND THEIR ARRAY IMPLEMENTATION

2.1
Introduction

Most computer applications manipulate data in one form or another. Usually the data involved are not random assortments of unrelated objects; on the contrary, the objects are grouped together precisely because they share certain properties. This chapter demonstrates how to store data efficiently by capitalizing on these common properties. The most frequently used data structures include stacks, queues, linked lists, and trees. We will emphasize pictorial representations of these data structures and their implementation in Pascal. The algorithms we will study can be programmed in any available programming language; we use Pascal because it has many advantages over other languages.

Before we begin discussing data structures, we should define two important terms. First, a *data type* specifies the kind of information or data a variable may contain. Examples of data types include integer, real, boolean, and char. Second, a *data structure* is a collection of data objects and a set of legal operations to be performed on them.

2.2
Linear Data Structures

2.2.1 Arrays

One of the simplest data structures is an *array,* which is a collection of data objects of the same data type. To declare an array in Pascal, we associate a name with it, define its permissible range of subscripts, and specify the type of its elements. For example,

---

13

FIGURE 2.1   (*a*) Uninitialized One-Dimensional Array.
(*b*) Initialized Array.

mathsatscores

1	
2	
3	
4	
5	
6	
7	
8	
9	
10	

(a)

mathsatscores

1	451
2	527
3	703
4	603
5	651
6	350
7	402
8	501
9	576
10	475

(b)

an array that contains the math SAT (Scholastic Aptitude Test) scores of 10 students (labeled 1, 2, . . . , 10) would be declared as follows:

mathsatscores : **array** [1 . . 10] **of** integer;

We can visualize this structure as in Figure 2.1*a*. Figure 2.1*b* represents the data structure after specific values (integers, in this case) have been stored in the array. One advantage of arrays is that they allow programmers to store related elements in one handy form and to refer to them with only one name. An array is a particularly simple and convenient data structure for storing "tabular" information.

The two operations associated with arrays are storage and retrieval. A storage operation enters a value into an array at the particular location defined by the subscript. A retrieval operation returns a value stored in a particular location in the array. The storage operation is usually effected by an assignment statement such as

mathsatscores[4] := 603

Both retrieval and storage operations will result in an error if the subscript is outside the prescribed range.

A simple, one-dimensional array can be generalized to an *n*-dimensional array, each

FIGURE 2.2 (*a*) Uninitialized Two-Dimensional Array.
(*b*) Initialized Two-Dimensional Array.

satscores

	1	2
1		
2		
3		
4		
5		
6		
7		
8		
9		
10		

(*a*)

satscores

	1	2
1	451	503
2	527	625
3	703	780
4	603	500
5	651	320
6	350	401
7	402	500
8	501	501
9	576	309
10	475	503

(*b*)

dimension of which has its own set of subscripts. An example of a two-dimensional array declaration in Pascal is

satscores : **array** [1 . . 10,1 . . 2] **of** integer;

We visualize this structure as in Figure 2.2*a*. Figure 2.2*b* represents an initialization of this array. The first column contains the math SAT scores of the 10 students; the second column contains their verbal SAT scores.

We could have used two one-dimensional arrays (one for math scores and the other for verbal scores), but the advantage of the two-dimensional array is that it enables the programmer to keep two related sets of data together. We have labeled the second subscript (column index) with the numbers 1 and 2. These numbers in themselves are meaningless and force programmers to remember that column 1 contains math SAT scores and column 2 contains verbal SAT scores. To enhance the readability of the program, it is preferable to declare the array as follows.

type
      scores   = (math,verbal);
var
      satscores   : **array** [1 . . 10,scores] **of** integer;

This is less taxing on the programmers' memory and will help any future users to understand the program.

Likewise, the first subscript can be replaced with a more meaningful name by adding a constant declaration to denote the maximum number of students; that is,

const
    maximumstudents   = 10;
type
    scores   = (math,verbal);
var
    satscores   : **array** [1 . . maximumstudents,scores] **of** integer;

The main advantage of using the constant declaration is that if it becomes necessary to change the number of students, this change can be effected in one step. Instead of going through the program and finding every relevant occurrence of the number 10, programmers need only assign a new value to the constant maximumstudents.

An understanding of how the computer actually stores data in its memory will help programmers to format data more efficiently. The basic problem is how to map any given data structure (e.g., a two-dimensional array) into a computer's memory, which can be visualized as a very large, one-dimensional array, as shown here.

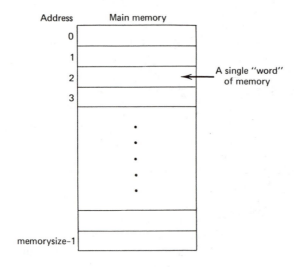

Notice that in this representation the first word of memory has an index (actually an address) of 0. There are "memorysize" words of memory in all and, therefore, the last word in memory is indexed "memorysize-1." The value of "memorysize" in binary computers is usually a power of 2.

We will now consider how one-dimensional and two-dimensional arrays are mapped into the computer's memory. This mapping should (1) ensure that retrieval of elements in the array is efficient and (2) determine the amount of memory needed to store the array.

For one-dimensional arrays, determining how much memory to allocate is simple. We will assume for now that each element of the array will require one word of memory. The total number of words required to store the array declared as follows:

var
    example   : **array** [lowerbound . . upperbound] **of** integer;

is

$$upperbound - lowerbound + 1$$

For the previous example of the one-dimensional array of math SAT scores, the number of words required is

$$10 \text{ (upperbound)} - 1 \text{ (lowerbound)} + 1 = 10$$

(Notice that the number of words required cannot automatically be assigned the same value as the upperbound. These two values are only identical when lowerbound equals 1, which is not always the case. Recall that in Pascal, *any* integer, negative, zero, or positive, can be used to represent the lowerbound.)

When an array a is stored in sequential memory locations, the location of the array element with subscript j is given by

$$loc(a[j]) = loc(a[lowerbound]) + j - lowerbound$$

Once the location of the lowerbound element is established, the location of all other elements is determined in relation to that. This formula applies only when the individual elements of the array each occupy *one* word of memory. However, it can be modified to accommodate array elements requiring more than one word. If each array element requires s words, the total number of words needed to store the array becomes

$$s * (upperbound - lowerbound + 1)$$

The location of the jth element of the array becomes

$$loc(a[j]) = loc(a[lowerbound]) + s * (j - lowerbound)$$

(We assume in this case that $loc(a[lowerbound])$ refers to the first word address in which the array is stored.)

To summarize, for a general one-dimensional array

a : **array** [l . . u] **of** element;

where each element requires s words, the total number of words occupied by the array is

$$s * (u - l + 1)$$

and the location of the jth element of the array is

$$\text{loc}(a[j]) = \text{loc}(a[l]) + (j - l) * s$$

Consider now how to map the two-dimensional array satscores into the one-dimensional memory of a computer.

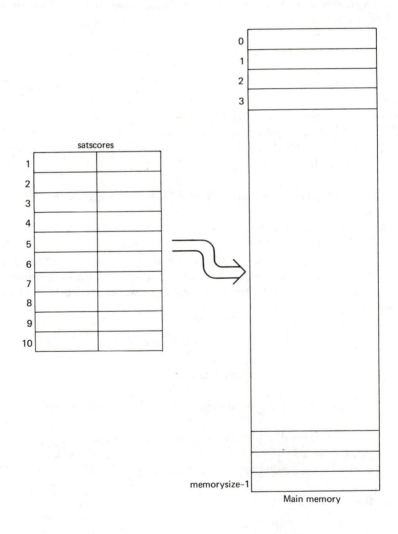

Main memory

There are two straightforward ways to accomplish this mapping. The first method is to store the first column of the array satscores, followed directly by the second column. This is called *column-major ordering*. The second method stores one row right after another, and this is called *row-major ordering*. The following picture should help clarify the distinction.

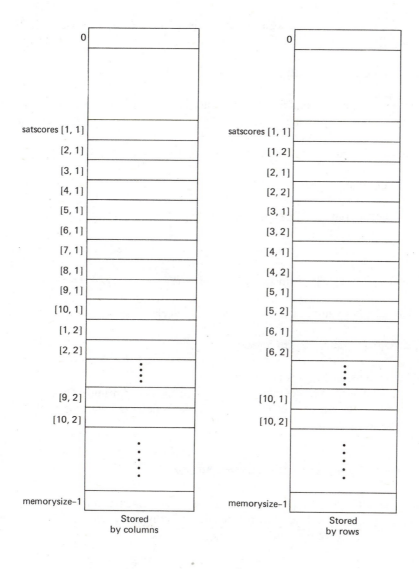

| | Stored
by columns | | | Stored
by rows |

To determine the location of the i, jth element of satscores if the array is stored by columns, we first establish the location of the first element of the array (loc(satscores[1,1])). Each column contains 10 elements. The location of satscores[i,1] would be

$$loc(satscores[i,1]) = loc(satscores[1,1]) + (i - 1)$$

Knowing the location of satscores[i,1], to compute the address of satscores[i,2], we simply add 10 to the loc(satscores[i,1]); that is

$$loc(satscores[i,2]) = loc(satscores[1,1]) + (i - 1) + 10$$

It is easy to see how to combine the previous two formulas into one that works for $j = 1$ or $j = 2$.

$$loc(satscores[i,j]) = loc(satscores[1,1]) + (i - 1) + 10 * (j - 1)$$

For a two-dimensional array declared

a   : **array** $[1 .. u_1, 1 .. u_2]$ **of** integer;

the preceding formula for computing $a[i,j]$ if the array is stored by columns would be

$$loc(a[i,j]) = loc(a[1,1]) + (i - 1) + u_1 * (j - 1)$$

We leave the derivation of formulas for arrays declared as

a   : **array** $[l_1 .. u_1, l_2 .. u_2]$ **of** integer;

and higher-dimensional arrays as exercises.

Arrays can be used to represent sequences of characters or strings. These characters can be stored in an array, and one might use the following data type to define the array's structure:

type
    string = **packed array** $[1 .. maxlength]$ **of** char;

In some programming languages the string is implemented as a primitive data type of the language. In Pascal, as shown here, the string is implemented using the array data type. The primitive operations on strings, such as

1. *Concatenation.* Merge two strings together into a single string.
2. *Length.* Determine the number of characters in a string.
3. *Pattern Match.* Find the occurrence of a special substring in a larger string.

4. *Substring Change*. Change all occurrences of one substring to another substring in a large string.

are therefore implemented as user-written procedures or functions operating on packed arrays. We will discuss the processing of strings extensively in the case study at the end of this chapter.

2.2.2 Records

In Section 2.2.1 we used two parallel, one-dimensional arrays (actually, a two-dimensional array) to contain the math and verbal SAT scores of 10 (maximumstudents) students. Each row represented two scores for one student. Pascal also offers another means of representing related data, the *record*. For our example we could put the math and verbal SAT scores into a record and then associate a record with each of the 10 students. We can associate a type name with the record as follows.

```
const
    maximumstudents      = 10;
type
    satscores            =
        record
            math         : 0 .. 800;
            verbal       : 0 .. 800
        end; { of record satscores }
```

Then, to indicate that there are 10 students, each with a math and verbal SAT score, we simply use an array of records.

```
var
    students      : array [1 .. maximumstudents] of satscores;
```

We now need a means of accessing the *fields* of the record (i.e., math and verbal). In Pascal we can accomplish this in one of two ways: through the dot notation or through the **with** statement. For example, to assign a math score of 603 and a verbal score of 550 to the first student, we could write

```
students[1] . math := 603;
students[1] . verbal := 550
```

or

```
with students[1] do
begin
    math := 603;
    verbal := 550
end
```

Inside the scope of the **with** statement we do not need to include the record variable name, only the field name. For records with many fields, the **with** statement provides a very convenient shorthand notation.

The previous example illustrated how to define arrays whose elements are records. You can also define records in which one or more fields are arrays. For example,

```
const
    maxnamelength       = 20;
type
    string              = packed array [1 .. maxnamelength] of char;
var
    students            : array [1 .. maximumstudents] of
            record
                math        : 0 .. 800;
                verbal      : 0 .. 800;
                name        : string
            end; { of record }
```

To select the first character of the third student's name, we could write

```
students[3] . name[1]
```

To write out a list of the names of the students (assuming all this information had already been initialized), we could write

```
for i := 1 to maximumstudents do
    with students[i] do
    begin
        write(' student ',i:2, ' ');
        for j := 1 to maxnamelength do write(name[j]);
        writeln
    end
```

It seems logical that you could nest records inside records. And, in fact, you can. For example,

```
var
    students                        : array [1 .. maximumstudents] of
            record
                math                    : 0 .. 800;
                verbal                  : 0 .. 800;
                name                    : string
```

```
dateofexam      :
    record
        month    : 1 .. 12;
        day      : 1 .. 31;
        year     : 1900 .. 2000
    end { of record dateofexam }
end; { of student element record }
```

To initialize the year in which the first student took the SAT, we could write

students[1].dateofexam.year := 1987

or

with students[1] **do**
    dateofexam.year := 1987

or

with students[1].dateofexam **do** year := 1987

Arrays and records are different methods of structuring data. The components of an array are all of the same type and are selected by subscripts. The components of a record need not all be the same type and are specified by field names. These two data structures can be combined in any fashion to construct complex data structures.

We will use records often in the programs and program segments in this chapter. To make you more familiar with them, we will discuss a few more examples of how to use records.

Recall that Pascal has two predefined types to express numbers: integer and real. But what if you needed to manipulate complex numbers (i.e., numbers of the form

$$a + b * i$$

where a and b are real numbers and i is the square root of -1). Unlike FORTRAN, Pascal has no predefined way of handling complex numbers. It is easy to remedy this situation with a user-defined type.

type
    complex   =
        record
            a   : real;   { real part }
            b   : real   { imaginary part }
        end; { of record complex }

(We do not need to represent the i.)

Now we can define variables to be of this new type.

var
    x   : complex;
    y   : complex;

Arithmetic operations can be performed on complex numbers. For example, the sum of the complex numbers

$$a + bi \quad \text{and} \quad c + di$$

is

$$(a + c) + (b + d)i$$

We can easily write a procedure to add two complex numbers.

procedure complexadd(x : complex; y : complex; **var** z : complex);
begin
    z.a := x.a + y.a;
    z.b := x.b + y.b
end; { of procedure complexadd }

The other arithmetic operations on complex numbers can also be treated easily.

As a second example of using records, consider the following problem. Design a data structure that will help the police department maintain a table of stolen cars by precinct. The following information is required: license plate number, car description (year and make), and whether or not the car was found. If you were to draw a picture of the information required by each precinct it might look like this:

	Car description		
License plate	Year	Make	Found

Now let us try to encode this step by step into a meaningful Pascal data structure. First, since we want the same structure for each precinct, we will declare a constant for the number of precincts:

const
    numberofprecincts   = 9;

and an array of records (or tables), one for each precinct:

type
    bigtable   = **array** [1 . . numberofprecincts] **of** precincttables;

Each precinct table will be an array that can accommodate up to some maximum number of stolen cars; hence,

const
    maxstolencars   = 100;
type
    precincttables   = **array** [1 . . maxstolencars] **of** cardescription;

Now all we need do is describe what information is required for each stolen car.

type
    alfa   = **packed array** [1 . . 10] **of** char;
    cardescription   =
        record
            licenseplate   : alfa;
            description   :
                record
                    year   : integer;
                    make   : alfa
               end; { of record description }
            found   : boolean
        end; { of record cardescription }

Then, to allocate the space for this data structure in memory, we write

var
    stolencars   : bigtable;

Unfortunately, we cannot just write down the description of the data structure the way we envisioned it because identifiers in Pascal must be declared before they are referenced. (See Chapter 3, however, for an exception to this rule.) Therefore the declarations for the stolen car data structure should read

const
    maxstolencars   = 100;   { max stolen cars per precinct }
    numberofprecincts   = 9;   { number of precincts in city }

```
type
    alfa                        = packed array [1 . . 10] of char;
    cardescription              =
        record
            licenseplate    : alfa;
            description     :
                record
                    year    : integer;
                    make    : alfa
                end; { of record description }
            found               : boolean
        end; { of record cardescription }
    precincttables              = array [1 . . maxstolencars] of cardescription;
    bigtable                    = array [1 . . numberofprecincts] of precincttables;

var
    stolencars                  : bigtable;
```

How do you set the year and make of the third stolen car in precinct 5 to 1971 and Pontiac, respectively? There are, of course, a number of ways.

```
stolencars[5][3].description.year := 1971;
stolencars[5][3].description.make := 'Pontiac

with stolencars[5,3] do
begin
    description.year := 1971;
    description.make := 'Pontiac
end { of with }

with stolencars[5] [3] do
    with description do
    begin
        year := 1971;
        make := 'Pontiac
    end
```

or

```
with stolencars[5,3].description do
begin
    year := 1971;
    make := 'Pontiac
end { of with }
```

The entire data structure would be laid out in the machine's memory as follows:

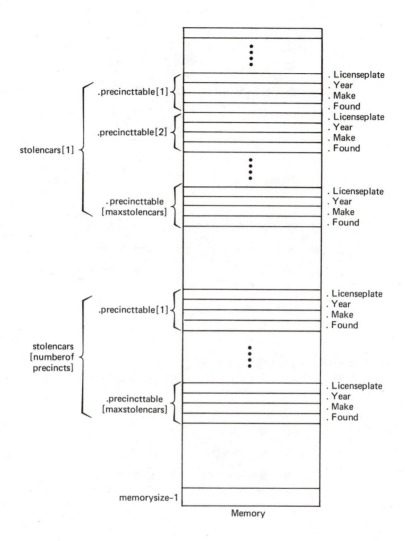

Memory

As a final example of the use of records, we will ask you to design a data structure to be used in playing a type of solitaire called Idiot's Delight. Represent the playing cards as records with one field for the suit and another for the rank.

Idiot's Delight is played by dealing cards face up from a shuffled deck onto a hand (or pile). Whenever the suit of the top card matches that of the fourth card in the pile, the two intervening cards are discarded; when the rank of the top card matches the rank of the fourth card in the pile, all four cards are discarded. The object of the game is to be left with no cards in the hand.

To make sure the rules are understood, we will play an abbreviated game. First, shuffle the deck. Then deal off four cards.

↑
top

Since there is neither a suit nor a rank match, we deal off another card

↑
top

Now, since 5 ♦ and 5 ♣ have the same rank, we discard the top four cards and are left only with the 8 ♥. We deal off three more cards and continue in the same manner.

↑
top

At this point, stop and try to write a program that plays, say, 1000 random games of Idiot's Delight. Keep a histogram to show the distribution of the number of undiscarded cards. The choice of a good data structure for the card pile in this program will greatly influence the clarity of the resulting solution. Once you have tried to write the program yourself, read through the following program, which is based on one written by the late Michael Machtey of Purdue University.

```
program IdiotsDelight(input,output);
const
    decksize        = 52;        { number of cards in a deck }
    suitsize        = 13;        { number of cards in a suit }
    widthmax        = 78;        { max number of chars across histogram }
```

type

suits	= (clubs,diamonds,hearts,spades);	
ranks	= (ace,two,three,four,five,six,seven,eight,nine,ten,jack, queen,king);	
card	=	
record		
suit	: suits;	
rank	: ranks	
end; { of record card }		
cards	= 1 . . decksize;	
deck	= **array** [cards] **of** card;	
histsize	= 0 . . decksize;	

var

cardnumber	: cards:	{ one of the fifty-two cards }
cardsleft	: histsize;	{ number of cards left }
column	: integer;	{ current column of histogram }
deckofcards	: deck;	{ the deck }
game	: integer;	{ the current game number }
hand	: deck;	{ deal cards from deck to hand }
histogram	: **array** [histsize] **of** integer;	
		{ keeps track of number of cards left after each game }
i	: integer;	{ index variable }
numberofgames	: integer;	{ number of games to play }
rankofcard	: ranks;	{ index variable }
suitofcard	: suits;	{ index variable }
top	: histsize;	{ points to top card of hand }
trying	: boolean;	{ true when legal game moves are possible }

{ random

    obtain a random number between 0 and 1;
    this function may be system dependent
}

function random : real; extern;

{ shuffledeck

    shuffle a deck of cards

    entry conditions:
        deckofcards   : array of records representing card deck

    exit conditions:
        the deck is shuffled
}

```
procedure shuffledeck(var deckofcards : deck);
var
    cardnumber          : cards;       { random card number }
    i                   : cards;       { temporary card index }
    temp                : card;        { card in deck }
begin
    for i := 1 to decksize do
    begin
        { select a random card in deck }
        cardnumber := trunc(decksize * random) + 1;

        { exchange that card with the ith card in deck }
        temp := deckofcards[i];
        deckofcards[i] := deckofcards[cardnumber];
        deckofcards[cardnumber] := temp
    end { of for }
end; { of procedure shuffledeck }

begin { program idiot's delight }
    { initialize the card deck }
    for suitofcard := clubs to spades do
        for rankofcard := ace to king do
        begin
            { convert a suit and rank into a cardnumber }
            cardnumber := ord(rankofcard) + 1 + ord(suitofcard) * suitsize;

            { initialize the suit and rank of this card }
            with deckofcards[cardnumber] do
            begin
                suit := suitofcard;
                rank := rankofcard
            end { of with }
        end; { of for }

    { initialize the histogram }
    for cardsleft := 0 to decksize do histogram[cardsleft] := 0;

    { read the number of games to play }
    writeln(' input the number of games to play (as an integer)');
    read(numberofgames);

    writeln(' I will now play ',numberofgames:1, ' games of idiot''s, delight. ');

    { play the games keeping the results in the histogram array }
    for game := 1 to numberofgames do
    begin
        { shuffle the deck at start of each game }
        shuffledeck(deckofcards);
```

```
{ play the game }
top := 0;
for cardnumber := 1 to decksize do
begin
    top := top + 1;
    hand[top] := deckofcards[cardnumber];
    trying := true;

    while trying and (top > = 4) do
    begin
        if hand[top].suit = hand[top − 3].suit then
        begin
            { suits match − discard intervening two cards }
            hand[top − 2] := hand[top];
            top := top − 2
        end
        else
        if hand[top].rank = hand[top − 3].rank then
        begin
            { ranks match − discard top 4 cards }
            top := top − 4
        end
        else trying := false
    end { of while }
end; { of for }
histogram[top] := histogram [top] + 1
end; { of for }

{ print the histogram }
writeln(' ':11,' out of ',numberofgames:1,' games of idiot''s delight played, ');
writeln(' ':11, ' the distribution of the number of undiscarded cards is:');
writeln;
writeln(' cards');
writeln(' left   frequency');
for cardsleft := 0 to decksize div 2 do
begin
    { recall that only an even number of cards can be left }
    write(cardsleft * 2:4,histogram[cardsleft * 2]:6);
    write(' ');
    column := 11; { 4 + 6 + 1 }
    for i := 1 to histogram[cardsleft * 2] do
    begin
        if column > = widthmax then
        begin { start overflow line }
            writeln;
            write(' ':11);
            column := 11
        end; { of line too long }
```

```
            write('*');
            column := column + 1
        end; { of for i }
        writeln
    end { of for }
end. { of program Idiot's Delight }
```

2.2.3 Stacks

Although arrays are simple and useful and an integral part of every programming language, they cannot solve every data structuring problem. Some data are more amenable to another data structure, the *stack*. A stack of data can be visualized very much like a stack of china plates. Imagine a dishwasher stacking the dishes after washing them, and a busperson taking dishes off the top as they are needed. Although data are not literally stacked in the computer, the effect is the same. As with the china plates, those on top of the stack are accessed first and those on the bottom, last (last in/first out). At any given point, the dish (or data item) at the top of the stack is the most important because it will be accessed next (see Figure 2.3). Figure 2.3a shows a stack with six elements. Figure 2.3b shows the same stack with one additional element added. Note that the top pointer always points to the most recently added element.

It is useful to keep this picture of a stack in mind. There are many ways to implement a stack, but the visual analogy with the china plates applies regardless of which implementation is used.

Stacks occur naturally in the execution of computer programs. Whenever a procedure or function is called, the computer must save the address of the instruction immediately following the procedure call statement (the return address) in order to return to that statement after executing the procedure. When a procedure is called, the return address is placed on an execution time stack. After the procedure is executed, the return address is removed from the stack, and control is transferred to that location.

FIGURE 2.3   (*a*) A Nonempty Stack. (*b*) Same Stack with One More Element.

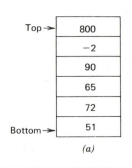
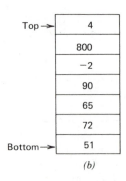

Stacks are especially useful when several procedures are used in succession (procedure *a* calls procedure *b*, which calls procedure *c*, etc.). In this case, the return addresses appear in the stack in the reverse order (*c*, *b*, *a*). After each procedure is executed, its return address is removed from the stack, and control is returned to this address. This process demonstrates the utility of the last-in/first-out property of stacks.

One way to implement a stack is with a one-dimensional array. In our example, the elements of the array will be of type char. There is a pointer (an index into the array) positioned at the topmost element of the stack. The declarations for the stack are

```
const
    stacklowerbound      = 1;              { lower bound of stack }
    stackupperbound      = 100;            { upper bound of stack }
    lowerminus1          = 0;              { stacklowerbound − 1 }
type
    stacklimits          = stacklowerbound .. stackupperbound;
    toplimits            = lowerminus1 .. stackupperbound;
    stackarray           = array [stacklimits] of char;
var
    stack                : stackarray;     { the stack }
    top                  : toplimits;      { top pointer }
```

Three operations can be performed on a stack: (1) *pushing* an element on top of a stack, (2) *popping* (removing) the topmost element from the stack, and (3) testing whether or not a stack is empty. The procedure to push an element on a stack must first check if the stack is full (i.e., if adding one more element will exceed the capacity of the stack). Likewise, the procedure to pop an element from a stack must first check if there is at least one element left to be removed. Obviously, the pop operation cannot be performed on an empty stack.

The push procedure is

```
procedure push(item : char; var stack : stackarray; var top:
        toplimits; upperbound : stacklimits; var flag : boolean);
begin
    if top < upperbound then      { space available in stack }
    begin
        top := top + 1;           { update top pointer }
        stack[top] := item;       { store item on top of stack }
        flag := true              { push operation successful }
    end
    else flag := false            { indicate overflow }
end; { of procedure push }
```

The stack is said to *overflow* when one attempts to push an item onto a full stack.

The pop operation is implemented as a procedure in which the top pointer is updated and the current top of the stack is returned through the parameter called item.

```
procedure pop(var item : char; stack : stackarray; var top:
      toplimits; lowerbound : stacklimits; var flag : boolean);
begin
      if top > = lowerbound then        { stack is not empty }
      begin
            item := stack[top];          { return top of stack }
            top := top − 1;              { update top pointer }
            flag := true                 { pop operation successful }
      end
      else flag := false                 { indicate underflow }
end; { of procedure pop }
```

With this implementation a stack is empty if $top = lowerbound - 1$; otherwise, it contains at least one element. Attempting to pop off a nonexistent item from the stack is referred to as *underflow*.

An alternative way of implementing a stack is to place all the information pertinent to the stack into a Pascal record. This method reduces to two the number of parameters to be passed into the push and pop procedures. The push procedure and its associated declarations become

```
const
      stacklowerbound         = 1;           { lower bound of stack }
      stackupperbound         = 100;         { upper bound of stack }
      lowerminus1             = 0;           { stacklowerbound − 1 }
type
      stacklimits             = stacklowerbound .. stackupperbound;
      toplimits               = lowerminus1 .. stackupperbound;
      stackarray              = array [stacklimits] of char;
      stackrecord             =
            record
                  stacked     : stackarray;    { the stack }
                  top         : toplimits;     { top pointer }
                  lowerbound  : stacklimits;   { stack lower bound }
                  upperbound  : stacklimits;   { stack upper bound }
                  successful  : boolean        { status of operation }
            end; { of record stackrecord }
var
      stack                   : stackrecord;
```

The procedure to push an item onto the stack then becomes

```
procedure push(item : char; var stack : stackrecord);
begin
      with stack do
      begin
            if top < upperbound then      { space available in stack }
```

```
      begin
          top := top + 1;              { update top pointer }
          stacked[top] := item;        { store item on top of stack }
          successful := true           { push operation successful }
      end
      else successful := false         { indicate overflow }
   end { of with stack }
end; { of procedure push }
```

The pop procedure is

```
procedure pop(var item : char; var stack : stackrecord);
begin
    with stack do
    begin
        if top >= lowerbound then
        begin
            item := stacked [top];       { remove item from top of stack }
            top := top - 1;              { update top pointer }
            successful := true           { pop operation successful }
        end
        else successful := false         { indicate underflow }
    end { of with stack }
end; { of procedure pop }
```

Before procedure push or pop can be called, the stack must be initialized by

```
with stack do
begin
    top := lowerminus1;
    lowerbound := stacklowerbound;
    upperbound := stackupperbound
end
```

2.2.4 Examples of Stacks

A stack can be used to recognize if a particular string is written in a language defined by some grammar. This is what a compiler does when it parses a program to determine if its input string (the program) is syntactically correct. For example, to recognize the set of strings defined by the rule

> some string, w, followed by the character ''c'',
> followed by the string w in reverse order

where w is a string of 0 or more characters and w reverse is the string read backward, we can employ a stack. In this language, the string 123c321 is legal, but the string 123c312 is not legal because it does not conform to the prescribed pattern.

To determine if a particular string is legal, we read it one character at a time, pushing each character on the stack until we reach the character c. At this point, we continue to read the string and pop off the top element of the stack as each character is read. If the character read is not identical to this top element, the string is illegal. If all the characters match and the stack is empty after the last character has been read, the string is legal.

The following Pascal program reads a string [which is followed by a dollar sign ($) to mark its end] and determines if the string is legal.

```pascal
program wcwreverse(input,output);
const
      stacklowerbound        = 1;              { stack lower bound }
      stackupperbound        = 100;            { stack upper bound }
      lowerminus1            = 0;              { stack lower bound − 1 }
type
      stacklimits            = stacklowerbound .. stackupperbound;
      toplimits              = lowerminus1 .. stackupperbound;
      stackarray             = array [stacklimits] of char;
      stackrecord            =
            record
                  stacked         : stackarray;
                  top             : toplimits;
                  lowerbound      : stacklimits;
                  upperbound      : stacklimits;
                  successful      : boolean
            end; { of record stackrecord }
var
      ch                     : char;           { character of string }
      match                  : boolean;        { true while string is ok }
      overflow               : boolean;        { true if stack overflow }
      stack                  : stackrecord;    { the stack }
      temp                   : char;           { temporary }
      underflow              : boolean;        { true if stack underflow }

procedure push(item : char; var stack : stackrecord);
begin
      with stack do
      begin
            if top < upperbound then
            begin
                  top := top + 1;
                  stacked[top] := item;
                  successful := true
            end
            else successful := false
      end { of with stack }
end; { of procedure push }
```

```
procedure pop(var item : char; var stack : stackrecord);
begin
    with stack do
    begin
        if top >= lowerbound then
        begin
            item := stacked[top];
            top := top - 1;
            successful := true
        end
        else successful := false
    end { of with stack }
end; { of procedure pop }

begin
    { initialization }
    with stack do
    begin
        top := lowerminus1;
        lowerbound := stacklowerbound;
        upperbound := stackupperbound
    end;
    overflow := false;
    underflow := false;
    ch := ' ';
    match := false;

    if not eof then read(ch);
    while (ch <> 'c') and (not overflow) and (not eof) do
    begin
        push(ch,stack);
        overflow := not stack.successful;
        read(ch)
    end; { of while }

    if (not eof) and (not overflow) then
    begin
        read(ch);
        match := true;
        while match and (ch <> '$') and (not eof) and (not underflow) do
        begin
            pop(temp,stack);
            underflow := not stack.successful;
            if not underflow then
                if temp <> ch then match := false else read(ch)
        end { of while }
    end; { of if }
```

```
        if match and (ch = '$') and (stack . top = lowerminus1) then
            writeln(' legal string ');
        if overflow then writeln(' stack overflow; increase stack space');
        if eof then writeln(' end of file encountered; did you leave off the $');
        if underflow or (not match) then writeln(' illegal string ')
end.
```

A more elegant way to solve the same problem is by using a *recursive* function (i.e., a function that calls itself). Before we write the recursive version of the program, we will briefly review a simple example of a recursive function—one to evaluate $n!$ (called n factorial). $n!$ is defined by

$$n! = n * (n - 1)!$$

with $1! = 1$
and $0! = 1$ by definition.

A Pascal function to evaluate $n!$ is

```
function nfactorial(n : integer) : integer;
begin
    if (n <= 0) or (n = 1) then nfactorial := 1
    else nfactorial := n * nfactorial(n - 1)
end; { of function nfactorial }
```

Execution of nfactorial(3) invokes another instance of nfactorial with an argument of 2, and this second invocation results in a call to nfactorial with the argument 1. The recursive calls stop at this point, since nfactorial(1) evaluates to 1. The second instance of the function (with $n = 2$) receives a value 1 from the third instance [nfactorial(1)], multiplies it by 2, and returns the product $2 * 1 = 2$ as the value of nfactorial(2) requested by the original instance of nfactorial with the argument 3. Hence, the final value of the function will be $3 * 2 = 6$.

In general, every recursive call to a procedure will require us to save the return address and restart execution of the same procedure. When we complete the execution of the procedure, we are not yet through. We must still complete any previously suspended invocations of this procedure, and we must finish them in the *reverse* order in which they were saved.

Thus, a stack is the ideal data structure to help us implement recursion in our language. A recursive procedure call [e.g., nfactorial(2) or nfactorial(1) from the preceding] will cause the following operation.

push ("the return address on the stack")

Whenever we complete execution of the procedure, we would execute the following:

if "stack is not empty" **then**
    pop ("a return address off the stack")

and continue execution of the procedure from that point.

It would be a good idea to go back and retrace the execution of nfactorial(3), keeping track of the state of the stack and the top pointer. We will have more to say about the subject of recursion in Chapter 5 and show many examples of recursive algorithms in Chapters 6 and 7.

Returning to the example of recognizing if a string is of the correct form, study the following program until you can convince yourself that the recursive function match will accept only legal strings. Try to trace through this program using the following strings:

aca$, 11c12$, abcdd$, and c$

program accept(input,output);

{ this is a recursive program to recognize a string of the form: w'c'm$
    where w is some string, 'c' is the character c, and m is the reverse of w. note
    that w may not contain the letter 'c' or a '$'

}

```
function match : boolean;
var
    ch1     : char;        { first char of a symmetric pair }
    ch2     : char;        { last char of a symmetric pair }
    t       : boolean;     { holds value returned by recursive call }
begin
    if not eof then
    begin
        read(ch1);
        if ch1 <> 'c' then
        begin
            t := match; { this is a recursive call }
            if t and not eof then
            begin
                read(ch2);
                match := (ch1 = ch2)
            end
            else match := false
        end
        else match := true { found a c }
    end
    else match := false
end; { of function match }
```

```
begin { program accept }
    if match then
    begin
        if input ↑ = '$' then writeln(' legal string')
        else writeln(' no dollar sign')
    end
    else writeln(' illegal string')
end. { of program accept }
```

Stacks are also used to convert expressions from infix notation to postfix notation. An infix expression is an algebraic expression in which the operators are located between the operands. In postfix notation the operator immediately follows the operands. Examples of infix expressions are

$$a * b, \quad f * g - b, \quad d / e * c + 2$$

The corresponding postfix expressions are

$$ab*, \quad fg*b-, \quad de/c*2+$$

Notice that the operands in a postfix expression occur in the same order as in the corresponding infix expression. Only the position of the operators is changed.

Some operators require two operands (e.g., $+$, $-$, $*$, and $/$). In a postfix expression these operands directly precede their operators. But, more important, the order in which the arithmetic operators are applied is explicit in the postfix expression. As an example, in the infix expression

$$a + b * c$$

the rules of Pascal dictate that the multiplication $b * c$ is performed before the addition. We say that multiplication takes precedence over addition. The corresponding postfix expression is

$$a \, b \, c * +$$

It is now clear that the multiplication operator applies to the operands b and c. The addition operation is then applied to the operand a and the result of $b * c$.

To convert an infix expression to a postfix expression, we use a stack to contain operators that cannot be output until their respective operands are output. In the exercises at the end of this chapter you will be required to design and write an infix to postfix program.

2.2.5 Queues

Queues are familiar from everyday life—we can hardly avoid waiting in a queue (or line). Queues develop whenever people, work, computer jobs, and the like, must wait for some service.

The first person to enter a queue is also the first to leave it. Hence, queues are often called first-in/first-out (FIFO) or first-come/first-served (FCFS) lists.

A queue is a linear list for which all insertions are made at one end. All deletions (and usually all accesses) are made at the other end.

This definition implies that two positions in a queue are especially important: the front and the rear. We identify these positions by pointers as in the following queue.

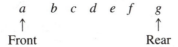

The next element to be deleted will be *a*, which would change the picture to

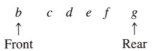

One way to implement a queue is with an array. For this implementation we must specify the maximum array length (maximum number of queued elements), the type of the queued elements (in this case, characters), and front and rear pointers (indices into the array). The necessary Pascal declarations follow.

```
const
    queuelowerbound          = 1;              { lower bound of queue }
    queueupperbound          = 100;            { upper bound of queue }
    lowerminus1              = 0;              { queue lower bound − 1 }
type
    limits                   = lowerminus1 .. queueupperbound;
    queuelimits              = queuelowerbound .. queueupperbound;
    queuearray               = array [queuelimits] of char;
    queuerecord              =
        record
            queued           : queuearray;     { the queue }
            front            : limits;         { front pointer }
            rear             : limits;         { rear pointer }
            lowerbound       : queuelimits;    { queue lower bound }
            upperbound       : queuelimits;    { queue upper bound }
            successful       : boolean         { status of operation }
        end; { of record queuerecord }
var
    queue                    : queuerecord;
```

An initially empty queue is represented by front = rear = lowerminus1.

Rear always points to the last element in the queue. Because of our previous assumption, we cannot let the front pointer point to the first element in the queue; otherwise, a one-element queue would have front and rear pointing to the same element—implying an empty queue. To resolve this, we will assume that front is always *one less* than the actual front of the queue. Our previous example would then have the following pictorial representation:

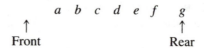

$$a \quad b \quad c \quad d \quad e \quad f \quad g$$

↑   ↑
Front   Rear

Enqueueing is the operation by which an element is added to a queue. Under our assumptions, the procedure is

```
procedure enqueue(item : char; var queue : queuerecord);
begin
    with queue do
    begin
        if rear < upperbound then
        begin
            rear := rear + 1;          { update pointer to rear of queue }
            queued[rear] := item;      { enter item on queue }
            successful := true         { successful enqueue operation }
        end
        else successful := false       { indicate overflow }
    end { of with queue }
end; { of procedure enqueue }
```

The operation to delete an element from a queue is called *dequeueing* and is implemented as follows:

```
procedure dequeue(var item : char; var queue : queuerecord);
begin
    with queue do
    begin
        if front <> rear then
        begin
            front := front + 1;        { update pointer to front of queue }
            item := queued[front];     { remove item at head of queue }
            successful := true         { successful dequeue operation }
        end
        else successful := false       { indicate underflow }
    end { of with queue }
end; { of procedure dequeue }
```

Before either procedure enqueue or dequeue is called, the queue must be initialized by the following operations.

```
with queue do
begin
     front := lowerminus1;
     rear := lowerminus1;
     lowerbound := queuelowerbound;
     upperbound := queueupperbound
end
```

Unfortunately, this implementation is seriously flawed. Since both front and rear migrate to the end of the array, it is possible for rear = queueupperbound when there may actually be space in the array to contain enqueued elements. For simplicity, let us see what happens to a queue of size 3 (i.e., the constants queuelowerbound and queueupperbound are set to 1 and 3, respectively). If we attempted to enqueue four elements in succession, the queue would overflow, which is exactly what we would want to happen.

But if, instead, we had the following sequence of operations:

```
enqueue('a',queue);
dequeue(item,queue);
enqueue('c',queue);
enqueue('f',queue);
enqueue('g',queue) { This will improperly cause an overflow }
```

we see that, in fact, there is a free location, pointed to by front, which could be used to contain the 'g'.

We could shift all elements "up" in the array whenever rear = queueupperbound and front<>queueupperbound and front<>queuelowerbound, but this is a time-consuming operation, especially if queueupperbound is large.

It is better to consider an alternative implementation in which we view the queue as a ring (see Figure 2.4). The elements of the queue are still stored in an array whose declarations may be

```
const
     queuelowerbound          = 0;        { queue lower bound }
     queueupperbound          = 100;      { queue upper bound }
type
     queuelimits              = queuelowerbound .. queueupperbound;
     queuerecord              =
          record
               queued         : array [queuelimits] of char;
               front          : queuelimits;
               rear           : queuelimits;
               lowerbound     : queuelimits;
               upperbound     : queuelimits;
               successful     : boolean
          end; { of record queuerecord }
var
     queue                    : queuerecord;
```

FIGURE 2.4   Queue Viewed as a Ring.

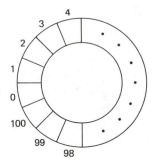

The procedures to add an element to the queue (enqueue) and remove an element from the queue (dequeue) are coded as follows:

```
function enqueue(item : char; var queue : queuerecord);
begin
    with queue do
    begin
        { Check whether queue is full }
        if ((rear = upperbound) and (front = lowerbound)) or
           ((rear+1) = front) then
        begin
            { Indicate queue overflow }
            successful := false
        end
        else
        begin
            { Advance the rear pointer to the next element }
            if rear = upperbound then
            begin
                { Wrap the rear pointer around the ring }
                rear := lowerbound
            end
            else
            begin
                { Move the rear pointer ahead one in the ring }
                rear := rear + 1
            end;

            { Add the element to the queue }
            queued[rear] := item;
```

```
                { Indicate successful enqueue }
                successful := true
            end
        end { of with queue }
end; { of function enqueue }


function dequeue(var item : char; var queue : queuerecord);
begin
    with queue do
    begin
        { Check whether queue is empty }
        if front = rear then
        begin
            { Indicate queue underflow }
            successful := false
        end
        else
        begin
            { Advance the front pointer to the first element in the queue }
            if front = upperbound then
            begin
                { Wrap the front pointer around the ring }
                front := lowerbound
            end
            else
            begin
                { Move the front pointer ahead one in the ring }
                front := front + 1
            end;

            { Remove the item from queue }
            item := queued[front];

            { Indicate successful dequeue operation }
            successful := true
        end
    end { of with queue }
end; { of function dequeue }
```

Before either procedure enqueue or dequeue is called, the queue must be initialized by

```
with queue do
begin
    front := queueupperbound;
    rear := queueupperbound;
    lowerbound := queuelowerbound;
    upperbound := queueupperbound
end
```

Notice that in this implementation we have allocated 101 elements for the array queued, but the maximum number of items in a full queue is 100.

2.2.6 A Queue-*t* Example

Consider the following problem. You are given a stack and asked to reverse its contents, as in the following example.

Top →	5	
	15	
	35	
	2	
	7	
	19	
	68	

Top →	68	
	19	
	7	
	2	
	35	
	15	
	5	

How would you accomplish this task? An elegant solution (although it requires more storage than is actually needed) employs a queue. You simply pop off elements of the stack one at a time and enqueue them. Then dequeue the elements one at a time and push them onto the stack.

```
while stack.top <> lowerminus1 do
begin
    pop(item,stack);
    enqueue(item,queue)
end; { of while }

while queue.front <> queue.rear do
begin
    dequeue(item,queue);
    push(item,stack)
end { of while }
```

2.3
Case Study—A Lexical Scanner

In Pascal a program is simply a string of characters. A Pascal compiler reads the string and determines if it is syntactically correct. To accomplish this, the compiler divides the input string into substrings (or *tokens*).

For example, in the program segment:

```
var
    i : integer;
```

begin
    i := 5
end

the compiler would collect the first string of characters (**var**) into a token. The next tokens the compiler finds as it processes the input text are

i, :, integer, ;, **begin**, i, := , 5, **end**,

The process by which a program (such as a compiler) processes strings into tokens is usually called *lexical analysis,* or *scanning.*

A lexical scanner has several purposes, including

1. The conversion from characters representing a number to the internal binary representation of that number; for our purposes the numbers may be integers, reals, or octal numbers.

2. Collecting together the characters of a nonnumeric string.

3. Processing single-character special strings (:, *, + , − , etc.) or double-character special strings (e.g., :=).

4. Recognizing literal strings surrounded by quotation marks.

5. Detecting and recovering from errors in processing illegal strings.

To see how integers are recognized and converted, consider the string:

$$1675$$

At this point you may be reading this as the number one thousand six hundred seventy five. But the compiler (or scanner) will read this line *one character* at a time. So it will read the *character* 1, not the *number* 1, the character 6, not the number 6, and so forth. The distinction between the character representation of a number and its numeric value is often blurred, but here it is crucial.

First, we consider this specific example (converting from the characters 1, 6, 7, and 5 to the number 1675). Later we will generalize the process. Assume that we declare

var
    ch   : char;
    number   : integer;

and issue

read(ch)

where ch = '1'. To convert the character '1' to the number 1, we could use

number := ord(ch) − ord('0')

where ord is a standard Pascal function that yields the ordinal number of the character passed as its argument; in ASCII:

$$ord(`0') = 48$$
$$ord(`1') = 49$$
$$ord(`2') = 50$$
$$ord(`3') = 51$$

.

.

.

$$ord(`9') = 57$$

Now you should be able to see why the numeric value of the character '1' can be determined using

$$ord(`1') - ord(`0') \qquad (49 - 48 = 1)$$

We can read the next character of the number by again executing

read(ch)

Now, if we execute

number := ord(ch) − ord('0')

as before, we lose the value of the previous digit. To retain it and its relative numerical value, we perform

number := 10 * number + ord(ch) − ord('0')

instead. We can continue in the same manner until the entire number has been converted. To recap, we can convert the characters 1, 6, 7, and 5 into the number 1675 by

```
read(ch); { ch = '1' }
number := ord(ch) − ord('0'); { number = 1 }
read(ch); { ch = '6' }
number := 10 * number + ord(ch) − ord('0'); { number = 16 }
read(ch); { ch = '7' }
number := 10 * number + ord(ch) − ord('0'); { number = 167 }
read(ch); { ch = '5' }
number := 10 * number + ord(ch) − ord('0'); { number = 1675 }
```

It should be obvious that an iterative procedure is called for. The iteration will terminate when we read a character that is not a digit. For now we assume we have a function that performs the following task.

numeric(ch) returns true if ch in '0' . . '9' and false otherwise

Then our iterative process might look like

```
read(ch);
if numeric(ch) then
begin
    number := 0;
    repeat
        number := 10 * number + ord(ch) − ord('0');
        read(ch)
    until not numeric(ch)
end
```

Do you see anything wrong with this program segment? If file input were empty, the first read(ch) would attempt to read past the end of file—which is a fatal run-time error. Since we do not want always to check the end-of-file status before reading the next character from the input file, we will assume that we have written a procedure getnextchar that does the checking for us; it will return the next character on the input file if there is one, or some type of nonnumeric, nonalphabetic character if the end-of-file or end-of-line has been encountered. A call to getnextchar(ch) would then replace calls to read(ch).

Next, assume that an octal number is followed by the letter b, as in

17b

This may seem acceptable since, once we fall out of the **repeat** loop, we can check if ch = 'b'. If it does, the value in the variable number will be interpreted as 17 *octal*, not 17 decimal. You might think the simple thing to do would be to write a conversion procedure that would convert the decimal value into an octal value. Unfortunately, this overlooks one major problem: octal numbers (base 8) can contain only the digits 0 to 7. Hence a number such as 1825b is illegal. Our scanner must be designed to recognize such illegal values. It would be nice if we could read the input file backward to see if the number had an 8 or a 9, but this is not possible.

A simple alternative is, once a digit is recognized, to place it and any succeeding digits into an array that will be rescanned after we know whether or not the string of digits is followed by a 'b'; that is,

```
getnextchar(ch);
if numeric(ch) then
begin
    i := 0;
```

```
repeat
    i := i + 1;
    { note : we are converting characters representing a digit to the digit
      itself here }
    digit[i] := ord(ch) − ord('0');
    getnextchar(ch)
until not numeric(ch);

number := 0;
if ch = 'b' then      { convert as an octal number }
begin
    k := 1;
    repeat
        if digit[k] in [8,9] then
        begin
            error := true;
            k := i
        end
        else number := 8 * number + digit[k];
        k := k + 1
    until k > i
end
else
begin
    k := 1;
    repeat
        number := 10 * number + digit[k];
        k := k + 1
    until k > i
end
end
```

Study this program segment, noting the difference between converting octal numbers and decimal numbers. After carefully reviewing the code, can you spot any other
potential problems? What happens if the numeric value of the number being scanned is
greater than maxint? A simple solution is to check that the value in the variable number
does not exceed maxint. Consult the full scanner program at the end of this chapter for
one way of doing this.

We have been describing a method for recognizing (and converting) integers and
octal numbers. The process can be diagrammed as

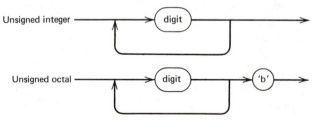

To be complete, our scanner must be able to recognize real numbers as well. Recall that the following are all legal real numbers.

$$1.0 \qquad 1.1E+5 \qquad 6.7E-6 \qquad 15E5$$

The diagram for real numbers looks like this:

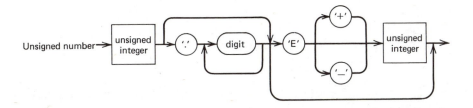

Because the techniques we use to recognize reals are very similar to the process just described for scanning integers and octal numbers, you should study the scanner program at the end of the chapter.

The scanner should also recognize tokens in the form of identifiers (i.e., alphabetic characters followed by 0 or more alphabetic or numeric characters).

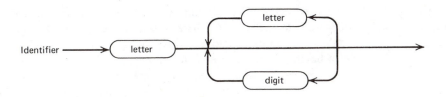

The scanner will return these characters in an array that is dimensioned to hold tokenlenmax characters.

```
const
    tokenlenmax    = 80;
var
    tokenbuffer    : packed array [0 .. tokenlenmax] of char;
    j              : 0 .. tokenlenmax;
```

If we assume the function alphabetic has been defined as

alphabetic(ch) returns true if ch in 'a' . . 'z', false otherwise

the portion of the scanner that recognizes identifiers is simple.

```
getnextchar(ch);
if alphabetic(ch) then
begin
    j := 0;
    repeat
        if j < tokenlenmax then
        begin
            j := j + 1;
            tokenbuffer[j] := ch
        end;
        getnextchar(ch)
    until not (alphabetic(ch) or numeric(ch))
end
```

Notice that if an identifier is longer than tokenlenmax characters, those characters will be read and ignored.

The scanner we have implemented incorporates an error flagging mechanism similar to that of the Pascal compiler. For example, any line containing errors will be printed followed by a line with arrows pointing to the symbols in error.

58b   17. 695   abc
↑   ↑

To accomplish this, we read each input line into a buffer (array) in the procedure getnextline. The procedure getnextchar takes characters from the line buffer and updates a pointer (or, in this case, an index into the array) for each character processed.

As before, instead of having many parameters to the scanner (the procedure called getnextsymbol), we use a record to collect all the information that the scanner needs.

The following program incorporates many of the preceding ideas. The scanner we have written actually is much more powerful and versatile than what we have been describing. The code is modular and, we feel, very easy to read and understand.

```
program scanner(input,output);
const
    debug            = false;      { debug flag }
    maxcharsperline  = 140;        { max characters per line }
    maxexponent      = 200;        { allowable exponent for real numbers }
    quote            = '''';       { for literal strings }
    tokenlenmax      = 80;         { token buffer size }
    version = ' scanner 0.4 — a basic lexical scanner. jon l spear, 03 mar 86';

type
    tokenclass   =
        (delimiter, identifier, integerconstant, literal, realconstant, tendoffile,
         tendofline);
```

```
tokenrec        =
    record
        blankptr         : 0 .. tokenlenmax;      { used to blank fill buffer }
        tbptr            : 0 .. tokenlenmax;      { index of last char added }
        tokenbuffer      : packed array [1 .. tokenlenmax] of char;
        case class       : tokenclass of
            integerconstant    : (integervalue : integer);
            realconstant       : (realvalue : real)
        end; { of case and record tokenrec }
errorclass      =
    (errnone, erroct, errnodigit, errbigint, errexposize, errexpochar,
    errmissingquote, errlongliteral, errlast);
lineindex       = 0 .. maxcharsperline;
linebufrec      =
    record
        ch              : char;         { the line buffer char }
        charptr         : lineindex;    { next char to be processed }
        echo            : boolean;      { true → echo each line to output }
        endoffile       : boolean;      { true → at end of file }
        endofline       : boolean;      { true → at end of line }
        errorline       : array [lineindex] of errorclass;
        errorset        : set of errorclass; { for the whole file }
        fileerror       : boolean;      { true if the file had an error }
        length          : lineindex;    { length of line }
        line            : array [lineindex] of char; { the one line buffer }
        linecount       : integer;      { counts input lines }
        lineerror       : boolean;      { set true if an error is found on the line }
        pfrac           : lineindex;    { ptr to first digit of frac part }
        pint            : lineindex;    { ptr to first nonzero char of number }
        pnum            : lineindex     { ptr to the first char of a number }
    end; { of record linebufrec }


var
    linebuffer                  : linebufrec;    { a one line buffer }
    token                       : tokenrec;      { holds a lexical token }


{ initialize

    initialize line buffer
}


procedure initialize(var linebuffer : linebufrec);
var
    i       : lineindex;    { loop index }
begin
    if debug then writeln(' initializing line buffer');
```

```
    with linebuffer do
    begin
        echo := true;      { we will echo the input lines }
        lineerror := false;
        linecount := 0;
        for i := 0 to maxcharsperline do
        begin
            line[i] := ' ';
            errorline[i] := errnone
        end; { of for }

        errorset := [ ];
        fileerror := false;
        endoffile := false;
        endofline := true;
        pnum := 0
    end { of with }
end; { of procedure initialize }

{ getnextline

    read a new line into the linebuffer
}

procedure getnextline(var linebuffer : linebufrec);

    { printline

        write a line and its line number to output

    }

    procedure printline(var linebuffer : linebufrec);
    var
        i    : lineindex;     { loop index }
    begin
        with linebuffer do
        begin
            write(linecount:6, ' ');
            for i := 1 to length do write(line[i]);
            writeln
        end
    end; { of procedure printline }

    { printerrorline

        print pointers to errors, add to errorset, clear lineerror
    }
```

```
procedure printerrorline(var linebuffer : linebufrec);
var
      column      : integer;    { output column number }
      i           : integer;    { loop index }
      j           : integer;    { loop index }
      num         : integer;    { ord(errclass) }
begin
      column := 0;
      with linebuffer do
      begin
            printline(linebuffer); { this could be removed later }
            write(' *****':6,' '); { space over line number }
            for i := 1 to length + 1 do
                  if errorline[i] <> errnone then
                  begin
                        errorset := errorset + [errorline[i]];
                        num := ord(errorline[i]); { errornumber }
                        if i > column then
                        begin
                              for j := column + 2 to i do write(' '); { tab }
                              write(' ↑ ');
                              column := i
                        end
                        else
                        begin
                              write(',');
                              column := column + 1
                        end;
                        write(num:1); { use a 1 or 2 char field }
                        column := column + 1;
                        if num > 9 then column := column + 1;
                        errorline[i] := errnone
                  end; { of if and for }
            writeln;
            lineerror := false;
            fileerror := true
      end { of with }
end; { of procedure printerrorline }

begin { of procedure getnextline }
   if debug then writeln(' getting new line');
   with linebuffer do
   begin
      if lineerror then printerrorline(linebuffer); { last line had errors }
      if not eof(input) then { read the line }
      begin
            length := 0;
```

```
    while not eoln(input) do { line overflow assumed impossible }
    begin
        length := length + 1;
        read(input,line[length])
    end;
    readln(input); { get next line so eof can be checked }

    { delete any trailing blanks }
    line[0] := '*';
    while line[length] = ' ' do length := length - 1;
    line[length + 1] := ' '; { ensure endofline returns blank }

    linecount := linecount + 1;
    if echo then printline(linebuffer);

    charptr := 1;
    ch := line[charptr];
    endofline := (charptr > length)
    end { not eof }
    else endoffile := true
    end { with }
end; { of procedure getnextline }

{ alphabetic

    function to determine if a character is a letter
}

function alphabetic(ch : char) : boolean;
begin
    alphabetic := ch in ['a' .. 'z']
end; { of function alphabetic }

{ numeric

    function to determine if a character is a digit
}

function numeric(ch : char) : boolean;
begin
    numeric := ch in ['0' .. '9']
end; { of function numeric }

{ getnextsymbol

    find next token in linebuffer
}
```

```
procedure getnextsymbol(var linebuffer : linebufrec; var token : tokenrec);

    { puterror

        place error message at the current buffer pointer

    }

    procedure puterror(error : errorclass; var linebuffer : linebufrec);
    begin
        with linebuffer do
        begin
            lineerror := true;
            errorline[charptr] := error
        end
    end; { of procedure puterror }

    { blankfill

        ensure that the token buffer is blank filled

    }

    procedure blankfill(var token : tokenrec);
    begin
        with token do
        begin
            while blankptr > tbptr do
            begin
                tokenbuffer[blankptr] = ' ';
                blankptr := blankptr − 1
            end;
            blankptr := tbptr
        end { of with }
    end; { of procedure blankfill }

    { getnextcharacter

        read next character from line buffer and advance pointer

    }

    procedure getnextchar(var linebuffer : linebufrec);
    begin
        with linebuffer do
        begin
            if endofline then
                if eof(input) then endoffile := true
                else getnextline(linebuffer)
            else
```

```
            begin
                charptr := charptr + 1;
                if charptr > length then endofline := true
            end;
            ch := line[charptr]
        end { of with }
    end; { of procedure getnextchar }

{ scanidentifier

    scan alphanumeric characters (copying them to tokenbuffer)
}

procedure scanidentifier(var linebuffer : linebufrec; var token : tokenrec);
begin
    if debug then writeln(' scanning identifier');
    with linebuffer , token do
    begin
        class := identifier;
        tbptr := 0;
        repeat      { first char is known to be alphabetic }
            if tbptr < tokenlenmax then
            begin
                tbptr := tbptr + 1;
                tokenbuffer[tbptr] := ch
            end;
            getnextchar(linebuffer)
        until not (alphabetic(ch) or numeric(ch))
    end { with }
end; { of procedure scanidentifier }

{ scannumber

    convert a decimal or octal number, or a real to internal form
}

procedure scannumber(var linebuffer : linebufrec; var token : tokenrec);
var
    i     : integer;

    { convinteger

        convert part of linebuffer to an integer (with no overflow)
    }

    procedure convinteger(var linebuffer : linebufrec; base : integer;
            maxint : integer; first, last : lineindex; var n : integer);
```

```
var
    digit      : 0 .. 9;       { holds a single digit's worth }
    i          : integer;      { loop index }
    x          : real;         { used to check for overflow }

begin
    n := 0;
    x := 0.0;
    i := first;
    while i < last do
    begin
        digit := ord(linebuffer.line[i]) − ord('0');
        if digit >= base then
        begin
            puterror(erroct,linebuffer);
            i := last { terminate loop }
        end;

        x := x * base + digit;
        if x <= maxint then n := n * base + digit
        else
        begin
            puterror(errbigint,linebuffer);
            i := last
        end;
        i := i + 1
    end { of while }
end; { of procedure convinteger }

{ scaninteger

    scan a decimal integer
}

procedure scaninteger(var linebuffer : linebufrec; var token : tokenrec);
begin
    with linebuffer , token do
    begin
        class := integerconstant;
        convinteger(linebuffer,10,maxint,pint,charptr,integervalue)
    end
end; { of procedure scaninteger }

{ scanoctal

    scan an octal number
}
```

```
procedure scanoctal(var linebuffer : linebufrec; var token : tokenrec);
begin
    with linebuffer , token do
    begin
        class := integerconstant;
        convinteger(linebuffer,8,maxint,pint,charptr,integervalue);
        getnextchar(linebuffer) { skip 'b' }
    end
end; { of procedure scanoctal }

{ scanreal

    scan a real number with/without exponent
}

procedure scanreal(var linebuffer : linebufrec; var token : tokenrec);
var
    expo       : integer;
    fac        : real;        { used to compute power of 10 }
    i          : integer;
    negexp     : boolean;     { true if exponent is < 0 }
    nexpo      : integer;     { normalized exponent }
    r          : real;        { used to compute power of 10 }
    scale      : integer;
    x          : real;        { accumulator }

begin
    if debug then writeln(' scanning real number ');
    with linebuffer , token do
    begin
        class := realconstant;

        { do integer part. overflow assumed impossible }
        x := 0.0;
        expo := 0;
        for i := pint to charptr − 1 do
            x = x * 10.0 + ord(line[i]) − ord('0');

        nexpo := charptr − pint;
        scale := 0;
        if ch = '.' then
        begin
            getnextchar(linebuffer); { skip '.' }
            pfrac := charptr;
            if numeric(ch) then
                repeat
                    scale := scale − 1;
```

```
            x := x * 10.0 + ord(ch) − ord('0');
            getnextchar(linebuffer)
        until not numeric(ch)
    else puterror(errnodigit,linebuffer);

    { check if we must find first nonzero digit }
    if nexpo = 0 then { integer part was zero }
    begin
        i := pfrac;
        while line[i] = '0' do i := i + 1;
        nexpo := pfrac − i { = trunc(log10(x)) }
    end
end; { fractional part }

{ do we have an exponent? }
if ch = 'e' then
begin
    negexp := false;
    getnextchar(linebuffer); { skip 'e' }
    if ch = '−' then
    begin
        negexp := true;
        getnextchar(linebuffer) { skip '−' }
    end
    else if ch = '+' then getnextchar(linebuffer);

    { build exponent }
    if numeric(ch) then
    begin
        repeat
            expo := expo * 10 + ord(ch) − ord('0');
            getnextchar(linebuffer)
        until not numeric(ch);

        { adjust scale and nexpo }
        if negexp then
        begin
            scale := scale − expo;
            nexpo := scale − expo
        end
        else
        begin
            scale := scale + expo;
            nexpo := nexpo + expo
        end
    end
    else puterror(errexpochar,linebuffer)
end; { exponent }
```

```
                    { compute 10**scale using right to left binary method }
            if abs(nexpo) <= maxexponent then
                    if scale <> 0 then { must adjust exponent }
                    begin
                        r := 1.0;
                        negexp := scale < 0;
                        scale := abs(scale);
                        fac := 10.0;
                        repeat
                            if odd(scale) then r := r * fac;
                            fac := sqr(fac);
                            scale := scale div 2
                        until scale = 0;
                        if negexp then realvalue := x / r
                        else realvalue := x * r
                    end { apply exponent }
                    else realvalue := x
            else puterror(errexposize,linebuffer)
        end { of with }
end; { of procedure scanreal }


begin { of procedure scannumber }
    if debug then writeln(' scanning number');
    with linebuffer , token do
    begin
        tbptr := 0; { reset token buffer pointer }
        pnum := charptr; { insures no read past eoln }

        { skip leading zeros }
        while ch = '0' do getnextchar(linebuffer);
        pint := charptr; { first nonzero char }

        { scan integer part }
        while numeric(ch) do getnextchar(linebuffer);

        if ch <> 'b' then
        begin
            if not ((ch = '.') or (ch = 'e')) then scaninteger(linebuffer,token)
            else scanreal(linebuffer,token)
        end
        else scanoctal(linebuffer,token);

        { copy number into token buffer }
        i := pnum;
        tbptr := 0;
        while (i < charptr) and (tbptr < tokenlenmax) do
```

```
        begin
            tbptr := tbptr + 1;
            tokenbuffer[tbptr] := line[i];
            i := i + 1
        end; { of copy }

        pnum := 0     { enable getnextline }
    end { with }
end; { of procedure scannumber }

{ scanliteral

    read in a literal string
}

procedure scanliteral(var linebuffer : linebufrec; var token : tokenrec);
var
    working    : boolean;     { true if the closing quote has not been found }
begin
    if debug then writeln(' scanning literal');
    with linebuffer , token do
    begin
        class := literal;
        tbptr := 0;
        getnextchar(linebuffer); { skip first quote }
        working := true ;
        while working and not endofline do
        begin
            if ch = quote then { is it two in a row? }
            begin
                getnextchar(linebuffer);
                { if ch is a quote, continue since it is an imbedded one }
                working := ch = quote
            end;
            if working then
            begin
                if tbptr < tokenlenmax then
                begin
                    tbptr := tbptr + 1;
                    tokenbuffer[tbptr] := ch;
                    getnextchar(linebuffer)
                end
                else { string too long }
                begin
                    puterror(errlongliteral,linebuffer);
                    while (ch <> quote) and not endofline do
                        getnextchar(linebuffer); { skip over string }
```

```
                       if ch = quote then getnextchar(linebuffer);
                         working := false
                     end { overflow }
                 end { of if working }
             end; { of while }
             if working then puterror(errmissingquote,linebuffer)
         end { with }
end; { of procedure scanliteral }


{ scandelimiter

      put ch into token buffer and advance
}


procedure scandelimiter(var linebuffer : linebufrec; var token : tokenrec);
begin
     if debug then writeln(' scanning delimiter');
     token.class := delimiter;
     token.tbptr := 1;
     token.tokenbuffer[token.tbptr] := linebuffer.ch;
     getnextchar(linebuffer)
end; { of procedure scandelimiter }


{ scanendofline

      return end of line status
}


procedure scanendofline(var linebuffer : linebufrec; var token : tokenrec);
begin
     if debug then writeln(' scanning end of line');
     token.class := tendofline;
     token.tbptr := 0
end; { of procedure scan endofline }


{ scanfileend

      return end of file status
}


procedure scanfileend(var linebuffer : linebufrec; var token : tokenrec);
begin
     if debug then writeln(' scanning end of file');
     token.class := tendoffile;
     token.tbptr := 0
end; { of procedure scanfileend }
```

```
begin { of procedure getnextsymbol }
    if debug then writeln(' getting next symbol. (ch = ',linebuffer.ch,')');
    if (token.class = tendofline) or (token.class = tendoffile) then
        getnextline(linebuffer);
    with linebuffer do
    begin
        { scan leading blanks }
        while (ch = ' ') and not endofline do getnextchar(linebuffer);

        { classify token based on its first char }
        if alphabetic(ch) then scanidentifier(linebuffer,token)
        else
        if numeric(ch) then scannumber(linebuffer,token)
        else
        if ch = quote then scanliteral(linebuffer,token)
        else
        if not endofline then scandelimiter(linebuffer,token)
        else
        if not endoffile then scanendofline(linebuffer,token)
        else
        if endoffile then scanfileend(linebuffer,token)
        else
            halt
    end; { with }
    blankfill(token)        { follow token with blanks }
end; { of procedure getnextsymbol }

{ reporterrors

    write a list of errors that have been found in the file
}

procedure reporterrors(var linebuffer : linebufrec);
var
    err     : errorclass;      { loop index }
begin
    writeln(' ***** errors in file:');
    writeln;
    for err := succ(errnone) to pred(errlast) do
        if err in linebuffer.errorset then
        begin
            write(ord(err):8, ' : ');
            case err of
                erroct              : write('digit 8 or 9 in octal constant');
                errbigint           : write('integer constant >',
                                        'maxint(=',maxint:1,')');
                errexposize         : write('abs(real exponent) >'
                                        'maxexponent(=', maxexponent:1,')');
```

```
                    errexpochar          : write('digit expected in exponent');
                    errnodigit           : write('digit expected after "." ');
                    errmissingquote      : write('no closing quote in literal');
                    errlongliteral       : write('literal too long (max is',
                                             tokenlenmax:1, ' chars)')
              end; { of case }
              writeln
         end; { of error and for loop }
      writeln;
      writeln(' end of error list')
end; { of procedure reporterrors }


begin { of program scanner }
      page(output);
      writeln(version);
      initialize(linebuffer);
      getnextline(linebuffer); { read the first line }
      if not linebuffer.endoffile then token.class := delimiter
      else token.class := tendoffile;
      token.blankptr := tokenlenmax;

      while token.class <> tendoffile do
      begin
          getnextsymbol(linebuffer,token);
          write(' ',token.tokenbuffer : 20, '→ ');
          with token do
              case class of
                  identifier           : write('ident');
                  integerconstant      : write('integer = ',integervalue);
                  realconstant         : write('real = ',realvalue);
                  delimiter            : write('delimiter');
                  literal              : write('literal');
                  tendofline           : write('end of line');
                  tendoffile           : write('end of file')
              end; { of case and with }
          writeln;
      end; { of while }
      writeln;
      if linebuffer.fileerror then reporterrors(linebuffer);
      writeln(' execution of scanner complete');
end. { program scanner }
```

Exercises for Chapter 2

*1. Derive an expression for the location of the i, jth element of an array with the following declaration:

var
>   a : **array** [l_1 . . u_1,l_2 . . u_2] **of** integer;

Assume the array is stored by columns; l_1, l_2, u_1, and u_2 are defined as constants with the following restrictions.

$$l_1 <= u_1 \quad \text{and} \quad l_2 <= u_2$$

*2.   Repeat Exercise 1 assuming that the array a is stored by *rows*.

3.   Generalize the results in Exercises 1 and 2 to handle n-dimensional arrays. That is

var
>   a : **array** [l_1 . . u_1,l_2 . . u_2, l_3 . . u_3, . . . ,l_n . . u_n] **of** integer;

4.   Given the declaration

var
>   students   : **array** [1 . . 100] **of**
>   **record**
>   math   : integer;
>   verbal   : integer;
>   name   : **array** [1 . . 10] **of** char
>   **end**; { of record }

derive an expression for

loc(students[i] . name[j])

where $1 <= i <= 100$ and $1 <= j <= 10$.

*5.   Write a complete Pascal declaration (using records) to describe the name, height, eye color, age, sex, and weight of a person.

6.   Write a Pascal declaration that contains information regarding a student's academic history. Include name, student number, courses taken, grades, and current address.

7.   Modify the Idiot's Delight program to output the rank and suit of the card at the top of the hand. Use an array to store the names of the ranks (ace, two, three, . . . kings), and suits (clubs, spades, hearts, diamonds).

*8.   Convert the following infix expression to postfix:

$$(a * b) * (c + d) \uparrow e * (f - g) \uparrow h - i - j * k / l$$

($\uparrow$ is used to denote exponentiation.)

*9.   Ackermann's function $A(m,n)$ is defined as follows:

$$A(m,n) = \begin{cases} n + 1, \text{ if } m = 0 \\ A(m - 1,1), \text{ if } n = 0 \\ A(m - 1,A(m,n - 1)), \text{ otherwise} \end{cases}$$

Write a recursive Pascal function to compute this function. What is the value of $A(3,2)$?

*10.   Binomial coefficients are common in mathematics. They are defined as

$$\binom{n}{m} = \frac{n!}{m!\,(n - m)!}$$

where integer $n \geq$ integer $m \geq 0$, and can be computed recursively using the following relation:

$$\binom{n}{m} = \binom{n - 1}{m} + \binom{n - 1}{m - 1}$$

Write a recursive Pascal function to evaluate binomial coefficients.

11.   The transpose of a given matrix is defined so that the i, jth element of the original matrix is placed in the j, ith element of the transpose matrix. For example,

$$A = \begin{bmatrix} 1 & 6 & 19 \\ 5 & 1 & 30 \\ 7 & 5 & 16 \end{bmatrix} \qquad A^T = \begin{bmatrix} 1 & 5 & 7 \\ 6 & 1 & 5 \\ 19 & 30 & 16 \end{bmatrix}$$

Notice that we are simply interchanging rows and columns. Write a Pascal procedure to compute the transpose of a matrix in place (i.e., use only the storage reserved for the original array).

12.   Modify the program scanner of Section 2.3 so that
   (a)   It accepts and correctly converts binary, or base 2, values. The syntax of these values is

$$dddd \ldots dy$$

   where "d" can be only the digits 0 or 1.
   (b)   It recognizes a special class of identifier called "reserved words." The list of reserved words is in a special table and, if one is found, the program prints out

$$\text{reserved word} =$$

   and the identifier.

CHAPTER 3

LINEAR DATA STRUCTURES AND THEIR LINKED LIST IMPLEMENTATION

3.1
Introduction

In Chapter 2 we discussed arrays and some of their uses (implementing stacks or queues, and manipulating strings). Although arrays are useful in many contexts, they are not appropriate for all situations. For example, arrays are not necessarily the best way to store an ordered list, especially if frequent insertions or deletions are necessary.

This data movement problem is caused by storing *logically* consecutive elements of an ordered list into *physically* consecutive storage locations. Conceptually, there is no reason for the elements of an ordered list to reside in consecutive locations. Assigning elements to arbitrary locations does present a problem: how do we preserve the *logical ordering?* The solution, as we will see, is to include explicit pointers to the next element in the logical sequence. Then any element may be accessed by following the links, provided we know the location of the *first* element. Storing an ordered list in this way eliminates data movement during insertion and deletion operations.

3.2
Linked Lists

In essence, a linked list data structure is an ordered list of nodes. The *first* node is accessed by a special pointer (often called the *head* pointer). The *last* node contains a *null* link field that indicates the end of the list. A general diagram of a linked list is shown in Figure 3.1 (d_i refers to elements in the data field of a node).

3.2.1   Pointers in Pascal
Storage locations for a linked list are usually created *dynamically* (i.e., while the program is executing). Usually, however, variables are declared and referenced by an

FIGURE 3.1   Linked List Diagram.

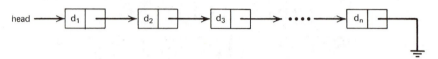

identifier name. For example,

var

    a   : integer;

    b   : real;   *global variables*

    c   : char;

declares three *static* global variables. Each global variable occupies one fixed (known) memory location.

    Suppose we want to set up a linked list with nodes that contain two fields, a social security number and a link field to point to the next node in the list. Pictorially, this can be shown as follows:

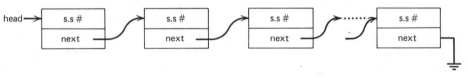

    The first step is to declare a type such as   *must be declared.*

type

    person   = ↑personrecord;   *define person as a pointer type*

which defines person as a *pointer type*. Each value of type person will be a pointer to an undetermined storage area that contains information of type personrecord. (Notice that personrecord has not been declared. This is an exception to the rule that all identifiers must be declared before they are used.) The item of type personrecord is a two-field node declared using the following **record** type:

type

    personrecord =

        record

            socialsecurity   : integer;

            next   : person

        end; { of record person record }

The field socialsecurity will contain a person's social security number stored as an integer, and the next field will contain a pointer to the next node in the linked list. This declaration has not allocated any space.

Each entry, or node, in the list (except the first) is referenced by a pointer from the previous node. To reference the first node, we must declare a variable (head):

var
    head   : person;

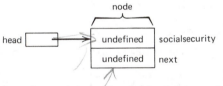

1st node

in which we can store a pointer to the first node.

This declaration creates a storage location for head *only;* its value is undefined. It does not point to any storage location.

The predefined Pascal procedure new is used to dynamically allocate storage locations to instances of data types. For example,

new(head)

new has already been defined.

creates a new node that is *referenced by* head:

node

head   → undefined   socialsecurity

                       undefined   next

We can store a value into the socialsecurity field of the newly created node by the following:

head ↑ socialsecurity := 123456789

head↑. socialsecurity := 123456789

Head ↑ is the first node, which is a record that has two fields. The field identifier socialsecurity is used to select the socialsecurity field of that record.

In Pascal the reserved word **nil** is used to set the final pointer in the last node of the list to point to nothing. We can assign the constant value **nil** to any *pointer* field, regardless of type.

We also use **nil** to denote empty lists with no entries or nodes. The following statement creates an empty list of personrecord.

head := **nil**

or

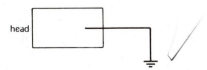

Thus, the name head refers to the actual value of the pointer variable, while head ↑ refers to either **nil** or the object being pointed at by head. The difference made by the ↑ cannot be overemphasized.

These ideas are now combined into a simple program that creates a linked list of social security numbers read from file input until an end of file is encountered.

```
program linkedlist(input,output);
type
    person                  =  ↑ personrecord;
    personrecord            =
        record
            socialsecurity    : integer;
            next              : person
        end; { of record personrecord }
var
    head                    : person;    { pointer to head of list }
    node                    : person;    { temporary }
    ssnumber                : integer;    { social security number }
begin
    { initialize list to be empty }
    head := nil;

    { process the social security numbers until an end of file }
    readln(ssnumber);
    while not eof do
    begin
        new(node);                          { allocate a new node }
        node ↑ .socialsecurity := ssnumber;  { initialize social security
                                              number }
        node ↑ .next := head;               { link new node to
                                              previous head of list }
        head := node ;                      { make new node the first
                                              in the list }
        readln(ssnumber)
    end; { of while }


end.
```

It is instructive to trace through this program statement by statement to see how it works. Assume file input is nonempty and contains the following data:

111111111
555555555
777777777

The first executable statement creates an empty list with the following picture:

Next 111111111 is read into ssnumber. Since we have not reached the end of file, we create a new node.

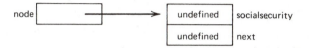

The next two assignment statements change the picture as shown:

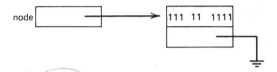

Then the assignment head : = node makes head point to the first (and only) element of the list.

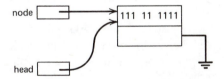

The next value is read into ssnumber and the **while** loop is executed again. Now the picture is updated to

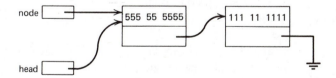

Finally, the last value is read and the picture will look like this:

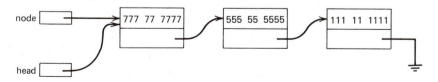

Before you read on, be sure you can trace through the execution of this program and understand how this list was formed. If you understand this example, what follows should be easy.

A typical operation on linked lists is to search for nodes with a particular attribute. As an example, there are two ways we can find the social security number 555555555. First, since we know what the linked list looks like, the node we are searching for is simply

```
head ↑ .next ↑
```

More generally (but still with the assumption that 555555555 appears in the list), we could access this node through another pointer variable.

```
var
     pointer                : person;
     .

     .

     .
     pointer := head;
     while pointer ↑ .socialsecurity <> 555555555 do
          pointer := pointer ↑ .next
```

When this **while** loop terminates, pointer will point to the node whose social security field contains 555555555.

The search method we have just described works only if the item is in the list. If we do not know if the item is in the list, the search procedure must be changed so as not to run off the end of the list. For example, to find a social security number (which is in the variable ssnumber) in the list, we could proceed in this way.

```
pointer := head;
while (pointer <> nil) and
     (pointer ↑ .socialsecurity <> ssnumber) do
          pointer := pointer ↑ .next
```

There is a bug in this algorithm; try to locate it before continuing. The problem is that Pascal will evaluate both alternatives of the conjunction. Hence, even when pointer = **nil** becomes true, making the first alternative false, Pascal will evaluate pointer ↑ .socialsecurity. But **nil** ↑ .socialsecurity does not exist. This will result in an execution time error that could be avoided by using a boolean variable.

```
pointer := head;
found := false;
while (pointer <> nil) and (not found) do
     if pointer ↑ .socialsecurity = ssnumber then found := true
     else pointer := pointer ↑ .next
```

When the **while** loop terminates, we can determine if ssnumber is in the list by
checking the value of the boolean variable found.

3.2.2   Stacks as Linked Lists

In Chapter 2 we saw that a stack can be implemented using an array. Sometimes it is
better to implement a stack using a linked list, as depicted here.

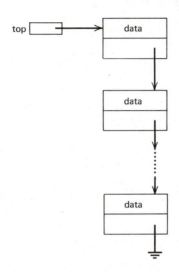

To do so, we first declare the type:

type
    stackpointer   =   ↑ stackelement;

which defines stackpointer to be a pointer type. Each element of the stack will have two
fields: a data field (for our purposes it will be used to hold items of type char) and a
pointer field used to contain a pointer to the next node in the stack.

type
    stackelement   =
        record
            data   : char;
            next   : stackpointer
        end; { of record stackelement }

The first entry in the stack is pointed to by the stack pointer top.

var
    top   : stackpointer;

Initially,

```
top := nil
```

is used to denote an empty stack. To push an item onto the top of the stack, we call the procedure push, which is modified to read

```
procedure push(item : char; var top : stackpointer);
var
    node                    : stackpointer;
begin
    new(node);              { acquire new element for stack }
    node ↑ .data := item;   { insert item into node }
    node ↑ .next := top;    { make this node point to old top }
    top := node             { establish new top of stack }
end; { of procedure push }
```

no overflow

Unfortunately, this approach does not handle stack overflow. We cannot ascertain whether the procedure new will be able to "find enough space" for the new node. There is no standard method in Pascal to determine if all the available space for new node creation has been exhausted. If we do run out of space, the procedure new will "blow up" instead of returning an error flag. That is, a postmortem dump will be produced, and the program will halt.

How do we pop an element off the stack? Try to write the procedure pop before you read further.

```
procedure pop(var item : char; var top : stackpointer;
        var successful : boolean);
begin
    if top <> nil then          { at least one element on stack }
    begin
        item := top ↑ .data;    { set item to element at top of stack }
        top := top ↑ .next;     { update top pointer }
        successful := true      { pop operation successful }
    end
    else successful := false    { indicate stack underflow }
end; { of procedure pop }
```

This procedure works, with one exception. Consider what happens when procedure pop is called on this list.

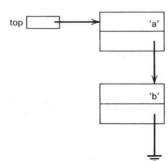

Since top<>**nil**, we execute the compound statement after the **then**. This will change the data structure (picture) to look like this.

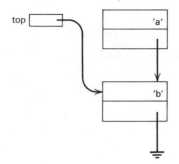

No problem? Look again. Now there is no way to reference the node whose data field contains the character a. Pascal permits us to return nodes like this to the list of allocatable nodes by using the predefined procedure dispose. To take advantage of this facility in the procedure pop, we declare the local variable:

var
      temp   : stackpointer;

and change the compound statement to read

begin
    item := top ↑ .data;   { set item to element at top of stack }
    temp := top;   { save pointer to top of stack }
    top := top ↑ .next;   { update top pointer }
    dispose(temp);   { return node to available space }
    successful := true   { pop operation successful }
end

The temporary is used to hold another pointer to the node to be disposed. (*Note:* Some Pascal compilers do not implement the procedure dispose.)

3.2.3 Queues as Linked Lists
We can also view a queue as a linked list.

It is easier to implement a queue with the linked list representation than with the array representation. Try it. The node structure is the same as for the stack, although we change the names of the (field) identifiers for clarity.

```
type
    queuepointer      = ↑ queueelement;
    queueelement      =
        record
            data      : char;
            next      : queuepointer
        end; { of record queueelement }
var
    front             : queuepointer;
    rear              : queuepointer;
```

An empty queue is initialized using

front := **nil**

The procedure to add a new element to the rear of the queue is

```
procedure enqueue(item : char; var front : queuepointer;
    var rear : queuepointer);
var
    node      : queuepointer;
begin
    { create new queue element and initialize its fields }
    new(node);
    with node ↑ do
    begin
        data := item;
        next := nil
    end;

    { add new node to rear of queue }
    if front = nil then                      { queue is empty }
    begin
        front := node;                       { front and rear will point }
        rear := node                         { to the only element in the queue }
    end
    else                                     { queue not empty }
    begin
        rear ↑ .next := node;                { add new node to rear of queue }
        rear := node                         { establish a new rear of queue }
    end
end; { of procedure enqueue }
```

The corresponding procedure to delete an element from the front of the queue is

```
procedure dequeue(var item : char; var front : queuepointer;
    var successful : boolean);
```

```
var
      node                          : queuepointer;
begin
      if front <> nil then          { nonempty queue }
      begin
            item := front ↑ .data;  { return item at head of queue }
            node := front;          { save pointer to head of queue }
            front := front ↑ .next; { update front pointer }
            dispose(node);          { return node to available space }
            successful := true      { dequeue operation successful }
      end
      else successful := false      { indicate queue underflow }
end; { of procedure dequeue }
```

3.2.4   Simple Operations on One-Way Linked Lists

The preceding sections showed two examples of using linked lists to implement stacks and queues; later sections will describe several other applications of linked lists. First, we will present some examples to help you gain more experience manipulating linked lists. For these examples, we will assume that the node structure looks like

where the data field is of type char and the next field contains a pointer to the next node in the list. We assume the following declarations:

```
type
      nodepointer                   = ↑ node;
      node                          =
            record
                  data              : char;
                  next              : nodepointer
            end; { of record node }
```

Suppose you are given two lists, as shown:

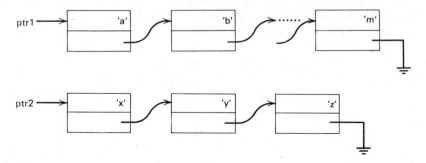

and are asked to concatenate them to produce one list that looks like

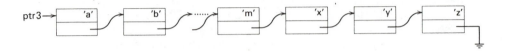

One possible solution is the following procedure of three parameters:

```
procedure concatenate(list1 : nodepointer; list2 : nodepointer;
    var list3 : nodepointer);
var
    ptr1        : nodepointer;      { pointer to nodes of list 1 }
begin
    { find last node of list1 }
    ptr1 := list1;
    while ptr1 ↑.next <> nil do ptr1 := ptr1 ↑.next;

    { note : ptr1 should now point to last node in list 1; link list 1 to list 2 }
    ptr1 ↑.next := list2;

    { return pointer to first list }
    list3 := list1
end; { of procedure concatenate }
```

Is this procedure robust? Hardly! It will work if presented with the preceding two lists, but what if list1 were the following empty list?

Then the condition in the **while** loop would generate a run-time error. It is vital always to check the boundary conditions of an algorithm. When working with lists, always check that an algorithm will work when presented with an empty list. Also, make sure that list algorithms work properly for the last node in a list.

Try to correct the concatenation procedure before looking at our revised version.

```
procedure concatenate(list1 : nodepointer; list2 : nodepointer;
    var list3 : nodepointer);
var
    ptr1        : nodepointer;      { pointer to nodes of list 1 }
begin
    if list1 <> nil then           { first list not empty }
```

```
begin
    list3 := list1;
    if list2 <> nil then       { second list not empty }
    begin
        { search for end of list 1 }
        ptr1 := list1;
        while ptr1 ↑ .next <> nil do ptr1 := ptr1 ↑ .next;
        ptr1 ↑ .next := list2
    end
end
    else list3 := list2            { return pointer to list 2 }
end; { of procedure concatenate }
```

(*Note:* This procedure may have an undesirable side effect; that is, the list pointed to by list 1 may be changed, even though list 1 is a value parameter. What can you do to eliminate this side effect?)

In this procedure the **while** loop is used to ''walk'' down a list until we come to the last node. This can be a very time-consuming operation when the list is long. To speed up such a search, it is often a good idea to keep a pointer to the last element in the list.

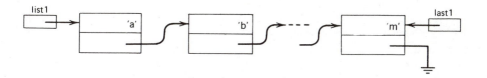

(We now have a structure identical to a queue, although we will be performing operations other than enqueue and dequeue on the structure.) It is not really necessary to have both pointers. Consider the following representation of the list.

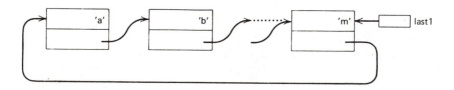

This defines a *circular list*. We no longer have an explicit pointer to the head of the list (although it is easy to locate, provided last1<>**nil**; then the first node in the list is last1 ↑ .next). Make the necessary modifications to the concatenation procedure to handle *circular lists* passed as parameters.

Now consider the problem of determining how many nodes there are in a circular list. If we are not careful, this procedure can easily run around in circles. (This is known as a dynamic halt.)

```
function numberofnodes(list : nodepointer) : integer;
var
    count        : integer;         { counts the number of nodes }
    lastnode     : nodepointer;     { holds pointer to last node }
    pointer      : nodepointer;     { used to walk through list }
begin
    { initialize }
    count := 0;

    if list <> nil then             { at least one node in list }
    begin
        { save pointer to last node in circular list }
        lastnode := list;

        { walk through list counting number of nodes }
        pointer := list;
        repeat
            count := count + 1;
            pointer := pointer ↑ .next
        until pointer = lastnode
    end;

    { return length }
    numberofnodes := count
end; { of function numberofnodes }
```

As a final example, suppose you are given the list

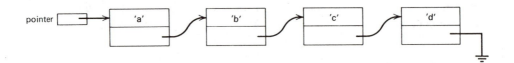

and are asked to reverse the links to produce

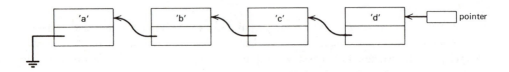

This is more challenging than it looks. Try it. We will develop the solution in the exercises at the end of the chapter.

3.3
Sentinel Nodes

When working with linked lists, we are often confronted with the problem of locating a record with a specific key in a linked list. If the key is not present, then we must add a new node to the list with this key value. As we have seen before, this requires searching the list until we encounter either a node with the correct key value or the end of the list. This task can be simplified if we know that the key is in the list. That is the idea behind using a *sentinel node*. Before searching the list for the key, we put the key value into a node (designated the sentinel node) that is the last node of the list. The data structure for an empty list would look like

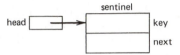

If we had to search for a node containing a key value of 10, the first step would be to put 10 into the sentinel node:

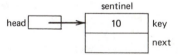

and then search the list starting at the node pointed to by head. If, after searching the list, we find the key in the sentinel node, we will add a new node to the list before the sentinel node.

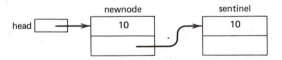

If later we tried to locate the key 20 in the list, we would first put 20 into the sentinel node:

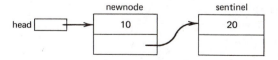

then search the list starting from its head. Since the search will find 20 in the sentinel node, we add a new node, as shown.

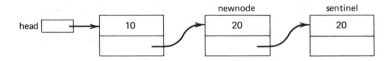

Try to set up the necessary declarations and write a search procedure that conforms to these specifications. Here is ours:

```
program find(input,output);
type
     nodepointer                   =  ↑ node;
     node                          =
         record
             key                   : integer;
             next                  : nodepointer
         end; { of record node }
var
     foundnode:                    : nodepointer;      { pointer to node with keyvalue }
     head                          : nodepointer;      { pointer to head of list }
     keyvalue                      : integer;          { key to search for }
     sentinel                      : nodepointer;      { pointer to sentinel node }

procedure search(keyvalue : integer; head : nodepointer;
     var currentnode : nodepointer; var sentinel : nodepointer);
var
     node                          : nodepointer;      { used to allocate new
                                                         node }
begin
     { put searched for key into the sentinel node }
     sentinel ↑ .key := keyvalue;

     {walk through the list searching for keyvalue }
     currentnode := head;
     while currentnode ↑ .key <> keyvalue do
         currentnode := currentnode ↑ .next;

     { if the keyvalue is in the sentinel node, then create another sentinel }
     if currentnode = sentinel then
     begin
         new(node);
         sentinel ↑ .next := node;                     { allocate new node }
         sentinel := node
     end { of if }
end; { of procedure search }
```

```
begin
    { initialize }
    new(sentinel);
    head := sentinel;

    { read in a key value; search for it in the list; stop reading when a negative
      value is encountered }
    read(keyvalue);
    while keyvalue >= 0 do
    begin
        search(keyvalue, head, foundnode, sentinel);
        read(keyvalue)
    end { of while }
end.
```

The use of sentinel nodes can reduce the number of special cases that must be checked to find an element in a list. We will be using sentinel nodes in many of our examples.

3.4
Doubly Linked Lists

forward and backward

The list structures we have discussed so far contain only one pointer field and generally look like this.

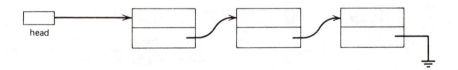

This type of structure allows us to move through the list only in the "forward" direction. If we are somewhere in the middle of a long list and perhaps need to look at a node three to the "left" of the current node, we would have to retraverse the list from the beginning to locate the node. A better solution is to design a data structure that includes both forward *and* backward links, such as,

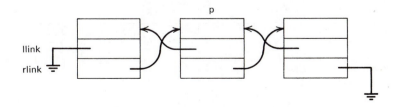

This node structure can be defined in Pascal as

type
```
    nodepointer      = ↑ node;
    node             =
        record
            data     : integer;
            llink    : nodepointer;
            rlink    : nodepointer
        end; { of record node }
```

We have named the two pointer fields llink (for pointers to nodes to the left of the current node) and rlink (which corresponds to our usual usage of a pointer field). Notice also that we now have two **nil** pointers in the list to indicate the two "ends" of the list.

In our previous diagram, we set up a pointer p to the middle node in the list. For this doubly linked structure the following condition holds:

$$p = p\uparrow.rlink\uparrow.llink = p\uparrow.llink\uparrow.rlink$$

A doubly linked list can be converted into a circular doubly linked list in this way:

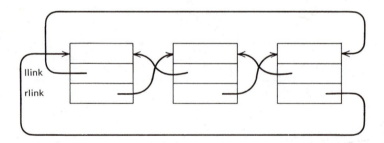

The previous condition now applies to the circular list, no matter which node p is pointing to.

Deleting a node from a doubly linked list is easy. Before a node deletion takes place, our list looks like

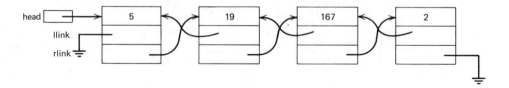

If we delete the node with data field 19, the resulting picture will be

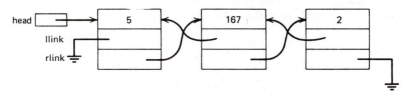

Given a pointer to the list head, write a procedure to delete an arbitrary node; then look at our solution. We assume the following declarations:

```
type
    nodepointer                 =  ↑ node;
    node                        =
        record
            data                : integer;
            llink               : nodepointer;
            rlink               : nodepointer
        end; { of record node }

procedure delete(ptr : nodepointer; var head : nodepointer);
begin
    if ptr <> head then { not deleting list head }
    begin
        { there must be node to left of current node }
        ptr ↑ .llink ↑ .rlink := ptr ↑ .rlink;

        { last node in list has rlink = nil }
        if ptr ↑ .rlink <> nil then
            ptr ↑ .rlink ↑ .llink := ptr ↑ .llink;
        dispose(ptr)
    end
    else
    begin
        if head ↑ .rlink <> nil then { make that node new head }
        begin
            head ↑ .rlink ↑ .llink := nil;
            head := head ↑ .rlink;
            dispose(ptr)
        end
        else
        begin
            dispose (ptr);
            head := nil
        end
    end
end; { of procedure delete }
```

As you can see, the procedure is complicated by many different special cases. We can simplify the procedure if we change the representation of our list. Let an empty list be denoted by a header node with the following structure:

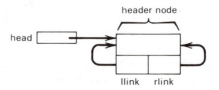

A nonempty list would be represented by

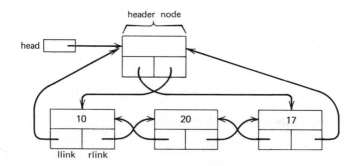

If p is a pointer to any node in this type of doubly linked list, then

$$p = p \uparrow .\text{rlink} \uparrow .\text{llink} = p \uparrow .\text{llink} \uparrow .\text{rlink}$$

Compare the previous deletion procedure with this one.

```
procedure delete(ptr : nodepointer; var head : nodepointer);
begin
    if ptr <> head then
    begin
        ptr ↑ .llink ↑ .rlink := ptr ↑ .rlink;
        ptr ↑ .rlink ↑ .llink := ptr ↑ .llink;
        dispose(ptr)
    end
end; { of procedure delete }
```

The simplicity of this routine is a result of including just one extra node (the header node) in an empty list.

3.5
Applications of Linked Lists

Linked lists can be used in many different applications. This section will describe some of them. In the exercises at the end of the chapter you will develop and implement algorithms for some of these applications.

Matrices have many applications in all branches of science. They occur naturally in the solution of simultaneous linear equations. For the following system of equations:

$$x + y = 1$$
$$2x + y = 0$$

the coefficients of the variables x and y are grouped together in a matrix.

$$\begin{bmatrix} 1 & 1 \\ 2 & 1 \end{bmatrix}$$

The matrix can be represented by a two-dimensional array.

Problems from physics might require solving systems with thousands of variables. A system of 1000 equations with 1000 unknowns could require a coefficient matrix with 1 million entries! This exceeds the main memory capacity of many large-scale computers.

Large systems often contain many zeroes. The corresponding matrices would also therefore contain many zeroes. Such matrices are called *sparse*. Instead of representing a sparse matrix with a two-dimensional array, we can design a data structure that would represent only the nonzero elements of the matrix. Our data structure will have one node per nonzero coefficient; we include in this node the row and column of the coefficient, as well as two link pointers:

Obviously this node should be linked to something. One method uses header nodes— one node for each column and row—and links the nonzero coefficient entries to other elements in a row or column list or to a header node. For example, the matrix

$$\begin{bmatrix} 3 & 2 & 0 \\ 0 & 1 & 6 \\ 1 & 0 & 4 \end{bmatrix}$$

might be encoded

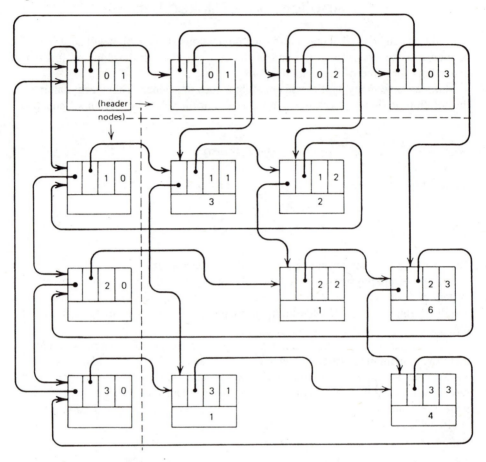

In the exercises you will be asked to write procedures that add and subtract sparse matrices and print the elements of the matrix in a readable form.

Another classic example of the use of linked lists is the symbolic manipulation of polynomials. A polynomial of the form

$$a_n x^n + a_{n-1} x^{n-1} + \ldots + a_1 x^1 + a_0$$

where the a_i are real coefficients, can be represented (term by term) by a linked list using the following node structure:

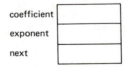

The polynomial

$$5x^3 + 2x - 5$$

would be represented by this linked list:

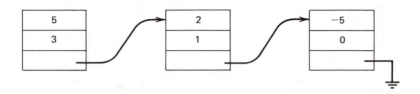

In the exercises you will be asked to implement algorithms to add, subtract, and multiply two polynomials using this linked list representation.

3.6
Conclusion

In this chapter we have described another widely used data structure: linked lists. The exercises reinforce and expand on the material presented. It is not essential to work out all the details of every exercise, but it is important to at least try to sketch out the data structure you would use to solve each problem.

An important point that we have made in the last two chapters bears repeating here. It is extremely important to have a good pictorial representation of a data structure. Draw the picture of the data structure before you try to use it. Study the picture to see if the operations to be performed on the data structure can be simplified if, for example, you were to use an extra pointer field or header node. Then use the picture to guide you in the implementation. The final picture of any data structure used in a program should always be included in the documentation (or user's manual) for the program.

Exercises for Chapter 3

*1. The following singly linked list represents a queue with front and rear pointers.

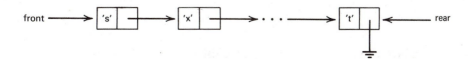

Show that only one of the pointers front and rear is necessary if the queue is represented as a singly linked *circular* list. Write a complete Pascal procedure to dequeue an element from the circular queue. Draw a picture first.

*2.   Write a Pascal function that counts the number of nodes in a list. The parameter to the function should be a pointer to some element in the list. Your function should work properly whether the list is circular or one-way with a **nil** pointer in the last node.

3.   Write a Pascal procedure Merge (p1,p2) that merges two ordered lists, pointed to by p1 and p2, respectively. The program should merge the nodes of p2 into p1 so that p1 remains an ordered list, as illustrated. Duplicate nodes in list p2 should not be merged into p1 but should remain in list p2. Thus, when the merge is complete, list p1 will be the union of lists p1 and p2, and list p2 will be the intersection.

Before merge:

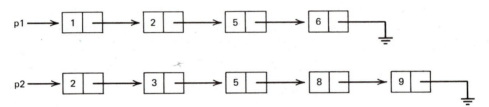

After merge:

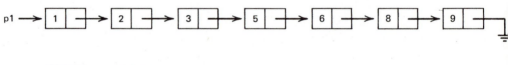

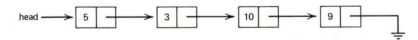

*4.   Write a Pascal procedure to reverse the order of nodes in a list with ptr as a pointer to the first node.

Before operation:

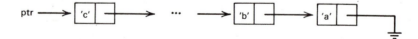

After operation:

(*Hint:* Use three pointers walking through the list.)

5.   Write a Pascal procedure to sort a list into increasing order.

Before operation:

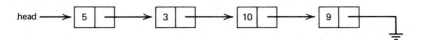

After operation:

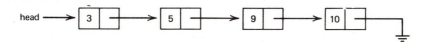

We have emphasized throughout this chapter that you must always check boundary conditions on list processing algorithms. Such checking can be reduced at the expense of a little storage by including appropriate head nodes and making lists circular. The following exercises ask you to rework some of the examples in the text by including head nodes.

*6.   Section 3.2.3 describes a procedure to enqueue an item in a queue represented as a linked list. Insert a head node in the data structure used to implement a queue. This implies that an empty queue will contain one node (the head node). Rewrite procedures enqueue and dequeue with this assumption.

7.   In the implementation of procedure dequeue we returned the contents of the data field of the node at the head of the list. Is it generally more desirable to return a pointer to the record removed from the queue?

*8.   Add a head node to the lists used in the concatenation procedure. Will this simplify the concatenation procedure? Does your head node contain two pointer fields?

9.   Section 3.3 described the use of sentinel nodes. An alternative to this is using a circularly linked list with a head node. Initially, it looks like this:

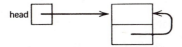

```
{ create an empty list }
new(head);
head ↑ .next := head
```

Searching for a node is simple.

```
head ↑ .data := item;      { head node used as sentinel }
ptr := head ↑ .next;
while ptr ↑ .data <> item do ptr := ptr ↑ .next
```

Ptr now points to a node containing the searched-for item (it may be pointing to the head node). Note that there are no special cases in this search. Write a procedure to insert a node into such a list if the node is not already there.

*10. Set up the data structure described in the text to represent an *n-x-n* sparse matrix (where $n = 50$).

11. Write a procedure that reads three numbers (two indices and a value) and constructs a new node with these three values. Write another procedure to link this node into the data structure at the appropriate place.

12. Write a procedure that will output the values in the sparse matrix. The output should be designed to be as readable as possible and take as little paper as possible.

13. Next, write a procedure to add two sparse matrices, *A* and *B*, and generate a third, *C*.

14. Repeat Exercise 13 performing a subtraction instead of an addition.

15. Using the node structure described in the text, build the data structure for the polynomial

$$x^3 + 2x^2 - x + 10$$

Write a procedure that inputs coefficient, exponent pairs (until eof) and builds the correct data structure.

16. Write a procedure that outputs the polynomial encoded in the data structure described in the text. Use ↑ to denote exponentiation.

17. Write a procedure to add two polynomials.

18. Write a procedure to subtract two polynomials.

19. Write a procedure to eliminate any unnecessary terms in the polynomials above. For example,

```
    eliminate      0x,   0x², . . etc.
and  change        1x ↑ 0 to 1
```

You should have only one constant term at the end of the polynomial.

20. Write a procedure to multiply two polynomials. Reduce your answer.

CHAPTER 4

ABSTRACT DATA TYPES

4.1
Introduction

This chapter describes a very powerful method of organizing programs and their associated data structures. The basic idea is to view a data structure as being manipulated only by a set of well-defined operations. In fact, the data structure should be thought of as being completely inaccessible except through use of these operations (see Figure 4.1). This notion may, at first, seem rather odd because up until this point the way in which you have structured your data has had a considerable effect on how you have written your programs.

Let us try to motivate the notion of an *abstract data type* and its *associated operations* by use of an example. In Chapters 2 and 3 we described how a stack could be implemented using either an array or a linked list. The operations *push* and *pop* were coded differently depending on which data structure was selected. In fact, even the argument lists to the two procedures were different depending on the data structure chosen. But no matter which data structure and, consequently, implementation you select, the function of the *push* and *pop* operations is the same. What is important to realize, then, is that the operations on a stack are the same, independent of the particular implementation of the stack data structure chosen. So, in a manner of speaking, it is more important that the *push* and *pop* operations have a specific functionality (or meaning) than it is to choose whether to use an array, linked list, or other data structure to implement the stack. In fact, if you were building a *module* (a collection of procedures and functions) that was to be used by another person writing a different program, you could envision defining the *push* and *pop* operations and not telling the other user whether you implemented the stack using an array or a linked list. You would then be *hiding* the underlying implementation data structure from that user,

95

FIGURE 4.1   Abstract Data Type Idea.

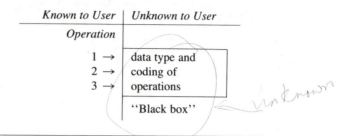

Known to User	Unknown to User
Operation	
1 →	data type and
2 →	coding of
3 →	operations
	"Black box"

unknown

but you would have to provide him or her with a complete *specification* for how your *push* and *pop* operations worked.

Figure 4.2 tries to illustrate these points. Notice that we have drawn a box surrounding the code and the data structures that one uses to implement the stack. Also notice that the only *interface* (or gateway) to this module is through the operations *push* and *pop* (which are denoted by arrows pointing to the box). These ideas may still seem hazy to you, but we hope they will become clearer as we reinforce them with detailed examples. Unfortunately, it is possible to become mired in the details of these examples without getting the "big picture" of what is happening. If this is the case for you, please do not hesitate to reread this chapter several times. We guarantee that it will be worth the effort!

Before proceeding, it is worth reminding you that you are already quite familiar with another type of abstraction, that is, *procedural abstraction*. With procedural abstraction we can study the high-level operations carried out by a procedure separate from the details of how it is implemented. As an example, if you were asked to sort a sequence of integers, you would (probably) immediately think of writing a procedure *sort* that accepts as arguments the sequence of integers and the number of elements in the sequence:

sort(sequence,n)

FIGURE 4.2   Stack Abstract Data Type.

Known to User	Unknown to User
push →	data structure used
	to implement stack
pop →	and coding of
	operations

At this point you can then start considering different algorithms to accomplish the sorting process (see, for example, Chapter 7). We are now asking you to do the same thing with data. Some people argue that procedural and data abstraction are two of the most powerful tools in programming!

4.2
Abstract Data Type—Stack Operations

In the previous discussion, we stressed the importance of the operations on a data structure and relegated the actual data structure implementation (an array versus linked list for the stack example) to "second place." Therefore, let us first informally describe the type of operations that a user of the "stack module" might require.

First, even before a *push* and *pop* operation can be performed, a stack must be created. Since the user of the stack module may require many different stacks in his or her program, we must dynamically create new instances of the stack data type, one per call to the *create* operation. This requirement already places a major constraint on the stack module, that is, the space for the stack cannot be statically allocated by the compiler but, instead, must be dynamically generated upon request. (If you are thinking already about the implementation, please stop! But if you insist on doing so, realize that this requirement does not preclude our using the array implementation of a stack.) The *create* operation does not require any parameters and its result should be the newly created empty stack. A possible invocation of the operation looks like the following:

stack := create()

This leads to one problem: the variable stack must be declared to be the same type as the result of the *create* operation. That would seem to imply that we cannot hide the type of our actual stack implementation (an array or linked list implementation). For the time being, rest assured that we have a solution to this dilemma and let us therefore continue to concentrate solely on the operations and not be distracted by Pascal's strong-typing feature. A user could establish another instance of an empty stack by issuing

stacknumber2 := create()

Clearly, the user can call on *create* to generate any number of stacks. For these reasons, the *create* operation is referred to as a *generator* of the type stack.

A second operation that a user of the stack module might find useful is a means for determining whether or not a stack is empty. Remember that the user does not know which data structure was chosen to implement the stack, so that this condition cannot be tested for by using top = **nil**, as would have been possible in the linked list implementation of the stack from Chapter 3. The empty operation clearly should return a boolean result and might be used like this:

```
if empty(stack) then
begin
     { Do something for the case in which the stack is empty }
end
else
begin
     { Do something else for the case in which the stack is not empty }
end
```

The argument to empty (the variable ''stack'') is the same variable that we used in the *create* operation when we said

```
stack := create()
```

A third operation that is in the same vein as *empty* is the *full* operation. This operation could be used to tell whether or not a stack is about to overflow. The *full* operation also returns a boolean result and takes as an argument a stack that was generated using *create;* for example, **if** full(stack) **then** . . . **else** . . . could be used in the user's program. The *full* and *empty* operations are referred to as *observers* of the type stack. Observers are usually predicates (functions that return a boolean result) that describe some condition about the state of the data object.

The next two operations are *top* and *pop*. The *top* operation permits us to inspect the top element of the stack. Recall from our previous implementations that the way we did this before was by issuing a *pop* operation. The *pop* operation not only returned the previous top of the stack but also reduced the number of elements on the stack by one (the one that was removed). Because these are two distinct operations, we are defining them as such in the present context. Hence, the *top* operation returns the element at the top of the stack and does not alter the stack in any way (see Figure 4.3*a*). In particular, then, if you issued two successive *top* operations on the same stack, you would receive the same element back. The *pop* operation is then defined to return a new stack (one with one fewer elements). So the result of the *pop* operation is the new stack and not the top of the stack (see Figure 4.3*b*). Accordingly, the *pop* operation is a *generator* of the type stack, and the *top* operation is an *observer* of the type stack.

The sixth operation on the stack is the familiar *push* operation. It takes as arguments an element to be added to a stack and the stack to which the element is to be added. The result of the *push* operation is a new stack, and hence the *push* operation is classified as a *generator* of the type stack.

4.2.1   Syntax and Semantics of Abstract Data Types
So far we have described the operations on the abstract data type stack. But we need a more rigorous method for defining them. The next two subsections, therefore, describe the syntax and semantic definitions we will use in discussing abstract data types.

FIGURE 4.3a   Operation of *top*.

Before *top* operation

Known to User	Unknown to User
push →	
pop →	15
empty →	
full →	21
top →	17
create →	

After *top* operation

Value of top operation = 21 and
"before picture" does not change.

FIGURE 4.3b   Operation of *pop*.

Before *pop* operation

Known to User	Unknown to User
push →	
pop →	15
empty →	
full →	21
top →	17
create →	

After *pop* operation

Known to User	Unknown to User
push →	
pop →	15
empty →	
full →	
top →	17
create →	

Pop operation has created a new stack

4.2.1.1   A Syntax for the Stack Operations   We now turn to a brief syntactic description of each of the aforementioned operations. This syntactic description is similar in spirit to the way in which Pascal defines new types. A few observations might make the distinction clearer. Whenever we are describing the abstract data type stack, we will be using all capital letters. This should reinforce the fact that we are not describing the actual Pascal data type implementation. Next, it is not necessary to describe the type of the elements that are to be manipulated by the stack operations. When we get around to the actual implementation, this issue will be treated; but for now in the description of the abstract data type stack the specific type of the stack elements is irrelevant.

We start, then, with a description of the operations on the abstract data type:

TYPE STACK[ELEMENT]

This declaration informs us that we are defining an abstract data type that is referred to by the name STACK and that this STACK will be composed of objects of type ELEMENT. (Do not be confused here by the use of the square brackets ([,])—we are not using them in Pascal's usual sense for an array reference.) We now turn to the syntactic definition of the stack operations.

The first operation to be performed is

CREATE() : STACK[ELEMENT]

This says that the *create* operation has no input parameters and returns as its value an instance of the abstract data type STACK. As mentioned previously, what is created is an empty stack.

The syntax of the *empty* and *full* operations are described as

FULL(STACK[ELEMENT]) : BOOLEAN
EMPTY(STACK[ELEMENT]) : BOOLEAN

The implication is that both operations take as arguments instances of the abstract data type STACK and return as their result a value of type BOOLEAN (which is the standard true and false).

The syntax of the *top* operation looks like

TOP(STACK[ELEMENT]) : ELEMENT

which says that *top* accepts as its argument an instance of the abstract data type STACK and returns as its result a value of type ELEMENT.

Finally, the syntax of the *push* and *pop* operations are defined as

PUSH(ELEMENT,STACK[ELEMENT]) : STACK[ELEMENT]
POP(STACK[ELEMENT]) : STACK[ELEMENT]

Both operations return an instance of the abstract data type STACK as their result. Both operations also accept an instance of the abstract data type STACK as an argument, and the *push* operation requires as its first argument the ELEMENT to be *push*ed. This completes the syntactic description of the operations.

4.2.1.2 Semantics of the Stack Operations   Now we turn to a semiformal description of what these six operations do. In this description of the *semantics* of each operation, we will again be using capital letters to reinforce the distinction between this description and a Pascal description. The following set of semantic definitions completely characterize the operation and functionality of a stack. The technique that we employ to describe the behavior of these operations is to consider the effect of each operation when it is applied to either a newly created stack or a nonempty stack. Some of the semantic definitions use a composition of operations. Recall that if you have two functions, f and g, the interpretation of

$$f(g(x))$$

is that function g is first performed on the argument x and the value of this function then becomes the argument of the function f.

Let's start with the easy definitions first and work our way to the more complicated ones. The interpretation of the *empty* operation is

```
EMPTY(CREATE()) = TRUE
EMPTY(PUSH(X,S)) = FALSE
```

The first definition says that if we apply the *empty* operation on a newly created stack, the result will be true; that is, a newly created stack is empty by definition. The second statement says that if the *empty* operation is applied to a nonempty stack, the result will be false. Notice that a way to guarantee that one has a nonempty stack is to push an element (X) onto an already existing stack (S), as in

```
PUSH(X,S)
```

The definition of the *full* operation is as follows:

```
FULL(CREATE()) = FALSE
FULL(S) = IF PUSH(X,S) = ERROR THEN TRUE ELSE FALSE
```

The first statement implies that a newly created stack will never be full. The second statement says that the *full* operation applied to an arbitrary stack (S) will return true whenever it is the case that adding one more element (X) into the stack (S) would result in an error (i.e., *stack overflow*); otherwise, the *full* operation returns false.

The definition of the *top* operation is

TOP(CREATE()) = NULL
TOP(PUSH(X,S)) = X

The first statement says that if one attempts to inspect the top element of a newly created stack, a NULL value is returned. The second statement implies that the top element of the stack S is the element X, where X is the last element pushed onto the stack.

Finally, the *pop* operation is defined as

POP(CREATE()) = CREATE()
POP(PUSH(X,S)) = S

The first rule says that if you try to apply the *pop* operation to a newly created empty stack, then this is the stack that will be returned as the result of the *pop* operation. Recall that *pop* is defined to return a stack and not the top of the stack. The second statement implies that if you push an element (X) onto a stack (S) and then immediately pop that stack, the result will be the original stack (S).

Consider the following example: we ask that you trace through steps 1 through 7 until you understand the effect of each operation:

1.   S ← PUSH(3,PUSH(4,PUSH(18,POP(PUSH(3,CREATE()))))))
2.   S ← PUSH(3,PUSH(4,PUSH(18,POP(PUSH(3,[])))))
3.   S ← PUSH(3,PUSH(4,PUSH(18,POP([3]))))
4.   S ← PUSH(3,PUSH(4,PUSH(18,[])))
5.   S ← PUSH(3,PUSH(4,[18]))
6.   S ← PUSH(3,[18 4])
7.   S ← [18 4 3]

Hence, all of the right-hand sides of steps 1 through 7 are, by definition, the same stack:

[18 4 3].

4.2.2   Pre- and Postconditions for the Stack Operations

In order to completely specify the interface to the stack module that we are defining, we must also include a description of what each operation expects before it is invoked (the precondition) and the effect of each operation once it is completed (the postcondition). These pre- and postconditions are largely a matter of common sense, but it is, nonetheless, important to describe them completely for the would-be user of the module. Included in this description will be an indication of any error that occurred as the result of invoking an operation. The errors that are possible with this module are

Message Type	Meaning
None	No error occurred on the last operation executed.
StackUnderFlow	A pop operation was applied to an empty stack.
StackOverFlow	No more room is available for an element.
TopOfEmptyStack	Attempt to return the top of an empty stack.

The precondition for the *create* operation is simple: there is none. It should be noted as well that there is no restriction on the number of stacks that can be created by *create*. The postconditions are that the stack is created, which will be denoted by

stack = [ ]

and that no error has resulted:

StackError = None

The precondition for the *pop* operation is divided into two separate cases corresponding to a nonempty and an empty stack. First, there is the case in which the stack is not empty:

$$\text{stack} = [x_1, x_2, \ldots, x_n] \qquad \text{where } n > 0$$

This condition implies that we are treating the elements of the stack as a sequence of elements $x_1, x_2, \ldots, x_n$. By convention, we assume that the top of the stack is x_n. Given this as the precondition, the corresponding postcondition for the *pop* operation is

$$\text{stack} = [x_1, x_2, \ldots, x_{n-1}] \text{ and StackError} = \text{None}$$

Notice that pop has returned a new stack with one less element. It is possible that the original stack had just one element, that is,

$$\text{stack} = [x_1], \{n = 1\}$$

In this case, the postcondition would simply be

$$\text{stack} = [\ ] \text{ and StackError} = \text{None}$$

From now on we will not treat a one-element stack as a special case. The only cases to consider, as mentioned earlier, are a nonempty stack and an empty stack. The other precondition then corresponds to an empty stack:

$$\text{stack} = [\ ] \{n = 0\}$$

In this case, the postcondition for the *pop* operation is

$$\text{stack} = [\ ] \text{ and StackError} = \text{StackUnderFlow}$$

The result of the *pop* operation applied to an empty stack is that the empty stack is returned and a stack error indication is set.

The preconditions for the *push* operation are

$$\text{stack} = [x_1, x_2, \ldots, x_n], \qquad \text{where } n > 0 \quad \text{or}$$
$$\text{stack} = [\ ], \qquad\qquad\quad n = 0$$

The first postcondition corresponds to the case in which there was sufficient room in the stack to contain the new item:

$$\text{stack} = [x_1, x_2, \ldots, x_n, x_{n+1}], \qquad \text{where } x_{n+1} = \text{item pushed,}$$
$$\text{StackError} = \text{None}$$

The other postcondition specifies what happens when there is no space left in the stack:

$$\text{stack} = [x_1, x_2, \ldots, x_n], \qquad n = \text{MaxStackSize,}$$
$$\text{and StackError} = \text{StackOverFlow}$$

This case arises because the value of n is equal to the maximum number of elements that can be stored in the stack (MaxStackSize). As a result of this operation, the original stack is returned and the stack error indication is set to StackOverFlow.

The *top* and *full* operations have exactly the same two preconditions as does the *push* operation. The corresponding postconditions for the *top* operation are

$$\text{top} = x_n, \qquad \text{where } n > 0, \qquad \text{StackError} = \text{None} \quad \text{or}$$
$$\text{top} = \text{NULL}, \qquad \text{when } n = 0, \qquad \text{StackError} = \text{TopOfEmptyStack}$$

Obviously, no error should result when inspecting a nonempty stack, and the value of the operation should be the top element of the stack (x_n). When *top* is invoked with an empty stack (the second statement) the stack error indication is set to TopOfEmpty-Stack. It is the responsibility of the program that called *top* to process this error indication in any way it sees fit. The corresponding postconditions for the *empty* operation are

$$\text{empty} = \text{false} \qquad \text{when } n > 0, \qquad \text{StackError} = \text{None} \quad \text{or}$$
$$\text{empty} = \text{true} \qquad \text{when } n = 0, \qquad \text{StackError} = \text{None}$$

These statements should be self-explanatory.

Finally, the preconditions for the *full* operation read as follows:

$$\text{stack} = [x_1, x_2, \ldots, x_n] \qquad \text{when } n = \text{MaxStackSize}$$
$$\text{stack} = [x_1, x_2, \ldots, x_n] \qquad \text{when } n < \text{MaxStackSize}$$

The corresponding postconditions are simple to derive:

full = true,   when n = MaxStackSize,   StackError = None   or
full = false   when n < MaxStackSize,   StackError = None

4.2.3 Auxiliary Operations

There are two more operations on the abstract data type stack that are defined simply as a matter of convenience. The first is called *size,* which returns the number of elements in the stack. The second is *scan,* which takes as arguments a stack and an operation; *scan* then performs the specified operation on each element in the stack. The use of these operations will be illustrated in the test program that we have devised to show the correctness of our implementation of the stack abstract data type.

4.2.4 Conclusion

To summarize what we have done, we have described an abstract data type called stack by specifying the following:

1. The domain of the objects manipulated by the stack.

2. The syntax of the operations on the stack.

3. The semantics of the operations on the stack.

4. The pre- and postconditions associated with the operations on the stack.

This is enough to allow a person to utilize the concept of a stack fully. Nothing that we have done so far requires an understanding of how you will actually *implement* the stack in Pascal. (Other texts may use different notational schemes in describing abstract data types, but the idea is always the same.)

4.3
The Interface to the Abstract Data Type Stack

We have spent a fair amount of time describing the notion of the abstract data type stack. It is now time to see how one actually implements this notion in Pascal.[1] We will gradually build up to the actual implementation in hopes that this will make the code more understandable.

---

[1] It should be noted that other programming languages allow you to implement abstract data types more directly than Pascal does.

4.3.1   Operation Interface

We start with a repetition of the syntax of the operations that we have defined on the abstract data type stack and also show the corresponding Pascal **function** declarations:

```
CREATE() : STACK[ELEMENT]
function create : StackType;

POP(STACK[ELEMENT]) : STACK[ELEMENT]
function pop(Stack : StackType) : StackType;

PUSH(ELEMENT,STACK[ELEMENT]) : STACK[ELEMENT]
function push(item : Element; Stack : StackType) : StackType;

TOP(STACK[ELEMENT]) : ELEMENT
function top(Stack : StackType) : ElementReferenceType;

EMPTY(STACK[ELEMENT]) : BOOLEAN
function empty(Stack : StackType) : boolean;

FULL(STACK[ELEMENT]) : BOOLEAN
function full(Stack : StackType) : boolean;
```

From inspection of these definitions, it is clear that the user of the stack module must know the definitions for the following three types: StackType, ElementReferenceType, and Element. StackType is the type that the user of the module must use to "refer" to the abstract data type stack. It is defined as follows:

```
StackType = ^StackTypeRecord;
StackTypeRecord =
      record
          { Implementation dependent }
      end { of record StackTypeRecord }
```

There appears to be something missing (like fields in the record), but in fact this is exactly the definition for this type that we want for now. Recall from the beginning of this chapter that we want to *hide* the specific data structure that is used to implement the stack from the user of the stack module. This requirement is met by this type definition.

ElementReferenceType is used to refer to the element that *top* returns; type Element specifies the actual structure of the elements manipulated in the abstract data type stack. These two types are defined as

```
ElementReferenceType = ^Element;
Element =
      record
          { whatever you want }
      end { of record Element }
```

As indicated, the actual specification for the record Element can be whatever you want; a particular example might be as follows:

```
Element =
    record
        letter : 'a' . . 'z';
        count : integer
    end { of record Element }
```

in which the elements to be added to the stack are characters (letter) and the number of times the characters have occurred (count). This particular definition of the **type** Element must also be included in our stack module.

This has the unfortunate ramification that our stack module cannot be *completely* general. In particular, if one wants to *push* elements of **type** Element that looked like the following:

```
Element =
    record
        digit : '0' . . '9';
        count : integer
    end { of record Element }
```

this would require a recompilation of the stack module. This is a concession that we have to make to our chosen implementation language, Pascal. In certain other programming languages we could have circumvented this problem.

In summary, what the user of the stack module needs to know are the following types and function definitions:

```
{ Pascal definition of the abstract data type stack }
StackType = ^StackTypeRecord;
StackTypeRecord =
    record
    end; { of record StackTypeRecord }

{ Pascal definition of the elements in the stack }
ElementReferenceType = ^Element;
Element =
    record
        letter : 'a' . . 'z';
        count : integer
    end; { of record Element }

{ Pascal definition of the operations on the abstract data type stack }
function create : StackType;

function pop(Stack : StackType) : StackType;
```

function push(item : Element; Stack : StackType) : StackType;

function top(Stack : StackType) : ElementReferenceType;

function empty(Stack : StackType) : boolean;

function full(Stack : StackType) : boolean;

This is what the user will see; he or she will not see the actual implementation of the operations.

4.4
Implementation of the Abstract Data Type Stack

At this point we have described what the user of our stack module will see. Our next task is to get on with the business of coding the stack module according to the specifications described in the previous sections. We will actually be coding two separate stack modules; the first one implements the stack using a *one-dimensional array* and the second one implements the stack using a *one-way linked list*. The user of our stack module will not be required to know this particular implementation detail.

We have also written a program that will test whether or not our implementations are correct. We emphasize here that *exactly* the same test program is used to test both implementations. Not a single line is changed in the test program. There is some code that is identical in the implementations of the stack module, and that is what we describe first.

4.4.1   Common Code between Implementations of Stack Module
The common code provides us with a uniform mechanism for determining whether or not an error has occurred. It is the responsibility of the programmer who is using our stack module to check after any operation that could possibly have generated an error, whether one actually did occur or not. For example, if the user of our module writes

```
push(x,stack);
y := top(stack)
```

it is possible that y will not contain the value x that was pushed onto the stack. This could occur if the *push* operation detected that no more space was available for the element (x) and hence the *push* operation could not add this element to the stack and instead set the StackError field to StackOverFlow. Since each operation has as its postcondition the setting of this StackError field, it is quite possible for an error (such as StackOverFlow) to go undetected unless the user of the stack module explicitly checks for such error conditions after each invocation of an operation. To facilitate this, the stack module implements one additional "visible" operation called *StackConditionCode*. Its use is shown below in a program segment that corrects our previously miscoded sequence of *push* and *top* operations:

```
push(x,stack);          { push x onto stack "stack" }
if StackConditionCode(stack) = None then
begin
     y := top(stack);      { retrieve element x }
     .
     .
     .

end
else
begin
     handle stack overflow in whatever way you want
end
```

The function *StackConditionCode* is coded as follows:

```
{ StackConditionCode—takes a stack and returns the condition code of the last
  operation on the stack }
function StackConditionCode(Stack : StackType) : StackErrorTypes;
begin
     { Retrieve the condition code of the last stack operation for this particular stack }
     StackConditionCode := Stack ^.StackError
end { of function StackConditionCode }
```

4.4.2   Implementation of Some of the Operations

At this point we are ready to discuss the implementation of the operations in our stack module. As stated earlier, we have implemented the stack module in two different ways: one implementation is based on an array and the other implementation is based on a one-way linked list. We will leave it to the reader to study most of the operations on his or her own and will describe only two operations in each implementation. For the array implementation of a stack, we consider the functions *push* and *pop*.

4.4.2.1   The Push Operation—Array Implementation   We start by describing the declarations required for the "representation view" of the abstract data type stack:

```
const
     LowerBoundOfStack        = -4;    { Lower bound of stack }
     UpperBoundOfStack        =  5;    { Upper bound of stack }
     LowerMinus1              = -5;    { LowerBoundOfStack - 1 }
```

```
type
    StackType                   = ^StackTypeRecord;
    StackRange                  = LowerBoundOfStack . . UpperBoundOfStack;
    StackIndex                  = LowerMinus1 . . UpperBoundOfStack;
    StackTypeRecord             =
        record
            StackElements       : array [StackRange] of Element;
            StackTop            : StackIndex;
            StackError          : StackErrorTypes
        end { of record StackTypeRecord }
```

Notice that we have now defined the StackTypeRecord that we intentionally left unspecified before. With these definitions in mind, the complete push function becomes

```
{ PUSH(ELEMENT,STACK[ELEMENT]) : STACK[ELEMENT]
  push—returns new stack created when an element is added to the old stack }
function push(item : Element; Stack : StackType) : StackType;
begin
    with Stack^ do
    begin
        { Check whether stack is full }
        if full(Stack) then
        begin
            { Set stack overflow error }
            StackError := StackOverFlow
        end
        else
        begin
            { Add an element to the stack }
            StackTop := StackTop + 1;
            StackElements[StackTop] := item;

            { No error on this operation }
            StackError := None
        end
    end; { of with Stack^ }

    { Return pointer to new stack }
    push := Stack
end { of function push }
```

This function may at first look quite complex, but in actuality it is quite straightforward. On entry to the function, we actually have a pointer to the representation view of the stack which we dereference using the **with** statement. Inside the **with** statement we first check whether the stack is full; this is accomplished by invoking one of our other visible operations, namely, *full*. If the *full* operation returns true, then we have no space to insert the current item into the stack and consequently we set the StackError field to StackOverFlow and do nothing else. Otherwise, we do have room so we increment our stack pointer by 1 and insert the item into the corresponding array location. Since the operation was successful in this case, we set the StackError field to None. The last statement of the function returns a pointer to the representation view of the stack. This pointer is returned to the invoking program as the value of the function push.

4.4.2.2 The Pop Operation—Array Implementation   After describing the push operation, the pop operation should be fairly simple to follow.

```
{ POP(STACK[ELEMENT]) : STACK[ELEMENT]
  pop—returns new stack that is the result of removing topmost element
  from the stack }
function pop(Stack : StackType) : StackType;
begin
     with Stack^ do
     begin
          { Check whether stack is empty }
          if empty(Stack) then
          begin
               { POP(CREATE()) = CREATE()
                 Set stack underflow error and return original stack }
               StackError := StackUnderFlow
          end
          else
          begin
               { POP(PUSH(X,S)) = S; Remove top element of stack }
               StackTop := StackTop - 1;

               { No errors on this operation }
               StackError := None
          end
     end; { of with Stack^ }

     { Return pointer to new stack }
     pop := Stack
end { of function pop }
```

Inside the **with** statement we check whether or not the stack is currently empty and, if it is, set the StackError field to StackOverFlow. Otherwise, a new stack is returned by decrementing StackTop by 1 and setting StackError to None. The last statement of the function returns a pointer to the representation view of the stack.

4.4.2.3 The Push Operation—Linked List Implementation   The only difference between the implementation of the *push* operation in the array implementation of the

stack and the linked list implementation is in the manner in which an element is entered into the stack; the relevant code is reproduced below:

```
else
begin
    { Allocate new element to be added to stack }
    new(StackElement);

    { Fill in fields in new stack element }
    with StackElement^ do
    begin
        member := item;
        next := StackTop
    end; { of with StackElement^ }

    { Link new stack element into stack }
    StackTop := StackElement;

    { No error on this operation }
    StackError := None
end
```

First, a new StackElement is generated by the call to procedure new. The "after" picture looks like this:

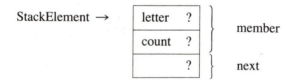

The **with** StackElement^ **do** dereferences the pointer. The assignment statement member: = item stores the record item (which is a parameter to the function), with its two fields letter and count, into the corresponding fields shown above. Then next: = Stack-Top sets the next field of the above record to point to the "previous" top of the stack. StackTop: = StackElement establishes the new top of the stack and StackError: = None indicates that nothing has gone wrong. Unfortunately, something may have gone wrong without us knowing it; the call to procedure new may have failed. However, since Pascal does not return control to the user program in such a case, if the new operation does not have sufficient space for the allocation of the new item, we can do nothing about this error condition.

4.4.2.4 The Pop Operation—Linked List Implementation

There is only one difference between the array and linked list implementation of the *pop* operation! This difference is in how the new stack is created (i.e., in how the element at the top of the stack is removed). The array implementation used

$$\text{StackTop} := \text{StackTop} - 1$$

whereas the linked list implementation uses

$$\text{StackTop} := \text{StackTop}\hat{}.\text{next}$$

The reader is asked to draw the appropriate picture needed to verify that this statement works as required.

4.4.2.5   Summary of Specifications and Implementations

The following table describes where the reader can find the specification and implementation of the stack and queue modules. Once the reader has understood the code for the stack modules, the queue modules should become quite easy to understand.

Section	Contents
4.4.2.5.1	Complete specification of Stack Module
4.4.2.5.2	Implementation of stack specification using arrays
4.4.2.5.3	Implementation of stack specification using linked lists
4.4.2.5.4	Test Program: Stacks
4.4.2.5.5	Complete specification of Queue Module
4.4.2.5.6	Implementation of queue specification using arrays
4.4.2.5.7	Implementation of queue specification using linked lists
4.4.2.5.8	Test Program: Queues

4.4.2.5.1   Complete Specification of Stack Module

Formal description of the legal operations on the data type stack.

TYPE STACK[ELEMENT]

SYNTAX

```
CREATE()                         : STACK[ELEMENT]
PUSH(ELEMENT,STACK[ELEMENT])     : STACK[ELEMENT]
POP(STACK[ELEMENT])              : STACK[ELEMENT]
TOP(STACK[ELEMENT])              : ELEMENT
FULL(STACK[ELEMENT])             : BOOLEAN
EMPTY(STACK[ELEMENT])            : BOOLEAN
```

SEMANTICS

```
POP(CREATE())                    = CREATE()
POP(PUSH(X,S))                   = S
```

```
TOP(CREATE())                    = NULL
TOP(PUSH(X,S))                   = X
FULL(CREATE())                   = FALSE
FULL(S)                          = IF PUSH(X,S) = ERROR THEN TRUE ELSE
                                   FALSE
EMPTY(CREATE())                  = TRUE
EMPTY(PUSH(X,S))                 = FALSE
```

END STACK[ELEMENT]

Pascal specification of stack data type syntax:

> *Elements:* Can be any type, for example integers, reals, characters, as
> well as structured types. We will use the type name element.
> *Structure:* A sequence of elements such that all insertions and deletions
> are made at one end of the list.
> *Operations:* Six operations on the structure are defined and divided into
> two categories—generators and observers.

The first three operations are classified as generators. As the name implies, these
operations generate instances of the data type stack.

GENERATORS:

| CREATE() | : STACK[ELEMENT] |

| function create | : AbstractStackType; |

| create | - returns an empty stack. |

| Precondition | : None. |

| Postcondition | : stack = [ ].
StackError = None |

| POP(STACK[ELEMENT]) | : STACK[ELEMENT] |

function pop(AbstractStack : AbstractStackType) : AbstractStackType;

| pop | - returns new stack that is the result
of removing topmost item from the stack. |

| Precondition | : stack = $[x_1, \ldots, x_n]$ when $n > 0$
OR
stack = [ ] when $n = 0$. |

Postcondition

: stack $= [x_1, \ldots ,x_{n-1}]$ when n-1 > 0,
StackError = None
OR
stack = [ ] when n = 0,
StackError = StackUnderFlow.

PUSH(ELEMENT,STACK[ELEMENT])   : STACK[ELEMENT]

function push(item : Element; AbstractStack : AbstractStackType)
  : AbstractStackType;

push

- returns new stack created when an
  element is added to the old stack.

Precondition

: stack $= [x_1, \ldots ,x_n]$ when n > 0
OR
stack = [ ] when n = 0.

Postcondition

: stack $= [x_1, \ldots ,x_n,x_{n+1}]$,
x_{n+1} = item, StackError = None
OR
stack $= [x_1, \ldots ,x_n]$ when
n = MaxStackSize,
StackError = StackOverFlow.

The remaining three operations are classified as observers. These operations observe information about instances of the data type stack. Note that the observer functions never change the contents of the stack.

OBSERVERS:

TOP(STACK[ELEMENT])   : ELEMENT

function top(AbstractStack : AbstractStackType) : ElementReferenceType;

top

- returns a pointer to the most recently
  inserted element.

Precondition

: stack $= [x_1, \ldots ,x_n]$ when n > 0
OR
stack = [ ] when n = 0.

Postcondition

: top $= x_n$, when n > 0,
StackError = None
OR
top = NULL, when n = 0,
StackError = TopOfEmptyStack.

EMPTY(STACK[ELEMENT])   : BOOLEAN

function empty(AbstractStack : AbstractStackType) : boolean;

empty	- returns true if the stack is empty and false otherwise.
Precondition	: stack = $[x_1, \ldots, x_n]$ when $n > 0$ OR stack = [ ] when $n = 0$.
Postcondition	: empty = false, when $n > 0$, StackError = None OR empty = true, when $n = 0$, StackError = None.

FULL(STACK[ELEMENT])   : BOOLEAN

function full(AbstractStack : AbstractStackType) : boolean;

full	- returns true if the stack is full and false otherwise.
Precondition	: stack = $[x_1, \ldots, x_n]$ when $n = MaxStackSize$ OR stack = $[x_1, \ldots, x_n]$ when $n < MaxStackSize$.
Postcondition	: full = true, when $n = MaxStackSize$, StackError = None OR full = false, when $n < MaxStackSize$, StackError = None.

AUXILIARY:

function size(AbstractStack : AbstractStackType) : integer;

size	- returns number of elements in the stack.
Precondition	: stack = $[x_1, \ldots, x_n]$ when $n > 0$ OR stack = [ ] when $n = 0$.

Postcondition   : size $=$ n, when n $>$ 0
                                             OR
                                             size $=$ 0, when n $=$ 0.

procedure scan(AbstractStack : AbstractStackType;
    procedure operation(item : Element));

scan   - perform the operation specified by the
                                        procedure (passed in as the second
                                        argument) to each element in the stack.

Precondition   : stack $=$ [$x_1, \ldots ,x_n$] when n $>$ 0
                                           OR
                                           stack $=$ [ ] when n $=$ 0.

Postcondition   : stream $=$ operation(x_i),
                                           for all i: $1 <= i <= n$.

4.4.5.2.2   *Implementation of Stack Specification Using Arrays*

```
{ Module that implements the abstract data type stack:
  (Array implementation)

  Tim Barry
  Steve Bruell
  6/1/86
}
```

program StackTypetest(output);
const
     LowerBoundOfStack $=$ -4;   { Lower bound of stack }
     UpperBoundOfStack $=$ 5;   { Upper bound of stack }
     LowerMinus1 $=$ -5;   { LowerBoundOfStack - 1 }

type
     { The possible stack errors }
     StackErrorTypes $=$ (None,StackUnderFlow,StackOverFlow,
                                         TopOfEmptyStack);

     { Representation data type declaration for stack }
     ElementReferenceType $=$ ˆElement;
     Element $=$
         record
             letter   : 'a' . . 'z';
            count   : integer
         end; { of record Element }

```
StackType                    = ^StackTypeRecord;
StackRange                   = LowerBoundOfStack .. UpperBoundOfStack;
StackIndex                   = LowerMinus1 .. UpperBoundOfStack;
StackTypeRecord              =
    record
        StackElements        : array [StackRange] of Element;
        StackTop             : StackIndex;
        StackError           : StackErrorTypes
    end; { of record StackTypeRecord }

{ StackConditionCode—takes a stack and returns the condition code of the last
  operation on this stack }
function StackConditionCode(Stack : StackType) : StackErrorTypes;
begin
    { Retrieve the condition code of the last stack operation for
      this particular stack }
    StackConditionCode := Stack^.StackError
end; { of function StackConditionCode }

{ IMPLEMENTATION: Stack of elements based on array }

{ CREATE() : STACK[ELEMENT]
  create—returns an empty stack }
function create     : StackType;
var
    Stack           : StackType;
begin
    { Create a new instance of a stack of type element }
    new(Stack);

    { Fill in the fields of the newly created stack }
    with Stack^ do
    begin
        StackTop := LowerMinus1;
        StackError := None
    end;

    { Return pointer to newly created stack }
    create := Stack
end; { of function create }

{ EMPTY(STACK[ELEMENT]) : BOOLEAN
  empty—returns true if the stack is empty and false otherwise }
function empty(Stack : StackType) : boolean;
begin
    with Stack^ do
    begin
        { EMPTY(PUSH(X,S)) = FALSE; EMPTY(CREATE()) = TRUE
          Return true if stack is empty and false otherwise }
        empty := StackTop = LowerMinus1;
```

```
                { Empty function cannot cause an error }
                StackError := None
        end
end; { of function empty }


{ FULL(STACK[ELEMENT]) : BOOLEAN
  full—returns true if the stack is full and false otherwise }
function full(Stack : StackType) : boolean;
begin
        with Stack^ do
        begin
                { FULL(CREATE()) = FALSE
                  FULL(S) = IF PUSH(X,S) = ERROR THEN TRUE ELSE FALSE
                  Return true if stack is full and false otherwise }
                full := StackTop = UpperBoundOfStack;

                { Full function cannot cause an error }
                StackError := None
        end
end; { of function full }


{ POP(STACK[ELEMENT]) : STACK[ELEMENT]
  pop—returns new stack that is the result of removing topmost element
  from the stack }
function pop(Stack : StackType) : StackType;
begin
        with Stack^ do
        begin
                { Check whether stack is empty }
                if empty(Stack) then
                begin
                        { POP(CREATE()) = CREATE()
                          Set stack underflow error and return original stack }
                        StackError := StackUnderFlow
                end
                else
                begin
                        { POP(PUSH(X,S)) = S; Remove top element of stack }
                        StackTop := StackTop - 1;

                        { No errors on this operation }
                        StackError := None
                end
        end; { of with Stack^ }

        { Return pointer to new stack }
        pop := Stack
end; { of function pop }
```

```
{ PUSH(ELEMENT,STACK[ELEMENT]) : STACK[ELEMENT]
 push—returns new stack created when an element is added to the old stack }
function push(item : Element; Stack : StackType) : StackType;
begin
    with Stack^ do
    begin
        { Check whether stack is full }
        if full(Stack) then
        begin
            { Set stack overflow error }
            StackError := StackOverFlow
        end
        else
        begin
            { Add an element to the stack }
            StackTop := StackTop + 1;
            StackElements[StackTop] := item;

            { No error on this operation }
            StackError := None

        end
    end; { of with Stack^ }

    { Return pointer to new stack }
    push := Stack
end; { of function push }

{ TOP(STACK[ELEMENT]) : ELEMENT
 top—returns a pointer to the most recently inserted element }
function top(Stack : StackType) : ElementReferenceType;
var
    ElementPointer      : ElementReferenceType;
begin
    with Stack^ do
    begin
        { Return top of stack if it exists, otherwise set error condition }
        if empty(Stack) then
        begin
            { TOP(CREATE()) = NULL }
            top := nil;

            { Set error indication that you are trying to
              inspect the top of an empty stack }
            StackError := TopOfEmptyStack
        end
        else
        begin
            { TOP(PUSH(X,S)) = X; Return top element of stack;
              Create space for new element }
            new (ElementPointer);
```

```
                { Make a copy of the top element of the stack }
                ElementPointer^ := StackElements[StackTop];

                { Return pointer to topmost element }
                top := ElementPointer;

                { No error on this operation }
                StackError := None
            end
        end { of with Stack^ }
end; { of function top }

{ scan—perform the operation specified by the procedure (passed in as the
  second argument) to each element in the stack }
procedure scan(Stack : StackType; procedure operation(item : Element));
var
    ElementPointer      : ElementReferenceType;
    SaveStackTop        : StackRange;
begin
    if not empty(Stack) then
    begin
            { Save pointer to the top of the array stack because scan destroys it }
            SaveStackTop := Stack^.StackTop;

            { Apply the operation to the topmost element of the stack }
            ElementPointer := top(Stack);
            operation(ElementPointer^);

            { Apply the operation to the stack less its topmost element }
            scan(pop(Stack),operation);

            { Reset stack's top pointer to top of array stack }
            Stack^.StackTop := SaveStackTop
    end
end; { of procedure scan }

{ size—returns the number of elements in the stack }
function size(Stack : StackType) : integer;
var
    SaveStackTop        : StackRange;
begin
    if empty(Stack) then
    begin
            { No elements in this stack }
            size := 0
    end
    else
    begin
            { Save pointer to the top of the array stack because size destroys it }
            SaveStackTop := Stack^.StackTop;
```

```
        { Determine the size of the stack by recursively calling size with
          the stack less its topmost element }
        size := 1 + size(pop(Stack));

        { Reset stack's top pointer to top of array stack }
        Stack^.StackTop := SaveStackTop
    end
end; { of function size }

{ test—minimally exercises the stack operations }
procedure test;
    { See subsequent section }
end; { of procedure test }

begin
    test
end.
```

4.4.5.2.3   Implementation of Stack Specification Using Linked Lists

```
{ Module that implements the abstract data type stack:
  (Linked list implementation)

  Tim Barry
  Steve Bruell
  6/2/86
}

program StackTypetest(output);
type
    { The possible stack errors }
    StackErrorTypes              = (None,StackUnderFlow,StackOverFlow,
                                    TopOfEmptyStack);

    { Representation data type declaration for stack }
    ElementReferenceType         = ^Element;
    Element                      =
        record
            letter               : 'a' .. 'z';
            count                : integer
        end; { of record Element }

    StackElementType             = ^StackElementTypeRecord;
    StackElementTypeRecord       =
        record
            member               : Element;
            next                 : StackElementType
        end; { of record StackElementTypeRecord }
```

```
StackType                    = ^StackTypeRecord;
StackTypeRecord              =
    record
        StackTop             : StackElementType;
        StackError           : StackErrorTypes
    end; { of record StackTypeRecord }
```

{ StackConditionCode—takes a stack and returns the condition code of the last
  operation on this stack }
function StackConditionCode(Stack : StackType) : StackErrorTypes;
begin
    { Retrieve the condition code of the last stack operation for
      this particular stack }
    StackConditionCode := Stack^.StackError
end; { of function StackConditionCode }

{ IMPLEMENTATION: Stack of elements based on linked list }

{ CREATE() : STACK[ELEMENT]
  create—returns an empty stack }
function create   : StackType;
var
        Stack   : StackType;
begin
    { Create a new instance of a stack of type element }
    new(Stack);

    { Fill in the fields of the newly created stack }
    with Stack^ **do**
    begin
        StackTop := **nil**;
        StackError := None
    end;

    { Return pointer to new stack }
    create := Stack
end; { of function create }

{ EMPTY(STACK[ELEMENT]) : BOOLEAN
  empty—returns true if the stack is empty and false otherwise }
function empty(Stack : StackType) : boolean;
begin
    with Stack^ **do**
    begin
        { EMPTY(PUSH(X,S)) = FALSE; EMPTY(CREATE()) = TRUE
          Return true if stack is empty and false otherwise }
        empty := StackTop = **nil**;
```
```

```
            { Empty function cannot cause an error }
            StackError := None
      end
end; { of function empty }


{ FULL(STACK[ELEMENT]) : BOOLEAN
  full—returns true if the stack is full and false otherwise }
function full(Stack : StackType) : boolean;
begin
      with Stack^ do
      begin
            { FULL(CREATE()) = FALSE
            FULL(S) = IF PUSH(X,S) = ERROR THEN TRUE ELSE FALSE
            Since the standard Pascal procedure 'new' gives no indication of
            when free space has run out, setting full to false is all that may be
            done for a dynamic allocation implementation of this stack }
            full := false;

            { Empty function cannot cause an error }
            StackError := None
      end
end; { of function full }


{ POP(STACK[ELEMENT]) : STACK[ELEMENT]
  pop—returns new stack that is the result of removing topmost element
  from the stack }
function pop(Stack : StackType) : StackType;
begin
      with Stack^ do
      begin
            { Check whether stack is empty }
            if empty(Stack) then
            begin
                  { POP(CREATE()) = CREATE()
                    Set stack underflow error and return original stack }
                  StackError := StackUnderFlow
            end
            else
            begin
                  { POP(PUSH(X,S)) = S; Remove top element of stack }
                  StackTop := StackTop^.next;

                  { No errors on this operation }
                  StackError := None
            end
      end; { of with Stack^ }
```

```
        { Return pointer to new stack }
        pop := Stack
end; { of function pop }
```

```
{ PUSH(ELEMENT,STACK[ELEMENT]) : STACK[ELEMENT]
  push—returns new stack created when an element is added to the old stack }
function push(item : Element; Stack : StackType) : StackType;
var
        StackElement        : StackElementType;
begin
    with Stack^ do
    begin
        { Check whether stack is full }
        if full(Stack) then
        begin
            { Set stack overflow error }
            StackError := StackOverFlow
        end
        else
        begin
            { Allocate new element to be added to stack }
            new(StackElement);

            { Fill in fields in new stack element }
            with StackElement^ do
            begin
                member := item;
                next := StackTop
            end; { of with StackElement^ }

            { Link new stack element into stack }
            StackTop := StackElement;

            { No error on this operation }
            StackError := None
        end
    end; { of with Stack^ }

    { Return pointer to new stack }
    push := Stack
end; { of function push }
```

```
{ TOP(STACK[ELEMENT]) : ELEMENT
  top—returns a pointer to the most recently inserted element }
function top(Stack : StackType) : ElementReferenceType;
var
        ElementPointer      : ElementReferenceType;
```

```
begin
    with Stack^ do
    begin
        { Return top of stack if it exists, otherwise set error condition }
        if empty(Stack) then
        begin
            { TOP(CREATE()) = NULL }
            top := nil;

            { Set error indication that you are trying to
              inspect the top of an empty stack }
            StackError := TopOfEmptyStack
        end
        else
        begin
            { TOP(PUSH(X,S)) = X; Return top element of stack;
              Create space for new element }
            new(ElementPointer);

            { Make a copy of the top element of the stack }
            ElementPointer^ := StackTop^.member;

            { Return pointer to topmost element }
            top := ElementPointer;

            { No error on this operation }
            StackError := None
        end
    end { of with Stack^ }
end; { of function top }


{ scan—perform the operation specified by the procedure (passed in as the second
  argument) to each element in the stack }
procedure scan(Stack : StackType; procedure operation(item : Element));
    { Same code as in array implementation }
end; { of procedure scan }


{ size—returns the number of elements in the stack }
function size(Stack : StackType) : integer;
    { Same code as in array implementation }
end; { of function size }


{ test—minimally exercises the stack operations }
procedure test;
    { Same code as in array implementation; see Section 4.4.5.2.4 }
end; { of procedure test }
```

```
begin
    test
end.
```

4.4.5.2.4   Test Program: Stacks

```
{ test—minimally exercises the stack operations }
procedure test;
var
    ElementPointer      : ElementReferenceType;
    i                   : integer;
    item                : Element;
    stack               : StackType;

    { DumpStack—output an item from a stack }
    procedure DumpStack(item : Element);
    begin
        with item do
            write(letter:1,'-',count:1,' ')
    end; { of procedure DumpStack }

begin { of procedure test }
    { Initialize:
      Create a new instance of a stack }
    stack := create;

    { Test the semantic:
            POP(CREATE()) = CREATE() }
    writeln('Trying to remove one element from an empty stack should',
        ' cause an error:');
    stack := pop(stack);
    if StackConditionCode(stack) = StackUnderFlow then
        writeln('Error: Tried to pop element from an empty stack.')
    else
        writeln('PANIC: Stack should show underflow error here!?');
    writeln;

    { Test the semantic:
            TOP(CREATE()) = NULL }
    writeln('Trying to remove the top element from an empty stack should',
        ' cause an error:');
    ElementPointer := top(stack);
    if StackConditionCode(stack) = TopOfEmptyStack then
        writeln('Error: Tried to access top element of an empty stack.')
    else
        writeln('PANIC: Stack should show top of empty stack error here!?');
    writeln;
```

```
{ Test the semantic:
        FULL(CREATE()) = FALSE }
writeln('Stack should not be full:');
if not full(stack) then
    writeln('Stack is not full.')
else
    writeln('PANIC: stack is full!?');
writeln;

{ Test the semantic:
        EMPTY(CREATE()) = TRUE }
writeln('Stack should be empty:');
if empty(stack) then
    writeln('Stack is empty.')
else
    writeln('PANIC: stack somehow has elements in it!?');
writeln;

{ Test the auxiliary semantic:
        SIZE(CREATE()) = 0 }
writeln('Stack should have a size of 0:');
if size(stack) = 0 then
    writeln('Stack has a size of 0.')
else
    writeln('PANIC: stack size is ',size(stack):1);
writeln;

{ Test the generator PUSH }
writeln('Now we will put some elements into the stack . . .');
writeln;
for i := 0 to 8 do
begin
    with item do
    begin
        letter := chr(ord('a')+i);
        count := i + 1
    end;
    stack := push(item,stack)
end;

{ Test the auxiliary semantic:
        SCAN(PUSH(X,S),OPERATION) = OPERATION(X) U SCAN(S,OPERATION) }
writeln('Before the pop operation the contents of the stack should',
    ' look like:');
writeln('[i-9  h-8  g-7  f-6  e-5  d-4  c-3  b-2  a-1  ]');
writeln;
writeln('The contents of the stack actually look like:');
```

```
write('[');
scan(stack,DumpStack);
writeln(']');
writeln;

{ Do another pop operation }
writeln('Perform a pop operation:');
writeln;
stack := pop(stack);

{ Retest the auxiliary semantic:
          SCAN(PUSH(X,S),OPERATION) = OPERATION(X) U SCAN(S,OPERATION) }
writeln('After the pop operation the contents of the stack should',
     ' look like:');
writeln('[h-8  g-7  f-6  e-5  d-4  c-3  b-2  a-1  ]');
writeln;
writeln('The contents of the stack actually look like:');
write('[');
scan(stack,DumpStack);
writeln(']');
writeln;

{ Test the semantic:
          POP(PUSH(X,S)) = S }
writeln('We will push the last element added to the stack back on');
writeln('the stack and then pop the stack');
writeln;
stack := pop(push(item,stack));
writeln('The stack should look like:');
writeln('[h-8  g-7  f-6  e-5  d-4  c-3  b-2  a-1  ]');
writeln;
writeln('The contents of the stack actually look like:');
write('[');
scan(stack,DumpStack);
writeln(']');
writeln;

{ Test the semantic:
          TOP(PUSH(X,S)) = X }
writeln('The top element of the stack should be:');
writeln('[h-8   ]');
writeln;
writeln('The top element of the stack actually is:');
ElementPointer := top(stack);
write('[');
DumpStack(ElementPointer^);
writeln(']');
writeln;
```

```
{ Test the semantic:
        FULL(S) = IF PUSH(X,S) = ERROR THEN TRUE ELSE FALSE }
writeln('Stack may be full:');
if not full(stack) then
    writeln('Stack is not full.')
else
    writeln('Stack is full.');
writeln;

{ Test the semantic:
        EMPTY(PUSH(X,S)) = FALSE }
writeln('Stack should not be empty:');
if not empty(stack) then
    writeln('Stack is not empty.')
else
    writeln('PANIC: stack is still empty!?');
writeln;

{ Test the auxiliary semantic:
        SIZE(PUSH(X,S)) = 1 + SIZE(S) }
writeln('Stack should have a size of 8:');
if size(stack) = 8 then
    writeln('Stack has a size of 8.')
else
    writeln('PANIC: stack size is ',size(stack):1,'!?');
writeln;

{ Now empty the stack }
writeln('Now remove all the elements from the stack . . .');
writeln;
for i := 1 to 8 do
    stack := pop(stack);

{ Retest the semantic:
        POP(CREATE()) = CREATE() }
writeln('Trying to remove one element from an empty stack should',
    ' cause an error:');
stack := pop(stack);
if StackConditionCode(stack) = StackUnderFlow then
    writeln('Error: Tried to pop element from an empty stack.')
else
    writeln('PANIC: Stack should show underflow error here!?');
writeln;

{ Retest the semantic:
        FULL(CREATE()) = FALSE }
writeln('Stack should not be full:');
```

```
if not full(stack) then
      writeln('Stack is not full.')
else
      writeln('PANIC: stack is full!?');
writeln;

{ Retest the semantic:
          EMPTY(CREATE()) = TRUE }
writeln('Stack should be empty:');
if empty(stack) then
      writeln('Stack is empty.')
else
      writeln('PANIC: stack somehow has elements in it!?');
writeln;

{ Retest the auxiliary semantic:
          SIZE(CREATE()) = 0 }
writeln('Stack should have a size of 0:');
if size(stack) = 0 then
      writeln('Stack has a size of 0.')
else
      writeln('PANIC: stack size is ',size(stack));
woriteln
end; { of procedure test }
```

4.4.5.2.5   *Complete Specification of Queue Module*

Formal description of the legal operations on the data type queue.

TYPE QUEUE[ELEMENT]

SYNTAX

CREATE()	: QUEUE[ELEMENT]
ENQUEUE(ELEMENT,QUEUE[ELEMENT])	: QUEUE[ELEMENT]
DEQUEUE(QUEUE[ELEMENT])	: QUEUE[ELEMENT]
FIRST(QUEUE[ELEMENT])	: ELEMENT
FULL(QUEUE[ELEMENT])	: BOOLEAN
EMPTY(QUEUE[ELEMENT])	: BOOLEAN

SEMANTICS

DEQUEUE(CREATE())	= CREATE()
DEQUEUE(ENQUEUE(x_k,Q[x_1, . . . ,x_n]))	= Q[x_2, . . . ,x_n,x_k]
FIRST(CREATE())	= NULL
FIRST(ENQUEUE(x_k,Q[x_1, . . . ,x_n]))	= x_1
FULL(CREATE())	= FALSE

FULL(Q)   = IF ENQUEUE(X,Q) = ERROR THEN
                                 TRUE ELSE FALSE
EMPTY(CREATE())   = TRUE
EMPTY(ENQUEUE(X,Q))   = FALSE

END QUEUE[ELEMENT]

Pascal specification of queue data type syntax:

> *Elements:* Can be any type, for example integers, reals, characters, as
>   well as structured types. We will use the type name element.
> *Structure:* A sequence of elements such that all insertions are made at one
>   end of the list and all deletions are made at the other.
> *Operations:* Six operations on the structure are defined and they are di-
>   vided into two categories: generators and observers.

The first three operations are classified as generators. As the name implies these operations generate instances of the data type queue.

GENERATORS:

CREATE()   : QUEUE[ELEMENT]

function create   : AbstractQueueType;

   create   - returns an empty queue.

   Precondition   : None.

   Postcondition   : queue = [ ], QueueError = None.

DEQUEUE(QUEUE[ELEMENT])   : QUEUE[ELEMENT]

function dequeue(AbstractQueue : AbstractQueueType) : AbstractQueueType;

   dequeue   - returns new queue that is the result
                                           of removing the first element from the
                                           queue.

   Precondition   : queue = $[x_1, x_2, \ldots , x_n]$, when $n > 0$
                                           OR
                                           queue = [ ] when $n = 0$.

   Postcondition   : queue = $[x_2, \ldots , x_n]$, when $n > 0$,
                                           QueueError = None
                                           OR
                                           queue = [ ] when $n = 0$,
                                           QueueError = QueueUnderFlow.

ENQUEUE(ELEMENT,QUEUE[ELEMENT])   : QUEUE[ELEMENT]

function enqueue(item : Element; AbstractQueue : AbstractQueueType)
  : AbstractQueueType;

enqueue	- returns new queue created when an element is added to the old queue.
Precondition	: queue = $[x_1, \ldots ,x_n]$, when $n > 0$ OR queue = [ ] when $n = 0$.
Postcondition	: queue = $[x_1, \ldots ,x_n,x_k]$, when $n > 0$, x_k = item, QueueError = None OR queue = $[x_1, \ldots ,x_n]$ when n = MaxQueueSize, QueueError = QueueOverFlow.

The remaining three operations are classified as observers. These operations observe information about instances of the data type queue. Note that the observer functions never change the contents of the queue.

OBSERVERS:

FIRST(QUEUE[ELEMENT])   : ELEMENT

function first(AbstractQueue : AbstractQueueType) : ElementReferenceType;

first	- returns a pointer to the first element of the queue.
Precondition	: queue = $[x_1, \ldots ,x_n]$, when $n > 0$ OR queue = [ ] when $n = 0$.
Postcondition	: first = pointer to x_1, when $n > 0$, QueueError = None OR first = NULL, when n = 0, QueueError = None.

EMPTY(QUEUE[ELEMENT])   : BOOLEAN

function empty(AbstractQueue : AbstractQueueType) : boolean;

empty	- returns true if the queue is empty and false otherwise.

Precondition	: queue = $[x_1, \ldots ,x_n]$, when $n > 0$ OR queue = [ ], when $n = 0$.
Postcondition	: empty = false, when $n > 0$, QueueError = None OR empty = true, when $n = 0$, QueueError = None.

FULL(QUEUE[ELEMENT])   : BOOLEAN

function full(AbstractQueue : AbstractQueueType) : boolean;

full	- returns true if the queue is full and false otherwise.
Precondition	: queue = $[x_1, \ldots ,x_n]$, when $n = $ MaxQueueSize OR queue = $[x_1, \ldots ,x_n]$, when $n <$ MaxQueueSize.
Postcondition	: full = true, when $n = $ MaxQueueSize, QueueError = None OR full = false, when $n <$ MaxQueueSize, QueueError = None.

AUXILIARY:

function size(AbstractQueue : AbstractQueueType) : integer;

size	- returns the number of elements in the queue.
Precondition	: queue = $[x_1, \ldots ,x_n]$, when $n > 0$ OR queue = [ ], when $n = 0$.
Postcondition	: size = n, when $n > 0$ OR size = 0, when $n = 0$.

procedure scan(AbstractQueue : AbstractQueue Type;
    procedure operation(item : Element));

scan   - perform the operation specified by
                                  the procedure (passed in as the
                                  second argument) to each element
                                  in the queue.

Precondition   : queue = $[x_1, \ldots ,x_n]$, when $n > 0$
                                  OR
                                  queue = [ ], when $n = 0$.

Postcondition   : stream = operation(x_i),
                                  for all i: $1 <= i <= n$.

4.4.5.2.6   Implementation of Queue Specification Using Arrays

{ Module that implements the abstract data type queue:
(Array implementation)

Tim Barry
Steve Bruell
6/3/86
}

program QueueTypetest(output);
const
    LowerBoundOfQueue   = -4;   { Lower bound of queue }
    UpperBoundOfQueue   = 5;   { Upper bound of queue }
    LowerMinus1   = -5;   { LowerBoundOfQueue - 1 }

type
    { The possible queue errors }
    QueueErrorTypes   = (None,QueueUnderFlow,QueueOverFlow,
              FirstOfEmptyQueue);

    { Representation data type declarations for queue }
    ElementReferenceType   = ^Element;
    Element   = real;

    QueueType   = ^QueueTypeRecord;
    QueueRange   = LowerBoundOfQueue . . UpperBoundOfQueue;
    QueueIndex   = LowerMinus1 . . UpperBoundOfQueue;
    QueueTypeRecord =
      record
        QueueElement   : **array** [QueueRange] **of** Element;
        Front   : QueueIndex;
        Rear   : QueueIndex;
        QueueError   : QueueErrorTypes
      end; { of record QueueType Record }

{ QueueConditionCode—takes a queue and returns the condition code of the last
   operation in this queue }
function QueueConditionCode(Queue : QueueType): QueueErrorTypes;
begin
    { Retrieve the condition code of the last queue operation for this
      particular queue }
    QueueConditionCode := Queue^.QueueError
end; { of function QueueConditionCode }

{ IMPLEMENTATION: Queue of elements based on array }

{ CREATE() : QUEUE[ELEMENT]
  create—returns an empty queue }
function create   : QueueType;
var
    Queue   : QueueType;
begin
    { Create a new instance of a queue of type element }
    new (Queue);

    { Set fields of the newly created queue }
    with Queue^ **do**
    begin
        Front := UpperBoundOfQueue;
        Rear := UpperboundOfQueue;
        QueueError := None
    end;

    { Return pointer to new queue }
    create := Queue
end; { of function create }

{ EMPTY(QUEUE[ELEMENT]) : BOOLEAN
  empty—returns true if the queue is empty and false otherwise }
function empty(Queue : QueueType) : boolean;
begin
    with Queue^ **do**
    begin
        { EMPTY(ENQUEUE(X,Q) = FALSE; EMPTY(CREATE()) = TRUE;
        Return true if queue is empty and false otherwise }
        empty := Front = Rear;

        { Empty function cannot cause an error }
        QueueError := None
    end
end; { of function empty }

{ FULL(QUEUE[ELEMENT]) : BOOLEAN
  full—returns true if the queue is full and false otherwise }

```
function full(Queue : QueueType) : boolean;
begin
    with Queue^ do
    begin
        { FULL(CREATE()) = FALSE
          FULL(Q) = IF ENQUEUE(X,Q) = ERROR THEN TRUE ELSE FALSE;
          Determine if the stack is full }
        full := ((Rear = UpperBoundOfQueue) and (Front = LowerBoundOfQueue))
            or ((Rear + 1) = Front);

        { Full function cannot cause an error }
        QueueError := None
    end
end; { of function full }


{ DEQUEUE(QUEUE[ELEMENT]) : QUEUE[ELEMENT]
  dequeue—returns new queue that is the result of removing the
  first element from the queue }
function dequeue (Queue : QueueType) : QueueType;
begin
    with Queue^ do
    begin
        { Check whether queue is empty }
        if empty(Queue) then
        begin
            { DEQUEUE(CREATE()) = CREATE()
              Set queue underflow error and return original queue }
            QueueError := QueueUnderFlow
        end
        else
        begin
            { DEQUEUE(ENQUEUE(xk,Q[x1, . . . ,xn])) = Q[x2, . . . ,xn,xk]);
              Remove first element of queue }
            if Front = UpperBoundOfQueue then
            begin
                { Wrap the front pointer around the ring }
                Front := LowerBoundOfQueue
            end
            else
            begin
                { Move the front pointer ahead one in the ring }
                Front := Front + 1
            end;

            { No error on this operation }
            QueueError := None
        end
    end; { of with Queue^ }
```

```
        { Return pointer to new queue }
        dequeue := Queue
end; { of function dequeue }
```

```
{ ENQUEUE(ELEMENT,QUEUE[ELEMENT]) : QUEUE[ELEMENT]
  enqueue—returns new queue created when an element is added to
  the old queue }
function enqueue(item : Element; Queue : QueueType) : QueueType;
begin
    with Queueˆ do
    begin
        { Check whether queue is full }
        if full(Queue) then
        begin
            { Set queue overflow error }
            QueueError := QueueOverFlow
        end
        else
        begin
            { Advance the rear pointer to the next element }
            if Rear = UpperBoundOfQueue then
            begin
                { Wrap the rear pointer around the ring }
                Rear := LowerBoundOfQueue
            end
            else
            begin
                { Move the rear pointer ahead one in the ring }
                Rear := Rear + 1
            end;

            { Add an element to the queue }
            QueueElement[Rear] := item;

            { No error on this operation }
            QueueError := None
        end
    end; { of with Queueˆ }

    { Return pointer to new queue }
    enqueue := Queue
end; { of function enqueue }
```

```
{ FIRST(QUEUE[ELEMENT]) : ELEMENT
  first—returns a pointer to the first element of queue }
function first (Queue : QueueType) : ElementReferenceType;
var
    ElementPointer      : ElementReferenceType;
```

```
begin
    with Queue^ do
    begin
        { Return first element of queue if it exists, otherwise set error condition }
        if empty(Queue) then
        begin
            { FIRST(CREATE()) = NULL }
            first := nil;

            { Set error indication that you are trying to inspect first element of an
              empty queue }
            QueueError := FirstOfEmptyQueue
        end
        else
        begin
            { FIRST(ENQUEUE(xk,Q[x1, . . . ,xn])) = x1;
              Return first element of queue; Allocate and define new element }
            new(ElementPointer);
            ElementPointer^ := QueueElement[Front];

            { Return pointer to first element }
            first := ElementPointer;

            { No error on this operation }
            QueueError := None
        end
    end { of with Queue^ }
end; { of function first }
```

{ scan—perform the operation specified by the procedure (passed in as the second
  argument) to each element in the queue }

```
procedure scan(Queue : QueueType; procedure operation(item : Element));
var
    ElementPointer      : ElementReferenceType;
    SaveQueueFront      : QueueRange;
begin
    if not empty(Queue) then
    begin
        { Save the queue's front pointer because scan destroys it }
        SaveQueueFront := Queue^.Front;

        { Apply the operation to the first element of the queue }
        ElementPointer := first(Queue);
        operation(ElementPointer^);

        { Apply the operation to the queue less its first element }
        scan(dequeue(Queue),operation);
```

```
                { Reset queue's front pointer }
                Queue^.Front := SaveQueueFront
        end
end; { of procedure scan }

{ size—returns the number of elements in the queue }
function size(Queue : QueueType) : integer;
var
        SaveQueueFront      : QueueRange;
begin
        if empty(Queue) then
        begin
                { No elements in this queue }
                size := 0
        end
        else
        begin
                { Save the queue's front pointer because size destroys it }
                SaveQueueFront := Queue^.Front;

                { Determine the size of the queue by recursively calling size with
                  the queue less its first element }
                size := 1 + size(dequeue(Queue));

                { Reset queue's first pointer }
                Queue^.Front := SaveQueueFront
        end
end; { of function size }

{ test—minimally exercises the queue operations }
procedure test;
        { See subsequent section }
end; { of procedure test }


begin
        test
end.
```

4.4.5.2.7 *Implementation of Queue Specification Using Linked Lists*

```
{ Module that implements the abstract data type queue:
  (Linked list implementation)

  Tim Barry
  Steve Bruell
  6/4/86
}
```

```pascal
program QueueTypetest(output);
type
    { The possible queue errors }
    QueueErrorTypes              = (None,QueueUnderFlow,QueueOverFlow,
                                    FirstOfEmptyQueue);

    { Representation data type declarations for queue }
    ElementReferenceType         = ^Element;
    Element                      = real;

    QueueElementType             = ^QueueElementTypeRecord;
    QueueElementTypeRecord       =
        record
            member               : Element;
            next                 : QueueElementType
        end; { of record QueueElementTypeRecord }

    QueueType                    = ^QueueTypeRecord;
    QueueTypeRecord =
        record
            Front                : QueueElementType;
            Rear                 : QueueElementType;
            QueueError           : QueueErrorTypes
        end; { of record QueueTypeRecord }
```

{ QueueConditionCode—takes a queue and returns the condition code of the last
  operation on this queue }

```pascal
function QueueConditionCode(Queue : QueueType): QueueErrorTypes;
begin
    { Retrieve the condition code of the last queue operation for this
      particular queue }
    QueueConditionCode := Queue^.QueueError
end; { of function QueueConditionCode }
```

{ IMPLEMENTATION: Queue of elements based on linked list }

{ CREATE() : QUEUE[ELEMENT]
  create—returns an empty queue }

```pascal
function create     : QueueType;
var
    Queue           : QueueType;
begin
    { Create a new instance of a queue of type element }
    new(Queue);
    { Set fields of the newly created queue }
    with Queue^ do
```

```
    begin
        Front := nil;
        Rear := nil;
        QueueError := None
    end;

    { Return a pointer to newly create queue }
    create := Queue
end; { of function create }
```

```
{ EMPTY(QUEUE[ELEMENT]) : BOOLEAN
  empty—returns true if the queue is empty and false otherwise }
function empty(Queue : QueueType) : boolean;
begin
    with Queue^ do
    begin
        { EMPTY(ENQUEUE(X,Q)) = FALSE; EMPTY(CREATE()) = TRUE;
          Return true if queue is empty and false otherwise }
        empty := (Front = nil) and (Rear = nil);

        { Empty function cannot cause an error }
        QueueError := None
    end
end; { of function empty }
```

```
{ FULL(QUEUE[ELEMENT]) : BOOLEAN
  full—returns true if the queue is full and false otherwise }
function full(Queue : QueueType) : boolean;
begin
    with Queue^ do
    begin
        { FULL(CREATE()) = FALSE
          FULL(Q) = IF ENQUEUE(X,Q) = ERROR THEN TRUE ELSE FALSE;
          Since the standard Pascal procedure 'new' gives no indication of
          when free space has run out, setting full to false is all that may be
          done for a dynamic allocation implementation of a queue }
        full := false;

        { Full function cannot cause an error }
        QueueError := None
    end
end; { of function full }
```

```
{ DEQUEUE(QUEUE[ELEMENT]) : QUEUE[ELEMENT]
  dequeue—returns new queue that is the result of removing the
  first element from the queue }
function dequeue(Queue : QueueType) : QueueType;
```

```
begin
    with Queue^ do
    begin
        { Check whether queue is empty }
        if empty(Queue) then
        begin
            { DEQUEUE(CREATE()) = CREATE();
              Set queue underflow error and return original queue }
            QueueError := QueueUnderFlow
        end
        else
        begin
            { DEQUEUE(ENQUEUE(xk,Q[x1, . . . ,xn])) = Q[x2, . . . ,xn,xk]);
              Remove first element of queue }
            Front := Front^.next;
            if Front = nil then
            begin
                { Queue is now empty }
                Rear := nil
            end;

            { No error on this operation }
            QueueError := None
        end
    end; { of with Queue^ }

    { Return a pointer to queue }
    dequeue := Queue
end; { of function dequeue }


{ ENQUEUE(ELEMENT,QUEUE[ELEMENT]) : QUEUE[ELEMENT]
  enqueue—returns new queue created when an element is added to
  the old queue }
function enqueue (item : Element; Queue : QueueType) : QueueType;
var
    QueueElement     : QueueElementType;
begin
    with Queue^ do
    begin
        { Check whether queue is full }
        if full(Queue) then
        begin
            { Set queue overflow error }
            QueueError := QueueOverFlow
        end
        else
```

```
    begin
        { Allocate new element to be added to queue }
        new(QueueElement);

        { Fill in fields in new queue element }
        with QueueElement^ do
        begin
            member := item;
            next := nil
        end;

        { Insert the new element into the queue }
        if empty(Queue) then
        begin
            { Front and rear point to single element }
            Front := QueueElement;
            Rear := QueueElement
        end
        else
        begin
            { Link new element into queue }
            Rear^.next := QueueElement;
            Rear := QueueElement
        end;

        { No error on this operation }
        QueueError := None
    end
  end; { of with Queue^ }

  { Return a pointer to new queue }
  enqueue := Queue
end; { of function enqueue }

{ FIRST(QUEUE[ELEMENT]) : ELEMENT
  first—returns a pointer to the first element of queue }
function first(Queue : QueueType) : ElementReferenceType;
var
    ElementPointer     : ElementReferenceType;
begin
    with Queue^ do
    begin
        { Return first element of queue if it exists, otherwise set error condition }
        if empty(Queue) then
        begin
            { FIRST(CREATE()) = NULL }
            first := nil;
```

```
              { Set error indication that you are trying to inspect first element of
                an empty queue }
              QueueError := FirstOfEmptyQueue
        end
        else
        begin
              { FIRST(ENQUEUE(xk,Q[x1, . . . xn])) = x1;
                Return first element of queue; Allocate and define new element }
              new(ElementPointer);
              ElementPointer^ := Front^.member;


              { Return pointer to first element }
              first := ElementPointer;


              { No error on this operation }
              QueueError := None
        end
      end { of with Queue^ }
end; { of function first }


{ scan—perform the operation specified by the procedure (passed in as the
  second argument) to each element in the queue }
procedure scan(Queue : QueueType; procedure operation(item : Element));
var
      ElementPointer       : ElementReferenceType;
      SaveQueueFront       : QueueElementType;
      SaveQueueRear        : QueueElementType;
begin
      if not empty(Queue) then
      begin
            { Save the queue's front and rear pointers because scan destroys them }
            SaveQueueFront := Queue^.Front;
            SaveQueueRear := Queue^.Rear;


            { Apply the operation to the first element of the queue }
            ElementPointer := first (Queue);
            operation(ElementPointer^);


            { Apply the operation to the queue less its first element }
            scan(dequeue(Queue),operation);


            { Reset queue's front and rear pointers because size destroys them }
            Queue^.Front := SaveQueueFront;
            Queue^.Rear := SaveQueueRear
      end
end; { of procedure scan }
```

```
{ size—returns the number of elements in the queue }
function size(Queue : QueueType) : integer;
var
    SaveQueueFront      : QueueElementType;
    SaveQueueRear       : QueueElementType;
begin
    if empty(Queue) then
    begin
        { No elements in this queue }
        size := 0
    end
    else
    begin
        { Save the queue's front and rear pointers }
        SaveQueueFront := Queue^.Front;
        SaveQueueRear := Queue^.Rear;

        { Determine the size of the queue by recursively calling size with
          the queue less its first element }
        size := 1 + size(dequeue(Queue));

        { Reset queue's front and rear pointers }
        Queue^.Front := SaveQueueFront;
        Queue^.Rear := SaveQueueRear
    end
end; { of function size }


{ test—minimally exercises the queue operations }
procedure test;
    { Same code as in array implementation; see Section 4.4.5.2.8 }
end; { of procedure test }


begin
    test
end.
```

4.4.5.2.8   Test Program: Queues

```
{ test—minimally exercises the queue operations }
procedure test;
var
    ElementPointer     : ElementReferenceType;
    i                  : integer;
    queue              : QueueType;
    r                  : Element;

    { DumpQueue—output an item from a queue }
    procedure DumpQueue(item : Element);
```

```
begin
    write(item:1,' ')
end; { of procedure DumpQueue }

begin { of procedure test }
    { Initialize:
      Create a new instance of a queue }
    queue := create;

    { Check whether created queue is empty }
    writeln('Queue should be empty:');
    if empty(queue) then
        writeln('Queue is empty.')
    else
        writeln('PANIC: queue somehow has elements in it!?');
    writeln;

    { Check whether size of queue is 0 }
    writeln('Queue should have a size of 0:');
    if size(queue) = 0 then
        writeln('Queue has a size of 0.')
    else
        writeln('PANIC: queue size is ',size(queue):1);
    writeln;

    { Check whether queue is not full }
    writeln('Queue should not be full:');
    if not full(queue) then
        writeln('Queue is not full.')
    else
        writeln('PANIC; queue is full!?');
    writeln;

    writeln('Now (possibly) overflow the queue!');
    writeln;
    for i := 1 to 9 do
    begin
        r := i;
        queue := enqueue(r,queue);
        if QueueConditionCode(queue) = QueueOverFlow then
            writeln('Queue is full')
        else
            writeln('Queue is not full');
        write('[');
        scan(queue,DumpQueue);
        writeln(']');
        writeln
    end;
    writeln;
```

```
writeln('Queue may have overflowed!!');
writeln;

{ Empty the queue }
writeln('Now empty the queue!');
writeln;
for i := 1 to 9 do
begin
    queue := dequeue(queue);
    write('[');
    scan(queue,DumpQueue);
    writeln(']');
    writeln
end;

{ Add some elements to the queue }
writeln('Now we put some elements into the queue . . . ');
for i := 1 to 4 do
begin
    r := i;
    queue := enqueue(r,queue);
    write('[');
    scan(queue,DumpQueue);
    writeln(']');
    writeln
end;

{ Remove the elements from the queue }
writeln('And now we remove those elements . . . ');
for i := 1 to 4 do
begin
    queue := dequeue(queue);
    write('[');
    scan(queue,DumpQueue);
    writeln(']');
    writeln
end;

{ Add the elements back into the queue }
writeln('Now we put elements back in the queue . . . ');
for i := 1 to 4 do
begin
    r := i;
    queue := enqueue(r,queue);
    write('[');
    scan(queue,DumpQueue);
    writeln(']');
    writeln
end;
```

```
{ Remove the elements once more }
writeln('And then remove them again!');
for i := 1 to 4 do
begin
    queue := dequeue(queue);
    write('[');
    scan(queue,DumpQueue);
    writeln(']');
    writeln
end;

{ Put the elements back again }
writeln('Put elements back');
for i := 1 to 4 do
begin
    r := i;
    queue := enqueue(r,queue);
    write('[');
    scan(queue,DumpQueue);
    writeln(']');
    writeln
end;

{ Test whether queue is empty }
writeln('Queue should not be empty:');
if not empty(queue) then
    writeln('Queue is not empty.')
else
    writeln('PANIC: queue is still empty!?');
writeln;

{ Test size of queue }
writeln('Queue should have a size of 4:');
if size(queue) = 4 then
    writeln('Queue has a size of 4.')
else
    writeln('PANIC: queue size is ',size(queue):1);
writeln;

{ Test whether queue is full }
writeln('Queue may be full:');
if not full(queue) then
    writeln('Queue is not full.')
else
    writeln('Queue is full.');
writeln;

{ Test first element of queue }
writeln('The first element of the queue should be:');
```

```
writeln('1.0 + e00');
writeln;
writeln('The first element of the queue actually is:');
ElementPointer := first(queue);
writeln(ElementPointer^:1);
writeln;
writeln('The contents of the queue should look like:');
writeln('[1.0 + e00 2.0 + e00 3.0 + e00 4.0 + e00 ]');
writeln;

writeln('The contents of the queue actually look like:');
write('[');
scan(queue,DumpQueue);
writeln(']');
writeln;

{ Empty the queue }
writeln('Now remove every element from the queue . . . ');
for i := 1 to 4 do
begin
    queue := dequeue(queue);
    write('[');
    scan(queue,DumpQueue);
    writeln(']');
    writeln
end;

{ Test whether queue is empty }
writeln('Queue should be empty:');
if empty(queue) then
    writeln('Queue is empty.')
else
    writeln('PANIC: queue somehow has elements in it!?');
writeln;

{ Test whether queue size is 0 }
writeln('Queue should have a size of 0:');
if size(queue) = 0 then
    writeln('Queue has a size of 0.')
else
    writeln('PANIC: queue size is ',size(queue));
writeln;

{ Test whether queue is full }
writeln('Queue should not be full:');
if not full(queue) then
    writeln('Queue is not full.')
```

else
     writeln('PANIC: queue is full!?');
writeln;

{ See what happens if we remove a nonexistent element from queue }
writeln('Trying to remove one element from an empty queue should');
writeln('cause an error:');
queue := dequeue(queue);
if QueueConditionCode(queue) = QueueUnderFlow **then**
     writeln('Error: Tried to dequeue a nonexistent element.')
else
     writeln('PANIC: queue should have been empty!?');
writeln
end; { of procedure test }

Exercises for Chapter 4

1.   Change the module that implements a queue as a one-way linked list to one that implements the queue as a doubly linked list. Note: The interface to the module does *not* change.

2.   Give a complete specification and implementation of a module that searches a linked list for a particular item. Your specification should be independent of the fact that the list could be a singly or doubly linked list.

3.   A *deque* (or double-ended queue) is a linear list in which insertions and deletions can occur at either end of the list. Alter the queue specification to accommodate this added feature. Then implement your specification.

4.   Even though an array is a Pascal data type, it can also be viewed as an abstract data type with operations store and retrieve. Describe the syntactic and semantic specifications of the abstract data type called array.

5.   Add the specifications of a new queue operation called ''cuts'' which places an element E into queue Q at position i, rather than at the end of the line.

6.   Implement the operation ''cuts'' using the linked list implementation of a queue.

CHAPTER 5

RECURSION

5.1
Introduction

This chapter deals with an important method that is used in the solution of many problems: recursion. *Recursion* is a problem-solving technique that defines a problem in terms of itself. A recursive solution to that problem, then, repeatedly divides the problem into a combination of one instance of the problem and a smaller subproblem until we reach a directly solvable (sub)problem. Once we obtain the subproblem's solution, we feed this solution back into the next larger subproblem, thus obtaining the solution to that problem, continuing on until we ultimately solve the original problem.

This approach to problem solving might seem strange at first, but careful study of different recursive algorithms will help show you its usefulness, power, and simplicity. Often this topic is mentioned in a first course in computer science, but the typical student gains only a vague understanding of recursion. The objective of this chapter is to provide a variety of examples of recursive functions and procedures as well as explanations that should make the reader much more comfortable in his or her ability to write and/or understand recursion. We have included mathematical examples, a formatted printing example, and examples using linked lists, although recursion may be (and often is) used to solve many other types of problems. We start by reconsidering the factorial example that we covered in a previous chapter.

5.2
Examples of Recursion

5.2.1   Example 1: Factorial
Most people have seen a definition for *n* factorial (denoted *n*!) before. Consider the following (incorrect) definition:

$$n! = n * (n - 1)!$$

This says that in order to obtain the value for $n!$ we take the number n and multiply it by $(n - 1)!$. To obtain the value for $(n - 1)!$, we use the above definition, substituting $n - 1$ for n; that is,

$$(n - 1)! = (n - 1) * (n - 2)!$$

Let's say we wanted to evaluate 2!. Our definition would lead to the following result:

$$
\begin{aligned}
2! &= 2 * (2 - 1)! \\
&= 2 * 1! \\
&= 2 * 1 * (1 - 1)! \\
&= 2 * 1 * 0! \\
&= 2 * 1 * 0 * (0 - 1)! \\
&= 2 * 1 * 0 * (-1)! \\
&\text{etc.}
\end{aligned}
$$

We can identify two major problems. The first, and most serious, is that there is no way to stop the recursion. The second problem is that under this definition of $n!$ we have generated a multiplicand of zero; thus, for $n > 0$, $n!$ will always evaluate to zero. This second problem is actually caused by the first problem, so if we find a solution to the first problem we will have solved the second one as well.

The first problem is common to all recursive algorithms, namely, there must be a mechanism to stop the recursion from continuing forever. To create such a mechanism, we must divide a recursive solution definition into two cases: a *base case* and a *general case*. The base case is where the recursion stops. The general case is the "recursive" part of the solution definition. In our example, the base case is defined as

$$0! = 1$$

Once the base case is defined, the general case is handled as follows:

$$n! = n * (n - 1)!$$

It is only when both cases have been defined that we should consider coding the recursive function.

To summarize, our definition of $n!$ thus far is

$$
\begin{aligned}
0! &= 1 && \text{(base case)} \\
n! &= n * (n - 1)! && \text{(general case)}
\end{aligned}
$$

However, there is still one more stipulation or condition that we must enforce before this definition is precise. Can you figure it out?

According to our definition, what would $(-1)!$ be?

$$-1! = -1 * (-2)!$$
$$= -1 * (-2) * (-3)!$$
etc.

Once again, we have fallen prey to an infinite recursion. The simplest fix here is to define factorials only on the whole numbers, that is, $0, 1, 2, 3, \ldots$. This can easily be done by augmenting the general case with the condition that $n > 0$. Now we have a precise, recursive definition of $n!$, namely,

$$0! = 1$$
$$n! = n * (n - 1)! \qquad n > 0$$

We are now ready for the implementation of $n!$. First, we define the type WholeNumbers to be

type
    WholeNumbers   = 0 . . maxint;

Using this type definition we can define the recursive function *nfactorial* as follows:

function nfactorial(n : WholeNumbers) : NaturalNumbers;
begin
    if n = 0
    { A } **then** nfactorial := 1
    { B } **else** nfactorial := n * nfactorial(n-1)
end; { of function nfactorial }

Notice that the result of nfactorial will always be in the range from 1 to infinity and, hence, nfactorial's value is of type NaturalNumbers, which we leave to the reader to define properly. Notice also that the **if** statement does not need to handle the case for $n < 0$ because we have defined the input parameter, n, to be of type WholeNumbers. It is instructive to trace the execution of the recursive function calls for this relatively straightforward example; for this purpose we have labeled the **then** and **else** parts of the **if** statement with an (A) and (B), respectively.

We refer to the first call to the nfactorial function as being at level 1. The next (recursive) call will be at level 2, the following recursive call will be at level 3, and so on. Therefore to evaluate nfactorial(3) we would proceed as follows:

    Level 1: nfactorial(3)
                    nfactorial := 3 * nfactorial(2)   from (B)
    Level 2: nfactorial(2)
                    nfactorial := 2 * nfactorial(1)   from (B)

Level 3: nfactorial(1)

nfactorial : = 1 ∗ nfactorial(0)   from (B)

Level 4: nfactorial(0)

nfactorial : = 1   from (A)

Once we have reached Level 4 (in this case) we have reached our base case and can finally evaluate nfactorial without resorting to another recursive call. At this point we start to "unwind" the recursion or, in other words, define values for the previously generated problems. We do this by evaluating nfactorial in reverse order as in the following:

Level 4: nfactorial(0) = 1 obtained from nfactorial : = 1
Level 3: nfactorial(1) = 1 obtained from nfactorial : = 1 ∗ nfactorial(0)
Level 2: nfactorial(2) = 2 obtained from nfactorial : = 2 ∗ nfactorial(1)
Level 1: nfactorial(1) = 6 obtained from nfactorial : = 3 ∗ nfactorial(2)

5.2.2 Example 2: Sum of the First n Natural Numbers

A different mathematical example might be helpful at this point. Consider how one could add the first n natural numbers:

$$\sum_{i=1}^{n} i = 1 + 2 + 3 + \ldots + n, \qquad n > 0$$

Another way to express this sum is by adding n to the sum of all terms up to and including $n - 1$ as in

$$\sum_{i=1}^{n} i = n + \sum_{i=1}^{n-1} i, \qquad n > 0$$

We have defined the sum of the first n natural numbers in terms of n and the sum of the first $n - 1$ natural numbers. Do you see that this has led to a recursive formulation of the problem? What would the base case be? In this example, the base case is the sum of the first n natural numbers when $n = 1$. Clearly, that sum is $1 (\sum_{i=1}^{1} i = 1)$. Hence, the complete specification for our problem is

$$\sum_{i=1}^{n} i = \begin{matrix} 1 & \text{if} & n = 1 \\ n + \sum_{i=1}^{n-1} i, & & n > 1 \end{matrix}$$

Before reading our Pascal function definition, try writing one on your own.

function SumOfFirstnNaturalNumbers(n : NaturalNumbers) : NaturalNumbers;
begin
    if n = 1
    then SumOfFirstnNaturalNumbers := 1
      else SumOfFirstnNaturalNumbers := n + SumOfFirstnNaturalNumbers(n-1)
end; { of function SumOfFirstnNaturalNumbers }

Before leaving this example we must point out that, although this problem has led to a simple recursive formulation, one should never really use it! The reason is that the $\sum_{i=1}^{n} i$ has a closed-form solution; in particular,

$$\sum_{i=1}^{n} i = \frac{n(n+1)}{2}$$

This formula (called Gauss's formula) arises in many different applications, and if you have not already done so, it is well worth your effort to learn it.

5.2.3 Example 3: Printing Whole Numbers

Next we consider the development of a recursive method for printing whole numbers digit by digit. Given a whole number between 0 and 9, contained in the variable number, we can obviously print it using

write(number:1)

If we have a number of two or more digits, how can we isolate the individual digits? For example if the number is 27, then to obtain the leading digit we can write

number **div** 10 (which yields 2)

and can write

number **mod** 10 (which yields 7)

So we are able to isolate the digits in a number with only two digits. Does this method work for a three-digit number? Not directly, as the following example illustrates:

number := 961
number **div** 10 = 96
number **mod** 10 = 1

Notice that using the first statement we can convert a three-digit number into one that has two digits. But we have already shown how we can isolate the digits in a two-digit number. This should instantly say to you that there is a recursive way to solve this problem!

What are the base and general cases for this problem? For the base case we can use our method for printing a number between 0 and 9, that is,

write(number:1)

If we call our recursive procedure (notice that we are using a procedure instead of a function) WriteWholeNumber, then the general case is a recursive call like

WriteWholeNumber(number **div** 10)

This call is made whenever the number has more than one digit. Putting our base and general cases together, our recursive procedure might look like the following:

```
procedure WriteWholeNumber(number : WholeNumber);
begin
    if number < 10
    {A} then write(WholeNumber:1)
    {B} else WriteWholeNumber(number div 10)
end; { of procedure WriteWholeNumber }
```

Let's try this procedure definition on three examples. First, what happens when this call is made

WriteWholeNumber(5)

Clearly, part (A) of the WriteWholeNumber procedure is executed and the digit "5" is printed. No recursive call is necessary here. But when we make the call

WriteWholeNumber(25)

we obtain

```
Level 1: WriteWholeNumber(25)   initial call
Level 2: WriteWholeNumber(2)    from (B)
         write(2:1) = 2         from (A)
```

Accordingly, the only character printed is the 2![1] Obviously, there is something wrong; rather than try to fix it quickly, it is instructive to see what happens when the following call is made:

WriteWholeNumber(625)

```
Level 1: WriteWholeNumber(625)  initial call
Level 2: WriteWholeNumber(62)   from (B)
```

[1] This is not 2 factorial!

FIGURE 5.1   Trace of WriteWholeNumber.

Level 1	Level 2	Level 3	Level 4

```
                          ⎧ argument:              ⎧ argument:              ⎧ argument:
                          │   number = 625         │   number = 62          │   number = 6
WriteWholeNumber(625) →   ⎨ WriteWholeNumber(62) → ⎨ WriteWholeNumber(6) →  ⎨ write(6:1)
       D ←                │ write(5:1) ←           │ write(2:1) ←           │    A
                          ⎩     C                  ⎩     B                  ⎩
```

Statement label:	A	B	C	D
Action	output 6	output 2	output 5	execute statement after WriteWholeNumber(625)

Level 3: WriteWholeNumber(6)   from (B)
                  write(6:1) = 6   from (A)

Once again only one digit is printed, and as before it is the leading digit of the number. Clearly, we have forgotten to process the remaining digits of the number. Can you see how to do this? Hint: Consider adding the statement

write((number **mod** 10):1)

somewhere in the code before reading on. The correct definition for the procedure follows:

```
procedure WriteWholeNumber(number : WholeNumbers);
begin
    if number < 10 then
        write(number:1)
    else
    begin
        WriteWholeNumber(number div 10);
        write((number mod 10):1)
    end
end; { of procedure WriteWholeNumber }
```

Try to step through this procedure using the following values: 5, 25, 625, and 1625. Figure 5.1 shows our trace of the call to WriteWholeNumber with an argument of 625. What would happen if the second write statement were converted into another recursive call as in

WriteWholeNumber(number **mod** 10)?

5.2.4   Example 4: The Number of Nodes in a One-Way Linked List
The remaining examples show how recursion can be used to process one-way linked lists; in Chapters 2 and 3 we concentrated on iterative processing of these linked-list

structures. The remaining examples illustrate the general pattern common to recursive algorithms that deal with linked lists. This pattern is

1. Process the current node.
2. Recursively process the remaining nodes.

In the previous chapter we wrote a function to count the number of nodes in a circular list. The exercises at the end of that chapter then asked you to make that function work when its input was either a one-way linked list or a circular list. Our next example shows how to determine the number of nodes in a one-way linked list recursively (a list that is terminated by a **nil** pointer).

The idea behind the recursive function, NumberOfNodes, is that the number of nodes in a one-way linked list can be computed by

$$1 + \text{NumberOfNodes(list with one less element)}$$

That is, visit a node (by this we mean add one to a running count) and then recursively process the remaining nodes in the linked list. The base case becomes what should be added to the running count when we fall off the end of the list (we add 0, obviously). Therefore, the recursive function is

```
function NumberOfNodes(list : NodePointer) : WholeNumbers;
begin
    if list = nil
    then NumberOfNodes := 0
    else NumberOfNodes := 1 + NumberOfNodes(list^.next)
end; { of function NumberOfNodes }
```

Notice how simple this function is and that there is no need for a temporary variable to contain the count.[2] The simplicity of this algorithm is a characteristic of most recursive algorithms! Notice also how this algorithm follows the general two-step pattern of "process the current node," then "recursively process the remaining nodes" that we mentioned earlier.

5.2.5 Example 5: Outputting the Data Fields of a One-Way Linked List

Let us assume that the data fields of the nodes in our linked list contain a single character. Think how you could write a recursive procedure to output these data fields, one character per line. The idea to follow is to output the character in the data field of the current node and then output the characters in the remaining nodes of the linked list. The base case is to not output anything once the end of the list is encountered. The procedure follows:

---

[2] We have used this function under another name, *size,* in the previous chapter on abstract data types.

```
procedure OutputNodesOfLinkedList(list : NodePointer);
begin
    if list <> nil then
    begin
        writeln(list^.data:1);
        OutputNodesOfLinkedList(list^.next)
    end
end; { of function OutputNodesOfLinkedList }
```

Notice once again how compact the recursive solution is and the fact that a **while** loop has been replaced, in effect, by the recursion. What would happen if the writeln statement and the call to OutputNodesOfLinkedList were interchanged in the previous example?

5.2.6   Example 6: Making a Copy of a One-Way Linked List

Our problem is this: given a linked list pointed to by List1, we want to make a copy of this list and return a pointer in List2 to the copy. The obvious base case is that a copy of an empty list is an empty list. The general case is to make a copy of the current node and then recursively copy the remaining nodes of the list. With these insights, it should not be difficult to understand the following procedure:

```
procedure CopyLinkedList(List1 : NodePointer; var List2 : NodePointer);
begin
    if List1 = nil then List2 := nil
    else
    begin
        { Create new node to be entered into List2 }
        new(List2);

        { Copy data field from List1 node }
        List2^.data := List1^.data;

        { Copy remaining nodes of List1 }
        CopyLinkedList(List1^.next,List2^.next)
    end
end; { of procedure CopyLinkedList }
```

We will trace the operation of this procedure on the following linked list:

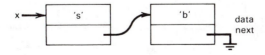

The procedure call might look like

CopyLinkedList(x,y)

The picture we will ultimately create looks like

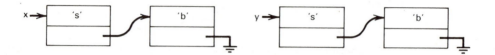

Since List1 (x) is not empty, we execute the **else** part of the **if** statement that says

new(List2)

which is actually equivalent to executing

new(y)

because the second parameter to the procedure is a reference parameter. The picture becomes

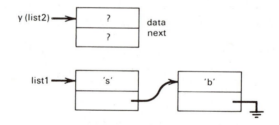

The next line says to copy the data field of the node pointed to by List1 (x) into this newly created node; hence the picture changes to

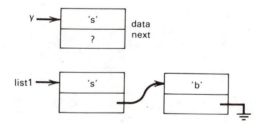

Finally, the recursive call to CopyLinkedList is executed; it would read as

CopyLinkedList(List1^.next,y^.next)

which is equivalent to having this picture after the call:

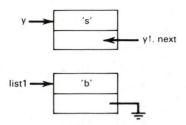

There are two points to notice here. The first is that y^.next evaluates to the next field in the newly created node. Therefore, when we enter the body of the procedure and execute new(List2) the pointer returned by new will be stored in the aforementioned next field. Second, the List1 pointer has changed to point to the only remaining node of that list.

Now, since List1 is still not empty, we execute the call to new with the resulting picture being

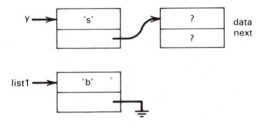

Copying the data is next and changes the picture to

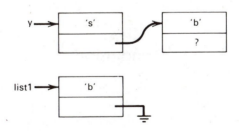

followed by the recursive call

CopyLinkedList(List1^.next,List2^.next)

List2^.next is the field with the ? in it above. List1^.next is **nil**. So the base case of the recursion applies. Hence, the field with the ? is replaced by **nil** and the final picture becomes the desired one:

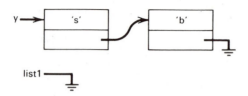

Please make sure that you can trace through this example on your own and then try to write it from scratch without looking at the text.

5.2.7 Example 7: Searching a Linked List

Our final example is as follows: given a pointer to a one-way linked list and an item to search for, write a function that returns true if the item is in the list and false otherwise. The base case for the recursion says that if we encounter the end of the list, then the item is not in the list. The general case says to check whether or not the item is in the current node; if it is return true, and otherwise recursively process the remaining elements in the linked list. With these ideas, the following recursive function should be obvious:

```
function SearchLinkedList(list : NodePointer; item : char) : boolean;
begin
    if list = nil then SearchLinkedList := false
    else
    begin
        if listˆ.data = item
        then SearchLinkedList := true
        else SearchLinkedList := SearchLinkedList(listˆ.next)
    end
end; { of function SearchLinkedList }
```

5.3
Conclusion

We hope that the previous seven examples have helped you to become more comfortable with recursive functions and procedures. The main points to remember in the construction of any recursive function or procedure are to specify the base case carefully and then specify the general case. The base case is what stops the recursion, and the general case is what subdivides a problem into a single instance of the problem (like processing one node in a list) and a smaller problem (like processing the remaining nodes in the list). The last four examples in the previous section show that the base case for a one-way linked list always handles the end-of-list condition (i.e., **nil**).

Although the examples we have presented could be done fairly easily without using recursion, there are many common problems for which a recursive solution is the only understandable or practical method for solving the problem. We have presented some of the easier examples of recursion to familiarize you with the technique itself. You will see some further examples of recursion in the next chapter and in the chapter on sorting and searching. Because of the power and elegance of recursive algorithms, you should practice developing recursive algorithms. Be forewarned, however, that a recursive solution to a problem may not always be the most efficient solution, as was illustrated in the second example.

Exercises for Chapter 5

*1. Write a recursive procedure that prints out the data fields of a one-way linked list in reverse order.

2. A palindrome is a string of characters that is the same whether read from left to right or from right to left. The following are examples of palindromes: radar, madam, xyaayx. Write a recursive procedure that takes a pointer to a one-way linked list of characters and prints out a palindrome containing twice as many characters as in the original string. For example,

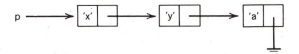

Output: xyaayx

3. A binomial coefficient is defined as follows:

$$\binom{n}{m} = \frac{n!}{(n - m)!m!}$$

It can also be recursively defined by

$$\binom{n}{1} = n$$

$$\binom{n}{n} = 1$$

$$\binom{n}{m} = \binom{n-1}{m-1} + \binom{n-1}{m} \qquad \text{for } n > m > 1$$

Write a recursive function that computes binomial coefficients using their recursive definition. Compare the results of your implementation with the results obtained by implementing binomial coefficients straight from the definition. (Use small values for m and n.)

*4. Ackermann's function $A(m,n)$ is defined as follows:

$$A(m,n) = \begin{cases} n + 1, & \text{if } m = 0 \\ A(m - 1,1), & \text{if } n = 0 \\ A(m - 1, A(m,n - 1)), & \text{otherwise} \end{cases}$$

Write a recursive Pascal function to compute this function. What is the value of $A(3,2)$?

5. Write a recursive function that counts the number of times a particular key appears in a one-way list.

6. In **procedure** WriteWholeNumber described at the end of Section 5.2.3 what would happen if the second write statement were converted into another recursive call as in WriteWholeNumber (number **mod** 10)?

7. In **procedure** OutputNodesOfLinkedList described in Section 5.2.5 what would happen if the writeln statement and the call to OutputNodesOfLinkedList were interchanged?

CHAPTER 6

TREES

6.1
Introduction

In this chapter we will study the hierarchical data structure called a *tree*. Trees are familiar from everyday life. Everybody has a family tree.

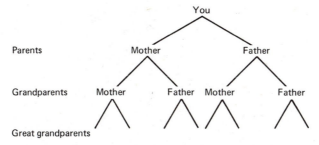

Sporting competitions are often displayed in a treelike manner.

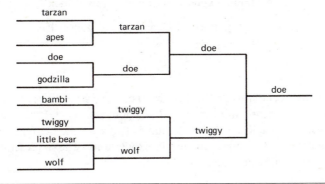

We are also familiar with parse trees.

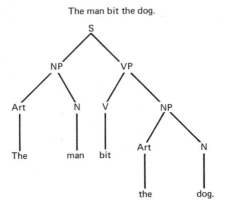

The man bit the dog.

Trees have many computer-related applications. For example, we can draw a parse tree for the expression $a * b + c$. (*Note:* even though the data we will be storing in the nodes of a tree will be of type char, to avoid cluttering the figures we will not surround the characters with single quotes.)

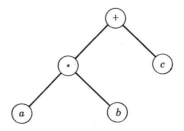

When a compiler parses a program to determine if it is syntactically correct, it can generate a parse tree. A simple expression grammar might look like

expr	: : =	term { (``+'' | ``−'') term }
term	: : =	factor { ``*'' factor }
factor	: : =	letter | ``('' expr ``)''
letter	: : =	``a'' | ``b'' | ``c''

where : : = means "is defined as," { } means 0 or more repetitions of the information enclosed inside the braces, and | means alternation, that is, selection of one of the alternatives. Symbols enclosed in double quotes ('') are called terminal symbols and these symbols are the only ones allowed in expressions. The expression $a * b + c$ would produce the following parse tree.

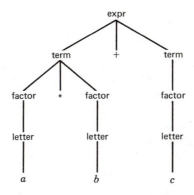

6.2
Definition

A tree has a precise mathematical definition that you are urged to study. As we describe some properties of trees, keep the following definition in mind:

> *Definition.* A tree T is a finite set of one or more nodes such that there is a specially designated node $t \in T$ (called the *root* of T) and $T - \{t\}$ is partitioned into disjoint subsets $T_1, T_2, \ldots, T_n$, each of which is itself a tree (called a *subtree* of the root t).

This definition implies that every node of a tree is a root of some subtree contained in the whole tree. Let us look at this definition more carefully using the following tree.

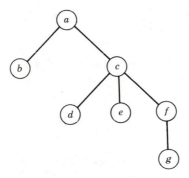

This tree is composed of seven nodes.

$$T = \{\, a, b, c, d, e, f, g \,\}$$

Its root is a. It has two subtrees.

$$T_1 = \{\, b \,\} \qquad T_2 = \{\, c, d, e, f, g \,\}$$

The number of subtrees of a node is called the node's *degree*. Hence node a is of degree 2. Nodes with no subtrees (b, d, e, g) are called *leaf* or *terminal nodes*. All others are *nonterminal nodes*. The nonterminal nodes are a, c, and f; they are often called *internal* or *branch nodes*.

In discussing trees we often use familial terms. For example, node a is the *parent* of nodes b and c, and nodes b and c are the *children* of node a.

Before we get mired in more terminology, we should consider how to implement a tree structure. For our example each node will have a char field to represent the node name ($a - g$) and from 0 to 3 pointer fields.

data	
ptr1	
ptr2	
ptr3	

This node structure is adequate for the present example, but not for:

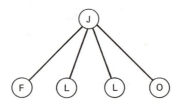

To avoid such representational problems, we will restrict our attention to a special type of structure called a *binary tree*.

6.3
Binary Trees

Binary trees are distinct from generalized trees in two important ways. Nodes in a binary tree have degrees less than or equal to 2 (i.e., have two or fewer children), and binary trees can be empty (contain no nodes at all). Consider how binary trees are defined.

> *Definition.* A *binary tree* is a finite set of nodes that is either empty or consists of a root and two disjoint binary trees called the *left* and *right* *subtrees*.

Here are some examples of binary trees:

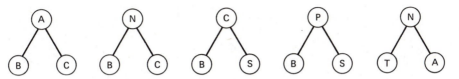

All these binary trees are identical except for their data fields. The following binary trees are *not* identical.

The binary tree on the left has an empty *right* subtree whereas the one on the right has an empty *left* subtree.

The definition of a binary tree is *recursive;* that is, it defines an object in terms of other objects of its class. As we will see, this recursive definition gives rise to many recursive algorithms dealing with these structures. It is important to observe that a binary tree is not a tree! Reread the definitions of a tree and a binary tree and notice that a tree must have at least one node whereas a binary tree can be empty.

We can use the following node structure to represent binary trees:

```
type
     nodepointer              = ↑ node;
     node                     =
         record
             data             : char;
             leftsubtree      : nodepointer;
             rightsubtree     : nodepointer
         end; { of record node }
var
     root                     : nodepointer;
```

Then the binary tree

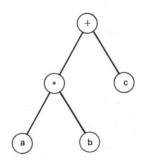

is represented by the following data structure:

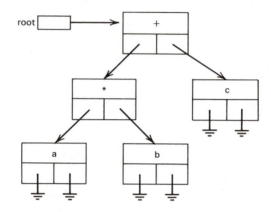

To determine the number of nodes in a tree, we will have to "walk through" the tree structure, counting the nodes as we go. This is known as *traversing* a tree, or *visiting* each node of the tree exactly once. (You should note that we have defined a similar operation on linked lists; in fact, our function NumberOfNodes "walked through" our linked list structure.)

There are a number of ways to visit each node. One method starts at the root and visits it; in our case we add one to a counter, keeping track of how many nodes we have visited so far. Next we have a choice: we can traverse either the nodes in the left subtree (*, *a*, *b*) or those in the right subtree (*c*). If we choose to traverse the left subtree first, we traverse it in the same way as the original tree. We visit the root (of the subtree) and then traverse all the nodes of the left subtree followed by all the nodes of the right subtree.

Let us see exactly what this means for our previous example.

1. Visit the root: ('+').
2. Traverse the left subtree: ('*' '*a*' '*b*').
3. Traverse the right subtree: ('*c*').

Steps 2 and 3 each involve traversing a subtree. We can visit each node of a subtree by reapplying all three steps:

1:	Visit the root ' + '.
2:	Traverse the left subtree.
2.1:	Visit the root '*'.
2.2:	Traverse the left subtree.
2.3:	Traverse the right subtree.
3:	Traverse the right subtree.
3.1:	Visit the root '*c*'.
3.2:	Traverse the left subtree.
3.3:	Traverse the right subtree.

When a subtree is empty (steps 3.2 and 3.3), we go on to the next step.

1:	Visit the root ' + '.
2:	Traverse the left subtree.
2.1:	Visit the root '∗'.
2.2:	Traverse the left subtree.
2.2.1:	Visit the root 'a'.
2.2.2:	Traverse the left subtree (empty).
2.2.3:	Traverse the right subtree (empty).
2.3:	Traverse the right subtree.
2.3.1:	Visit the root 'b'.
2.3.2:	Traverse the left subtree (empty).
2.3.3:	Traverse the right subtree (empty).
3:	Traverse the right subtree.
3.1:	Visit the root 'c'.
3.2:	Traverse the left subtree (empty).
3.3:	Traverse the right subtree (empty).

You may think that all of this will be difficult to program, but it is actually a trivial application of a recursive procedure.

```
procedure preorder(root : nodepointer; var count : integer);
begin
    if root <> nil then
    begin
        { visit the root }
        visit (root);
        count := count + 1;

        { traverse the left subtree }
        preorder(root ↑ .leftsubtree, count);

        { traverse the right subtree }
        preorder(root ↑ .rightsubtree, count)
    end
end; { of procedure preorder }
```

Take a few minutes to step through the actions of this procedure on the example tree. The base case handles what to do in case an empty binary tree is passed into the procedure; as you can see, the procedure simply returns without changing the value in count. The general case is to visit the root, add 1 to the count, traverse the nodes in the left subtree, followed by traversing the nodes in the right subtree. If you understand how the recursion is working, you will have no problem understanding how any other algorithm in this chapter works.

Often the following picture is useful in describing operations on binary trees:

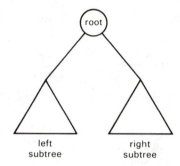

For example, the preorder traversal method can clearly be visualized using this picture (visit the root of the tree, traverse nodes in the left subtree, traverse nodes in the right subtree). There are a number of other ways to traverse a tree. As you might have guessed from the procedure name, the traversal scheme we have been describing is called *preorder traversal*. It walks through the tree by doing the following.

1. Visiting the root.
2. Traversing the left subtree.
3. Traversing the right subtree.

Other traversal methods can be arrived at by permuting the order of the preceding operations. Two permutations of the most interest result in *postorder traversal:*

1. Traverse the left subtree.
2. Traverse the right subtree.
3. Visit the root.

and *inorder traversal:*

1. Traverse the left subtree.
2. Visit the root.
3. Traverse the right subtree.

There is a natural correspondence between the preorder, postorder, and inorder traversals of a tree and the prefix, postfix, and infix forms of an expression. Using our previous tree and assuming that "visit the root" means to output the contents of the following data field:

Prefix expression for $a*b + c$: $+ *abc$ (operators precede operands)
Preorder traversal of tree: $+ *abc$

Postfix expression for $a*b + c$: $ab*c +$ (operators follow operands)
Postorder traversal of tree: $ab*c +$

Infix expression for $a*b + c$: $a*b + c$ (operators in between operands)
Inorder traversal of tree: $a*b + c$

For completeness we will write the postorder and inorder traversal procedures; we code the step "visit the root" as a call on procedure visit with a pointer to the root.

Notice in each case that left subtrees are traversed before right subtrees. In conjunction with this observation, the following pattern can be used as an aid in remembering the steps of the traversal methods:

Traversal Method	When Root Is Visited	
*Pre*order	*Before*	Traversing left and right subtrees
*In*order	*In between*	Traversing left and right subtrees
*Post*order	*After*	Traversing left and right subtrees

```
procedure postorder(root : nodepointer);
begin
    if root <> nil then
    begin
        { traverse the left subtree }
        postorder(root ↑ .leftsubtree);

        { traverse the right subtree }
        postorder(root ↑ .rightsubtree);

        { visit the root }
        visit(root)
    end
end; { of procedure postorder }

procedure inorder(root : nodepointer);
begin
    if root <> nil then
    begin
        { traverse the left subtree }
        inorder(root ↑ .leftsubtree);

        { visit the root }
        visit(root);

        { traverse the right subtree }
        inorder(root ↑ .rightsubtree)
    end
end; { of procedure inorder }
```

There is another convenient way to remember the order in which nodes are visited in each of the traversal methods. We start by "tracing out" the form of the tree as indicated.

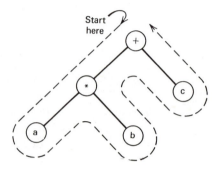

For a preorder traversal, we visit a node as we pass it on the left, tracing out the tree. Hence the nodes will be visited: $+*abc$.

For a postorder traversal we visit a node as we pass it on the right going up. Hence the nodes will be visited: $ab*c+$.

Finally, for an inorder traversal we visit a node as we pass underneath it. Hence the nodes will be visited: $a*b+c$.

Now consider the following problem. You are given pointers to two binary trees. Determine if they are equal, that is, if they have the same structure, and if the contents of the data field of corresponding nodes in the trees are the same. By this definition, these two trees are equal:

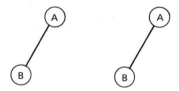

but these two trees are not:

Try to write a recursive algorithm to solve this problem. Remember the boundary condition. If you need help solving this problem, look at the exercises at the end of this chapter.

As another instructive exercise, consider the problem of making an exact copy of a binary tree. Given a pointer to the tree to be copied:

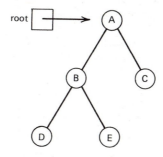

make an exact duplicate of it, letting root1 point to the copy.

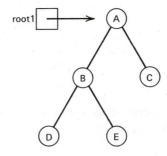

We will use a modified postorder traversal of the original tree; it works like this:

1. Copy the left subtree.
2. Copy the right subtree.
3. Allocate a new node.

```
procedure copy(root : nodepointer; var root1 : nodepointer);
var
        lefttree                : nodepointer;
        righttree               : nodepointer;
begin
        root1 := nil;
        if root <> nil then
        begin
            { copy left subtree-lefttree will point to left subtree of node being
              copied }
            copy(root↑.leftsubtree,lefttree);
```

{ copy right subtree-righttree will point to right subtree of node being
  copied }
copy(root ↑ .rightsubtree,righttree);

{ allocate a new node and set its fields }
new(root1);
root1 ↑ .leftsubtree := lefttree;
root1 ↑ .rightsubtree := righttree;
root1 ↑ .data := root ↑ .data
end
end; { of procedure copy }

We strongly urge you to trace through this procedure with the following tree:

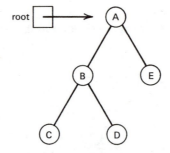

to see exactly how the copy operation accomplishes its task. If you are having problems with this, go back and study Example 6 of Chapter 5 on making a copy of a one-
way linked list.

6.4
Threaded Binary Trees

With the representation we have chosen for binary trees there are many **nil** pointers. If
there are n nodes in a tree, there will be $2n$ link fields; $n + 1$ of these will contain **nil**
pointers, which can be used to point to other nodes in the tree. These new pointers are
called *threads*. In particular we will let the leftsubtree field point to the predecessor of
the current node in an inorder traversal and the rightsubtree field point to the successor
of the current node in an inorder traversal. Using this scheme, the tree

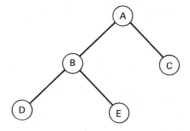

would have the following representation:

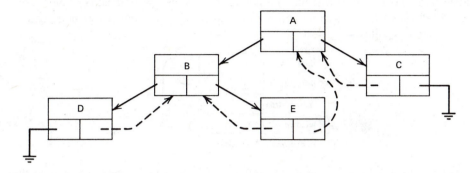

where we have represented the threads by dashed links. Unfortunately, this suffers from one simple flaw: the program cannot determine when a link field contains a pointer or a thread. To distinguish these two cases, we will add two "bit fields" (i.e., boolean) to resolve the problem. The node structure will look like the following:

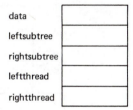

where

    leftthread = true if leftsubtree field contains a thread, false otherwise

and

    rightthread = true if rightsubtree field contains a thread, false otherwise

To save space and ensure that the leftthread and rightthread fields do not occupy one word apiece, we will use a **packed record** to implement the node structure.

type
```
    node                                =
        packed record
             data                        : char;
             leftsubtree                 : nodepointer;
             rightsubtree                : nodepointer;
             leftthread                  : boolean;
             rightthread                 : boolean
        end; { of packed record node }
```

If you look back at the internal representation of the binary tree, you will see that there are still two nodes containing **nil** pointers. As before, we will add one more node (the head node) to the tree structure. An empty tree will contain this node and be represented as follows:

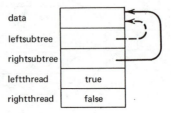

The leftsubtree field of the head node will point to the root of a nonempty tree, as this picture suggests.

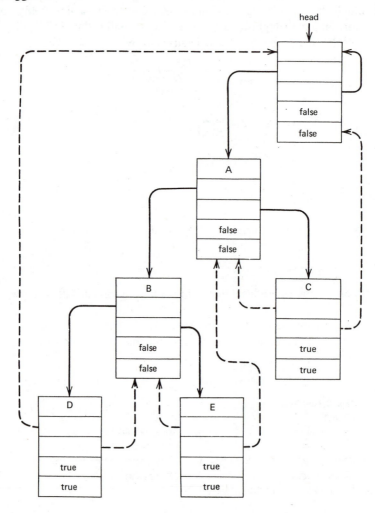

The exercises will explore a nonrecursive method for traversing a threaded binary tree in inorder.

6.5
Binary Tree Representation of Trees

We have covered binary trees in such depth because every tree can be represented as a binary tree. As an example, consider this tree:

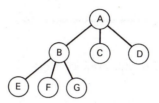

Recall that a node in a binary tree has only two link fields: one to point to the leftsubtree of that node and the other to point to the rightsubtree of that node. In this tree consider removing all but the leftmost pointer of a node, as shown. Now we use the "free" rightsubtree pointers to link nodes on the same "line."

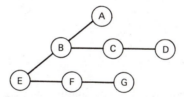

This may not look like a binary tree, but it is. (Try tilting the figure 45 degrees.)

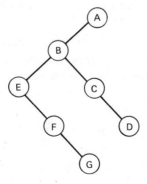

This simple transformation scheme is significant because it circumvents the problem of not knowing how many link fields to allocate in a node used in a tree. Using this technique, we can always convert any arbitrary tree to a binary tree.

6.6
Conclusion

Trees have many applications in computer science. In this chapter we were interested only in presenting a basic overview of this important topic. In later courses you will encounter many of the interesting properties of trees.

Exercises for Chapter 6

*1. What are the terminal and nonterminal nodes in this binary tree?

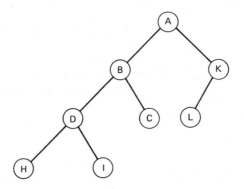

2. Design and implement a method of inputting and constructing a binary tree.

3. In the tree in Exercise 1, node A is at *level* 1; nodes B and K are at level 2; nodes D, C, and L are at level 3; and nodes H and I are at level 4. Write a Pascal procedure to output the nodes of a binary tree by increasing level number. Try to write it recursively.

*4. Write a procedure that counts the number of leaf nodes in a binary tree.

*5. Two binary trees are "equal" if they have the same structure and if the contents of the data field of corresponding nodes in the tree are the same. Write a function of two arguments that traverses each binary tree in preorder. The function returns true if the trees are equal and false otherwise.

*6. Given a threaded binary tree, write a procedure to find the inorder successor of any node in the tree.

*7. Using your procedure from Exercise 6, write a nonrecursive algorithm to traverse a threaded binary tree in inorder.

CHAPTER 7

SORTING AND
SEARCHING
ALGORITHMS

7.1
Introduction

This chapter describes two of the most frequently used operations in all of computer programming: sorting and searching. To appreciate the importance of these two operations, consider searching for the phone number of John Doe in the New York City telephone directory if it were not sorted in alphabetical order! It has been estimated that the world's computers spend more than half their time searching or sorting data! It is for this reason that many different algorithms have been developed for each of these two operations. Much effort has also been expended in determining the properties of these algorithms, such as how time- and space-efficient they are. (We will have more to say about this topic in Chapter 17.) For sorting algorithms, the "best choice" algorithm depends both on the amount of data to be sorted and on the type of data. For searching algorithms, the "best choice" algorithm for a particular problem also depends on several factors, such as whether or not the data are already sorted, the amount of data, and whether the data are stored in a random-access memory. The purpose of this chapter is not to enumerate all of the different sorting and searching techniques in use today, but instead to provide a unified and coherent description of a few of the most popular methods.

7.2
Sorting

Most textbooks that have described sorting algorithms have used virtually the same organization. They start with what seems to be the simplest method for accomplishing the task and then proceed to develop the more "difficult" algorithms. We have chosen to adopt a newer method of presentation of sorting algorithms that is based on the work reported in an article by Susan Merritt entitled "An Inverted Taxonomy of Sorting Algorithms" (*Communications of the ACM,* Vol. 28, No. 1, 1985, pp. 96–99). Her work leads to a "top-down" approach to the problem of sorting, rather than the more traditional "bottom-up" approach.

Any sorting algorithm can be cast into the following general mold. The elements to be sorted form a sequence. Throughout our discussion of sorting algorithms we assume that the data to be sorted are integers. It is a relatively straightforward task to change these algorithms to sort other types of data, for example, the names in a phone book. Therefore, we will be working with a *sequence of integers.* For the purposes of illustrating the operation of the algorithms, we will consider a specific sequence, denoted by the letter S, whose elements are

$$S = \{7,29,2,11,3,170,1,55,349,41\}$$

If we wish to sort such a sequence S, one general approach that we can take is to *split* S into two *nonoverlapping* subsequences and then sort those two subsequences individually. We will denote the two subsequences by the letters T and U. (At this point you should be thinking that we are describing the sorting process in terms of itself and therefore should expect to see recursive algorithms for accomplishing the task.) After the subsequences T and U have been sorted into T' and U' we can *join* the results in a way that produces the final sorted sequence, which we will denote by SS (for sorted sequence). The overall sorting process is graphically depicted in Figure 7.1.

Merritt's taxonomy of sorting algorithms divides sorting algorithms into two general categories that she refers to as easysplit/hardjoin and hardsplit/easyjoin. As the names imply, a sorting algorithm is classified according to how difficult the *splitting* and *joining* operations are for that particular algorithm. Figure 7.2 illustrates her hierarchy of sorting algorithms. We will describe most of these algorithms and their implementation in this chapter, leaving BubbleSort to be covered in the exercises at the end of the chapter.

Before describing the sorting algorithms, we should mention that the general technique we have described, which takes a problem and divides it into smaller, similar subproblems, is called the *divide and conquer* technique. Divide and conquer algorithms use the solutions to the subproblems to create the solution to the larger problem.

The general pattern for a divide and conquer sorting algorithm looks like

```
Sort(sequence, newsequence)
      if |sequence| > 1 then      { number of elements in the sequence is >1 }
      begin
          Split sequence into T and U
          Sort(T,T')
          Sort(U,U')
          Join(T',U')
      end
```

FIGURE 7.1 High-Level View of Sorting Process (cf. *CACM* 28, p. 97).

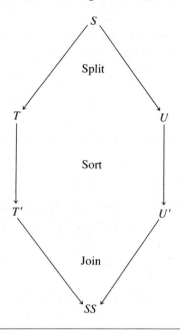

FIGURE 7.2 Taxonomy of Sorting Algorithms (cf. *CACM* 28, p. 98).

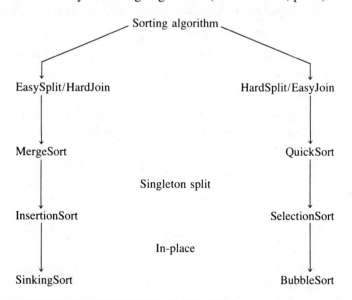

Notice the recursive calls to Sort. The MergeSort and QuickSort algorithms that we will describe next are good examples of this technique. In each of the two algorithms we divide the sequence of elements to be sorted into two subsequences at each step of the algorithm. We then reapply the divide and conquer algorithm to each of these subsequences. Eventually, we will reach sequences with either no elements or only one element; these sequences are obviously easy to sort.

7.2.1 MergeSort

The high-level description of the MergeSort algorithm is exactly the same as the general sorting process shown in Figure 7.1, which was to

1. Split the data into two sequences that are approximately equal in length.
2. Separately sort each of these two sequences.
3. Join these two sorted sequences to produce the final sorted sequence.

Let's see how MergeSort works on our sequence S. In step 1, S splits into

$$T = \{7,29,2,11,3\} \quad \text{and} \quad U = \{170,1,55,349,41\}$$

After step 2, subsequences T and U have been sorted into

$$T' = \{2,3,7,11,29\} \quad \text{and} \quad U' = \{1,41,55,170,349\}$$

Step 3 then joins these sequences T' and U' to obtain the sorted sequence SS. To do this we repeat the following two steps until all the elements in one of T' and U' are exhausted:

a. Select the smaller of the first elements of T' and U' and add it to the sequence SS.
b. Remove the selected element from the sequence to which it belonged (either T' or U').

When we reach the point where all elements of either T' or U' are completely exhausted, we can then simply copy the remaining elements of the other sequence directly into SS.

According to this scheme the sorted sequence SS would be constructed by selecting the element 1 from U', then elements 2, 3, 7, 11, and 29 from T', and finally 41, 55, 170, and 349 are copied from U' into SS. The result is the sorted sequence

$$SS = \{1,2,3,7,11,29,41,55,170,349\}$$

7.2.1.1 MergeSort Implementation   Now let's look at how we might implement MergeSort. The splitting done in step 1 is actually quite simple. If the numbers to be sorted were in an array that was defined as

```
const
    SizeOfArrayToBeSorted        = 100;
type
    IndexRange                   = 1 . . SizeOfArrayToBeSorted;
    ArrayToBeSorted              = array [IndexRange] of integer;
var
    NumbersToSort                : ArrayToBeSorted;
```

Then given a subrange of the elements in the array from FirstElementPtr to LastElementPtr, the midpoint of this range could be computed using

$$\text{MiddleElementPtr} := (\text{FirstElementPtr} + \text{LastElementPtr}) \ \textbf{div} \ 2$$

Therefore, we have partitioned the array to be sorted into subarrays with indices ranging from FirstElementPtr to MiddleElementPtr and MiddleElementPtr + 1 to LastElementPtr.

Step 2 requires that we separately sort the elements in the subdivided array: NumbersToSort[FirstElementPtr . . MiddleElementPtr] and NumbersToSort[MiddleElementPtr + 1 . . LastElementPtr]. We could accomplish this by using any sorting algorithm that we know. Rather than developing a different algorithm, we are instead going to use the algorithm we are currently developing recursively! This means that we will be using step 1 again (and again) to subdivide portions of an array into smaller and smaller portions. We will eventually come to the point at which the number of elements in a portion is just one element. But a sequence with one element is a trivial example of a sorted sequence.

Step 3 then merges the elements in the two sorted sequences obtained in step 2. We described this step earlier using our sequence S.

Figure 7.3 illustrates one coding of the complete MergeSort algorithm. From this code it should be clear why MergeSort is classified as an easysplit/hardjoin algorithm. Figure 7.4a shows how the original sequence S is partitioned into subsequences that are eventually sorted by MergeSort. Figure 7.4b then shows the result of the Merge operation on these subsequences.

7.2.2 QuickSort

The next sorting method, known as QuickSort, expends more effort (than MergeSort) in the splitting step and less effort in joining the subsequences together again. The QuickSort algorithm selects one element from the sequence and refers to this element as the *pivot* element. Quicksort then splits the sequence into two subsequences, where all the elements in one subsequence are less than the pivot element and all the elements in the other subsequence are greater than the pivot element. These two subsequences may or may not be the same size. Ideally, about half of the elements in the sequence will be less than the pivot element, and half of the elements will be greater than the pivot element. These two subsequences are then sorted (using the same idea) and, finally, we combine the subsequences together to form the sorted sequence.

FIGURE 7.3   The MergeSort Algorithm.

```
program mergesort(input,output);
const
    SizeOfArrayToBeSorted        = 10;
type
    ArrayToBeSorted              = array [1 . . SizeOfArrayToBeSorted] of integer;
var
    S                            : ArrayToBeSorted;

procedure Merge(var NumbersToSort : ArrayToBeSorted; FirstElementPtr : integer;
    MiddleElementPtr : integer; LastElementPtr : integer);
var
    FirstHalfPtr                 : integer;
    SecondHalfPtr                : integer;
    TempNumbersToSort            : ArrayToBeSorted;
    TempPtr                      : integer;
begin
    { Initialize }
    FirstHalfPtr := FirstElementPtr;
    SecondHalfPtr := MiddleElementPtr + 1;
    TempPtr := FirstElementPtr;

    { Perform merge }
    while (FirstHalfPtr <= MiddleElementPtr) and
          (SecondHalfPtr <= LastElementPtr) do
    begin
        if NumbersToSort[FirstHalfPtr] <= NumbersToSort[SecondHalfPtr] then
        begin
            TempNumbersToSort[TempPtr] := NumbersToSort[FirstHalfPtr];
            FirstHalfPtr := succ(FirstHalfPtr)
        end
        else
        begin
            TempNumbersToSort[TempPtr] := NumbersToSort[SecondHalfPtr];
            SecondHalfPtr := succ(SecondHalfPtr)
        end;
        TempPtr := succ(TempPtr)
    end;

    { Empty the remaining elements }
    if FirstHalfPtr <= MiddleElementPtr then
    begin
        for FirstHalfPtr := FirstHalfPtr to MiddleElementPtr do
        begin
            TempNumbersToSort[TempPtr] := NumbersToSort[FirstHalfPtr];
            TempPtr := succ(TempPtr)
        end
    end
```

FIGURE 7.3 *(Continued)*

```
    else
    begin
        for SecondHalfPtr := SecondHalfPtr to LastElementPtr do
        begin
            TempNumbersToSort[TempPtr] := NumbersToSort[SecondHalfPtr];
            TempPtr := succ(TempPtr)
        end
    end;

    for TempPtr := FirstElementPtr to LastElementPtr do
        NumbersToSort[TempPtr] := TempNumbersToSort[TempPtr]
end; { of procedure Merge }

procedure MergeSort(var NumbersToSort : ArrayToBeSorted;
    FirstElementPtr : integer; LastElementPtr : integer);
var
    MiddleElementPtr          : integer;
begin
    if FirstElementPtr <> LastElementPtr then { we have something to sort }
    begin
        MiddleElementPtr := (FirstElementPtr + LastElementPtr) div 2;
        MergeSort(NumbersToSort,FirstElementPtr,MiddleElementPtr);
        MergeSort(NumbersToSort,MiddleElementPtr+1,LastElementPtr);
        Merge(NumbersToSort,FirstElementPtr,MiddleElementPtr,LastElementPtr)
    end
end; { of procedure MergeSort }

procedure PrintSortedList(SortedArray : ArrayToBeSorted;
    FirstElementPtr : integer; LastElementPtr : integer);
begin
    for FirstElementPtr := FirstElementPtr to LastElementPtr do
    begin
        write(SortedArray[FirstElementPtr]:5,' ');
        if (FirstElementPtr mod 5) = 0 then writeln
    end;
    writeln
end; { of procedure PrintSortedList }

begin
    S[1] := 7; S[2] := 29; S[3] := 2; S[4] := 11; S[5] := 3;
    S[6] := 170; S[7] := 1; S[8] := 55; S[9] := 349; S[10] := 41;
    MergeSort(S,1,10);
    PrintSortedList(S,1,10)
end.
```

FIGURE 7.4a   MergeSort: Generation of Subproblems.

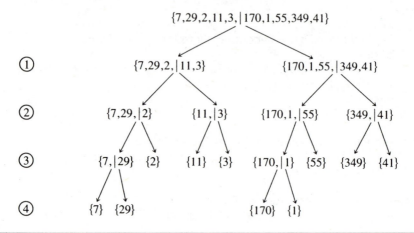

FIGURE 7.4b   MergeSort: Result of Merge Operations.

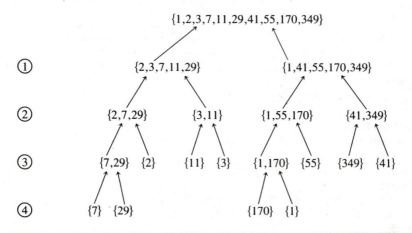

The idea behind partitioning the sequence around the pivot element is to make sure after each partitioning that the pivot element ends up in its correct position in the overall sorted sequence. Thus, once a pivot element is chosen and a partitioning performed around that pivot element, the pivot element is correctly placed for the final sorted sequence; we will not need to consider that pivot element again.

The high-level description of the QuickSort algorithm is as follows:

1. Select the pivot element.
2. Partition the sequence into two sequences, one with numbers less than the pivot element and the other with numbers that are greater than the pivot element.

3. Place the pivot element in its correct final location in the sorted sequence.

4. Separately sort each of the two sequences obtained in step 2.

An example is in order. We start with the original sequence S:

$$S = \{7,29,2,11,3,170,1,55,349,41\}$$

Now we must somehow choose the pivot element. For simplicity, we choose the first element of the sequence to be the pivot element; hence, our first pivot element is 7.

To implement the partitioning we use two pointers called LeftPtr and RightPtr. The RightPtr scans the sequence backward from the rightmost element to the beginning of the sequence until we find an element that is less than or equal to the pivot element. The LeftPtr scans the sequence forward from the leftmost element to the end of the sequence until we find an element that is greater than the pivot element. The elements found are then interchanged and the scan is continued until the two pointers cross each other—that is, LeftPtr $\geq$ RightPtr. The scan terminates when the pointers cross because we have then considered all elements in the sequence.

For example, the scan of S will interchange 29 and 1, then 3 and 11. At this point S looks like

$$S = \{7,1,2,3,11,170,29,55,349,41\}$$

When the scan terminates, we must place the pivot element in its correct place in the overall sequence. To do this, we interchange the pivot element with the last element in the subsequence of elements less than the pivot element. In our example, we interchange the pivot element, 7, with 3. Now 7 is in its correct sorted place in S (the fourth element) and S has been partitioned into

$$T = \{3,1,2\} \quad \text{and} \quad U = \{11,170,29,55,349,41\}$$

We are now faced with sorting T and U, which we do by reapplying the algorithm to both T and U individually. From the sequence T we choose the pivot element 3, and consequently the sequence T is partitioned into the sequence $\{2,1\}$ with pivot element 3. The sequence $\{2,1\}$ has a pivot element of 2 and the partitioned sequence of $\{1\}$. We then merge the sequence $\{1\}$ with the pivot element 2 to obtain the ordered sequence $\{1,2\}$, which is then merged with the previous pivot element 3 to obtain $\{1,2,3\}$. We now go back to the chore of sorting the sequence U. The pivot element is 11, which partitions the sequence U into the pivot element 11 and the sequence

$$\{170,29,55,349,41\}$$

and proceed as we did with sequence T. Figure 7.5a shows the complete picture of how the sequence S is partitioned along with the corresponding pivot element that is circled. Figure 7.5b shows how trivial the "merge" operation becomes.

FIGURE 7.5*a*   QuickSort: Generation of Subproblems and
Pivot Elements (Circled).

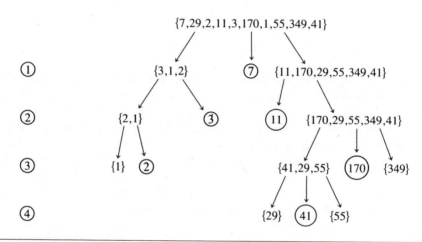

FIGURE 7.5*b*   QuickSort: Result of Merge Operations.

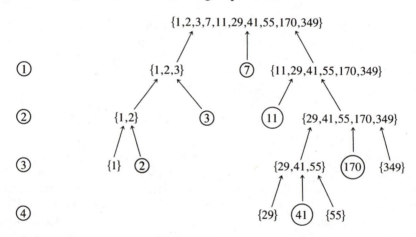

7.2.2.1 QuickSort: Implementation

Figure 7.6 illustrates one coding of the complete QuickSort algorithm. From this code and the previous figures, it should be clear why QuickSort is classified as a hardsplit/easyjoin algorithm.

7.2.3 InsertionSort

The basic idea of InsertionSort is to start with a sorted sequence containing one element, then successively insert elements into that sequence, keeping the sequence sorted. We first build a one-element sorted sequence using the first element of S. Then we "insert" a second element of S into the correct position in the one-element sorted sequence to form a sorted two-element sequence. We then "insert" the third element of S into the correct position in this two-element sorted sequence to form a sorted three-element sequence, and so on.

The high-level description of the InsertionSort algorithm is

1. Start with the first element of the sequence. This sequence is trivially in sorted order.
2. For i in the range 2 to N, where N is the number of elements in the sequence, assume that we have already sorted the first $i - 1$ elements. Take element i and search for its correct place in the sequence of $i - 1$ elements. Once the correct place is found, insert element i in that place. Now we have an i-element sorted sequence.

As an example of how InsertionSort works, let's once again consider our sequence:

$$S = \{7,29,2,11,3,170,1,55,349,41\}$$

To build the sorted sequence SS we start with

$$SS = \{7\}$$

Next we consider 29; because it is greater than 7, we do not need to do anything with either 7 or 29. Now we have

$$SS = \{7,29\}$$

Next we consider 2; to insert 2 into its proper place, we first move 29 to the third location, then 7 to the second location, and finally insert 2 as the first element in SS. At this point we have

$$SS = \{2,7,29\}$$

and we continue by inserting 11, then 3, and so on until we have inserted the last element, 41. Figure 7.7 shows a trace of this process for the entire sequence S.

7.2.3.1 InsertionSort: Implementation

The previous description forms the basis of the nonrecursive InsertionSort algorithm as coded in Figure 7.8.

FIGURE 7.6   The QuickSort Algorithm.

```
program quicksort(input,output);
const
    SizeOfArrayToBeSorted      = 10;
type
    ArrayToBeSorted            = array [1 . . SizeOfArrayToBeSorted] of integer;
var
    S                          : ArrayToBeSorted;


procedure Partition(var NumbersToSort : ArrayToBeSorted;
    FirstElementPtr : integer; var MiddleElementPtr : integer; LastElementPtr : integer);
var
    LeftPtr                    : integer;
    RightPtr                   : integer;
    SaveNumber                 : integer;
begin
    { Initialize }
    LeftPtr := FirstElementPtr;
    RightPtr := LastElementPtr;


    { Search for position to place FirstElementPtr }
    while LeftPtr < RightPtr do
    begin
        { Search array from right to left for an element greater than
          FirstElementPtr }
        while NumbersToSort[RightPtr] > NumbersToSort[First ElementPtr] do
            RightPtr := pred(RightPtr);


        { Search array from left to right for an element less than or
          equal to FirstElementPtr }
        while (LeftPtr < RightPtr) and
            (NumbersToSort[LeftPtr] <= NumbersToSort[FirstElementPtr]) do
            LeftPtr := succ(LeftPtr);


        { Interchange values found provided that searches have not crossed }
        if LeftPtr < RightPtr then
        begin
            SaveNumber := NumbersToSort[LeftPtr];
            NumbersToSort[LeftPtr] := NumbersToSort[RightPtr];
            NumbersToSort[RightPtr] := SaveNumber
        end
    end; { of while }


    { Put FirstElementPtr in correct location }
    MiddleElementPtr := RightPtr;
    SaveNumber := NumbersToSort[MiddleElementPtr];
```

FIGURE 7.6 *(Continued)*

```
        NumbersToSort[MiddleElementPtr] := NumbersToSort[FirstElementPtr];
        NumbersToSort[FirstElementPtr] := SaveNumber
end; { of procedure Partition }

procedure QuickSort(var NumbersToSort : ArrayToBeSorted;
        FirstElementPtr : integer; LastElementPtr : integer);
var
        MiddleElementPtr            : integer;
begin
        if FirstElementPtr < LastElementPtr then { we have something to sort }
        begin
                Partition(NumbersToSort,FirstElementPtr,MiddleElementPtr,LastElementPtr);
                QuickSort(NumbersToSort,FirstElementPtr,MiddleElementPtr-1);
                QuickSort(NumbersToSort,MiddleElementPtr+1,LastElementPtr)
        end
end; { of procedure QuickSort }

procedure PrintSortedList(SortedArray : ArrayToBeSorted;
        FirstElementPtr : integer; LastElementPtr : integer);
begin
        for FirstElementPtr := FirstElementPtr to LastElementPtr do
        begin
                write(SortedArray[FirstElementPtr]:5,' ');
                if (FirstElementPtr mod 5) = 0 then writeln
        end;
        writeln
end; { of procedure PrintSortedList }

begin
        S[1] := 7; S[2] := 29; S[3] := 2; S[4] := 11; S[5] := 3;
        S[6] := 170; S[7] := 1; S[8] := 55; S[9] := 349; S[10] := 41;
        QuickSort(S,1,10);
        PrintSortedList(S,1,10)
end.
```

7.2.3.2 InsertionSort as a Special Case of MergeSort It may not be apparent to you that InsertionSort follows the general sorting pattern mentioned at the beginning of this chapter, where the sequence S splits into T and U, which are then sorted and joined together to form the sorted sequence SS. However, InsertionSort does fit this pattern when we think of InsertionSort as a special case of MergeSort in which S is partitioned into two sequences such that one of those sequences always contains only one element and the other sequence contains all the remaining elements. (Remember that in MergeSort the partition results in two sequences of approximately equal length.) In

FIGURE 7.7   Trace of Operation of the InsertionSort Algorithm.
(Arrows are used to show point at which new element is
inserted into the sequence; circled elements show subsequences
of elements that are currently in sorted order.)

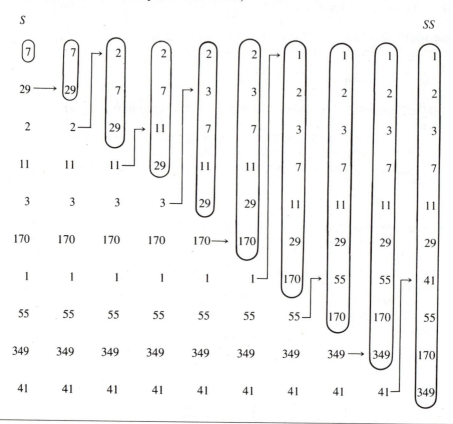

FIGURE 7.8   The InsertionSort Algorithm.

```
program insertionsort(input,output);
const
    SizeOfArrayToBeSorted       = 10;
type
    ArrayToBeSorted             = array [1 .. SizeOfArrayToBeSorted] of integer;
var
    S                           : ArrayToBeSorted;

procedure InsertionSort(var NumbersToSort : ArrayToBeSorted;
    FirstElementPtr : integer; LastElementPtr : integer);
```

FIGURE 7.8 (*Continued*)

```pascal
var
    CurrentPtr                  : integer;
    Found                       : boolean;
    Ptr                         : integer;
    SaveNumber                  : integer;
begin
    for CurrentPtr := FirstElementPtr + 1 to LastElementPtr do
    begin
        { Initialize }
        SaveNumber := NumbersToSort[CurrentPtr];

        { Move elements greater than SaveNumber down one position }
        Ptr := CurrentPtr − 1;
        Found := false;
        while (Ptr >= FirstElementPtr) and (not Found) do
        begin
            if SaveNumber < NumbersToSort[Ptr] then
            begin
                NumbersToSort[Ptr + 1] := NumbersToSort[Ptr];
                Ptr := Ptr − 1
            end
            else Found := true
        end;

        { Insert SaveNumber in correct position }
        NumbersToSort[Ptr + 1] := SaveNumber
    end
end; { of procedure InsertionSort }


procedure PrintSortedList(SortedArray : ArrayToBeSorted;
    FirstElementPtr : integer; LastElementPtr : integer);
begin
    for FirstElementPtr := FirstElementPtr to LastElementPtr do
    begin
        write(SortedArray[FirstElementPtr]:5,' ');
        if (FirstElementPtr mod 5) = 0 then writeln
    end;
    writeln
end; { of procedure PrintSortedList }

begin
    S[1] := 7; S[2] := 29; S[3] := 2; S[4] := 11; S[5] := 3;
    S[6] := 170; S[7] := 1; S[8] := 55; S[9] := 349; S[10] := 41;
    InsertionSort(S,1,10);
    PrintSortedList(S,1,10)
end.
```

FIGURE 7.9a   InsertionSort Derived from MergeSort.

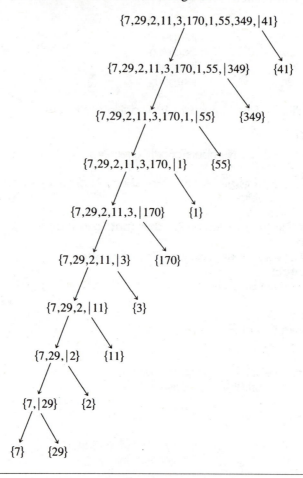

InsertionSort, the singleton sequence is formed using the "last" element of the sequence S. The tree of subproblems generated by this special case of MergeSort and the resulting merge operations are illustrated in Figure 7.9a and b.

7.2.4 SelectionSort

In the discussion of InsertionSort you might have noticed one striking inefficiency. Say that we have successfully sorted most of the elements of the sequence and we have the last few left. Let's also assume that these last elements are less than any of the elements in the previously sorted sequence. Then to insert these elements in their rightful places in the sequence requires that we move all of the previously sorted elements. Further-

FIGURE 7.9*b*   InsertionSort Idea.

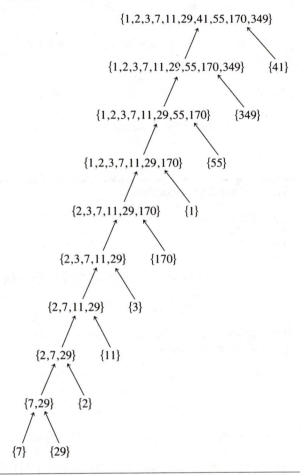

more, all the moves made by InsertionSort are made one position at a time. This can be extremely time-consuming for large sequences.

The idea behind the next sorting algorithm, SelectionSort, is to avoid these unnecessary move operations, although we still must make as many comparisons as we do in InsertionSort. In particular, whenever it is necessary to move an element, we will move it immediately to its correct, sorted position. We start by examining all the elements and putting the smallest one in the first location. We then find the minimum of the second through the *n*th elements and put this one in the second location. We continue in this manner until finally we find the smaller of the $(n - 1)$st element and the *n*th element and put it in the $(n - 1)$st location. We now have obtained the sorted sequence.

The high-level description of the SelectionSort algorithm is then

1. For *i* ranging from the first element of the sequence to the next to the last element of the sequence, do the following two steps.

2. Locate the smallest entry in the sequence between element *i* and the last element.

3. Interchange the element located in step 2 with the element at position *i*.

7.2.4.1 SelectionSort: Implementation
This idea forms the basis of the nonrecursive SelectionSort algorithm, the code for which is shown in Figure 7.10a. Figure 7.10b traces through the operation of the SelectionSort algorithm when applied to our sequence *S*.

FIGURE 7.10a   The SelectionSort Algorithm.

```
program selectionsort(input,output);
const
    SizeOfArrayToBeSorted      = 10;
type
    ArrayToBeSorted            = array [1 . . SizeOfArrayToBeSorted] of integer;
var
    S                          :  ArrayToBeSorted;

procedure SelectionSort(var NumbersToSort : ArrayToBeSorted;
    FirstElementPtr : integer; LastElementPtr : integer);
var
    CurrentPtr                 : integer;
    SaveNumber                 : integer;
    SmallestPtr                : integer;
begin
    for FirstElementPtr := FirstElementPtr to LastElementPtr − 1 do
    begin
        { Find smallest element in sequence starting from current FirstElementPtr }
        SmallestPtr := FirstElementPtr;
        for CurrentPtr := FirstElementPtr + 1 to LastElementPtr do
            if NumbersToSort[CurrentPtr] < NumbersToSort[SmallestPtr] then
                SmallestPtr := CurrentPtr;

        { Interchange smallest element with current FirstElementPtr,
          if necessary }
        if SmallestPtr <> FirstElementPtr then
        begin
            SaveNumber := NumbersToSort[FirstElementPtr];
            NumbersToSort[FirstElementPtr] := NumbersToSort[SmallestPtr];
            NumbersToSort[SmallestPtr] := SaveNumber
        end
    end
end; { of procedure SelectionSort }
```

FIGURE 7.10*a*   (*Continued*)

```
procedure PrintSortedList(SortedArray : ArrayToBeSorted;
    FirstElementPtr : integer; LastElementPtr : integer);
begin
    for FirstElementPtr := FirstElementPtr to LastElementPtr do
    begin
        write(SortedArray[FirstElementPtr]:5,' ');
        if (FirstElementPtr mod 5) = 0 then writeln
    end;
    writeln
end; { of procedure PrintSortedList }

begin
    S[1] := 7; S[2] := 29; S[3] := 2; S[4] := 11; S[5] := 3;
    S[6] := 170; S[7] := 1; S[8] := 55; S[9] := 349; S[10] := 41;
    SelectionSort(S,1,10);
    PrintSortedList(S,1,10)
end.
```

FIGURE 7.10*b*   Trace of the Operation of the SelectionSort Algorithm.
(Arrows indicate which elements are interchanged; circled elements
show sets of elements that are in correctly sorted order.)

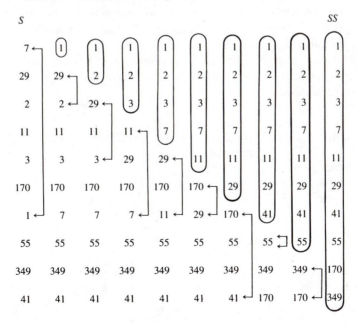

7.2.4.2 SelectionSort as a Special Case of QuickSort Earlier we showed how InsertionSort could be derived as a special case of MergeSort. Using a similar idea of splitting off a singleton sequence, can you discover how SelectionSort can be derived from QuickSort?

7.2.5 Taxonomy of Sorting Algorithms

Figure 7.2 illustrates the hierarchy of sorting algorithms that we have described so far as well as two other sorting algorithms that will be covered in the exercises. The figure shows the two broad classifications of sorting algorithms and the relationships between representative algorithms in each classification. Remembering these two general classifications should help you in recalling the major ideas behind each of the sorting algorithms discussed.

7.3
Searching

A number of sorting algorithms have been presented. It is now appropriate to turn our attention to the process of searching for an element (or key) in a list (or sequence). The key could correspond to a person's name and we might be searching for that name to display some information about that person. This information (e.g., an address or telephone number) could be grouped together in a record that is tagged by the name.

We will discuss three searching methods—sequential search, binary search, and hashing. Of these three methods, sequential searching is the simplest and usually the slowest method. Binary search is appropriate only for sorted data and is much faster than a sequential search. Hashing is a very fast method of finding data that need not be sorted; however, to perform well, hashing typically requires roughly twice as much memory as the other searching methods.

Throughout our coverage of searching algorithms we will assume that the data to be searched through comprise a sequence of records. Therefore, we define the following Pascal **type** declaration:

```
type
    TypeOfKey    = ;    { possible types include characters (to represent names)
                          or numbers }
    InfoRecord   =
        record
            key    : TypeOfKey;
            .      :  .      { information associated with key }
            .      :  .
            .      :  .
        end { of record InfoRecord }
```

If the data are stored in an array, we assume that the following declarations have also been made:

```
const
    TableSize      = ;       { size of array }
type
    TableType      = array [0 . . TableSize] of InfoRecord;
```

7.3.1 Sequential Search

The simplest method of determining if a key belongs to a list of elements is to do a sequential search, scanning each successive element until we reach the one we are looking for. We treat two sequential search procedures: the first searches an array of elements and the second a list of elements.

7.3.1.1 Sequential Search (of an Array)

A successful search returns the position where the key was found in the list and zero otherwise. The algorithm begins by inserting the key in the 0th location of the table to be searched; notice that we are employing the idea of a sentinel node described in the chapter on linked lists. The sequential search then starts with the last element (indexed by TableSize), checks whether it matches the key, and returns TableSize if the match is successful. Otherwise, the search proceeds to the element indexed TableSize-1 and the process is repeated. As long as a match for the key does not occur, the search is continued at the next element in the list. We are guaranteed to eventually find the key in the list because we inserted it in the 0th location. The Pascal procedure to perform a sequential search is quite straightforward:

```
procedure SequentialSearch(key : TypeOfKey; Table : TableType;
    var TableIndex : integer; TableSize : integer);
begin
    { initialize }
    TableIndex := TableSize;
    Table[0] := key;

    { search }
    while Table[TableIndex] <> key do
        TableIndex := pred(TableIndex)
end { of procedure SequentialSearch }
```

7.3.1.2 Sequential Search (of a Linked List)

Performing a sequential search when the data are organized as a linked list of records is equally easy. We assume that the linked list is a one-way list and that a pointer to the head of the list is passed into the procedure as a parameter. The procedure changes this parameter to point to the list element in which the key was found or it returns **nil** to denote an unsuccessful search. We assume that each record contains an additional field (the next field) to point to the next element in the list and that the next field of the last element of the list contains **nil**. Hence, the Pascal procedure looks like

```
procedure SequentialSearch(key : TypeOfKey; var ptr : PointerType);
var
    done      : boolean;
begin
    { initialize }
    done := false;

    { search }
    while (ptr <> nil) and (not done) do
    begin
        if key = ptr^.key
        then done := true
        else ptr := ptr^.next
    end { of while }
end; { of procedure SequentialSearch }
```

7.3.1.3 Sequential Search: Analysis

It should be clear that even though the data may be stored in two different ways (in an array or in a linked list) both of the algorithms perform the same basic operation. This operation is the comparison to determine whether or not the key is present in the record currently being inspected. Let us assume that the list we are searching contains n elements (n = TableSize in the algorithm based on the array). It should then be clear that, if the key was present in the first position in the list, one comparison must have been made to determine this. Likewise if the key was in the last position in the list, n comparisons must have been performed. This tells us something about how the algorithm performs in the best and worst cases, but what can we say about how this algorithm performs *on average?*

To obtain the average behavior of the sequential search algorithm, we must assume that each element in the list is as likely as any other element in the list to be searched for. Hence, to determine the average number of comparisons required in a successful sequential search on a list of size n, we must first sum up the number of comparisons necessary to find each possible element and then divide that number by n. Since finding the first element requires one search, finding the second element requires two searches, and so forth, the sum is $1 + 2 + 3 + \ldots + n$. Back in the chapter on recursion we mentioned that this sum is known as Gauss's formula and equals $n(n + 1)/2$. Hence, the average number of comparisons required in a successful sequential search on a list of size n is

$$\frac{n(n + 1)/2}{n} = (n + 1)/2$$

This implies that, on the average, to find a key in the list requires that about half of the list must be searched. For large values of n, $(n + 1)/2$ is approximately $n/2$. The average search time is then proportional to n, the size of the table. This implies that if the table size is doubled, the average search time will also be doubled.

7.3.2 Binary Search (of an Array)

If the data to be searched are sorted on a key value (say, in increasing order), then we can use a much faster searching algorithm than sequential search called *binary search*. Binary search takes its name from the fact that after each comparison the amount of data remaining to be searched decreases by half.

The simplest binary search algorithm compares the sought for key against the key value of the middle element in the table. Based on the result of this comparison, one of the following three conditions must be true:

1. If the key is less than the middle element, then we know that the upper half of the table cannot contain the key and therefore does not have to be searched.

2. If the key is greater than the middle element, then the lower half of the table can be excluded from the search.

3. If the key equals the middle element, we have found the key being searched for.

The same technique is then repeatedly applied on the nonexcluded portion of the table until the key is either found or we have excluded all elements from the search, that is, the key is not in the table. As you can see, we reduce the search space by half each time we make a simple comparison of the key value to a middle element. The binary search procedure is depicted in Figure 7.11.

7.3.2.1 Binary Search: Analysis

Since each invocation of the binary search procedure eliminates half of the table it is searching, successive calls to Binary Search deal in turn with tables of size TableSize, TableSize/2, TableSize/4, TableSize/16, and so on. Again, let n = TableSize. Then the maximum number of times the table can be divided in half is equal to the smallest integer k such that

$$2^k \geq n$$

In other words, k is the least integer greater than or equal to $\log_2 n$. So the *maximum* number of comparisons necessary to either find the key or determine that the key is not in the table is approximately $\log_2 n$, where n is the number of elements in the table. This is much faster than even the *average* case for a sequential search, which you may recall required approximately $n/2$ comparisons.

7.3.3 Hash Search

In searching for a name in the telephone book you may actually use a combination of the binary search and sequential search algorithms. Binary search would be used to zero in on the page that contains the name you are looking for and then you might do a sequential search starting from a certain entry on that page. The next searching algorithm is quite different from either of these two methods and would not be used by a person in locating a name in the phone book. But it has the distinct advantage that it is "easy" for a machine to perform because it uses the ability of machines to perform arithmetic computations quickly.

FIGURE 7.11   The Binary Search Algorithm.

```
procedure BinarySearch(key : TypeOfKey; Table : TableType;
      var MiddleElementofSearch : integer; TableSize : integer);
var
      done                          : boolean;
      LeftMostElementofSearch       : integer;
      RightMostElementofSearch      : integer;
begin
      { Initialize }
      LeftMostElementofSearch := 0;
      RightMostElementofSearch := TableSize + 1;
      MiddleElementofSearch :=
            (LeftMostElementofSearch + RightMostElementofSearch) div 2;
      done := MiddleElementofSearch = LeftMostElementofSearch;

      { Search }
      while not done do
      begin
            { Compare }
            if Table[MiddleElementofSearch] = key then done := true
            else
            begin
                  if Table[MiddleElementofSearch] > key
                  then RightMostElementofSearch := MiddleElementofSearch
                  else LeftMostElementofSearch := MiddleElementofSearch
            end;
            MiddleElementofSearch :=
                  (LeftMostElementofSearch + RightMostElementofSearch) div 2;
            done := MiddleElementofSearch = LeftMostElementofSearch
      end
end; { of procedure BinarySearch }
```

The main idea behind computing a *hash value* of a key is to transform the key into a number that is used as an index into the search table. Given a key we apply a function (referred to as a *hash function*) on the key to obtain a value x:

$$x = h(key)$$

that is used to locate the key in the data structure. (We will see shortly what to do if several key values are the same.) As an example of how to calculate a key value, suppose we have names for keys. To obtain the hash value of a given name, we could associate a number with each letter in the name; for example, the letter "a" might have the value 1, the letter "b" might be equivalent to 2, and so on. Using the numeric values of each letter we apply some mathematical function to obtain a single value that is known as the "hash value" of that name.

To see how this idea works, consider the following example. Let's say that we have a table of size 256 with key values that are names (alphabetic characters). Then we would like each element stored in the table to hash into a value between 1 and 256. The mathematical function could be as simple as adding up the values for each letter in the key and taking that sum modulo 256. This would generate a value between 0 and 255, so we would then add 1 to obtain a value in the correct range. Therefore, for the key "cookie" we would perform the following:

$$
\begin{aligned}
\text{'c'} &= 3 \\
\text{'o'} &= 15 \\
\text{'o'} &= 15 \\
\text{'k'} &= 11 \\
\text{'i'} &= 9 \\
\text{'e'} &= 5 \\
\hline
\text{sum} &= 58 \\
58 \bmod 256 &= 58 \\
58 + 1 &= 59
\end{aligned}
$$

The key "cookie," then, hashes to the value 59. We could now go directly to location 59 of our table to find the record whose key is "cookie."

Now that the idea behind a simple hash function should be clear, let us consider the problem of how the data elements are actually entered into the table that will later be searched. For the data elements to be found eventually by their hash address, it should be obvious that they must have initially been stored in the table using this hash address (in other words, the data elements are hashed into the table). Stated in another way, the problem is that of storing, say, m keys in a table of size n. In the typical case, m is less than or equal to n; otherwise there would not be enough room in the table for all the keys. We denote the hash function by the letter h and a typical argument (a key) by the letters x and y. Thus, given a key x, $h(x)$ is the hash address of the key x and will be a number between 1 and n. A good hash function has the property that if x and y are distinct words, then $h(x)$ will not equal $h(y)$. Unfortunately, even the best hash functions can generate *collisions;* that is, for $x <> y$, $h(x) = h(y)$. For example, using the hash function described above the key "phone" hashes to the same value as the key "cookie." Collisions like this are typically unavoidable because the domain of possible keys can be very large.

How can we handle such collisions? The simplest scheme to handle collisions is to sequentially search through locations $h(x)$, $h(x) + 1$, $h(x) + 2$, and so on until one finds either the key x or an unused location. The search can wrap around the end of the table and is unsuccessfully terminated if it returns to location $h(x)$ without finding either an empty position or the key being sought.

7.3.3.1 **Hash Search: Analysis** In the best case, a hash search requires only one comparison for a successful search. In the worst case, we may have to search the entire table to discover whether or not a key value is present; in this worst case, the hash search becomes a sequential search. For the average case, the number of comparisons required for a successful search depends on how full the table is; it is probably obvious to you that as the table gets fuller, the chances of a collision are more likely. We will not go into the details of calculating the average search time here, but will simply mention the result. If we denote the fraction of the table entries already in use by *LF* (for load fraction), then the average number of comparisons in a hash table search is given by

$$\frac{1}{1 - LF}$$

For example, if our table is half full (*LF* = 0.5), we will require on average 1/(1 − ½) = 2 searches. Compare this with a binary or sequential search applied to a table with 100,000 elements. This explains why hashing is such a popular technique.

<h2 style="text-align:center">7.4
Conclusion</h2>

We have described four sorting and three searching algorithms. Because sorting and searching arise in so many applications, many different algorithms have been developed for each process. In fact, entire books have been written on the subject of sorting and searching. The most authoritative and complete reference is still *The Art of Computer Programming,* Volume 3, *Searching and Sorting,* by Donald Knuth (Addison-Wesley, 1973).

On most computers, ''canned programs'' are available for both of these operations. Often it is wise to use these thoroughly tested programs rather than write your own algorithms. The purpose of this chapter has been to expose you to some of the ideas underlying sorting and searching techniques.

Exercises for Chapter 7

1. The BubbleSort algorithm differs from the SelectionSort algorithm in that BubbleSort interchanges elements immediately if it finds that these elements are out of order. This will cause the smallest element to ''bubble up'' to the beginning of the sequence. Modify the SelectionSort algorithm so that it becomes the BubbleSort algorithm.

2. Implement a hash function as described in the text.

3. Modify the linked-list version of the sequential search procedure to add the key to the list if it is not found in the list.

4. We described the binary search algorithm for data stored in an array. If the data were, instead, in a ''sorted'' tree with the root node containing the ''median'' value, how would you modify binary search to find a key in such a tree?

5. Can the sorting algorithms described in this chapter be implemented to handle data stored in linked lists?

CHAPTER 8

FILES

8.1
Introduction

In this chapter we discuss sequential and random access files. Any program that uses input or output statements also uses files. The read statement reads data from a file named input, and the write statement writes data to a file named output. Pascal allows you to create and manipulate files other than input and output, as we will see next.

8.2
Sequential Files

Like an array, a *sequential file* in Pascal contains components of the same type. But there are two important differences between arrays and files:

1. An array has a fixed size. A file may initially contain zero components and expand as more components are added. (The number of components in a file is called its length.)

2. Elements of an array can be accessed in any order. For a file, however, components must be accessed sequentially.

We visualize a file like this:

Component

1   2   3   4   5   6   7

Several operations can be performed on files including reading and writing. A *file pointer* is associated with each file. If the file pointer is positioned as shown:

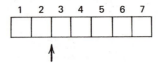

the third component will be read by the next read operation on the file. You cannot read past the last component in a file. After reading the seventh component, the picture looks like this:

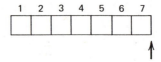

Attempting another read operation on this file causes a run-time error (attempt to read past the end-of-file, eof). The boolean function eof determines if the file pointer is at the end-of-file.

The situation is different for the write operation. Here the file pointer always points to the current end-of-file (unless the file has been reset) because a write operation on a sequential file always adds the new record at the end of the file.

The next write operation adds a fifth component and also moves the file pointer.

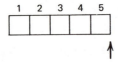

Every file in Pascal except input and output must be defined in a **var** declaration. The file is given a name and a type in this declaration (as any other variable). Its type is

file of componenttype

where componenttype specifies the type of the components of the file. Here are some example file declarations:

var
    temp   : **file of** char;
    x   : **file of** integer;

```
y              : file of real;
z              : file of array [1 . . 10] of real;
```

Files input and output are predefined text files and should not appear in **var** declarations. We can associate a type name with the file type as follows:

```
type
    text        = file of char;
var
    temp        : text;
```

In Pascal the name text is a predefined type identifier with the preceding meaning. Hence, files input and output are of type text.

The components of a file need not be restricted to simple types, as the following example illustrates.

```
type
    employeerecord      =
        record
            name        : array [1 . . 20] of char;
            age         : 0 . . 150;
            sex         : (male,female)
        end; { of record employeerecord }
var
    workers                     : file of employeerecord;
```

Files other than input and output must be prepared for writing or reading by *rewrite* and *reset* operations. These are predefined procedures.

Before writing the first component to a file called f, we must execute the following operation:

```
rewrite(f)
```

This prepares file f for subsequent write operations. After the rewrite operation, file f will have zero components; that is, it will be an empty file. To write components to the file, we use a modified form of the write statement.

```
write(f,x)
```

Notice that the first parameter to the procedure is the file name (if the file name is omitted from the argument list of procedure write, output is assumed). This statement appends a component (whose value is that of the expression x) to the end of file f. The type of the expression x must be compatible with the declared component type of file f.

The effect of the write operation is as follows:

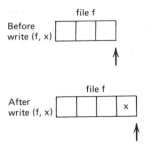

More than one component can be added to a file using the write statement.

write(f,a,b,c,d)

The updated file now looks like this:

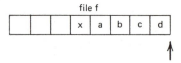

A file created by a program can be read by the same program (or other programs). Before issuing the first read statement, we must execute the reset operation.

reset(f)

This prepares file f for subsequent read operations. After the reset operation, the file pointer will point to the first component of the file.

To read the first component from the file, we use a modified form of the read statement.

read(f,x)

The first parameter to the procedure is the file name. If the file name is omitted from the argument list of procedure read, the file name input is assumed. The read statement copies the next component of file f into the variable x and moves the file pointer past this component. The type of the variable x must be compatible with the declared component type of file f.

The effect of the read operation is illustrated by the following diagram.

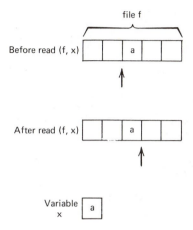

Files that are listed in the program header of a Pascal program either already exist (before the program is run) or are created by the program and are to be retained after it terminates (in some system-dependent manner). Any other files that are used as temporary (or scratch) files need not be listed in the **program** statement. All files other than input and output must be declared in the **var** declaration.

8.2.1 The File Buffer Variable

Every file has a special variable associated with it, called the *buffer variable*. For a file named f, the buffer variable is called f ↑ . (On some systems the "up-arrow" character, ↑ , may be replaced by the "caret" (^), and the buffer variable would be represented as f^.) The buffer variable can be used just like any other variable. When a file is read, the buffer variable contains the component immediately to the right of the file pointer. For example, if file f is reset by

reset(f)

a picture of file f might look like the following:

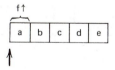

Then the value of f ↑ is a. Notice that the reset operation has automatically defined a value for f ↑ . The file pointer can be moved one position to the right by using a get operation on the file. The syntax of the get operation is:

get(f)

Its effect is as follows:

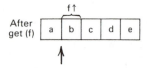

Now the value of f ↑ is b. The read operation is defined in terms of the get operation and the buffer variable.

```
read(f,x)    =    begin
                      x := f ↑ ;
                      get(f)
                  end
```

This definition for read can sometimes lead to problems. When data are read from a file, the file pointer is positioned at the component following the one just read. If there is no component there, the file pointer will be pointing to the end-of-file. As a result, if a program is structured in such a way that an eof test is performed after a read statement, a valid data item from the file may not get processed.

We can append a component to a file by using the buffer variable and a put operation. For example, assume the buffer variable has been assigned a value using the following assignment statement:

f ↑ := a

Then this value may be appended to the file f by using the put(f) command, which writes the contents of the buffer variable to the end of the file.

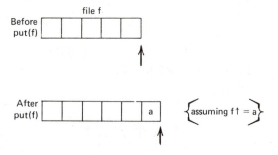

After the put operation, the value of the buffer variable (f ↑) is undefined.

It should be clear that the write statement is equivalent to:

```
write(f,x)   =    begin
                      f ↑ := x;
                      put(f)
                  end
```

8.2.2 Text Files

Any file to be printed on a line printer must be of type text. Recall that the definition of type text is:

type
    text   = **file of** char;

Text files have a distinctive property. They are composed of *lines* terminated by an *end-of-line* (eoln) marker. The end-of-line marker can be tested for by the boolean function eoln(f), where f is the name of some text file. (If no file name is specified, input is assumed.) The function returns true if the file pointer is positioned at the end-of-line marker. In the following example, we let eoln stand for the end-of-line marker. A text file can be pictured as follows:

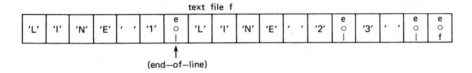

text file f

(end—of—line)

To read the first character from the file f, we perform

reset(f);   { which positions the file pointer to
                  the left of the first character and fills
                  the buffer variable }

read(f,ch)   { which sets ch = 'L' and moves the
                  file pointer to the left of the second
                  character }

If the file pointer is currently positioned at an eoln marker then the value of the eoln predicate is true. If the following read operation is performed:

read(f,ch)

a blank is placed into the variable ch (ch = ' '), the file pointer is shifted past the eoln marker, and the value of the eoln predicate is false.

The effect of the readln(f) operation is to move the file pointer past the *next* eoln marker in the file. Hence f ↑ will contain the first character of the next line (if there is one).

Eoln markers can be inserted in text files that are being written by issuing a

writeln(f)

This appends the eoln marker to the text file and updates the file pointer in the usual manner. An eoln marker can be tested for by using the boolean function eoln(f).

The following program shows how to make a copy of a text file:

```
program copy(file1,file2,output);
var
    ch      : char;     { temporary }
    file1   : text;     { file to be copied }
    file2   : text;     { will be a copy of file1 }
begin
    { prepare to read from file1 }
    reset(file1);

    { prepare to write to file2 }
    rewrite(file2);

    { loop through file1 reading (and writing) one line at a time }
    while not eof(file1) do
    begin
        { copy next line }
        while not eoln(file1) do
        begin
            read(file1,ch);
            write(file2,ch)
        end; { of while }

        { read past eoln marker }
        readln(file1);

        { mark eoln on file2 }
        writeln(file2)
    end { of while }
end.
```

The Pascal predefined procedure readln(f), used in the above program is defined in the following way:

```
readln(f)    =    while not eoln(f) do
                      get(f);
                  get(f)
```

8.3
Comparison between Sequential and Random Access Files

Files can be classified broadly as either *sequential* or *random*. Sequential files correspond to those that we have been using throughout this text, and which we just discussed in the preceding sections of this chapter. The properties of a sequential file are analogous to those of a cassette music tape:

Cassette Tape	Sequential File	Pascal Operation
Playing tape to listen to pre-recorded music	Reading file to process data	read(x), file = input read(f,x), file = f get(f), file = f
Recording music on tape for later listening	Writing data into file for later processing	write(x), file = output write(f,x), file = f put(f), file = f
Rewinding tape so that one can either listen to old music or record new music	Rewinding file so that one can either reread the data or write new data into file	reset(f), file = f rewrite(f), file = f prepare file for writing

To understand the properties of random access files, consider an analogy with laser disks. With a laser disk containing, say 10 songs, you can selectively play any subset of songs, and with some laser disk players you can also play these selections in any order. For example, you might listen to songs 2, 5, and 9 in the order 9, 2, and 5. That is to say that you are *randomly accessing* the music from the laser disk. This same idea carries over to a random access file, wherein you can randomly access different blocks (think of these as being the songs) of data rather than having to access them sequentially as in a sequential file. In addition, with a random access file, you can randomly write any block of data rather than having to always append to the end of a file as in a sequential file.

8.4
Random Access Files

Unfortunately, there is no widely available ''standard'' method for dealing with random access files in Pascal, and every compiler will have a slightly different set of operations to create and manipulate these files. For this reason we will not use them in this book. Nonetheless, we will provide you with a general model of random access files that should help you in understanding any specific implementation of such files at your site.

A random access file can be envisioned as being composed of blocks of data. These blocks are generally each of the same size. Moreover, each block is numbered, say starting with block 1 (some systems will start their block numbering from 0). A random access file allows you to access (read or write) any block of the file at any time. For example, if the file contained 22 blocks, you could read block 5 and then write into block 17. You can interleave operations in any order that you please.

Operations to support random access files usually fall into two categories: read and write. [There is usually no need for a reset (rewind) operation or a rewrite operation.] The read operation might look like

read(file,blocknumber,buffer)

The buffer would be declared as a one-dimensional array and contain at least as many elements as the block size of the random access file. The write operation might appear as

write(file,blocknumber,buffer)

You obviously must have stored some data into the buffer before you can use this operation.

For example, using our syntax, the operation

read(f,103,x)

would read the contents of block number 103 of random access file f into the buffer variable x. This operation would be done directly, regardless of where the previous operation on file f had been positioned. The operation

write(f,299,y)

would write the contents of y into block number 299 of random access file f.

Using this same underlying model of a random access file, we can define an alternative method for accessing the data that more closely resembles the sequential processing of a file. This method uses an operation called seek

seek(file,blocknumber)

to first position the file to the desired blocknumber before we read or write. To read the data from this block, we would then execute

read(file,buffer)

This command would then read the data from the "current" blocknumber into the buffer. If another read operation were performed (without executing another seek operation), then the next block from the file would be read (i.e., the block whose address is blocknumber + 1). The same type of operations allow you to write arbitrary blocks on the file. First, seek to the desired block

seek(file,blocknumber)

and then write your data at that point with

write(file,buffer)

For example, the previous operations which we showed could also be written in the following way:

```
seek(f,103);
read(f,x)

seek(f,299);
write(f,y)
```

With this model as a guide, we suggest that you explore the implementation of random access files on your system. It is quite possible, though, that your Pascal compiler does not support random access files.

8.5
Logical versus Physical Organization of Data

Before leaving this topic, it might be helpful to consider an example that illustrates the importance of being able to access large amounts of data on a disk randomly. Consider a payroll system for an organization with tens of thousands of employees. The employees can each be assigned a unique identifying number, which is referred to as a *key*. This key can then be used as a block index in a random access personnel file. All information about employee 19812 could (we hope) be stored in block 19812 of the file. With one read operation we could potentially access all the information stored in the system about this employee and display it in a formatted fashion on a CRT. This would certainly be much faster than rewinding the file and reading sequentially through the first 19,811 employees before locating the desired information!

Even though we might "logically" think that we are accessing block 19812 of our file, that does not mean that the actual "physical" address of that block of data is block 19812 on the disk. In fact, it would be extremely unlikely for this to be the case! The machine's operating system is responsible for allocating data on the disk; consequently, the operating system must maintain a mapping between the user's logical view of the file based on keys (like block 19812) and the actual physical location of the data on the disk.

Other computer science classes will teach you about other types of file formats, such as IBM's Indexed Sequential Access Method (ISAM). Courses on such subjects as database systems, operating systems, or file organization should contain a wealth of information on these topics.

8.6
Files and External Sorting

The previous chapter described several algorithms to sort data stored in a computer's memory. Frequently, the amount of data to be sorted exceeds the capacity of a computer's internal main memory but can easily be stored in the machine's secondary storage system (e.g., on a disk). Sorting algorithms applied to data on external storage devices are referred to as *external* sorting algorithms, as opposed to the *internal* sorting algorithms described in the last chapter.

One popular external sorting technique is based on the internal MergeSort algorithm. Consider that the external disk file contains the numbers

| 7 29 2 11 3 170 1 55 349 41 |

Obviously, these data could be sorted using any internal sorting method; we use this small example only so that we can more clearly illustrate the operation of the external MergeSort algorithm.

The algorithm proceeds in two distinct steps. First, regions of the input file are individually sorted by using any internal sorting algorithm, where a *region* is defined as a subset of the file which can fit into memory. Say that these regions each contain three elements (or records). The first region of the file is read into memory, sorted, and written onto another file stored on the disk. This process of reading, sorting, and outputting sorted data onto the other file is continued until all of the data from the original file are processed. For our example, the first phase would like like this:

Region 1	Region 2	Region 3	Region 4
7 29 2	11 3 170	1 55 349	41

Region	Original Data Read into Memory	Data Sorted in Memory	Data Appended on Disk File
1	7 29 2	2 7 29	2 7 29
2	11 3 170	3 11 170	2 7 29 | 3 11 170
3	1 55 349	1 55 349	2 7 29 | 3 11 170 | 1 55 349
4	41	41	2 7 29 | 3 11 170 | 1 55 349 | 41

The sorted regions on the second disk file are known as *runs*. In each case, the length of the run is three records except for the last run, which contains only one record.

The second phase of the algorithm takes the runs generated by phase 1 and merges them together, two at a time, until the end of the data file is reached. It is important to note that this merge operation does not require that entire runs be in memory! In particular, only the first element or record of each of the two runs must be in memory. These two runs are merged and output perhaps onto a third file (or over the original file). As an example, after phase 1 of the algorithm, we have a file with the indicated runs:

Run 1	Run 2	Run 3	Run 4
2 7 29	3 11 170	1 55 349	41

The first two runs are merged by comparing 2 with 3 and outputting 2, comparing 7 with 3 and outputting 3, comparing 7 with 11 and outputting 7, and so on. At the end of this process, the intermediate file contains

| 2 3 7 11 29 170 |

FIGURE 8.1   Operation of External MergeSort Algorithm.

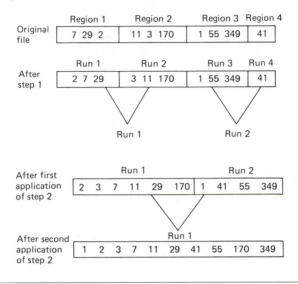

which is a file containing a run of length 6. The next two runs are merged and output; this process is continued as often as is necessary to sort the entire file.

The complete process is illustrated in Figure 8.1. The program is left as an exercise for the reader.

8.7
Conclusion

We have described two major file organizations: sequential and random access. All systems will be able to handle sequential files, but not all accommodate random access files. Since there is no generally accepted standard implementation of random access files in Pascal, we have described a general model that can help in understanding any implementation of random access files. This chapter also described one external sorting technique based on the internal sorting technique studied earlier: MergeSort.

Exercises for Chapter 8

1. Files can be composed of records as in

type
    studentrecords   =

```
        record
            lastname        : packed array [1 . . 10] of char;
            firstname       : packed array [1 . . 10] of char;
            age             : 0 . . 150
        end;
var
    x                       : file of studentrecords;
```

Explain how to create a file x with 25 students. How do you access the last name of the tenth student on the file? The age of the twentieth student?

2.   Given two files of integers sorted into increasing order, write a complete Pascal program that merges the two files into a third file in sorted order.

*3.   Write a Pascal procedure that counts the number of components in a file.

*4.   What is on file f after the following segment is executed?

```
var
    f     : file of integer;
    i     : 1 . . 10;
begin
    for i := 1 to 10 do
    begin
        if odd(i) then rewrite(f);
        write(f,i)
    end
        .
        .
        .
```

5.   Write a Pascal program that "reverses" the components of a file. That is, make the first component the last one on the new file, make the second component the second to the last one on the new file, and so on. Do not test your program on any large file!

6.   Write a Pascal procedure MergeSort that implements the Merge Sort technique described in Section 8.6. Try it on a file with 100 components and regions of 20 elements. (Disregard the fact that such a small file could probably be sorted using internal sorting methods!)

7.   Investigate how your Pascal system handles random-access files.

8.   Let f be any file. What will happen if you do the following:

```
reset(f);
while not eof(f) do
    reset(f)
```

9.   What happens if you try the following on file f:

```
reset(f);
get(f);
put(f)
```

10.   What does the following code do?

```
reset(f);
while not eof(f) do
    get(f);
put(f)
```

Try it!

Bibliography for Part One

Aho, A. V., J. E. Hopcroft, and J. D. Ullman. *Data Structures and Algorithms.* Reading, Mass.: Addison-Wesley, 1983.

Findlay, W., and D. A. Watt. *Pascal—An Introduction to Methodical Programming.* Potomac, Md.: Computer Science Press, 1978.

Harrison, M. *Data Structures and Programming.* Glenview, Ill.: Scott, Foresman, 1973.

Horowitz, E., and S. Sahni. *Fundamentals of Data Structures.* Potomac, Md.: Computer Science Press, 1976.

Jensen, K., and N. Wirth. *Pascal User Manual and Report,* 2nd ed. New York: Springer-Verlag, 1974.

Knuth, D. E. *The Art of Computer Programming,* Volume 1, *Fundamental Algorithms.* Reading, Mass.: Addison-Wesley, 1968.

Lewis, T. G., and M. Z. Smith. *Applying Data Structures.* Boston: Houghton Mifflin, 1976.

Merritt, S. "An Inverted Taxonomy of Sorting Algorithms," *Communications of the ACM 28,* Vol. 1, January 1985, pp. 96–99.

Peterson, J., and A. Silberschatz. *Operating System Concepts.* Reading, Mass.: Addison-Wesley, 1983.

Tanenbaum, A. S. *Structured Computer Organization,* Englewood Cliffs, N.J.: Prentice-Hall, 1976.

Tremblay, J., and P. G. Sorenson. *An Introduction to Data Structures with Applications.* New York: McGraw-Hill, 1984.

Wirth, N. *Algorithms + Data Structures = Programs.* Englewood Cliffs, N.J.: Prentice-Hall, 1976.

PART TWO

PROGRAM DEVELOPMENT

CHAPTER 9

AN OVERVIEW OF THE PROGRAM DESIGN PROCESS

9.1
Introduction

In this portion of the text we begin our investigation of the topic of *program design*—the overall process of developing and writing sequences of instructions to solve problems on a computer system. We will be studying this topic in its very broadest sense, as "the entire sequence of steps needed to solve a given problem on a computer, from the initial rough problem statement, to the finished, verified, and documented computer program."

Too often students treat computer programming in a much, much narrower sense; they view it only as coding statements in some high-level computer language, typically BASIC, FORTRAN, COBOL, PL/1, or Pascal. Once given a problem statement, they immediately begin writing programming language statements on a coding sheet or entering them at their terminal. They continue writing or typing until they have a complete program and then hope that they have produced a valid solution. If it is incorrect, their first reaction is immediately to add more statements, hoping these statements now make the program a correct solution. Invariably it is not, and all the student ends up with is a logical and structural mess that does not come close to solving the original problem.

Where the student went wrong is in failing to understand the enormous amount of preparatory work that must be done *before* you can actually begin to code statements in a programming language. Programming is somewhat unusual in this respect because with most other complex tasks people recognize the importance of "laying the groundwork" before they begin the actual implementation work. For example, when writing a term paper, you would (hopefully!) not start by putting a clean, white sheet of paper in the typewriter and trying to type a finished, polished document. You must obviously precede that phase with a great deal of preparatory work researching your topic, developing an outline, and writing one or more rough drafts. Then, and only then, would you feel ready to produce the final manuscript. And, given the planning work already done, this typing phase should be quite simple and mechanical. It is concerned solely with putting on paper, in a correct and visually pleasing format, the thoughts and ideas you have developed.

Similarly, you would not build a house by immediately picking up hammer, nails, and wood, and proceeding to erect walls. This approach leads immediately to chaos. Again, a great deal of preparatory work is needed to ensure the consistency, safety, and beauty of what you are going to construct. This time, the preparatory work involves architectural designs, engineering blueprints, and contracting agreements with electricians, plumbers, masons, and others. When this preparatory work has been done well, the construction phase, again, is a straightforward, mechanical procedure. The truly creative work in designing the building will have already been completed.

Why, then, if we recognize the complex of steps involved in such diverse tasks as writing term papers and building a house, do we frequently not see the same needs in the area of computer programming? Why is the important preparatory work of specifying, designing, planning, and organizing a solution frequently deemed unimportant and skipped over? Why is the coding phase (which is analogous to the relatively mechanical steps of typing a paper or constructing a house) improperly viewed as the truly creative part of programming?

The answer to these questions generally has to do with the *size* of the programming projects and homework assignments solved in introductory programming classes. These programs are extremely, and unrealistically, small. The initial programs that students are asked to design and write are usually no more than 25 to 30 lines long. Even by the end of their first course, it is still unusual for students to write programs that are more than a few hundred lines in length.

This is a totally unrealistic value. "Real-world" programs are one, two, or even three orders of magnitude longer and more complex. Most programs that solve interesting problems require thousands or tens of thousands of lines of code, and truly large complex software systems, such as the NASA space shuttle control system, may require the development of programs with more than a million lines of code!

Figure 9.1, reproduced from Fairley (1985), *Software Engineering Concepts* shows a typical categorization of software products based on their size, the number of professionals needed to implement them, and the duration of implementation.

Notice that virtually all of the programs developed by undergraduate computer science students would be classified as "trivial." Even the larger independent projects done by seniors or graduate students would still likely fall into the "small" category of Figure 9.1. However, most of the software products developed for the marketplace are neither trivial nor small and would fall instead into the "medium" or "large" category, occupying a dozen or so programmers for a few years and resulting in tens of thousands of lines of code. The "very large" and "extremely large" categories, typified by such products as Military Command and Control Systems, or operating systems for networks of large mainframe computers, are some of the largest enterprises being produced, requiring as much as 5000 to 50,000 man-years of effort to imple-

FIGURE 9.1   Size Categories for Software Products.

Category	No. of Programmers	Duration	Product Size
Trivial	1	1–4 weeks	500 lines of code
Small	1	1–6 months	1K–5K
Medium	2–5	1–2 years	5K–50K
Large	5–20	2–3 years	50K–100K
Very large	100–1000	4–5 years	1M
Extremely large	2000–5000	5–10 years	1M–10M

ment. With problems of that size and complexity, it would be quite impossible to write a program immediately that could solve the problem without extensive planning, organizing, and design. In fact, with programs on the scale of tens or hundreds of thousands of lines of code, the specification and design phases will require 30 to 40% of the overall effort while coding will typically occupy less than 20%. (The remaining time is involved with debugging, testing, documentation, etc.) It is only with small toy problems that one sees in introductory programming classes in which it might be feasible to skip the necessary preparatory work, go directly into coding, and still get the programming working correctly.

The same is true for the two examples we referred to earlier—writing a paper and building a house. With a one-paragraph memo, it is usually not necessary to prepare an outline and then write one or two rough drafts. Similarly, one would probably not hire an architect to prepare blueprints for a doghouse! But a one-paragraph memo and a doghouse are special cases, and courses in creative writing or architecture do teach the student all the necessary steps to complete a large, complex writing or design project successfully. Students follow these steps on all classroom projects, regardless of size, so they are ready to handle the large, complex tasks they will encounter in real life.

The same approach should be used in learning programming. The simple 50 to 100-line programs you are asked to write must be recognized as special cases, not at all representative of programming projects you will encounter later. The fact that, for these small projects, you may be able to pick up pencil and paper and immediately write a correct BASIC, FORTRAN, or Pascal program does not mean that you will be able to do this for bigger problems. In fact, this "coding first" approach quickly collapses when the student attempts, without any prior planning or organization, to write his or her first large programming project (e.g., on the order of 1000 or more lines of code). These attempts are rarely successful and the student is left with an incorrect program and few ideas on how to get it working properly.

This inability to effectively manage the correct development of large, complex programming systems is frequently referred to in computer science as the *software crisis*. This term generally refers to the ever-increasing proportion of time and money involved in software development as a percentage of overall system cost. Programmer productivity, measured in the number of lines of correct code produced per unit time, has not increased significantly in the last 10 years. During that time, however, hard-

FIGURE 9.2 Comparison of the Steps Involved in Writing a
Term Paper and a Computer Program.

Writing a Term Paper	*Writing a Computer Program*
1. Developing a topic and a thesis statement	1. Developing the problem specification document
2. Outlining the paper	2. Developing the program design document
3. Doing library research of the topic and selecting the key points to cover	3. Selecting the best algorithms and data types for the problem
4. Writing a rough draft	4. Writing a computer program
5. Reviewing the rough draft and preparing succeeding drafts	5. Debugging the program and preparing new versions, if necessary
6. Sending the manuscript out for critical review	6. Verifying that the finished program is indeed correct
7. Preparing the final, finished version, including index, bibliography, cover page, etc.	7. Preparing the necessary user and technical documentation to support the program

ware speeds have increased 1000-fold and costs have come down dramatically. In addition, the quality and reliability of much software in the marketplace is significantly lower than the quality and reliability of the hardware on which it runs. When we buy a computer system, we generally expect it to operate uninterrupted for weeks or months. When it does fail, we expect it to be repaired and returned quickly to its original level of operation.

Unfortunately, the same cannot be said for software. It is not rare to encounter programs that do not do what they say they will, contain numerous bugs, and are not adequately documented. One very popular microcomputer software package contains the following disclaimer printed in large boldface type on page 1 of its *User's Manual:*

> . . . Company X does not warrant that the functions contained in the software and described in this *User's Manual* will operate error free or that all software defects will be corrected. Except as set forth in the licensing agreement, there are no warranties, expressed or implied, on any phase of this product.

Essentially, what the company is saying is that they are not sure if the package will work and they will not guarantee to fix it if it does not!

In this textbook we introduce and discuss the phases involved in the development of correct and efficient computer programs. This includes the work that must go on *prior* to the actual coding of the program, such as specification, organization, and design; the work involved *during* coding; and the work that must go on *after* the program is implemented, such as verification, documentation, and maintenance. Figure 9.2 compares the steps involved in writing a term paper and those involved in developing a computer program in order to reinforce the notion of programming and problem solving as a complex series of operations involving a number of distinct steps.

Every problem you solve and every program you write, regardless of size, should follow the steps we will be introducing here and in future chapters. As much time and effort should be put into these preparatory phases as into coding. Do not cut corners because the problem seems simple. It is important to initially develop good programming habits and to become familiar with and knowledgeable of all phases of programming, not just coding. By following the steps we will be outlining, you should be able to handle *all* programming projects, regardless of size, and you will be a programmer in the fullest sense of the word.

In the next section, we will briefly review the steps involved in writing a computer program. Each of these steps (except the first) will be discussed at greater length in the upcoming chapters.

9.2
The Steps Involved in Programming

In the previous section we continually referred to "the steps involved in computer programming." Let's be more specific and list these nine steps.

Step 1: The Feasibility Study
Too often, people want to use a computer to solve a problem, even when it is not the appropriate tool for the job. Even though costs of computer hardware are coming down dramatically, computers are still not cheap, typically costing $2000 to $5000 for a small but complete home or business microcomputer system. Large minicomputer systems capable of supporting 8 to 16 users can easily cost $25,000 to $100,000. However, added to the purchase price of the hardware are the hidden costs of software, maintenance, and the salaries of any analysts, consultants, programmers, and data entry personnel operators you may need to hire. Typically, these other costs can be as much as (if not more than) the original purchase price of the computer system, as shown in Figure 9.3. Thus, the overall cost of a computer system to solve one's problem can be surprisingly higher than expected and cost more than the value of the information the program provides.

The first phase of any programming project should therefore be directed at answering one critical question: "Is it worth it for me to buy a computer and write or buy a program to solve my problem? Is the information that I will get worth the cost, in terms of money and/or my time?" It is very important to realize early on that not every problem you encounter should use or needs to use a computer system, and for many simple problems a sophisticated computer program is definitely overkill. Perhaps the best system for storing and retrieving kitchen recipes is not an expensive relational database management system, running on a personal computer, but a box of 3 by 5-inch index cards stored in a small metal box! In addition, there are the social costs to consider, including the possible loss of jobs, the retraining of personnel, and

FIGURE 9.3   Changes in the Cost of Computer System Components.

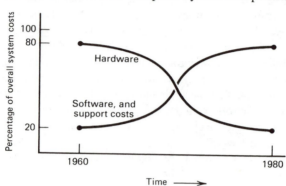

the upheaval caused by a major shift in the way we manage information and do business.

The feasibility study, then, is concerned with evaluating and comparing costs and benefits of a computer system. The output of this phase is called a *feasibility document* and is simply a recommendation to the user to proceed or not to proceed with the development or purchase of a computer program and any necessary hardware. The development of such a document is an extremely complex process and involves subject matter well beyond computer science alone, including business, management, economics, industrial psychology, and accounting. Because of this, we will not discuss this topic further and will assume that for every program in this text, a recommendation has already been made that it is a worthwhile undertaking and should be designed and built. We mention the feasibility study phase only to make you realize that a computer is simply a tool, and like any tool we first need to decide whether or not it can be useful in solving a given problem. That is, is it the right tool for the job? Only when that question has been answered "yes," do we decide how best to use it.

Step 2: Problem Specification Phase

Problem specification, sometimes called *requirements specification*, involves developing a clear, concise, and unambiguous statement of the exact problem to be solved. It seems somewhat silly to include this as a separate step because it is obvious that we need to know what to do before we can do it. However, it is surprising how often programmers will begin to solve a problem that is incompletely described, fraught with ambiguities, and sometimes even contradictory in places. Problems to be solved by a computer program must be described in extreme detail, typically much more detail than we include when describing problems to other people. In addition, the specifications must contain enough information for the programmer to anticipate and handle *all* possibilities, not just the expected ones.

The process of changing the rough problem statement initially posed by a user into a clear, concise, and exact *problem specification document* will be addressed in Chapter 10. This document will be an exact description of the problem to be solved and generally marks the end of the user's involvement with the problem until the finished product is delivered.

Step 3: Program Design Phase

Any large, complex project must first be divided into a set of smaller and less complex subtasks in order to be managed and completed effectively. Otherwise the job would be much too large and unwieldy to understand and to follow. This is why, for example, a large book (like this one) is not written as one long document but is divided into parts, chapters, and sections, each of which is researched and written separately.

The program design phase involves decomposing the problem statement from step 2 into a set of simpler modules and data structures, which, if they existed, would correctly solve the problem. For example, a problem to input student test scores, compute the test average, and write out the average may be more easily understood if it is not viewed as a single monolithic task but as composed of an abstract data type called ScoreTable and the following four separate subunits:

1. *Input module.* A program to input test scores, store them in the ScoreTable, and signal us when all data have been read.

2. *Validation module.* A program to check whether the test scores in ScoreTable are correct, or whether one or more of them are illegal, that is, out of range.

3. *Averaging module.* A program to compute the average of all legal scores in ScoreTable and to disregard illegal scores.

4. *Report writer module.* A program to print, in a nice readable format, the average test score.

The original problem will likely be easier to understand and implement in terms of these four simple tasks rather than in terms of a single large problem statement.

The result of this decomposition will be a *program design document* that lists

1. Every module used in the solution.

2. The structural relationship of that module to other modules (i.e., who calls whom).

3. The interface specifications of that module (i.e., the face it shows to the rest of the program).

4. The operations and functions carried out by these modules.

5. The abstract data types that will be used.

6. The operations that will be performed on these abstract data types.

The program design phase will be described in detail in Chapter 11.

As we mentioned earlier, some of the early programs that will be developed in this text are quite small and are composed of only a single module. For these, the program design phase is not really necessary. Remember, however, that these single-module programs are special cases and program design is a critically important step in the overall programming process.

Step 4:   Module Design

Once we know exactly what pieces are needed to solve the problem, we can begin to implement the modules one by one. Our first step is to select the *method* for solving the problem and the *internal representation* of the abstract data types that we have specified.

An *algorithm* is a formal step-by-step method for solving problems. It is one of the most important concepts in computer science and one that occupies a central place in any first programming course. (In fact, one of the definitions of computer science is the study of the design, representation, and analysis of algorithms.) For some problems, there is only a single technique and the selection is easy. For example, the method used for computing averages is the well-known formula

$$\text{average} = \frac{\text{sum of all legal scores}}{\text{number of legal scores}}$$

and we could use this technique to implement the averaging module referred to in the earlier discussion. Sometimes, the choice of an algorithm is not so obvious, because either dozens of techniques exist, and we must choose one, or no known method currently exists.

In addition to choosing the algorithm to use in implementing a module, we must select the internal representation for our abstract data types. For example, our input module referred to earlier must read in test scores. Will these scores be integers (e.g., 0–100), decimal quantities (e.g., 0.00–100.00) or letter grades (e.g., A, A−, B+, B, . . .)?

Similarly, our abstract data type called ScoreTable may be represented internally as a one-dimensional real array, a record structure, or a linked list. The topic of abstract data types and their internal realization was the central issue addressed in Part One of the text. We will now see how to use those ideas within the context of the overall problem-solving process.

Once we have selected our algorithm, sketched it in some suitable pseudocode notation, and selected the internal data representations for all data types, we have effectively completed the design of an individual module. Chapter 12 will introduce and discuss the evaluation of *module characteristics,* and how to distinguish a well-designed module from a poor one.

Step 5:   Coding

This is the step that most people immediately think of when they think of programming, and it was the primary topic of discussion in the first programming course. However, as we have shown, a great deal of important preparatory work precedes this step. In fact, if this preparatory work has been done well, then coding simply becomes the mechanical translation of algorithmic statements within a module into the syntax of some programming language. For example,

Algorithm: Divide the sum of the legal scores by the number of legal
   scores to determine the average.

```
Pascal:   average := sum/number;
BASIC:    Let A = S/N
FORTRAN:  average = sum/number
COBOL:    divide sum by number giving average
APL:      average ← sum ÷ number
```

Algorithm: Print out the average.

```
Pascal:   writeln(average);
BASIC:    print A
FORTRAN:  write (6,100) average
            100 format (i5)
COBOL:    write average
APL:      □ ← average
```

As you can clearly see, there are minor differences in syntax between languages, but conceptually they all carry out the same operation. The most creative part of programming is determining what operations are needed to be done, not determining how to write it out.

In this text we will be using the language called Pascal.[1] The language syntax and its correct use are the central topics of the first course in computer science. Chapters 13 and 14 will introduce some additional material concerning the "elegant" and "proper" use of the language as well as the design of *structured code*—the creation of programs using only nested single-entry, single-exit blocks.

Figure 9.4 lists some other well-known programming languages that are in widespread use today.

It is quite likely that during your career you will code in more than one of the languages shown in Figure 9.4. Similarly, it is quite likely that many of the languages contained in that figure will fall out of favor and into disuse while new languages will be developed to take their place. (Pascal was virtually unknown 15 years ago.) This is not a problem, though, because almost all of the issues addressed in this text, such as problem specification and program design, are *language independent* in that they hold true regardless of the language you choose for implementing your program. A programming language and its associated syntax, so important to the first programming course, are far, far less important issues now.

---

[1] Pascal is *not* an acronym and therefore is not written out in capital letters. It was named in honor of the French mathematician and religious philosopher Blaise Pascal (1623–1667).

FIGURE 9.4   Survey of Some Widely Used Computer Languages.

Language	Approximate Date of Introduction	General Application Areas
FORTRAN	1957	Numerically oriented language; most applicable to scientific, mathematical, and statistical problem areas; very widely used and very widely available.
ALGOL	1960	Also a numerically oriented language but with new language features; widely used in Europe
COBOL	1960	The most widely used business-oriented computer language
LISP	1961	Special-purpose language developed primarily for list processing and symbolic manipulation; widely used in the area of artificial intelligence
SNOBOL	1962	Special-purpose language used primarily for character string processing; this includes applications such as text editors, language processors, and bibliographic work
BASIC	1965	A simple interactive programming language widely used to teach programming in high schools and colleges
PL/1	1965	An extremely complex, general-purpose language designed to incorporate the numeric capabilities of FORTRAN, the business capabilities of COBOL, and many other features into a single language
APL	1967	An operator-oriented interactive language that introduced a wide range of new mathematical operations that are built directly into the language.
Pascal	1971	A general-purpose language designed specifically to teach the concepts of computer programming and allow the efficient implementation of large programs
Modula-2	1980	A language that builds on the ideas of Pascal but adds facilities for modularization and data abstraction
Ada	1981	A new systems implementation language designed and built for the Department of Defense
Prolog	1982	A nonprocedural language built on the concepts of the first-order predicate logic

Step 6:   Debugging

Once the code has been written, you would like to think you are almost done. Unfortunately, this is not the case. Time studies on large software projects show that about 45 to 55% of the overall time is spent on simply implementing the code on a computer system, after it has been written.

As a first step, you must begin to *debug* your program—locate and correct all errors that cause the program to produce incorrect results or perform improper actions. This has always been one of the most frustrating, agonizing, and time-consuming steps in the overall programming process. The reason for this is related to the issue we have been mentioning all along—the lack of time spent on carefully planning, organizing, and structuring the solution. When insufficient time is spent on planning, the result is usually a structural mess with convoluted, hard-to-understand "spaghetti-type" logic. In this type of environment it is easy for bugs to occur and very hard for them to be located and corrected. An important point to remember about debugging is

> The very best technique for debugging is to *avoid* making mistakes in the first place.

Much of what we are going to describe about program specification and design is directed at getting the program correct *the first time,* so that the debugging phase becomes less time-consuming. Errors do occur, however, and formal methods for locating and correcting them will be discussed in Chapter 16.

Step 7:   Testing, Verification, and Benchmarking

Even though a program works correctly on 1, 5, or 1000 data sets, how do we know that it is indeed correct? The testing and verification phase involves demonstrating that the program is theoretically correct and will work properly on *all* data, even those that have not been explicitly tested. There are two basic and quite different techniques for doing this—called *empirical testing* and *formal verification.*

With empirical testing we carefully select a large number of test cases and run the program using these data. If the program produces correct results for this collection of test data, we can say that it will work properly on *all* test data.

With verification techniques we argue in a more formal mathematical or logical sense to prove that the program P will produce the correct output O, for all input data I. We treat the program and its individual statements as mathematical entities and formally prove that they have certain characteristics or properties. Naturally, verification is much more complex than simple testing, but it allows us to make much stronger claims about the correctness of the program. Both techniques for determining correctness will be introduced and discussed in Chapter 16.

In addition to simply testing the program for correctness we may also choose, at this time, to measure the *efficiency characteristics* of the nearly completed program. How fast does it run? How much memory space does it occupy? Does it operate as required by the specification document? This is sometimes termed *benchmarking* the program. If our measurements indicate that the processing speed (or some other measure) is not quite up to specifications, then we will likely have to do some fine tuning of the code to speed it up. If we are way off the mark in terms of run time (i.e., hours versus seconds), fine tuning will likely be inadequate, and we will probably need to go back and redesign entire sections of the program. (If you are this far off specifications, however, it usually indicates poor planning in the first place.)

The topics of program efficiency and benchmarking are treated in Chapter 16.

At the completion of the testing and verification stage, we should have a correct, working, and reasonably efficient program. It is extremely important that this phase be done thoroughly and precisely. One of the most important quality characteristics of a program is *reliability*—its ability to operate uninterrupted and error free over long periods of time. An unreliable program will not be used.

Step 8: Documentation Phase

Programmers are often more comfortable with formal languages like Pascal or BASIC than with natural language such as English. However, it does no good to have an elegant and powerful computer program if a user does not know how to use it correctly. Documentation involves developing and writing the supporting manuals and on-line assistance, which the user will need to understand and use the finished program effectively. Failure to do a good job at this stage can invalidate all the good work done up till now. (How often have you become frustrated with using something and thrown it away because you could not understand the instruction booklet!)

You do not start writing documentation after the program is finished. In fact, much of the information you need has already been written during previous phases:

Step 1. The Feasibility Document
Step 2. The Specification Document
Step 3. The Design Document
Step 4. The Algorithms and Abstract Data Types
Step 5. Program Listings and Comments
Step 6. Benchmark Results and Sample Test Data

Your job now is to bring this material together into finished documents that clearly explain to users and other programmers how to use this program properly and effectively. It is not enough for a programmer to be able to communicate with a machine; he or she must also be able to communicate with other people!

Documentation standards and guidelines, both printed and on-line, will be discussed in Chapter 18.

Step 9: Program Maintenance

Programs are *not* static entities that, once completed, never change. Because of the expense involved in developing software (see Figure 9.3), programs are generally used for quite a long time. It is not unusual to see a program still being used 5, 10, or 15 years after it was originally written. In fact, the typical life-cycle for a medium-to-large software product is 2 to 3 years in development and 5 to 15 years in use in the marketplace. The overall cost of maintaining the software over its effective life will typically exceed the initial cost of development by a factor of 2:1. During this long period of use new errors may be uncovered, new hardware may be purchased, user needs will change, laws and regulations may change, and the whims of the marketplace will fluctuate. Because of this, the original program will need to be modified to meet these new needs. *Program maintenance* is the operation of adapting a program to keep it correct and current with changing specifications and new equipment. If the program has been well organized and well planned, has been carefully designed as a set of independent modules, has been well coded, and is clearly documented so that we know what it does, then program maintenance will be a less difficult task. In fact, it could be

FIGURE 9.5   Approximate Percentage of Time on Each
Phase of Programming.

Phase	Approximate Percentage of Time
Specification/design/planning	30–40
Coding	15–20
Testing/reviewing/fixing	30–40
Documenting	10–15

quite similar to the job of a TV repairperson who checks the components one by one, locates the defective one, unplugs it, and snaps in a new one. Much of our concern for the careful planning and designing of computer programs is to ensure that program maintenance is *not* a difficult task.

9.3
Conclusion

As we have tried to show in this chapter, there is much, much more to programming than coding. Recent studies on the time spent by programmers in various stages of initial program development show that a relatively small amount of time is spent on the coding phase. Figure 9.5 describes the approximate amount of time spent by programmers on the major phases in program development.

The point that this chapter has tried to make is that programming is an extremely complex task made up of many phases, each of which is important and each of which contributes to the overall solution of a problem. Do not confuse the topics of programming and coding. When developing your own programs, remember that the coding phase must be preceded by a great deal of preparatory work clarifying, planning, and organizing your solution. Failing to understand and follow this principle is the first and greatest mistake you can make in computer programming.

The field of computer science that involves the study and development of methods for managing the systematic implementation of correct, efficient, and reliable software products is called *software engineering*. It is an extremely important area of computer science, and an important subject of advanced study.

In the upcoming chapters we will expand on each of the topics introduced here and begin our detailed study of the topic of program development.

Exercises for Chapter 9

1.   Go to a computer store and look at the user's manual of any popular software package (e.g., a word processor or educational package). See if there is a warranty

disclaimer like the one shown on page 230. Why do you feel that it is necessary to put that there? How does it make you feel about using this package?

2.   Assume that a new microcomputer and printer could be purchased for $2000. Try to do an informal feasibility study on whether or not it would be worth it for your school to purchase a computer and write a program to allow teachers to keep student records on the system—that is, names, test scores, and homework grades. (Sort of like an electronic grade book.) What useful information could the computer give to the teacher? Would it save any time? Do you think it would be worth the cost?

3.   The average student program is approximately 25 to 200 lines of Pascal code. Go to a computer store and talk to a technical specialist to find out the size (in terms of lines of high-level code) of some popular computer programs such as a game, a graphics package, a word processor, or an integrated business software system. What category do they fall into, using the notation of Figure 9.1. Discuss the problems that you might have writing programs of this size without adequate planning and organization.

4.   One common misconception that people have is that overall computer system costs will decline continuously because hardware costs are dropping. Why does Figure 9.3 refute that argument?

5.   Talk to the director of the computer center at your institution and determine the approximate percentage of the overall computer services budget that is allocated to

Hardware purchases/maintenance/staff
Software development/purchase/maintenance
User services staff/documentation

How does this compare with the values shown in Figure 9.3?

*6.   Why would it be more difficult to specify a problem that will be programmed on a computer than it is to specify a problem that will be given to a person and solved manually?

*7.   Why is outlining a term paper very similar in concept to the program design phase?

8.   An algorithm is not simply a concept in computer science. Algorithms occur frequently in everyday life (although they are rarely ever called that). Describe algorithms that would occur outside the context of computer programs.

9.   Looking over the languages listed in Figure 9.4, which language do you think you might select for implementing each of the following applications:
   a.   A payroll system.
   b.   A statistics library package, such as SPSS (Statistical Package for the Social Sciences).
   c.   A Pascal compiler.
Give some general reasons for your choice.

*10.   We have repeatedly said that poorly planned, poorly organized, and sloppy programs are difficult to get working correctly and difficult to maintain. The following sequence of instructions was intended to try to find which of three given numbers—x, y, z—is the largest and to write it out.

Step	Instruction
1	if x is bigger than y then go to step 4
2	if y is bigger than z then go to step 8
3	go to step 10
4	if x is greater than z then go to step 6
5	go to step 8
6	set the biggest value to x
7	go to step 11
8	set the biggest value to y
9	go to step 11
10	set the biggest value to z
11	write out the biggest value
12	you are done

Does it do what it is supposed to do? If not, locate and correct the bug. What was there about the structure of this set of instructions that made it difficult to follow? Write out a sequence of instructions that is clearer and easier to follow.

11. Try to find out the total development time and the release date of the original version of the Pascal compiler and operating system used at your installation. What is the ratio of development time to maintenance time for these software products? What version number are they on? How many updates and/or new releases have there been for these software products?

12. Talk to a professional programmer and see how much time is spent on the different programming phases we have described in this chapter. Is it similar to the values given in Figure 9.5? Do they perform additional steps that were not described in this chapter?

CHAPTER 10

THE PROBLEM SPECIFICATION PHASE

10.1
Introduction

Most problems begin as extremely rough and very incomplete ideas in the minds of an individual. They are nowhere near ready to form the basis for the design of a rather complicated program. These rough problem statements represent the initial thoughts of a user who has an information-based problem but who is not exactly sure what needs to be done or how to do it. Typical examples of such initial problem statements would include the teacher who "wants help with recording and averaging student test scores"; the scientist who "wants to collect and analyze laboratory instrument data"; the business person who "wants a program to calculate and print out my 90-day receivables." All these areas represent valid applications of computers, but none of these statements can, in its present form, serve as the basis for the design and implementation of a program.

The problem specification phase is concerned with the refinement of a rough problem statement, replete with omissions, inconsistencies, ambiguities, and uncertainties, into a finished *problem specification document,* which is a complete and unambiguous statement of the problem to be solved. The term "problem specification document" is not standard, and this item may variously be termed a *system specification,* a *software requirements document,* or a *user-needs inventory.* However, regardless of the title, they will all contain very similar information.

What is contained in such a document? What information is needed by the programmer to continue the development of the program? What information is not yet needed and can effectively be postponed until later stages? These are the questions we will answer in the remainder of this chapter.

243

10.2
Contents of the Problem Specification Document

Essentially a problem specification document is an *input/output document*. It specifies exactly what inputs are coming into the program and exactly what actions or outputs are produced by the program. It says nothing at all about *how* the program will convert the input values into the desired results, that is, what algorithms it will use or what data types will be selected. The program specification document treats the program to be developed as a "black box," in the sense that its only concern is what goes in and what comes out, not what happens inside. This situation is diagrammed in Figure 10.1.

This is exactly as it should be, because users generally do not care about how a program works as long as it produces the desired results in a reasonably efficient manner. In fact, including technical details about how to solve the problem would likely confuse the user and make the specification document much more difficult to read.

To completely specify the input to a program, we need to provide the following five pieces of information:

1. Exactly what values will be provided to the program and in what order? The meaning of these input values must be clear and unambiguous.
2. How many input values will there be, or, phrased another way, how will we know when there is no more input?
3. What is the exact format of the input data including type, accuracy, and units?
4. From what class of input device will these values be provided—on-line keyboard, input file, voice input, or some other device?
5. Is there a legal range of allowable values for the input? Is there some upper bound on the plausible range of values?

To specify the output of a program completely, we need to include answers to the following four questions:

1. Exactly what results do you want the program to produce? The meaning of these output values must be clear and unambiguous.
2. What format do you want for these values, including type, accuracy, and units?
3. On what class of output device should we produce the output—printed copy, CRT, plotter, graphics, or some other device?
4. Exactly how do you wish these values to be displayed, including spacing, headings, titles, and layout?

Together, the input and output specifications represent the major (although not the only) component of the program specification document.

Let's do a simple example. Let's say your Latin professor approached you with the problem shown in Figure 10.2. We certainly have a good idea of what is wanted, but

FIGURE 10.1   Pictorial View of a Program Specification Document.

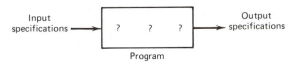

this extremely rough problem statement is much too incomplete to form the basis of a program design. Looking at the statement in Figure 10.2, we see that in its current form it does not contain answers to any of the following questions:

1. What is the format of the test scores—numbers such as 72, 99, or letters such as C+, A−, F?

2. How many students were in the class?

3. What is the order of the data—the test 1 scores for the entire class followed by all test 2 scores followed by test 3, or, alternatively, the test 1, test 2, and test 3 scores for each student entered as 3-tuples (Figure 10.3)?

4. What is the legal range of scores on the test?

5. Exactly how should the output appear? Should the values be printed in alphanumeric form or graphed?

6. What accuracy would you like for the mean and the standard deviation?

We must get answers to these questions before continuing on with program development. Therefore, a key part of the specification phase involves *interviewing* the user in order to determine exactly what he or she wants or needs. It is the job of the programmer to identify what is missing or contradictory in the problem specification, suggest alternative ways to implement these missing features, and, where necessary, provide technical advice. The user may then select the approach that appears best for him or her and that comes closest to providing the desired results.

Sometimes the programmer may be unfamiliar with either the area of application or other specialized subject areas that come up during specification (e.g., statistics). In this case, the programmer may need to call in one or more technical specialists in these

FIGURE 10.2   Rough Problem Statement for a Test Scoring Problem.

Every student in my Latin class took three tests during the semester. I would like a program that would give me the mean and standard deviation for each test.[1]

---

[1] Interestingly enough, a feasibility study would probably show that, unless the class was quite large, we probably should not bother to use a computer for this problem. Paper and pencil, or at most a hand calculator, would most likely be cheaper and faster!

FIGURE 10.3   Example of Differing Input Formats.

```
XXX ⎫                      Test 1    Test 2    Test 3
  ·  ⎪                        ↓         ↓         ↓
  ·  ⎬  Test 1              XXX,      XXX,      XXX   ←student 1
  ·  ⎪                      XXX,      XXX,      XXX   ←student 2
XXX ⎭                         ·

XXX ⎫          or             ·
  ·  ⎪                        ·
  ·  ⎬  Test 2
  ·  ⎪
XXX ⎭

XXX ⎫
  ·  ⎪
  ·  ⎬  Test 3
  ·  ⎪
XXX ⎭
```

---

areas. The interview will now go on between the user, the programmer, and the technical specialists, each contributing ideas and soliciting answers in order to flesh out a detailed specification.

Assume, for example, that we interviewed our Latin professor and got answers to all the questions previously listed. For technical questions such as number 5, in which the professor was unsure of what to do, we provided sufficient explanation to allow an informed and reasonable selection to be made. Figure 10.4 shows a possible first draft of a specification document for this problem. After this first draft has been written, it is the job of both the programmer and the user to carefully review what has been written and see if the program, as described, is exactly what is wanted. It is quite easy to make changes at this stage in the programming process, since no code has been written. But at a later time, after we have begun the design, coding, and testing phases, changes become much more time-consuming and expensive.

Software engineering studies have shown that it is approximately ten times more expensive to make a significant change in a program during the coding stage than during specification. That ratio may go up as high as 50:1 if the change is made during the final stages of testing. Last minute changes to a specification will require rewriting the specification document, redoing portions of the design, and recoding and debugging selected modules. This involves significantly more effort. The moral here is "get it right initially."

Figure 10.5, reproduced from Fairly, (1985) summarizes the relative costs involved in making a change at various points in the overall software life cycle.

Referring back to the problem specification draft in Figure 10.4, the programmer may decide that it describes a highly inflexible program without much generality. As it

FIGURE 10.4   First Draft of the Problem Specification
Document for the Test Scoring Problem.

I have 34 students in my Latin class, each of whom took three tests during the semester. The test scores are numbers in the range 0 to 100. I would like a program that would allow me to input at my computer terminal the test scores in the following order:

T_1, T_2, T_3 (the three test scores of student 1)
T_1, T_2, T_3 (the three test scores of student 2)
.
.
.
T_1, T_2, T_3 (the three test scores of student 34)

After all the input has been entered, the program should print the following six lines of output on a hard-copy output device that I can take with me.

The mean of all test 1 scores is *xxx.x*.
The mean of all test 2 scores is *xxx.x*.
The mean of all test 3 scores is *xxx.x*.

The standard deviation on test 1 is *xx.x*.
The standard deviation on test 2 is *xx.x*.
The standard deviation on test 3 is *xx.x*.

FIGURE 10.5   Relative Cost to Make a Change.

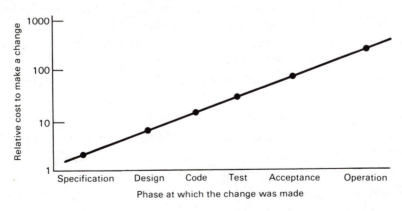

currently stands, it always assumes a class size of 34 students and legal test scores in the range 0 to 100. There is no provision for changing any of these three values. Next semester the teacher may have only 28 students or may give 50-point quizzes. The programmer suggests a modification that will allow the program to work for any range of test scores. The change would involve having the user enter, prior to the test scores, one additional line of data containing the following three values:

1. The number of students in the class.
2. The lowest legal test score.
3. The highest legal test score.

Once the program inputs these values, it can use them in all subsequent calculations. Thus, the modified program would work for both a Latin class of 34 taking 100-point tests and a chemistry class of 25 taking a 50-point quiz. This change would significantly widen the generality of the finished program.

Similarly, the professor, after reviewing the first draft, may decide that it would be much easier to input all the test 1 scores first, followed by all test 2 and then all test 3 scores, rather than as described in Figure 10.4. The three different tests were recorded on three different pages of the grade book, and this latter approach will minimize page flipping and facilitate the task of input. After discussing and accepting these changes, we produce the second draft of the specification document shown in Figure 10.6.

This development process would continue, possibly through a third or fourth draft—each time making sure that we were giving the user exactly what information he or she needs in exactly the form he or she wants. For example, looking back at Figure 10.6, we might wish to discuss any or all of the following issues with the user as possible modifications to the problem:

1. Would you like a program that works for any number of tests, rather than specifically for three? As it now stands, the program lacks complete generality because of its fixed requirement of exactly three tests per student.
2. Would you like the input to come from a data file rather than the terminal, so you do not have to reenter the data each time the program is run?
3. Would you like to include the students' names and/or ID numbers on the input as well as their test scores?
4. Would you like us to echo print the examination scores on the output report?
5. Are there any other statistical measures you would like to have, such as the median, mode, or range?
6. Would you like the scores printed in sorted sequence?
7. Would you like graphical rather than printed output (e.g., bar charts or graphs)?

Depending on the responses to these questions, we may wish to revise the draft shown in Figure 10.6 and incorporate any changes that have been suggested.

As well as suggesting improvements and enhancements, it is also the job of the programmer to inform the user about things that would be either impossible or ex-

FIGURE 10.6   Second Draft of the Problem Specification
Document for the Test Scoring Problem.

I would like a program that would allow me to input the three examination scores of students
in my class and determine the mean and standard deviation of those scores. All input to the
program will be through the terminal keyboard. The first line of input will contain the following three values, in this order:

1.   The number, N, of students $1 \leq N \leq 500$.

2.   The lowest legal test score, LOW.

3.   The highest legal test score, HIGH where HIGH $\geq$ LOW.

All succeeding input will be the three test scores in the following order:

T_1
T_2
.
.
.   The N scores on test 1, each score must be in the
            range LOW to HIGH
T_N

T_1
T_2
.
.
.   The N scores on test 2, each score must be in the
            range LOW to HIGH
T_N

T_1
T_2
.
.
.   The N scores on test 3, each score must be in the
            range LOW to HIGH
T_N

After all input has been entered, the program should produce, on a hard-copy output device,
the following seven lines of output:

Number of students $= xx$ Possible Range of Test Scores $xxx–xxx$.

The mean of all test 1 scores is $xxx.x$.
The mean of all test 2 scores is $xxx.x$.
The mean of all test 3 scores is $xxx.x$.

The standard deviation on test 1 is $xx.x$.
The standard deviation on test 2 is $xx.x$.
The standard deviation on test 3 is $xx.x$.

tremely difficult to do well on a computer and should probably *not* be part of the program. For example, if our Latin professor had asked us to include in the program the ability to assign letter grades—A, A−, B+, B, B−, C+, and so on—to each test, we should probably inform him or her that this type of qualitative decision making and higher-level evaluation of data is difficult to program and would be better done manually. The same thing may be true for such judgmental operations as determining exactly where the student is strong or weak and planning a set of remedial training exercises (unless the professor can describe this in explicit algorithmic terms). It is important for a user to learn that some things are better done by people than by programs and probably should not be included in the problem specifications.

The point of this extended example has been to show you that a problem specification document is not something done once and never changed. It is a highly dynamic document that typically evolves over many drafts as meetings are held, alternatives are discussed, and suggestions are made. Each one of the people involved in these meetings—users, programmers, specialists—contribute their expertise to ensure that the system being designed gives the user all the necessary information. As we mentioned earlier, it is very important to get it right now because future changes will be significantly more expensive and time-consuming. This situation is analogous to redesigning a new house. If the suggestions are made to the architect during the design phase it is relatively easy—only involving the redrawing of some blueprints. However, if the changes are suggested after the contractors have arrived, dug the foundation, and put up the walls, the difficulty and costs increase manyfold.

10.3
Exception Handling

If nothing ever went wrong, we would have finished our discussion. You would simply write out the input/output specifications of the program exactly as discussed in the previous section. However, a specification document must describe the actions to take for *every possible input,* including those that are implausible, illegal, or even impossible. The problem specification document must include a third section, in addition to input and output, called "special handling" (or exception handling), which describes out-of-the-ordinary events that violate the normal and expected specifications of the problem. These special conditions can be caused by any of the following:

1. Input that falls outside the legal range.
2. Too much input.
3. Not enough input.
4. Input that is in the improper format (e.g., letters instead of digits).
5. Input that would lead to an illegal arithmetic operation (e.g., dividing by 0).

We must anticipate all of these circumstances and include in our specification document exactly what response to take for each condition. If we do this, our "black box" program will be able to take meaningful actions under all conditions, not just the

FIGURE 10.7   Complete Pictorial View of a Program
Specification Document.

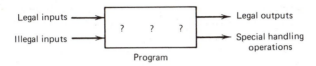

Program

expected ones, as shown in Figure 10.7. This special handling section of the
specification document is the easiest place for a programmer to overlook things and
omit important details. The reason for this omission is that this type of information is
usually not included in instructions given to people because they have common sense.
When giving instructions to people we usually assume that they will be able to figure
out what to do when faced with unanticipated conditions or unexpected circumstances.
For example, when preparing instructions on how to start a car, we do not usually
specify what to do if you have lost your keys or the car was stolen! We assume that an
intelligent adult can determine the proper actions to take in either case. However,
computer programs do not have common sense. Responses to such unusual happenings
must be planned for, specified, and explicitly included in the program.

Looking back at the second draft of the specification document in Figure 10.6, we
see that it does not tell us what to do if any of the following special conditions occur:

1.   No one took the tests ($N = 0$).
2.   Too many people took the tests ($N > 500$), and the computer cannot store all the
     data values in memory.
3.   The test score range is meaningless (LOW > HIGH).
4.   A test score T is not an integer value.
5.   A test score T is a number outside the range LOW to HIGH.

We must talk to the user again to find out what he or she would like done for each of
these special conditions. Should they not be sure exactly what response to take, we
may suggest some possibilities. Typical ways to deal with erroneous input data would
include the following operations:

1.   Produce a descriptive error message and allow the user to reenter the correct data.
2.   Go into an on-line assistance mode, provide help to the user, and then reenter the
     correct data.
3.   Use a special default value in place of the illegal one. Inform the user of the use of
     this default value.
4.   Skip over the incorrect value entirely. Solve the problem using only $N - 1$ pieces
     of data rather than N.
5.   Terminate the program with an error message indicating the reason for termina-
     tion.

FIGURE 10.8 Third Draft of the Problem Specification
Document for the Test Scoring Program.

I would like a program that would allow me to input the three examination scores of students
in my class and determine the mean and standard deviation of those scores. All input to the
program will be through the terminal keyboard. The first line of input will contain the following three values, in this order:

1. The number, N, of students $1 \leq N \leq 500$.
2. The lowest legal test score, LOW.
3. The highest legal test score, HIGH, where HIGH $\geq$ LOW.

Should the value of N be either nonnumeric or outside the range 1 to 500, print the following
message:

**Error: The number of students must be in the range 1–500, please reenter
the previous line using a legal value.**

Should the value for either LOW or HIGH be nonnumeric or should LOW $>$ HIGH, print
the following message:

**Error: The test score range provided is illegal. Please reenter the previous
line using legal values.**

If either or both of these messages has been printed, the program should ask the user to
reenter a new first line containing all three values. When the first line of input has been
entered correctly, the user should input the test scores in the following order:

T_1
T_2
.
.   The N scores on test 1, each score must be in the
.   range LOW to HIGH
T_N

T_1
T_2
.
.   The N scores on test 2, each score must be in the
.   range LOW to HIGH
T_N

T_1
T_2
.
.   The N scores on test 3, each score must be in the
.   range LOW to HIGH
T_N

FIGURE 10.8 *(Continued)*

Should any test score T_i be nonnumeric or outside the range LOW-HIGH discard it and print the following message:

Error: The last test score was not in the range *xxx–xxx*. Please reenter that score.

where *xxx–xxx* represents the range LOW to HIGH. After all input has been legally entered, produce the following seven lines of output:

Number of students $= xx$ Possible Range of Test Scores *xxx–xxx*.

The mean of all test 1 scores is *xxx.x*.
The mean of all test 2 scores is *xxx.x*.
The mean of all test 3 scores is *xxx.x*.

The standard deviation on test 1 is *xx.x*.
The standard deviation on test 2 is *xx.x*.
The standard deviation on test 3 is *xx.x*.

In any case, we must make a decision now on how to respond to each of the above error conditions and include the appropriate actions in our specification document. A third draft of the test-scoring problem, which addresses the above special handling conditions, is shown in Figure 10.8. Looking over the description contained in Figure 10.8, we see how far we have come from the original rough problem statement in Figure 10.2, and the first draft of our specification document in Figure 10.4.

However, because it is so important to get the problem specification document correct now, we should not simply stop when we have a good specification. We must develop an excellent specification that minimizes future problems and changes. We should carefully review all aspects of the problem to ensure that we have accounted for all possibilities, no matter how unlikely. For example, if we look in the instructor's grade book, we may notice that some students were excused from one or more of the tests, and this missing grade should not be included in the test average. Unless we plan for the concept of *missing data* right now, here is what might happen later on (assume an examination score in the range 1 to 100):

?Please enter next test score
0   (Assume we try to put in a 0 for the missing grade)
Error: The last test score was not in the range 1-100. Please reenter that score.
   (Now we try a blank)
Error: The last test score was not in the range 1-100. Please reenter that score.
help
**Error: The last . . .

Now we realize our problem, and we will have to do a major redesign and recoding of significant portions of the program to eliminate this oversight. How much easier it would have been to solve this problem during the specification phase. (Exercise 1 at the end of the chapter asks you to modify the specification document in Figure 10.8 to provide for the concept of missing data.)

Notice that nowhere in Figure 10.8 did we say anything about *how* this problem will be solved. This is because the user generally does not care about the algorithm we choose to solve the problem, as long as it works, is reasonably efficient, and produces the desired results. It is in the next two programming steps that we will begin to select the algorithms and data types for solving the problem. Thus, we were able to write a successful specification document even though we may currently be unsure of how to compute a standard deviation (or even what it is!).

If the user is now satisfied with the problem as described in the current draft, he or she signs off on the problem specification document. This means that he or she certifies that the problem, as described in that document, is exactly what is wanted and agrees not to make any future changes without accepting the time delay and expense involved in making those changes. Similarly, the programmer agrees to design and build a program that performs exactly as described in the specifications. In a sense, this document becomes a contract between user and programmer certifying exactly what task must be done. This generally ends the user's role in the project, until the final system is delivered for checkout and acceptance testing.

The input–output specifications of Section 10.2 and the special handling operations of Section 10.3 together constitute what are called the *functional specifications* of the proposed program. They describe, for every possible combination of inputs, the behavior (i.e., functions) the program will display. The functional specifications are the most important part of the problem specification document.

In an academic environment, the problem specification phase is generally not seen by the student. This is not because it does not exist, but because it has already been done for the student by the instructor who thinks up a problem, refines and clarifies it through a number of drafts, and, finally, prepares it in a nice readable format. This document spells out, quite explicitly, exactly what problem is to be solved. Thus, in an academic environment the problem specification document is better known as a *homework assignment!* In real life, however, problems rarely start out with such clarity and accuracy. It is up to the programmer to extract from the user adequate information to produce a document, similar to Figure 10.8, which can form the basis for the next stage of program development, called program design.

EXAMPLE

1. Rough problem statement:

    I would like a program that would tell me if a given number is or is not prime.

2. Problem specification document:

Definition:

   You are to write a program to determine whether an integer value N, $N > 1$ is or is not prime. A number is defined to be prime if it is not evenly divisible by any whole number, other than 1 and itself.

Input:
  The program should accept as input from the terminal a single whole number, N,. greater than 1.

Output:
  The program should then determine if the number just input is or is not prime. If the number is prime, the program should produce the following output:

  "N" is a prime number

where "N" is replaced by the input data. If the number is not prime, the program should produce the following output:

  "N" is not a prime number, "M" is a factor

where "N" is replaced by the input data and "M" is replaced by the numeric value of any factor of N. That is, M is a positive whole number, other than 1 or N, which divides evenly into N.

Special Handling:
  If the quantity N is illegal, that is, either nonnumeric or $N \leq 1$, then print out the following error message:

  ***Error--The input value is incorrect. It must be a whole number greater than 1. Please reenter this value**

Then allow the user to reenter this value. After the program has completed the processing of a single correct input value, it should print out the following line:

  **End of program--Thank you

and terminate.

10.4
Performance Specifications

For some problems the functional specifications described in the two preceding sections are the only information needed. However, one additional class of information can be highly useful to include in problem specification document—the topic of *performance specifications*. These are specifications of the minimal operating characteristics required of the finished program. Remembering that the specification document is a user-oriented document rather than a technical one, these performance specifications should be expressed in terms of quantities that a user can understand, observe, and measure, rather than internal technical measures understandable only to a programmer. Therefore, performance criteria such as the following (although they may be highly appropriate at later stages in the program design) would be totally inappropriate in a specification document:

> Execution of at least 10,000 machine language instructions per second.
> No more than 100 bus interrupts per second.
> At least 5000 disk accesses per minute.

Better to specify something like

> The program must process at least 100 data sets per second.

This is a statement that the user can easily verify.

Performance metrics, as they are frequently called, must be detailed and quantitative rather than subjective and qualitative. The performance conditions contained in the specification document will be used to judge the quality and acceptability of the finished program. Subjective measures such as the following are too vague to serve as good acceptance measures:

> The program must be extremely quick in processing data.
> It must be robust.
> It must respond fast enough so that users do not get angry.

(One person may get angry after waiting 3 seconds, while another is content to sit for 3 minutes and not get upset.) Measures must be phrased in exact and unambiguous quantitative terms like the following:

> The average response time to an input query must be less than 2.0 sec-
> onds, and no single response must ever require more than 5.0 seconds.
> The program must process 99% of the data sets in under 10 seconds.

Performance metrics generally address the following six areas of program performance (although there could be many others):

1. *Speed.* How fast can the program operate, typically in terms of response time to a query, total time to produce a given result, or worst-case behavior for the largest possible data set.

2. *Throughput.* How much information can be "pushed through" the program in a given time unit. Typically measured in completed data sets/time unit.

3. *Availability.* A measure of the percentage of time the system is up and available for processing; usually used as a hardware metric, but can also measure the availability and robustness of software products.

4. *Capacity.* A measure of the maximum number of data items that can be handled by the program.

5. *Precision.* The accuracy with which the final results can be produced, typically given in terms of *maximal error bounds.*

6. *Equipment Needs.* A specification of the maximal resources (memory, I/O) that will be needed to run the completed program. These should be expressed in nontechnical terms and be directed toward ensuring that the finished product will run on the user's equipment.

Looking back at the problem specification document in Figure 10.8, we see that it contains two performance metrics. The finished program must be able to successfully process any number of students up to and including 500, and it must be able to determine the mean and standard deviation to one-decimal-place accuracy. To this, we may wish to add other performance criteria such as

> The program must be able to accept a LOW-HIGH test score range anywhere in the range 0 to 10,000.
>
> The program must be able to accept a 500-element data set and complete all processing of that data set in 5 seconds or less.
>
> The completed program must be able to run on an IBM-PC/AT computer system with 640K of memory and a 10-Mbyte hard disk.

These performance criteria serve two important purposes: they ensure that the finished product will be not only *correct* but also *useful*. After all, a correct answer is meaningless if it is not provided quickly enough to be of any use to us or it requires equipment that we do not have. Second, these performance measures will be used during the final *acceptance testing* of the finished program. A program will be said to be correct and ready for delivery when it meets both the (a) functional specifications, as laid out in the input, output, and special handling sections, and the (b) performance specifications, as laid out in the performance metrics section, of the problem specification document. This is another reason why completeness, thoroughness, and exactness are very important in a problem specification document. Not only is this document used to describe the problem to be solved, it is an important component in determining when the program has been successfully finished.

To write a problem specification document well, it is important to realize that describing the functional and performance characteristics of a program is quite similar to describing exactly how the completed program works, that is, writing the *user's manual*. Frequently, programmers believe that the user's manual is written at the very conclusion of a software project and, indeed, our chapter on documentation (Chapter 18) comes at the very end of the book, reinforcing that idea. However, this is not the case in practice. More and more, the user's manual is written *prior* to the development of the software product itself. This gives the user an exact description of the operational characteristics of the software *before* it has been started and serves the role of the specification document that we have been describing. As we mentioned in the previous chapter, you should not think of documentation as something to be done only when the program has been completed successfully. Documentation is a process that can go on *during* and even *prior to* the design and coding stages.

10.5
Formal Specification Method

Throughout this chapter we have stressed the need for clarity, completeness, and exactness as essential characteristics of good specifications. Every possible combination of inputs must be anticipated and dealt with, and there must be no confusion or ambiguity in determining what actions are to be taken for each. However, we have then

FIGURE 10.9   Quadrants of a Decision Table.

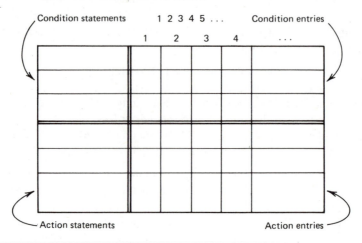

used natural language, that is, English, to express these specifications. This is a poor choice of notations, because all natural languages suffer from the problems of ambiguities, context sensitivity, multiple meanings, unintended meanings, and shades of interpretation. Natural languages were never intended to have the clear and precise notational characteristics of mathematics or formal language. For example, if I say

Check if Tom or Bill is in and if so, give him the money.

Who does "him" refer to—Tom or Bill—or does it not matter? Similarly, when I say

If Tom comes in the front door or Bill goes out the back door, then call me immediately.

what do we do if *both* Tom comes in the front *and* Bill goes out the back? The Pascal concept of *or* is well defined as meaning inclusive-OR, but in English the word *or* can mean either an inclusive-OR or exclusive-OR, depending on the context.

For this reason, a good deal of software engineering research is being carried out in the area of *formal representation methods* for problem specification documents. These formal methods are not intended to replace natural language documents (e.g., the user's manual) but to be used in conjunction with them to help make them more complete and exact. There are many formalized techniques, and we will describe only one—called *decision tables*.

A decision table is a two-dimensional matrix structure that is divided into quadrants, each of which contains a number of rows and columns. The columns of the decision table are called *decision rules*. The overall structure of a decision table is shown in Figure 10.9.

FIGURE 10.10 Partial Decision Table.

		2		4	
x is odd	...	Y	...	N	...
$y \geq 500$	...	Y	...	N	...
$z = 0$		N		—	
Action 1		X			
Action 2					
Action 3		X		X	

A *condition statement* is a boolean condition that may or may not be met by a specific set of input data. Examples of condition statements include the following:

The value of x is in the range 1 to 100.
The size of the data set exceeds 500 elements.
The value for score is nonnumeric.
There are four entries in this input set.

There are as many condition statements in the decision table as it takes to describe all the characteristics of the input.

The *condition entries* describe, for a specific decision rule, whether a data set does or does not meet the condition described in the condition statement. Generally, the following three symbols are used:

Y = Yes. For this decision rule, the data satisfy this condition.
N = No. For this decision rule, the data do not satisfy this condition.
— = For this decision rule, it does not matter whether the data do or do not meet this condition. This is equivalent to writing (Y or N).

The condition entries will all be set to Y, N, or —.

The *action statements* are simply declarative statements that describe operations to perform, results to compute, or output to be provided. The *action entries* are simply indicators that specify whether, for this decision rule, we should or should not take this action. Usually we simply put an X in the box to indicate that this action statement should be carried out and leave it blank if it should not be.

The meaning of the entries in a decision table is now fairly obvious. If a set of input satisfies all of the conditions specified in column i of the decision table, then perform all of the actions marked by an X in the action entries of column i. For example, referring to Figure 10.10, if we read in an input set with $x = 3$, $y = 600$, $z = 1$, then decision rule 2 applies, and we would take both action 1 and action 3 in response to this input set. If the input were $x = 2$ and $y = 400$ and $z = 0$, then rule 4 would apply, and we would take only action 3.

Table 10.1

	1	2	3
c_1	F	F	T
c_2	F	T	F

The decision rules of a decision table must satisfy two conditions for the decision table to be valid. First, they must be *complete*—every possible combination of (Y, N) values for the input must be accounted for, and every input set must match at least one decision rule. Table 10.1 is incomplete. If both conditions c_1 and c_2 are true, this table does not specify what actions to take. It will require at most 2^k decision rules to completely specify a decision table with k condition statements. (It may require less than this because of the existence of the "—" entry.)

The decision table must also be *unambiguous*. An input set must not match more than one decision rule. Otherwise the actions we are to take would be nondeterministic. Table 10.2 is ambiguous. If condition c_1 is true and condition c_2 is false, both rules 3 and 4 are satisfied, and we would be unsure whether to take action a_1 or action a_2. Together, the characteristics of completeness and unambiguousness can be expressed in the following way:

> Every set of inputs to the program must match one and only one decision rule. The actions to take in response to that input are all action statements marked by an X in the decision rule which was matched.

A decision table is a highly formalized way to express the input–output characteristics of a program, rather than the natural language technique we employed in the previous section.

Figure 10.11 is a decision table for the prime number problem whose natural lan-

Table 10.2

	1	2	3	4
c_1	F	F	T	T
c_2	F	T	F	—
a_1	X		X	
a_2		X		X

FIGURE 10.11   Decision Table for the Prime Number Problem.

The input value N is nonnumeric	T	F	F	F
The input value $N \leq 1$	—	T	F	F
N is legal and prime	—	—	T	F
Print out "N is prime"			X	
Print out "N is NOT prime"				X
Print out "M is a factor"				X
Print error message	X	X		
Print the goodbye message			X	X
Input a new value	X	X		
Terminate			X	X

guage specification is contained on page 254. A comparison of the two examples will clearly demonstrate the difference between these two specification methods.

The exercises at the end of the chapter contain a number of additional problems in designing and using decision tables.

Decision tables are one of the simplest, easiest, but least powerful techniques for formal specification. One variation, which we will mention only briefly, is the use of a *finite state automaton,* also called a *finite state machine.*

One of the main problems with the decision table just described is that there is only one table. If our input matches decision rule i, then we will always take action i, regardless of the previous history of inputs and the current *situation* or *state* that we are in. For example, we may be developing a program in which the first time you make an input error the program simply prints out an error message and lets you reenter the data. However, the second time the mistake is made something different happens— perhaps you automatically enter an on-line help program or a warning message is flashed to the operator (as might be done with an incorrect password being entered a second time).

A convenient way to specify this would be to have *two* decision tables. The first one would be the one to use if the user has not yet made an error; the second one would be used if the user has previously made an input error. We would now use the decision table that corresponded to the proper state we were in. In addition to specifying what action to take in response to our input, our tables would also have to contain action entries that specified when to switch and start using the other decision table, as shown in Figure 10.12. Essentially, what we are saying in Figure 10.12 is that the output to be produced by a program depends not only on the inputs to the program, but on the *current state* of the program as well. This is exactly what a finite state machine (FSM)

FIGURE 10.12   Using Multiple Decision Table.

Input value is correct	T	F
Accept value	X	
Print error message		X
Reenter value		X
Start using decision Table 10.2		X

Decision Table 10.1
("No Errors")

Input value is correct	T	F
Accept value	X	
Take special action		X
Go back to using decision Table 10.1	X	

Decision Table 10.2
("One Error")

allows us to describe. An FSM is a collection of states $(S_1, S_2, \ldots)$, inputs $(I_1, I_2, \ldots)$ and actions or outputs $(A_1, A_2, \ldots)$. The following notation

$$\left(S_1\right) \xrightarrow[A_1, A_2, \ldots]{I_1, I_2, \ldots} \left(S_2\right)$$

means that if you are currently in state S_1 and you receive either input I_1, I_2, or $\ldots$, then you are simultaneously to make a *state transition* to state S_2 and perform all actions A_1, A_2, $\ldots$. A collection of states, inputs, outputs, and transitions is also called a *state diagram*.

In a sense, each individual state of a state diagram can be thought of as a separate decision table since it has a set of inputs and actions to take in response to those inputs. However, by adding the concept of multiple states and state transitions, we have added a memory to our decision table. We can keep track of previous inputs and actions taken by our program and base our next actions not only on the current input but on the previous history of inputs.

For example, assume that we generalized the decision table of Figure 10.12 so that we allowed the user to make up to *three* input errors, without penalty. However, if the user made the same mistake a fourth time, he or she would be transferred to a special error state, where something different happened. This four-step process would be cumbersome to describe using decision tables, because we would need four relatively large tables, along with indicators to move us back and forth between the table. With a finite state machine, however, it becomes a simple task. A finite state machine to accomplish this task is shown in Figure 10.13.

There are a great number of other formal specification methods, including predicate logic, multivalued decision tables, Petri nets, algebraic notation, and functional mapping diagrams. Future courses in software engineering will expand on this topic at much greater length and introduce you to some of these other specification methods.

FIGURE 10.13 Finite State Machine.

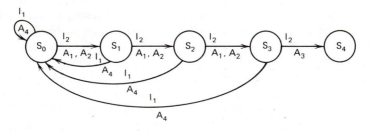

States	Inputs	Actions
S_0 : No error state	I_1 : Legal input	A_1 : Print error message
S_1 : One error state	I_2 : Illegal input	A_2 : Get new input
S_2 : Two error state		A_3 : Print "Going into special error state"
S_3 : Three error state		A_4 : Perform normal processing operations
S_4 : Special "Error State"		

10.6
Conclusion

This chapter has introduced you to the topic of the *problem specification document*. This is a critically important document that is used to ensure that the problem to be solved is well understood and unambiguously specified. In addition, it will be used to test and validate the completed system. This document is composed of at least the following two major sections:

1. Functional specifications
   Input
   Output
   Special handling
2. Performance specifications
   Speed
   Throughput
   Availability
   Capacity
   Precision
   Equipment needs

The document will not be short and simple, like the one in Figure 10.8, but a long complex document possibly running to hundreds of pages and comprising both formal and informal notational techniques.

In this part of the text we will assume that we have a clear, concise, unambiguous problem specification document describing the problem we are working on. We will never have to guess what operations should be performed by the program; it should always be clearly spelled out in this document. If the information we need to know is not there, we have not done a thorough job on this phase of the problem-solving task.

Even though, as we said earlier, a specification document is rarely developed in an academic environment, get in the habit, early on, of looking at any "finished" problem statement you are given with a thorough and picky eye. Examine it carefully to ensure that all possible input conditions are included, the output is clearly described, and all special cases are covered. If there are any omissions, ambiguities, or discrepancies, get them cleared up now, before you begin the next phase of programming, program design, which we discuss in the next chapter.

Exercises for Chapter 10

1. Rewrite a new draft of the specification document shown in Figure 10.8 that adds the following four features that the user has asked for:
   a. The program should allow *any* number of tests per student, rather than exactly three.
   b. All input data come from a permanent file, rather than the terminal.
   c. For each test, the teacher wants not only the mean and standard deviation, but also the *range,* that is, the highest and lowest score actually received.
   d. The instructor wants to allow a student to be excused from a test. He would like to be able to use the value -1 to indicate that a student was legally excused from a test. The computation of means, standard deviations, and ranges should *not* include the excused tests.

2. Rewrite a new draft of the specification document for the prime number problem shown on pages 254–255. The new draft should incorporate the following changes.
   a. The program should not terminate after processing one correct input value, but should ask the user if he or she wants to input another value. Do not stop until the user indicates he or she wants to stop.
   b. If a number is not prime, print out *all* factors.
   c. If the user enters a value $N < 0$, determine whether the value $|N|$ is or is not prime, rather than treating it as an error.

*3. Here is a specification document describing the problem of evaluating quadratic equations using the quadratic formula. It includes only a description of the normal input/output to the problem. As it stands, it does *not* include any special circumstances:

> Your program will be given as input three real values, a, b, c, in that order, which correspond to the three coefficients of the following quadratic equation:

$$ax^2 + bx + c = 0$$

You should determine the two roots of this quadratic equation using the quadratic formula

$$\frac{-b \pm \sqrt{b^2 - 4ac}}{2a}$$

and then print out the two answers in the following format:

The first root is = xxx.xxx
The second root is = xxx.xxx

and then stop.

Describe exactly what errors or special situations could occur in this problem, and then rewrite the specification document so that we know exactly how to respond to each condition.

4.   Here is a specification for a table look-up problem:

You will be given as input a two-column list of 20 character names and seven-digit phone numbers ($xxx\text{-}xxxx$), in the following format:

name   phone #
name   phone #
.

.

.

name   phone #

There are 1000 (name, phone number) pairs. You will then be given a single name. Look up that one name in the list of 1000 names. When you find the name, produce the following line of output:

The phone number for this person is xxx-xxxx

where "xxx-xxxx" is the phone number in the corresponding phone number column for that person.

Again, this specification document omits the errors or special conditions that could occur in this problem. Describe these error conditions and rewrite the specifications so we know how to handle them.

5.   The following are very rough problem statements. Using the instructor or a fellow student as the user, ask the questions you think are needed to produce a clear,

unambiguous problem statement, and then write the specification document. Remember to include all the error conditions!

    *a.   I'd like a program to sort a list of N numbers into order.

    b.   I'd like a program to find roots of equations. That is, if I give it an equation $f(x)$, it will give me all values of x for which $f(x) = 0$.

    c.   I'd like a program that would tell me how much I would have to pay each month for different sized mortgages at differing interest rates.

    d.   I'd like a program that would tell me the day of the week on which my birthday would fall for any year.

    e.   I'd like a program that would look through some English-language text and locate every occurrence of the character string "Pascal."

    f.   I'd like a program that would tell me which stock to buy in order to make some money.

  6.   Closely review the third draft of the test scoring program in Figure 10.8 and see if you feel it is complete and unambiguous. Also, would you make any suggestions to the user on how the program must be improved or made a little more flexible? Produce a fourth draft that reflects the improvements you suggested.

  *7.   For each of the following performance metrics, state whether you think it is sufficiently descriptive to be included in a problem specification document.

    a.   The finished program should be able to run on a personal computer.

    b.   The finished program should be able to run on an IBM-PC personal computer.

    c.   The program should run most data sets in under 1 second.

    d.   The program should run all data sets in under 1 second.

    e.   The program should run 95% of all data sets in under 1 second.

    f.   The program must successfully sort any table up to and including 5000 elements in length.

    g.   The file must be large enough to hold 30,000 unique patient records.

    h.   The name field must be large enough to hold the longest name without truncation.

    i.   All answers must be accurate to within 0.001%.

    j.   All answers must contain at least three significant digits.

    k.   The program must be available 100% of the time.

  *8.   What is wrong with the decision table shown in Table 10.3 on page 267? What needs to be added or removed to make it correct?

  9.   Develop a decision table for the following problem:

We are to read in a part number and an amount ordered from the terminal. We then look up that part number in an inventory file containing part numbers and amounts on hand. If the part number is not found in the file, then we print an error message that the part number was not found and ask the person to reenter it. If the part number is found, we input the value of amount on hand from the inventory file. If we have enough on hand to satisfy the amount ordered, we send out the order

Table 10.3

$x > 0$		T	F	F	T	T
$y > 0$		T	T	T	F	F
$z > 0$		—	F	T	F	T
Compute r/x		X			X	X
Compute r/y		X	X	X		
Compute r/z				X		X
Print error message			X	X	X	X

and update the amount on hand field of the inventory file. If we do not
have enough on hand, we send out what we do have, mark the rest as
back ordered, and update the amount on hand field of the inventory
file. In either case, when we are done we go back and get the next
input request. We stop when the last part number input is 00000.

Compare the ease and exactness of developing specifications in a natural language
versus a decision table.

10.   Develop a decision table for the modified prime number problem as described in
Question 2. Your decision table should include all three modifications described in that
question. Compare the advantages and disadvantages of the two different ways for
representing specifications.

11.   Develop a decision table for your modified quadratic equation program from
Question 3. Your decision table should address all of the special handling conditions
that you added to the specification statement of Question 3.

12.   Develop a decision table for the third draft of the test-scoring problem contained
in Figure 10.8.

*13.   Given the following finite state machine

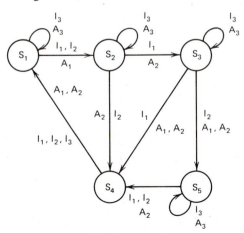

assume that we start in state S_1. Given the following sequence of inputs

I_1, I_3, I_2, I_2, I_2, I_1, I_3

what state will we end up in, and exactly what operations will be performed?

*14.   Assume that we are writing a program to input a series of characters that comprise a signed integer value. The syntax of the number is an (optional) + or − sign, followed by one to four digits in the range 0 to 9, followed by either a blank or carriage return. Develop a finite state machine that determines whether some given input does or does not meet the specification just described. The FSM should perform the action of printing out either of the following messages:

Valid number
Invalid number

Furthermore, if the syntax is valid, the FSM should take the action of converting it to an integer. Use the type of notation shown in Figure 10.13.

CHAPTER 11

PROGRAM DESIGN TECHNIQUES

11.1
Introduction

We are now at the point where we have a clear, concise, and unambiguous problem statement, and we are ready to design and build a program to solve that problem. The user is no longer directly involved in the project. He or she cares only that we successfully complete the program on time (and under budget!).

At first it may seem that our next step would be to select the algorithms and data structures needed to solve the problem. For example, to implement the examples of the previous chapter, we would need to select reasonably efficient algorithms that determine if a number is prime and compute the mean and standard deviation of a set of test scores.

However, for a "real-world" programming problem this would most decidedly *not* be the next step. There is one very important phase that must precede the selection and representation of algorithms and data types. This step is called *program design*. Program design involves the intellectual and administrative techniques for managing the overall development of large software products.

The reason for the inclusion of this design stage in the development of computer programs has to do with their size and complexity. As shown in Figure 9.1, real programs are 100 to 1000 times larger than those typically given as student assignments. In addition, interesting programs are not composed of a single task, but of many, many interrelated tasks that, when integrated into a single system, solve the complete problem.[1]

For example, a payroll system for a large company would most definitely not be a

---

[1] Remember our earlier comment that this statement may not be true for some simple programs done in a first programming class. Here we are describing the general case.

single program, but would be composed of dozens of separate program units (let's call these pieces *subprograms* or *modules* for now), which would handle such diverse tasks as

1. Describing the layout of the data structures used in the payroll file and the employee's time card.
2. Finding the employee's pay record in the payroll file.
3. Handling the error condition of no existing payroll record for a given employee.
4. Converting clock times (e.g., 8:30 A.M. to 4:45 P.M.) to hours and fractions of hours (e.g., 8.25 hours).
5. Computing weekly pay based on hours worked, pay rate, and overtime rate.
6. Determining deductions, such as federal tax, state tax, and social security.
7. Printing out the worker's pay check.
8. Updating the employee's pay record in the payroll file to include this week's pay information.

Even the relatively simple test scoring program we described in the previous chapter would likely not be implemented as a single unit but as approximately five separate and independent modules for handling the following tasks:

1. Reading student test scores into a score table.
2. Validating that all test scores in the table are correct.
3. Computing the mean of a test.
4. Computing the standard deviation of a test.
5. Printing out the results.

(In reality, there may be many more than just these five. For example, there may be a number of modules for handling errors.)

Any realistic program, P, you encounter will likely be composed of a large number of modules $P_1, P_2, P_3, \ldots, P_n$, which, when implemented correctly and executed in the proper order, will solve problem P.

Therefore, our next step in the programming process is not to start coding but, instead, to take the problem described in the problem specification document and decompose it into a collection of simpler subproblems. In a sense, we are using a design technique called *divide and conquer,* which says it is easier to solve many small, simple problems than to solve one extremely large and complex one.

The alternative "design technique" used by many students in a first programming class—to start writing code immediately—may work adequately for small programs, but it quickly collapses when applied to longer efforts. Confusion usually occurs when beginning students attempt their first large programming project without any planning or organization (e.g., a project on the order of 1000 or more lines of code). These attempts are rarely successful.

Specifically, the following are just some of the problems encountered when attempting a large programming project.

1. We find ourselves totally engulfed in detail. There is so much to do and remember that we forget to perform certain operations, miss key completion dates, or omit critical sections from the code. We cannot keep details in our head or on scratch paper and hope to remember them. We easily lose track of what has already been done and what still needs to be done.

2. Debugging and testing become extremely complex. The programs are so large that looking for an error can be like searching for the proverbial needle in a haystack.

3. It is difficult to predict all the ramifications of an early decision. The programs are so large that the effect of a decision may not become evident for days, weeks, or even months. Unless we have planned carefully, it may be difficult to undo its effects, and we are stuck with our early choice, even though it may not be the best one.

Careful planning and a good program design technique can effectively overcome these and other problems and lead to the successful completion of quite large programs, even those on the scale of the large and very large projects of Figure 9.1.

Our approach is certainly not unique to programming. The partitioning of problems into smaller subproblems is a technique used to manage any large system or to complete any large writing task. As an example, this textbook addresses literally hundreds of issues including Pascal syntax, programming style, data abstraction, program design, and testing methods. To manage this monstrously large writing task, it is essential to first decompose the book into simpler subtasks—in this case, ''chapters.'' For each chapter we decide what issues it will address and how it will fit in with other chapters of the book. If it is a particularly complex chapter, we will likely repeat this process one or more times, breaking the chapter down into yet simpler pieces, called ''sections,'' ''subsections,'' or ''sub-subsections.'' Thus, the task of writing an extremely long and complicated book becomes one of writing many small sections, each of which is clearly defined and simpler to implement.

What we have quite obviously described is the familiar operation called *outlining* a paper, and the program design phase can be thought of as the stage in which we ''outline the program.'' When this outlining technique is applied to programming, it is generally called *top-down program design*.

11.2
Top-Down Program Design

Top-down program design involves starting from the broadest and most general description of *what* needs to be done—that is, the problem specification document—and then subdividing the original problem into collections of one or more modules. Each of these lower-level modules is generally smaller and simpler than the original task and begins to get more and more involved with the details of *how* to solve the problem. We proceed from overall high-level goals to detailed low-level solution methods.

We can represent this top-down design approach pictorially by using the following notation. If a program P can be subdivided into simpler modules—P_1, P_2, and P_3—we represent that pictorially as shown in Figure 11.1.

FIGURE 11.1   Pictorial Representation of the Program
Design Method.

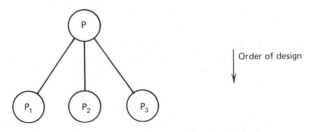

The structure shown in Figure 11.1 is called a *tree,* and when a tree structure is used
to show both the modules needed to solve a problem and the interrelationships between
modules, it is typically called a *program development tree.* However, this is just one of
many popular ways of representing program designs, and we could have used a number
of other representational techniques, including the outline format with which you are
quite familiar:

I.   Program P

    A.   Module P_1

    B.   Module P_2

    C.   Module P_3

The important point to realize is that the specific pictorial format you choose is not
important as long as it clearly shows the structural relationship between a program unit
(P in this case) and the component modules of that unit (P_1, P_2, and P_3).

In this section, we will use the development tree model, as shown in Figure 11.1, to
display the structure of our proposed design. In Section 11.3.1 we will discuss the
issue of other, more formalized notational conventions.

There is another important aspect of top-down program design. In our earlier discussion on outlining a book, we started by dividing the book into a series of chapters.
However, we also said that some or all of the chapters may still be too large and
complex to write directly and will themselves have to be further decomposed and
simplified.

Top-down program design is most definitely not the one-step process shown in
Figure 11.1. The decomposition and simplification task is performed over and over
again, first on the original problem and then on the successive submodules, until finally
we are left with a task that is so elementary it need not be simplified any further. The
repeated decomposition and simplification of a task into a collection of simpler subtasks is called *stepwise refinement* and leads to the more interesting and realistic
development tree shown in Figure 11.2.

Each of the tasks in Figure 11.2 represents a separate program unit needed to solve

FIGURE 11.2   Example of a More Realistic Program Design.

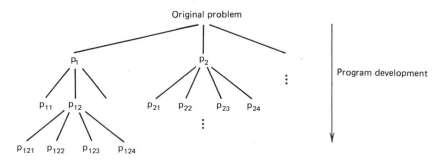

the original problem. The development tree of Figure 11.2. which shows (1) what program units are needed (P, P_1, P_2, P_3, P_{11}, P_{12}, . . .) and (2) how they are related to each other, is a central component of the *program design document,* which we will discuss in detail in Section 11.3.

In addition to the program modules, the data structures are also developed in a top-down fashion as we proceed from generalized descriptions of classes of abstract data types to determining what operations are performed on these types to their internal implementation.

For example, early on in a program design we may decide that we need a first-in/first-out waiting line data structure in which people are placed at the end of the line and leave from the front. That level of data structure specification may be enough for us to begin to design some of our early modules. Later, we may need to add the specifications of additional operations performed on our waiting line, such as

> *Initialize (line).* Sets the initial waiting line length to 0.
> *Linelength (line).* Returns the current length of the line.
> *Cuts (person, line, i).* Allows a person to cut into line just in front of
> person *i*.

Near the completion of the design phase, we will have to decide on the internal structure to use for our abstract data type waiting line. Perhaps an array of person-records:

type
    waitingline = **array** [1 . . maxlength] **of** personrecords;

Finally, at some point we will need to specify the actual internal structure for the data type called personrecord as well as select a constant value for maxlength.

Let's take this highly theoretical discussion, and put it into more concrete terms by doing a specific example—the test scoring program or "electronic grade book" whose specifications were given in Figure 10.8. The purpose of this example will *not* be to show you how to select and evaluate a design. Rather, our purpose here will simply be to show you one possible design, introduce the types of information that would be contained in the design document, and explain why it is beneficial to approach a problem in this fashion. We will postpone until Chapter 12 the more complex issues of how to approach a problem in the first place and how to evaluate the resulting design for beauty, organization, and structure.

A top-level solution to the electronic grade book program of Figure 10.8 can be expressed as follows:

```
Program "Electronic Grade Book"
    Use input-1 to get N, LOW, HIGH
    Repeat 3 times
        Use input-2 to get the N scores and place them in ScoreTable
        Use ComputeMean to determine the mean score of values in ScoreTable
        Use ComputeStandardDeviation to determine the standard deviation of
            values in ScoreTable
        Use Output to print the results
    End of loop
End of program
```

This top level solution created the following five lower-level modules:

Module	Responsibility
1. Input-1	This module requests the user to input values for the three quantities N, LOW, HIGH. It then validates that they are syntactically valid and fall within the ranges given in the specification document. If they are not correct, it asks the user to reenter them. It will continue asking for input and validating it until the user finally enters these values correctly. It then returns to the calling program legal values for N, LOW, and HIGH.
2. Input-2	This module is given, as input, legal values for N, LOW, HIGH as well as an empty Score-Table. It then proceeds to ask the user to input test scores. It checks each test score to make sure it is in the range LOW to HIGH. If it is, it stores the test score in the next empty slot of the ScoreTable. If it is not in the correct range, it does not store the score but asks the user to reenter the score. It will continue to ask the user to reenter a score until it is correct. It will stop when it has input

Module	Responsibility
	N legal scores and will return all *N* legal test scores properly stored in the ScoreTable.
3. ComputeMean	This module is given an *N*-element ScoreTable filled with valid test scores and computes and returns the arithmetic mean of all tests contained in the table.
4. ComputeStan-dardDeviation	This module is given both an *N*-element ScoreTable filled with valid test scores and the mean, and it computes and returns the standard deviation of all tests contained in the table.
5. Output	This module is given *N*, LOW, HIGH, and the mean and standard deviation of a single test. It prints the results in the format shown in the specification document.

In addition to these five modules, we also need an abstract data type called *Score-Table*. ScoreTable is a structure that must be capable of performing the following two operations:

Store(score,ScoreTable,i) Store an examination score in slot *i* of the ScoreTable. The table must be capable of holding at least 500 scores. If *i* is not in the range 1 to 500, this operation is undefined.

Retrieve(score,ScoreTable,i) Retrieve the score stored in slot *i* of the ScoreTable, if a score has been entered there. Otherwise this operation is undefined.

We have now defined the original problem in terms of one abstract data type and five simpler subproblems, which, when activated in the proper order, would solve the original problem. This completes the first level of design of the test scoring program.

Our job now is to ask ourselves if each of these five modules is so simple that there is really no need to refine it further or, alternatively, whether one of these tasks is still so complex that we would benefit by simplifying it further.[2] For example, we might decide that the module called input-2 is really a higher-level problem that needs to be further decomposed.

---

[2]In reality, the former is true. As described, each of the five modules is very simple to write and would require no more than 10 to 15 lines of code. Our further refinements of this problem are just to show how it would be done, not because it is actually needed.

Module   Input-2

```
i := 0
Repeat until we have N good scores
    Getdata(score,switch)
    if switch is "GOOD" then
        i := i + 1
        store(score,ScoreTable,i)
    else { switch was "BAD" }
        Errorhandler
End of the loop
```

End of Module Input-2

This refinement of module input-2 uses two lower-level routines called *getdata* and *errorhandler*. Their specifications are given below.

Module	Responsibility
1. Getdata	This module requests the user to input a single test score. It checks that score to see that it is (1) numeric and (2) in the range LOW to HIGH. It returns the unmodified test score and a switch with the value "GOOD" or "BAD" specifying whether the score did or did not meet both conditions.
2. Errorhandler	This module is activated if an illegal test score has been input. It performs all error handling operations and the printing of error messages.

In addition, we need to decide whether or not we now wish to select an internal representation for the abstract data type called *ScoreTable*. We could choose to implement it as an array of integers or, possibly, a linked list. Our choice between these two alternatives might be based on concerns of efficiency, implementation, or programming language constraints. Alternatively, we could decide to postpone this decision until later in the design process and leave *ScoreTable* as an abstract data type, still defined in terms of only the two operations called *store* and *retrieve*.

This completes the second refinement of the test scoring problem. The development tree for this level of refinement is shown in Figure 11.3. When we are done refining each module as far as we wish to go, we will have created a large number of simple modules and a collection of data structures, defined in terms of the information they contain and the operations that can be performed on them. Together, these module and data structure descriptions constitute the major components of the program design document, which will be described in the next section.

FIGURE 11.3   Development Tree for the Electronic Grade
Book Program.

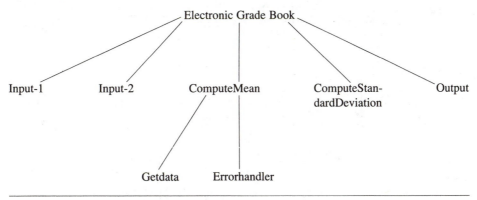

11.3
The Program Design Document

The *program design document* enumerates the individual components contained in the program and specifies the structural relationships between these components' relationship to each other. Specifically, it contains three major sections:

1. *The structure chart.* This is a pictorial representation of the structural relationship between modules and between modules and data structures.

2. *The module specification.* For every module contained in the structure chart there must be a specification that describes the external interface that that module presents to the rest of the program.

3. *The data dictionary.* For every major data structure we must describe the information fields contained in that structure and the operations that can be performed on that data structure.

In the next sections, we will describe each of these three components separately.

11.3.1   The Structure Chart

In Figure 11.2, we used a tree structure to display the relationship between modules in a program. This is a reasonable technique and development trees, like Figure 11.2, are used frequently in program design documents. However, a tree suffers from one major problem—not all designs can be fit within the rigidly hierarchical structure of a tree. For example, a very low-level routine, such as a random number generator, might be called by a great number of other modules throughout the system, as follows:

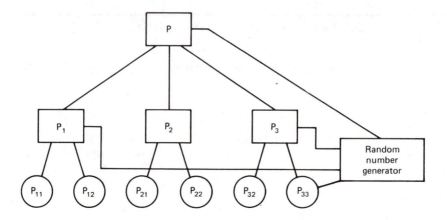

This diagram, although a reasonable one, violates the hierarchical structure used in forming a tree. For this reason, there are, just as with the problem specification document, a great many other methodologies for displaying the overall design structure of a piece of software. They are known by such diverse terms as *data flow diagrams, bubble charts, HIPO* (hierarchy-input-process-output) *charts, procedure templates,* and *decision tables* (as discussed in Chapter 10). A great deal of ongoing research is being carried out in the area of program design techniques, and advanced courses in software engineering will introduce you to one or more of these formalized design methods.

The technique we will introduce here is a highly simplified version of some of the above-named techniques and uses a *directed graph* to represent the overall design. With a directed graph, we are no longer restricted to the rigidly hierarchical relationships imposed by the development trees of Figure 11.2. Any module may be linked to any other module in the solution, not just its immediate parent or child. The notation we will use for our structure chart is shown in Figure 11.4. For example, the following notation

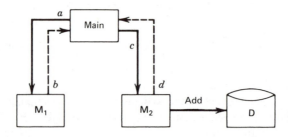

would represent a program structure containing three modules, called Main, M_1, and M_2. Modules M_1 and M_2 are activated by Main and return to it. M_1 is given the value of

FIGURE 11.4   Notation for Use in Structure Charts of
Program Design Documents.

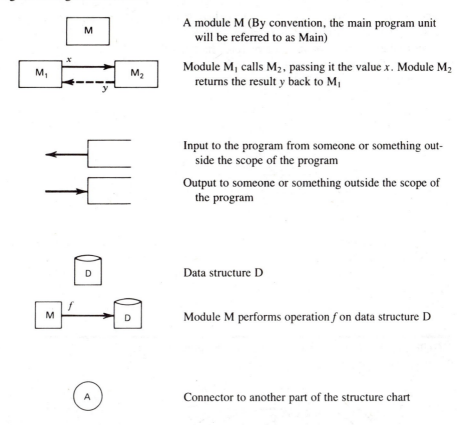

A module M (By convention, the main program unit
will be referred to as Main)

Module M_1 calls M_2, passing it the value x. Module M_2
returns the result y back to M_1

Input to the program from someone or something outside the scope of the program

Output to someone or something outside the scope of
the program

Data structure D

Module M performs operation f on data structure D

Connector to another part of the structure chart

a and returns the result b. M_2 is passed the input value c and returns the result d.
Module M_2 also performs the abstract operation termed *add* on data structure D.
Neither Main nor M_1 operate on D, and M_1 and M_2 do not directly invoke each other.

   This type of structure chart may seem superficially similar to the *flowchart* frequently used to represent algorithms in introductory programming courses. However,
it is quite different in at least two respects. A structure chart contains no control or
looping information, as found on flowcharts. The notation

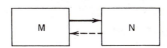

does not imply that module M must necessarily call module N during its execution or that it will call module N only once. It simply says that in describing the overall logic of module M, there will be included, somewhere within M, a call to module N. When, if, and exactly how many times N will be called depends on the actual data being used, and this is not part of the structure chart.

A second difference between a structure chart and flowchart is that a structure chart contains no *temporal information*. It does not imply the order or sequence in which operations must be done. The notation

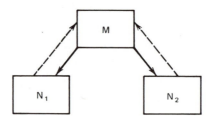

does not imply that module N_1 will necessarily be invoked before module N_2. Again, it merely says that the specification of the characteristics of module M includes activations of both modules N_1 and N_2. The order in which they are invoked will be part of the implementation of modules M, N_1, N_2.

Figure 11.5 shows a possible structure chart for the first refinement of the test-

FIGURE 11.5 Structure Chart for the First Refinement of the Text Scoring Program.

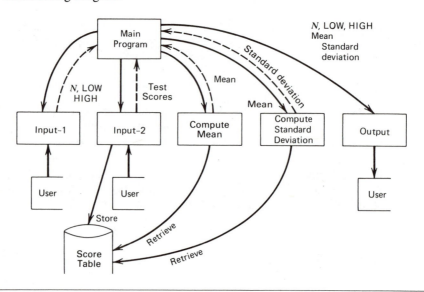

scoring program example of Section 11.2. As can be seen from Figure 11.5, a structure chart for an interesting program can be quite large and contain many, many components. For this reason, structure charts are rarely displayed as a single unit and, instead, are divided into separate charts over many separate pages using the following *connector* symbol:

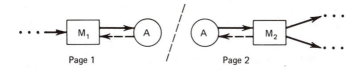

For example, Figure 11.6 shows a very small portion of the design of an on-line inventory control program. The part shown is the "Part Number Look-up" section. It is assumed that another portion of the program (labeled A) has already selected a part number. The portion of the structure chart shown in Figure 11.6 invokes a look-up module to find that part number in the inventory file. If the look-up operation is successful, it will return the complete inventory record for that part. (Notice that the specific look-up algorithm being used by the look-up module is not part of this diagram.) If the module cannot find the part number in the file, it activates an errorhandler module, which itself activates a logger routine to log an entry in a special error file. The errorhandler also activates a bellringer module, which rings a bell on the operator's console, to warn of the error. A real inventory control program might typically have 100 to 500 separate modules, one or two dozen major data structures, and a chart of its overall design may run to well over 100 pages!

FIGURE 11.6   Portion of the Structure Chart of an
Inventory Control System.

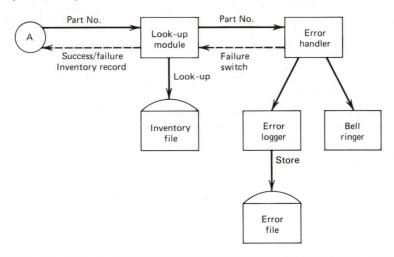

The finished structure chart serves a number of important purposes. First, it gives us a pictorial overview of the entire solution (the "big picture") and shows us the magnitude of the programming task ahead of us. In addition, it is needed by the other two sections of the design document—the module specifications and data dictionary. For every module included in the structure chart, we must include a written specification in the program design document. Similarly, every major data structure shown on the structure chart must be included in the data dictionary. Therefore, the structure chart iself need not contain extensive and detailed descriptions of its components; those will come later. Rather, it is simply a pictorial representation of the relationship between components in the proposed solution.

Finally, the structure chart will be of use to us during implementation. By showing the relationships between segments of the program, we can gather together related elements and implement them as a group. For example, referring to Figure 11.5, if we wanted one programmer to be responsible for all decisions related to I/O, the structure chart shows that we should have him or her code the three modules Input-1, Input-2, and Output. Similarly, the chart shows that the programmer who selects the internal implementation of ScoreTable and codes the two operations store and retrieve will work most closely with the people who are implementing the modules Input-2, ComputeMean, and ComputeStandardDeviation and will be relatively uninvolved with the implementor of the module called Output. Structure charts, then, can show interrelationships, areas of cooperation, and "spheres of influence" that can be very important during the implementation phase. They can help us coordinate the implementation of related modules, facilitate communication between programmers working on common pieces of information, and allocate personpower in the most efficient manner. We will have much more to say about implementation issues in both Section 11.4 and in Chapters 16 through 18.

11.3.2   Module Specifications

We have used the term *module* informally and intuitively. We will now define it formally.

A *module* is an independent program unit that satisfies the following four constraints:

1. It is a *named* entity.
2. It can be *activated* or *invoked* by name from other modules in the system. At the time of activation, information can be passed into or out of the module.
3. When invoked, the module can *create* new data objects and/or *perform* executable statements.
4. It can be *compiled* separately from other modules and stored independently in a module library.

The most familiar modules are the well-known functions, subroutines and procedures of high-level languages such as FORTRAN, BASIC, COBOL, and Pascal.

However, the concept is much wider than that and includes such units as the Modula-2 *module* and the Ada *package* (these last two are program units that encapsulate descriptions of abstract data types and operations on those data types); the *generic* concept of Ada (models to describe a general class of subprogram); the *task* in Ada, C, and PL/1 (program units that execute in parallel with each other); and the *coroutine* (symmetric procedures) of Modula-2. All of these fit the definition of a module given above, and we will always try to use the term module in this broader sense.

There are two parts to a module specification: the *external interface* and the *internal structure*. The external interface must always be included in the module specification. However, there is a good deal of disagreement over whether or not the internal structure should be included in the design document, and it may or may not be present. If not present, it will be postponed until the next phase of programming—the coding stage.

The external interface is simply a complete and thorough description of exactly what can be seen of the module by other modules in the system. This will include the following type of information:

1. Module name.
2. Module type (e.g., procedure, package, task, etc.).
3. General description of its function.
4. Calling sequence (how to activate it).
5. Entry conditions (the state of the system when the module is activated).
6. Exit conditions (the state of the system when the module has been completed).
7. Side effects (effects on any other global objects in the program).
8. Possible error conditions, unusual behavior, or abnormal terminations.

In addition to this information, designers may choose to add other information that could be of help during the implementation phase, such as the approximate size of the completed module, the library where it will be stored, or other modules that are closely related to this one and that will be implemented jointly.

Figure 11.7 shows a module specification for the module named ComputeMean from the structure chart of Figure 11.5. This specification includes only the eight pieces of information listed above. Notice that the specification of Figure 11.7 describes only those external aspects of the module that can be seen by the rest of the system.

The *internal structure* of the module (sometimes called the *internal specifications* or the *detailed design*) shows exactly *how* the module will solve the problem. It describes the algorithm to be used and sketches out, in either pseudocode or flowchart notation, the top-level control structure of the module. If we chose to include the internal structure as part of the module specification, we would include something like the following pseudocode within the specifications of Figure 11.7.

FIGURE 11.7   Module Specification for ComputeMean.

1. Module name: ComputeMean

2. Module type: Pascal procedure

3. Purpose: To compute the arithmetic mean of a series of examination scores stored in ScoreTable

4. Calling sequence: ComputeMean(ScoreTable, N, Mean);

5. Entry conditions:

   ScoreTable: Has been defined and validated. It contains N valid scores (in the range LOW to HIGH) in the first N slots of ScoreTable.
   N: Has been defined and validated. It is set to an integer value in the range 1 to 500, which specifies exactly how many entries there are in ScoreTable.
   Mean: Undefined

6. Exit conditions:

   ScoreTable and N are unchanged by ComputeMean
   Mean: Has been set to the arithmetic mean of the N scores in ScoreTable, where the arithmetic mean is a real value defined as follows:

   $$\text{Mean} = \frac{\sum_{i=1}^{N} \text{retrieve}(\text{score}, \text{ScoreTable}, i)}{N}$$

7. Other side effects: None

8. Possible error conditions: None.

---

9. Internal module structure.

```
initialize sum to 0
for i = 1 to N do
      retrieve (T,ScoreTable,i)
      add T to sum
end { of for loop }
set mean to sum/N
```

Most program designers feel that the internal structure of a module more properly belongs to the coding rather than the design stage and is inappropriate and too detailed to be included in the program design document. We generally agree with this position and, in any future examples, will not include the control structure of a subprogram in its specifications, leaving that instead for the next stage of development.

11.3.3 The Data Dictionary

The data dictionary summarizes the external characteristics of every major data structure that has been included on the structure chart. These characteristics would include the following items of information:

1. Data type name.
2. General description of that data type.
3. Information fields contained within the data type.
4. Operations that can be performed on that data structure. For each operation we must describe the state of the data structure prior to and after the operation has been performed.
5. What modules access this structure; what modules define or redefine this structure.
6. Limitations or restrictions on this data type.

Notice that, as with the module specification of Section 11.3.2, we generally do not need to include the internal realization of this data structure, unless it is a type that is directly supported by the language (e.g., array, record, set, file). This information is generally not needed during the design stage, and can be left to the programmer to decide during implementation based on such technical issues as availability of memory, language features, or the need for efficiency.

Figure 11.8 shows a sample data dictionary entry for the data structure called ScoreTable from Figure 11.5.

Together, these three components—the structure chart, module specifications, and data dictionary—constitute the essential elements of the program design document.

As we mentioned in our earlier discussion about the problem specification document, a real-world design document for a large program will contain a great deal more material than we have described here and may run to literally hundreds of pages. This additional technical information may address concerns such as implementation schedules, benchmark tests, on-line assistance, and user-interface specifications. It may also include discussions of such nontechnical matters as budgets, staffing needs, staff training, equipment selection, and needed support tools.

Once the design document is completed, it will serve as our guide to the next stage of programming, called *implementation*. Each of the individual module specifications and data structure operations will be given to a programmer to code and test. When that component is thoroughly validated and certified to be correct, only then do we integrate it into the overall structure of the developing program, exactly as specified in the structure chart.

11.4
Implementation Issues

The issues relating to program implementation (e.g., debugging, testing, efficiency, documentation) will be discussed thoroughly in Part Three of this text. In this section,

FIGURE 11.8   Sample Data Dictionary Entry.

1. Data type name: ScoreTable

2. General description: A linear one-dimensional random access data structure that holds N examination scores of students, where $N \geq 1$.

3. Information contained: Integer examination scores in the range LOW to HIGH.

4. Operations:

   retrieve(score,ScoreTable,*i*)

   If $1 \leq i \leq N$, then the value of score is the value of the ith score in ScoreTable (where the first score is considered 1, the second score 2, etc.). If $i < 1$ or $i > N$, then retrieve is undefined. ScoreTable and i are unchanged by the operation.

   store(score,ScoreTable,*i*)

   If $1 \leq i \leq N$, then the value of the store operation is a new ScoreTable with the integer value score stored in the ith slot of ScoreTable. Whatever was previously in the ith slot of ScoreTable has been overwritten and lost. If $i < 1$ or $i > N$, then the store operation is undefined. Both i and score are unchanged by this operation.

5. Modules that access (A) or change (C) this structure:

   Input-2 (C)
   ComputeMean (A)
   ComputeStandardDeviation (A)

6. Limitations or restrictions: ScoreTable must be capable of holding at least 500 examination scores.

---

we want to mention briefly some implementation issues that are closely related to the topic of program design.

11.4.1   Phased Implementation/Testing

During the design phase, we develop the specifications for all modules in the program. We generally complete much or all of the design phase before going on to implementation. However, when implementing the modules and data structures, we do not work in the same fashion. We do *not* develop the flowcharts and code for all modules in the system and only then begin to debug and test what we have written. Instead, we proceed in a *phased* manner alternating between coding and testing. We implement a higher-level module and then thoroughly test and verify it. Only when it is certified to be correct, do we move down to the next lower level and begin coding those modules. For example, given the following structure chart from our program design document:

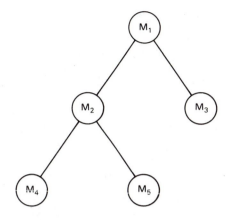

(Assume that we have also developed the external specifications of module $M_1, \ldots, M_5$)

we might begin our implementation by first coding module M_1. Before coding any additional units, we would thoroughly debug and test M_1 and continue to work on it until it is correct. (The guidelines for testing and verifying individual modules will be presented in Chapter 16.) Only when it is completely correct should we consider coding modules M_2 and/or M_3. We would continue moving down through the development tree in this alternating coding/testing fashion.

There is an important reason for this phased approach to implementation, and it has to do with our need and desire to *localize* any errors. If we were to code all five modules at once ($M_1, M_2, \ldots, M_5$), and only then begin testing, when the inevitable error occurred we would have no idea which might be the offending module. The error might be anywhere in the system since none of the modules had as yet been tested. Our debugging task would be enormous because we have little or no idea where to look.

However, if we were to alternate our implementation and testing stages, our job would be considerably easier. Assume that we have coded and tested module M_1 and removed all errors. We now implement both modules M_2 and M_3, integrate them with module M_1 and run them. If an error occurs, we know that the error must either be in module M_2 or M_3, or the M_1–M_2 or M_1–M_3 interface. It should not be in module M_1, because that unit has already been tested.

In general, if modules $1, 2, \ldots, i-1$ have been written and tested, and an error occurs when you add module i, the error is localized to either (1) module i itself or (2) the interface between i and some other module $j, j = 1, \ldots, i-1$. This greatly reduces the area in which we must look for the error and makes the debugging task significantly easier. One should always write a relatively small number of modules (preferably only one or two) and then test what has been written. Writing hundreds upon hundreds of lines of code, and then trying to get it working correctly is a serious programming error that will significantly increase the time and cost of program development.

There is one problem, however, with this phased approach to implementation. The top-down program design method we are using always describes a solution in terms of lower-level procedures that are as yet *unwritten*. For example, assume we are planning to debug and test the following module.

```
Program primechecker(input,output);
var
      factor              : integer;
      goodswitch          : boolean;
      N                   : integer;
      primeswitch         : boolean;
begin
      getinput(N);
      validate(N,goodswitch);
      if goodswitch then
      begin
            checkifprime(N,primeswitch,factor);
            if primeswitch then
                  writeln(N, 'is prime')
            else
                  writeln(N, 'is not prime', factor, 'is a factor')
      end { then clause }
      else
            errorhandler
end. { program primechecker }
```

The program primechecker has been implemented in terms of four lower-level routines called *getinput, validate, checkifprime,* and *errorhandler.* How will it be possible to test primechecker when none of these four routines has yet been written?

The answer is that we will test our program using *stubs*. A stub is a dummy procedure included in a program to allow compilation and execution to proceed mean-ingfully. Stubs do as *little* as possible. They usually carry out only the following three operations:

1. Write out a message that you have reached this procedure. This guarantees that we are correctly linking to the procedure.

2. Write out the value of any input parameters passed to the procedure, to ensure that they are being passed correctly.

3. If the calling program references a value that is defined by this procedure, the stub must also define that value in order to prevent a run-time error caused by an undefined variable.

So, for example, a reasonable stub for getinput might be

```
procedure getinput(var N : integer);
begin
      writeln('We are now in getinput and would prompt the user for input',
            'Not yet completed');
      N := 5 { must give N a value to prevent an error }
end;
```

A reasonable stub for validate could be the following:

```
procedure validate(N : integer; var sw : boolean);
begin
     writeln('Now in validate and would check for correctness of the input',
          'Not yet completed');
     writeln ('The value of N which arrived here is ', N);
     sw := true { Must give sw a value }
end;
```

We would continue in this fashion, writing stubs for all lower-level routines referenced by the modules being tested. When all of the stubs are in place, we can test our code, at least as far as we have progressed. Of course, the program will not yet operate exactly as described in the problem specification document, but at least we can compile and test the logic of the code developed so far. For example, the execution of the program primechecker (with the stubs shown) might lead to the following output:

```
We are now in getinput and would prompt the user for input
     Not yet completed
Now in validate and would check for correctness of the input
     Not yet completed
The value of N which arrived here is 5
Now in checkifprime to see if value is or is not prime
     Assume it is. Not yet completed
5 is prime
```

and, up to this point, everything seems to be operating properly. When we are thoroughly satisfied that program primechecker is indeed correct, we will proceed to implement the modules at the next level.

   If, for example, we chose to code getinput next, we would discard the temporary stub shown above and write the actual code following the specifications given in the program design document. One possibility might be:

```
procedure getinput(var N : integer);
begin
     writeln('Please enter the input data →');
     readln(N);
     CursorToHome { moves the cursor back to row 1, col 1 of the screen }
end;
```

After coding the module we again must test it.[3] We now include in our program the actual code for both primechecker and getinput along with the stubs for validate,

---

[3] The refinements we are showing are unrealistically small. It would not really be necessary to test this three-line module separately! We are talking about the general case, not this simple example.

checkifprime, and errorhandler. If the code for getinput referenced any new lower-level routines (e.g., the screen handler program called CursorToHome), we would include stubs for those as well. We are now in a position to test this new level of implementation.

Thus, the development of our program will continue downward through a tree of tasks from the most general to the most detailed. One by one the "do-nothing" stubs will be replaced by fully functional program units that perform the operations described in the module specification section of the program design document. Slowly but surely the functionality of the program is increasing, and it begins to perform more and more meaningful operations, until, when the last piece is put in place, it should perform exactly as described in the problem specifications document!

In this section we talked only about the *order* in which modules are tested and why the implementation and testing phases are alternated with each other. In Chapter 16 we will present the specific techniques for testing and verifying individual modules.

11.4.2 Top-Down versus Bottom-Up Implementation

Program design always proceeds in a top-down fashion, exactly as we have described in the first sections of this chapter. The previous section on phased implementation/testing may lead you to believe that implementation also proceeds in exactly the same fashion—always moving from general high-level routines to more detailed lower-level routines. Although this may sometimes be the case, it is not necessarily true.

When developing high-level applications-oriented routines, we will almost certainly need to make frequent reference to a number of simple, ordinary low-level modules that do everyday "housekeeping"-type tasks. These tasks may not be directly related to the application on which we are working. They are simply procedures to perform rather elementary and quite universal processing operations. Good examples of these might include a procedure to clear a CRT screen or a function to change a lowercase character to the corresponding uppercase character. Such routines are typically quite short—both of the above modules would probably be one line long. It would be as much trouble to write a stub for these routines as it would be simply to write the routine itself. In addition, without these fundamental elementary routines, we have no "bedrock" on which to build our high-level applications modules. They will be unable to display much useful behavior until the very end, when these basic routines are finally coded.

Therefore, implementation may not be only top-down, but *bottom-up* as well. Prior to the implementation stage, the program designer will need to identify a set of essential low-level routines that would be both important and helpful to have available as early as possible. These modules, frequently called *primitives,* or *utility routines* would then be implemented initially, in parallel with or even preceding the development of the first high-level modules. When tested and completed, these utilities are put into a *program development library* and are then available as *programming tools* to all professional staff for the duration of the implementation. When the most critical low-

FIGURE 11.9   Dual Top-Down/Bottom-Up Approach to
Implementation.

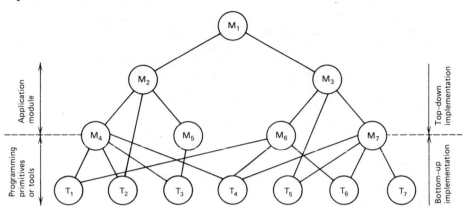

level primitives are finished, the designer may identify other low-level routines that
would also be highly desirable to have available as tools to aid in the development of
applications modules. Thus, implementation generally proceeds in *both* directions—
top-down for the implementation of high-level applications-oriented modules, and
bottom-up for the development of low-level programming tools to support applications
development. This dual approach is diagrammed in Figure 11.9.

It is not possible to give, out of context of a specific application, a list of exactly
what tools would need to be developed first. Figure 11.10 is a list of the general types
of elementary routines that are useful to have available in a program development
library and would probably be candidates for early development in any large programming project. Chapter 18 will discuss more about programming environments and
program support packages.

11.5
The Advantages of Top-Down Program Design

As we showed in Figure 9.1, an average real-world program may easily be 5000 to
50,000 lines long and be composed of from 100 to 500 separate modules! Larger
programs may be composed of literally thousands of separate program units. With a
problem of this scale, it would be sheer folly to leap in immediately and start writing
code. We need a way to manage this welter of detail, this enormous amount of
information, and this scale of complexity. We need a way to know what we are
currently working on, how it fits into the overall problem, and what will need to be
done next.

FIGURE 11.10   Typical Primitive Modules.

Screen Management
Clear a CRT screen.
Move the cursor to row i, column j.
Turn on/off the blink field.
Turn on/off the reverse video feature.
Turn on/off the half-intensity feature.

Output
Convert lowercase to uppercase.
Convert uppercase to lowercase.
Ring the bell.
Eject a page.
Turn off echo printing.

File Management
Seek key i.
Rewind file to beginning.
Go to end of file.
Return length of file.

Numeric/Seminumeric
Random number generator.
Sort package.
Convert character to integer.
Convert integers to characters.
Convert characters to real.
Convert reals to characters.

Miscellaneous
Convert calendar date to Julian date.
Convert regular time to "24-hour" time.
Interval timers.

The top-down design philosophy brings this to software development. The problem is solved from the most generalized goals to the more specific details. So we are always seeing the "big picture." We always know what we have done and where we are going. We never have to address a detailed, picky question until we have first answered all the important questions leading up to it. This is termed *delayed decision making*. For example, in the following program design:

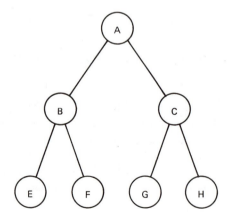

if I am trying to decide how to handle some low-level aspect of program unit E, I will have already completed the design and module specification of both program units A and B. Delaying this decision should make the answers to my questions about unit E much easier to determine. If, instead, I had immediately started to produce the specifications for module E, I would have become mired in very low-level details in the very early stages of program development and without knowing what other higher-level modules will be affected by this decision. This intellectual manageability has been achieved through two fundamental cognitive processes—*abstraction* and *modularization*.

Abstraction refers to dealing with an operation from a general viewpoint only, while disregarding its detailed substructure. It is abstraction that allows us, for example, to understand a large, complex map of the world. Initially, we ignore the many low-level details and concentrate on higher-level structures such as continents and countries. Only later, when we have understood these higher-level concepts, do we narrow our focus to the details of any specific country. In our development of computer programs, our approach is the same. We can manage the development of large, complex, multimodule programs by disregarding, at first, all lower-level details and concentrating on a few higher-level constructs. Only when we feel that we have a thorough understanding of these points do we begin to investigate and develop the lower-level details that were originally "abstracted away."

In *procedural abstraction* we initially think only about the highest-level functions and procedures needed to solve the problem. The specification of low-level routines is postponed until later. Each successive refinement of the design, then, adds additional details to the developing solution.

With *data abstraction*, we initially view a data structure only in terms of the external interface it displays to the user—that is, the operations that can be performed on that structure. Only later do we begin to concern ourselves with the underlying details of the implementation of that data type in a given programming language. (The issue of data abstraction was discussed extensively in Chapter 4.)

Procedural abstraction and data abstraction, as provided by the top-down program design method, are the fundamental tools for managing the implementation of large programs.

Modularization is the formal term for the informal idea earlier called divide and conquer. It allows one to compartmentalize a large problem into collections of related smaller units, which address simpler and coherent subproblems. Modularization also brings with it a number of distinct benefits.

First of all, modularization provides us with a way to create a rational, organized *implementation plan*. After the design phase has been completed, we are ready to begin implementation. The question is, "What do we do first?" "What do we do next?" "How do we create a plan for actually writing the tens of thousands of lines of code that we have specified?" By modularizing the overall problem and creating a structure chart that shows the relationship between these modules, we have the means to create such an implementation plan.

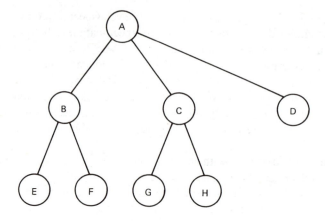

For example, given the above development tree, after coding module B, it would make sense to then implement units E and F, in order to get the entire (B, E, F) cluster working properly. Following that, we might choose to implement C and then G, H, and get the (C, G, H) cluster working. A second approach might be to implement all high-level modules first, leaving the lower-level routines for later. If we choose that strategy, then we might implement the modules in the order A, B, C, D, E, F, ... Finally, as mentioned in the previous section, we may choose to go at it in both ways. One group might work on high-level unit A, whereas another group works on the low-level routines E, F.

The point is that having modularized the problem and developed it in a top-down fashion, we have a choice of ways to approach the implementation of a large number of program units logically. While working on one unit we will know what unit we should work on next and which ones can be effectively postponed until later. Without this plan of action, we might write pieces of code in some unplanned random order and will not have pieces that work together or that can be tested as an entire unit.

Another advantage of modularization is that we *validate* each program unit for correctness as it is developed, not after the entire program is completely coded. The number of individual statements is not the only factor that affects debugging time. The effects of *interactions* between statements also contribute to the problem. This means that the time, *t*, needed to debug a program consisting of *n* lines will not increase at the same rate as program length but will do so *faster*. The relationship between *t* and *n* is

$$t \approx n^k, \qquad k > 1$$

As programs get longer, debugging time increases dramatically, eventually becoming the dominant step in the entire programming project. Reports show that on large projects with inadequate program management and organization, debugging consumed almost 50% of the overall project hours and, even then, the programs were not completely free of bugs.

It is definitely to our advantage to debug and test a program as a series of smaller units rather than as one large "lump." The top-down design method, which develops a program as a hierarchical set of tasks, defines a natural set of small subunits that can be individually tested, verified, and integrated into the overall solution.

11.6
Programming Teams

There has been a great deal of academic and industrial concern about the optimal organization and management of *programming teams*. Gone are the days of the "lone wolf" programmer who disappears for six months and emerges with a working program. Now programs are the result of coordinated team effort involving customers, managers, designers, programmers, coders, and clerical staff. The reasons for this are

1. Most software projects are too complex to be handled by a single programmer.
2. More than one person will have technical knowledge of a piece of software. Users will not be at the mercy of the employment whims of a single individual.
3. Responsibilities can be separated and specialized. One person would no longer have to handle such diverse tasks as program specification, design, coding, data entry, and documentation.

In the early days of software development, the basic approach to programming teams was the "army of ants" philosophy; keep throwing bodies at a problem and you will eventually solve it. Teams might include 50, 100, or even 500 programmers. At its peak, in 1965, the programming team involved with designing IBM's 360 Operating System numbered more than 1000. However, more recent research into team structure and programmer productivity has shown that more is not always better. At some point, the time and effort spent attempting to coordinate and manage such a large group can cause an actual *decrease* in overall group productivity.

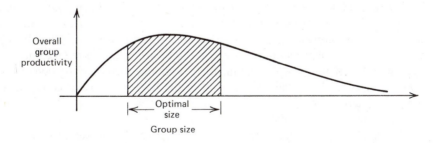

During the early 1970s, case studies in team organization began to develop models, or *paradigms,* for the structure of a programming team. One of the most famous of these models is called the *Chief Programmer Team (CPT).*[4] The CPT philosophy is

---

[4]F. T. Baker, "Chief Programmer Team Management of Production Programs," *IBM System Journal,* Vol. 11, No. 1, 1972.

based on the program design concepts discussed in this book and includes the following elements:

1. Top-down program design.
2. Adherence to the principles of structured coding (discussed in Chapter 13).
3. Validation of individual modules through stubs and structured walkthroughs (discussed in Chapter 16).

However, the CPT also has a very specific *functional organization* based on a rigidly assigned set of responsibilities. Like a crack surgical team (which was its model), all members of the CPT must know his or her exact responsibility and carry it out flawlessly. The CPT is made up of 3 to 10 members who have the following titles and responsibilities:

1. *Chief Programmer.* The technical manager of the project. He or she must have extensive programming experience and has responsibility for all high-level program design decisions and for coding and testing critical program units. The chief programmer assigns the work of implementing individual modules to other members of the team, manages the acceptance testing of the code, and integrates their completed work into the overall solution.

2. *Assistant Chief Programmer.* A senior-level programmer who is totally familiar with all phases of the developing project. He or she assists the chief programmer and will be able to move into the role of chief programmer if it becomes necessary.

3. *Programmers.* Depending on the complexity of the project, there may be none to five additional junior or senior-level programmers. They implement and code the algorithms and modules designed by both the chief and assistant chief programmers.

4. *Librarian.* A nontechnical clerical person responsible for maintaining the *Program Production Library* (*PPL*). The PPL consists of both *on-line,* machine-readable information (source code, test data files, object code) and *external information* (binders containing up-to-date module specifications, program listings, and output). The librarian allows the team to clearly separate the technical and clerical duties of program development. In addition, there may be none to two lower-level clerical assistants who report to the librarian and handle other nontechnical details such as
   a. Entering and editing data.
   b. Filing results in chronological order and keeping all external documents current.
   c. Preparing progress reports and memoranda.
   d. Delivering and picking up output and tapes.

The organizational structure of a typical CPT is summarized in Figure 11.11.

There are a number of other organizational models similar to the CPT model shown in Figure 11.11. They all have the same objective—the effective management of human resources to solve a programming project. Students should realize that real-

FIGURE 11.11   The CPT Model.

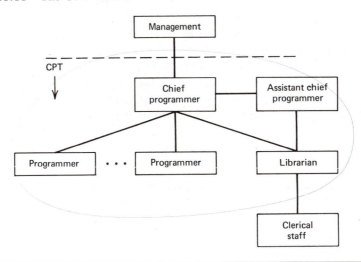

world programming is not an individual effort, but a cooperative effort usually involving up to a dozen specialists.

At the end of Chapter 15 (the completion of the program design portion of the text) we have provided a number of large programming assignments that would be appropriate to design and implement with a group of two to five students. We hope that every student will have the educational experience of working as part of a programming team, if not in this course then in a later one. It is an important experience because of the introduction it provides to the *human* issues involved in program design and implementation. These issues include

1. The importance of clear, concise written and oral communication.

2. The need to coordinate and cooperate with other technical specialists.

3. The need to manage the differences in ability and temperment of different team members.

4. The need to be able to suppress one's own ego or pride for overall team success.

Texts such as this one dwell mostly on such technical concerns as decision tables, design documents, and module specifications. Working as a member of a programming team will expose you to the important problem of working with and for people and introduce you to the *human* as well as the technical issues in program design.

11.7
Conclusion

In this chapter we have presented the idea that the process of designing a program is really one of dividing up the original program into a collection of smaller and simpler modules and data structures, which, when put together, solve the original problem. Without this divide-and-conquer step all but the most trivial problems would be too intellectually complex to implement and get working correctly. That is why the subprogram and data definition facilities of a programming language are so critically important to the overall programming process.

However, not all program designs are of the same worth, just as not all paper outlines or architectural blueprints are equally beautiful or elegant. In Chapter 12 we will take a look at the overall program design to learn how to evaluate its structure and goodness and the effects of a particular design on the overall software life cycle.

Exercises for Chapter 11

1. Comment on whether or not you would have divided the electronic grade book program into the five first-level modules shown on page 274. If not, propose an alternative design.

2. Assume that we felt the module called input-1 on page 274 was still too complex to implement as described. Propose a refinement of that module into three simpler modules that separately handle the following jobs:
    a. Getting a value for N and validating it.
    b. Getting values for LOW and HIGH and validating them.
    c. An errorhandler, which is activated if the user made a mistake when entering either N, LOW, or HIGH. It prints an appropriate error message, which tells the user what mistake was made.

Do you think this refinement helped and improved the design or made it unnecessarily complicated?

*3. Design the prime number program whose specification is contained on pages 254–255. Draw the structure chart and write out module and data specifications for all entries on the structure chart.

4. In the design of the electronic grade book program we left the data type called ScoreTable unspecified except for the two operations called store and retrieve. Discuss the advantages/disadvantages of implementing ScoreTable using
    a. An array of integers.
    b. A file of integers.
    c. A linked list.

Implement the two functions store and retrieve assuming we select each of the above internal representations. Assuming that we changed our minds on selection of an internal representation of ScoreTable, what affect would that change have on the other modules in the system?

*5. Given the following structure chart:

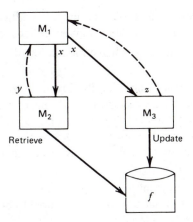

What (if anything) is wrong with the following statement: "M_1 first calls M_2 to retrieve a value from f and then calls module M_3 to update f"?

*6.   Given the following structure chart:

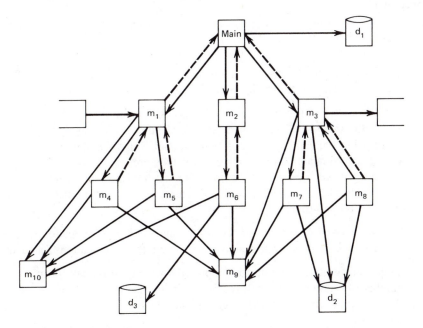

a.   In a pure top-down design, what would be the likely order of specification of the modules?

b.   In a mixed top-down/bottom-up implementation, in what order would we most likely implement the module?

c.   Identify "spheres of influence" in the sense of modules that are related by a common characteristic and that might be implemented jointly.

7. Write a module specification for the module entitled Input-2 of Figure 11.5. Follow the module specification guidelines given in Section 11.3.2.

*8. Write a module specification for the module entitled "Look-up" on the structure chart of Figure 11.6.

9. Write a data dictionary entry for the inventory file data structure shown in Figure 11.6. Assume the data structure is made up of part records containing the following information: part number, part name, amount on hand. Describe the typical operations that would be carried out on this data structure. (Just because we have used the term *file* in the name of the data structure, we are not implying that it must necessarily be implemented using the Pascal *file* type.)

10. Write a data dictionary entry for the error file data structure shown in Figure 11.6. Determine, yourself, what information it should contain and what operations should be defined for this data structure.

*11. Why would a for loop not be considered a module, according to the definition in this chapter?

12. Write stubs for the following modules referred to by the primechecker program of Section 11.4.1.
    a.   checkifprime.
    b.   errorhandler.
    c.   CursorToHome.

*13. What is poor about the following description of a module called SORT which was included as part of a design document?

> Module SORT is given as input a list of 100 integer values. It is the job of the module SORT to sort that list of numbers into ascending order using the technique called "bubble sort" in which adjacent values are compared and interchanged if they are out of order. The module will keep making passes over the list until no interchanges have been made. The module should return, as a result, the list sorted into ascending order.

14. Propose a possible design for the following problem specification. List what modules you are including in your design and write out the specifications for each one:

> You are to write a program to compute the weekly gross pay for a number of workers. You will receive as input a series of 50 time cards containing names (1 to 20 characters) and hours worked (hours and minutes).

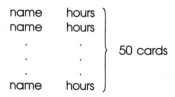

You are to compute take-home pay in the following manner: The individual is paid $4.00/hour for the first 40 hours and $6.00 for all hours beyond that. This is net pay. From this is deducted federal tax and social security tax, which are computed according to the rules specified by the federal government. The gross pay is then the net pay less all deductions.

For each employee, produce the following line of output:

Name   Net Pay   Federal Tax   Soc. Sec.   Gross Pay

If the hours worked are not in the range 0 to 60 (60 hours is the maximum allowed) print an error message:

**Error—illegal time card

and do *not* compute the gross pay.

15. Propose a possible design for the following problem specification. List what modules you are including in your design and write out the specifications for each module.

You are to read in values for LOW and HIGH, where LOW and HIGH are positive decimal values such that $0 <$ LOW $\leq$ HIGH. If LOW $>$ HIGH or either value is negative or zero, then print an error message:

**Error—illegal range provided, please reenter.

and get new value for LOW and HIGH.

When you have correct values, generate a table of values for x, x^2, and $1/x$ rounded to three-decimal-place accuracy, beginning at LOW, and proceeding in increments of 0.1 until you have reached (or exceeded) HIGH. Thus, if LOW were 0.1 and HIGH were 5.0, your program should produce the following output:

	x	x^2	$1/x$
(LOW)	0.1	0.010	10.000
	0.2	0.040	5.000
	.	.	.
	.	.	.
	.	.	.
	4.9	24.010	0.204
(HIGH)	5.0	25.000	0.200

16. Propose a design for the following problem specification. Draw the structure chart, and write out the module specifications and data dictionary.

You will be given a file of textual material. The file contains a series of words separated from each other by one or more blanks. The words are collected together into lines from 1 to 80 characters in length, with the end of each line marked by a carriage routine. The layout of the file is

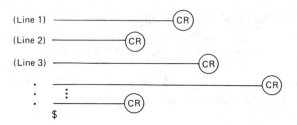

The end of all text is denoted by a line whose first character is '$'. You are to design a program to produce a *concordance*—an alphabetized list of every unique word that occurred in the text, along with every line on which that word occurred. Thus, if the text file contained the following lines:

See Spot run. (CR)

See Jane run. (CR)

See Spot bite Jane. (CR)
$

the output from your program would be the following:

Word	Line Reference
bite	3
Jane	2, 3
run	1, 2
see	1, 2, 3
Spot	1, 3

Disregard punctuation and differences of case (i.e., See, see). If a word occurs twice on the same line, include only one reference to it.

CHAPTER 12

DESIGN EVALUATION

12.1
Introduction

In Chapter 11 we introduced the concepts of top-down program design and stepwise refinement. At each stage in the design process, we flesh out the details of one program module and may, in the process, define the specifications for a number of new lower-level modules. The solution develops in the classic downward-growing-tree pattern shown in Figure 11.2.

In that chapter we motivated the importance of using this (or a similar) design methodology when developing large programs, intellectual manageability being high among these reasons. However, nowhere in that discussion did we talk about methods for the *qualitative evaluation* of a given design. Depending on how you view a problem, what you see as high-level operations, and the order in which you carry out the refinements, you may end up with a very different design from someone else. Given the same problem, one designer may end up with six modules, $M_1, M_2, \ldots, M_6$, structurally grouped into a three-level hierarchy, as follows:

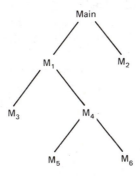

A second designer may view the problem in quite a different way, specifying only three modules—M_5, M_6, M_7, all of which are much larger and at the same level in the overall design:

The central question now is, does it matter? Are both designs equally good as long as they are correct and solve the original problem? Is there any way to judge the goodness, beauty, and elegance of both a design document and a program's overall structure? The answer is a most emphatic yes, and in the remainder of this chapter we will introduce some of the criteria needed to make this evaluation.

An excellent program design is one in which the individual modules specified in the design document all display highly desirable characteristics.[1] Therefore, design evaluation is really a question of knowing and understanding the most desirable properties of program modules.

Chapters 12 through 14 will discuss the topics of module characteristics and their desirable properties. In this chapter we will introduce those characteristics that measure how a single module is affected by and interacts with the other modules in the program. In Chapters 13 and 14 we will look at the stylistic and run-time characteristics of the individual modules themselves.

The three characteristics to be discussed in this chapter are

1. Logical coherence
2. Independence
3. Module size

12.2
Logical Coherence

A module is said to be *logically coherent* (also called *cohesive* or *functionally strong*) if it addresses only a single task and all the operations it performs are very closely related to each other. Informally, we can say that logical coherence means that a module does only one thing, and does it well. Looking back at the design of the test-scoring program in Figure 11.5, we see that all modules in the design meet this criterion. For example, Input-1 has the responsibility to get the problem parameters (N, LOW, HIGH); ComputeMean does everything related to computing an arithmetic mean and nothing else; Output has the responsibility for printing all reports. Within a single unit, all operations are closely related and highly homogeneous.

---

[1] In addition, an excellent design also produces data structures and abstract data type specifications that display desirable characteristics. The topic of data structure design was covered extensively in Part One of the text; here we will concentrate more on module characteristics.

FIGURE 12.1   Overlapping of Task Responsibility.

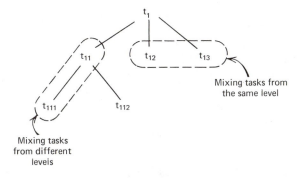

A good example of a module that is *not* logically coherent is the following:

Module M computes the frequencies of a series of test scores and displays them graphically on a terminal.

Obviously, the two operations of statistically determining frequencies and producing graphical output are quite distinct and not closely related to each other. We would say that this module is *logically incoherent* or *functionally weak*.

Another example would be a single module M, which takes as input a matrix A_1, inverts it to produce matrix A_2, and transposes it to produce matrix A_3. Although the operations of matrix inversion and matrix transposition are loosely related by being matrix operations, they are not generally considered related enough to be directly coded into a single module. We would again say that M is functionally weak.

When designing logically coherent program modules, we must be careful to avoid including unrelated tasks, either from the *same level* or from *different levels* within the design. For example, referring to Figure 12.1, when coding procedure t_{11}, we could err in two ways—by including aspects of tasks t_{12} or t_{13} or by including lower-level details from task t_{111} or t_{112}.

It is an easy mistake to include in a single module operations from related but distinct peer level tasks. For example, in Figure 12.1, tasks t_{11} and t_{12} are both required to perform task t_1; therefore, they will probably be related in some manner. It is incorrect, however, to necessarily conclude that the two related tasks are actually one operation that can be handled within a single program module.

For example, the following pairs of tasks are obviously related to one another:

1.   Read in the input. Validate the input for legality.
2.   Read in a string. Search a string for a specific pattern.
3.   Compute the mean. Compute the coefficient of variation.
4.   Sort a list. Merge two sorted lists.

In almost all situations, however, these pairs of tasks represent two distinct operations that should be implemented as separate and distinct program units.

The first pair of modules listed above (read, validate) display what is frequently called a *temporal relationship,* in that the second operation is started immediately after the first one has been completed. (We almost always validate immediately after completing the input.) Other examples of temporal relationships might include initialization operations or error recovery procedures.

The second and third pairs of modules above display what is termed *logical* or *application-oriented relationships,* in that the two modules address tasks drawn from the same area of application. The second pair (read, search) are both string-oriented tasks, and to that list we could have added modules for concatenation, string length determination, or substring replacements. The third pair are both statistically based computations, and that list could be enlarged to include literally hundreds of other statistical routines.

Finally, the fourth pair above (sort, merge) display what is called a *shared-data relationship.* This simply refers to two or more modules, which perform tasks on a common data structure—in this case, a list. Other examples of shared data relationships might include routines to open and close a file, or enter and remove entries from a queue.

However, neither temporal, applications-oriented, nor shared data relationships, in and of themselves, are sufficient to warrant grouping two or more operations together into a single module. That grouping should be done only when the two operations being considered demonstrate a stronger interaction, called a *functional relationship,* in which every aspect of both operations is directed at solving very closely related tasks. For example, the following three operations

1. Validate that LOW > 0.
2. Validate that HIGH < 1000.
3. Validate that HIGH $>$ LOW.

display a strong functional relationship, as they are all addressing the single task of validating the test score range [LOW..HIGH]. Putting these three operations into their own separate modules would be inappropriate and, in fact, would create unnecessary complexity.

There are a number of important reasons for keeping modules logically coherent; the most important has to do with *modification* and *program maintenance.* Problem specifications and users' needs change. Supporting these changes usually requires program modification. To minimize errors during the modification process, we should change as little of the code as possible. The sections of the code that are unaffected by new specifications should not be affected by the modification process. One way to ensure this is to isolate each indivisible operation into its own separate module.

For example, assume that I have a single module that both inputs and sorts data. From our previous discussion we would say that this module is functionally weak since the operations of input and sorting are not very closely related to each other. Let's say that I now want to rewrite this module to implement a newer and faster sorting algorithm. In the process of rewriting the sorting code, I may introduce a mistake in the input section, even though ideally the input part of the module should be unaffected by the proposed change. (For example, I may accidentally modify a variable in the sorting section also used in the input section.) If, instead, I had two separate and independent modules called *input* and *sort,* then a change in the sorting module could not in any way affect the process of input. Separating a task into its own module allows you to put "a wall around it" and protect it from accidental modification. During the design phase, you must ask yourself whether an operation represents a single, uniform, and coherent operation. If the answer to that is no, then consider splitting the proposed module into two or more separate units that isolate related tasks. Isolation of responsibility enhances and facilitates change.

   Aside from the advantages to be gained during modification, we can also benefit significantly during the testing phase. Assume that we have task A with m distinct control paths and task B with n distinct paths. If we write a procedure that incorporates both tasks into a single unit, we need at least $(m * n)$ unique data sets to test exhaustively all possible paths through this program unit (see Figure 12.2). But if we coded it

FIGURE 12.2   Testing of Program Modules. (*a*) mn Unique
Paths through This Program Unit. (*b*) m + n Total Paths
through the Two Separate Program Units.

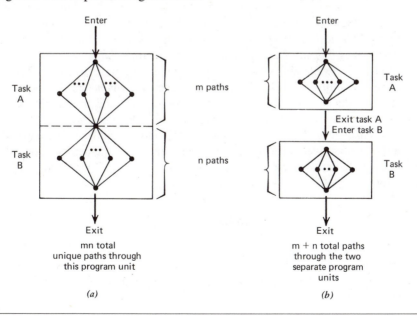

as two separate tasks, it would require only *m* cases to test A and *n* cases to test B—a total of $(m + n)$ data sets. For any $m,n > 2$, $(m + n) < (m * n)$. It is obviously useful to develop and test a program using short, simple procedures.

We have established the importance of maintaining logical coherence between tasks at the same level. Of equal importance is logical coherence between tasks at *different levels* (see Figure 12.1). Including unnecessary and inappropriate lower-level details in a higher-level module can obscure the purpose and function of a program unit.

For example, look at the following program fragment that reads in a string of characters:

```
i := 0;
while (i < arraymax) and (not eoln) do
    begin
    i := i + 1;
    read(ch);
    if (ch >= 'a') and (ch <= 'z') then
        ch := chr(ord(ch) - 32);
    if (ch = '[') or (ch = '{') then ch := '(';
    if (ch = ']') or (ch = '}') then ch := ')';
    if ((ord(ch) >= 0) and
        (ord(ch) <= 31)) or
        (ord(ch) > 127) then ch := '?';
    text[i] := ch;
    write(ch)
    end { of the while loop }
```

The logic of the loop is actually quite simple. It reads characters coded in the ASCII code set (see Appendix B), stores them in an array called text, and then echo prints them. What makes this simple loop so difficult to interpret is the presence of several messy lower-level details about how to handle certain special characters. The first **if** statement converts all lowercase characters to uppercase characters, the next two **if** statements map the braces and brackets into parentheses, and the last **if** statement makes all nonprinting characters (which in ASCII are 0–31 and 128–255) and sets them to the character ''?''. However, these details are certainly not essential to an understanding of the overall input operation, and the entire fragment would be much more lucid if these items were relegated to a logically separate, lower-level procedure, as in the following:

```
i := 0;
while (i < arraymax) and (not eoln) do
    begin
    i := i + 1;
    read(ch);
    FixUpChar(ch);       { correct certain special characters }
    text[i] := ch;
    write(ch)
    end { of the while loop }
```

By including a welter of inappropriate lower-level details in a given module, we defeat the advantages gained by means of the concept called *abstraction,* which we introduced in the last chapter. In the first of the modules shown above, we must immediately become aware of and knowledgeable of the detailed rules for character modification. However, in the second example the designer has effectively collected together this detail and placed it in the abstract entity called FixUpChar. We no longer need to think about this information until we feel that it is appropriate in the design and implementation of the overall program.

When designing a module, ask yourself whether particular details are or are not central to an understanding of the task being performed, or whether they are peripheral and may actually confuse and complicate an understanding of the logic. If the latter, consider putting this detail into a separate lower-level module, whose specification and implementation can be postponed until the appropriate time.

Naturally, deciding which operations are logically coherent and therefore deserving of a distinct module will depend on the specific problem we are trying to solve. However, the general rule still applies; each procedure should do *one* thing and do it well. If you are unsure about how to decompose a task, err on the side of defining a greater number of shorter procedures, it is much better stylistically to have many short procedures than to have a few large, complex, highly interrelated units. The former will usually be easier to work with, understand, test, and modify.

12.3
Independence

A program module is said to be *independent* (also referred to as *self-contained* or *decoupled*), if it does not need to know anything at all about the inner workings of any other module in the program to perform its task successfully. Specifically, it does not need to know the following:

1. The exact source of the input passed to the module.
2. The disposition of the output.
3. Which modules were activated prior to it.
4. Which modules will be activated after it.
5. How other modules are internally implemented.

The ideal specification for a module will go something like the following:

> I don't know anything else about the program other than if you give me
> data value *x* I'll produce result *y* and return. Period.

This type of specification does not depend on knowing where the input parameter *x* came from, how the result *y* will be used, or what other modules exist in the program. It simply does a task, by itself, and produces a result. It has no other unexpected impact on the overall behavior of the system.

If we design program units like this, we can treat them much like circuit boards. We can remove one procedure and "plug in" in a different one without affecting the remainder of the program, as long as the interface specifications for the two procedures are identical. We use this approach with Pascal's library routines when we code the following assignment statement.

```
y := sin(theta) − 1.0
```

We do not care at all what algorithm is used to evaluate the sine function. Whether it uses a Taylor Series Expansion or the "Modified Gliebowitz Technique" is immaterial (and it is even immaterial to us if the method changes during the life of our program) as long as the function being used has these characteristics:

1. It accepts one real parameter, x, whose units are radians.
2. It returns a real value, v, such that $v = \sin(x)$ to a sufficient level of accuracy.
3. It does it in a reasonable amount of time.
4. It has no other effects on the program being executed.

Failure to develop independent modules results in what is called the *ripple effect*. This occurs when a change to one program unit causes unexpected changes to a number of other units throughout the program. This severely complicates the program modification process, turning minor changes into major undertakings.

For example, suppose that we are asked to design a module to compute the root of an equation to five-decimal-place accuracy. Let's also say that we know the output module of this program was displaying the results on a plotting device that was not very precise and could only draw accurately to two significant places. We might be tempted to implement a compute module that (in violation of the specifications) automatically stopped evaluating when it had two significant digits, knowing that the output routine would be satisfied and any additional accuracy was unnecessary. The program would work; however, we would have a very poor design. If we ever buy a new plotter (or we switch to another output device), we will not only have to rewrite the output module (which we expected) but will also have to rewrite the compute module (which we did not expect!). Thus, what should have been a simple change has become unexpectedly more difficult because of the dependence of one module on the inner workings of another.

Computer scientists frequently call this characteristic *information hiding*—a module should hide what it does from all other modules in the system. All that these other modules should see is what goes in and what comes out. Then, if we change the inner workings, it cannot possibly cause problems because no other module could see them in the first place. If we practice the principle of information hiding, then the fact that the output module needs only two-place accuracy would not be known to any other module in the system.

This type of loosely coupled design greatly facilitates the task of program maintenance—keeping a program current and correct. Fixing or updating a program becomes as easy as fixing a TV set. We remove the old module, and insert the new one, just as the TV repairman pulls out the failed component and plugs in the new one. However, dependencies between modules in a program are like wires "jury-rigged" between components of our TV:

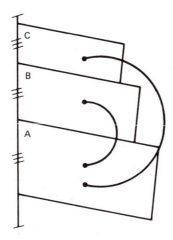

In this case, it is no longer easy to insert a new component A because of its *ad hoc* relationship to components B and C. All those interconnecting wires must be unplugged and reconnected in exactly the same fashion, with a quite high likelihood of error. This kind of a design, whether it be in TV sets or computer programs, is not good.

The best design is one in which, to the greatest extent possible, every module is independent of every other module in the system. The best way to achieve module independence is by

1. Not referencing or modifying global variables, thus making the procedure free of undesirable *side effects*.

2. Declaring all temporary variables or data structures local to the procedure in which they occur.

3. Avoiding changes to input parameters that were passed by reference because of memory space limitations. Whenever possible, input parameters should be passed by value so they cannot be modified.

4. Making no assumptions whatever about the internal structure or internal logic of other modules.

5. Adhering exactly to the calling sequence as described in the program design document.

These rules clearly indicate that, as viewed by the outside world, a procedure should affect only its call-by-reference parameters. All other values outside the scope of the procedure should be unaffected and hidden from view.

The following procedure is supposed to find the location (i.e., array subscript) of the largest element in array *A* of length *N*:

```
procedure findlargest (A: arraytype; N : integer; var location : integer);
var
      i : integer;
begin
    for i := 1 to N do
        if A[i] > big then
            begin
              big := A[i];
              location := i
            end
end; { procedure findlargest }
```

This module makes one very dangerous and inappropriate assumption, namely, that some other module in the system will properly initialize the global variable called *big*, as follows:

```
big := −maxint;
```

If the module where this initialization is performed were ever changed, and the above statement accidentally changed or removed, then findlargest may no longer work properly, even though the module itself was not modified in any way. (It could terminate abnormally at line 7 with a reference to an undefined quantity.)

A much better way to code this module would be to declare big as a local variable and initialize it within the module findlargest. Now the existence of the variable big and its initial value are hidden from view and cannot be affected by changes to other units.

As a second example, assume we are to implement a sort procedure, which will take as input a list of *n* numbers in the range 0 to 10. Some entries in the list have the value − 1, which represents missing data. The procedure sort should sort the values in the list into ascending order, but with the − 1s placed at the end of the list, as follows:

Input	Output
10	3
3	5
9	8
− 1	9
5	10
− 1	− 1
8	− 1

A ''too-clever'' programmer might reason that if the − 1s were instead set to + 11s, the sort algorithm would naturally place them at the end of the list without any extra work. The result might be the sort procedure shown in Figure 12.3.

FIGURE 12.3   Bubble Sort Procedure with Improper Side Effects.

```
procedure sort(var list : arraytype; n : integer;
    var m : integer);

{ procedure to sort a "list" of n values in the range 1–10 into ascending order using
  a bubble sort. Missing data are indicated by a −1. These items are placed at
  the end of the sorted list. }

var
    i           : integer;      { for loop index }
    sorted      : boolean;      { flag to test if list is sorted }
    temp        : integer;      { temporary used for interchanging items }

begin
    m := 0;
    for i := 1 to n do
        if list[i] = −1 then
            begin
            m := m + 1;
            list[i] := +11      { bad,bad,bad }
            end; { of if }

    { now do the bubble sort. The 11's will naturally percolate to the end }

    repeat
        sorted := true;
        for i := 1 to n − 1 do
            if list[i] > list[i + 1] then
                begin
                sorted := false;
                { exchange the items that are out of place }
                temp := list[i];
                list[i] := list[i + 1];
                list[i + 1] := temp
                end { of if statement }
    until sorted
end; { of procedure sort }
```

This procedure does sort a list into ascending order. However, the procedure has a disastrous side effect. Any other procedure using the list which is the output of sort will work improperly if it still assumes that the missing data symbol is a − 1. Now we must search through every module activated subsequent to sort to see if there are any references to the missing data constant − 1 and change them to refer to the new value + 11. Even worse, if at some time in the future we change procedure sort to utilize a faster algorithm, we must ensure that the new procedure changes the missing data indicator in precisely the same way, from a -1 to a $+11$. Otherwise, we will again be forced to go through every module, making changes to procedures that should be totally unaffected by a change in the sorting method. This is a classic example of the ripple effect in action.

Another important technique for enhancing program independence is the process of *localizing a data structure*. A data object (integer, array, pointer, etc.) should be declared in the innermost (i.e., most local) module possible. Assume that we have the following program structure:

Furthermore, assume that procedure A creates and manipulates a data structure called DS. B builds DS; C searches DS. Even though no other module in the program references DS, we could legally declare DS in either Main or procedure A. However, declaring the data structure DS in Main also makes it available, through the scope rules of Pascal, to modules D, E, and F (unless they declare a structure of the same name), and they could accidentally access and/or modify DS. Placing the declaration of DS in module A makes this impossible, since modules D, E, and F are outside the scope of the declaration of DS. In addition, if we should decide to modify DS, we can be certain that only modules A, B, and C could possibly be affected. The data structure modification cannot possibly affect either Main, D, E, or F, since they are independent of DS.

This is another example of the concept of information hiding. By declaring the data structure in module A, rather than in Main, we are hiding the existence of that object from modules D, E, and F and ensuring that they cannot be affected by changes to it.

This discussion indicates why the powerful scope rules of languages such as Algol, Pascal, Modula-2, or Ada are so important to proper program design. These scope rules allow us to declare a data object at the most appropriate level in the design hierarchy and hide it from modules that should not logically be aware of its existence. The same is true for the call-by-value parameter passing mechanism, which prevents unauthorized changes to parameters. In a sense, the language itself is providing tools to encourage and support the design of independent program modules. Languages without these features, such as BASIC or FORTRAN, must rely more on a programmer's proper behavior and good intentions to ensure module independence. Newer programming languages go even further than Pascal in providing explicit language features to support the development of highly independent program units.

The final point we will mention about achieving module independence is the importance of adhering exactly to the interface specifications for that module (i.e., the calling sequence) as laid out in the program design document. Ideally, the inner workings of a module are hidden from all other units, which see only the standardized interface. If the principles discussed in this section have been followed, a change in the internal structure of one module should have no effect on other modules. We emphasized this point when we discussed how we use a library routine, such as sine, while being totally unaware of its internal implementation:

```
y := sin(theta) − 1.0;
```

This independence is achieved through the use of *standardized interfaces*—a common external calling sequence regardless of the internal implementation. A change to the internal implementation should have no effect. However, a change to this external interface has drastic consequences.

Suppose, for example, we decided to add to the sine function an output parameter that signaled the existence of an error condition:

```
function sin(x : real; var switch : boolean) : real;
```

Now every single program that makes use of the sine function will have to be changed to reflect this new calling sequence. This may involve literally thousands of changes. Even the apparently small modification of changing parameter units from radians to degrees could cause massive upheaval. Every existing call to the sine function will need to be preceded by a new assignment statement, which converts radians to degrees.

```
newtheta := theta * (180.0/pi);
y := sin(newtheta) − 1.0
```

The point to realize is that one way program independence is achieved is through agreements of standardized modules interfaces. Programmers are quite free in their selection of the internal algorithm and data structures to use within a module, but must follow exactly the external calling sequences specified in the program design document. Changes there can have drastic consequences throughout the program.

In summary, program *independence* defines a set of modules constructed in such a way that a module is unaware of the internal structure of any other module, and a change in any one module does not cause an unexpected change in any other module in the program.

12.4
Module Size

The third desirable characteristic of program modules, namely, the proper size, is not an isolated characteristic; instead it is the result of closely adhering to the two guidelines just introduced—logical coherence and independence. If you design your modules to do only one logically coherent task and to be independent of other modules within the system, they will naturally be quite small, and, in the area of computer programming, "small is beautiful." Small modules are easier to debug, easier to verify, and much easier to understand.

The time needed for debugging and testing a program unit does not grow linearly as a function of program length. (Linear growth means that it would be twice as hard to debug a program that is twice as long, three times as hard to debug a program that is three times as long, etc.) In fact, most studies have shown that the difficulty factor in debugging a program grows exponentially as a function of program length; that is, the difficulty factor will grow at a rate proportional to k^x, for some constant k. For example, it may be twice as difficult to debug a program that is twice as long, 8 times more difficult to debug a program 3 times longer, and 32 times harder to debug a program whose length has increased by a factor of 5! Therefore, it is always to your advantage to keep your modules small and compact. It will result in an enormous savings in total debugging time.

Although there is no absolute guideline as to what constitutes small in computer programs, most professional programmers adopt the convention that no single module in a program should be longer than about 50 to 60 lines. There is a decidedly nontechnical reason for this value. It is approximately the number of lines that will fit on one page of printed computer output. Thus, if you use a 50- to 60-line limit, you can look at a module in its entirety without having to flip pages, as shown in Figure 12.4a. Some programmers use an upper limit of about 100 lines of code per module, since that would allow them to see the entire module on two pages of an open notebook, as shown in Figure 12.4b. Others may limit their units to about 25 lines so they can see the entire unit displayed on one screen of a CRT.

The point to remember is that the critical characteristic we are striving for is not smallness, per se, but logical coherence. If you find yourself writing program units that are quite large—many hundreds of line codes—you should really rethink your design. You are most likely performing two or more operations that should be separated and each placed into their own unit. Or it is possible that you are incorporating inappropriate low-level details into a higher-level module. This low-level detail should be hidden in its own module and invoked as needed by the higher-level routine. It always results

FIGURE 12.4 Proper Module Size. (*a*) About 50 to 60 Lines. (*b*) About 100 Lines.

About 50–60 lines

About 100 lines

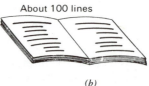

(*a*) (*b*)

in a better design to implement a program as a collection of many simpler components rather than fewer larger ones.

In this text we adopt the convention that no individual module should exceed 60 lines in length.

12.5
Conclusion

In this chapter we have presented an initial set of criteria for evaluating and judging the quality of a program design. Here we have been interested in the characteristics and properties of the relationships *between* components, that is, how the modules of the proposed design communicate, interact, and affect each other. By far, the two most important qualitative measures of module interaction are the following:

1. *Logical cohesion.* A measure of the strength of the functional relationship between the tasks carried out within a single module.

2. *Independence.* A measure of the amount of dependency of one module on the internal structure or implementation details of another module.

The best design is one in which, to the greatest extent possible, all modules display both a very high level of cohesion and independence.

While cohesion and independence are the most important system characteristics by which to judge the overall design, they are by no means the only ones. One other characteristic that deserves brief mention is called *connectivity*. It is a measure of the degree of interconnectedness of modules in the design, that is, for each module M, how many other modules invoke or are invoked by M. For example, a design containing 10 separate units could be implemented in two ways as shown in Figure 12.5.

In Figure 12.5a there is a high degree of connectivity since the module labeled Main has direct connections to nine other modules labeled $M_1, \ldots, M_9$. In Figure 12.5b there is a much lower level of connectivity. Now the module called Main is connected

FIGURE 12.5   Examples of Different Levels of Connectivity.

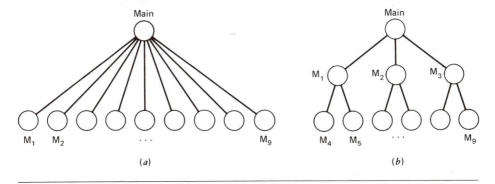

(a)   (b)

to only three other modules labeled M_1, M_2, and M_3. Each of those three second-level modules is connected to at most two other third-level modules.

The type of structure displayed in Figure 12.5a, sometimes called *high fan-out*, is generally less desirable than the structure shown in Figure 12.5b, sometimes called *low fan-out*. The reason for this is similar to many of our previous discussions—it simplifies any future maintenance and change. A change to the interface of Main would directly affect nine modules given the structure of Figure 12.5a, but the same change would affect only three modules given the structure of Figure 12.5b. Again, this is consistent with the goals presented throughout this chapter—to localize and isolate program operations to the fewest number of modules so that the effects of an error, a change, or an update do not propagate throughout the system. If we can do this, then we will greatly reduce the time (and the cost) involved with debugging, testing, and maintaining our program.

The characteristics of the interrelationships between modules is not the only criterion for evaluating a proposed design. We must also look at the individual modules them-selves, independent of any other units in the design. In the next two chapters we will be developing quality guidelines for evaluating the implementation of individual modules. These quality guidelines are generally referred to collectively as guidelines for *programming style*.

Exercises for Chapter 12

1. Take a program you wrote for another course and judge its design by the module standards discussed in this chapter. If you feel that the design was poor, propose an alternative and better design.

2. Propose a program design for the following problem specification:

> Assume that we have a file called dictionary, which contains word pairs with the first word in English and the second word its Spanish equivalent. There are approximately 5000 pairs of words with exactly one blank be-tween the pair. The end of the file is signaled by the character pair $ $. Thus, the file looks like this:

> how como
> if si
> then entonces
> you usted
> are esta
> hello hola
> good bueno
>
> .
> .
> .
>
> $ $

Your program should input one line of English text and do a simple word-for-word replacement of each English word by its Spanish equivalent taken from the dictionary. If the English word cannot be found in the dictionary, leave it untranslated. When the line has been translated and printed out, request a new English input line. The program should terminate when the input line entered is the character $ followed by a carriage return.

EXAMPLE

    Input: How are you?
           Como esta usted?
    Input: Who are you?
           Who esta usted?
    Input: If $a = b$ then $c := 1$
           Si $a = b$ entonces $c := 1$
    Input: $

Prepare a program design document. Then evaluate each module contained in the design using the cohesion and independence criteria proposed in this chapter.

*3.   Propose a program design for the following problem specification:

    Input a value n from the user, where n is an integer in the range 1 to 25. Then read in a line of English text. Now perform a *substitution cipher,* in which each letter of the encoded message is replaced by the letter n positions ahead of it in the alphabet. (For example, if $n = 2$, then a would be replaced by c, b would be replaced by d, . . . , z would be replaced by b.) In addition, the letters are regrouped together in units of five characters followed by a space, regardless of their original grouping structure. After each line has been encoded and regrouped, it is printed out. We then wait for another line of input. The program ends when the input line contains only the single character '@'.

EXAMPLE

    ?$n = 3$
    Input: This is an encoded message.
    Output: WKLVL VDQHA FRGHG PHVVD JG.
    Input: So is this.
    Output: VRLVW KLV.
    Input: @

Prepare a program design document. Then evaluate each module in the design using the cohesion and independence criteria proposed in this chapter.

4.   Propose a program design for the following problem specification:

    We have a two-dimensional file of diseases and symptoms. For hundreds of diseases d_1, d_2, d_3, . . . , d_n we have indicated (using a simple yes/no scheme) whether a specific symptom is or is not present with the disease. Seventeen possible symptoms are maintained in the file.

File: **Disease   Symptoms**

	S_1	S_2	S_3	$S_4 \ldots S_{17}$	
d_1	X		X		
d_2		X		X X	(X = Yes
d_3		X		X	blank = No)
.					
.					
.					
d_n	X	X	X		

You are to design a program that takes as input a list of symptoms and produces as output:

a.   A list of diseases whose symptoms match exactly the given list of input symptoms.

b.   A list of diseases whose symptoms match the given list of input symptoms in all places but one. The invalid symptom should be printed out.

EXAMPLE

Input: s_2, s_4
Output: Disease d_3 matches exactly.
Disease d_2 matches except for the presence of symptom s_{17}.
Input: s_1, s_2, s_3, s_4
Disease d_n matches except for the absence of symptom s_4.

Prepare a program design document. Then evaluate each module in the design using the cohesion and independence criteria proposed in this chapter.

*5.   For each of the following pairs of operations discuss whether or not you feel that they should be placed in the same program module.

a.   Computation of hours worked per week from time cards. Computation of pay rates from hours worked, hourly salary, and overtime rules.

b.   The conversion of clock time (e.g., 7:30 A.M., 8:15 P.M.) to a 24-hour-based decimal value (7.5, 20.25). The determination of the fractional interval between two time values (e.g., 7:30 A.M. to 8:15 P.M. is 12.75 hours).

*6.   Comment on the design of the following module:

```
type deck = array [1 .. 52] of card;
         .
         .
         .
procedure shuffle (var D : deck);
    { this procedure shuffles a deck using a random number generator }
```

```
const
    seed = 314159;
       a = 16807;
       M = 2147483647;
var
    temp : card;
    i, z, random : integer;
    R : real;
begin
    z := seed;
    for i := 1 to 52 do
        begin
        z := (a * z) mod M;
        R := z/M;
        random := round (51 * R + 1);
        { now do the interchange of the cards at positions i and random }
        temp := D[i];
        D[i] := D[random];
        D[random] := temp
        end
end;
```

If you feel that it is poorly done, redesign it, creating any additional modules you feel are necessary.

*7.   Comment on the design of the following module:

```
procedure CountNegative (L : listtype; var count : integer);
var
    i : integer;
begin
    { count the number of negative values in the list L }
    for i := 1 to listsize do
        if L[i] < 0 then
            count := count + 1;
    writeln ('Final count is ', count : 10)
end;
```

If you feel that it is poorly done, redesign it.

8.   Give other examples of operations that can cause undesirable dependencies between two or more program units. For each one, list an alternative approach that can eliminate the problem.

*9.   Comment on the following statement:

The problem with the bubble sort procedure in Figure 12.3 can be completely solved by simply changing the $+1$s back to -1 when you have finished sorting. Then we will have no problem and the module design can be considered excellent.

10. Some languages have a different set of scope rules from those of Pascal. For example, in some languages variables declared in an outer block are not automatically available in an inner block unless they are explicitly *imported* into the block. For example:

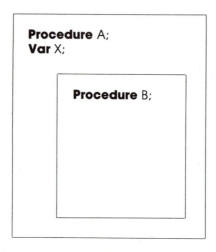

Variable *x* would not automatically be available in procedure B unless we said something like:

import x

Discuss how such a feature would or would not enhance module independence.

11. Some programmers get lazy about the scope rules of Pascal and put every declaration in the outermost block, that is, the main program. Discuss what negative characteristics this could have on the program's design.

12. Some languages directly support the idea of an abstract data type, as discussed in Chapter 4. They let you hide the underlying implementation of an abstract type. For example,

type stack **is** private;
var S: stack; top : integer;
    .
    .
    .

private
    type stack **is array** [1 . . 100] **of** integer;

The compiler would prevent you from making any references to the underlying implementation of the stack called S. All of the following would be marked as syntactically illegal:

```
S[1] := 0;
S[top] := S[top – 4]
```

Discuss how such a feature would or would not enhance module independence.

13.   Get the listing for a major software product that you are using (e.g., compiler, utility program, library routine) and measure the average and maximum length of the modules. Are they within the length guidelines proposed in this chapter? If not, look at some of the longer modules and see if their greater length significantly decreases your ability to comprehend them.

CHAPTER 13

PROGRAMMING STYLE: PROGRAMS THAT LOOK NICE

13.1
Introduction

Chapters 13 and 14 will introduce and develop an important concept called *programming style*. This refers to the entire set of conventions, guidelines, aids, and rules that make program modules easier *for people* to read, work with, and understand. The phrase *for people* is central to the definition of programming style. Computer programs are used by both machines and people—a fact that is too often overlooked. The long litany of syntactic rules and restrictions that define a programming language ensures that a *computer* can properly accept and execute a program. The style rules and restrictions that we will now present ensure that *people* can properly and easily read, understand, and work with that same program. We should stress that, from the machine's point of view, these style rules are completely unnecessary. As long as we adhere to all the language rules of Pascal, it is immaterial to the computer (actually, to the compiler) how that program was prepared or how it looked originally. As an extreme example, Figure 13.1 shows two program fragments that utilize very different styles. From the computer's viewpoint, these two fragments behave identically and, given the same input data, would produce the same results. However, for a person trying to understand the purpose of these program units, they are hardly identical; the second example would almost certainly be considered more difficult to read and understand. Although this is an extreme case, it illustrates the importance, *to people,* of developing and using pleasing, helpful, and effective stylistic guidelines.

It is often difficult for students in an academic environment to appreciate the importance of good programming habits. The academic environment is very different from the real-world, production programming environment, where programming style and expression are critical. In an academic environment, working programs are typically

FIGURE 13.1   Example of Two Identical Program Pieces
Using Differing Styles.

```
found := false;
i := 0;
while (i < tablesize) and (not found) do
    begin
    i := i + 1;
    if table[i] = key then found := true
    end;
```

(a)

```
a := 0; i := 1; 97: if t[i] = k then
goto 98; if i >= tsz then goto 99;
i := i + 1; goto 97; 98: a := 1;
99:
```

(b)

run only once and are almost never changed or modified after that final run. These programs are rarely examined in detail by anyone other than those already familiar with the problem—the teacher who designed it or the student who coded it. Usually neither of these people leaves the project (i.e., the class) prior to completion of the program. Finally, no one is paying any salaries or "real money" to develop this piece of software, and there are no budget restrictions to worry about. Taken together, these characteristics make for a most unrealistic situation.

In a production environment, computer programs are used for fairly long periods of time—possibly longer than the employment period of the original author of the program. In addition, programs are most definitely not static; they change frequently in response to changes in things such as tax laws, federal or state regulations, accounting policies, management priorities, new product lines, and consumer demands as well as the inevitable selection of a new computer. These two characteristics—program longevity and frequent change—mean that *program maintenance,* the process of keeping programs current and correct, is commonly done by someone who is unfamiliar with the original program. In this environment, the importance of clear, readable, and understandable program modules becomes obvious.

Likewise, most production programs are large software systems, not the small 100- or 200-line toy programs used in programming classes. These large, real-world projects are usually not the effort of one person but of a programming team of 3 to 10 people. The team members cooperate in program development, design, and coding and can pick up the work of another teammate who has left the project. Again, this necessitates software that is clear and readable and can be understood quickly and easily by various people.

Another reason that good program design and style habits are important is the enormous *decrease* in hardware costs and a concomitant *increase* in people costs: salaries and benefits. Ten or twenty years ago, when every computer was a multimillion dollar investment (not even counting the expensive computer rooms, air conditioning, etc.), the guiding philosophy in programming was to avoid wasting precious computer time. Today, however, complete microcomputer systems sell for as little as $1000, and even a sophisticated, medium-sized computing facility capable of handling 16 simultaneous users may cost only $20,000 to $50,000. If we assume a life expectancy of five years, the average annual cost for the hardware will be $4000 to $10,000—less than a few months' salary of a single programmer! Studies on the overall cost of computing systems show that the people costs of developing and maintaining software are now 50 to 70% of the overall costs, and they are still increasing!

So the new philosophy in programming is to avoid wasting precious programmer's time by writing unintelligible programs. The way to achieve this is to develop program design methods and style guidelines for creating software that is *initially* free of bugs, easy to read and understand, and subsequently easy to maintain. We always want to avoid software like that shown in Figure 13.1*b*. Such programs, even though they may be technically correct, are extremely conducive to errors that will cost time and money to locate and correct; the inevitable updating of such programs will be an expensive and time-consuming task as we try to interpret intricate, obtuse, and confusing logic.

There is one final point that we must mention. A discussion of programming style and expression can present only guidelines, not rules. Unlike syntax rules, there are no absolute rights or wrongs of programming style—only personal judgments and subjective evaluations. While we can say with absolute certainty that $i = i + 1$ is an incorrect assignment statement and that $i := i + 1$ is correct, there are no clear-cut answers to stylistic questions. For example, which of the two following indentation schemes for the **if**/**then**/**else** is superior:

```
if boolean-expression then
     begin
         . . .
     end
else
     begin
         . . .
     end
```

or

```
if boolean-expression
     then begin
             . . .
         end
     else begin
             . . .
         end
```

Of course, there is no answer to that question. Like many issues we will raise, this is a debatable point based on personal taste.

We will be presenting numerous examples of what we feel are useful stylistic guides. However, as readers become more experienced, they will develop personal programming styles that may differ somewhat from ours but with which they feel more comfortable. Remember that the "bottom line" on programming style is not to make your programs look exactly like ours but to make them easy for people to read, understand, and work with.

Programming style and expression will be considered in the next two chapters. The remainder of this chapter will discuss how to develop program modules that *look* nice (i.e., that are easy to read and understand). Chapter 14 will talk about program modules that *behave nicely* (i.e., whose execution time behavior is beneficial to either the end-user or other programmers who must work with that program).

13.2
Stylistic Guidelines

13.2.1 Clarity and Simplicity of Expression

Often programmers pride themselves on having designed a particularly intricate piece of code. The feeling is that a solution that looks difficult is better than one that is simple and clear. Nothing could be more untrue.

Look at the program in Figure 13.2, for example. Twenty-six lines and four loops— surely something important must be going on! But eight lines and one loop are all that is really needed to sum the positive and negative values in the list, as shown below:

```
positivesum := 0;
negativesum := 0;
for i := 1 to n do
    if list[i] >= 0
    then positivesum := positivesum + list[i]
    else negativesum := negativesum + list[i];
writeln(' sum of all positive values = ',positivesum);
writeln(' sum of all negative values = ',negativesum)
```

The program in Figure 13.2 was actually submitted as an example of "programmer expertise" and cleverness. The student who wrote it was proud of his exotic approach (the code sorts the list into ascending order, using a bubble sort, and then traverses it until the sign changes); it served his personal purposes and did wonders for his ego. To him it did not matter that the code was confusing and *unnecessarily* complicated. And it also did not matter that the code was *wrong!* The program in Figure 13.2 will not work properly unless the list contains at least one positive and one negative value. This points out another key fact: it is very easy for errors to slip unnoticed into confusing and complex programs.

This type of programming behavior should not really be admired or even tolerated. Programmers must always remember that the code they develop will be read and

FIGURE 13.2   Example of Unnecessary Complexity
in a Program.

```
sw := false;
while not sw do
begin
    { sort list using bubble sort }
    sw := true;
    for i := 1 to n − 1 do
        if list[i] > list[i + 1] then
        begin
            temp := list[i];
            list[i] := list[i + 1];
            list[i + 1] := temp;
            sw := false
        end
end;
sum := 0;
i := 1;
repeat
    sum := sum + list[i];
    i := i + 1
until list[i] > 0;
writeln (' sum of all negative values =',sum);
sum := 0;
repeat
    sum := sum + list[i];
    i := i + 1
until i > n;
writeln(' sum of all positive values =',sum)
```

studied by others and must therefore clearly and directly reflect the operation that it is carrying out. When choosing among alternative methods of coding a programming task, don't sacrifice clarity of expression for cleverness of implementation. Do it the simple and straightforward way. If you are tempted to break this rule, be sure you are doing it for a good reason (e.g., unusual conditions, special circumstances).

Another example of misplaced priorities is the effort to reduce execution time at all costs. If we were to learn that, on our computer, a floating-point addition could be carried out in 1.6 microseconds while a floating-point multiplication took 18.0 microseconds, some programmers might actually be tempted to code the operation $a = b * n$ as

```
a := 0.0;
if n <= 11
then for i := 1 to n do a := a + b
else a := b * n
```

The gains to be made with this optimization (if any) will usually be measured in thousandths or millionths of a second. But the loss in programmer time caused by repeated use of confusing code fragments could be measured in hours, days, and weeks! Don't sacrifice clarity for minor reductions in machine execution time. (However, this does not imply that we would tolerate *gross* inefficiencies only to achieve elegance of code. The trade-offs between machine efficiency and programming style will be discussed more fully in Chapter 17.)

Finally, look at the following statement:

```
y := x − (x div n) * n
```

You will probably determine, after some effort, that it says the same thing as

```
y := x mod n
```

but with considerably more bombast. Where possible, avoid the use of programming tricks whose intent will not be immediately obvious to readers.

In summary, programmers will need to learn to take personal satisfaction in simplicity and clarity: The biggest or the most complex is not necessarily the best. The goal is not to impress fellow programmers but to enlighten the end-users and facilitate program maintenance. The overriding and motivating factor in all program modules is *simplicity* and *clarity;* say exactly what you mean.

13.2.2 Names

Nothing contributes as much to a program's clarity and readability as the simple expedient of choosing good *mnemonic names*. For example,

```
m := s / (n − b)
```

gives no clue to the purpose of the operations that we are performing. However,

```
average := sum / (count − invalid)
```

is quite clear, even when presented out of context. The syntax of identifiers in Pascal does not limit the number of characters in a name, nor does it require the selection of a specific initial character to guarantee a specific data type. The only requirement is to select a name that is immediately recognizable and helpful to someone looking at the code. In most cases this is quite easy.

```
root, profit, sumsquared, mean, stepsize, score, date
```

are all easily recognized and quite appropriate. A programming technique that can be helpful is to use a common prefix (or suffix) to identify a group of variables that are logically related within the program. For example, if we were computing individual weekly payrolls and then carrying the totals along in a year-to-date (ytd) file, we might choose to preface our variables with weekly and ytd to identify this relationship.

weeklygross   ytdgross
weeklyfica   ytdfica
weeklynet   ytdnet

Likewise, the suffix "file" can quickly identify all the files used in the program:

masterfile   transactionfile   updatefile

Standard versions of Pascal do not allow blanks, hyphens, or underscores to be included as part of a name, as in

cost-per-fluid-ounce   date_of_purchase

Because of this some names, when written without spacing, can be very difficult to read.

costperfluidounce   dateofpurchase

A nice stylistic aid is to utilize the uppercase and lowercase abilities of the character set and to use capitalization as a visual delimiter to help in reading long names.

AmountInStock   AverageScore
CostPerFluidOunce   DateOfPurchase

There are some very important *do nots* related to name selection:

1. Do not use nonstandard, personally invented abbreviations that are not immediately clear:

    dlds   (days lost due to sickness)
    inclmtx   (increment limit of x)
    mxdspn   (maximum dispersion)

    It is well worth the effort to use the few extra characters needed to create meaningful names. Abbreviated or shortened identifiers are acceptable only as long as they are unambiguously recognizable and still carry sufficient mnemonic value. Therefore,

    freqtable   instead of frequencytable
    maxvalue   instead of maximumvalue

    seem to be reasonable names, whereas ft, mv, ftab, or maxv would most likely be unacceptable. Remember, when selecting a name, your goal is not to minimize keystrokes but to maximize clarity.

2. Be very careful about choosing two names that might be confused. Be especially cautious about confusing 0 and o, 1 and i, 2 and z.

positionmax	xxyz	kkk	interestrate
positionmax2	xxy2	kkkk	interstate

The eye can easily gloss over the minimal differences in these pairs.

3. In some languages you are forced into misspellings because of restrictions on data types or identifier length. Pascal does not impose these restrictions, so there is no need to create ''cute'' misspellings or unnecessary abbreviations that can lead to trouble when the person attempts to use the correct spelling:

kount	(instead of count)
averag	(instead of average)
matrx	(instead of matrix)
xnumber	(instead of number—a hangover from other languages)

One bad habit closely related to this is the selection of cute names that form a joke or a play on words:

if (puss **in** boots) **then** . . .
while boolexp **do** wackadoo := . . .

This may be funny, but it is not good programming.

Finally, there are two places where the selection of a name is particularly critical as a legibility aid. The first is the assignment of a symbolic name to a scalar constant. By themselves, constants have no mnemonic value (except for a few special ones such as 3.14159 and 2.71828). Therefore the appearance of a constant in an expression does not in any way assist us in understanding the purpose of the expression. For example,

credit := (0.0525 * balance) − 5.00

may leave us bewildered as to the purpose of the constants 0.0525 and 5.00. In Pascal, the **const** declaration allows us to overcome this limitation by assigning a helpful name to a scalar constant:

const
InterestRate	= 0.0525;	{ the annual interest paid on the account balance }
AnnualCharge	= 5.00;	{ the fixed $5.00 annual charge against all accounts }

This assignment statement becomes

```
credit := (InterestRate * balance) − AnnualCharge
```

From the compiler's point of view we have added nothing, since InterestRate and AnnualCharge are still constants. But from the user's point of view, we have made the purpose of the assignment much more obvious.

The second place where name selection is especially critical is with procedures and functions. If we are careful in our choice of procedure names, we should be able to determine what a program does merely by looking at the main program, which calls the various procedures. The following example illustrates this point quite clearly:

```
ReadData(list);
Validate(list,ok);
if ok then
    begin
        ComputeMean(list,mean);
        ComputeVariance(list,variance);
        PrintResults(mean,variance)
    end
else ErrorHandler
```

This fragment of a main program is extremely lucid, partly because of our choice of descriptive names for the various procedures: ReadData, Validate, ErrorHandler, and the like. It should be sufficient to look at the main program to determine *what* the program is doing. The only reason we have to scan the procedures is to determine *how* they actually perform that task.

13.2.3   Comments

Most students treat comments as something to be added after a program has been completed, to guarantee that they receive full credit. Again, this is because of the environment in which the students operate; the programs, usually quite short, are seen only by the authors, and only when they are fresh in their minds. In addition, the program never requires maintenance. Taken together, these characteristics result in an unnatural situation. Contrast this with the production environment discussed at the beginning of this chapter, where *proper* commenting is absolutely essential for correct program utilization. Notice the emphasis on the word *proper*. Not all comments are helpful, and certain commenting styles can even be detrimental to program understanding.

The single most important comment in a program is the *preface* or *prologue* comment, which should appear near the beginning of each program unit. Just as the preface of a book introduces its contents and purpose, the prologue comment should introduce the program unit to follow. The exact nature of the information in a prologue comment depends on the specific program or on specific policy, but it generally contains the following types of information:

1. A brief summary of what the program does and the method it uses.
2. The name(s) of the programmer(s).
3. The date it was written.
4. A reference to the written technical and user documentation manuals that give additional information about this program.
5. A brief history of all modifications to the program and why they were necessary.

For a procedure or function subprogram, a useful prologue comment should probably include the following two points:

1. *The entry conditions.* The initial state of the subprogram and what initial values are passed into it.
2. *The exit conditions.* What values are returned on completion and whether the state of the program has changed in any other way.

Figure 13.3 shows a typical prologue comment.

In a way, the declaration section itself can be thought of as a prologue or introduction to the entire program. Therefore, closely related to the prologue comment are comments explaining each individual item in either a **const**, **type**, or **var** declaration, making these declarations act almost as a table of contents for the rest of the program.

```
const
    high        = 999;          { highest valid flight number }
    low         = 1;            { lowest valid flight number }
    max         = 1000;         { the maximum length of the flight tables }
type
    flightrange = low . . high;
    list        = array [1 . . max] of flightrange;
var
    available   : integer;      { the number of seats currently available on
                                   this flight }
    flights     : list;         { list of all flight numbers going in or
                                   out today }
    found       : boolean;      { switch indicating whether flight was found }
    i           : integer;      { loop index }
    j           : integer;      { loop index }
    key         : flightrange;  { flight number we are searching }
    tally       : integer;      { if found was true, tally will be the number of
                                   passengers holding confirmed reservations }
```

If the declarations section has been commented in this fashion, we can determine the purpose of any variable by referring to the **var** declaration (always in a fixed and known location) and reading the comment about that variable.

To make the declaration section even easier to use, it is good stylistic practice to alphabetize the names in the **const**, **var**, and **type** declarations. As we have stressed repeatedly, real-world programs can be large, containing thousands of statements and

FIGURE 13.3   Sample Prologue Comment.

```
program example(input,output);

{

This program reads in student quiz scores, computes the mean score, and out-
puts the test scores, the mean, and the letter grade a, b, c, or f based on the
mean. The program does extensive error checking and will detect improper stu-
dent scores.

Author: G. Michael Schneider

Date: January 1, 1987

Refer to the book Advanced Programming and Problem Solving in Pascal,
2nd ed., John Wiley and Sons, for further specifications and details. }
```

hundreds of variables. Alphabetizing this list can significantly reduce the time needed
to locate a specific declaration and its comment. We will follow this practice in our
larger sample programs.

Another very useful set of comments are those that *paragraph* the program (i.e.,
identify and introduce blocks of code that perform a single task). The comment can
explain the purpose of the upcoming segment and mark the beginning and end of the
individual segments.

```
{ data input section }
n := 0;
while not eoln do
begin
    n := n + 1;
    read(string[n])
end;
readln;
read(ch);

{ guarantee that the character just read is alphabetic }
if ch in ['a' .. 'z'] then

    { count frequency of character in the input text }
    begin
    count := 0;
    for i := 1 to n do
        if ch = string[i] then count := count + 1;
```

```
      { output the character and its frequency count }
      writeln(' input character =',ch);
      writeln(' frequency count =',count)
   end
else writeln(' *** error—character must be alphabetic, please resubmit *** .')
```

When dividing a program into paragraphs, it is helpful to have an explanatory comment to introduce each new paragraph. However, even a series of comments consisting of nothing more than *blank lines* can be helpful. Although they do not explain anything, they still visually isolate groups of related statements.

```
read(x,y,z);
read(theta);

first := sqr(x) + theta;
second := sqr(y) + theta;
third := sqr(z) + theta;

writeln;
writeln(first,second,third)
```

Another very helpful class of comments are those that identify matching *pairs* of reserved words. This is especially important in matching the beginning and end of nested loops or large, compound statements. It is very common to have a number of compound statements (within loops or conditionals) end near one another.

```
         end
      end
      . . .
end
```

Although the indentation will give us a clue, a comment attached to each **end** can also help us identify the matching **begin-end** or **case-end** pairs, as in the following:

```
      end { of inner while loop }
   end { of else clause for negative parameters }
   . . .
end; { of procedure readfile }
```

Surprisingly, the least useful types of comments are those that annotate a single line of code. If we adhere to the stylistic guidelines that are being presented here, most individual lines of code will be quite clear and self-documenting. Comments that simply restate the obvious intent of a Pascal statement are usually worthless. For example,

```
{ input the date }
read(day,month,year);

{ validate day and month }
if (day > 31) or (month > 12) then
```

However, this does not mean that all such comments are unnecessary. The purpose of some individual statements may not be immediately obvious and, for those, a comment can be quite useful, even essential. For example, if we were searching for a match between a string of length m within some text of length n ($m \leq n$), the last possible starting position for such a match (assuming the array was indexed from 1) would be the subscript $n - m + 1$. However, to a first-time reader, the reason for the upper limit in this loop construct—for i := 1 to ($n - m + 1$) do—would probably not be immediately clear. It would have been much better to say

```
{ position n − m + 1 is the last possible place a successful match can start }
for i := 1 to n − m + 1 do
```

Closely related to the unnecessary comment is the *cryptic* comment. The code should tell us *how* an operation is to be done. The comment should enlighten us about *why* we are doing it. Avoid the unclear, technical, and jargon-filled comment.

```
{ check the 2 link fields in the doubly linked list to see if they are pointing to the
  same node element }
if head ↑ = tail ↑ then ...
```

How much nicer it is to say

```
{ determine if we have come to the end of the list }
if head ↑ = tail ↑ then ...
```

So far we have concentrated on which comments should (and should not) be placed in a program. Another important stylistic point is that comments should be written along with the code, as it is being developed, *not after*. Programmers should treat the comment as a Pascal statement (much as the assignment or if/then/else) and "code" with it right from the start. If you fail to do this, you will have to comment an entire (possibly large) program all at once. What will probably result is a grossly undercommented program, with brief comments that are only marginally helpful. Also, if there is a significant time lapse between the writing of a code section and the commenting of that section, the comment may be either inappropriate or less detailed than it would have been if we had done it immediately. Time can quickly dim even the best of memories.

Finally, after all comments are written, our job is still not finished. As we perform the job of program maintenance, it is critical that we modify the comments to reflect the new intent of any modified code. Programmers rely heavily on comments to explain what is going on. Incorrect or outdated comments can thus be ruinous to a proper understanding of the program. If we say

{ Here we compute the median score of all who completed the test. }

but then later rewrite the code to calculate the average instead, we must also change the above comment to describe the new operation being performed. If we fail to keep the comments current, we could completely mislead someone who is trying to understand what our program does. When you change a section of a program, simultaneously change all necessary comments to reflect the change. Incorrect or misleading comments are worse than no comments at all.

13.2.4   Indentation and Formatting

As we indicated in Figure 13.1*b*, Pascal is a free-format language (with the minor exception that it does not allow splitting constants and identifiers between two lines). The selection of guidelines for both horizontal and vertical spacing of programs is totally a matter of style.

The question of vertical spacing—blank lines—was treated in the previous section under the topic of blank comments. The question of horizontal spacing, usually termed *indentation,* will be treated here.

As we have stressed repeatedly, Pascal programs will always be written as a series of properly nested control constructs. The depth of this nesting is usually called the *level* of a statement. All programs initially begin at level 0.

Each time we enter either a loop or an alternative of a conditional statement, we enter the next level. The major use of indentation guidelines is as a *level indicator*—as a visual aid in determining the nesting structure of the program we are reading or writing.

Although there are a number of different indentation styles (and their proponents still have heated arguments about which is best), the best style is still determined by which indentation scheme most clearly highlights the hierarchical structure of a program. Figure 13.4 shows one possible, and quite legible, set of indentation guidelines. In all cases the process of proceeding from level i to level $i + 1$ is clearly delineated by an appropriately indented space; all statements at the same level will always be aligned. The result is good visual interpretation. The actual number of spaces to indent between levels is a matter of personal taste, and this is usually based on things such as the printing characteristics of a particular output device or the width of the paper being used. Three to five spaces usually give enough good visual clues and avoid one major problem—indenting so far to the right margin that there is barely enough room left for the statement itself.

The procedure sort in Figure 13.5 clearly illustrates the advantages of a good indentation scheme. There is no difficulty at all in determining the scope of any of the loops or conditions within the procedure, even though the procedure reaches a nesting depth of five levels.

FIGURE 13.4   Indentation Guidelines on Pascal Control
Statements.

```
while bool-exp do
    begin
    s1;
    s2;
    ...
    sn
    end { of while }

repeat
    s1;
    s2;
    ...
    sn
until bool-exp

for j := initial-exp to final-exp do
    begin
    s1;
    s2;
    ...
    sn
    end { of for }

if bool-exp then
    begin
    s1;
    s2;
    ...
    sn
    end { of then clause }
else
    begin
    s1;
    s2;
    ...
    sn
    end { of if }

case exp of
    caselabels : s1;
    caselabels : s2;
    ...
    caselabels : sn
end { of case }
```

FIGURE 13.5   Selection Sort Procedure—an Example of
Good Indentation Habits.

```
procedure sort (var list : arraytype; firstelement : arrayindex;
      lastelement : arrayindex; lowerbound : arrayindex;
      upperbound : arrayindex; var success : boolean);

var
      big           : integer;        { largest item of sublist }
      i             : arrayindex;     { loop index }
      j             : arrayindex;     { loop index }
      location      : arrayindex;     { position in sublist of big }
      temp          : integer;        { used to exchange two array elements }

begin
      if (firstelement >= lowerbound) and (lastelement <= upperbound)
            and (firstelement <= lastelement) then
            begin
            success := true;
            for i := firstelement to lastelement − 1 do
                  begin
                  big := list[i];
                  location.:= i;

                  { find the largest item in sublist beginning at position i+1 }
                  for j := i + 1 to lastelement do
                        if list[j] > big then
                              begin
                              big := list[j];
                              location := j
                              end; { of if and for j }

                  { now interchange the largest item with the one at position i }
                  temp := list[i];
                  list[i] := list[location];
                  list[location] := temp
                  end { of for i }
            end { of then clause }
      else success := false
end; { of procedure sort }
```

It is important to remember, however, that indentation only *highlights* structure, it does not *cause* it. Regardless of whether or not we indent statements, execution will be unaffected, and the program will have the same number of levels. This point is demonstrated by the following program fragment:

	Level
while not eof **do**	1
begin	2
readln(n);	2
for i := 1 **to** n **do**	2
begin	3
read(ch);	3
write(ch)	3
end	3
end;	2
write(n)	1

This fragment represents a nesting depth of two levels, regardless of the fact that we have (improperly) chosen not to indicate that.

Aside from the use of indentation to indicate levels, the other indentation guidelines are of significantly less importance. Two that should be mentioned concern multiple statements per line and multiple lines per statement.

Pascal does allow you to place more than one statement on a line; however, there are two good reasons to avoid this. First, we may miss a statement altogether as our eye naturally follows down the margin of aligned statements.

```
initialvalue := 0; i := 1;
read(final);
median := (initialvalue + final) / 2.0
```

We may, on a quick and casual reading of the preceding statements, miss the initialization of i. Second, when a statement appears on a single line, its nesting level is not indicated by indentation level. This can be important if you attempt to place two control statements on a single line—usually a bad practice.

```
If a = 0 then if b <> 0 then c := b else c := a
```

However, we will not adhere to this restriction too rigidly and will occasionally place more than one noncontrol statement on a line, especially if they are logically related or if we wish to describe both with a single comment.

```
z := 0; y := 0;     { initialize the cartesian coordinates }
read(x);
writeln(' x = ',x)
```

If a statement is too long to fit on a single line, we should position the next (or continuation) line so that structurally related parts of the statement are aligned.

```
if ( (a < 0) or (a > 99) ) and
   ( (b < 0) or (b > 99) ) and
   ( (c < 0) or (c > 99) )
then ...
```

13.2.5 Unburdening the User

Pascal contains a set of precedence rules that allow us to determine unambiguously the order of execution of arithmetic or logical operations within an expression. Using these rules, we could determine, for example, that in the assignment statement

```
b := x − a div 2
```

a **div** 2 is to be evaluated before the subtraction. However, we want to avoid, whenever possible, writing a program that requires recall of specific syntactic or semantic rules— in this case, the precedence rules of the language. Instead, we would add our own stylistic rule that says to parenthesize for both order of evaluation and clarity of expression. Parenthesize expressions so that the order of evaluation is obvious on a first reading.

```
b := x − (a div 2)
```

Nothing has been changed (from the compiler's point of view), but now readers of the program cannot possibly misinterpret the meaning of the statement. Of course, there is a point of diminishing returns, where overparenthesizing can actually make an expression *more* difficult to read. This usually does not occur, however, until the nesting depth reaches three or four levels. In most cases, the intelligent use of a limited number of extra grouping symbols will enhance a program's clarity.

A second example of the same problem is the ''dangling **else**'' problem. The statement

```
if x > 0 then
   if y > 0 then root := y
   else root := x
```

although indented reasonably, could still confuse a reader as to which **then** the **else** belongs to. An extraneous **begin-end** could completely alleviate this problem and avoid having a program that relies on the user's (possibly faulty) memory.

```
if x > 0 then
begin
   if y > 0 then root := y
   else root := x
end { of if x > 0 }
```

There are numerous other situations in which this can occur; the general rule is to help users by unburdening them from having to remember a specific syntactic rule to interpret properly a statement or piece of data. If it means having to add unneeded symbols—( ), **begin end**, or blank spaces—that is insignificant. What is important is what we have been stressing and striving for in this chapter: clarity of expression.

13.3
Structured Coding

13.3.1   Introduction

The final stylistic guideline we will introduce in this chapter concerns the programming technique called structured coding. *Structured coding* involves constructing individual program units using only three types of statements: sequential, conditional, and iterative.

A *sequential statement* performs an operation and then continues on to the next statement in the program. The flow of control of any sequential statement, s, can be represented visually by the diagram shown in Figure 13.6*a*. Examples of sequential statement types in Pascal are the assignment, input, output, compound, and procedure calls.

A *conditional statement* performs a test to decide which statement to execute next. In general, the model of a conditional statement is diagrammed in Figure 13.6*b*. The **if/then/else** and **case/end** are examples of two-way and multiway branch conditionals, respectively.

Finally, an *iterative statement* repetitively executes a number of statements (called the *loop body*) until a specific condition is met. In general, either statement in Figure 13.6*c* is valid. The Pascal **while**, **repeat**, and **for** are examples of iterative control statement.

A well-structured program unit contains only those three statement types: sequence, conditional, and iterative. The flowchart of any well-structured code fragment can be written as a properly nested series of sequence, conditional, and iterative boxes of the type shown in Figures 13.6*a, b,* and *c*.

In Pascal a well-structured program module is constructed using only the following high-level control structures:

begin/end
if/then/else
case/end
while/do
repeat/until
for/do

Specifically excluded are the **goto** construct and statement labels. The most fundamental characteristic of structured code is that it is composed of properly nested code segments that are entered only at the top and exited only from the bottom. These are called *single-entry, single-exit blocks*. The preceding statements and the flowcharts in Figure 13.6 all exhibit this characteristic.

FIGURE 13.6   Allowable Operation Types Using Structured
Code (*a*) Sequence (*b*) Conditional (*c*) Iterative.

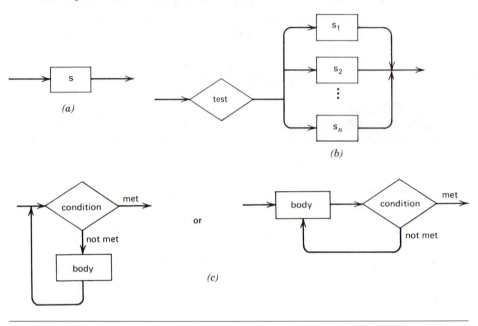

In 1966 C. Boehm and G. Jacopini formally demonstrated that any well-behaved computer program (i.e., one without an infinite loop) could be constructed using only the **if/then/else** and **while/do** control statements and the appropriate sequential operations (assignment, input, and output).[2] Therefore, in any programming language that contains those two control statements (e.g., Pascal, Modula-2, Ada, C), the **goto** statement is theoretically unnecessary. During the early work on structured coding, the **goto** statement became the center of a major debate called the "**goto** controversy." Misuse of the unconditional branch was blamed for a wide range of programming errors and crises, and the inclusion of even a single **goto** anywhere was considered to be the mark of a poor programmer.

Today, things have quieted down and most people recognize that the emphasis should not be on preaching against a particular construct such as the **goto** but on explaining why certain programming characteristics are desirable. Striving to attain those desirable characteristics will result naturally in programs that have few, if any, unconditional branches.

[2]C. Boehm and G. Jacopini, Flow diagrams, Turing machines, and languages with only two formation rules. *Communications of the ACM*, May 1966.

The basic problem with the **goto** is that it is too *primitive* and *low level*. (It is closely related to the unconditional branch in machine language that is executed directly by the hardware.) The **goto** and **if/then** are, in a sense, low-level building blocks to create more sophisticated and higher-level control statements. Languages like Pascal, Modula-2, and Ada already provide these higher-level constructs, and there is no reason to duplicate this work. The use of the **if/then** and **goto** to synthesize high-level control statements defeats the purpose of including them in the language. It is similar to building a house from mud, clay, and water when finished bricks are readily available.

The unrestricted use of the **goto** can result in a program that is difficult to read and understand and, consequently, difficult to work with and maintain. The fragment in Figure 13.7 shows a program module that is poorly structured and violates almost all the stylistic guidelines introduced in this chapter. Study this program in order to experience firsthand the difficulty in attempting to work with and understand the logic of a poorly structured program. In addition, we have intentionally included some bugs (that you should try to find) to impress on you the difficulties involved in getting poorly written programs to work properly. We will rewrite this program according to structured coding guidelines in the following section. (The bugs in Figure 13.7 are listed at the conclusion to this chapter.)

13.3.2 Example of Structured Coding

Let us rewrite the merge example of Figure 13.7 using the structured coding guidelines presented in the previous section. The formal specifications of the merge problem are as follows.

You are given two lists of integer values—alist and blist of size $m > 0$, and $n > 0$, respectively. The lists are sorted into ascending order. Merge alist and blist into a new list, called clist, of length $(m + n)$, which is also sorted into ascending order. This new list should contain all the items from both alist and blist. For example,

5	3	3
9	5	5
10	5	5
13	11	5
	13	9
		10
		11
		13
		13
alist	blist	clist

Let us assume that alist and blist, and their lengths, now called asize and bsize for clarity, were defined previously. First, we must verify that the values provided for asize and bsize are meaningful, that is, there must be something to merge. We must also check that the total length of the final merged list (asize + bsize) does not exceed the capacity of the clist array.

FIGURE 13.7   Example of a Poorly Written Unstructured
Program Unit.

{ Assume that the arrays a1,b1 and the integer variables a, as, b, bs, c, i have
  been previously defined. This program will attempt to merge two sorted lists, a1
  and b1, of length as and bs, respectively, and produce a single merged list, c1.
  The merged list should contain every item in either list a1 or b1 and should be
  sorted into ascending order. }

```
begin
        if (as < 0) or (bs < 0) or (as + bs > maxcsize) then goto 7;
        a := 1;
        b := 1;
        c := 1;
4:      if (a > as) then goto 1;
        if (b > bs) then goto 1;
        if (a1[a] < b1[b] then goto 2;
        goto 3;
2:      c1[c] := a1[a];
        a := a + 1;
        goto 9;
3:      c1[c] := b1[b];
        b := b + 1;
9:      c := c + 1;
        goto 4;
1:      if b > bs then goto 5;
        i := b;
6:      c1[c] := b1[b];
        i := i + 1;
        c := c + 1;
        if i <= bs then goto 6;
        goto 7;
5:      i := a;
8:      c1[c] := a1[a];
        i := i + 1;
        c := c + 1;
        if i <= as then goto 5;
7:
end.
```

```
if ((asize > 0) or (bsize > 0)) and (asize + bsize <= maxcsize) then
    begin
    { the data are valid, so solve the problem }
    end
else
    writeln('error in the size of the lists')
```

We can now concentrate on solving the problem for valid list sizes. Let us use the variables a, b, and c as indexes pointing to the next item in alist, blist, and clist, respectively. To merge the two lists, we find the current top item of each list, determine which is smaller (we are sorting into ascending order), move it to clist, and adjust the pointers of the appropriate lists. We continue this operation as long as there is at least one item in each list. The beginning of our solution is

```
{ these initializations assume the arrays are indexed beginning at 1 }
a := 1;
b := 1;
c := 1;
while (a <= asize) and (b <= bsize) do
    begin
    if alist[a] < blist[b] then
        begin
        "move an item from alist to clist"
        end
    else
        begin
        "move an item from blist to clist"
        end
    end { of while }
```

Moving an item from one list to another involves copying that item and updating the index. For example, to move an item from alist to clist:

```
clist[c] := alist[a];
a := a + 1;
c := c + 1
```

A similar set of operations applies for blist.

This works until we run out of items from one of the two lists (i.e., until a > asize or b > bsize). Then the comparison alist[a] < blist[b] becomes meaningless. When this happens, we should copy the remaining items in the unfinished list over to clist directly, without performing a comparison.

```
if a > asize then
    begin
        "move the remaining blist items to clist"
    end
else
    begin
        "move the remaining alist items to clist"
    end { of it }
```

If we exhaust alist first, the remaining items in blist are those between the current position of the pointer (b) and the end of the list (bsize), inclusive.

```
for i := b to bsize do
    begin
        clist[c] := blist[i];
        c := c + 1
    end { of for }
```

The identical reasoning applies if blist is exhausted first.

The entire program fragment is shown in Figure 13.8. Comparing the code fragments of Figures 13.7 and 13.8 should clearly demonstrate the increase in clarity and readability that results from following the stylistic and structured coding guidelines discussed in this section.

13.3.3 Advantages of Structured Coding

The main purpose of structured coding is to achieve clarity and readability within individual program modules and thus increase the maintainability of that module. However, that is not the only reason for coding in this fashion.

One of the most important advantages of structured coding is that it brings *intellectual manageability* to the coding of individual program modules. Instead of coding randomly and haphazardly, we take advantage of the hierarchy of properly nested blocks. We code the statements in the outer block first and work our way inward. Each successive block allows us to narrow our focus and concentrate on finer and finer details of the program. We work from the general aspects of the code to the more specific.

This is exactly the same advantage we talked about in Chapter 11 in the context of the design of entire programs. In fact, structured coding is really the application of the principles of top-down design and stepwise refinement to the implementation of individual program modules. All the advantages of top-down design—for example, abstraction, modularization, and delayed decision—have now been brought to the coding phase.

The characteristics of structured code are also critically important during the debugging and testing of individual program units. If a block of code has a single entry and a single exit, it is relatively easy to test whether or not that block is correct. We merely write out the values of all important variables on entering and exiting the block.

FIGURE 13.8   Structured Code Fragment for the Merge Operation.   349

```
if ((asize > 0) or (bsize > 0)) and
      (asize + bsize <= maxcsize) then
    begin { the merge operation }
    a := 1;
    b := 1;
    c := 1;

    { This while loop merges alist and blist so long as there is at least one item in each
      list. }
    while (a <= asize) and (b <= bsize) do
        begin
        { see which list has the smaller item on top }
        if alist[a] < blist[b] then
            begin { select the next item from alist }
            clist[c] := alist[a];
            a := a + 1;
            c := c + 1
            end
        else
            begin { select the next item from blist }
            clist[c] := blist[b];
            b := b + 1;
            c := c + 1
            end
        end; { of while }

    { We arrive here when we have exhausted one of the two lists.
      First see which one is empty. }
    if a > asize then
        begin
        { We have copied all elements from alist to clist. Copy the
          remaining items of blist into clist. }
        for i := b to bsize do
            begin
            clist[c] := blist[i];
            c := c + 1
            end
        end
    else
            begin
            { We have copied all elements from blist to clist. Copy the
              remaining items of alist into clist. }
            for i := a to asize do
                begin
                clist[c] := alist[i];
                c := c + 1
                end { of for }
            end { of else clause }
    csize := c - 1
    end { of then clause testing for valid data }
else
writeln ("error in list size—cannot merge")
```

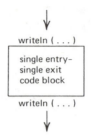

If the values were correct on entering the block but incorrect coming out, the error must be in the block itself, since there is no other means of entry into the block. If, however, we allow arbitrary branching at any point in the program,

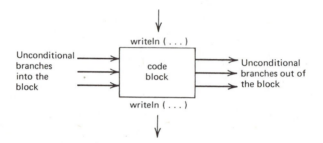

we cannot be sure of the exact site of the error. It may be in the block itself, or in any one of the other blocks linked to it by a transfer of control. This will significantly increase the complexity of the debugging task. (We will say more about this in Chapter 16.)

There is an important technique in programming called *program verification* that attempts to verify the correctness of programs in a quite different way. Instead of empirically testing a number of discrete data sets, we attempt to prove, using *formal mathematical* methods, that the program will produce correct values for all input. In program verification we think of the problem specification, p, as a function, with input, x, and output, y.

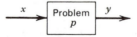

We now attempt to show that our program, P, is a correct realization of the formal specifications, p. That is, if for any input, x, the program produces a value y, $y = P(x)$, we then show that the value y is correct with respect to the specifications of the problem—that is, $y = p(x)$. Verification offers an exciting new alternative to the sometimes hit and miss approach to testing that presently exists. However, for formal verification to be realistic the program being verified must contain properly nested blocks, each of which exhibits well-known mathematical and logical properties. (We will also have more to say about program verification in Chapter 16.)

13.4
Example Program

We will now write a complete Pascal program which illustrates the stylistic characteristics that we have been stressing throughout this and previous chapters. The program will read in examination scores, and produce seven values:

1. A list of scores with illegal scores flagged as errors.
2. The number of valid scores.
3. The arithmetic mean, or average.
4. The mode and its frequency. The mode is the individual score that occurred with the greatest frequency. (If two or more scores have the same frequency, print the highest mode.)
5. The lowest and highest scores.
6. A histogram, giving for each valid score a bar whose length is proportional to the number achieving that score.
7. The total number of illegal scores.

For the following input:

```
 6   5   2   4
 3   3   1   0
 2   4   1   2
 2   4   2   3
17   6   5   3
```

the desired output (for an assumed examination score range of 0 to 6) is as follows:

The list of all scores:

```
 6   5   2   4
 3   3   1   0
 2   4   1   2
 2   4   2   3
17   6   5   3
```

Number of good scores = 19
Mean = 3.05
Mode = 2   Frequency = 5
Lowest score = 0
Highest score = 6
Score frequency:

```
6    **
5    **
4    ***
3    ****
2    *****
1    **
0    *
```

Number of illegal scores = 1

The complete program to produce the preceding output is shown in Figure 13.9.

FIGURE 13.9   Sample Program for Elementary Statistics.

program Statistics(Input, Output);
{ This is a program to input test scores and produce as output the mean,
  the mode, the lowest and highest scores, the number of valid and invalid
  scores, and a histogram of all scores.

  AUTHORS:
      G. Michael Schneider
      Steven C. Bruell
      Scott Chapman
      Macalester College
      St. Paul, Minnesota

  Date: January 1, 1987 }

const
    HeaderSize   = 10;   { Length of header for histogram }
    High   = 6;   { Highest Score }
    LineSize   = 132;   { Maximum output line width in characters
                                     for our line printer }
    Low   = 0;   { Lowest test score }
    PrintChar   = '*';   { Histogram printing character }

type
    ScoreRange   = Low .. High;   { Possible score range }
    ScoreArray   = **array** [ScoreRange] **of** integer;   { Data structure to hold
                                       all scores }

var
    Count   : integer;   { Count of all valid scores }
    Freq   : ScoreArray;   { Frequency count of test scores }
    Illegal   : integer;   { Count of all invalid scores }
    MaxScore   : ScoreRange;   { Highest legal score read }
    MinScore   : ScoreRange;   { Lowest legal score read }
    PrintSize   : integer;   { Number of spaces left for printing the
                                       histogram after we have printed the
                                       header }
    Sum   : real;   { Sum of all valid scores }

procedure Initialize(**var** ScoreFreq : ScoreArray; **var** ScoreSum : real;
    var ScoreCount, IllegalScores, PrinterSize : integer);

{ This procedure will initialize appropriate variables. }

FIGURE 13.9 *(Continued)*

```pascal
var
    i                       : integer;              { For loop index }
begin
    for i := Low to High do
        ScoreFreq[i] := 0;
    ScoreCount := 0;
    IllegalScores := 0;
    ScoreSum := 0.0;
    PrinterSize := LineSize - HeaderSize        { The header for each line of the
                                                  histogram is headersize characters }
end; { of procedure Initialize }

procedure GetScores(var ScoreFreq : ScoreArray; var ScoreCount : integer;
    var ScoreSum : real; var IllegalScores : integer);

{ This procedure will start reading data and making some initial
  statistical calculations. }

var
    Score      : integer;      { Temporary score for tallying }

begin
    writeln(' Enter list of all scores : ');
    while not eof do
    begin
        read(Score);
        writeln(Score:HeaderSize);
        if (Score >= Low) and (Score <= High) then
        begin
            ScoreSum := ScoreSum + Score;
            ScoreCount := ScoreCount + 1;
            ScoreFreq[Score] := ScoreFreq[Score] + 1;
        end { of then }
        else
        begin
            IllegalScores := IllegalScores + 1;
            writeln('The above score is illegal and is not included',
                    ' in the following statistics.');
        end; { of else }
    end; { of while }
end; { of procedure GetScores }

procedure CalculateMean(ScoreSum : real; ScoreCount : integer);

{ This procedure will calculate the mean value of all the scores read
  by dividing the number read by the total number read. }
```

FIGURE 13.9 *(Continued)*

```pascal
var
    Mean      : real;      { Average of all valid scores }

begin
    Mean := ScoreSum / ScoreCount;
    Writeln('Mean = ',Mean:HeaderSize:2)
end; { of procedure CalculateMean }


procedure CalculateMode(ScoreFreq : ScoreArray);

{ This procedure will determine the mode by finding the most frequently
  occurring score. }

var
    Mode          : ScoreRange;      { Score with highest frequency }
    MaxCount      : integer;         { Holds the most frequent score thus far. }
    i             : integer;         { For loop index }

begin
    MaxCount := 0;
    for i := Low to High do
        if ScoreFreq[i] >= MaxCount then
        begin
            MaxCount := ScoreFreq[i];
            Mode := i
        end; { of if and for }
    writeln('Mode = ',Mode:HeaderSize div 2, ' Frequency = ',
        ScoreFreq[Mode]:HeaderSize div 2)
end; { of procedure CalculateMode }


procedure FindHighLow(ScoreFreq : ScoreArray; var Max, Min : ScoreRange);

{ This procedure will calculate the highest and lowest scores read. }

begin
    Min := Low;
    while ScoreFreq[Min] = 0 do Min := Min + 1;

    Max := High;
    while ScoreFreq[Max] = 0 do Max := Max - 1;

    writeln('Lowest Score = ',Min:HeaderSize div 2,' Highest Score = ',
        Max:HeaderSize div 2)
end; { of procedure FindHighLow }
```

FIGURE 13.9 *(Continued)*

```pascal
procedure PrintHistogram(ScoreFreq : ScoreArray; Max, Min : ScoreRange;
    IllegalScores : integer);

{ This procedure will print out the appropriate histogram for the scores read. }

var
    i,j     : integer;      { for loop indexes }

begin
    writeln(' Score':HeaderSize div 2,' Frequency');

    for i := Max downto Min do
    begin
        { Print the header for this line }
        write(i:HeaderSize div 2, ' ':HeaderSize div 2);

        { First check to see that the length of the bar to be printed on the
          histogram exceeds the length of a line. If so, print it on multiple lines. }

        while ScoreFreq[i] > PrintSize do
        begin
            { Print a full line }
            for j := 1 to PrintSize do write(PrintChar);
            writeln;
            write(' ':HeaderSize);      { Skip header on continuation line }
            ScoreFreq[i] := ScoreFreq[i] − PrintSize
        end;

        { Print the partially filled last line }

        for j := 1 to ScoreFreq[i] do write(PrintChar);
        writeln
    end; { of for i }

    { Finish up the report with illegal score count. }

    writeln('Number of Illegal Scores = ',IllegalScores:HeaderSize div 2)

end; { of procedure PrintHistogram }

begin

{ Main Program }
```

FIGURE 13.9   (*Continued*)

```
Initialize(Freq,Sum,Count,Illegal,PrintSize);
GetScores(Freq,Count,Sum,Illegal);
if count > 0 then      { If there were legal values read. }
begin
    CalculateMean(Sum,Count);
    CalculateMode(Freq);
    FindHighLow(Freq,MaxScore,MinScore);
    PrintHistogram(Freq, MaxScore, MinScore, Illegal)
end { of if }

end. { of main program }
```

The errors in Figure 13.7 are: 1) The statement labeled 6: should read 6: $c1[c] :=$ $b1[i]$; 2) the statement labeled 8: should read $c1[c] := a1[i]$ and 3) the next to last line should read **if** $i <=$ as **then goto** 8.

Exercises for Chapter 13

*1.   The following program reads a value for x and computes an approximate value for e^x using the following formula.

$$e^x \approx 1 + x + \frac{x^2}{2!} + \frac{x^3}{3!} + \ldots \frac{x^n}{n!}$$

```
program ex(input,output);
var i : integer;
    x,s,n,d : real;
begin
readln(x);
s := 0.0;
n := 1.0;
d := 1.0;
i := 0;
repeat
s := s + n / d;
n := n * x;
i := i + 1;
d := d * i
until (n/d > (-0.01)) and (n/d < 0.01) or (i > 10);
writeln(s)
end.
```

Discuss what you feel are poor stylistic habits displayed in this program. Rewrite the program so that it achieves the same result but in a way that is easier to read and understand.

*2.   The following procedure computes the first and third quartile of a list of examination scores. Discuss which comments you feel are helpful to understanding the program and which you feel are not very helpful. Discuss which comments actually interfere with your understanding of the program. Rewrite the procedure to meet your own commenting standards and other stylistic concerns.

```
procedure quartile(list : arraytype; n : integer;
     var fq, tq : integer; var fail : boolean);

{ This procedure takes a list of examination scores, 'list,' of length 'n,' and returns
  the first and third quartiles in 'fq' and 'tq,' respectively. The first quartile is the
  score at which 25% did worse and 75% did better. The third quartile is the score
  at which 75% did worse, 25% did better. If we were unable to compute the
  quartiles, the parameter 'fail' is set to true; otherwise, it is set to false. }

var   errflag :    boolean;      { a flag returned by the sorting routine to determine
                                   whether or not it worked properly }
      fqindex :   integer;      { the subscript position in list of where the first quartile
                                   score is located }
      tqindex :   integer;      { the subscript position in list of where the third quartile
                                   score is located }

begin
     { first we must sort the list into ascending order }
     sort(list, n, errflag);
     { check the flag to see if there was any error encountered during the sorting
       operation }
     if errflag then
          { set the switch to true }
          fail := true
     else
          begin
          { set switch to false }
          fail := false;
          { Now we will compute the quartiles. First accurately determine the position
            in the list of the third quartile }
          fqindex := round (n/4.0);
          { Now determine the position of the first quartile }
          tqindex := round (3.0 * n/4.0);
          { Now set the parameters to the appropriate value. First fq }
          fq := list [fqindex];
          { and now tq }
          tq := list [tqindex]
          end { of the else no error clause }
end; { of procedure quartile }
```

3. Modify the statistics program in Figure 13.9 so that, in addition to what it now does, it also computes and prints the *standard deviation*. The standard deviation, σ, of a list of n values, $x_1, \ldots, x_n$, is defined as

$$\sigma = \sqrt{\frac{\sum_{i=1}^{n} (x_i - M)^2}{n}}$$

where M is the mean of the scores x_i. Discuss how you feel the style of the program helped or hindered you in understanding and modifying the program.

4. Modify the procedure sort in Figure 13.5 so that it
   a. Sorts into ascending order.
   b. Sorts only the first m items into place, $m \le n$. The remaining $n - m$ items can be left unsorted at the end of the list. That is, if $m = 7$, $n = 10$, procedure sort will correctly sort the first seven items in the list. The values in list[8] ... list[10] are not affected by the procedure.

Again, discuss how you feel the coding style and structure helped you with the maintenance task.

5. Write a complete Pascal program to solve the following problem. Given a series of data records on the physical characteristics of men and women in the following format:
   a. Sex code: "m" or "f".
   b. Age (in years).
   c. Height (in inches).
   d. Weight (in pounds).

produce a report in the following format.

Age	Average Height for Men (in.)	Average Height for Women (in.)	Average Weight for Men (lb)	Average Weight for Women (lb)
0–17	xx.x	xx.x	xxx.x	xxx.x
18–29	.	.	.	.
30–39	.	.	.	.
40–49	.	.	.	.
Over 50	.	.	.	.

Discuss the stylistic aspects of your program with regard to mnemonic names, indenting, commenting, and parenthesizing. If you have developed personal stylistic habits that differ from those presented in this chapter, discuss why you feel your presentation format is an improvement.

6. Write a Pascal procedure called *roman* that takes a character array containing Roman numerals and returns the corresponding decimal value. The end of the Roman numeral is indicated by a blank. The valid characters that may appear in the Roman numeral are I (1), V (5), X (10), L (50), C (100), D (500), and M (1000). Thus, if the array contained

```
roman[1] = 'C'
roman[2] = 'C'
roman[3] = 'L'
roman[4] = 'I'
roman[5] = 'X'
roman[6] = ' ' (blank)
```

the procedure should return the decimal value 259.

7.   Take a program you wrote in an earlier programming class before you were introduced to the material in this chapter. Review your own early programming style and discuss its weak and strong points. In what ways did you follow the guidelines presented here? In what ways was your style different? How do you think it can be improved?

8.   Rewrite the following fragment so it achieves the same results without using **goto** statements.

```
var
    hand       :    array [1 .. 13] of cards;
    cards      :    record
                        rank : 1 .. 13; { j = 11, q = 12, k = 13 }
                        suit : (spade,heart,diamond,club)
                    end;
    points,i   :    integer;
        .
        .
        .
{ count the points in the hand using the following point values: ace = 4 pts,
  k = 3, q = 2, j = 1 }
    points := 0;
    i := 1;
3:  if hand[i].rank = 1 then
    begin
        points := points + 4;
        goto 2
    end;
    if hand[i].rank = 13 then
    begin
        points := points + 3;
        goto 2
    end;
    if hand[i].rank = 12 then
    begin
        points := points + 2;
        goto 2
    end;
    if hand[i].rank = 11 then points := points + 1;
```

```
2:   i := i + 1;
     if i <= 13 then goto 3;
     writeln('total points in the hand = ', points)
```

Discuss how the fragment could also be improved through the use of symbolic constants.

9. Extend your rewritten fragment from Exercise 8 so that it also awards points for distribution according to the following rules:

Three points if you have no cards of a suit (*void*).
Two points if you have one card in a suit (*singleton*).
One point if you have two cards in a suit (*doubleton*).

10. Rewrite the following **repeat** loop so that all conditions for loop termination are specified directly in the **repeat** statement.

```
{ Find the vowel pair 'ae' in the current line. The characters of the current line are
  stored in line[1], . . . , line[max]. A period encountered in the line should also stop the
  scan. }

     i := 0;
     repeat
         i := i + 1;
         if line[i] = '.' then goto 2;
         if i >= max then goto 2
     until (line[i] = 'a') and (line[i + 1] = 'e');
2:        .
          .
          .
```

*11. Rewrite the following **for** loop, using either a **repeat** or a **while** statement, so that it achieves the same effect but without the **goto**.

```
{ Generate a table of function values, f(x), for x = 0, 1, . . . , 500. However stop if the
  value of f(x) ever exceeds the upper bound called limit, for any x. }

for x := 0 to 500 do
    begin
    value := f(x);
    if value > limit then
        begin
        writeln('value of function unacceptable at the point',x);
        goto 1
        end { of then clause }
    else table(x) := value
    end; { of for loop }
1:
```

12.   Try modifying the unstructured program fragment from Figure 13.7 so that it eliminates *duplicates* between lists a1 and b1. That is, if a value occurs in both lists, move just one value to the merged list c1 and discard all other identical values. Keep track of the time and effort involved. Now try making the identical change to the fragment in Figure 13.8. Discuss how the program's structure and style facilitated this modification.

13.   Code the following problems as a well-structured, elegant Pascal procedure called path.

   a.   You will be given, as input, a two-dimensional matrix called connection that is $n \times n$. Connection$(i,j) = 1$ if there is a direct physical path (i.e., a road, a bridge, a connection) from node i to node j. Otherwise, connection$(i,j) = 0$. For example,

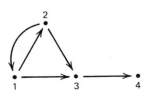

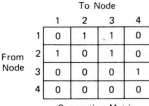

	To Node			
	1	2	3	4
1	0	1	1	0
From Node 2	1	0	1	0
3	0	0	0	1
4	0	0	0	0

Connection Matrix

   Your procedure should take as input the matrix called connection along with the index of any two nodes i,j; $i,j = 1, \ldots, n$. The output of the procedure should be a boolean value that is true if there is a path that eventually leads from node i to node j and false otherwise. For example, referring to the preceding chart:

   Path (1,4) is true $(1 \rightarrow 2 \rightarrow 3 \rightarrow 4)$ or, alternatively, $(1 \rightarrow 3 \rightarrow 4)$.
   Path (4,3) is false.
   Path (3,1) is false.
   Path (4,4) is false.

   b.   Modify the procedure of part a so that, in addition to telling you that a path exists, it also returns what that path is. That is, it returns the exact sequence of nodes $a_1, a_2, \ldots, a_k$ such that $a_1 = i$, $a_k = j$ and such that there is a connection from a_i to a_{i+1}, $i = 1$ to $k - 1$.

CHAPTER 14

PROGRAMMING STYLE: PROGRAMS THAT BEHAVE NICELY

14.1
Introduction

In Chapter 13 we presented guidelines for developing program modules that are *clear, readable,* and *well structured.* But clarity alone is not enough. To maximize utility and flexibility, the run-time characteristics of programs must also conform to certain stylistic constraints and guidelines. Each program module must not only "look nice," it must also "behave nicely" when executed.

Too often, however, programmers believe that *correctness* is the only important runtime attribute. Of course, a program must produce proper results, but correctness is not the only important characteristic. This chapter will discuss many other desirable qualities.

14.2
Robustness

A *robust* program will produce meaningful results from any data set, regardless of how illegal, implausible, improper, or "pathological" it may be. Notice that we said meaningful results, not correct answers. For most problems there will be data sets for which we cannot produce an answer or apply an algorithm. But we can always perform certain operations that are meaningful and helpful to the user. This could include printing an appropriate error message, explaining why the operations cannot be executed, and, if possible, supplying details about how to correct and resubmit the data. Under certain conditions, the program could also reset data items within allowable limits (after informing the user).

```
if n > maximum then
    begin
        n := maximum;
        writeln ('The list was too large. It will be reset to',maximum)
    end { of if }
```

Robustness guidelines require that under *no* circumstances will a program terminate abnormally during execution. Terminations should occur only at the end of the main program, and the output produced should be a meaningful result directly related to the input data provided.

14.2.1 Input Validation

The most important operation a programmer can perform to ensure robustness is a complete and thorough validation of all input. Errors in input data are common and can be caused by any of the following:

1. Data entry errors when typing in the data (hitting a 7 instead of a 1).

2. Improper ordering of the data items on a line or of the lines themselves.

3. A misunderstanding of what type of value to enter [e.g., entering a date as June 10, 6/10, or 161 (the number of days since January 1)].

There is a popular phrase in programming: GIGO (garbage in/garbage out). If improper data values are accepted by a program, unpredictable and meaningless operations may result, regardless of the care we have taken to write a good program.

Input values must first be validated for *legality*. They must be within the bounds set by either the problem specification or physical reality. For example, the specifications of a payroll program may state that the following bounds apply:

$$0 < \text{ID number} \leq 99999$$
$$0 \leq \text{Dept number} \leq 99$$
$$\$3.35 \leq \text{Payrate}$$
$$0 \leq \text{Exemptions}$$

To this we could add the following constraints based on natural physical limits:

$$0 \leq \text{Daily hours worked} \leq 24$$
$$0 \leq \text{Days worked this week} \leq 7$$

and check that all input falls within this range.

```
type
    errortype = (iderror, depterror, payerror, exemerror, hourserror, dayerror);
```

```
var
    error      : set of errortype;
        .
        .
        .
begin
    error := [ ];
    if (id <= 0) or (id > 99999) then
        error := error + [iderror];
    if (dept < 0) or (dept > 99) then
        error := error + [depterror];
    if payrate < 3.35 then
        error := error + [payerror];
    if exemptions < 0 then
        error := error + [exemerror];
    if (hours < 0) or (hours > 24) then
        error := error + [hourserror];
    if (days < 0) or (days > 7) then
        error := error + [dayerror];
        .
        .
        .
    if error = [ ] then "process the data"
    else "invoke error procedure"
```

This example illustrates another important point about input validation; in case of an error, we should gather enough information to be able to tell the user exactly what the error was and where it occurred. In the preceding example we made a separate entry in the variable error for each of the six possible types of error. Now the error procedure we write can produce detailed messages of the form:

```
** error in the hours-worked field of this record
** value must be an integer in the range 0-24 **
```

simply by checking the variable error

```
if iderror in error then
    writeln (' ** error in id field. value must ',
        'be in the range',low,'to',high);
if hourserror in error then
    begin
    writeln(' ** error in the hours-worked field of ',
        'this record.');
    writeln(' ** value must be an integer in ',
        'the range 0-24 ** ')
    end
```

If we had made error a boolean value with, say, false signifying no errors and true signifying one or more of the preceding six error types, the most we could say is

** Error on this data record **

We would have no additional information about the error because of the data type selected. Always try to relate an error message to the mistake that caused it. All-inclusive error messages should generally be avoided as they are less helpful to the user.

Validating input for legality is not sufficient. We should also validate for *plausibility*. When a data value is highly unlikely (although not impossible), we should identify it for special (manual) processing. Many values provided to a program have no preestablished upper bound that we can check. For instance, in the previous example, what is the maximum pay rate allowed? (Some consultants may earn $200 an hour.) What is the maximum number of exemptions allowed? If there were no way to validate this type of value, we would develop programs that accept hourly pay rates of $123,456 or a claim of 35,000 dependents—certainly suspicious! To prevent this, during the problem specification phase we should develop *plausibility bounds* in conjunction with the end-user. Then we can verify within the program that all values are legal and also plausible.

```
{ do not accept pay rate over $30 }
if payrate > 30.00 then error := error + [overpayerror];

{ do not accept 20 or more dependents }
if exemptions > = 20 then error := error + [overexempterror]
```

If we do not wish to mark them as erroneous and activate an error handler, we should at least print out some type of warning message to the user to inform them of a suspicious and potentially incorrect data item.

```
if exemptions > = 20 then
    writeln (' ** Warning: This input data contained a value of ', exemptions, ' in the
        exemption field. Please verify and resubmit if incorrect ');
```

These cases cannot be automatically considered input errors because the values might be correct, albeit unusual. However, users will at least be made aware of the suspicious value and can rely on their own judgment instead of on the program to determine if the data item is correct.

Finally, even if improper input slips through our checks for legality and plausibility, we have one final checkpoint—the user. By always *echo printing* the input data, we allow the user to locate incorrect data before utilizing the output. Always include, somewhere in the output, the input data that produced those results.

```
read(x);
writeln(' x-coordinate = ',x)
```

Exactly where this is to be printed will naturally depend on the problem specifications. However, regardless of exactly where it is to be placed, the output should include an exact copy of the input file as one of its reports.

Between echo printing and validating for legality and plausibility, the input validation phase can be quite long. It is not unusual, especially for commercial and business-oriented problems, for the input and input checks to account for 20, 30, or even 40% of the statements in the program. Your program should be protected against *all* improper data, no matter how pathological. The number of lines it takes to achieve that level of security is not important. A well-known maxim of programming states that the error you do not check for is the one that will occur!

14.2.2 Defensive Programming

A *run-time error* causes a program to terminate abnormally during execution. Such an error may be caused by improper input data, or even by data that are perfectly legal and plausible. For example, even if we validate that $0° \leq \theta \leq 360°$, $\tan(\theta)$ is still undefined at $\theta = 90°$ and $270°$, and any attempt to use those values will cause the program to abort. Obviously, protection against run-time errors is necessary in addition to input validation to guarantee program robustness.

In Pascal, the most common run-time errors are caused by

1. Array subscript out of bounds.
2. Subrange out of bounds.
3. Real to integer conversion with the absolute value of the real $>$ maxint.
4. Case statement expression not matching one of the case labels.
5. Improper argument for a function.

sqrt(x)	x < 0
ln(x)	x <= 0
chr(x)	x < 0 or x > maximum number of characters
succ(x)	where x is the last entry in the scalar data type
pred(x)	where x is the first entry in the data type

6. Input errors: illegal input syntax or attempts to read past the end-of-file.
7. Referencing a data object before it is defined.
8. Division by zero.

To prevent an operation from aborting (even in spite of our input checks), we should include tests in the program that insure that all necessary preconditions are met before we perform that operation. Inclusion of these precautions is usually termed *defensive programming*—anticipating potential trouble spots and guarding against them. Defensive programming ensures that when we perform an operation, we know that operation is well defined and will complete successfully. [There is one notable exception. Most implementations of the read and readln procedures will automatically abort the program if they encounter an error during input (e.g., a nonnumeric character punched in an integer field). Users cannot prevent this loss of control except by choosing not to use the read or readln procedures.]

For example, the following assignment statement computes one root of a quadratic equation using the well-known quadratic formula (assume we have already checked that $a \neq 0$):

```
root1 := (−b + sqrt(sqr(b) − 4.0∗a∗c)) / (2.0∗a)
```

However, if $sqr(b) - 4.0*a*c < 0.0$, there is a complex root, and the preceding statement will attempt to find the square root of a negative value, causing the program to terminate. It is better to say

```
discriminant := sqr(b) − (4.0 ∗ a ∗ c);
if discriminant >= 0.0 then
    begin
        root1 := (−b + sqrt(discriminant)) / (2.0 ∗ a);
        root2 := (−b − sqrt(discriminant)) / (2.0 ∗ a)
    end
else complexroots { procedure to compute complex roots }
```

Another example is the following method for counting the frequency of each letter in the input.

```
var
    freq    : array ['a'. .'z'] of integer;

        .
        .
        .

begin
    read(ch);
    freq[ch] := freq[ch] + 1
```

This code works properly only as long as we can guarantee that all characters in the text are in the range 'a' to 'z'. The occurrence of a single out-of-range character will abort the entire program with an array subscript out of bounds. A better way to code that operation would be

```
read(ch);
if (ch < 'a') or (ch > 'z') then illegal := illegal + 1
else freq[ch] := freq[ch] + 1
```

Another common cause of run-time errors is the failure to handle the null case properly. The *null case* is the empty data set (e.g., no input, no legal values, or a list of length 0). If we are not careful, it is easy to write code that works properly only when there is one or more valid pieces of data. This harmless-looking loop:

```
i := 0;
repeat
    i := i + 1;
    readln(table[i])
until (i = listsize) or eof
```

will "blow up" if the input file is *initially* empty. We will attempt to perform a readln operation while eof is true and will terminate with a fatal error. Likewise,

```
sum   := 0;
i     := 0;
repeat
    i     := i + 1;
    sum   := sum + table[i]
until i = listsize
```

is correct only if listsize > 0. If we are ever presented with a table of length 0, this fragment will abort with an array index out of bounds (i.e., table[1]).

Referring to the code fragment in Figure 13.2, we can see one more example of the failure to handle the null case. That program attempted to sum up separately the positive and negative values contained in a list. However, it fails to handle the special case of a list without either one positive or one negative value. (It either produces a wrong answer or terminates abnormally with an array reference out of bounds.)

When writing a loop, immediately ask yourself if any null cases are possible and, if so, check to see if the loop as written will properly handle those cases.

Finally, be particularly careful with the **case** statement in Pascal. Failure to match a case label with the value of the selector expression can be a fatal error.

```
case yearinschool of
    1,2 : processlowerclassman;
    3,4 : processupperclassman;
    5   : processgraduate
end { of case }
```

If we cannot guarantee that yearinschool will always be an integer in the range 1 to 5 (possibly from an earlier input check), the preceding statement is very risky. It is much safer to write

if (yearinschool $>=$ 1) **and** (yearinschool $<=$ 5) **then**
    case yearinschool **of**
        1,2 : processlowerclassman;
        3,4 : processupperclassman;
        5   : processgraduate
    end { of case }
else
    errorhandler

As the previous examples clearly indicate, programmers must think defensively by anticipating and preventing problems. A run-time error is a sure sign of a poorly designed and poorly written program.

14.2.3 Protecting against Representational Errors

On any machine, we can represent exactly all scalar data types except real. With any positional numbering system—binary or decimal—we may incur a *round-off error* in attempting to represent a real value with a finite number of decimal places. We are all familiar with this limitation in our own decimal notation.

$$1/3 = 0.33333. . .$$
$$1/7 = 0.1428571428. . .$$

The same thing happens in the *binary*, or *base 2*, numbering system used by almost all computers:

$$\frac{1}{5}_{10} = 0.001100110011. . ._2$$

Because of this round-off error we should never expect a real number to be exactly equal to a particular value. For example, when $\frac{1}{5}$ is represented on a computer with eight binary place accuracy, we get the following representation:

$$\frac{1}{5} \doteq 0.00110011_2 \doteq 0.1992$$

Therefore, the apparently true relationship

$$\frac{1}{5} + \frac{1}{5} + \frac{1}{5} + \frac{1}{5} + \frac{1}{5} = 1$$

would actually be false. (It would be approximately 0.996 on our eight-place machine.)

The implications of this in our programming is that we should never test for exact equality between elements of the real data type. We should either use an ordinal data type that does not suffer from round-off error (integers, character, user-defined) or write our programs in such a way that they are not sensitive to round-off errors in the real values. In a way, this can be viewed as simply another type of defensive programming technique. Only this time we are not just defending against a possible abnormal termination but also against incorrect answers caused by the finite internal representation of the computer system.

For example, the following code was intended to process values of x in the range 0.0 to 2.0 in steps of 0.2, a total of 11 iterations.

```
x := 0.0;
while x <> 2.2 do
      begin
      .
      .
      .
      { process this value of x }
      .
      .
      .
      x := x + 0.2
      end { while loop }
```

This code is highly dangerous, however, and could very well result in an infinite loop. Because of round-off errors the value of x after the eleventh iteration may not be exactly 2.2 but $2.2 - \epsilon$, where ϵ is some small, positive value. (For example, on our 8-bit machine mentioned earlier, the value of x after 11 iterations would be about 2.1912.) This slight difference will cause the inequality test to remain true and the loop to execute repeatedly. A better way to structure the above code would be

```
x := 0.0;
while x <= 2.0 do
      begin
      .
      .
      .
      { process this value of x }
      .
      .
      .
      x := x + 0.2
      end { while loop }
```

Now the loop will correctly execute 11 times, even in the presence of a small round-off error in the value of x.

Another source of trouble can come about through the use of what are called *iterative algorithms*. These are techniques that do not give an answer directly, but in which a formula is applied repeatedly and we *converge* on the answer in an infinite number of steps. For example, the roots of the equation

$$x^2 - 3x - 10 = 0 \qquad \text{(roots are } -2, +5\text{)}$$

can be found by a repeated execution of the following iterative formula:

$$x_{i+1} = x_i - \left(\frac{x_i^2 - 3x_i - 10}{2x_i - 3}\right) \quad i = 0,1,2, \ldots$$

The formula (based on a technique called *Newton's method*) will ultimately converge to one of the roots of the preceding formula (which root it finds will depend on the starting point x_0). If $x_0 = 10$ the formula will generate the following sequence of values (to three-place accuracy):

$$x_0 = 10.000$$
$$x_1 = 6.471$$
$$x_2 = 5.218$$
$$x_3 = 5.006$$

and we are obviously converging on the root $+5$. If we were to run the process a great many more times, we would get much closer to the correct answer but, at least theoretically, would never get the exact result because of the small round-off errors present in the representation of each individual x_i. Therefore, whenever programming any type of iterative process that converges on the desired result, we cannot use the criteria of exactness as the termination of the process. If we do, we will likely get an infinite loop as the program attempts an impossible task. Instead, we must check to see if the last two values in our sequence are ''close enough'': that is, if the *absolute truncation error* is acceptably small. For example,

```
{ see if we have converged to the root }
if abs (x[i+1] − x[i]) <= epsilon then . . .
```

would work given an appropriate value for epsilon. An alternative way to perform the check is to test the size of the *relative truncation error:*

```
if abs ((x[i+1] − x[i]) / x[i]) <= epsilon then . . .
```

This latter way is preferred. This is because it may be extremely difficult in certain cases to achieve an absolute level of accuracy. If epsilon were 0.0001 and our root were near 1, then we would need about four significant digits to satisfy the termination test. However, if the root were near 1 million we would need about 10 significant digits. This may be beyond the accuracy capabilities of our machine. A relative accuracy test with $\epsilon = 0.0001$ simply says that the last two values must be within 0.01% of each other, regardless of their absolute magnitudes.

In summary, one must be very careful when using the real data type. Unlike the ordinal types, all real values cannot be represented exactly. Checking for equality of real quantities or expecting exactness of real results can produce a program that may work properly for certain cases but exhibits incorrect or abnormal run-time behavior on others, and this is precisely the flaw we want to avoid.

14.2.4 Graceful Degradation

So far this section has been concerned with detecting errors and preventing them from ruining our program. If an error does occur, what should we do? The answer is that we should do as much as possible to recover and keep going on with meaningful processing.

The worst thing about run-time errors is that they cause the program to lose control. A cryptic error message is produced (see Section 16.1.2) and the program is terminated whether or not there is still useful work that can be done. By checking for run-time error conditions, we can maintain control and take the actions we feel are appropriate, not the actions provided automatically by the system.

Aside from producing a meaningful error message, a program should generally apply the following rules in the following order.

1. Make a reasonable assumption about the erroneous item that allows continued processing of that item. Inform the user about this assumption.

2. Discard the erroneous item but continue if possible to process the remainder of the current record.

3. Discard the current record containing the erroneous item but, if possible, continue to process the current file, until eof.

4. Discard the file containing the erroneous item but, if possible, process any subsequent files until the end of all information.

Only if it is impossible to apply one of these rules do we come, as a last resort, to rule 5.

5. Die gracefully. Produce useful, meaningful messages that will allow the user to properly rerun the program and then exit by the end of the main program.

This process of checking for errors, and either continuing on with whatever meaningful work can be accomplished or bringing the system down in a way that will allow the user to easily restart it, is called *graceful degradation*.

14.2.5 Example

Figure 14.1 shows a program that converts dates in the form mm/dd/yy into dates of the form nnn—01/01/88 = 001, 01/02/88 = 002, . . . , 12/31/88 = 366. (The program should probably be developed as a procedure, but we are writing it this way to make a point.)

Notice that we validate $00 \leq$ year ≤ 99; $1 \leq$ month ≤ 12; and $1 \leq$ day ≤ 28, 29, 30, or 31, depending on the month and year. If an error makes it impossible to compute the result, we terminate that data case and go on to the next one. We also check the format of the data to ensure that a "/" appears between the month, day, and year. However, since this error does not preclude a correct date (it may have been entered as mm-dd-yy), we will continue to process that data set after warning the user.

The program in Figure 14.1 clearly illustrates a point we made earlier. Almost 50% of the code in that program is there to prevent incorrect results. The program is robust. Regardless of how many statements it takes, try to make your code impervious to bad data.

FIGURE 14.1   Program to Do Date Conversion.

program dateconversion(input,output);

{ this program converts dates of the form mm/dd/yy into an integer date
  of the form nnn, where nnn is between 001 and 366 }

const
     separator   = '/';   { separator between portions of date }

type
     months   = 1 .. 12;

var

ch1	: char;	{ separator between month and day }
ch2	: char;	{ separator between day and year }
day	: integer;	{ input data }
daycount	: 0 .. 366;	{ the date as an integer }
days	: **array** [months] **of** 1 .. 31;	{ number of days in each month }
error	: boolean;	{ error flag for input data }
leapyear	: boolean;	{ true if year is a leap year }
m	: months;	{ loop index }
month	: integer;	{ input data }
year	: integer;	{ input data }

begin
     { initialization section }
     days[1] := 31; days[2] := 28; days[3] := 31; days[4] := 30;
     days[5] := 31; days[6] := 30; days[7] := 31; days[8] := 31;
     days[9] := 30; days[10] := 31; days[11] := 30; days[12] := 31;

while not eof **do**
     begin
     error := false;
     readln(month,ch1,day,ch2,year);
     writeln('input date: ',month,ch1,day,ch2,year);

     { now validate the input }
     if (ch1 <> separator) **or** (ch2 <> separator) **then**
          writeln('illegal date format. it should be mm',
              separator,'dd',separator,'yy');

     if (month < 1) **or** (month > 12) **then**
          begin
          error := true;
          writeln('error in month field—must be 1 .. 12.')
          end; { of if }

FIGURE 14.1   *(Continued)*

```
    if (year < 0) or (year > 99) then
        begin
        error := true;
        writeln('error in year field—must be 0 . . 99.')
        end; { of if }

    if not error then
        begin
        leapyear := ((year mod 4) = 0) and (year <> 0);
        if leapyear then days[2] := 29
        else days[2] = 28;
        end;

    if (day < 1) or (day > days[month]) then
        begin
        error := true;
        writeln('error in day field—must be 1 . . ',days[month], 'for
            month', month);
        end; { of if }
    end; { of input validation }

    { start date computation }
    if not error then
        begin
        daycount := 0;
        for m := 1 to (month − 1) do
            daycount := daycount + days[m];
        { finally add on days in current month }
        daycount := daycount + day;
        writeln('the corresponding integer date = ',daycount)
        end { of if not error }
    else
        writeln('This data will be skipped')
    end { of while not eof }
end. { of program dateconversion }
```

14.3
Proper and Elegant Use of Procedures and Functions

The proper use of subprograms (procedures and functions) is critical to the development of programs of any reasonable size and complexity. The ability to write each type of subprogram is central to good programming and in this section we will discuss the stylistic guidelines for usable, effective subprograms.

14.3.1 Parameter Passing Mechanisms

In some programming languages (most notably FORTRAN and BASIC), there is only one way to pass parameters between a calling program and a procedure. In Pascal, however, there are two ways to manage this exchange, and it is extremely important to select the proper technique for each parameter. Choosing the wrong parameter passing mechanism can lead to either wrong answers or programs with poor run-time characteristics.

The first type of parameter passing mechanism is *call-by-reference,* indicated by the reserved word **var** before the formal (or dummy) parameter. This method functions as if every occurrence of the formal parameter in the procedure were replaced by the actual parameter in the procedure invocation.

```
procedure sample(var x,y : integer);
begin
     x := x + 1;
     y := y + 1
end;



    .
    .
begin
     a := 5;
     b := 10;
     sample(a,b);
     writeln(a,b)
     .
     .
end.
```

In this example, every occurrence of the name *x* is replaced by the name *a*, and every occurrence of *y* is replaced by *b*. (Actually, *addresses* are being replaced, but we can think in terms of names.) The assignment statements in the procedure actually modify the variables *a* and *b*, and the output produced by the writeln command would be

6 11

The second method of parameter passing is *call-by-value* and is indicated by omitting the reserved word **var** before the parameter name. With call-by-value, we make *local copies* of all dummy parameters and initialize those local copies to the current value of the actual parameters.

```
procedure sample(x,y : integer);
begin
    x := x + 1;
    y := y + 1
end;
    .
    .
begin
    a := 5;
    b := 10;
    sample(a,b);
    writeln(a,b)
    .
    .
end.
```

Now the dummy parameters x, y are call-by-value. The call to sample will create a local variable x that is automatically initialized to the current value of a and a local variable y that is automatically initialized to the current value of b. Except for this initialization, the variables a and b are inaccessible to the procedure. Now the assignment statements in the procedure modify not a and b, but the local copies of x and y. The variables a and b will be *unaffected* by the procedure, and the output produced by the writeln will be

5 10

By way of analogy, we can think of two different ways to pass a file of information to an office worker. First, the key to the filing cabinet could simply be passed from one person to another. Now the second person has complete access to the original information and can add, change, or delete any details as desired. Any changes made to the file are permanent. This method is analogous to *call-by-reference*.

Second, we could open the file cabinet, remove the needed information, duplicate it, put the original back in the file cabinet (and lock it), and give the *duplicate* to the other person. That person now has access to the needed information, but any changes affect only that duplicate copy. The original is inaccessible and therefore immune to change. This is analogous to *call-by-value*.

Call-by-reference creates a two-way path between a calling program and a procedure. Information can flow both into and out of a procedure. Thus, *result* or *output parameters*, which will be returned to the calling program, must be made call-by-reference. *Input parameters* (the values that need only to be passed into a procedure) should be made *call-by-value*. This will make the value available to the procedure but will prevent any accidental (or intentional) change to that value.

The proper use of the call-by-value feature will guarantee the security of a variable and enhance the robustness of a program. Avoid the tendency to automatically make all parameters call-by-reference simply because that is the method you learned first. (FORTRAN supports only call-by-reference.)

There is one important exception to these guidelines. As we indicated, with call-by-value the system will make a local copy of the dummy parameter. This is fine for scalar variables or small structured types. But for large, complex data types such as

var
     x : **array** [0. .5000] **of** integer;

this copy operation can be very expensive in terms of memory. Passing the preceding array by value will require the system to create a local 5001-element integer array, possibly exceeding the total memory capacity of the computer. So, even though security will always be our primary concern, we may also have to consider the availability of memory when selecting parameter passing mechanisms. If memory is a critical resource, we may have to pass large data structures such as the previous one by reference, not by value.

14.3.2 Global Variables versus Parameters

The *scope* of a variable is the set of all blocks in which that variable is known and can be accessed. In Pascal the scope of a variable is the block in which it is declared and all blocks contained therein. Referring to Figure 14.2, the *scope* of the variable x is blocks a, b, c, and d; the scope of y is b and c; and the scope of z is d.

A variable (or any declaration) is said to be *global* to a procedure if it was not declared inside that procedure but inside a procedure (or program) declared at a higher level. In Figure 14.2, x is global to b, c, and d, and y is global to c. Looking back at Figure 14.2, procedures b and d could exchange information through the global variable x to which both have access. In fact, carried to the extreme, parameters could be omitted entirely by declaring all variables in the outermost block of the program and letting each procedure access these global variables directly.

However, whenever possible, *avoid* using global variables for exchanging information between program units. Global variables impart some extremely negative run-time behavior characteristics to programs that use them.

1.   The procedure is *bound* to use of a specific variable name that cannot be replaced by other actual parameters at invocation time. That is, if we write a procedure called sort to sort a list called table, where table is a global variable, we are bound to sorting only that object. To use sort on other lists with other names would first involve copying into the variable called table.

2.   The use of global variables requires close coordination between the person writing the outer block and the person writing the procedure. Specifically, they both must be aware of and agree to the common name to be used for a variable.

3.   Since we access by common name, a change to an outer block declaration could require changes to all procedures that access that object (and vice versa).

4.   Global variables cannot be used for external procedures.

FIGURE 14.2   Scope of a Variable.

```
program a;
var
    x      : integer;

    procedure b;
    var
        y      : integer;

        procedure c;
        begin { of procedure c }
            .
            .
            .
        end; { of procedure c }
    begin { of procedure b }
        .
        .
        .
    end; { of procedure b }

    procedure d;
    var
        z      : integer;
    begin { of procedure d }
        .
        .
        .
    end; { of procedure d }

begin { of main program a }
    .
    .
    .
end. { of main program a }
```

In general, the use of global variables risks program anarchy. We effectively open our entire program name space to every procedure, allowing any and all changes with no limits imposed. We lose all security. The seemingly innocuous procedure call

proc;

can erroneously change any variable. The use of global variables is considered stylistically so bad that the pejorative term *side effect* is used for the modification of any global variable by a procedure during its execution.

In general, it is best to write procedures that operate without any side effects. Pass all information into or out of a procedure using either value or reference parameters.

14.3.3 Local Variables versus Global Variables

A variable is said to be *local* to a block if it is declared within that block. Thus, referring again to Figure 14.2, we would say that y is local to procedure b, and z is local to procedure d.

In almost any procedure, we will need to use variables that are not passed in or out as parameters but are used only within the procedure itself. For example,

Temporary variables for operations (temp)	temp := a; a := b; b := temp
Loop indices (*i*):	**for** i := 1 **to** n **do** ...

Theoretically, these variables could be declared in any block containing the preceding statements, including the outermost block—the main program. The variables temp and i would then be global to the procedure containing these statements. However, that is a very poor practice to follow. All variables should be declared *local* to the block where they are used. Specifically, temporary variables should always be declared local to the procedure in which they are needed to prevent the accidental modification of any variable outside the procedure.

As an example, look at the following fragment, which sums each row of an $n \times n$ matrix called table using a call to a procedure called rowsum:

```
for i := 1 to n do
    rowsum(table, n, i, sum)
```

If we write rowsum the following way, with i as a global variable:

```
procedure rowsum(matrix : tabletype; size,row : integer;
    var sum : integer);
begin
    sum := 0;
    for i := 1 to size do
        sum := sum + matrix[row,i]
end; { of procedure rowsum }
```

then the loop index i referenced within the procedure rowsum is the same variable as the loop index used in the calling program. Each call to rowsum will improperly modify the loop count being kept by the outer **for** loop—a disastrous side effect. If we instead had written the procedure using a local variable as the index:

```
procedure rowsum(matrix : tabletype; size,row : integer;
    var sum : integer);
var
    i      : integer; { local variable used for loop index }
begin
    sum := 0;
    for i := 1 to size do
        sum := sum + matrix[row,i]
end; { of procedure rowsum }
```

there would be no problem because of Pascal's *name precedence rule.* When two variables of the same name are declared in different blocks, any reference to that name will always refer to the *innermost,* or *most recent,* declaration of that variable. In procedure rowsum, any reference to *i* will be to the local *i* declared within the procedure. Outside of procedure rowsum, references to *i* will be to the other (global) *i.* By always declaring variables local to the current block, programmers are free to code modules independently, without worrying about name conflicts or accidental modifications of variables outside the scope of the procedure they are writing. By using a global variable, we will develop programs that may or may not work correctly, depending on the actions of other programmers—a very uncomfortable prospect.

To eliminate side effects and minimize errors caused by the interaction of two or more program units, all data either defined or referenced by a procedure should be one of the following three types of objects:

1. Call-by-value parameter.
2. Call-by-reference parameter.
3. Local variable.

14.3.4 Signal Flags

In response to our demand for robustness in programs (Section 14.2), we would probably not write rowsum as we did in the previous section. If rowsum were given a row index outside the range 1. .size, the program would ''blow up'' because of an array index out of bounds. Our first reaction might be to add the following statement as the first line of procedure rowsum:

```
if (row >= 1) and (row <= size) then
    begin
        .   { solve the problem just as before }
        .
    end { of if }
else writeln('Error in row index passed to rowsum')
```

Although this would prevent a run-time error in rowsum, it represents an extremely poor programming technique and a misunderstanding of the purpose of procedures.

While rowsum knows that the procedure did not complete properly, the calling program does *not*. If the calling program contained the following code segment:

```
for i := first to last do
      begin
      rowsum(table,n,i,sum);
      writeln(' sum of row ',i,' = ',sum)
      end { of for }
```

we would again have created the possibility of a run-time error caused by attempting to write out a value (sum) that was not properly defined.

One of the most important output values produced by a procedure is a *signal flag* (sometimes called a *status variable*). This is an output parameter that indicates the status of the computation carried out by the procedure (i.e., whether or not it was successful) and which of several special cases occurred. The signal flag parameter can be tested by the calling program to determine the outcome of a procedure before attempting to use the results of that procedure.

```
procedure rowsum(matrix : tabletype; size,row : integer;
      var sum : integer; var success : boolean);
var
      i      : integer;
begin
   If (row >= 1) and (row <= size) then
         begin
         success := true;
         sum := 0;
         for i := 1 to size do
               sum := sum + matrix[row,i]
         end { of then }
      else success := false
end; { of procedure rowsum }
```

Any procedure that might fail to complete the operations for which it was invoked must be able to return that information to the calling program through a signal flag passed as a call-by-reference parameter. Likewise, to ensure robustness, any program that invokes a procedure that returns a signal flag should check that flag *before* referencing any of the other output parameters.

```
rowsum(table,n,i,sum,correct);
If correct then { carry on with the computation }
            else { invoke error recovery methods }
```

Since we are now able to return the status of a computation, we can eliminate two other approaches to handling errors within procedures that generally represent poor programming habits:

if "error condition" **then** halt

or

if "error condition" **then** writeln "error message"

The termination of execution within a procedure violates the graceful degradation characteristic discussed earlier. If execution is halted within the procedure, the calling program cannot analyze what caused the error and, if possible, recover. In addition, by deciding at this point to produce a specific error message, we lose the flexibility of having the calling program analyze the output and determine if an error message should be produced and what type of message it should be. In fact, a procedure should generally not do output of any kind unless it is specifically an output procedure. This is consistent with our discussion in Chapter 12 about logically coherent modules. When we include output commands directly within the procedure, we again lose the flexibility of allowing the calling program to decide if we will print a value and, if so, in what format. (For example, what if the line printer was currently loaded with blank payroll checks!)

A well-written procedure should do no more than perform its computation and return the results and status of that computation to the calling program. All further decisions about how to use those results and how to continue should be done outside the procedure.

14.3.5 Example Program

Figure 14.3 shows a procedure to *integrate* a function numerically using the *trapezoidal rule*. The integral of a function f on the interval $[a,b]$ is the area under the graph of that function between the two points, a and b, and is written as

$$\int_a^b f(x)$$

This is illustrated in Figure 14.4a. The trapezoidal rule approximates that area by placing a set of trapezoids under the curve f and summing up their area as shown in Figure 14.4b. The more trapezoids used, the better the approximation.

The formula for the area, i, under the curve, f, using the trapezoidal rule is given by the following formula.

$$i = \Delta * [(1/2)f(a) + f(a + \Delta) + f(a + 2\Delta) + \ldots + f(a + (n - 1)\Delta) + (1/2)f(b)]$$

where a and b are the endpoints of the integration, Δ is the width of each individual trapezoid, n is the number of trapezoids to use in the approximation, and $f(x)$ is the value of f at the point x. Given a, b, and n, Δ can be determined by the following formula:

$$\Delta = (b - a) / n \qquad \text{for } b > a \text{ and } n > 0$$

FIGURE 14.3   Procedure to Integrate Using the
Trapezoidal Rule.

{ trapezoidrule

  Procedure to integrate functions using the trapezoidal rule.

  Entry conditions:
      f   : the formal function to be integrated
      a   : lower bound of integration
      b   : upper bound of integration
      n   : the number of trapezoids to use (n > 0)

  Exit conditions:
      result   : the result of integration, if flag is true, otherwise undefined
      flag   : returned true if operation was successful, false otherwise
}

procedure trapezoidrule(**function** f(x : real) : real; a : real; b : real;
      n : integer; **var** result : real; **var** flag : boolean);
var
      delta   : real;   { the step size along the axis }
      i   : integer;   { loop index }
      sum   : real;   { accumulates intermediate results }
      temp   : real;   { temporary variable }
      x   : real;   { will range from a to be in steps of delta }

begin
      If n >= 1 **then**
            begin
            flag := true;
            if a <> b **then**
                  begin
                  if b > a **then**
                        begin
                        { the integral from a to b = the integral from b to a.
                          let's switch the limits. }
                        temp := a;
                        a := b;
                        b := temp
                        end; { of if b > a }

                  delta := (b − a) / n;
                  sum := 0.0;
                  x := a;

FIGURE 14.3   *(Continued)*

```
{ first sum the intermediate terms f(a + i*delta), i = 1 .. n − 1 }
for i := 1 to n − 1 do
    begin
    x := x + delta;
    sum := sum + f(x)
    end; { of for }

{ add in the end terms 0.5*f(a) + 0.5*(b) and multiply by delta
    to complete the computation }
    result := (0.5 * (f(a) + f(b)) + sum) * delta
    end { of if a <> b }
else result := 0.0 { integral from a to a of f(x) is 0 }
    end { of if n >= 1 }
else flag := false
end; { of procedure trapezoidrule }
```

Our procedure, called trapezoidrule, uses four value parameters: the function *f*, and *a*, *b*, and *n*. The procedure returns two reference parameters: the result and a boolean flag. The flag is set to false on detection of the one fatal error condition: *n* < 1. If the procedure detects the condition *a* > *b*, it will simply interchange the two values, since the area from *a* to *b* is the same as the area from *b* to *a*. (Remember, wherever possible, keep going and get meaningful results.) Finally, all other values that are not parameters but are needed by the procedure are declared *local* to the procedure. The complete procedure is shown in Figure 14.3.

FIGURE 14.4   The Meaning of Integration. (*a*) The Value of $\int_a^b f(x)$. (*b*) Its Approximation Using Two Trapezoids.

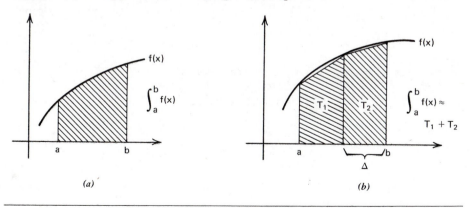

(*a*)   (*b*)

14.4
Generality

Generality means that a program unit is free from dependence on any specific data set. That is, the program can operate properly on many different data sets without requiring change to the code itself. Generality is a very desirable property because it reduces the need for program modification as the needs of the end-user change. Modifications take time and can induce errors. As an example of inflexible, nongeneral code, look at the following.

```
count := 0;
sum := 0;
for i := 1 to 25 do
    if (score[i] >= 0) and (score[i] <= 100) then
        begin
        count := count + 1;
        sum := sum + score[i]
        end; { of if }
mean := sum / count
```

(The code is also not very robust, since the last statement could possibly cause a division by 0.)

   To work properly, this code requires a data set containing exactly 25 items, and it will produce the correct values only when the legal range of the items is exactly 0 to 100. Any change to those two conditions will require a search through the code to find every occurrence of the constants 25, 0, and 100 and change them to the appropriate values. If even one occurrence of any of those constants is overlooked, it will almost certainly introduce a bug into the code. (Actually, the problem is even worse, because we only want to change the occurrence of the constants 0, 25, and 100 used for this purpose. A value of 25 that refers to some other aspect of the code must be left unchanged. The likelihood of inducing errors into the program during this type of modification is obviously very high.) A first pass at making the code more general might be

```
const
    datasets    = 25;      { number of data items }
    high        = 100;     { max range of valid scores }
    low         = 0;       { min range of valid scores }

        .
        .
        .

count := 0;
sum    := 0;
error  := false;
for i   := 1 to datasets do
    if (score[i] >= low) and (score[i] <= high) then
```

```
        begin
        count := count + 1;
        sum   := sum + score[i]
        end;
if count > 0 then mean := sum / count
else error := true
```

This approach is an improvement because it localizes the change to a single statement. It is no longer necessary to read through the entire program searching for constants. Now we need only change a single declaration. This significantly reduces the possibility of introducing an error during the modification process.

However, the preceding change may not be sufficient. If items such as datasets, high, and low change often enough, declaring them as constants requires the program to change on virtually every run. Values such as these that may change from one data set to another should always be made *variables*, not constants. This will make the code independent of any specific values.

```
var
        datasets, low, high    : integer;
            .
            .
            .
readln (datasets, high, low);
```

This code will now find the sum of any number of scores over any range of values. The generality has been increased significantly.

There is a similar stylistic guideline for writing generalized procedures. Any value that may change from one procedure invocation to another should be made a *parameter* to the procedure instead of a local variable or constant.

The following procedure for reading strings of characters into a packed array exhibits the same lack of generality as our earlier example.

```
procedure stringread(var list : string);
var
        ch     : char;        { input character }
        i      : integer;     { loop index }
begin
    i := 0;
    read(ch);
    while (not eoln) and (i < 80) and (ch <> '.') do
        begin
        i := i + 1;
        list[i] := ch;
        read(ch)
        end { of while }
end; { of procedure stringread }
```

The procedure will read a set of characters until end-of-line, the specific terminating character "." , or an upper bound of 80 characters is encountered. There is no way, short of changing the procedure, for the user to specify either a maximum character string length other than 80 characters or a terminator character other than "." . By adding the appropriate parameters, however, we can generalize the procedure and eliminate these shortcomings.

```
procedure stringread(var list : string; var size : integer;
     max : integer; terminator : char);
const
     maxstringlength    = 80;
begin
     if max > maxstringlength then max := maxstringlength;
     size := 0;
     read(ch);
     while (not eoln) and (size < max) and (ch <> terminator) do
          begin
          size := size + 1;
          list[size] := ch;
          read(ch)
          end
end; { of procedure stringread }
```

The procedure will now allow the user to read any string of characters up to a length of 80 or until the first occurrence of any user-designated character. This procedure could now be used, *without change*, to process any of the following fields:

A last name of up to 20 characters ending with a "," .
A first name of up to 20 characters ending with a " " .
A comment of up to 80 characters ending with a "}" .

As a final example of program generality, look at the following skeleton of a program.

```
begin
     initialize all values;
     read data;
     if data is valid then process data
     else error;
     write out results
end
```

This is a reasonable outline for a program that operates on only a single data set to produce only a single set of results. As it now is coded it cannot accept or run a second data set. However, with the following change:

```
while not eof do
    begin
        initialize for this data set;
        read this data set;
        if data is valid then process data set
                        else error;
        write out results
    end { of while }
```

The code now works on any arbitrary number of data sets—0, 1, or more. This marked increase in generality was achieved with virtually no increase in program complexity and little change to the code itself.

These last few examples illustrate a fundamentally important point concerning program generality. Generality is not merely *coded* into a program; it is *designed* in. During the development of the module specification, we should attempt to anticipate variations that could occur in future modification or with different end-users. We should then incorporate sufficient generality into our design, using the techniques just discussed, to accommodate these variations.

Figure 14.5 shows a generalized pattern matching procedure that will attempt to locate a pattern (up to length n) within a string of text of length $\leq n$. The attempted match can begin at any location within the text, and the procedure will return either the location of the match of 0 if no match is found. In addition, the special character "$\wedge$" will match any single character within the text. Given the following input stream:

> Text: "d x f h e f g d z f g c e k"
> Pattern: "d $\wedge$ f g"

the procedure will return an 8, the index of the first column of the match between Pattern and Text.

This example illustrates a very generalized program unit, but it still could be further generalized. For example, we could include yet another parameter called direction of type (left,right), that would indicate to the procedure the direction in which we would attempt to perform the match, left to right for text in English, French, Russian, and so forth, or right to left for languages such as Hebrew and Arabic. (Exercise 12 at the end of this chapter proposes additional changes.) Naturally, we would need to know more about the proposed use of this procedure to determine whether this feature (or others) would be useful enough to warrant the additional effort. From the very first stages of program design, always look for useful ways to increase generality in the programs and procedures you develop.

14.5
Portability

While generality makes a program independent of any particular data set, *portability* implies program independence from the hardware, or a specific operating system or

FIGURE 14.5   A Generalized Pattern Matching Procedure.

```
{ patternmatch

  procedure to do generalized pattern matching.

          text          : the string of characters in which we will look for
                          the match. (arraytype)
          size          : the actual length of text. 1 <= size <= max.
          start         : the starting location in text to begin the match.
                          1 <= start <= 1 + size − length.
          pattern       : the object string of the search. (arraytype)
          length        : the length of the character stream in pattern.
                          1 <= length <= max.
          found         : if no match is found, - found - will return 0. if the
                          pattern is matched, the first position of the match
                          (1 . . size) will be returned.
          error         : returns - errnone - if all input parameters are
                          correct, otherwise returns - errbound -,
                          - errsize -, or - errstart - to indicate the presence
                          of one of these classes of errors.
    the following global declarations are assumed:
          const  max = nnn;      /for some integer nnn/
          type   arraytype       = packed array [1 . . max] of char;
                 errortype       = (errnone,errbound,errsize,errstart);
}

procedure patternmatch(text : arraytype; size : integer; start : integer;
    pattern : arraytype; length : integer; var found : integer;
    var error : errortype);


const
    anymatch           = '∧';            { the character that matches anything }


var
    lastmatchplace     : integer;        { last possible position in text where a
                                           successful match can occur }

    matched            : boolean;
    p                  : integer;        { index into pattern }
    t                  : integer;        { index into text }


begin
    error := errnone;
    lastmatchplace := size − length + 1;
```

FIGURE 14.5   (*Continued*)

```
{ error checking }
if (size < 1) or (size > max) or (length < 1) or
    (length > max) then error := errbound;
if length > size then error := errsize
else
    if (start < 1) or (start > lastmatchplace)
    then error := errstart;

if error = errnone then
    begin
    repeat { loop to look through all possible match locations }
        p := 1;       { to index through pattern }
        t := start;   { to index through text }
        matched := true;

        repeat { loop to check a match at a specific location }
            if (pattern[p] <> anymatch) and (pattern[p] <> text[t])
            then matched := false
            else
                begin
                p := p + 1;
                t := t + 1
                end
        until (p > length) or not matched;

        if not matched then start := start + 1
    until (start > lastmatchplace) or matched;

        if matched then found := start
                   else found := 0
    end { of else error = errnone }
end; { of procedure patternmatch }
```

compiler. A portable program is independent of any particular *machine environment*. Because computer changes are so rapid and frequent and because programmers exchange and share programs, portability is a critical characteristic. We would like to avoid significant reprogramming efforts for new machines to keep costs down and minimize new errors in the programs during the change. Programs that require little or no change as environments change will certainly cause fewer problems during their lifetimes.

The most important guideline in writing portable programs is strict adherence to the *standard version* of a programming language. Many people are unaware that some

FIGURE 14.6   Language Standards.

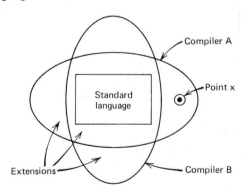

programming languages, like electrical voltages, radio frequencies, and screw sizes, are standardized by international conventions. The group that directs most of these standardization efforts is the International Standards Organization (ISO), an agency of the United Nations. ISO publishes a programming language standard that specifies the *syntax* of statements in the language and the action (called the *semantics*) taken by each of those statements. A *standard compiler* for a language accepts and correctly compiles the standard language. It may also accept additional nonstandard features (called *extensions*). In Figure 14.6 compilers A and B would be standard compilers, because they include the entire language standard as a subset.

By using only the standard version of a language, we ensure that our program will be immediately movable to any other standard compiler for that language. But if we use a language feature that is a local extension to our compiler (e.g., point x in Figure 14.6), there is no guarantee that our programs will run when moved.

Most Pascal compilers contain local extensions, and it is often very tempting to use them; after all, they are usually added to provide a shorter way of performing some common operation. All of the following (and many, many others) have been proposed and implemented as extensions to standard Pascal.

1. A *value* declaration (like a data statement in FORTRAN).
2. An *otherwise* clause in the **case** statement as the default match.
3. An exponentiation operator.
4. Dynamic array bounds.
5. A string data type with the basic string operations—concatenate, pattern match, delete substring.
6. Extensions of the procedure read to read arrays, records, and user-defined scalars.
7. Random-access files.

When using any such nonstandard language feature, be aware that it may not be possible to transfer your program to other systems without a massive reprogramming effort. This fact must be carefully weighed against the programming advantages to be gained from using these features.

We must also try to avoid other machine-dependent features that could prevent our program from running on another computer system. Where possible, try to avoid:

1. Machine-dependent constants. Avoid constants that are specific to one machine. For example, use maxint instead of $2^{48} - 1$ and ord('a') instead of 141 (base 8). These values may not be the same on a different system.

2. Machine-dependent collating sequences. Do not make any assumptions about the collating sequence of a particular code set except the following:

$$'A' < 'B' < \ldots < 'Z'$$
$$'a' < 'b' < \ldots < 'z'$$
$$'0' < '1' < \ldots < '9'$$

You must check all other assumptions. For example, do not assume that 'a' . . 'z' are contiguous without gaps (BCD and ASCII-true, EBCDIC-false). Instead, check whether

$$\text{ord}('z') = \text{ord}('a') + 25$$

and take the appropriate action for each case.

At times it may be impossible to avoid using machine-dependent features. When that occurs, *localize* the machine-dependent information to a single place within the program and identify it clearly as information that must be changed when the program is moved, as in the following:

```
{ The following parameters apply to the VAX-11/782. They should be reset when
   moved to a new machine.}
const
    wordsize = 32;
    bytesize = 8;
    codeset = 'ASCII';
```

Taken together, the programming techniques introduced in Chapters 12, 13, and 14—coherence, clarity, readability, good structure, robustness, generality, portability—all contribute to a centrally important overall characteristic of programs called *maintainability*. This simply refers to programs that require fewer changes over their lifetimes and, when changes do need to be made, can be implemented more quickly and with fewer errors. A maintainable program will be much more usable and cost significantly less over its lifetime.

14.6
User-Friendliness

Most of the stylistic guidelines we have described in Chapters 12, 13, and 14 have been directed at helping the people who must read, understand, and modify a computer program—that is, the *maintenance programmers*. Much of this (logical coherence, naming conventions, parameter passing mechanisms) is irrelevant to the end-user.

To end-users, a program is not unlike a black box. They know what goes in and what comes out but nothing about what goes on inside. To end-users, the stylistic guidelines we follow, the elegance of our design, and the beauty of our code may be unimportant. What does matter is the interface between the users and the program, the program's *input* and *output behavior*. A beautifully structured program that produces confusing and poorly formatted output will probably end up in the wastebasket. We should have as much concern for elegance of input/output as for elegance of code.

When working interactively, we should identify the input we are requesting, either with a *prompt:*

Please Enter ID:

or a *screen template*—preset information on a CRT screen identifying what must be provided.

```
name: _____
address:
city:
state:
zip:
```

Never write a program that simply waits for some unidentified input:

?

First-time users of this program will be thoroughly confused. (See Exercise 15.)

However, once familiar with a program, users may wish to avoid the wordiness of either of the preceding user aids. A good program allows users to *suppress* aids, such as prompts, if desired. This facility will allow us to develop a program useful to both the novice and the expert.

Be careful not to write a program with an infinite ''input-error'' loop that gives the user no clue as to how to either correct the error or get help.

```
? 123
error—please reenter
? 123.
error—please reenter
? 123,
error—please reenter
? help
error—please reenter
```

Programs should always provide, along with the error notice, some clear, unambiguous statement about what caused the error and how it can be corrected.

```
? 123
    error—the input value must be of the form nnn.n, please reenter.
```

In more complex programs, where the explanation cannot be provided in only a single sentence, the explanation may be in the form of *on-line assistance,* also called *help mode.* This is simply on-line user documentation that the user can browse through, with the end of the program, to locate the information needed to solve a problem or correct an error.

```
? 123
    error—type help for assistance or reenter the value.
? help
    please type the single letter corresponding to the type of information you desire
        F for information on input data formats.
        T for information on terminal characteristics and settings.
        R for information on the legal range of values.
        Q to quit help mode and return to the program.
? F
    all input values must be real numbers entered in the following format
        .
        .
        .
```

Regardless of which approach you choose, the important point is that error messages must be user oriented and be directed at informing the user, in simple nontechnical terms, of what caused the error and how to recover.

Another poor I/O technique is to ask end-users to perform operations that the computer can and should do for them. For example, never terminate data files (except the very smallest ones) by an explicit user-supplied count field. Always use either *eof* or a special *signal card.* Why ask a person to count a set of data cards (and risk the chance of an erroneous count) when computers can count much more quickly and reliably? Similarly, do not require users to employ the internal representation scheme of the computer. The following illustrates this kind of thinking.

```
enter 0 = yes 1 = no
```

Wouldn't it make more sense simply to say

```
enter yes or no
```

and let the program perform the translation?
The following output line

```
Smith, John    85    93    −1    75    60
```

from a finished report of student test results might leave us wondering how a student could possibly receive a -1 on a test. Only after looking at the code might we discover that a -1 was used by the program as a flag to indicate missing data. [The -1 was probably chosen so that we could distinguish between a missing score, -1, and a valid test score (0 . . . n)]. However, just because the program uses a value internally does not mean that we must output the value in precisely that format, especially if it will be unclear or misleading to end-users. The following statement could greatly improve the clarity of the output:

if item[i] $=$ -1 **then** write(' * missing * ')

.

.

.

The output would then look like this:

Smith, John   85   93   * missing *   75   60

Request and provide information in a format that is best for end-users.

Closely related to this is the idea of requesting and providing information in a *medium* that is best for end-users. For the first 30 or so years of computing, there were precious few ways for a user to interact with a computer system—punch cards, paper tape, and keyboard was about it. However, the last few years have seen an explosion in the number and type of peripheral devices that can be used to collect or display information to and from a user, for example,

Input	Output
Touch screen	Two-dimensional graphics
Touch pad	Three-dimensional graphics
Mouse	Plotters
Voice input	Voice output
Digitizer	Microfilm
	Sound

If your computer system has any of these devices available, consider them as alternatives to the more traditional keyboard/screen/line printer for interacting with the user. They may be more natural, convenient, and friendly for the user.

In Section 14.2.1 we talked about validating input for both legibility and plausibility. However, there are incorrect values that are both legal and plausible. Our last line of defense against erroneous input are the users themselves. *Echo printing* the input allows users to check input and locate improper data values. Avoid programs that produce output such as

the result is 11

but do not identify the input values that led to this result. Users have no way of knowing if the input is correct or if the output can be trusted. (Remember: garbage in/garbage out.)

Be sure to select input formats that are easy and natural to prepare, proofread, and verify. Input fields that are run together, broken between lines, or encoded with some cryptic representation are highly prone to errors and extremely difficult to proofread, verify, and correct. Input data prepared in the following format:

```
Smith101893401101011020203201
Jones138962301102012010203201
```

will almost certainly be the cause of significant grief during the life of the program. Although it may be a convenient format for the program, it is highly unnatural to typical end-users and will be difficult to verify visually. The programmer has improperly traded a reduction in programming effort for an increase in user effort. This is another example of catering to the machine instead of to the people using it. How much nicer to prepare the preceding data in the following way:

```
Smith     101893 sr
math      101
math      102
cs        201
/
Jones     138962 jr
          .
          .
          .
```

Input errors will be much easier to locate and correct.

Finally, there is the problem of requiring users to provide too much data. In Section 14.4 we encouraged designing generality into all programs. One way that generality can be achieved is by allowing greater user control over input values. However, carried to the extreme, generality would require users to provide literally dozens of input values to customize a very generalized program to their specific needs. This would result in much duplication of effort. *Default values* can reduce the user's burden. A default value is a value set by the program to be used *unless* the user specifies otherwise. For example, the following assignments:

```
speed := 2400;         { terminal speed in bits per second }
linesize := 80;        { characters per line }
pagesize := 57;        { lines per page }
code := ascii;         { code set }
eol := '.';            { end of line character }
missingdata := −1;     { the missing data indicator flag }
rubouts := 0;          { used for delays during carriage returns }
      .                      .
      .                      .
      .                      .
```

set default values for terminal description parameters needed within a typical word processing program. Instead of providing dozens of parameters, users need only supply the values for which the defaults do not apply. This could be done, for example, with *self-identifying input*.

linesize = 132

The preceding input line indicates that the linesize parameter is to be reset to 132, while all other values remain set to their defaults. Thus, the user need provide only one piece of data, rather than dozens.

Overall, a program that has convenient methods of input, is tolerant and forgiving of mistakes, produces helpful and easy-to-understand error messages, has on-line assistance, and produces its results in a natural, convenient format and medium would be said to be *user-friendly*. From the user's point of view this characteristic is, after correctness, probably the most important quality measure of a piece of software.

The placement of this section on I/O behavior at the very end of the discussion on programming style is very appropriate. During the program design, coding, and debugging phases, we really should not be concerned with the elegance of our input or output as long as we can understand what the program is doing. End-users do not see the program during this phase, so our *first* concern should be with correctness, coherence, independence, readability, code structure, robustness, generality, and portability. Most books on programming and style include the following rule:

> Make it correct before you make it pretty.

In following the guidelines we have presented, we would add the following related rules, among others:

> Make it readable before you make it pretty.
> Make it robust before you make it pretty.
> Make it general before you make it pretty.

But we add one final important corollary:

> Eventually, *do* make it pretty!

14.7
Conclusion

Chapters 12, 13, and 14 have discussed guidelines for producing programs and program units that are easy to use for the *programmers* who will work with and maintain them and for the *end-users* who will use the results from them. Programs and procedures that follow these guidelines could help reduce the skyrocketing costs associated with software development and maintenance. They will also nurture an idea that should be a commandment to every programmer. The two most important elements of any computer system are the *people* who use the computer (not the computer itself), and

Table 14.1
Differences between Academic and
Production Programming Environments

Academic Assignments	Production Programs
1. Once working are typically run once or twice and then discarded	1. Once working are run on a regular basis for many years
2. Are short, rarely exceeding 500 to 1000 lines of code	2. May be quite long, 1000 to 10,000 lines is not unusual and 25,000 to 100,000 lines is not unheard of
3. Are done alone	3. Are done in groups or teams of 3 to 10 members
4. Are started and completed by the same individual	4. May have many different programmers in charge over the life of the program
5. Are rarely changed after they work correctly	5. May be updated frequently over the life of the program
6. If maintenance is ever required it is typically done by the original programmer	6. Maintenance is frequently handled by someone other than the original programmer
7. The program is never looked at except by those intimately familiar with the problem—the instructor and the student	7. The code may be looked at by levels of management not immediately familiar with the structure of the program
8. The end-users of the program are only those who are intimately familiar with the problem	8. The end-users may be totally naive in the area of computers or the specific program
9. No salaries are paid to the student programmers when they do their homework; lower productivity does not result in decreased profits	9. Real money is being paid to the programmers for all work performed, whether useful or not
10. If the program does not perform up to specifications, the student will receive a lower grade	10. If the program does not perform up to specifications, a significant financial loss may be suffered, possibly including the programmer's job

the useful *information* we provide to those people (not the raw data on which we perform the computations).

There is one final comment about the guidelines presented in Chapters 12 through 14. In an *academic* environment, many of the techniques we have discussed may seem unnecessary, excessive, or out of place. This is not because the techniques are wrong, but because the environment in which students work is different from the *production* environment in which they will someday be working. This point was raised in the beginning of Chapter 13 and is presented in greater detail in Table 14.1. A quick glance through the table indicates one major difference: in a production environment, a wide range of people with a wide range of ability and familiarity with the problem will come in contact with that program during its lifetime. These people will be looking at, reading, correcting, updating, and modifying the program and will need to understand its purpose quickly and correctly. The design and implementation guidelines we have discussed will ensure that these people can perform their work properly and keep costs down. Even if you do not immediately see the need to develop such "beautiful" homework assignments, remember that the programming habits you are developing now will be of critical importance throughout your career.

Exercises for Chapter 14

1. Under what conditions could the following fragments terminate abnormally? Rewrite the fragments to avoid this problem.

*a.
```
{ Compute the average of scorecount number of exams in the range
    low. .high. Assume scorecount and exam have been defined }
bad := 0;
i    := 0;
sum := 0.0;
while i < scorecount do
    begin
    i := i + 1;
    if (exam[i] < low) or (exam[i] > high) then
        bad := bad + 1
    else
        sum := sum + exam[i]
    end; { of while loop }
average := sum/(scorecount − bad)
```

*b.
```
var
    salaryclass : (salaried, hourly, piecework, temporary);
    .
    .
    .
{ get payroll information on all regular employees }
readln(salaryclass,dept,name,payrolldata);
case salaryclass of
    salaried   : salariedproc(dept,name,payrolldata);
    hourly     : hourlyproc(dept,name,payrolldata);
    piecework  : pieceproc(dept,name,payrolldata)
end { of case }
    .
    .
```

c.
```
{ The end of data is marked by the special signal card 999. The signal
    value will be stored in the last position of the item list }
i := 0;
repeat
    i := i + 1;
    readln(item[i]);
    processdata(item[i])
until (item[i] = 999)
```

d.   { read all the transactions that occurred this week and merge them into
the master file }
repeat
readln(number,name,amount);
merge(number,name,amount);
writeln(number,name,amount)
until eof

*e.   p := succ(p)   { p is some user-defined data type }
f.   upperbound := 0.5 * sqr(ln(0.25 * (a + b)))

2.   In Exercise 6 of Chapter 13 you were asked to write a program to translate
Roman numerals to decimal quantities. Discuss the robustness of that program with
regard to the following problems:

a.   The total maximal length (in characters) of the Roman numeral.
b.   An invalid character (i.e., not I, V, X, L, C, D, or M) encountered during
translation.
c.   An illegal sequence of characters encountered (e.g., LLL instead of CL).
d.   The handling of the null case—a Roman numeral with 0 characters.

Rewrite the procedure Roman so that it correctly handles these special circumstances.

*3.   Write a procedure *validate* that, given a real matrix M, of size $n \times n, n \geq 1$,
validates that

a.   All entries of M are nonnegative.
b.   At least one diagonal element of M is nonzero.
c.   The matrix is not upper triangular (i.e., all elements to the right of the
diagonal are not zero).

If any of these conditions occur, the procedure should set the parameter called errorflag
to one of the following:

(negative, diagonal, triangular).

4.   Write a program to generate *mailing labels*. The input to the program will be
three data lines in the following format:

Last, first	Where first and last names are 1 to 20 characters in length
City, state zip	Where city and state are 1 to 10 characters in length, and zip is an integer 0 to 99999
Month/year	Month and year of expiration $1 \leq$ month ≤ 12 $87 \leq$ year ≤ 99

Your program should output a four-line mailing label of the form:

Expiration date
Firstname lastname
City, state
Zip

if and only if the month and year of expiration are chronologically *after* the current month and year. After writing the program, determine what percentage of this typical "business-oriented" program is devoted to

    a.   Input and input validation.
    b.   Processing.
    c.   Output.

  5. Rewrite the program in Figure 14.1 so that the input is in the form:

    mmm. dd, 19yy

where mmm is the three-letter abbreviation for the current month and is selected from the following data type:

type months = (jan, feb, mar, apr, may, jun, jul, aug, sep, oct, nov, dec);

Perform the same types of validation on this new input that you did on the input in Figure 14.1.

  *6. Given the following procedure:

```
procedure example(a : integer; var b : integer);
var c : integer;
begin
    a := 20; b := 30; c := 40
end;
```

what is the result of executing these statements in another program unit?

```
var
    a,b,c : integer;
    .
    .
    .
a := 5; b := 10; c := 15;
example(a,b); writeln(a,b,c);
example(c,b); writeln(c,b,a);
example(b,c); writeln(a,b,c)
```

  7. Rewrite the date conversion program in Figure 14.1 so that it is a Pascal *function*. Be sure to consider and handle the following problems:

    a.   Signal flags.
    b.   Output statements.
    c.   Local variables/global variables.
    d.   Parameters and proper parameter-passing mechanisms.

Now show a mainline program, which uses the date conversion function, to read in dates entered from a terminal in mm/dd/yy format and print them out in Julian format. The main program should continue until end-of-file.

8. Write a complete Pascal procedure to compute the *determinant* of a 3 × 3 matrix M. The determinant of M, called $D(M)$ is defined as

$$M = \begin{bmatrix} a_{11} & a_{12} & a_{13} \\ a_{21} & a_{22} & a_{23} \\ a_{31} & a_{32} & a_{33} \end{bmatrix}$$

$$\begin{aligned} D(M) = & (a_{11}\,a_{22}\,a_{33} + a_{12}\,a_{23}\,a_{31} + a_{13}\,a_{21}\,a_{32}) \\ & - (a_{13}\,a_{22}\,a_{31} + a_{12}\,a_{21}\,a_{33} + a_{11}\,a_{32}\,a_{23}) \end{aligned}$$

If the determinant is 0, M is *singular*. Return a special flag called singular that is true if this condition exists and false otherwise.

Use the preceding procedure to find the solution to the 3 × 3 system of equations:

$$\begin{aligned} a_{11}x_1 + a_{12}x_2 + a_{13}x_3 &= b_1 \\ a_{21}x_1 + a_{22}x_2 + a_{23}x_3 &= b_2 \\ a_{31}x_1 + a_{32}x_2 + a_{33}x_3 &= b_3 \end{aligned}$$

using *Cramer's rule*. Cramer's rule states that the solution to the preceding problem can be found by building an *augmented matrix* M_i by replacing the ith column of M with the constants b_1, b_2, and b_3. The value of x_i at the solution point is simply

$$x_i = \frac{D(M_i)}{D(M)}$$

For example, to find the value of x_1:

$$x_1 = \frac{D\begin{bmatrix} b_1 & a_{12} & a_{13} \\ b_2 & a_{22} & a_{23} \\ b_3 & a_{32} & a_{33} \end{bmatrix}}{D\begin{bmatrix} a_{11} & a_{12} & a_{13} \\ a_{21} & a_{22} & a_{23} \\ a_{31} & a_{32} & a_{33} \end{bmatrix}}$$

(if $D(M)$ is not singular)

and similarly for x_2 and x_3. Write a program that reads in the values for a_{ij} and b_i and solves the resulting 3 × 3 system of equations. Be concerned with the style and organization of all procedures and functions used.

*9. Write a function called power(a,b) that will compute, for any real values a,b: a^b by using the relation $a^b = \exp[b*\ln(a)]$. However, this will only work for $a > 0$. Write a function that also works for $a \le 0$.

*10. Look at Exercise 5 in Chapter 13. Is there any reason for which you would criticize the program for a lack of *generality?* If so, rewrite it to make it more generally applicable to a wider range of problems.

*11.   What would happen to the procedure trapezoidal if it attempted to evaluate the function $f(x)$ at the point where it is undefined? For example,

$$f(x) = \frac{1}{x - 2}$$

at the point $x = 2$. Rewrite the example from Figure 14.3 assuming that the function $f(x)$ returns the value ($\pm$ maxint) if it is undefined at the point x. Your procedure should now take the proper recovery action and inform the user about what has happened.

12.   Rewrite the generalized pattern matching procedure from Figure 14.5 so that
    a.   It can match from right to left or left to right based on the value of a parameter called direction.
    b.   It will delete the string if it is found and if a parameter called delete is set to true.

13.   The program fragment:

```
var
     x : alfa;
     y : integer; value 1;
     w,z : integer;

          .

          .

          .
     readln(x,z);
     if x = 'all done     ' then
          begin
          writeln('program completed');
          halt
          end;
     w := z + y;
     case w of
          1,2 : proc1;
          3,4 : proc2;
          else : proc3
     end { of case }
end. { of program }
```

uses the following nonstandard Pascal features:
    a.   A type alfa that is predefined to be a **packed array** [1. .10] **of** char.
    b.   A **value** clause that initializes a variable to a value at compile time.
    c.   A procedure halt that terminates program execution.
    d.   An **else** clause in the case to handle the situation in which the selector expression did not match any label.
    e.   A direct comparison between a variable of type alfa and a ten-character string constant.

Rewrite this fragment so that it does not use any nonstandard features and would be acceptable to any standard Pascal compiler.

14.   Examine the syntactic specifications of the Pascal compiler at your installation and, if possible, find five or more local extensions provided by your compiler but which are not part of the official Pascal standard. For each one, describe why it is useful but also how you could achieve the same effect with only standard features of the language.

15.   Write a *screen handler* procedure. This is a program unit that puts up preset information on a CRT screen and then allows the user to input data at specific locations on the screen. The preset information typically comes from a *screen file,* which contains specifications about the text to place on the screen and the location and type of the response fields that the user will provide. For example,

		Preset Headers		Response Field			
Screen File:	Text	Row	Column	Row	Column	Length	Type
	Name:	1	10	1	16	20	String
	Age:	2	10	2	15	2	Unsigned number

This file would cause us to put up the characters ''Name:'' and ''Age:'' in rows 1 and 2, column 10, respectively:

```
                    Column
                 10
          1  ┌──────────────────────────┐
             │    Name:  —              │
Row       2  │    Age:                  │
             │                          │
             │                          │
             │                          │
             └──────────────────────────┘
```

The cursor would now be positioned on row 1, column 16 as we wait for a 1 to 20-character response. When the user enters it and hits return, the value is validated that it is of the correct type and then stored in a file. The cursor is now placed on row 2, column 15 as we wait for a one- or two-character response for the age field, which must be an unsigned number. When all responses have been entered, validated, and properly stored, the procedure prints ''Thank You,'' and returns.

Discuss this form of input in terms of ease of use, and simplicity for the end-user.

16.   Check what ''nontraditional'' I/O peripherals are available on the computer system at your installation—that is, something other than an alphanumeric keyboard screen or printer. Learn about the programming conventions of that particular device and discuss what particular end-user applications would be best suited for input/output using these new techniques.

CHAPTER 15

CASE STUDY IN PROGRAM DESIGN

15.1
Introduction

In this chapter we will follow the design and development of a large, complex program. While not as large as the real-world program sizes quoted in Figure 9.1, it will certainly be large enough to illustrate the importance of the program design concepts presented in Chapters 9 to 14.

This case study will involve the construction of a *simulation model*—specifically, a model of a terminal room for computer science students. Computer simulation is a well-known and popular technique for studying the behavior of complex systems. There are other ways to study system behavior, but they are often impractical or impossible.

1. *Study the actual system.* With existing systems, this approach is often either unsafe or prohibitively expensive. It obviously does not apply in cases in which we want to determine if the system is unstable *before* we build it.

2. *Study a physical model of the system.* This is done with wind tunnel tests of airplane and rocket models. But how does one build a miniature student?

3. *Study a mathematical model of the system.* If the system can be described in terms of explicit mathematical formulas, solving the formulas will explain the behavior of the system. For large, complex systems this is often difficult or impossible.

Simulation is a useful tool that frequently provides good results when the preceding techniques cannot.

The system we will be simulating is shown in Figure 15.1. Students enter the terminal room; they either go directly to one of the k identical terminals, if one is available, or they enter a waiting line (called a *queue*) to wait for an available terminal.

FIGURE 15.1   The Terminal Room System to Be Simulated.

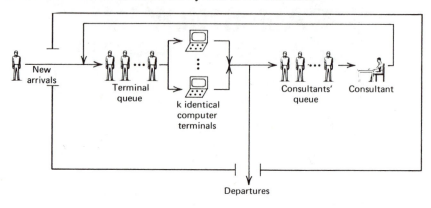

There are no special priorities in the queue; students are given a terminal according to when they arrived. (This is called a *first-come/first-served* (FCFS) queueing discipline.)

After working on the terminal, the students will either finish their work and leave the room or they will encounter some difficulty. In the latter case, they stand in another FCFS queue waiting for assistance from a programming consultant. After getting the help they need, they get back in line and wait for another terminal.

Our purpose in building this simulation model will be to determine, for a given number of terminals, the average time that a student will wait before a terminal becomes free. This information will be used to determine the optimum number of terminals to place in the terminal room to maximize student satisfaction and, at the same time, minimize cost.

The problem specification document for our simulation program is shown in Figure 15.2. Assume that this document is the culmination of a number of meetings between the programmers, the computing center staff, students, and consultants, and that all the people involved in the project are satisfied with and have signed off on this document. Our task is now to solve the problem described in that document.

15.2
The Top-Level Design

The technique we will use to simulate this system is called *discrete event simulation*. With this method we do not simulate the continuous behavior of a system, only a very specific class of *events* in the life of the system. We will observe only the events that *change* the state of the system. A special data structure, called a *calendar*, contains a

FIGURE 15.2 Problem Specification Document.

You are to design and build a program that accurately models the behavior of the students' terminal room as diagrammed in Figure 15.1.

The user must provide two pieces of input:

1. The simulated number of terminals to place in the room. This is an integer value greater than or equal to 1.
2. The simulation time. This is the total time to run the simulation model. The value is real and the units are minutes. For example, an input value of 200.0 would cause the model to simulate 200.0 minutes (e.g., 3 hours, 20 minutes) of operation of the terminal room.

If either input value has been entered incorrectly, the program should print an appropriate error message and allow the correct value to be correctly reentered.

The user must also supply to the programmer the following four statistical values:

1. The arrival rate at which students enter the room (students/minute).
2. The average length of a terminal session (in minutes).
3. The percentage of students who use the consultant.
4. The average length of a consulting session (in minutes).

The user must provide to the programmer accurate measures for all four of the above parameters.

When the simulation model has been run for the desired time period, the program should produce as output the following five quantities:

1. Average waiting time for a terminal (in minutes).
2. Percentage utilization of all terminals.
3. Average time spent waiting in line to see the consultant.
4. Percentage utilization of the consultant.
5. Total time spent by an average student in the terminal room.

After producing this output, the program should ask if the user wishes to run the program again. If yes then the program should begin again, allowing new input for both the number of terminals and the simulation time. If the user responds no, the program should print a message that the program is finished and then terminate.

list of all the events to be processed and keeps them sorted by the time they occur—for example,

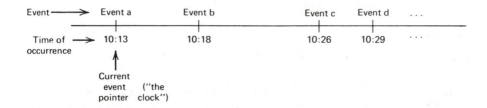

The highest level design of our simulation program can be explained in terms of a calendar and its events. We move the current event pointer (sometimes called the simulation clock) to the next event on the calendar and process that event by changing the system according to the specifications of that event. We continue this until either there are no more events on the calendar or the time on the clock exceeds some preset upper bound. For example, in the preceding diagram, after completing event a we would move the current event pointer to 10:18 and begin processing event b. We would not model the behavior of the system between 10:13 and 10:18.

After reviewing the terminal room model of Figure 15.1, we determine that the three events that will change the state of our terminal room system are as follows:

1. *Arrival event.* A new student walks in and either goes to a terminal or is placed in a waiting line for one.

2. *Terminal completion event.* A student finishes using a terminal and either leaves the room or goes to the consultant for assistance.

3. *Consultant completion event.* A student finishes talking to the consultant and reenters the terminal queue; the consultant becomes free to help the next person in line.

These three events will be part of the top-level design of our simulation model.

Another detail about simulation will affect the top level of our program. Simulation is a design tool. This means that we do not know beforehand how to set certain parameters so the system will behave properly. First, we try a set of parameters, note how the system behaves, and adjust the parameters accordingly. This is done repeatedly, always with the goal of improving performance.

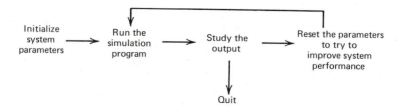

Our simulation program must therefore be able to run frequently, with a different set of parameters each time. Initially, let us assume that the only design parameters we wish to change are *nterms,* the number of terminals in the room, and *maxtime*, the total time (in minutes) for which we will run the simulation. In real life we would allow the user a great deal more control over the parameters that could be modified. For example, in a more powerful program we might allow the user to modify any or all of the following model parameters:

1. The number of consultants.
2. The rate at which students enter the room.
3. The average time that students sit at the terminal.
4. The priority with which students are given free terminals.
5. The percentage of students who go to the consultant.
6. The average time that students spend with the consultant.

We have not provided these capabilities in order to keep the program to a manageable size. (See Exercise 10 for modifications to provide some of these capabilities.)

To avoid having to pass around dozens of parameters from procedure to procedure or, even worse, refer to them globally (and possibly have disastrous side effects throughout our program), we will define two important **record** structures. The **record** variable *simstate* will contain all variables related to the status of the simulation. By simply passing around *simstate,* we can make the entire status of the simulation available to a procedure. The definition of simstate will, for now, look like this (it is only partially defined as yet; later refinements will add other necessary fields):

```
type
    staterec            =
        record
            calendar    : ?          { not sure yet what it will look like }
            clock       : real;      { the running time, from 0.0 to maxtime }
            maxtime     : real;      { total time to run the simulation }
            nterms      : integer    { number of terminals in the room }
        end; { of record staterec }


var
    simstate            : staterec;  { state of the simulation }
```

The second basic **record** structure will be *stats,* which will carry around all of the statistics that we are accumulating about the behavior of the system. Again, by passing only one **record** variable, we can make all the necessary information available to a

FIGURE 15.3   Top Level of the Simulation Program.

```
begin { program simulator }
    writeln(' Welcome to the terminal room simulator ');

    repeat
        repeat
            writeln(' Please enter values for the number of terminals,');
            writeln(' and the total simulation time in minutes');
            readln; { get user response }
            read(simstate.nterms,simstate.maxtime);

            if (simstate.nterms >= 1) and (simstate.maxtime > 0.0) then
            begin
                gooddata := true
            end
            else
            begin
                gooddata := false;
                writeln(' *** You made an error in the input. The number of terminals
                    must be >= 1');
                writeln(' *** and the time must be real and non-negative.');
                writeln(' *** Please try again')
            end { of else }
        until gooddata;

        { Initialize will put the first event on the calendar, set clock to 0, and clear all
          statistics }
        initialize(simstate, stats);

        { now we run the simulator for as long as the user specified }
        while (simstate.clock <= simstate.maxtime) do
        begin
            { getnextevent will pick off the next event from the calendar, and
              return the type and the time of occurrence }
            getnextevent(simstate.calendar,eventtype,eventtime);
            simstate.clock := eventtime;

            { now simply call the appropriate routine for this event type }
            case eventtype of
                arrival : arrivalevent(simstate,stats); { process arrival event }
                consult : consultevent(simstate,stats); { consultant
                                                          completion event }
                error : errorhandler; { something bad happened }
                term : termevent(simstate,stats) { terminal completion event }
            end { of case }
        end; { of while loop to handle one complete simulation }
```

FIGURE 15.3   *(Continued)*

```
      { We have finished one run. Throw everyone out of the room, produce
        the results and see if the user wants to try again }
      everybodyout;
      reportwriter(stats);
      writeln(' Do you wish to run the simulation again for a different');
      writeln(' number of terminals or time value? y(es) or n(o)');
      readln;
      read(response); { we will read only the first character }
      done := (response = 'n')
  until done;

      { We will go through the above repeat loop as many times as the user
        wants. We will exit here only when he/she is completely finished }
      writeln(' Exiting from the simulator program. Thank you')
end. { of program simulation }
```

procedure. However, since we have not decided anything at all about statistics, we can say nothing more about this data structure than simply

```
type
    statsrec         =
        record
                { this will be filled in later in the development }
        end; { of record statsrec }

var
    stats            : statsrec;     { the accumulated statistics }
```

This is a good example of what we earlier termed a delayed decision. We will postpone until later in the design, when we have more information, the specification of the data structure called stats. For now, we will simply leave it a stub, as shown above.

Finally, we need a user-defined data type to define the possible types of events that can occur.

```
type
    eventclass       = (arrival, consult, term, error);
var
    eventtype        : eventclass;
```

We are now in a position to specify the top level of our simulation program. The code is shown in Figure 15.3.

The top-level logic is quite easy to describe. First, the program prompts the user for the two input values *nterms* and *maxtime*. Following that, it goes into a loop where it repeatedly performs the following three operations:

1. Gets the next event off of the calendar data structure.

2. Resets the current event pointer (i.e., the master clock) forward to the time of this event.

3. Calls a routine to model that specific event. The routine will modify the state of the system (i.e., the terminal room) in accordance with the rules associated with that event type.

The simulation ends when the clock reaches the maximum simulation time specified by the user.

Before proceeding, we should point out a few important characteristics of the program in Figure 15.3:

1. The program unit defines a total of eight second-level modules:
   a. Initialize.
   b. Getnextevent.
   c. Arrivalevent.
   d. Consultevent.
   e. Errorhandler.
   f. Termevent.
   g. Everybodyout.
   h. Reportwriter.

2. The program unit consists of 45 lines of code, which is well within our guidelines for proper module length.

3. The program hides both the details of event processing and the internal representation for the calendar data structure. The details will come later, when we refine the eight lower-level procedures.

4. Our program adheres to the stylistic guidelines presented in Chapters 13 and 14 with respect to the following:
   a. Mnemonic names.
   b. Commenting standards.
   c. Indentation.
   d. Control structure.
   e. Input validation.
   f. Robustness.
   g. Output presentation.

We now must write out detailed module specifications for each of the eight modules created during the top-level design, as well as a data dictionary description for our abstract data type called calendar. In Figure 15.4 we have shown the module specification for "getnextevent." Specifications for the other seven are left as an exercise for the reader.

Before continuing with the development of the program, we should thoroughly test and validate what we have written in Figure 15.3 using stubs for those routines not yet written. We will omit this set of operations in our case study in order to concentrate on the program development process. However, we will say more about testing and verification methods in Chapter 16.

FIGURE 15.4   Specifications for the Module Getnextevent.

1. *Module name:* Getnextevent.

2. *Module type:* Procedure

3. *General description:* It is the job of getnextevent to search the calendar data structure
    and locate the next event, where next is defined as the event whose time of occurrence is
    closest to the current simulation time contained in the clock. When it is found, this pro-
    cedure removes that event from the calendar and returns two pieces of information about
    that event to the calling program—namely, the event type and the event time.

4. *Calling sequence*

    procedure getnextevent (**var** calendar : calendartype;
        var eventtype : eventclass; **var** time : real);

    where
    Calendar: The data structure containing a list of one or more event records.
    Eventtype: The event type (arrival event, terminal event, consult event) of the next
        event on the calendar.
    Time: The time of the next event.

5. *Entry conditions*

    Calendar: Contains n event records, $n \geq 1$.

6. *Exit conditions*

    Calendar: Contains $(n - 1)$ event records. The event with the time field closest to the
        simulation clock has been removed from the calendar.
    Eventtype: If calendar was not empty, it contains the type of the next event. Otherwise it
        contains the special value "error."
    Time: Contains the time of this event, if the calendar was not empty. Otherwise it is
        undefined.

7. *Side effect:* None

8. *Error conditions:* If the calendar is empty when getnextevent is called, then event type is
    set to error and time is left undefined and must not be referenced.

15.3
The First-Level Refinement

Now let's proceed to flesh out the details of these eight lower-level routines and some
of the as yet unspecified data structures.

First, let us look at the three event-processing routines—arrivalevent, termevent,
and consultevent. Before we can begin to code these routines, we must make an
important decision. Exactly what *output results* do we want our simulation model to
produce? What *statistics* do we need to understand the behavior of our system? There

are many possible values we could produce, but we will limit ourselves to the five which were listed on the specification document:

1. Average waiting time in the terminal queue.
2. Percentage of utilization of all *nterms* terminals.
3. Average waiting time in the consultant queue.
4. Percentage of utilization of the one consultant.
5. Total average time in the room for each student.

These five measures should allow us to characterize the behavior of the terminal room in terms of usage, bottlenecks, and wasted resources.

To determine these quantities we will need to add the following eight fields to the record variable call *stats,* which is as yet unspecified:

1. Termwait: The total waiting time of all people in the terminal queue (in minutes).
2. Termcount: The total number of people who entered the terminal queue.

Together, these two fields will allow us to determine the average terminal queue waiting time.

3. Totaltermtime: The total time that all terminals have been in use (in minutes).
4. Consultwait: The total waiting time of all people in the consultant queue (in minutes).
5. Consultcount: The total number of people who entered the consultant queue.

These last two fields will allow us to determine average consultant queue waiting time.

6. Total consulttime: The total time the consultant was busy (in minutes).
7. Finished: The total number of students who completed their work and left the terminal room.
8. Totaltime: The total time spent in the terminal room by all students who completed their work.

These last two fields will allow us to determine the average time in the room for each student.

This decision will also allow us to begin designing other necessary data structures. Each student who enters the terminal room will be represented by a single **record** containing the following two pieces of information:

(t_1) *Time of arrival.* Time the student first entered the terminal room (from the simulation clock).

(t_2) *Time in queue.* Time the student was initially placed in the current queue (either terminal or consultant).

```
type
    studentptr     = ↑ student;      { pointer to a student record }
    student        = record
        timeofarrival     : real;
        timeinqueue       : real
        { additional fields may be added here later }
                      end; { of student record }
```

We will also need two queues—a *terminal queue* for students waiting for the terminal, and a *consultant queue* for students waiting to talk to the consultant. A *queue* will simply be an ordered list of student records managed in such a way that the first student in the queue is the first student to leave the queue.

There are numerous ways to implement a queue in Pascal, including an array, a record, or a linked list. For now we will not worry about the underlying implementation of our two queues and leave them as abstract data types using the abstract queue operations that we developed in Chapter 4.

Enqueue (s, Q) If Q is a queue of length n, $n \geq 0$, this operation adds the student record s to the end of the queue. The length of Q is now $n + 1$.

Dequeue (s, Q) If Q is a queue of length n, $n > 0$, this operation removes the first item in Q and stores the information in s. The new length of Q is $n - 1$. If the length of Q is initially 0, this operation is undefined.

Empty (Q) If the length of Q is 0, Empty is true, otherwise Empty is false.

These last comments illustrate clearly the power and flexibility of the abstract data type concept. We have been able to carry out this first-level refinement in terms of high-level operations without worrying about the details of implementation. Furthermore, should the underlying implementation change at some point (e.g., from an array to a linked list) it will have no affect on what we have done so far, because the actual queue structure has been hidden inside these three routines.

At this point in the design we can also specify the high-level operations that can be performed on the abstract data type called *calendar*. Calendar is simply a time-ordered list of event records. These event records record the event type (e.g., the arrival of a student) and the time the event will occur. The calendar is the central data structure of our model and drives the entire simulation. Looking back at Figure 15.3, we can see that the top-level code consists of simply getting the next event off the calendar. carrying it out, and repeating that process over and over again.

There are many ways to implement a calendar structure but these detailed implementation considerations are inappropriate at this point in the implementation. For now we will concern ourselves only with the operations that can be performed on this abstract type. The physical structure of calendar will be hidden within these routines.

Getnextevent (C,e,t) If C is a calendar of event records of length n, $n > 0$, then this operation searches C to find the next (i.e., time-ordered) event. The type of that next event is returned in e and its time is returned in t. That event record is then removed from the calendar, and the final length of C is $n - 1$. If $n = 0$ initially (i.e., C is empty to start with), this operation is undefined.

Schedule (C,e,s,t) If C is a calendar of length n, $n \geq 0$, this operation adds an event of type e, for student s, at time t to the calendar. The final length of C is $n + 1$.

With this level of detail we can continue developing the problem. Later in the design we can select internal implementations for both the queue and calendar abstract data types.

We also need to add the following two fields to our record structure called *simstate,* which is maintaining the overall state of the simulation model:

Ntermsinuse   At any given time, this variable records the number of terminals actually being used by students. $0 \leq$ ntermsinuse $\leq$ nterms.

Helperbusy   A boolean variable, which is true if the consultant is currently helping a student and false otherwise.

These are only the first of a number of state variables that will be added to the simstate record to help us monitor the state of the simulation.

Finally, we must decide what causes new events to be placed on the calendar. So far only a single event has been put on the calendar, corresponding to the very first student who walks into the room. (It will be placed there by the procedure initialize.) How are other events created? The answer is that each event we have defined will spawn one or more additional events so that new events are constantly being created. In fact, one of the major purposes of the event procedures will be to schedule new events and place them on the calendar. Thus, the simulation will terminate not by running out of events but by running past the preset time limit called *maxtime.*

In our system the creation of new events will proceed as follows:

1. Each arrival event procedure will determine the interval until the next person enters the room and schedule an arrival event for that time.

2. If an arriving student can get on a terminal immediately, we will determine the length of the terminal session and schedule a terminal completion event for that time.

3. The terminal completion event procedure will check if a student is waiting in the terminal queue and, if so, give the terminal to that student and schedule another terminal completion event.

4. In addition, if the terminal completion event procedure determines that the current student will go to the consultant and if the consultant is idle, the procedure will determine the length of the consulting session and schedule a consultant completion event.

5. Finally, the consultant completion event will send that student back to a terminal (if one is available) and schedule a terminal completion event. It will also check if anybody is in line and, if so, schedule another consultant completion event.

The summary of the event-scheduling process is shown in the following diagram.

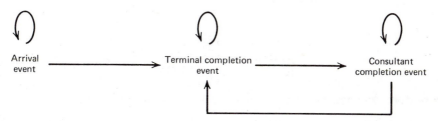

Placing the first arrival event on the calendar is like knocking over the first domino in that it indirectly creates all other events that will be processed by our system.

Now that we have decided on abstract data structures for the calendar and queues and have specified the event generation sequence, we are ready to encode the three second-level event processing routines defined earlier. The code for these routines is shown in Figure 15.5.

Again, let us make a few observations about this code:

1. The three modules are about 32, 36, and 46 lines long, respectively; they are nice and small and readily understood. They also adhere to the style and structure guidelines of Chapters 13 and 14.

2. These three second-level modules have defined a total of four new third-level modules. These new modules are all statistical procedures that characterize the behavior of the system.

   Nextarrival. Computes student interarrival times.
   Uselength. Computes how long students use the terminal.
   Needhelp. Computes what percentage of students use the consultant.
   Helplength. Computes how long students talk to the consultant.

   In addition, we are utilizing the following five operations on our abstract data types queue and calendar. All operations will ultimately have to be implemented:
   a. Operations on queues
      Enqueue
      Dequeue
      Empty
   b. Operations on the calendar
      Schedule
      Getnextevent

FIGURE 15.5   Second-Level Event Processing Procedures.

{ arrival event

    Handle a student who just arrived, giving him or her a terminal if one is available or putting him or her in line if one is not.

    entry conditions:
            simstate   : current state of the simulation
            stats   : current statistics

    exit conditions:
            simstate   : updated appropriately
            stats   : also updated appropriately
}

procedure arrivalevent (**var** simstate : staterec; **var** stats : statsrec);

var
    newp   : studentptr;   { temporary student pointer }
    t   : real;   { temporary variable used for scheduling }

begin { procedure arrivalevent }
    { schedule the next arrival event after this one }
    nextarrival(t); { procedure which determines interarrival time }

    { schedule next arrival event for t minutes from now }
    schedule(simstate.calendar,arrival,**nil**,simstate.clock + t);

    { now create the new student who just arrived and set initial parameters }
    new(newp);
    newp ↑ .timeofarrival := simstate.clock; { when student first walked in }

    { see if there are any terminals free }
    if simstate.ntermsinuse = simstate.nterms **then** { all busy }
    begin { put student in the terminal queue }
        enqueue(newp,simstate.termqueue);
        newp ↑ .timeinqueue := simstate.clock { when student started waiting }
    end { of if busy }
    else
    begin { give student one of the free terminals }
        { determine length of this terminal session }
        uselength(t);

FIGURE 15.5   (*Continued*)

```
        { schedule terminal completion event }
        schedule(simstate.calendar,term,newp,simstate.clock + t);
        simstate.ntermsinuse := simstate.ntermsinuse + 1;
        stats.termcount := stats.termcount + 1; { this is the number of
                                                    terminal sessions }
        stats.totaltermtime := stats.totaltermtime + t { total time a terminal
                                                          has been in use }
    end; { of else clause }

    stats.totalstudents := stats.totalstudents + 1
end; { of procedure arrivalevent }
```

{ consultant completion event

Take student p away from the consultant and give him or her a terminal if one is open, putting him or her in line if there are none. If anyone is waiting, that person will now be allowed to see the consultant.

```
entry conditions:
        p               : points to student who is done being helped
        simstate        : current state of the simulation
        stats           : accumulated statistics

exit conditions:
        p               : given a terminal or put on terminal queue
        simstate        : updated appropriately
        stats           : updated appropriately
}
```

```
procedure consultevent (p : studentptr; var simstate : staterec;
    var stats : statsrec);

var
    newp            : studentptr;     { temporary student pointer }
    t               : real;           { temporary used for scheduling }

begin { procedure consultevent }
    { first put the student who is finished with the consultant back in line for a terminal }
    if simstate.ntermsinuse = simstate.nterms then { all terminals busy }
    begin
        enqueue(p,simstate.termqueue); { wait in the terminal queue }
        p↑.timeinqueue := simstate.clock
    end { of if terminals full }
    else
```

FIGURE 15.5 *(Continued)*

```
    begin { give student a free terminal }
        uselength(t); { determine how long student will use terminal }
        { schedule the terminal completion event }
        schedule(simstate.calendar,term,p,simstate.clock + t);
        simstate.ntermsinuse := simstate.ntermsinuse + 1;
        stats.termcount := stats.termcount + 1;
        stats.totaltermtime := stats.totaltermtime + t
    end; { of else get an open terminal }

    { now see if anybody else wants to talk to the consultant }
    if empty(simstate.consultqueue) then { nobody is waiting }
        simstate.helperbusy := false
    else
    begin { somebody wants to see the consultant }
        dequeue(newp,simstate.consultqueue);
        { collect statistics about this person's wait in line }
        stats.consultwait := stats.consultwait
            + (simstate.clock − newp↑.timeinqueue);
        stats.consultcount := stats.consultcount + 1;

        { schedule completion event of consultant }
        helplength(t);
        schedule(simstate.calendar,consult,newp,simstate.clock + t);
        stats.totalconsulttime := stats.totalconsulttime + t
    end
end; { of procedure consultevent }

{ terminal completion event

Remove student p from the terminal. If he or she needs help, send him or her to the
consultant. If anyone is waiting for a terminal, it will be given to the first person
in line.

entry conditions:
        p           : points to the student who is done with the terminal
        simstate    : current state of the simulation
        stats       : accumulated statistics

exit conditions:
        p           : will either leave the room or go to the consultant
        simstate    : will be updated appropriately
        stats       : will be updated appropriately
}

procedure termevent(p : studentptr; var simstate : staterec;
    var stats : statsrec);
```

FIGURE 15.5   (*Continued*)

```
var
    newp              : studentptr;      { temporary student pointer }
    t                 : real;            { temporary used for scheduling }
    leaving           : boolean;         { true if a student is going to leave the
                                           room, false if he or she is going to the
                                           consultant }

begin { procedure termevent }
    { determine whether this student needs help or will leave the room }
    needhelp(leaving);
    if leaving then { collect statistics about this student }
    begin
        stats.finished := stats.finished + 1;
        stats.totaltime := stats.totaltime + (simstate.clock − p↑.timeofarrival);
        dispose(p) { say goodbye to student }
    end { of if leaving }
    else
    begin { he or she is going to the consultant }
        if simstate.helperbusy then { wait in line }
        begin
            enqueue(p,simstate.consultqueue);
            p↑.timeinqueue := simstate.clock
        end { of if helperbusy }
        else
        begin { consultant is available }
            simstate.helperbusy := true;
            helplength(t); { determine length of consultation }
            { schedule the consultant completion event }
            schedule(simstate.calendar,consult,p,simstate.clock + t);
            stats.consultcount := stats.consultcount + 1;
            stats.totalconsulttime := stats.totalconsulttime + t
        end { of else helper not busy }
    end; { of else person goes to consultant }

    { now see if anybody else wants the terminal just freed up }
    if empty(simstate.termqueue) then { no one is in line }
        simstate.ntermsinuse := simstate.ntermsinuse − 1
    else
    begin
        dequeue(newp,simstate.termqueue); { get next person from queue }
        { determine how long this person waited, adding it to total }
        stats.termwait := stats.termwait + (simstate.clock − newp↑.timeinqueue);
        stats.termcount := stats.termcount + 1;
        uselength(t); { determine length of terminal session }
        { schedule terminal completion event }
        schedule(simstate.calendar,term,newp,simstate.clock + t);
        stats.totaltermtime := stats.totaltermtime + t
    end
end; { of procedure termevent }
```

FIGURE 15.6   Current Development Tree for the Simulator.

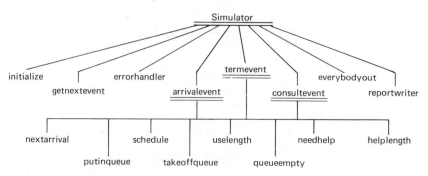

The overall development tree to this point is summarized in Figure 15.6. The underlined procedures are those that have already been developed.

3. Even though we have come a long way in the development of our program, a good deal of detail is still hidden in lower-level procedures. For example, we have not even begun to select an internal representation for the calendar. That level of detail is currently hidden in the modules called Getnextevent and Schedule. Also, we have not yet specified the algorithms for searching or sorting the calendar. Similarly, the queue structure has been hidden in the three lower-level routines called Enqueue, Dequeue, and Empty.

4. Each of the three modules specified by the preceding refinement adhere to our guidelines for coherence and independence. Each of the three modules addresses one and only one event type and performs operations associated only with that event. In addition, the modules do not access any global variables and affect only their reference parameters. They have no unexpected or unanticipated side effects.

As mentioned earlier, before we develop any of the unwritten modules listed in Figure 15.6, we must test our three new modules for correctness. We will again omit this step to concentrate on the issues related to program development and come back to the topics of testing and verification in Chapter 16.

15.4
Succeeding Refinements

We will now begin to specify and code some of the other modules on data structures shown in Figure 15.6. Exactly what order in which we approach this task is not critical, as long as we follow the principles of top-down design and adhere to the module characteristics described in Chapters 12 through 14.

Let us now develop the two calendar handling routines: getnextevent, which takes the next event from the calendar, and schedule, which puts a new event on the calendar in the proper (i.e., time-ordered) sequence. This will require us to select an internal implementation for the abstract data type called calendar.

In some programming languages the implementation details (i.e., type declarations, procedure, function declarations) of an abstract data type are placed in a separate program unit called an *implementation module* or *package body*. By placing them in a special unit, the compiler can enforce the separation of the visible part of the abstract data type from the hidden part—its implementation. Any attempt by another module to reference these hidden details would be caught by the compiler and flagged as an error. Unfortunately, Pascal does not have this capability, and our implementation of the abstract data type called calendar will use the normal **type, procedure,** and **function** declaration mechanism.

An array is probably an inappropriate internal structure for a calendar, since we have no prior knowledge of how many events may be on the calendar at any one time. If we declared the calendar array [1. .500], what would we do if there were 501 scheduled events (a fatal error)? Therefore, a *linked list structure* is the best way, in this situation, to represent a calendar. It will consist of a linked list of events sorted by increasing value in the time field.

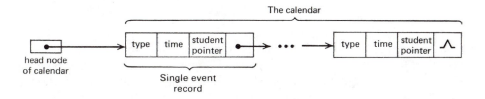

This structure can be created through the following declarations:

```
type
    eventptr            = ↑event;
    event               =
        record
            eventtype   : eventclass;       { the type of event }
            eventtime   : real;             { time the event will occur }
            studptr     : studentptr;       { pointer to the student who
                                              caused the event. }
            link        : eventptr          { pointer to next event record }
        end; { of event record }
var
    calendar            : eventptr;         { head of the calendar }
```

With our internal data structure decision made, we can better understand the purpose of the two new routines we are about to write.

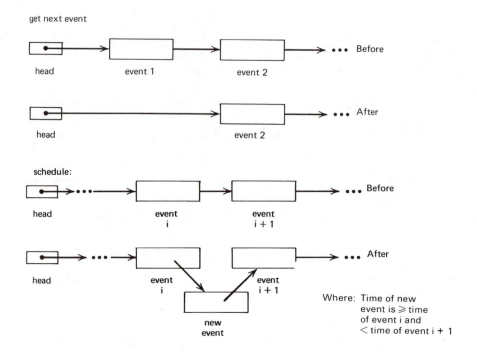

get next event

head   event 1   event 2   ••• Before

head   event 2   ••• After

schedule:

head   event
              i   event
                             i + 1   ••• Before

head   event
              i   event
                             i + 1   ••• After

new
event

Where: Time of new
       event is ≥ time
       of event i and
       < time of event i + 1

We can now write these routines, which are shown in Figure 15.7.

Neither of these routines defines any lower-level routines (both new and dispose are procedures that are part of standard Pascal), so we can immediately begin coding some of the other lower-level routines already specified.

Let us similarly select the underlying internal implementation of our two queue structures, termqueue and consultqueue. Currently they are defined only in terms of the three operations, enqueue, dequeue, and empty. (The queue structure and its internal implementations were discussed at length in Chapter 4, and you may wish to go back and review that section.)

An array would again be a poor choice for constructing a queue because we have no idea of the maximum number of people in line at any one time. A better structure would be, as with calendar, a linked list. A *queue* can be implemented as a linked list of individual student records.

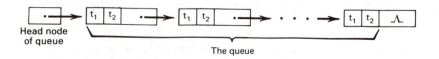

Head node
of queue

t_1 t_2 t_1 t_2 t_1 t_2

The queue

This structure can be created using the following declarations:

type
    studentptr   = ↑ student;
    student   =
        record
            timeofarrival   : real;
            timeinqueue   : real;
            next   : studentptr;
        end; { of student record }

var
    termqueue   : studentptr;   { pointer to the head of the
                                               terminal queue }
    consultqueue   : studentptr;   { pointer to the head of the
                                               consultant queue }

The queue handling routines—enqueue, dequeue, and empty—are somewhat similar to the calendar routines just developed. They both manage (add, delete, search) these linked list data structures. However, queue management is simple by comparison, since we never insert items in the middle of the data structure. Because we are using a first-come/first-served queueing discipline, we will always add items to the end of the list and take items from the beginning. There is one problem, though. If we look at the internal definition of the queue data structure that we selected, we see that it is a most inefficient selection based on the types of operations we will be doing. The queue structure we set up looked like this:

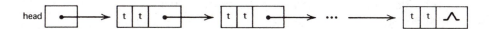

This is fine for taking items from the front of the list, but what about adding items to the end? Given the current internal definition, we would have to walk through the entire queue, following the links, until we came to the end. We could theoretically code enqueue this way, but it would be a most inefficient procedure.

Instead, we should implement pointers to both the *head* and *tail* of the queue.

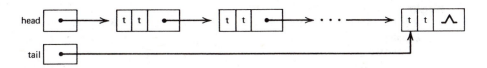

FIGURE 15.7   Calendar Handling Routines.

{ schedule

Search through the calendar to determine where a new event should be placed. Then add this new event to the calendar, keeping the calendar ordered by time field.

entry conditions:
    calendar   : pointer to a list of 0 or more events
    evtype   : type of the event to be scheduled
    sptr   : pointer to the student involved (may be nil)
    evtime   : time that event is to be scheduled

 exit conditions:
        the event is inserted into the calendar list, preserving the ordering by time field.
}

procedure schedule (**var** calendar : eventptr; evtype : eventclass;
    sptr : studentptr; evtime : real);

var
    done   : boolean;   { true when searching should stop }
    eventp   : eventptr;   { temporary for node creation }
    oldp   : eventptr;   { temporary used for calendar search }
    p   : eventptr;   { temporary used for calendar search }

begin { procedure schedule }
    { first build a new event node with the proper values }
    new(eventp);
    with eventp ↑ **do**
    begin
        eventtype := evtype;
        eventtime := evtime;
        studptr := sptr
    end; { of with }

    { now see where this new node should be placed on the calendar and reset the links }
    p := calendar;
    if p <> **nil then**
    begin
        if p ↑ .eventtime <= evtime **then** { we must search through the list }
        begin
            repeat
                oldp := p;
                p := p ↑ .link;

FIGURE 15.7   (*Continued*)

```
            { see if we are done without doing a nil pointer reference }
            if p <> nil then done := (p ↑ .eventtime > evtime)
            else done := true
        until done;

        { now insert the new item }
        eventp ↑ .link := p;
        oldp ↑ .link := eventp
    end { of search and insert new item }
    else
    begin { it goes at the head of the list }
        eventp ↑ .link := calendar;
        calendar := eventp
    end { of else }
end { of if p <> nil }
else
begin { calendar is empty }
    eventp ↑ .link := nil;
    calendar := eventp
end { of else empty calendar }
end; { of procedure schedule }

{ getnextevent

Get the next item from the calendar, removing it from the head of the list.

entry conditions:
        calendar      : pointer to the list of 1 or more events

exit conditions:
        calendar      : has had it's first event removed
        evtype        : returns the type of the event.
                        If the calendar list was empty, error is returned.
        sptr          : returns a pointer to the student involved
        evtime        : returns the time this event is to take place
}

procedure getnextevent (var calendar : eventptr; var evtype : eventclass;
        var sptr : studentptr; var evtime : real);

var
        newlink               : eventptr;     { temporary used for updating links }
```

FIGURE 15.7 *(Continued)*

```
begin { procedure getnextevent }
    if calendar <> nil then
    begin
        with calendar ↑ do
        begin
            evtype : = eventtype;
            evtime : = eventtime;
            sptr   : = studptr
        end; { of with }

        { now adjust the links and discard that node }
        newlink : = calendar ↑ .link;
        dispose (calendar); { dispose is a built-in Pascal procedure }
        calendar : = newlink
    end { of if calendar <> nil }
    else evtype : = error { calendar empty }
end; { of procedure getnextevent }
```

We can set up this new queue structure in the following way:

```
type
    queue          =
        record
            head     : studentptr;
            tail     : studentptr
        end; { of record queue }


var
    termqueue        : queue;    { the terminal waiting line }
    consultqueue     : queue;    { the consultant waiting line }
```

This change in the internal realization of the queue data structure will not change the procedures we have written so far because all details of queue operations were hidden in the abstract operations called enqueue and dequeue which we are about to write. This is a perfect example of the advantage of using abstract data types and separating the external operations on that abstract type from the internal implementation of that type. A major change in that internal implementation (for purposes of increasing efficiency) is totally transparent to all other routines and has caused us no problems at all.

With our new declarations in place, the responsibilities of the queueing procedures can be represented as follows:

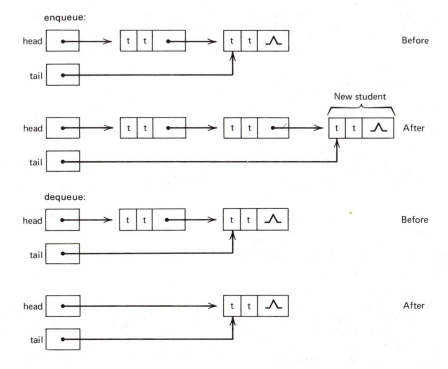

The three queue management routines are coded and shown in Figure 15.8.

We want to stress that our decision to implement both the calendar and queue data types at this point in the design was not mandatory. We could have postponed the selection of an internal representation for both until much later in the design, possibly gaining additional information that would help us in our selection. The use of abstract data types allows us to separate out the physical implementation and delay its selection for as long as we desire.

Again, these routines did not define any new low-level routines to be added to the development tree. Looking back at what we have done, we see that we have coded 9 of the 17 modules so far defined and written about 250 lines of code (about 350 lines, including comments). Despite the size of the program we are developing, it is clear and understandable (except possibly for some problems understanding the basics of simulation). We have a good idea of where we are going and what tasks still need to be done. It might not be a bad idea to review what we have developed and imagine trying to write the same program without any planning or organization! (Remember that this program is still very small compared with most real-world applications programs.)

We will now start coding the four statistical routines that characterize system behavior—nextarrival, uselength, needhelp, and helplength. More than any other routine we will write, these four modules will determine the ultimate overall accuracy of our simulator. It is imperative that our statistical assumptions about arrival rates, terminal session lengths, and the like closely match the actual values in the real system (the

FIGURE 15.8   Queue Handling Routines.

{ enqueue

Put student p at the end of queue q.

entry conditions:
    p   : points to the student being placed in line
    q   : points to a queue of 0 or more students

exit conditions:
    p   : the next field of p is set to nil since they are at the
                 end of the line
    q   : has had student p put at the end of this queue
}

```
procedure enqueue (p : studentptr; var q : queue);
begin { procedure enqueue }
    if q.tail <> nil then { queue is not empty }
    begin
        q.tail ↑ .next := p;
        p ↑ .next := nil;
        q.tail := p
    end { of add to nonempty queue }
    else
    begin { queue is empty }
        q.head := p;
        q.tail := p;
        p ↑ .next := nil
    end { of add to empty queue }
end; { of procedure enqueue }
```

{ dequeue

Take the first student p from queue q. Abort the entire program if queue is empty.

entry conditions:
    q   : points to a queue of 1 or more students

exit conditions:
    p   : points to the student who was first in line
    q   : has had its first entry removed
}

FIGURE 15.8   (*Continued*)

```
procedure dequeue (var p : studentptr; var q : queue);
begin
    if q.head <> nil then { there is at least one item in the queue }
    begin
        p := q.head;
        { now remove that item and reset pointers }
        if p↑.next <> nil then
            q.head := p↑. next { remove from list }
        else
        begin { the queue had only one item and is now empty }
            q.head := nil;
            q.tail := nil
        end { of else }
    end { of queue was not empty }
    else halt(' dequeue called with empty queue')
        { This will abort if the programmer is careless enough not to check if the
          queue is empty before calling this routine. This is a questionable
          stylistic practice and a future modification may wish to change this
          operation. }
end; { of procedure dequeue }

{ empty

Determine if queue q has any students left in it

entry conditions:
        q                 : points to a queue of 0 or more students

exit conditions:
        function returns true if the queue is empty, false otherwise.
}

function empty (q : queue) : boolean;
begin { function empty }
    empty := (q.head = nil)
end; { of function empty }
```

terminal room). If they do not, our entire simulator is an exercise in futility, and our results will be meaningless. (Remember: garbage in, garbage out.) The user will be required to collect these data and provide them to us prior to the design and implementation of these routines (see Figure 15.2). If the terminal room did not yet exist, the user would have to make reasonable estimates for these values. If the room actually existed, they could sit by the door and time the arrivals and terminal sessions with a stopwatch to get accurate empirical observations. We would then try to fit our observations to one of a number of well-known statistical distributions (e.g., exponential, normal, and uniform) that could then be coded into our procedures.

However, since this is only a case study and we cannot assume an understanding of statistics, we will use some very simple and unrealistic numerical values to describe the behavior of our system. These statistics are summarized in Figure 15.9.

Using the data from Figure 15.9, we can code the four statistical routines. We will use a random number generator that produces uniformly distributed random numbers between 0.0 and 1.0. Then, using the frequencies in the second column of Figure 15.9, we can determine the appropriate category and, with a second call to the random number generator, can find the exact value.

For example, to determine the length of a terminal session (Table B of Figure 15.9), we can generate a random number in the range 0.0 to 1.0. If the value were between 0.000 and 0.250, we would say the session lasted between 0 and 15 minutes. We could then generate a random number between 0.0 and 15.0 to get the exact length in minutes. If the original random number were 0.250 to 0.800, we would say the session lasted 15 to 30 minutes and generate a second random value from 15.0 to 30.0 to determine the length. If the original random number were between 0.800 and 0.980, we would generate a random value between 30.0 and 60.0. Finally, if the original random number exceeded 0.980, we would generate a second random value between 60.0 and some reasonable upper bound.

Notice that the four routines in Figure 15.10 create the need for yet another lower-level routine called random(x,y). This function will generate a random real number, r, in the range $x \leq r \leq y$. As with all our other procedures, we must add this one to the tree of procedures and eventually code it. This low-level procedure called random is typical of the type of utility routine that would not be coded near the end of a project, as we are doing here, but near the very beginning, as we discussed in Section 11.4.2. Anyone who has worked in the area of discrete event simulation is aware that the technique makes a good deal of use of random numbers. Therefore, as part of a programmer's "tool kit" we would provide to our programming staff, we would certainly include a range of routines for generating uniform, exponential, and normally distributed random numbers. These routines would be designed and coded very early in the project and placed, along with other useful utility routines, in a *program library* for everyone to use. Since we never want to duplicate useful work, we would always opt to use such a library routine if it were available. We could do this through an *external declaration*. (*Note:* The syntax of external declarations is not standardized.)

```
function random(x , y : real) : real; extern;
```

FIGURE 15.9   Statistical Tables Describing the System.

A.   *Interarrival Distribution*

Interval (minutes)	Percentage of Students
0–1	12
1–2	24
2–4	35
4–8	20
8–15	7
Over 15	2

B.   *Length of Terminal Session*

Time (minutes)	Percentage of Sessions
0–15	25
15–30	55
30–60	18
Over 60	2

C.   *Length of Consulting Sessions*

Time (minutes)	Percentage of Sessions
0–5	50
5–10	33
Over 10	17

D.   *Percentage of Students Who Use the Consultant = 30%*

The preceding declaration states that the function random will not be contained within the body of the program but will be found in an external library. If the routine were not available in some library, we would merely replace the preceding external declaration with the actual code for the function. (Since our library did not include a random number generator in exactly the form we needed, we wrote our own. It is shown in the listing of the entire program at the end of this chapter.)

The last four routines left to code are ones that appear at the beginning and end of the program: the initialize procedure, the errorhandler, the cleanup routine called everybodyout, and the output procedure called reportwriter. These routines are usually done last because only when we are finished with all *other* routines do we know for certain exactly what values to initialize and what values should be presented as output.

For initialize, we must go through all the modules and determine which data values should be initialized and to what values.

Also, at this late stage we cannot do a sloppy job of printing the results in the procedure reportwriter. All the time and hard work will be wasted (from the end-user's standpoint) if the output of our program is difficult to interpret or incomplete. We must put as much care and effort into the final output procedure as we have into any of the

FIGURE 15.10   Statistical Procedures.

```
{ helplength

  Compute length of consulting session based on the distribution in Figure 15.9

    entry conditions:
          none

    exit conditions:
          time          : set to the length of a consulting session
}

procedure helplength (var time : real);
var
      r                 : real;    { a pseudorandom number }
begin { procedure helplength }
      r := random(0.0,1.0);
      if r <= 0.50 then time := random(0.0,5.0)
      else
      if r <= 0.83 then time := random(5.0,10.0)
      else time := random(10.0,15.0)
      { assume maximum consulting time is 15 minutes }
end; { of procedure helplength }

{ uselength

  Determine the length of a terminal session based on the distribution in Figure 15.9.

    entry conditions:
          none

    exit conditions:
          time          : set to the length of a terminal session
}

procedure uselength (var time : real);
var
      r                 : real;    { a pseudorandom number }
begin { procedure uselength }
      r := random(0.0,1.0);
      if r <= 0.25 then time := random (0.0,15.0)
      else
      if r <= 0.80 then time := random(15.0,30.0)
      else
      if r <= 0.98 then time := random(30.0,60.0)
      else time := random(60.0,180.0)
      { assume nobody sits at a terminal for more than three hours }
end; { of procedure uselength }
```

FIGURE 15.10   (*Continued*)

{ needhelp

    Determine if a student does or does not go to the consultant based on the distribu-
tion shown in Figure 15.9

    entry conditions:
        none

    exit conditions:
        exit   : true if the student will go to the consultant, false otherwise.
}

procedure needhelp (**var** exit : boolean);
var
    r   : real;   { a pseudorandom number }
begin { procedure needhelp }
    r := random(0.0,1.0);
    exit := (r <= 0.70)
end; { of procedure needhelp }

{ nextarrival

    Determine how long until the next student arrives based on the distribution shown in
Figure 15.9.

    entry conditions:
        none

    exit conditions:
        time   : set to the length of time before the next student arrives.
}

procedure nextarrival (**var** time : real);
var
    r   : real;   { pseudo-random number }
begin { procedure nextarrival }
    r := random(0.0,1.0);
    if r <= 0.12 **then** time := random(0.0,1.0)
    else
    if r <= 0.36 **then** time := random(1.0,2.0)
    else
    if r <= 0.71 **then** time := random(2.0,4.0)
    else
    if r <= 0.91 **then** time := random(4.0,8.0)
    else
    if r <= 0.98 **then** time := random(8.0,15.0)
    else time := random(15.0,30.0)
    { assume that the maximum interarrival time is one half hour }
end; { of procedure nextarrival }

other modules. (This point was stressed in Section 14.6 on user-friendliness and the input-output characteristics of programs.)

Our errorhandler need handle only one case—an empty calendar. This should never happen and would indicate a significant flaw in the system. We will inform the user of this fact and then halt.

Finally, the routine everybodyout will clean up all the memory space used for student records and queues and return it to the main memory pool. This is necessary in Pascal to ensure that we do not run out of memory when we execute the simulator over and over again. This cleanup is done using the standard Pascal procedure dispose, which frees memory that had previously been allocated to a particular data structure.

The final four procedures of our simulator are shown in Figure 15.11.

FIGURE 15.11   Initialize, Errorhandler, Reportwriter, and
Everybodyout Procedures.

{ errorhandler

Handle an error by halting the program. In future versions of the program we might try to recover from the error.

entry conditions:
        none

exit conditions:
        the program will be halted
}

procedure errorhandler;
begin { procedure errorhandler }
    writeln(' *** Fatal error -- we encountered an empty calendar.');
    writeln(' *** Dump followed by a system halt');
    halt(' empty calendar')
end; { of procedure errorhandler }

{ initialize

Initialize the state of the simulation and zero out statistics.

entry conditions:
        none

exit conditions:
        simstate   : all fields are initialized except nterms and maxtime
                        which have been read from input
        stats   : all fields are set to zero
}

FIGURE 15.11   (*Continued*)

```
procedure initialize (var simstate : staterec; var stats : statsrec);
begin { procedure initialize }
    with simstate do
    begin
        clock := 0.0;
        { put first arrival event on the calendar for time 0.0 }
        calendar := nil;
        schedule(calendar,arrival,nil,0.0);
        { set the queues to be empty }
        termqueue.head := nil;
        termqueue.tail := nil;
        consultqueue.head := nil;
        consultqueue.tail := nil;
        { initially all terminals are free, and consultant is idle }
        ntermsinuse := 0;
        helperbusy := false
    end; { of with simstate }
    with stats do
    begin { zero all totals used for gathering data }
        consultcount := 0;
        consultwait := 0.0;
        finished := 0;
        termcount := 0;
        termwait := 0.0;
        totalconsulttime := 0.0;
        totalstudents := 0;
        totaltermtime := 0.0;
        totaltime := 0.0
    end { of with stats }
end; { of procedure initialize }


{ reportwriter

  Produce the finished report.


  entry conditions:
        nterms        : the number of terminals used in the simulation
        duration      : the time in minutes that the simulation ran
        stats         : the record containing all statistical data about the simulation


  exit conditions:
        the report will be written to output
}
```

FIGURE 15.11   (*Continued*)

```
procedure reportwriter (nterms : integer; duration : real; stats : statsrec);
var
      consultpercent      : real;      { consultant utilization level }
      termpercent         : real;      { terminal utilization level }
begin { procedure reportwriter }
      writeln;
      writeln;
      writeln(' Results of the simulation run');
      writeln(nterms:8,' terminals were available');
      writeln(duration:8:2,' minutes simulation time');
      with stats do
      begin
          writeln(totalstudents:8,' students entered the terminal room');
          writeln(finished:8,' students exited during the simulation');
          if termcount > 0 then
          writeln(termwait / termcount :8:2,' average minutes (per student)',
              ' spent waiting for a terminal')
          else writeln(' ':8,' No terminals were used');
          if consultcount > 0 then
              writeln(consultwait / consultcount :8:2,' average minutes',
                  ' (per student) spent waiting for the consultant')
          else writeln(' ':8,' Nobody saw the consultant');
          if finished > 0 then
              writeln(totaltime / finished :8:2,' average minutes (per student)',
                  ' spent in the terminal room');

          { Compute the fraction of usage of the terminals and consultant.
            Recall that zero length simulations cannot be requested }
          termpercent := (totaltermtime * 100.0) / (nterms * duration);
          consultpercent := (totalconsulttime * 100.0) / duration
      end; { of with stats }

      { It is possible to get terminal or consultant utilizations beyond 100% because we
        tally the last few sessions even though they may extend past closing time. To
        avoid confusing the reader, these values will be reset to 100. }
      if termpercent > 100.0 then termpercent := 100.0;
      if consultpercent > 100.0 then consultpercent := 100.0;

      writeln(termpercent:8:1,' percent usage made of all terminals');
      writeln(consultpercent:8:1,' percent usage made of the consultant')
end; { of procedure reportwriter }
```

{ everybodyout

It is closing time so all students will be asked to leave, freeing space to be used for
the next simulation. This procedure disposes of all the space allocated to this
program.

FIGURE 15.11 *(Continued)*

entry conditions:
>   calendar   : points to a list of 0 or more events
>   consultqueue   : points to a queue of 0 or more students
>   terminalqueue   : points to a queue of 0 or more students

exit conditions:
>   all nodes remaining in the above lists are returned to available storage
>   by disposing them, and the pointers are set to nil.

}

```
procedure everybodyout (var calendar : eventptr; var consultqueue : queue;
    var termqueue : queue);
var
    evptr      : eventptr; { used to scan calendar }

    { escortq

    Quietly escort those still waiting in line to the nearest exit!

    entry conditions:
        q    : points to a queue of 0 or more students
    exit conditions:
        all nodes in the queue are disposed, and the pointers set to nil
    }

    procedure escortq (var q : queue);
    var
        studentp      : studentptr; { the current deadbeat }
    begin { procedure escortq }
        while not empty(q) do
        begin
            dequeue(studentp,q);
            dispose(studentp)
        end; { of while loop to remove a student }
    end; { of procedure escortq }

begin { procedure everybodyout }
    while calendar <> nil do
    begin
        if calendar ↑ .studptr <> nil then dispose(calendar ↑ .studptr);
        evptr := calendar ↑ .link;
        dispose(calendar);
        calendar := evptr
    end; { of while loop emptying calendar }

    escortq(consultqueue);
    escortq(termqueue)
end; { of procedure everybodyout }
```

FIGURE 15.12   Results of the Simulation Model.

Number of Terminals	Average Waiting Time for a Terminal (min)	Utilization of Terminals (%)	Utilization of Consultant (%)
1	617	100.0	6.6
2	544	100.0	12.0
3	425	100.0	25.7
4	321	100.0	27.1
5	204	100.0	37.4
6	191	99.9	40.4
8	64	97.0	52.8
10	5	86.6	57.3
15	0.03	54.4	55.9
20	0	43.3	56.8
50	0	16.8	58.7

This completes our case study. By textbook standards, this is a monumental program—spanning 18 pages and containing 21 different procedures with approximately 500 lines of code (with comments, about 700 lines).[1] But, more than anything else in this text, this case study graphically illustrates the fundamentals of programming. It demonstrates the critical need for a management policy to handle large, complex programs. It exemplifies the top-down design of programs and data structures. It illustrates procedure modularity, independence, and logical coherence. Finally, it again demonstrates the importance of clarity of expression. A program of this size would have been much more difficult to follow if we had not adhered to the style and expression guidelines presented in earlier chapters.

15.5
Results

After spending all that time designing and coding, we would be remiss if we did not present the results of our simulation program. The program just developed was coded and run on a VAX-11/782; some results are presented in Figure 15.12. Before we can analyze the data and say what the proper number of terminals is, we must decide on acceptable limits for waiting times, waiting lines, and utilizations in our terminal room. For example, using our data, if we do not want students to wait more than 5 minutes on the average for a terminal, we would need at least 10 terminals in the room. If we wanted the waiting time to be just a few seconds, we would need about 15 terminals. The data in Figure 15.12 show clearly how important it is to study the behavior of this system thoroughly *before* we buy terminals. For example, if we had

[1] Although, interestingly enough, by the standards of Figure 9.1 this program would be classified as trivial!

purchased only three terminals for the room, the average waiting time would be about 7 hours!

We will leave it to the interested student (drawing on his or her own frustration with trying to find a free terminal the day before homework is due!) to analyze the data in Figure 15.12 further and decide how many terminals we should purchase.

A complete listing of the simulator program developed in this chapter appears in Figure 15.13.

FIGURE 15.13   The Completed Simulation Program.

program simulator(input,output);

```
{
 This is a program to simulate the behavior of a computer terminal room using
 discrete event simulation. The system is described in Chapter 15 of the second
 edition of Advanced Programming and Problem Solving by G. M.
 Schneider, S. C. Bruell.
}
```

```
const
    version                    = ' 3.1, last mod 1 jan 87';
type
    eventclass                 = (arrival, term, consult, error);

    studentptr                 = ↑ student;
    student                    =
        record
            timeinqueue        : real;         { time when inserted }
            timeofarrival      : real;         { to terminal room }
            next               : studentptr    { points to next person in
                                                  queue }
        end; { of student record }

    eventptr                   = ↑ event;
    event                      =
        record
            eventtype          : eventclass;
            eventtime          : real;         { time of occurrence }
            studptr            : studentptr;
            link               : eventptr
        end; { of event record }

    queue                      =
        record
            head               : studentptr;
            tail               : studentptr
        end; { of queue record }
```

FIGURE 15.13 *(Continued)*

```
statsrec                          =
    record { all statistical data are kept in this record structure }
                consultcount          : integer;     { counts consultations }
                consultwait           : real;        { accumulates time students
                                                       waited for a consultation }
                finished              : integer;     { counts students leaving
                                                       terminal room }
                termcount             : integer;     { counts terminal events }
                termwait              : real;        { accumulates student
                                                       waiting time }
                totalconsulttime      : real;        { accumulates consultation
                                                       times }
                totalstudents         : integer;     { counts student arrivals }
                totaltermtime         : real;        { accumulates useful
                                                       terminal time }
                totaltime             : real         { accumulates time spent in
                                                       room }
        end; { of statsrec record }

staterec                          =
    record { the current state of the simulation }
                calendar              : eventptr;    { head of calendar list }
                clock                 : real;        { the running time. starts at
                                                       0.0, up to maxtime, and is
                                                       reset to eventtime for each
                                                       new event }
                consultqueue          : queue;       { points to ends of
                                                       consultant queue }
                helperbusy            : boolean;     { true if the consultant is
                                                       busy, false otherwise }
                maxtime               : real;        { total time to run the
                                                       simulation }
                nterms                : integer;     { number of terminals in
                                                       room }
                ntermsinuse           : integer;     { number of terminals being
                                                       used }
                termqueue             : queue        { points to ends of terminal
                                                       queue }
        end; { of staterec record }
var
    done                              : boolean;     { boolean flag to signal
                                                       completion }
    eventtime                         : real;        { the time of the next
                                                       calendar event }
    eventtype                         : eventclass;  { the type of the next
                                                       calendar event }
```

FIGURE 15.13 *(Continued)*

gooddata	: boolean;	{ boolean flag used to validate input }
p	: studentptr;	{ student involved in current event }
response	: char;	{ user response about continuation }
simstate	: staterec;	{ state of the simulation }
stats	: statsrec;	{ accumulates statistics }

{ schedule

Search through the calendar to determine where a new event should be placed. Then add this new event to the calendar, keeping the event list ordered by the time field.

entry conditions:
      calendar   : pointer to a list of 0 or more events
      evtype   : type of the event to be scheduled
      sptr   : pointer to the student involved (may be nil)
      evtime   : time that event is to be scheduled

exit conditions:
      the event is inserted into the calendar list, preserving the ordering by time field.
}

```
procedure schedule(var calendar : eventptr; evtype : eventclass;
        sptr : studentptr; evtime : real);
var
    done        : boolean;     { true when searching should stop }
    eventp      : eventptr;    { temporary for node creation }
    oldp        : eventptr;    { temporary used for calendar search }
    p           : eventptr;    { temporary used for calendar search }
begin
    { first build a new event node with the proper values }
    new(eventp);
    with eventp ↑ do
    begin
        eventtype := evtype;
        eventtime := evtime;
        studptr := sptr
    end; { of with }
```

FIGURE 15.13 (*Continued*)

```
{ now see where this new node should be placed on the calendar and reset the
  links }
p := calendar;
if p <> nil then
begin
    if p↑.eventtime <= evtime then { we must search through the list }
    begin
        repeat
            oldp := p;
            p := p↑.link;

            { see if we are done without doing a nil pointer reference }
            if p <> nil then done := (p↑.eventtime > evtime)
            else done := true
        until done;

        { now insert the new item }
        eventp↑.link := p;
        oldp↑.link := eventp
    end { of search and insert new item }
    else
    begin { it goes at the head of the list }
        eventp↑.link := calendar;
        calendar := eventp
    end { of else }
end { of if p <> nil }
else
begin { calendar is empty }
    eventp↑.link := nil;
    calendar := eventp
end { of else empty calendar }
end; { of procedure schedule }

{ getnextevent

Get the next item from the calendar, removing it from the head of the list.

entry conditions:
    calendar      : pointer to the list of 1 or more events

exit conditions:
    calendar      : has had its first event removed
    evtype        : returns the type of the event.
                    if the calendar list was empty, error is returned.
    sptr          : returns a pointer to the student involved
    evtime        : returns the time this event is to take place
}
```

FIGURE 15.13 *(Continued)*

```
procedure getnextevent(var calendar : eventptr; var evtype : eventclass;
    var sptr : studentptr; var evtime : real);
var
    newlink               : eventptr; { temporary used for updating links }
begin
    if calendar <> nil then
    begin
        with calendar ↑ do
        begin
            evtype := eventtype;
            evtime := eventtime;
            sptr := studptr
        end; { of with }

        { now adjust the links and discard that node }
        newlink := calendar ↑ .link;
        dispose(calendar); { dispose is a built-in Pascal procedure }
        calendar := newlink
    end { of if calendar <> nil }
    else evtype := error { calendar empty }
end; { of procedure getnextevent }
```

```
{ random

Get a random number in the specified range from a uniform distribution. This is
a system-dependent routine in that it makes use of the local library routine called
ran.

entry conditions:
        low         : lower bound of range
        high        : upper bound of range

exit conditions:
        the function returns a number on the interval (low,high).
}
```

```
function random (low, high : real) : real;

    { ran is a local library routine which returns a uniform random value in the range
      (0.0,1.0). Check on the availability of this routine at your installation. }
    function ran : real; extern; { a local VAX-11/782 library routine }

begin
    random := ran * (high − low) + low
end; { of function random }
```

FIGURE 15.13 *(Continued)*

{ helplength

Compute the length of the consulting session based on the distribution in Figure 15.9.

entry conditions:
    none

exit conditions:
    time   : set to the length of a consulting session
}

```
procedure helplength(var time : real);
var
    r                       : real;    { a pseudorandom number }
begin
    r := random(0.0,1.0);
    if r <= 0.50 then time := random(0.0,5.0)
    else
    if r <= 0.83 then time := random(5.0,10.0)
    else time := random(10.0,15.0)
    { assume maximum consulting time is 15 minutes }
end; { of procedure helplength }
```

{ uselength

Determine the length of a terminal session based on the distribution in Figure 15.9.

entry conditions:
    none

exit conditions:
    time   : set to the length of a terminal session
}

```
procedure uselength(var time : real);
var
    r                       : real;    { a pseudorandom number }
begin
    r := random(0.0,1.0);
    if r <= 0.25 then time := random(0.0,15.0)
    else
    if r <= 0.80 then time := random(15.0,30.0)
    else
    if r <= 0.98 then time := random(30.0,60.0)
    else time := random(60.0,180.0)
    { assume nobody sits at a terminal for more than three hours }
end; { of procedure uselength }
```

FIGURE 15.13   (*Continued*)

{ needhelp

Determine if a student does or does not go to the consultant based on the distribution shown in Figure 15.9.

entry conditions:
         none

exit conditions:
         exit   : true if the student will go to the consultant, false otherwise.
}

```
procedure needhelp(var exit : boolean);
var
     r                      : real;      { a pseudorandom number }
begin
     r := random(0.0,1.0);
     exit := (r <= 0.70)
end; { of procedure needhelp }
```

{ nextarrival

Determine how long until the next student arrives based on the distribution shown in Figure 15.9.

entry conditions:
         none

exit conditions:
         time   : set to the length of time before the next student arrives.
}

```
procedure nextarrival(var time : real);
var
     r                      : real;      { pseudorandom number }
begin
     r := random(0.0,1.0);
     if r <= 0.12 then time := random(0.0,1.0)
     else
     if r <= 0.36 then time := random(1.0,2.0)
     else
     if r <= 0.71 then time := random(2.0,4.0)
     else
     if r <= 0.91 then time := random(4.0,8.0)
     else
     if r <= 0.98 then time := random(8.0,15.0)
     else time := random(15.0,30.0)
     { assume that the maximum interarrival time is one half hour }
end; { of procedure nextarrival }
```

FIGURE 15.13 *(Continued)*

```
{ enqueue

  Put student p at the end of queue q.

  entry conditions:
          p              : points to the student being placed in line
          q              : points to a queue of 0 or more students

  exit conditions:
          p              : the next field of p is set to nil.
          q              : has had student p put at the end of this queue
}

procedure enqueue (p : studentptr; var q : queue);
begin
    if q.tail <> nil then { queue is not empty }
    begin
        q.tail ↑ .next := p;
        p ↑ .next := nil;
        q.tail := p
    end { of add to nonempty queue }
    else
    begin { queue is empty }
        q.head := p;
        q.tail := p;
        p ↑ .next := nil
    end { of add to empty queue }
end; { of procedure enqueue }

{ dequeue

  Take the first student p from queue q. Abort the entire program if queue is empty.

  entry conditions:
          q              : points to a queue of one or more students

  exit conditions:
          p              : points to the student who was first in line
          q              : has had its first entry removed
}

procedure dequeue(var p : studentptr; var q : queue);
begin
    if q.head <> nil then { there is at least one item in the queue }
    begin
        p := q.head;
```

FIGURE 15.13 (*Continued*)

```
        { now remove that item and reset pointers }
        if p↑ .next <> nil then
            q.head := p↑ .next { remove from list }
        else
        begin { the queue had only one item and is now empty }
            q.head := nil;
            q.tail := nil
        end { of else }
    end { of queue was not empty }
    else halt(' dequeue called with empty queue')
        { This will abort the program if the programmer is careless enough not to
        check if the queue is empty before calling this routine }
end; { procedure takeoffqueue }

{ empty

Determine if queue q has any students left in it.

entry conditions:
        q                 : points to a queue of 0 or more students

exit conditions:
        function returns true if the queue is empty, false otherwise.
}

function empty(q : queue) : boolean;
begin
    empty := (q.head = nil)
end; { of procedure empty }

{ arrival event

Handle a student who just arrived, giving him or her a terminal if one is available or
putting him or her in line if one is not.

entry conditions:
        simstate          : current state of the simulation
        stats             : current statistics

exit conditions:
        simstate          : updated appropriately
        stats             : also updated appropriately
}
```

FIGURE 15.13 *(Continued)*

```
procedure arrivalevent(var simstate : staterec; var stats : statsrec);
var
    newp                : studentptr;      { temporary student pointer }
    t                   : real;            { temporary time for scheduling }
begin
    { just schedule the next arrival event after this one }
    nextarrival(t); { determines interarrival time }

    { schedule next arrival event in t minutes }
    schedule(simstate.calendar,arrival,nil,simstate.clock + t);

    { now create the new student who just arrived and set initial parameters }
    new(newp);
    newp ↑ .timeofarrival := simstate.clock; { when student first walked in }

    { see if there are any terminals free }
    if simstate.ntermsinuse = simstate.nterms then { all busy }
    begin { put student in the terminal queue }
        enqueue(newp,simstate.termqueue);
        newp ↑ .timeinqueue := simstate.clock
    end { of if busy }
    else
    begin { give student one of the free terminals }
        { determine length of this terminal session }
        uselength(t);

        { schedule terminal completion event }
        schedule(simstate.calendar,term,newp,simstate.clock + t);
        simstate.ntermsinuse := simstate.ntermsinuse + 1;
        stats.termcount := stats.termcount + 1;
        stats.totaltermtime := stats.totaltermtime + t
    end; { of else clause }

    stats.totalstudents := stats.totalstudents + 1
end; { of procedure arrivalevent }
```

{ consultant completion event

Take student p away from the consultant and give him or her a terminal if one is open, putting him or her in line if there are none. If anyone is waiting, that person will now be allowed to see the consultant.

```
entry conditions:
        p            : points to student who is done being helped
        simstate     : current state of the simulation
        stats        : accumulated statistics
```

FIGURE 15.13 (*Continued*)

```
exit conditions:
        simstate        : updated appropriately
        stats           : updated appropriately
}

procedure consultevent(p : studentptr; var simstate : staterec;
        var stats : statsrec);
var
        newp            : studentptr;       { temporary student pointer }
        t               : real;             { temporary time for scheduling }
begin
        { first put the student who is finished with the consultant back in line for a
          terminal }
        if simstate.ntermsinuse = simstate.nterms then { must wait }
        begin
                enqueue(p,simstate.termqueue);
                p ↑ .timeinqueue := simstate.clock
        end { of if terminals full }
        else
        begin { give student a terminal }
                uselength(t); { determine length of terminal session }
                schedule(simstate.calendar,term,p,simstate.clock + t);
                simstate.ntermsinuse := simstate.ntermsinuse + 1;
                stats.termcount := stats.termcount + 1;
                stats.totaltermtime := stats.totaltermtime + t
        end; { of else get an open terminal }

        { now see if anybody else wants to talk to the consultant }
        if empty(simstate.consultqueue) then { nobody is waiting }
                simstate.helperbusy := false
        else
        begin { somebody wants to see the consultant }
                dequeue(newp,simstate.consultqueue);

                { collect statistics about this person's wait in line }
                stats.consultwait := stats.consultwait + (simstate.clock −
                        newp ↑ .timeinqueue);
                stats.consultcount := stats.consultcount + 1;

                { schedule completion event of consultant }
                helplength(t);
                schedule(simstate.calendar,consult,newp,simstate.clock + t);
                stats.totalconsulttime := stats.totalconsulttime + t
        end
end; { of procedure consultevent }
```

FIGURE 15.13 *(Continued)*

{ errorhandler

Handle an error by halting the program. In future versions of the program we might try to recover from the error.

entry conditions:
    none

exit conditions:
    the program will be halted
}

procedure errorhandler;
begin
    writeln(' *** Fatal error -- we encountered an empty calendar.');
    writeln(' *** Dump followed by a system halt');
    halt(' empty calendar')
end; { of procedure errorhandler }

{ terminal completion event

Remove student p from the terminal. If he or she needs help, send him or her to the consultant. If anyone is waiting for a terminal, it will be given to the first person in line.

entry conditions:
    p   : points to the student who is done with the terminal
    simstate   : current state of the simulation
    stats   : accumulated statistics

exit conditions:
    p   : will either leave the room or go to the consultant
    simstate   : will be updated appropriately
    stats   : will be updated appropriately
}

procedure termevent(p : studentptr; **var** simstate : staterec;
    var stats : statsrec);
var
    leaving   : boolean;   { true if a student is going to leave the room,
                                    false if he or she is going to the consultant }
    newp   : studentptr; { temporary student pointer }
    t   : real;   { temporary time for scheduling }
begin
    { determine whether this student needs help or will leave the room }
    needhelp(leaving);
    if leaving **then** { collect statistics about this student }

FIGURE 15.13   *(Continued)*

```
    begin
        stats.finished := stats.finished + 1;
        stats.totaltime := stats totaltime + (simstate.clock − p↑.timeofarrival);
        dispose(p) { say goodbye to student }
    end { of if leaving }
    else
    begin { he or she is going to the consultant }
        if simstate.helperbusy then { wait in line }
        begin
            enqueue(p,simstate.consultqueue);
            p↑.timeinqueue := simstate.clock
        end { of if helperbusy }
        else
        begin { consultant is available }
            simstate.helperbusy := true;
            helplength(t); { determine length of consultation }
            schedule(simstate.calendar,consult,p,simstate.clock + t);
            stats.consultcount := stats.consultcount + 1;
            stats.totalconsulttime := stats.totalconsulttime + t
        end { of else helper not busy }
    end; { of else person goes to consultant }

    { now see if anybody else wants the terminal just freed }
    if empty(simstate.termqueue) then
        simstate.ntermsinuse := simstate.ntermsinuse − 1
    else
    begin
        dequeue(newp,simstate.termqueue); { get next person from queue }
        { determine how long this person waited, adding it to total }
        stats.termwait := stats.termwait + (simstate.clock −
            newp↑.timeinqueue);
        stats.termcount := stats.termcount + 1;
        uselength(t); { determine length of terminal session }

        { schedule terminal completion }
        schedule(simstate.calendar,term,newp,simstate.clock + t);
        stats.totaltermtime := stats.totaltermtime + t
    end
end; { of procedure termevent }

{ initialize

Initialize the state of the simulation and zero out statistics.

entry conditions:
        none
```

FIGURE 15.13 *(Continued)*

```
exit conditions:
        simstate        : all fields are initialized except nterms and
                          maxtime which have been read from input
        stats           : all fields are set to zero
}

procedure initialize(var simstate : staterec; var stats : statsrec);

begin
    with simstate do
    begin
        clock := 0.0;
        { put first arrival event on the calendar for time 0.0 }
        calendar := nil;
        schedule(calendar,arrival,nil,0.0);
        { set the queues to be empty }
        termqueue.head := nil;
        termqueue.tail := nil;
        consultqueue.head := nil;
        consultqueue.tail := nil;
        { initially all terminals are free, and consultant is idle }
        ntermsinuse := 0;
        helperbusy := false
    end; { of with simstate }

    with stats do
    begin { zero all totals used for gathering data }
        consultcount := 0;
        consultwait := 0.0;
        finished := 0;
        termcount := 0;
        termwait := 0.0;
        totalconsulttime := 0.0;
        totalstudents := 0;
        totaltermtime := 0.0;
        totaltime := 0.0
    end { of with stats }
end; { of procedure initialize }

{ reportwriter

Produce the finished report.

entry conditions:
        nterms          : the number of terminals used in the simulation
        duration        : the time in minutes that the simulation ran
        stats           : the record containing all statistical data about the simulation
```

FIGURE 15.13   *(Continued)*

```
 exit conditions:
        the report will be written to output
}

procedure reportwriter(nterms : integer; duration : real; stats : statsrec);
var
      consultpercent       : real;      { consultant utilization level }
      termpercent          : real;      { terminal utilization level }
begin
     writeln;
     writeln;
     writeln(' Results of the simulation run');
     writeln(nterms:8,' terminals were available');
     writeln(duration:8:2,' minutes simulation time');
     with stats do
     begin
         writeln(totalstudents:8,' students entered the terminal room');
         writeln(finished:8,' students exited during the simulation');
         if termcount > 0 then
             writeln(termwait / termcount :8:2,' average minutes (per student)',
                   ' spent waiting for a terminal')
         else writeln(' ':8,' No terminals were used');

         if consultcount > 0 then
             writeln(consultwait / consultcount :8:2,' average minutes',
                   ' (per student) spent waiting for the consultant')
         else writeln(' ':8,' Nobody saw the consultant');

         if finished > 0 then
             writeln(totaltime / finished :8:2,' average minutes (per student)',
                   ' spent in the terminal room');

         { Compute the fraction of usage of the terminals and consultant recall that
           zero length simulations cannot be requested }
         termpercent := (totaltermtime * 100.0) / (nterms * duration);
         consultpercent := (totalconsulttime * 100.0) / duration
     end; { of with stats }

     { It is possible to get terminal or consultant utilizations beyond 100% because we
       tally the last few sessions even though they may extend past closing time.
       To avoid confusing the reader, these values will be reset to 100. }
     if termpercent > 100.0 then termpercent := 100.0;
     if consultpercent > 100.0 then consultpercent := 100.0;

     writeln(termpercent:8:1,' percent usage made of all terminals');
     writeln(consultpercent:8:1,' percent usage made of the consultant')
end; { of procedure reportwriter }
```

FIGURE 15.13 *(Continued)*

{ everybodyout

It is closing time so all students will be asked to leave, freeing space to be used for the next simulation. This procedure disposes of all the space allocated to this program.

entry conditions:

calendar	: points to a list of 0 or more events
consultqueue	: points to a queue of 0 or more students
termqueue	: points to a queue of 0 or more students

exit conditions:
  all nodes remaining in the above lists are returned to available storage by disposing them, and the pointers are set to nil.
}

procedure everybodyout(**var** calendar : eventptr; **var** consultqueue : queue;
    var termqueue : queue);
var
    evptr   : eventptr;   { used to scan calendar }

    { escortq

    Quietly escort those still waiting in line to the nearest exit!

    entry conditions:
        q   : points to a queue of 0 or more students   }

    procedure escortq(**var** q : queue);
    var
            studentp   : studentptr;   { the current deadbeat }
    begin
        while not empty(q) **do**
        begin
            dequeue(studentp,q);
            dispose(studentp)
        end; { of while loop to remove a student }
    end; { of procedure escortq }

begin { procedure everybodyout }
    while calendar <> **nil do**
    begin
        if calendar ↑ .studptr <> **nil then** dispose(calendar ↑ .studptr);
        evptr := calendar ↑ .link;
        dispose(calendar);
        calendar := evptr
    end; { of while loop emptying calendar }

FIGURE 15.13 *(Continued)*

```
        escortq(consultqueue);
        escortq(termqueue)
end; { of procedure everybodyout }

begin { program simulator }
    writeln(' Welcome to the terminal room simulator version ',version);

    repeat
        repeat
            writeln(' Please enter values for the number of terminals,');
            writeln(' and the total simulation time in minutes:');
            readln; { get user response }
            read(simstate.nterms,simstate.maxtime);

            if (simstate.nterms >= 1) and (simstate.maxtime > 0.0) then
            begin
                gooddata := true
            end
            else
            begin
                gooddata := false;
                writeln(' *** You made an error in the input. The number of terminals
                    must be >= 1');
                writeln(' *** and the time must be real and nonnegative.');
                writeln(' *** Please try again.')
            end { of else }
        until gooddata;

        initialize(simstate,stats); { put the first event on the calendar and
            clear all queues }

        { now we run the simulator for as long as the user specified }
        while (simstate.clock <= simstate.maxtime) do
        begin
            getnextevent(simstate.calendar,eventtype,p,eventtime);
            simstate.clock := eventtime;

            { now simply call the appropriate routine for this event type }
            case eventtype of
                arrival : arrivalevent(simstate,stats); { process arrival event }
                consult : consultevent(p,simstate,stats); { consultant completion }
                error : errorhandler; { something bad happened }
                term : termevent(p,simstate,stats) { terminal completion }
            end { of case }
        end; { of while loop to handle one complete simulation }
```

FIGURE 15.13   *(Continued)*

```
        { We have finished one run. Produce the results and see if the user wants to try
          again }
        with simstate do
              everybodyout(calendar,consultqueue,termqueue);
        reportwriter(simstate.nterms,simstate.clock,stats);

        writeln(' Do you wish to run the simulation again for a different');
        writeln(' number of terminals or time value ? y(es) or n(o)');
        readln;
        read(response); { we will read only the first character }
        done := (response = 'n')
      until done;

      { We will go through the above repeat loop as many times as the user wants. We
        will exit here only when he or she is completely finished }
      writeln(' Exiting from the simulator program. Thank you')
end. { of program simulation }
```

In the next part of the text we will begin to focus on the details of program *implementation,* getting large complex software products, like this simulator, to work correctly and efficiently. In that part we will study the programming steps that must be carried out *after* the code has been written, including

    Debugging
    Testing
    Verification
    Benchmarking (efficiency studies)
    Documentation
    Maintenance

Even though we have come a long way in the program development process, our task is still not yet completed!

Exercises for Chapter 15

1.   Write the module specifications for the seven other second-level modules listed on page 414. Follow the module specification guidelines given in Chapter 11.

2.   Write the data dictionary entries for
      a.   Calendar
    *b.   Terminal queue
      c.   Consult queue

Follow the data dictionary specification given in Chapter 11.

3.   Redraw the simple tree diagram of Figure 15.6 into a formal structure chart using the notation of Figure 11.4.

*4.   We chose a linked list technique for implementing the calendar data structure. What would be the advantages/disadvantages of using an array structure such as the following to implement the calendar?

type
    calendar = **array** [1 . . maxsize] **of** event;

Rewrite the two routines schedule and getnextevent to utilize this new internal implementation. Were any other modules affected by this change?

5.   We chose a linked list technique for implementing the queue data structure. What would be the advantages/disadvantages of using the following record structure to implement our two queues?

type
    queue   = **record**
        line   : **array** [1 . . maxqueue] **of** student;
        front   :0 . . maxqueue;
        back   :0 . . maxqueue
        end; { queue record }

Rewrite the routines Enqueue, Dequeue, and Empty to utilize this new internal implementation. Were any other modules affected by this change?

6.   Comment on how the routine Dequeue does or does not meet the criterion of graceful degradation and helpfulness as discussed in Section 15.2.4. If you feel that it is not well designed, suggest improvements that could be made.

7.   Comment on how the following four statistical routines do or do not meet the guidelines for module generality as discussed in Section 15.4:

    Helplength
    Uselength
    Needhelp
    Nextarrival

If you feel that they are not well designed, suggest improvements that could be made.

8.   Comment on how the routine initialize does or does not meet the criterion of logical coherence as discussed in Section 12.2. If you feel that it is not well designed, suggest improvements that could be made.

9.   Review the entire design of the simulator program contained in Figure 15.13. Using the module guidelines presented in Chapter 12, discuss the good and bad points of the overall design of that program. Suggest changes that you think would improve the overall design. Would you have approached the problem in a significantly different way?

10. Rewrite the terminal room simulator developed in this chapter so it correctly handles the following changes.

    a.   Instead of allowing only one consultant, users may specify a value for n, the number of consultants to be used in the simulation.

    b.   Instead of having a single queue of people waiting for terminals, set up three separate queues with the following priority:

Faculty	(highest priority)
Graduate students	↓
Undergraduates	(lowest priority)

The queueing discipline is always to take a person from the highest-priority queue before taking one from a lower-priority queue. Within a queue the priority is still FCFS. The simulator should produce the average waiting time for each of the preceding three classes.

    c.   The average arrival intervals, average service time, and average consulting times should not be given explicitly by a table such as those in Figure 15.12 but should be assumed to be exponentially distributed with values $1/n_1$, $1/n_2$, and $1/n_3$, respectively. The values of n_1, n_2, and n_3 are input to the simulator. You may assume that there is a function to generate exponentially distributed random numbers of the form:

function exprandom (lambda : real) : real; extern;
{ generate exponentially distributed random numbers with expected value lambda }

After a change has been implemented, discuss how the overall design of the program did or did not facilitate making the desired change. Did any modules other than the ones being modified require changes? Did you encounter the "ripple effect" when making any changes?

11. Write a program that uses discrete event simulation to determine the optimum number, n, of elevators in a building of k stories. The input should consist of the average arrival rate of people to the elevator for each of the k floors, their destination (a value $1, \ldots, k$), and the capacity, c, of each elevator. Generate a table of average waiting times for an elevator as a function of n. (Assume k and c are fixed quantities that cannot be changed by the user.) Determine the value of n so that the average waiting time for an elevator is less than 1 minute.

    When coding the program, follow the implementation guidelines presented in this chapter. Develop the program as a series of independent, logically coherent modules without side effects.

The following projects are all quite large and intended not for individuals but as *team assignments* in groups of two to four students. The projects could involve only the design document or, if sufficient time is available, both the full design and implementation.

After the project has been completed, write a report that discusses the following points:

A. How much time was spent by the group on each phase of the programming project: specification, design, coding, debugging, testing? How does this division of time compare with the way you utilized your time on smaller programs written in introductory classes?

B. Discuss your design in terms of coherence, independence, modularity, robustness, generality, user-friendliness, and overall maintainability.

C. What difficulties were encountered in working on a problem with a group of one to three other individuals rather than alone? Discuss what problems you had in effectively organizing and utilizing the available manpower, scheduling meetings, managing personality and ability differences, orally communicating with each other, and trying to coordinate and integrate the work of two to four individuals into a single piece. How might you do things differently in your next group effort?

12. Develop a program to do *text formatting*. The input will consist of text lines, intermixed with formatting commands.

```
.l n    set the left margin to column n
.r n    set the right margin to column n
.p      terminate the current line and begin a new paragraph
.s n    skip n blank lines
```

The output of the program should be the input text printed with left and right margins aligned according to the formatting commands. For example, the following input:

```
.l 1
.r 10
Now is the time
for all good men
.s 1
Anonymous
```

should produce this output:

```
Now is      the
time        for
all     good
men.

Anonymous
```

Set up your program so that new commands can be added easily later. After your text formatter is working properly for the preceding four commands, think about what other commands might be useful in the preparation of pleasing text. Add these new commands to the next formatter.

13. Write a program that finds its way through a maze (**program** rat?). The program should read in an n-by-n matrix containing the values 0, 1, and 2: 1 represents a wall that cannot be penetrated, 0 represents open space, and 2 represents the goal to be reached (a pellet of food, perhaps). The program should then read in the x, y coordinates of the starting position and attempt to find the *shortest* path to the goal. (Assume that there is only a single 2 located in the maze.)

For example, in the following maze:

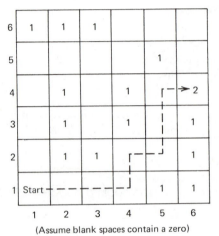

(Assume blank spaces contain a zero)

if the starting point were (1,1) then the output would be the path indicated by the dotted line

$$(1,1) \rightarrow (1,2) \rightarrow (1,3) \rightarrow \ldots \rightarrow (4,6)$$

Your program should be careful about the following situations:
  a. Going off the edge of the maze.
  b. Going around in an infinite circle [i.e., $(1,1) \rightarrow (1,2) \rightarrow (2,2) \rightarrow (2,1) \rightarrow (1,1)$ etc.].
  c. Trying hopelessly to find a path where none exists.

14. Develop a program to produce a *cross-reference table* of a Pascal program. A cross-reference table is a list of every user-defined identifier (type name, variable, constant, module name, etc.) appearing in the program along with every line on which it occurred. The list should be alphabetized and, if a name appears more than once on a line (e.g., $n := n + 1$), there should only be one reference to it. Finally, the letter "d" (for defined) should be appended to those line numbers in which a name is being assigned a value (e.g., read in, **const**, left side of an assignment operator, **for** loop control variable). Two other rules to follow in producing the cross-reference table are

a.   Do not include reserved words such as **begin**, **end**, and **if**. However, do include standard identifiers.

b.   Do not include names appearing within comments.

The output of your program should look something like this:

Name	References
amount	15, 31, 32, 50d, 160
bill	22, 23d
bundle	1, 2, 11d, 15d, 308
.	.
.	.
.	.

For input data, try running the cross-referencing program on itself!

15.   Develop a system that will allow you to do *plotting* on a line printer. The plotting should be done *vertically* on the page so that the plot can be as long as desired. For example, $y = \sin(x)$ might look like this:

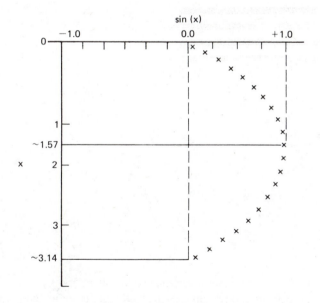

The input to your system will be a function $f(x)$ and a set of limits a, $b (b > a)$. Your system should plot the value of $f(x)$ from a to b. You should scale the horizontal axis so that all function values will fit on the page properly. You should also scale the vertical axis so the overall plot takes no more than 200 lines, or about four pages. That is, the step size on x should be no more than $(b - a)/200$. Other features you may want to include are

a.   The ability to plot more than one curve on a single graph.

b. The ability to let users set certain system values, such as the plotting character (x in the preceding example) and the width of the output device in
columns.

Be sure to handle the special case of a function that becomes *undefined* at a point x,
$a < x < b$. The plot should be able to be continued past point x.

16. Write a program that simulates the behavior of a *hand-held calculator*. The
program will interactively accept commands in two forms.

expression
variable ← expression

In the first case, the program will simply print out the value of the expression. In the
second case it will assign the variable the value of the expression. The syntax of
the expressions will follow the same rules as in Pascal, although you may change the
precedence rules for determining the order of evaluation of operators if desired. For
example, the following might be a typical dialogue with such a program. (The output
from the program is set in boldface type.)

```
    3 + 3
6
    a ← 1
    a + 3
4
    b ← 2
    a + (b * 2)
5
    50 div (a + 14)
3
    1 div 0
error
    1 + (2 + (3 + (4 + (5 + (6)))))
21
    b ← 3
    b
3
```

Initially begin with just the integer data type and the operators $+$, $-$, $*$, **div**, **mod**, and
( ). Then, if time permits, allow some of the following to be included in your expressions:

a. Standard functions.
b. Real data type and the / operator.
c. The boolean data type and the **and**, **or**, and **not** operators.
d. The character data type.
e. Some operators that do not exist in Pascal, such as ↑ (exponentiation) and
xor (exclusive-**or**).

17.   Write a program to simulate the playing of the game called *blackjack,* also called *twenty-one.* (If you do not know the rules, look in any good book of games.) The game should be played between a dealer and from one to *n* players. Each player should be able to bet from one to *m* chips against the dealer on each hand. The game should be played using a single deck of cards.

type
    cards = **record**
                rank : 1 . . 13;
                suit   : (spades,hearts,diamonds,clubs)
          end;

    deck = **array** [1 . . 52] **of** cards;

You should shuffle the deck, place your bets, and deal out the cards to the dealer and all the players according to the rules. Continue to play until you determine whether each player has won or lost. This constitutes a round. Have your program play some number, *k,* of rounds and then print out how much each player has won or lost and how much the house (the dealer) has won or lost. Determine what the advantage to the house is in the game of blackjack.

    Also try different types of betting and playing strategies to see if you can reduce the house advantage or even turn the advantage to the players against the house.

18.   Write a set of procedures to do *infinite precision arithmetic.* In infinite precision computations, each digit or character is individually stored in a separate position of an array. Thus, the quantities 53 and 12.56 would be stored as follows:

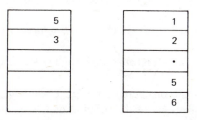

and the result of adding them together would be as follows:

6
5
.
5
6

Therefore, the only limit to the size of our numbers is the size of our arrays. This will usually allow numbers with thousands of digits and virtually ''infinite'' accuracy.

Write a set of procedures to do the following operations.

    a.   Read a real or integer number of arbitrary length into the preceding array representation. The value may occupy one or more lines of output and is terminated by the first blank.

    b.   Validate that the number just read in is syntactically valid in that it contains only the characters $+$, $-$, $.$, and $0 . . 9$ and follows the syntax rules for integers and reals of standard Pascal.

    c.   Write procedures to add and subtract two infinite precision values.

    d.   Output a value in infinite precision representation. The value may occupy one or more lines in the output file.

Try out your procedures with the following values:

π = 3.14159265358979323846264338327950288841972
e = 2.718281828459045235360287 4

and print out the values of 2π, $\pi + e$, $\pi - e$, and $e - \pi$.

Bibliography for Part Two

Aron, J. *The Program Development Process*. Reading, Mass.: Addison-Wesley, 1974.

Baker, F. T. Chief programmer teams. *Datamation*, Vol. 19, No. 12, December 1973.

Brooks, F. P. *The Mythical Man-Month: Essays in Software Engineering*. Reading, Mass.: Addison-Wesley, 1975.

Cassel, D. *The Structured Alternative: Program Design, Style, and Debugging*. Reston, 1983.

Dahl, O., E. Dijkstra, and C. A. R. Hoare. *Structured Programming*. New York: Academic Press, 1972.

Dijkstra, E. *A Discipline of Programming*. Englewood Cliffs, N.J.: Prentice-Hall, 1976.

Dijkstra, E. *Goto* statement considered harmful. *Communications of the ACM*, Vol. 11, No. 3, March 1968. (One of the original papers on structured coding.)

Fairley, R., *Software Engineering Concepts*. New York: McGraw-Hill, 1985.

Freeman, P., and A. Wasserman. *Tutorial on Software Design Techniques*, 3rd ed. IEEE Publications (Catalog No. EHO-161-0), IEEE Computer Society, 1980.

Gilbert, P. *Software Design and Development*. SRA, 1983.

Hughes, R., and M. Michtom. *A Structured Approach to Programming*. Englewood Cliffs, N.J.: Prentice-Hall, 1977.

Jackson, M. *System Design*. Englewood Cliffs, N.J.: Prentice-Hall, 1983.

Knuth, D. Structured programming with *Goto* statements. *ACM Computing Surveys*, Vol. 6, 1974.

McGowan, C., and J. Kelly. *Top-Down Structured Programming Techniques*. New York: Petrocelli, 1975.

Page-Jones, M. *The Practical Guide to Structured System Design*. Yourdon Press, 1980.

Shooman, M. L. *Software Engineering*. New York: McGraw-Hill, 1983.

Stevens, W., *Using Structured Design: How to Make Programs Simple, Changeable, Flexible, and Reusable*. New York: Wiley-Interscience, 1981.

Weinberg, V. *Structured Program Analysis*. Englewood Cliffs, N.J.: Prentice-Hall, 1979.

Wirth, N. *Algorithms + Data Structures = Programs*. Englewood Cliffs, N.J.: Prentice-Hall, 1976.

Yourdin, E., and L. Constantine. *Structured Design: Fundamentals of a Discipline of Computer Programming and Systems Design*. Englewood Cliffs, N.J.: Prentice-Hall, 1979.

PART THREE

PROGRAM
IMPLEMENTATION
CONCERNS

CHAPTER 16

DEBUGGING, TESTING, AND FORMAL VERIFICATION

16.1
Introduction

In this section of the text we begin our study of the issues concerned with *program implementation*—getting code such as the simulation program of Figure 15.13 working correctly. *Correctness,* as it relates to program implementation, is most definitely not a two-step process in which a program is "not correct," some operations are performed on it, and it suddenly becomes "correct." Rather, program correctness should be viewed as a multistage process with the program traversing a number of levels of partial correctness or partial reliability. At each stage, the program is displaying more reasonable behavior and becoming more reliable, but it is not yet totally correct. The eight levels shown in Figure 16.1, numbered 0 to 7, are typical of the stages (called *levels of reliability*) that a program goes through during the implementation phase.

As we begin the implementation phase we are at level 0. We have a program module that has been coded in some high-level programming language, and that we claim will behave exactly as described in the module specifications of the program design document. The *debugging phase* is concerned with getting us to reliability level 4, in which the program displays some amount, however small, of correct behavior and no error conditions are observed. The *testing phase* is designed to get us to reliability level 6, in which the program produces correct answers for a great number of carefully selected test cases and can be said to be *empirically* or *observably correct.* Finally, *formal verification* methods allow us to proceed to level 7 and make the strongest claim of all—that the program is *provably correct,* namely, that for every combination of inputs $x_1, x_2, \ldots, x_n$ the program P will produce the result $y = P(x_1, x_2, \ldots, x_n)$, where y is the value stated in the specification document.

473

FIGURE 16.1   Levels of Reliability of a Computer Program.

Stage	Level of Reliability
0	The program module is coded in a high-level programming language but has not yet been run on a computer.
1	The program module does not compile correctly and produces one or more syntax errors.
2	The program module compiles correctly, begins execution, but terminates abnormally with a fatal run-time error.
3	The program module compiles correctly, executes through to normal termination, but produces incorrect results.
4	The program module produces correct results for one (or a small number of) test case(s).
5	The program module produces correct results for a very large number of valid pieces of test data.
6	The program module produces correct results for a very large number of valid, extremal, and invalid pieces of test data.
7	The program module produces correct results for every possible combination of input data.

In this chapter we will discuss in detail these three phases of program implementation: debugging, testing, and verification.

16.2
Debugging

Debugging is the process of locating and correcting errors in a program in the presence of explicit and demonstrated incorrect behavior. That is, during debugging we have evidence of the presence of an error and our task is to find and remove it.

Debugging can be painfully slow unless proper guidelines are followed from the outset of the coding phase. Studies of the time required to implement large programs indicate that sometimes *more than half* of a programmer's time is spent finding and correcting errors. Although we do not claim that following our guidelines will result in error-free programs, we do believe it will significantly decrease the amount of time spent debugging.

Sometimes bugs are so deeply ingrained in a program that frustrated programmers despair of ever finding and correcting them. Instead, they incorporate into the documentation of the program methods to avoid these bugs. In extreme cases programmers have decided to rewrite entire programs from scratch because a bug could not be corrected effectively or economically. These costly mistakes can and should be avoided.

There are three primary reasons that debugging is so time-consuming. First, many programmers honestly believe they can write error-free code that will work properly the first time and therefore do not prepare for the occurrence of bugs during the early stages of coding. This is a myth, albeit a seductive one. Even with the most careful programming, coding errors are inevitable. The best way to find these bugs is to include appropriate tools, such as well-placed write statements, in strategic places throughout the code as you develop the program. When the program is executed, you will be able to follow exactly what is happening and determine why things go awry. Debugging is not something that begins after the coding phase has been completed. Rather it is something you plan for from the earliest stages of specification and design.

Second, debugging is considerably easier if the program is clearly written. We have consistently emphasized the importance of style and clarity of expression. Programs with complex, intricate, and "jumpy" logic are difficult not only to read but also to debug. (Figure 12.6 should have convinced you of that.) For example, see how long it takes you to locate and fix the bug(s) in the following program fragment. [The purpose of the fragment was to find a key in a list of integers and to write out the index (location) of the first occurrence of the key in the list.]

```pascal
label
      10,20;
const
      listsize    = 20;
var
      i            : 1 .. listsize;
      key          : integer;
      list         : array [1 .. listsize] of integer;
      temp         : 1 .. listsize;
begin
      { initialize all elements of the array list }
      .
      .
      .
      key := 5; i := 1;
10:if list[i] = key then begin
          temp := i; goto 20
      end else begin
      i := i + 1; if i = listsize then goto 20; goto 10 end;
20:writeln(' the key ',key,' was found in the ',
             'list at location ',temp);
      .
      .
      .
```

There are two bugs in this program segment: (1) it will not work if the key does not appear in the list—in which case temp is undefined and (2) it will not find the key if it is the last item in the array list. Program segments like this are difficult to debug because of their cumbersome style and structure.

When programs contain hundreds or thousands of lines of code, it becomes extremely difficult, if not impossible, to follow the flow of control. Using too many **goto** statements creates more logical paths than the mind can follow. It is much easier to locate bugs when control structures and systematic indentation delineate the control paths. For example, consider the previous program segment coded instead with a **while** statement, which corrects the first error listed above but leaves in the second.

```
{ declarations and initializations }

found := false;
key := 5;
i := 1;
while (i <> listsize) and (not found) do
    if list[i] = key then
        found := true
    else
        i := i + 1;
if found then
    writeln(' the key ',key,' was found in the ',
        ' list at location ',i);
```

Now it is easier to find the remaining bug because the flow of control in the program is made obvious by the **while** statement. The style and structured coding conventions of Chapters 13 and 14 represent some of the most powerful debugging tools available to a programmer. By increasing the legibility and readability of a module, and by clarifying the program structure and flow of control, they make it easy to spot and eliminate errors during the coding phase. Thus, they are prevented from ever having the chance to corrupt your program. One of the most important things to remember about debugging is

> The best debugging tool in the world is the *avoidance* of bugs from the beginning. The easiest bug to correct is the one that never got into your program in the first place.

Much of our earlier discussions on program style and structure can now be seen as information directed at simplifying the debugging task.

The third main reason that debugging is so problematic is that it has not been taught systematically, as have other aspects of programming. Most introductory programming classes include an extensive discussion on algorithms and their formal properties. Similarly, coding techniques and language syntax issues are usually presented in a well-organized sequence and include such formalized concepts as problem-solving techniques, pseudocode, flowcharts, and syntax diagrams. Debugging, however, is often taught in a haphazard manner, if at all. Students rarely received formal instruction about exactly what sequence of operations to perform when their programs fail. This can have especially frustrating consequences when there are no error messages or other clues about what went wrong.

Our objective in this section is to classify the approaches to debugging so that you will have a logical, organized method for dealing with any errors you encounter. The following sections treat syntax errors, run-time errors, and logic errors.

Before we cover these topics, we will mention one approach to debugging that is habit forming and *wrong:* trying something mindlessly because you do not know what else to do. We are all guilty of fixing the first bug we think we see and quickly resubmitting the program. Rushing through the program and trying quick fixes makes the program needlessly confusing and seldom corrects the original errors. Bugs can be tracked down in a logical manner. It makes no sense to change or rerun a program until you have spotted the cause of the error and determined the proper correction to make.

One final comment: ignore any suggestion to rerun a program without change because the problem may have been a "machine error." Such errors are rare. It might be comforting to blame the machine, but it is almost always a waste of time.

16.2.1 Syntax Errors

A *syntax error* is any violation of the syntactic rules of the language. Syntax errors are very common and relatively easy to correct. For example, in Pascal there are two possible ways to write an **if** statement. Their syntax is

if boolean expression **then** statement

or

if boolean expression **then** statement **else** statement

The expression placed between the **if** and the **then** must evaluate to either true or false (a type boolean result). The statement may be any legal Pascal statement (including another **if** statement). If two or more statements appear after the **then** or the **else**, they must be surrounded by a **begin/end** pair. All of the following are examples of violations of these syntactic rules:

```
var
    a     : boolean;
    b     : boolean;
    c     : real;
    d     : real;
begin
    .
    .
    .
    if a then writeln(' a is true');
    else writeln(' a is false')
        { misplaced semicolon }
    .
    .
    .
```

If a **and** b **then** c := 10; d := 5 **else** c := 7
    { 2 statements placed where only 1 is allowed }

.

.

.

If c + d **then** writeln(' c + d = ',c + d)
    { real expression used instead of boolean expression }

.

.

.

end.

Syntax errors are easier to correct than other errors because they often result in a helpful error message from the compiler when it translates the program into machine language. The compiler usually produces messages indicating where and what the mistakes may be.

Figure 16.2 is a listing of a Pascal program containing numerous syntax errors. It shows how errors are printed in one particular Pascal system. You may be using a Pascal compiler that prints error messages in a different manner, but the information should be comparable.

Figure 16.2 highlights most of the important points to consider when locating and correcting syntax errors.

1. Some of the error messages provided by Pascal are quite clear and point directly to the source of the error. For example, error message 55 appearing after line 10 says, " 'to' or 'downto' expected." Recalling the syntax of the **for** statement:

   for v := initial-value **to** (or **downto**) final-value **do** statement

   it should be clear that we have neither a **to** nor a **downto** in line 10. Error message 104 ("identifier not declared") occurs every time the variable found appears in the program. The problem is that the variable found has been misspelled in the variable declaration (we typed a zero instead of the letter "oh").

2. Unfortunately, many error messages produced by the compiler are not as clear and as easy to understand. This is because the error has masked our intentions and prevented the compiler from determining what type of statement we wanted. Some messages tell us nothing more than that an error exists. For example, on line 15, error message 6 ("unexpected symbol") is pointing at the reserved word **else**, which is actually legal, but not in this context. To determine what is wrong, we should first compare, element by element, the statement in question with the syntax of a statement of that type (an **if** statement). Usually this will lead us directly to the error. Here the problem is that we put a semicolon before the **else**. (Recall that semicolons in Pascal are used only to separate statements from each other.)

   Line 19 of Figure 16.2 contains the cryptic phrase "incomplete program." Can

FIGURE 16.2   Sample Pascal Program with Syntax Errors.

```
 1   program find(input,output);
 2   const
 3        listsize     = 20;
 4   var
 5        f0und       : boolean;
 6        i           : integer;
 7        key         : integer;
 8        list        : array [1 .. listsize] of integer;
 9   begin
10        for i := 1 , listsize do list[i] := i;
***                      ↑6      ↑55
11        found := false;
***             ↑104
12        key := 5;
13        i := 1;
14        while (i <= listsize) and (not found) do
***                                      ↑104 ↑135
15            if list[i] = key then found := true; else i := i + 1;
***                               ↑104             ↑6
16        if found then
***             ↑104
17            writeln(' the key ',key,' was found in the ',
18                    'list at location ',i)
19   end;
***           ↑6
***   incomplete program
```

compiler error message(s):

```
  6   : unexpected symbol.
 55   : 'to' or 'downto' expected.
104   : identifier not declared.
135   : type of operand must be boolean.
```

you spot the syntax error on this line? (Compare the program of Figure 16.2 with the legal structure of a Pascal program shown in Appendix A.)

3. Sometimes error indicators point to statements with no errors. If this occurs, you should check the statement immediately preceding the one supposedly in error. Many syntax errors are the result of incorrectly terminating a statement (omitting a required semicolon).

    If this still does not identify the syntax error, check all other statements or elements related in any way to the one in error. For example, check all the pertinent **var** declarations. Also check for matching comment delimiters, **begin/ end** pairs, **repeat/until** pairs, or **then** and **else** clauses of **if** statements.

For example, if I had an error message pointing at the following (apparently) correct **while** statement:

```
while i < listsize do { compute the sum }
    begin
        sum := sum + X[i];
        i := i + 1
    end
```

I would immediately check the following related structures:
a.   The **var** declarations for *i, listsize, sum,* and *X*.
b.   Matching comment delimiters, to make sure that the ''}'' is not accidentally closing off the wrong comment.
c.   Matching **begin/end** declarations in this unit to make sure that the **end** is not being matched with the wrong **begin**.

4.   There is usually not a one-to-one correspondence between error messages from the compiler and corrections to be made. Often a single error will generate multiple error messages. For example, line 10 has two error messages, but we can correct both at once by changing the comma to the reserved word **to**. Our error in declaring the variable found resulted in four error messages, one each time the variable found was used in the program.

Be aware that many error messages will have already been taken care of by earlier corrections of other syntax errors.

5.   Frequently, the compiler overlooks a syntax error because of the presence of other syntax errors on the same line. Therefore, it may require more than one additional run to eliminate all of them. However, after the second or third run, all original syntax errors should be eliminated from the program unit.

We have now successfully passed level 1 of Figure 16.1 and are ready to tackle level 2.

16.2.2   Run-Time Errors

Even when a program unit is syntactically correct, there is still the possibility of a *run-time error,* which causes abnormal program termination.

In Chapter 14 (Section 14.2.2) we discussed the concept of *defensive programming*—anticipating trouble spots and including statements in our program to guard against them. For example,

If (count <> 0) **and** ((sum **div** count) > minimum) **then** . . .

is syntactically correct. However, if count has the value zero, the program will be terminated during execution due to a division by zero. In the **if** statement, both alternatives are evaluated. To avoid the run-time error, we should instead write

if count $<>$ 0 **then**
    if (sum **div** count) $>$ minimum **then** . . .

Now, the second **if** will not be evaluated if count $=$ 0.
  Other common run-time errors include the following:

1. Using a variable before assigning a value to it.
2. Assigning values outside the prescribed bounds of the declared type of a sub-range variable.
3. Using an index outside the prescribed bounds of the array's lower and upper bound.
4. Failing to ensure that the value of a case expression corresponds to one of the case labels.
5. Passing illegal parameters to standard functions [e.g., $x < 0$ for sqrt(x) or ln(x)].
6. Converting a real number, x, to an integer when round[abs(x)] $>$ maxint.
7. Dividing by 0.
8. Using a set size larger than the implementation-defined maximum.
9. Performing a read or readln when eof is true.
10. Reading a piece of input data whose syntax is improper for the declared data type of the variable in the read list (e.g., a letter within an integer value).

  Run-time errors generally produce an error message and a *postmortem dump,* which help programmers determine what happened. Although the format of this dump may vary from one system to another, it usually includes a message indicating what caused the run-time error, the statement, and program unit in which the error appeared, and the names and current values of all (simple) variables in the main program and any procedures and/or functions activated from the main program.
  The identification of run-time errors is greatly facilitated by the postmortem dump. As an example, consider the program and the dump it produced shown in Figure 16.3.
  By studying the information in the postmortem dump, we can locate the source of the error. The postmortem dump of Figure 16.3 contains two distinct types of informatin that are particularly helpful in this case:

1. *Control information.* This specifies what line we are on, what module we are in, and exactly how we got to this module (i.e., the order of invocation of other modules).
2. *Symbol table.* This specifies the current value of all variables in this module at the point of termination. The information is presented in symbolic terms rather than as memory addresses.

The control information states that we were executing line 20 within the module called init, that is, the following assignment statement:

arrayname[i,j] := i − 1

FIGURE 16.3   Sample Pascal Program with a Run-Time
Error.

```
1   program post(input,output);
2   const
3       lowerbound      = 1;
4       upperbound      = 10;
5   type
6       bounds          = lowerbound .. upperbound;
7       arraytype       = array [bounds,bounds] of bounds;
8   var
9       i               : bounds;
10      j               : bounds;
11      matrix          : arraytype;
12
13  procedure init(var arrayname : arraytype);
14  var
15      i               : bounds;
16      j               : bounds;
17  begin
18      for i := lowerbound to upperbound do
19          for j := lowerbound to upperbound do
20              arrayname[i,j] := i − 1
21  end; { of procedure init }
22
23  begin
24      init(matrix);
25      for i := lowerbound to upperbound do
26      begin
27          for j := lowerbound to upperbound do
28              write(matrix[i,j]:5);
29          writeln
30      end
31  end.
```

program terminated at line 20 in procedure init.
value out of range.

--- init ---

   i =   1   j =   1

init was called from line 24 in program post.

--- post ---

   i =   undef   j =   undef

Looking at the symbol table, we see that, at the time of termination the value of i and j were $i = 1$, $j = 1$, and the formal parameter arrayname has been bound to the argument called matrix. Therefore, the assignment statement on line 20 was trying to perform the following operation:

```
matrix[1,1] := 0
```

Checking the declaration of matrix on lines 7 and 11 reveals, however, that matrix may only contain values in the range [1 . . 10]. This caused the run-time error message "value out of range."

This is generally the procedure to use in correcting a run-time error condition. Use the control information in the postmortem dump to locate the offending statement, and then use the symbol table data to determine the value of all data objects and the time the system attempted to execute the offending statement.

If a postmortem dump does not provide you with sufficient information to locate the error, you may wish to use a powerful debugging tool called a *symbolic debugger*.

A good interactive symbolic debugger would provide all of the information shown in Figure 16.3 and more. For example, the symbolic debugger on the UCSD (University of California—San Diego) Pascal system displays the following information on the screen when this program is executed.

```
value range error
invalid value was 0, outside range of [1 . . 10]
in source line: arrayname[i,j] := i − 1
variables in module init:

    i := 1          j := 1
```

Thus, users have the essential information for diagnosing the problem. After displaying this information, the symbolic debugger prompts users with the following line:

```
dump:  up  top  down  edit  file  quit
```

Users can select one of the listed commands by entering the first letter of the command. The up, top, and down commands are used to traverse the chain of procedure and function calls active at the time of the error. These commands permit users to trace the execution of a program back to the main program, inspecting variables that are local to each procedure or function. The edit and file commands activate the editor or filer program, respectively.

We will have more to say about debugging tools in our discussion in Chapter 18 on programming support environments, but it is important to mention now that on-line debuggers are one of the most important and powerful debugging aids available. If your installation has one, learn how to use it; it could save you a great deal of time, effort, and grief.

The preceding discussion explained how Pascal helps you to recover from abnormal run-time errors. However, it is a poor technique to expect either Pascal or the run-time system to help you recover. You should *prevent* run-time errors in the first place by using the defensive programming techniques introduced in Chapter 14. Generally speaking, the occurrence of a run-time error is usually a sign of a poorly written program.

By preventing run-time errors, we can recover in the program itself and continue processing instead of stopping irrevocably. Looking back at the discussion on graceful degradation in Section 14.2.4, we see that we usually want to try to continue on with useful processing. Complete termination of the program is the *last* option we want to consider. Even if the program does nothing more than write an appropriate error message before stopping, it will usually be easier to determine what went wrong because we will be interpreting our own clear, helpful error message, not some cryptic message printed by the system. This is especially true when the program is used by someone other than the original author.

One of the worst things that can happen to a novice user is to encounter a run-time error that abruptly terminates the program with some technical (and usually incomprehensible) error message:

```
*** program alert
*** memory trap at loc 177560, called from main psw register overflow
777777   pc = 001
```

The user will throw up his or her hands in frustration and vow never to use this program again!

How much nicer to check for these dangerous conditions in your program and print clear, helpful messages yourself, instead of relying on the system.

```
*** Warning. There is an insufficient amount of memory for the program to
     complete the operation you have requested, and the program will be
     terminated. Please call the User Help Hotline at 555-1212 for assistance. ***
```

Certainly much more friendly! Always program so that run-time errors cannot occur.

When all run-time errors have been eliminated, we have reached the third level of reliability listed in Figure 16.1.

16.2.3 Logic Errors

Another kind of error you will almost certainly encounter is the *logic error*. This is an incorrect translation of either the problem statement or the algorithm which causes the program to produce incorrect results. These errors can be extremely difficult to locate, certainly much more difficult than the syntax and run-time errors mentioned so far.

A good example of a logic error is the following translation of the formula for computing the two roots of the quadratic equation in the form

$$ax^2 + bx + c = 0$$

The roots are

$$roots = \frac{-b \pm \sqrt{b^2 - 4ac}}{2a}$$

```
discriminant := sqr(b) − 4.0 * a * c;
if (discriminant >= 0.0) and (a <> 0.0) then
begin
    r1 := −b + sqrt(discriminant) / (2.0 * a);
    r2 := −b − sqrt(discriminant) / (2.0 * a)
end
```

The syntax is correct, but the logic is flawed. The order of evaluation of the operators does not properly translate the quadratic formula. The formula, as written, evaluates the following:

$$roots = -b \pm \frac{\sqrt{b^2 - 4ac}}{2a}$$

This is the typical behavior of a program containing a logic error. It executes through to normal termination but produces wrong answers.

Another example of a logic error is the following Pascal segment that sums the numbers from 1 to 100, inclusive.

```
sum := 0;
i := 1;
repeat
    sum := sum + i;
    i := i + 1
until i >= 100
```

Do you see the error? (What happens when i $=$ 100?)

Both examples demonstrate why logic errors can be difficult to correct. Usually there is no clue as to what went wrong, except that the program produced an incorrect result. The first thing we could do is *hand-simulate* the erroneous program unit—that is, play computer and execute the code ourselves, step by step, using paper and pencil to record the value of all data objects. Hand-simulating a program, also called *code tracing,* may help locate problems, but this can be a very time-consuming process. Unfortunately, hand-simulation often does not uncover the problem either because the program is too complex or the mistake is too subtle. It is very frustrating to spend hours poring over a listing without finding any good reasons for the incorrect results.

The best and simplest way to uncover problems in a program is to use a number of well-placed write statements, preferably included when the program was first written. This technique is called *program tracing.* A convenient method for initially tracing the flow of control in a program is to include write statements as the first and last statements of each procedure. It also helps to write out the values of any procedure parameters on entry and exit. For example,

procedure exchange(**var** p1 : integer; **var** p2 : integer);

```
     .
     .
begin
    if debug then writeln(' exchange entered with p1 = ', p1,' p2 = ' ,p2);
     .
     .
     .
    if debug then writeln(' exchange exited with p1 = ', p1,' p2 = ' ,p2)
end; { of procedure exchange }
```

In this case we assume there is a global boolean flag called *debug* that is set to true whenever we want the computer to perform the trace, and it is set to false when we temporarily do not need this information. This programming technique is a good habit to develop because constantly entering and removing these debugging commands can itself introduce errors into the program. Also, we are never really sure when to remove these commands because we are never sure when new errors may appear. Therefore, leaving them in the program permanently and having them turned on and off by this simple assignment:

debug := true

or

debug := false

can be very useful. This type of built-in debugging aid is frequently called a *debugging instrument* or a *debugging tool*.

By writing out the values of all variables both on procedure entry and exit, we should be able to identify the program unit that is in error through simply seeing whether or not the values going into the procedure were correct but the values coming out were wrong. Our next step in the process is to locate the individual statement(s) within that module that are causing the error.

As discussed in Chapter 13, all well-written Pascal programs and procedures are composed of single-entry, single-exit program segments called blocks. There are no jumps into or out of the middle of a block. Blocks can be nested, but each one must follow the single-entry, single-exit restriction.

When you are searching for an error, the first step is to narrow its location to a specific block. This can be accomplished by initially bracketing a few of the larger outer blocks with write statements. All important variables defined and referenced should be written out before and after the block has executed.

For example,

```
if debug then writeln(. . .);
        begin
            [②
    ① [③
            [④
        end;
if debug then writeln(. . .)
```

If all values are correct going into block 1, but there are errors upon exiting block 1, we have definitely localized the error to block 1. This is because of the single-entry, single-exit characteristic of the block. There is no way to jump into (**goto**) a point in the middle of the block; we must enter through the writeln at the top. Depending on the size of block 1, we might now decide to hand-simulate the code contained in that block, using the evidence produced by the write statements during the tracing operation. If localizing the error to block 1 does not pinpoint the error, we can simply repeat the process by bracketing some of the inner blocks (2, 3, or 4) with writeln commands to see if they are correct. We work our way down, narrowing the possible location of the error to smaller and smaller program segments until we have limited it to such a small area that we can easily spot it by a visual check or hand-simulation.

This ability to approach debugging in an orderly top-down fashion is one of the reasons it is so important to follow the rules of structured coding laid down in Chapter 13.

For example, the procedure in Figure 16.4 was supposed to validate that the n items in the array called X all fell in the range [low . . high]. If any elements fall outside that range, the procedure is to tally them in the variable called badcount and reset that array element to the special indicator value -1. Our first step in checking the correctness of the unit would be to write out the values of X, n, low, and $high$ on procedure entry (line 7.5) and write out the values of X and badcount on procedure exit at line 18.5. Assume that we put in these output commands and got the following results:

```
Entry: X = 5   8   13   9   12
       n = 5
       low = 0   high = 10

Exit: badcount = 0
      X = 5   8   13   9   12
```

We obviously have an error within the program unit since there are two bad values contained in X (13 and 12) but badcount has the value 0. If an inspection of the code does not reveal what the error is, then we should follow the precepts laid down in this section and place output commands within some of the inner program blocks. For example, we could place a writeln on entry to the **then** clause (line 14.5) and upon

FIGURE 16.4   Sample Pascal Program with a Logic Error.

Line

```
 1   procedure validate (var X : arraytype; n : integer;
 2              low,high : integer; var badcount : integer);
 3   const
 4       badindicator = −1;
 5   var
 6       i : integer;
 7   begin
 8       badcount := 0;
 9       i := 0;
10       while (i <= n) do
11           begin
12           i := i + 1;
13           if not (X[i] >= low) and (X[i] <= high) then
14               begin
15               badcount := badcount + 1;
16               X[i] := badindicator
17               end { if }
18           end { while }
19   end; { procedure }
```

completion of the **while** loop (line 17.5). Assume that we do that and get the following output:

```
(Line 17.5) Exit: i = 1   X[1] = 5   badcount = 0
(Line 17.5) Exit: i = 2   X[2] = 8   badcount = 0
(Line 17.5) Exit: i = 3   X[3] = 13 badcount = 0
(Line 17.5) Exit: i = 4   X[4] = 9   badcount = 0
(Line 17.5) Exit: i = 5   X[5] = 12 badcount = 0
```

Comparing what was produced with what we expected shows that the value of *i* is being correctly incremented but badcount is not, and *X* is not being reset. Quite obviously we are not entering the **then** clause on lines 14–17 when we should. This is confirmed by the fact that the write we placed between lines 14 and 15 never produced any output. The error must be in the boolean expression on line 13. A closer check of that statement shows that our precedence was incorrectly expressed. The boolean expression should have been written as

if not ((X[i] >= low) **and** (X[i] <= high)) **then** . . .

or

if (X[i] < low) **or** (X[i] > high) **then** . . .

This example demonstrates the approach you should follow during debugging. Using your knowledge of what the program should do and how it is structured, carefully place a few strategic output commands to collect valuable information. Compare what was produced with what you expected and, in the great majority of cases, you should be led directly to the source of the error.

Two other guidelines should be followed when inserting write statements in a program.

1. Immediately echo-print all input data. Your program may be producing incorrect results not because it is wrong, but because you are inputting bad data. Although some of the debug output statements may eventually be removed or turned off when the program is complete, the echo-print statements should remain. They will associate a particular result with the data set that produced it.

2. Avoid placing output statements in loops that are executed many times. You may be inundated with so much output that meaningful values are buried or overlooked. If a write statement is necessary in a loop, you may consider printing a value every nth iteration.

```
for i := 1 to 5000 do
    begin
    if ((i mod 50) = 0) and debug then writeln(. . . .);
    .
    .
    .
    end { of for }
```

As we mentioned, most Pascal compilers have one built-in debugging aid—the postmortem dump—that activates whenever a program terminates abnormally. An example of the output produced by a postmortem dump was shown in Section 16.2.2. Some versions of Pascal include a *halt* procedure that terminates the program and produces a postmortem dump. Some Pascal compilers allow users to call the postmortem dump facility as a procedure, in which case the program is not terminated. This type of dump is usually called a *snapshot dump* because it gives you a picture of your program at one point in time and then keeps going.

Another useful debugging tool is the *automatic trace* facility available on some systems. In effect, the system automatically inserts write statements after every Pascal statement, producing a complete trace of program execution. Since this may result in excessive output, the system gives users a method of toggling into and out of trace mode with statements such as *trace* (*true*) and *trace* (*false*). We will talk more about these debugging tools in Chapter 18.

When all the logic errors have been located and corrected (at least for this one data set), we will finally see some correct answers. We have now reached level 4 in the reliability index of Figure 16.1, but we are far from done. The fact that we have been able to demonstrate correct behavior for one or two cases is not nearly enough evidence to state that the program is indeed correct and will work properly for all cases. That is part of the next phase of implementation called program testing.

16.3
Program Testing

Program testing (also called *empirical testing*) involves determining the correctness of a program by trying it on a large number of carefully chosen data sets and then seeing if it produces correct answers in all those cases. If it does, we argue that the likelihood of there being an error in the program after all those tests is so small that we can effectively assume the program is correct. Of course, our assumption could be wrong. We may have failed to test a section of the program containing an error; there may be two errors that offset each other; or the error may not have been demonstrated by the particular data sets we chose to use. However, if we are careful, systematic, and thorough in our test procedures and our selection process for test cases, the overwhelming majority of errors in our program will be uncovered and our assumption about correctness will generally be true. Therefore, the most important aspect of program testing is the careful selection of the data sets that will be used to test the program. In the next section we will present a systematic approach to this selection process.

If debugging can be said to be the process of "finding the error you know is there," then testing can be viewed as "finding the error you don't know is there."

16.3.1 Module Testing

In this section we will describe the four classes of testing—functional, extremal, error, and volume—that must be carried out on each individual program unit. In the subsequent section we will describe the testing procedures needed to integrate these separate modules into a correctly functioning whole.

16.3.1.1 Functional Testing   The first group of test cases are designed to test the common, everyday functions of the program unit; that is, we choose legal data values on which the program unit was normally meant to operate. We do not need to choose an enormous number of test cases to carry out functional testing. In fact, too often *quantity* of test data is accepted in place of *quality*. The mere fact that a program works on 500 test runs means nothing if those 500 sets were not chosen carefully. In fact, if all 500 test cases exercised the same logical part of the program, all we would know is that the specific part works. We could not say anything at all about the remainder of the code. Our objective must be to select values that cause the execution of all *flow paths* through the program, where a flow path is defined as a unique execution-time path through a program unit. For example, the following code fragment:

```
S₁
If B then
    begin
    S₂; S₃
    end
else
    S₄;
S₅
```

has two flow paths: s_1, s_2, s_3, s_5 and s_1, s_4, s_5. These independent flow paths are most easily identified when we have written our program using the structured coding conventions discussed in Chapter 13. This is another important argument for writing well-structured code.

Every **if**, **while**, and **for** statement in a program creates two distinct paths:

if *be* **then** s_1 **else** s_2 $\qquad$ $\left\{ \text{execute } s_1 \text{ or } s_2 \right\}$

while *be* **do** *s* $\qquad$ $\left\{ \text{either skip or execute } s \right\}$

for $v := e_1$ **to** e_2 **do** *s* $\qquad$ $\left\{ \text{either skip or execute } s \right\}$

and a **case** creates *n* unique paths, where *n* is the number of alternatives within the **case** statement. As programs get larger, the number of paths grows exponentially. In fact, the number of flow paths through a program is approximately 2^k, where *k* is the number of control statements (**while, if, for**) in the module. For small values of *k* such as 3, 4, and 5 the number of test cases needed to test every flow path is quite small—about 8, 16, or 32. However, in very large modules, with a great deal of decision logic, *k* may be 10 or 15, and it will require thousands of data sets to test every flow path. We will probably not be able to test the program unit adequately, and bugs may creep into the finished product.

This is another reason for keeping modules short and testing each module as it is developed rather than attempting to test a large program all at once.

Our first group of test cases therefore, must be sure to test every flow path in the

FIGURE 16.5   Sample Pascal Program.

```
procedure paycheck (hours : real; payrate : real; var pay : real;
                    var error : boolean);
begin
    if (hours < 0.00) or (payrate < 3.75) then
        error := true
    else
        begin
        error := false;
        if hours <= 40 then
            pay := hours * payrate
        else
            if hours <= 58 then
                pay := (40.0 * payrate) + (hours − 40.0) * payrate * 1.5
            else
                begin
                    writeln('Excessive overtime hours, will only be paid for 18');
                    pay := (40.0 * payrate) + (18.0 * payrate * 1.5)
                end
        end
end;
```

program, preferably a couple of times each. For example, the procedure in Figure 16.5 computes a worker's pay based on the number of hours worked, the hourly pay rate, and the overtime bonus of 150% for all hours above 40. In addition, no workers may work more than 18 hours of overtime; if they do, they are paid only for 18 hours. Finally, if either hours or pay rate contains an erroneous value, an error flag is set to true. During functional testing we must select one or more data sets from each of the following three cases:

Case 1: Hours worked $\leq$ 40 (no overtime).
Case 2: $40 <$ hours worked $\leq$ 58 (overtime).
Case 3: $58 <$ hours worked (excessive overtime).

Choosing sets from each of these three cases will ensure that every statement in the **else** clause of the first **if** statement will be executed at least once.

As a second example, the simple table lookup program in Figure 16.2 should (after the syntax errors are fixed) be tested with at least the following:

1. One data set where the key is found.
2. One data set where the key is not found.
3. One data set where listsize = 0.

Finally, looking at the generalized pattern-matching procedure in Figure 14.5, we would want to be sure to test the following cases:

1. No match between the pattern and the text.
2. A partial match between the pattern and the text (i.e., a match in the first k characters where $k <$ length).
3. A match that does not use the special "anymatch" character.
4. A match that does use the "anymatch" character.

These examples show that thorough functional testing does not require thousands upon thousands of test sets to be done right. If a module is small and well structured, 10 to 30 well-chosen data sets will likely suffice to test all normal module functions; as we have said, the amount of data is not as critical as how well it has been selected.

16.3.1.2 Extremal Testing   One subset of normal test cases is so critical that testing them should be a separate, identifiable stage. This subset includes those data sets that fall at the very extremes or limits of a range of legal values or at the crossover point between two distinct classes of test cases. These data sets are called *extremal cases* or *boundary cases*.

One of the most common errors in programming is called the *off-by-one* error, in which we do not correctly handle boundary or termination conditions. Whenever your program includes statements of the following form:

while i $<=$ limit **do** . . .
if (x $>$ 0.0) **or** (x $<$ 10.0) **then** . . .

it is critically important to test your program with boundary values such as:

$$i = \text{limit}$$
$$x = 0.0$$
$$x = 10.0$$

Other examples of extremal testing would include

1. Storing something in the first and last element of an array structure.
2. Retrieving something from the first and last position of an array structure.
3. Filling an array exactly to its declared capacity.
4. Testing a module using the largest or smallest legal value.
5. Creating the longest and shortest possible string allowed on your system.

For example, in the paycheck program of Figure 16.5, we would definitely want to add the following four extremal cases to our test plans:

Case 4: Hours $=$ 0.0 (the lower boundary for legal hours).
Case 5: Pay rate $=$ 3.75 (the lower boundary for a legal pay rate).
Case 6: Hours $=$ 40.0 (the crossover point between overtime/no overtime).
Case 7: Hours $=$ 58.0 (the upper limit for overtime hours).

In the pattern-matching program, a typical boundary case would be the pattern occurring at the very beginning or very end of the text.

pattern = abc   text = abcxxx . . . or . . . xxxxabc

Another boundary condition might be searching for a pattern whose length is exactly equal to the length of the text.

A related aspect of extremal testing is testing your program on the *null case*. Make sure that your program works correctly for the degenerate case of "nothing to do." Where appropriate, check your program with test cases such as an empty file, an empty table, an array of length 0, and a pointer value of **nil**. We should definitely test our pattern-matching procedure of Figure 14.5 with a pattern of length 0 and a text of length 0.

16.3.1.3 Error Testing

The first two phases of our test procedures were directed at ensuring that the program works properly for the legal and expected data cases. The third aspect of testing now moves into the area of *illegal data*. These illegal data items can fall into three categories, each of which should be included in this phase of testing:

1. Data that violate the specification of the problem as given in the problem specification document.
2. Data that violate physical law or real-world constraints (e.g., 25 hours per day, 8 days per week).
3. Data that violate the date type restrictions imposed on a value by the program declarations (e.g., a boolean value of "maybe"; an integer value of 2.561).

For all illegal cases, no matter how pathological, your program should do something meaningful and not terminate abnormally. If possible, try to carry on with program execution. If that is impossible, produce an instructive error message and terminate gracefully.

With our paycheck program, we would first want to include the following two test cases, which check how the program handles real values that fall outside the legal range:

> Case 8: Hours < 0.0 (an illegal value for hours).
> Case 9: Pay rate < 3.75 (an illegal value for pay rate).

We could then check to see what would happen if the input values violated the syntax of the real data type:

> Case 10: Hours nonreal (e.g., "forty").
> Case 11: Pay rate nonreal (e.g., "$5.00").

As a second example, in the pattern-matching program of Figure 14.5, we should include the following three error cases:

1. A pattern of illegal size (length outside the range [1 . . max]).

2.   A text of illegal size (length outside the range [1 . . max]).

3.   A starting point for the search that does not lie within the boundaries of the text.

Failure to test error handling adequately can lead to a very unforgiving and "user-unfriendly" program. As soon as the user makes an error, either by hitting the wrong key or misunderstanding the type of input requested, the program behaves erratically and/or terminates abnormally. This violates the graceful degradation guidelines presented in Section 14.2.4.

16.3.1.4   Volume Testing

The very last set of test cases, called *volume testing,* is one that is generally not appropriate for small student assignments because of time and cost constraints, but it is a very important aspect of testing in the real world. With volume testing, we test the program's behavior under the stress of extreme conditions in either its operating environment or the quantity of data we provide. We test the program under such conditions as

1.   Excessive quantities of input data.

2.   Large amounts of data entered in a very short period of time.

3.   A great number of simultaneous input operations.

4.   A great number of individuals using the program at the same time.

5.   Running the program on a heavily overloaded computer system.

The reason for including this last set of test cases is that some flow paths in a program are designed to handle only the rarest of circumstances—those that occur under the most extreme of conditions. Only if we correctly simulate these extreme conditions can we force the execution of the flow path and be sure the program will work properly when faced with this situation. To force these conditions to occur, we must typically stress the program with excessive amounts and rates of input.

For example, a program may have a block of code to deal with the condition that the system is completely out of available memory. This is a rare occurrence that would not be observed or tested under normal working conditions. We may have to set up a test case that simulates the occurrence of thousands of simultaneous requests for memory to force this condition to occur.

In a student program, you may have a 500-element array and a procedure that is activated when the array overflows. You will need at least one test case with 501 values to force the invocation of this procedure. Another example might be an errorhandler routine that is invoked only when our file storage is completely filled. We will need at least one test case that forces this unusual occurrence.

Volume testing is by far the most difficult class of test cases to perform because it may be quite hard to set up test data in a way that forces a particular flow path to be executed. However, it is critically important that it be done, because if a particular flow path is never executed, we can never really be sure of the execution-time behavior of that sequence of code.

The importance of testing programs in short, compact units becomes clear when we look back at our selection of test cases for both paycheck and pattern match. Both of these were quite short modules, about 10 to 30 lines in length. However, adequate testing of these short modules still requires about 10 to 12 distinct classes of test cases. As modules grow in size to 100, 200, or more lines, the number of cases needed to test them grows even more rapidly, and soon it is no longer feasible to apply the systematic procedures presented here. Untested program statements are very likely to have undetected bugs, and the result is an incorrect program. Without testing, the bug(s) may not be detected until a user supplies a data set that activates the bug and causes the program to "bomb out."

16.3.2   System Testing and Integration

In the previous section, we described the testing procedures that apply to an individual program module. This phase of testing is typically referred to as *unit testing*. However, the fact that each new module works properly does not guarantee that the overall program will work correctly. Errors may exist in the *interface* between two modules, and this fact may not become apparent until they are combined and tested as a complete unit. Therefore, additional testing of the overall program is essential for determining whether the correct individual modules fit together properly into a correct whole. This phase of testing is typically called *system testing* or *system integration*.

Typically, system integration will proceed in stages, with modules being tested in small clusters, which are in turn integrated with other clusters, until the entire program has been completely assembled. For example, given the following program development tree:

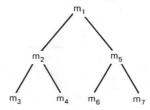

we might first carry out unit testing on modules M_1, M_2, M_3, and M_4 to make sure they are correct. We might then choose to test the (M_2, M_3, M_4) cluster. Similarly, we might do unit testing on M_5, M_6, and M_7 followed by system testing on the (M_5, M_6, M_7) cluster. Only after both clusters have been thoroughly tested might we integrate and test all seven modules operating as a single program.

What kinds of errors would be discovered in system testing that would not be discovered by unit testing?

1.   Errors in the interface between two modules.
2.   Errors or misunderstandings in interpreting the specifications of a module.
3.   Errors caused by the side effects of a module.

As an example of this last class of errors, look back at the sorting procedure of Figure 12.3, which had the side effect of changing the missing data indicator from -1 to $+11$. Unit testing would not uncover the error. In fact, it would show that it was working exactly as the programmer had designed it to work. The disastrous side effect would not be discovered until that procedure was integrated and tested with the other units that used the results of the sort procedure:

```
sort (list, n, missing);
for i := 1 to n do
    { print out only the nonmissing data items }
    if list[i] <> −1 then writeln(list[i]);
```

The program would now fail and the error would be discovered.

This last class of errors—those caused by a program module's side effects—should not occur in any well-written program because it would violate the independence guidelines laid down in Section 12.3. There, we specified that modules should not modify global variables or have any other unexpected side effect on any other module in the program. Therefore, if these principles are followed the only types of errors that should be uncovered during system testing are numbers 1 and 2 above—interface problems or a misunderstanding of specifications. (In fact, these are really quite similar and might be regarded as two variations of the same problem.)

Interface errors are inconsistencies between the invocation of a program unit and its declaration, and they generally fall into one of the following categories:

1. Incorrect number of parameters.

2. Incorrect order of parameters.

3. Incorrect data type for one or more parameters.

4. Improper parameter passing mechanism (i.e., value, reference).

5. Improper module type (e.g., function, procedure).

Some languages, such as BASIC or FORTRAN, will let these errors pass undetected and they will need to be caught during system testing. In other languages, especially strongly typed language such as Pascal, Modula-2, or Ada, the compiler will catch some of these interface inconsistencies at compile time and they will be flagged as syntax errors. Even in strongly typed languages, however, it is possible to have interface errors when using independently compiled library routines stored as relocatable object modules. Thus, the first phase of system testing is directed at simply making sure the program units all fit together properly.

We may have our interfaces in order and still have problems, if there was a misunderstanding about how to determine the value of a specific output parameter. This would be termed a *specification error*. For example, the person writing a function to evaluate some complex trigonometric formula might assume the function result is to be returned as a real number whose units are radians. The person invoking this function may assume that the result is real and the units are degrees. Each will test his or her own unit under his or her own (possibly incorrect) assumption and determine that it is correct. Only when these two routines are put together will the incompatibility be detected. Specification errors will be minimized if we have a clearly written design document and each programmer adheres exactly to the module calling sequence described in that document.

Thus, if we write our individual units exactly as described in the module specification and adhere to the guidelines of independence and logical coherence, the difficulty of carrying out the system-level testing operations will be greatly reduced.

16.3.3   Acceptance Testing

The very last phase of testing is called *acceptance testing*, and this is where we determine whether or not the program is considered finished and can be released for general use.

Acceptance testing differs from unit testing and system testing in two very important ways:

1.   It is typically done by the end-user, not the programmer.
2.   It is carried out without knowledge of the internal structure and organization of the program.

The user was last involved in the project in helping to develop the problem specification document, which we described in Chapter 10. Since that point, the design, implementation, debugging, and initial testing phases have all been carried out by the programming team without direct user assistance. It is now time for the user to become involved in acceptance testing to determine if the software product, as it now stands, is indeed correct.

The user brings an important, nontechnical perspective to the testing operation. In selecting data to use in checking the program, users can draw on their specialized knowledge of the applications area, the environment in which it will operate, and the characteristics and habits of the user community. Special situations or conditions that were ignored by the technical staff but which are important in this area will likely be anticipated and more thoroughly tested by users. Thus, acceptance testing is not simply *more* testing but testing from a different viewpoint, which can more extensively check such aspects of the program as user-friendliness, robustness, and on-line assistance.

A good example of this different perspective was an incident during the design of a data entry software package to be used by clerical personnel. Previously the staff had prepared the necessary forms using manual typewriters. The unit/system level testing by the programming staff showed that the program worked exactly according to specifications. However, very early in the acceptance testing the following dialogue took place at the terminal:

Please enter the expiration year: 1987
*** Error—An illegal character was entered in this field ***

This left the individual totally confused, as the quantity "1987" seemed correct. The problem was that the typist, drawing on previous experiences with manual typewriters, had used a lower case "ell" to represent the digit "1," a very common practice among clerical staff, especially when the "1" key is removed and used for another character. Naturally, this violated program specifications, which said a year field can contain only digits within the range [0 . . . 9]. The program had operated according to specification but was inappropriate for the needs of the user community. This problem was unanticipated by the technical staff, and it was not caught until acceptance testing. (The program was modified so that in a numeric field a lower case "ell" is converted to the digit "1.") This incident shows how acceptance testing tests not only the program, but the users and the environment in which the program will operate.

The other major difference is that acceptance testing is carried out in ignorance of the internal structure of the program.

Unit and system-level testing is typically called *white box testing*, which means that we carry out the testing procedure with complete knowledge of the internal design of the program. We typically choose a test case to test a specific flow path, module, or cluster of modules. Our test data act much like probes, examining the correctness of individual components of the program.

Acceptance testing, however, is *black box testing*, in that the user is totally unaware of this internal structure. In fact, the user is most likely totally naive about programming and computers in general. All he or she has available is the original problem specification document, which shows exactly what output should be produced for given inputs. The specification document may list exactly what test cases should be tried during acceptance testing, or the users may simply select their own test cases based on knowledge of the application. The point is that the users are not concerned about making sure they have tested every flow path or module but simply that the program operates according to specifications.

When the program has passed acceptance testing, it is deemed correct and released for general use. We have now reached level 6 in our levels of reliability chart shown in Figure 16.1. This is as far as we can go using the methods of empirical testing. To do any better than this, and to be able to make stronger claims, we must use a different technique entirely, called *formal verification*.

16.4
Program Verification

When we have completed the testing procedures described in Section 16.3, what can we say about the program? As mentioned at the beginning of that section, we cannot say that it is absolutely correct. Testing can only detect the presence of errors; it can never prove their absence. All we can say about the program is that for a wide range of carefully chosen data cases it has worked properly and, from this experience, we extrapolate to the statement that the program will work correctly under all circumstances, even for those test cases that were not explicitly tested. This extrapolation is

FIGURE 16.6 Problems in Proving Correctness Using
Empirical Observations.

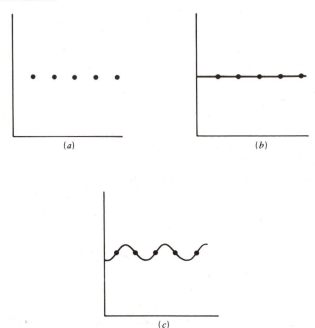

(a)   (b)

(c)

really a "leap of faith" that is not based on either mathematical formalities or physical laws but on empirical observation and human judgment.

This is a very weak form of correctness, which is quite different from the type of correctness proven in such classical disciplines as mathematics or physics. If a mathematician wished to study the formal properties of a function, he or she would not do it by empirically observing the value of that function at a few carefully selected points $(x_0, y_0)(x_1, y_1)(x_2, y_2), \ldots$, as shown in Figure 16.6a. He or she knows that it would not be possible to make any reliable assertions about the function's behavior at points not explicitly observed, and that the function could demonstrate very different and unanticipated characteristics, as shown in Figures 16.6b and c. Instead of random observations, the mathematician would express the function in a closed form that described its continuous behavior over the entire range of its definition: $y = f(x)$. This would allow the mathematician to make very powerful assertions about the formal properties of the function f.

Some computer scientists are trying now to show that computer programming can utilize the principles of and the power of mathematics and logic. Just as mathematicians prove that a theorem is correct, so should programmers prove that a program is correct. A program, P, could be treated much like a function with inputs $x_1, x_2, \ldots,$ x_n, and we could make *assertions* about the output, y, of program, P, for any arbitrary input, that is, $y = P(x_1, x_2, \ldots, x_n)$. Of course, the most important assertion is that y is the output given in the specification document for input $x_1, \ldots, x_n$.

This formal approach to correctness would allow us to make much stronger claims about program P. Instead of observing its instantaneous behavior at a few selected points, as in Figure 16.6a, we could assert its correctness over the entire range of defined inputs. This would allow us to reach level 7 of Figure 16.1, the highest level of reliability possible. It would essentially allow us to make the claim, "The program is provably correct."

Program verification is a complicated and controversial technique, but recent developments are simplifying it somewhat. New programming languages devised with program verification in mind include special features and formalized semantics that will make the verification process easier. Theoretical computer scientists believe that correctness should be an integral part of a program's design. This constructive approach to verification is very promising, especially for programs in which computations can be carried out in parallel as opposed to the more usual case of sequential execution.

In the following section we will briefly introduce some of the characteristics and methods of formal verification. The interested reader should refer to some of the books in the Bibliography at the end of this section for more material on this interesting subject.

The technique of formal verification is based on describing, for every statement S in a programming language, what conditions we know to be true before S is executed, called the *preconditions*, and what conditions we know to be true after S has been executed, called the *postconditions*. This is usually written as follows:

$$\{P\}\ S\ \{Q\}$$

where

P are the boolean preconditions
Q are the boolean postconditions
S is any statement in the language

Together $\{P\}$ and $\{Q\}$ are called *assertions* because they assert that a given condition is true at a given point in a program. The important thing, however, is not to make an assertion about the behavior of a single statement, but to study the behavior of entire programs. This can be done by using the composition laws of boolean logic, which say that

$$\{P\}\ S_1\ \{Q\} \text{ and } \{Q\}\ S_2\ \{R\} \text{ implies}$$
$$\{P\}\ S_1; S_2\ \{R\}$$

Thus, by knowing the preconditions and postconditions associated with individual statements, we can begin to make claims about what happens when sequences of statements are executed—that is, when we run a program. In the above example, if we know that the boolean predicate $\{P\}$ is initially true, then when we execute the "program" $S_1; S_2$ we know that condition $\{R\}$ will be true upon completion.

For example, if we had the assignment statement $a := b + 5$, and if we knew that when we reached this statement b was positive, then we would know (by the formal semantics of the assignment statement) that when the operation is complete a will be greater than 5 and b will be unchanged. We would write this as

$$\{b > 0\}$$
$$a := b + 5$$
$$\{b \text{ unchanged and } a > 5\}$$

In general, though, we are more interested in going in the reverse direction from that shown above. Most of the time we know what we want to end up with, and we are concerned with what initial conditions need to be set up to achieve this desired result.

Given the assignment statement $v := e$ and some postconditions $\{Q\}$, how do we go about determining the necessary preconditions $\{P\}$ so that $\{P\}$ $v := e$ $\{Q\}$? If we think about the semantics of the Pascal assignment operation, we realize that it makes e and v "equivalent" in the sense that after the assignment is completed the value of the expression e is the same value stored in the location associated with the variable v. Therefore, if $\{Q\}$ is true using the value v after execution of $v := e$, then it must have been true using the value of the expression e before execution. Thus, the precondition $\{P\}$ can be derived from $\{Q\}$ by simply replacing every occurrence of v in $\{Q\}$ with e. The precondition that results is frequently called the *weakest precondition* of $\{Q\}$. For example,

$$\{P\}$$
$$disc := (b * b) - (4.0 * a * c)$$
$$\{b = 10 \text{ and } disc > 0\}$$

The weakest precondition would be determined by replacing *disc* by $b^2 - 4ac$ in the given postcondition, resulting in

$$(b^2 - 4ac) > 0$$

Since we also know that $b = 10$,

$$100 - 4ac > 0$$
$$ac < 25$$

and the desired precondition is

$$\{b = 10 \text{ and } ac < 25\}$$
$$disc := b * b - 4.0 * a * c$$
$$\{b = 10 \text{ and } disc > 0\}$$

Next, let's look at the formal properties of the **if/then/else** statement in Pascal.

{ P } **if** B **then** S₁ **else** S₂ { Q }

If *B* is true, we execute statement S_1; otherwise we execute statement S_2. If we write the above as

{ P } **if** B **then** { P₁ } S₁ { Q₁ } **else** { P₂ } S₂ { Q₂ } { Q }

then we can say that when we have completed execution of the statement the following postcondition {*Q*} is true:

$$\{Q\} = (B \text{ and } \{Q_1\}) \text{ or } (\text{not } B \text{ and } \{Q_2\})$$

For example, consider a simple conditional statement that determines the absolute value of a variable *x*:

```
if x >= 0
then y := x
else y := -x
```

We assume nothing about the value in the variable *x* (except that it is defined before the **if** statement is performed). From the semantics of the **if** statement, we can easily derive the preconditions for the **then** and **else** clauses.

```
{ true }
if x >= 0 then
begin
    { x >= 0 }
    y := x
end
else
begin
    { not (x >= 0) }
    y := -x
end
```

(Notice that we have added **begin–end** pairs for clarity only.) The postconditions are derived as they were for assignment statements.

```
{ true }
if x >= 0 then
begin
    { x >= 0 }
    y := x
    { (x >= 0) and (y = x) }
end
else
begin
    { not (x >= 0) }
    y := -x
    { (not (x >= 0)) and (y = -x) }
end
```

The postcondition for the **if** statement is obtained by noting that only one branch of the **if** is ever executed. Therefore one of the two postconditions must be true. The final postcondition becomes

$$\{[(x \geq 0) \text{ and } (y = x)] \text{ or } [\text{not } (x \geq 0)] \text{ and } (y = -x)\}$$

which is the same as

$$y = \text{abs}(x)$$

Finally, we come to the looping statements of the language:

$\{P\}$ **while** B **do** $S; \{Q\}$

These are the most difficult statements about which to make assertions, for two reasons:

1. Because we do not know how many times the loop will execute (0, 1, 5000, etc.), the postcondition $\{Q\}$ must be independent of how many times we will go through the loop. Specifically, it must be true on loop entry (since the loop may execute zero times) and it must be true whenever we exit the loop. Because of these requirements, postconditions on loops are frequently called *loop invariants*.

2. It is not enough to simply say that $\{Q\}$ will be true upon loop exit. We must also prove that the loop will actually terminate in finite time. For example,

    $\{a > 0\}$ **while** true **do** $a := a + 1; \{a > 0\}$

    The postcondition is true, but that is immaterial, since the loop is infinite and will never terminate.

Probably the single most important aspect of formal program verification is determining the proper loop invariant for each loop included in the program. For example, given the following program fragment to find the maximum element in an array $x[1]$, ..., $x[N]$.

```
{ N ≥ 1 }
i := 1;
big := X[1];
while (i < N) do
    begin
    i := i + 1;
    if big > X[i] then big := X[i]
    end
```

A study of the loop shows that when i has the value k, $k = 1, \ldots, N$, then the variable big contains the largest of the first k values in the array X. This is true upon loop entry since $k = 1$ and big $= X[1]$. It is also true every time through the loop. Thus, the loop invariant can be expressed as

```
{ N ≥ 1 }
i := 1;
big := X[1];
{ i = k, big = max[X₁, ... , Xₖ], 1 ≤ k ≤ N }
while (i < N) do
    begin
    i := i + 1;
    if big > X[i] then big := X[i]
    { i = k, big = max[X₁, ... , Xₖ], 1 ≤ k ≤ N }
    end
```

We must also show that the loop terminates. In this case, it is easy and relies on the fact that between any two integers i, j there are only a finite number of other integers. We begin at $i = 1$ and proceed to the value N, $N \geq 1$, by adding 1. This operation will terminate after a finite number of additions. Given the semantics of the **while** loop:

while B **do** S

we know that, if the loop terminates, the condition not B must be true. Since we have just shown that the preceding loop will terminate, we know that the negation of the boolean condition, $i < N$, will be true. This condition is $i \geq N$. Thus, we have written out a loop invariant predicate we know to be true, have shown that the loop must terminate, and have developed the condition that must be true upon loop termination:

$$\{ Q \} = \{ \underbrace{i \geq N}_{\substack{\text{loop} \\ \text{termination} \\ \text{condition}}} \text{ and } \underbrace{i = k, 1 \leq k \leq N, \text{big} = \max[X_1, \ldots, X_k]}_{\text{loop invariant}} \}$$

Together, these two clauses imply that $i = N$, and therefore

$$\{Q\} = \{big = max[X_1, \ldots, X_N]\}$$

and the program has been proven correct.

This is the strongest possible form of correctness. We have not merely examined the behavior of the code for a few selected cases but are stating that for *any* data set for which the preconditions are true $\{N \geq 1\}$, the program will end up with the desired postcondition $\{big = max(X_1, \ldots, X_N)\}$.

Verification is a highly complex and somewhat controversial technique. To be done properly, it requires a good deal of mathematical sophistication in the areas of symbolic logic, predicate calculus, mathematical induction, and axiomatic semantics. If you look through the literature, you will see that the overwhelming majority of proofs have been carried out on simple 15- to 30-line "toy" programs, such as finding the sum of N numbers, the greatest common divisor, or, as we did here, the biggest of N numbers. The reason for that is quite obvious; the proofs of program correctness are quite long, frequently longer than the program itself! Proofs of more interesting and more realistic programs would run to many dozens of pages and can be enormously difficult to follow. This is one of the main arguments people use against verification as a realistic programming tool. They feel that the proofs are so long and complicated that there is as much likelihood of an error in the proof as there is of an error in the original program.[1]

Although this appears to be an attractive and somewhat convincing argument, it is not completely true. A number of developments in the area could make it much more likely that formal verification will become an important and practically usable tool.

The first is the development of languages whose structure is designed to facilitate the verification process. Early languages like FORTRAN and COBOL with their **goto** statements, common variables, and weak typing rules made proof development virtually impossible. Newer procedural languages such as Pascal and Modula-2, with their improved control structure, reduced side effects, and rigidly enforced scope rules, have eased this task somewhat. Nonprocedural fourth-generation languages such as Prolog, which are based entirely on the principles of symbolic logic, can simplify this task even further.

However, even more important will be the development of *automated program verifiers*. These are programs that will attempt to carry out mechanically the proof we did manually. The input to a program verifier would be another program along with some formalized representation of a specification document that describes what the program is supposed to do, perhaps represented as a decision table or a finite state

---

[1] Interestingly enough, they are generally correct. Most of the long, intricate proofs published in computer science journals or texts are later found to contain a number of typos, simple arithmetic mistakes, or outright mathematical errors!

automation, as described in Chapter 10. The output of a verifier would be a statement that the program is or is not correct according to the given specifications.[2]

No reliable and general-purpose program verifiers are currently available, but research work on this is being carried out, and the development of such programs would make formal verification a much more realistic proposal. Since verification will likely become a more and more important tool in the near future, it will be important for programmers to have the necessary mathematical background in logic, discrete mathematics, and predicate calculus and to familiarize themselves with the basic concepts of verification, including preconditions, postconditions, and loop invariants.

Until formal verification of every program unit becomes a practical reality, there is one other thing that programmers can learn from these techniques and use in their own modules—the idea of *informal verification*. Informal verification means that you argue and rationalize the correctness of your program as it is being written (just as with formal methods), but without necessarily using the mathematical notations and proof techniques of formal verification. Instead, you make use of natural language to argue and convince yourself of the correctness of what you have written. Informal verification represents a middle ground between the difficulties of the complex verification methods discussed earlier and avoiding the problem altogether. Too often, programmers will not even bother to think or reason about their programs as they are being written. They assume that if they make a mistake, it will be caught and corrected during the testing phase, so why worry now. This is an extremely poor approach that greatly increases the time and difficulty of the debugging task. (Remember our earlier comment that the easiest bug to correct is the one that *did not* get into the code!)

As an example of this type of thinking, assume that we were writing the following fragment to sum up the first N elements in a list:

```
i := 1;
sum := 0;
while i ? N do { not sure what is the correct relational operator }
    begin
        sum := sum + X[i];
        i := i + 1
    end
```

We are not completely sure right now whether the test condition in the loop should be $i < N$ or $i <= N$. A lazy way would be simply to write out whichever one you think is correct, knowing that boundary testing will detect an error if we are wrong. Although that is true, if this is done often enough it is possible for a large number of bugs to creep

---

[2] As an interesting aside, we should note that this problem cannot be solved for an arbitrary program, P. There will always exist some programs for which the verifier will not be able to decide the question of correctness. This result comes from the area of computability theory and will be discussed in other computer science courses.

into the program, and some of them may be overlooked. Certainly it will add greatly to the time spent in the debugging phase.

The discussion on verification has shown that it is possible to reason logically about the behavior of programs. We can use this form of logical reasoning to argue the correctness of our code, even if we do not use the formal notation of symbolic logic. The reasoning that could be done about the previous code fragment might go something like the following:

> .When we enter the loop the value of i is 1. We add $X[1]$ to *sum*, set i to 2, and end this iteration. After one pass, we have added one item from X and i is 2. After two passes, I see that we have added in two items from X and i is 3. Therefore, it must be the case that after k passes through the loop, we will have added $X[1], \ldots, X[k]$ to *sum* and i will have the value $k + 1$. Thus, if I want to stop when I have correctly computed $X[1] + \ldots + X[N]$, then I will want to end the loop when i has the value $N + 1$ at the end of the loop. The correct condition to write in the while loop must be **while** $i <= N$.

Even though this reasoning has been expressed in natural language rather than mathematical notation, this type of informal reasoning can be a powerful tool in helping you write correct programs. Every time you write out a loop or other control structure, stop and reason about the code you have just written. Convince yourself of the correctness of the logic by trying to explain its behavior in terms of the state of the computation. A good habit to get into is to include your *assertions* about the behavior of the program as comments in the code, as shown in Figure 16.7.

These assertions, even if they are informally stated and not part of an explicit proof, can be an important component of the finished program. They represent a written statement of one's thinking and reasoning about the program's behavior. The assertions can be checked later, by yourself or with others, to verify that your reasoning is sound and that all of the stated claims are indeed true.

An important verification technique developed recently is the "formalization" of the process of checking the informal assertions and claims made about program correctness. Instead of reasoning logically only to one's self, this arguing is done in a much more formal presentation to a group of one's peers and team members. This presentation is sometimes called a *structured walkthrough*.[3]

In this presentation you try to argue and convince all listeners of the correctness of your work. The arguments follow a very similar form to the one we gave earlier and should be based on the principles of logic and mathematics, rather than just intuition or common sense. The audience acts much as a devil's advocate, trying to find flaws in the reasoning and uncover errors or inconsistencies in the logic. They pick and probe until they are satisfied that the basic design is sound and the assertions about the program's behavior are correct.

---

[3] Note that this type of presentation technique need not be used only to argue the correctness of code. It is also used frequently to argue the correctness of both problem specifications and program design.

FIGURE 16.7   Including Assertions as Comments
in the Code.

```
i := 1;
sum := 0;
{ assertion : The following will only work correctly if N, X[1], . . . , X[N] are defined }
while i <= N do
    begin
    sum := sum + X[i];
    i := i + 1
    { assertion : At this point sum will always contain X[1] + . . . + X[k], where k = i − 1 }
```

Thus, even though formal verification may not, at the present time, be a completely feasible tool for widespread use, there are still a number of realistic things that can be done to minimize the number of bugs that get into the code:

1.   Reason logically about the behavior of code *as it is being written*. Convince yourself of its correctness immediately, rather than waiting until testing.

2.   Include, as comments in the code, your assertions about the program's behavior, and the reasoning you used to justify the correctness of the code.

3.   Show these assertions to one or more professional computer scientists and convince them, by reviewing your arguments, that your assertions are indeed correct.

These steps, along with a well-planned and well-organized empirical testing scheme, will go a long way toward eliminating bugs before they occur, quickly and efficiently removing the few that are present, and ensuring the correctness of the finished software product.

This has been only a brief introduction to this most important area. Later courses in both mathematics and computer science will go into a much more thorough discussion of this topic. The interested reader should refer to either the text by Edsger Dijkstra, *A Discipline of Programming*, or the book by David Gries, *The Science of Programming*. Both are listed in the Bibliography for Part Three.

Exercises for Chapter 16

*1.   For each of the following statements determine whether or not there is a syntax error in the statement by comparing it with the formal syntax charts given at the end of the book.

a.   **if** (a = 1) **or** (b = 2) **then** writeln(a,b)

b.   **while** true **do** a := 1

c.   **for** i := j + 7 **downto** k * 5 **do** k := k − 1
d. read (?)   *null*
e.   **if** a = 1 **then else** writeln (a)

*2.   For each of the following statements explain how a run-time error could occur. Write the necessary statements to prevent these errors from occurring.

var x : **array** [1..10, 1..10] **of** integer;
    y : 1 .. 10;

a.   x[i,j] := x[i−1, j+1] + 1
b.   readln(num); y := num
c.   **case** y **of**
        1,2,3,4 : proc1(a,b,c);
        5,6,7,8 : proc2(a,b,c);
            9 : proc3(a,b,c)
    end
d.   a := sqrt (b + 1.5);
e.   principle := (1 + i * N) / periods

3.   One of the problems with the read and readln procedures is that they "bomb out" if presented with data whose format is incompatible with the type of the variable in the read list. For example,

var x : integer;

read(x)

if we now enter "true," or the character string "x = 1" the program will terminate abnormally with the message "Illegal symbol encountered in digit field." Write three procedures which will read in a sequence of characters ending with a blank, determine if they are syntactically correct, and, if so, convert those characters to the proper data type and return a flag value of true:

a.   Getinteger(x,flag).
b.   Getreal(x,flag).
c.   Getboolean(x,flag).

If they are incorrect, flag is set to false and x is undefined. So, for example, if presented with the four characters " − ", "1", "2", "b", (b is a blank) Getinteger would return

x = −12
flag = true

If presented with the characters "X", "1", "Y", "b", Getinteger would return

x = undefined
flag = false

4.   Assume there is a bug in the program for doing date conversion shown in Figure 13.1. Where would you place debugging statements to locate the problem?

5.   What type of test data would you use to demonstrate that the pattern-matching procedure in Figure 14.5 works as documented? List all cases, including functional, extremal, error, and volume testing.

*6.   Repeat Exercises 4 and 5 with the sort procedure from Figure 13.5.

7.   Repeat Exercises 4 and 5 with the integration procedure from Figure 14.4.

8.   Find the bug(s) in the following fragment to read in characters comprising a signed integer value and convert it to a number.

```
if input ↑ = '−' then
begin
    sign := −1;
    get(input)
end
else
if input ↑ = '+' then
begin
    sign := 1;
    get(input)
end
get(input);
while not eoln do
begin
    number := 10 * number + ord(input ↑ ) − ord('0');
    get(input)
end
```

Show exactly where you would place the debugging output and describe the test cases you selected.

*9.   The following procedure is supposed to transpose (interchanges the rows and columns of) an *n*-by-*n* array. Is it correct? If not, explain how to go about debugging it systematically.

```
procedure transpose (var a : arraydef; n : nbounds);
var
    i : nbounds;
    j : nbounds;
begin
    for i := 1 to n do
        for j := 1 to n do a[j,i] := a[i,j]
end; { of procedure transpose }
```

no

*10.   Given the following skeletal outline of a Pascal program (where all S_i are legal Pascal statements) how many test cases would it take to test every flow path in the program.

```
if B₁ then      { Bᵢ is a boolean expression }
      S₁
else
      if B₂ then
            S₂
      else
            begin
            while B₃ do S₃;
            S₄
            end;
S₅;
if B₄ then S₆
```

11.   What would happen to program paycheck in Figure 16.5 if we ran it with a pay rate that included the character "$"? Modify the program so that the program will work properly if the pay-rate value is preceded by the character "$".

*12.   In the following code fragment identify the extremal and boundary tests that should likely be conducted.

```
var
      a : array [1 .. 100] of integer;
      .
      .
      .
read (i, x);
if (i < 1) or (i > 100) then
      writeln (' Error')
else
      if (i <= 50) then
            a[i] := x
      else
            repeat
                  x := x + delta;
                  i := i + 1
            until (i >= 90)
```

13.   Using the SORT program in Figure 13.5, develop a logical argument to prove (informally) that the program is correct according to the specifications given in Chapter 13.

14.   Using the integration program in Figure 14.4, develop a logical argument to prove (informally) that the program is correct according to the specifications given in Chapter 14.

15.   The following program fragment implements integer division by repeated subtraction:

```
{ computes a ÷ n by repeated subtraction, to
  get quotient, q, and remainder, r. a >= 0, n > 0 }
q := 0;
r := 0;
while a >= n do
    begin
    q := q + 1;
    a := a − n
    end;
r := a
```

Prove, formally, that this code is correct if the necessary preconditions are met.

CHAPTER 17

PROGRAM EFFICIENCY AND THE ANALYSIS OF ALGORITHMS

17.1
Introduction

Program efficiency is a measure of the amount of resources a program requires to produce correct results. Programmers and end-users are both interested in measurements that evaluate and rank programs. Programmers are concerned with designing programs that are fast enough to meet design specifications, while end-users are concerned with getting programs that are cheap to operate.

However, there has been a significant change in recent years concerning how programmers and users feel about the concerns of efficiency. This change in attitude has occurred in three main areas.

1. What are the important resources we should try to optimize?
2. Where are the important efficiency gains to be made?
3. How important is efficiency in the first place?

A few years ago, the only resources we measured and optimized were *machine resources:* processor time, memory space, and mass storage. Program efficiency was measured by running standardized test cases (called *benchmarks*) and analyzing how long they took to execute and how much memory they required.

Today, however, efficiency is defined in much broader terms that encompass human as well as machine resources and that divide machine efficiency into two categories: the inherent efficiency of the method itself and the efficiency of its use in a specific program on a specific computer system. We are now dealing with a much wider scope of measurement than simply "how many milliseconds did it take to run?"

The four major components of efficiency are

1. *User efficiency.* The amount of time and effort users will spend to learn how to use the program, how to prepare the input, and how to interpret and use the output.

2. *Maintenance efficiency.* The amount of time and effort maintenance programmers will spend reading a program and its accompanying technical documentation in order to understand it well enough to make any necessary modifications.

3. *Algorithmic complexity.* The inherent efficiency of the method itself, regardless of which machine we run it on or how we code it. For example, a sequential search through an N-element table will take, on the average, $N/2$ searches to find what it is looking for, and this quantity cannot be reduced by programming cleverness or newer and faster computers. A method that creates a two-dimensional n-by-n array to store a table will require at least n^2 cells, even if we do not use most of these spaces.

4. *Coding efficiency.* This is the traditional efficiency measure. Here we are concerned with exactly how much processor time and memory space a computer program requires to produce correct answers.

Section 17.2 will discuss points 1 and 2—*the human aspects of efficiency.* Sections 17.3 and 17.4 will discuss points 3 and 4—the *machine aspects of efficiency.*

17.2
The Human Aspects of Efficiency

In the area of efficiency, there has been a significant shift in focus away from the machine and toward the programmer and the user. The clever programmer who could reduce the execution time of a loop by 345 microseconds or eliminate 40 memory locations by means of the intricate redesign of program logic is no longer always considered an invaluable resource. In fact, that programmer's operations may not even be cost-effective. They may reduce overall efficiency because of the time spent on achieving these reductions and the possible increase in programmer time necessary to make future modifications.

The reason for this change in attitude is simple: money! Ten or 20 years ago, the most expensive aspect of programming was computer costs. Consequently, we tended to optimize for the machine. Today, however, the greatest costs involved in program development are not those gray boxes in the corner but the two-legged creatures who use them. Figure 17.1 compares the trends in starting salary for programmers and average medium-scale machine costs over the last 15 years.

At today's prices, a medium-size commercial installation might pay $100,000 to $250,000 for hardware with a 5-year life expectancy. If that same installation has a data-processing staff of five (one DP director, three programmers, and one technical/clerical person) the salaries over that same five-year period could total about $600,000—more than double the hardware costs. Most studies indicate that "people costs" in a typical computer center are 50 to 75% of overall costs. As another example,

FIGURE 17.1   Trends in Hardware and Personnel Costs in Programming.

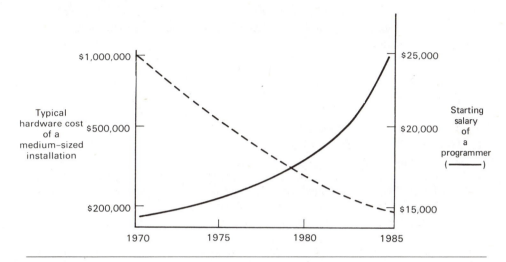

consider the case of the programmer earning $15 per hour and the large computer that rents for $12 per minute (both typical values). If the programmer works to save 500 microseconds per loop execution in a loop executed 1000 times, execution time will be reduced by ½ second, resulting in a processor cost savings of 10¢. Even if the program is run weekly, the annual savings will be about $5—approximately 20 minutes of programmer time. If the programmer spent days or even hours on that optimization, the result would be a net loss. Excessive programmer time spent on small gains in machine time is usually a losing proposition.

The best way to reduce costs is not to make minor reductions in machine time but to make major reductions in people time. Programmers cost more money in the long run than hardware, and any discussion of efficiency that considers only the machine and its resources is missing this fundamental point.

Computer programs should be written with these goals in mind:

1.   To be correct and reliable.

2.   To be easy to use for its intended end-user population.

3.   To be easy to understand and easy to change.

Point 1 is crucial and too often forgotten. People want programs that work properly under all conditions and keep working properly for a long time. Correctness is essential; efficiency is not. As Van Tassel's law observes: If the program need not be correct, it can be made as efficient as desired![1]

[1]D. Van Tassel, *Program Design, Style, Efficiency, and Testing.* Englewood Cliffs, N.J.: Prentice-Hall, 1978.

Point 2 refers to *end-user efficiency*. After correctness, the most important characteristic of a program is ease of use. An end-user is not going to be impressed by a program with poor documentation, confusing input/output formats, and inadequate results—regardless of how fast it runs. The extra time spent by that user in figuring out how to use the program and its results is certainly more important and valuable than small reductions in execution time.

Key aspects of end-user efficiency discussed in this text are

a.   Program robustness (Section 14.2).

b.   Program generality (Section 14.4).

c.   Portability (Section 14.5).

d.   User-friendliness (Section 14.6).

e.   Good-quality user documentation (Section 18.2).

Another significant human cost is point 3—the programmer time needed to maintain and modify an existing program (*maintenance efficiency*). A complex, logically contorted program that executes rapidly but is difficult to modify will almost certainly cost more over the life of the program. The salaries of the programmers spending time trying to understand and change the program will probably far exceed the savings in machine costs. (Remember the time you spent debugging the small program fragment in Figure 13.7.)

The key points in achieving maintenance efficiency are

a.   A clear, readable programming style.

b.   Adherence to structured coding conventions.

c.   A well-designed, functionally modular solution.

d.   A thoroughly tested and verified program with built-in debugging and testing aids.

e.   Good quality technical documentation.

In summary, the Schneider–Bruell corollary to Van Tassel's law is as follows: cater to people, not machines. You can worry about the machine later!

However, we would be remiss if we did not acknowledge some important exceptions to our corollary. There are special situations in which we must write the fastest, smallest, most efficient program we can, regardless of its effect on usability or maintenance. Three major examples stand out:

1.   *Real-time programs* must produce answers in a specified time period or else the results are worthless. Most often these programs are used to control ongoing physical processes (e.g., assembly lines, check-out counters, nuclear power plants). In these programs, time is critical. For example, a program automatically controlling the flight path of the space shuttle would continuously monitor altitude, position, pitch, yaw, and other values and then, if necessary, compute how to adjust engine thrust to correct these errors. If the program could not compute the necessary actions in time, the shuttle could go into an irreversible roll or spin. In

this case we would have to sacrifice any program characteristic, except correctness, to reduce running time.

2. Programs that do not fit into the memory space available on your computer. All computers have some fixed, finite memory capacity into which each program must fit. If your computer has N words of memory but your program requires more, it probably will not run.[2] The only alternative, short of buying more memory or a newer computer, is to "squeeze" the program down and make it shorter—again, without too much regard for its effect on the end-user or the maintenance programmer.

3. Programs that are run very often are likely candidates for extensive machine-level optimization. However, "very often" in computer terms does not mean weekly or even daily but, more likely, tens, hundreds, or even thousands of times a day. Programs with these rates of usage are most likely *systems programs* and are used by the computer itself and not by the end-user. Examples might include a Pascal compiler that translates hundreds of programs each day, or a computer's accounting system that may log in and bill thousands of interactive users daily. With this type of program, even small reductions in running time, when multiplied by the number of times the program is used, can result in very significant savings.

These cases, however, are special and, in general, we would state the following: Do not worry initially about the machine-level efficiency of the program you are writing. Choose a good method that solves the problem and write a clear, readable, and correct program that both the user and the maintenance programmer will find easy and efficient to use.

17.3
The Analysis of Algorithms

When we start discussing the topic of efficiency of a computer program, we must approach it from two different points—the inherent efficiency of the algorithm itself and the efficiency of a program that implements that algorithm. As we will see, the former is significantly more important than the latter.

The most obvious way to measure the efficiency of an algorithm is to run it for a specific set of data and measure how much processor time and memory space is needed to produce a correct solution. However, this would produce a measure of efficiency for only one very special case and would probably be inadequate to predict how the algorithm will perform with a different set of data. An algorithm for finding a name in a telephone book by searching sequentially from A to Z would work well for a book with 50 to 100 entries but would be totally unacceptable for use with the New York City directory.

---

[2] Some computers will still execute programs that are larger than the available memory capacity. They use sophisticated memory management techniques called *overlays* or *virtual memory*. However, we are not considering the existence of such techniques when making this point.

We need a way to formulate generalized guidelines that allow us to state that, for any arbitrary data set, one particular method will probably be better than another. In the previous phone book example, a more helpful piece of information than the performance of the algorithm on a specific directory would be a general guideline that says "Never use sequential lookup with any moderate-size or large telephone book."

Specifically, we would like to associate a value n (the *size* of the problem) with either t (the processing *time* needed to get the solution) or s (the total memory *space* required by the solution). The value, n, is a measure of the size of the problem we are attempting to solve. For example, if we are searching or sorting a list, the size n would most likely be the number of items in the list. If we were inverting an $r \times r$ matrix, the size of the problem would be r—the dimensions of the matrix.

The relationships between n, t, and s can sometimes be given in terms of explicit formulas:

$$t = f(n)$$
$$s = g(n)$$

If we had such a formula, it would allow us to plug in a value for n and determine exactly how many seconds it will take (or memory cells will be used) to solve a problem of size n. Given that information, we could immediately select the algorithm that would run most quickly (or with the least memory) on problems of that given size.

However, such explicit formulas are rarely used. First, they are difficult to obtain because they often rely on machine-dependent parameters that we may not know. Second, we usually do not care to use $f(n)$ and $g(n)$ to compute exact timings of specific data cases. We simply want a general guideline for comparing and selecting algorithms for arbitrary data sets.

We can get this type of information by using what is called *O-notation*.

$t \approx O[f(n)]$ {this is read "t is on the order of $f(n)$" or "t is proportional to $f(n)$"}
$s \approx O[g(n)]$

where the function $f(n)$ is called the *time complexity* or *order* of the algorithm and $g(n)$ is called the *space complexity*.

Formally, O-notation states that there exist constants M and $n*$ such that if $t \approx O[f(n)]$, then $t \le Mf(n)$ for all $n > n*$. This formidable definition is not as difficult as it looks. It simply states that the computing time (or space) requirement of the algorithm grows no faster than a constant times the function $f(n)$. That is, as n increases (i.e., the problem gets bigger), the time (or space) needed to solve that problem increases at a rate that is of the order of the function $f(n)$. If the order of the algorithm were, for example, $O(n^3)$, as the size of the problem doubled, the time to solve the new problem could increase about eightfold (2^3). The *order* of an algorithm is proportional to the solution time or space needs, and it approximates the amount of resources necessary to solve a problem as the size of the problem gets larger.

For reasonably large problems we want to select algorithms of the lowest order

FIGURE 17.2   Comparison of Three Complexity Measures.

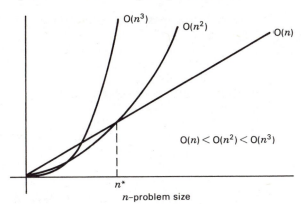

possible. If algorithm A is $O[f(n)]$ and algorithm B is $O[g(n)]$, then algorithm A is said to be of a *lower* order than B if $f(n) < g(n)$ for all n greater than some constant k. So, for example $O(n^2)$ is a lower order algorithm than $O(n^3)$ since $n^2 < n^3$ for all $n > 1$. Similarly $O(n^3)$ is a lower order algorithm than $O(2^n)$ because $n^3 < 2^n$ for all $n > 10$. We will not know exactly how much time or space is required to obtain a solution, but we will know that as the size of the problem increases there will always exist a point ($n*$) at which our lower-order method will always take less time (or space) than a method that is of a higher order. And, as the problem gets bigger, the gains become even more significant. Figure 17.2 shows this quite vividly for the orders $O(n)$, $O(n^2)$, and $O(n^3)$. For problems of size $n < n*$, the choice of algorithm is not too critical. However, as n becomes much larger than $n*$, the $O(n)$ algorithm is always superior to both the $O(n^2)$ and $O(n^3)$ algorithms, and it becomes better and better as n increases.

This is the general guideline for which we have been looking, and this is why O-notation is the fundamental technique for describing the efficiency properties of algorithms.

Let us look at some specific examples. The simple sequential search procedure of Figure 17.3 looks at every entry in an n-item list to locate a specific key. On the average, the comparison test within the while loop will be carried out $n/2$ times before we locate the desired key, and we could say that the average time complexity of the sequential search algorithm is $O(n/2)$. However, when dealing with complexity functions, we generally do not care about any constants associated with the leading terms of the complexity equations. Of course, these constants will affect the exact running time of a problem, but they will not change the basic characteristics of the algorithm. (Another way to view this statement is that these constants may change the exact location of the point $n*$ in Figure 17.2, but they will not change either the shape of the curves or the conclusion that we reached about the efficiency of the methods themselves.) Thus, we would say that the sequential search method is $O(n)$—a *linear*

FIGURE 17.3   Sequential Search Procedure.

{ Procedure to sequentially search a list for a specified key

entry conditions:
      list   : n element array of integers
      n   : size of the list, n >= 1
      key   : integer value we are searching for

exit conditions:
      position   : 0 if the key was not found; 1 . . n to denote the location of the first
                              occurrence of the key
}

procedure sequential(list : arraytype; n : integer; key : integer;
      var position : integer);
var
      found   : boolean; { to control loop termination }
      i   : integer; { array subscript }
begin
      found := false;
      i := 1;

      while (not found) **and** (i <= n) **do**
            begin
      if list[i] = key **then** found := true
                       else i := i + 1
            end { of while };

      if found **then** position := i **else** position := 0
end; { of procedure sequential }

---

growth function with respect to table size. If the list were to double in size, the average time required to search it would double, and so would the amount of space needed to store it.

However, if the list is already sorted, we can do much better than O(*n*) using the *binary search* technique.

The binary search algorithm works by comparing the key we are searching for with the item located in the middle position of the list. If it matches, we have found our item. If not, we discard the half of the list that cannot contain the desired key and repeat the process. We will eventually find what we are looking for or discard the entire list. A binary search program is shown in Figure 17.4.

With each comparison we halve the size of the list under consideration. Therefore, the list will be ½, ¼, ⅛, . . . its original size. In the worst case the process will continue until the list is empty. We can rephrase this by saying that the greatest number

FIGURE 17.4   Binary Search Procedure.

{ This procedure searches an n element list for a specified key. The entry and exit
  conditions are identical to those listed for the procedure sequential shown in
  Figure 17.3
}

```
procedure binary(list : arraytype; n : integer; key : integer;
    var position : integer);
var
    bottom      : integer;      { subscript into list }
    found       : boolean;      { to control loop termination }
    middle      : integer;      { subscript into list }
    top         : integer;      { subscript into list }
begin
    bottom := 1;
    top := n;
    found := false;

    while (not found) and (bottom <= top) do
        begin
        middle := (top + bottom) div 2;
        if list[middle] = key then found := true
        else
            if list[middle] > key then top := middle - 1
            else bottom := middle + 1
        end; { of while }

    if found then position := middle else position := 0
end; { of procedure binary }
```

of comparisons required by the binary search method will be the value k, where k is the
first integer, such that

$$2^k \geq n \text{ (the size of the list)}$$

Another way to write this is

$$k \geq \log_2 n$$

and we say that the time complexity, or order, of the binary search method is $O(\log_2 n)$.
The time needed to find an element in a list using binary search is proportional to the
logarithm of the list size, rather than proportional to the list size itself, as with
sequential search. This is a lower-order algorithm than the $O(n)$ sequential search
because the function $\log_2 n$ grows more slowly than n itself.

The larger a list (i.e., the greater the value of n), the more time is saved by using the

FIGURE 17.5   Comparison of $O(n)$ and $O(\log_2 n)$ Algorithm Performance.

	Average Number of Comparisons	
n	$O(n)$	$O(\log_2 n)$
10	5	3
100	50	7
1,000	500	10
50,000	25,000	16
800,000	400,000	20

binary search. For example, look at the table in Figure 17.5. We see that for small values of n the gains are not significant. (In fact, without knowing anything about constant values or lower-order terms, it is possible that, for small n, the sequential search may actually perform better.) However, for large lists, the improvements can be monumental. A list with 800,000 items will require, on the average, 400,000 comparisons using sequential lookup, while the binary search will never need more than 20— an improvement factor of 20,000!

We can do better still when looking up items in a table. Using the *hash coding algorithms* first presented in Chapter 7 we can reduce the time needed to locate a specific key in a table to $O(1)$. That is, we can locate the key in a single operation, independent of the size of the table.[3]

Similarly, in Chapter 7 we introduced and analyzed a number of sorting techniques. These algorithms generally display two different classes of time complexities.

$O(n^2)$:   Selection sort
   Bubble sort
   Exchange sort

$O(n \log_2 n)$:   Quicksort
    Radixsort
    Heapsort

Figure 17.6 gives the average number of operations needed to sort lists of different sizes using these two classes of sorting techniques—$O(n^2)$, and $O(n \log_2 n)$. Again, as with binary search, when n is quite small (e.g., $n < 100$) the differences between the behavior of the different classes of algorithms are small, and the choice of which type of sorting method to use is relatively unimportant. As n gets larger, however, the speed advantages of the $O(n \log n)$ algorithms become more and more apparent. When

---

[3] Hashing is only $O(1)$ if the table is quite empty. The time to locate a key increases as the table density increases.

FIGURE 17.6   Comparison of $O(n^2)$, $O(n^{3/2})$, and $O(n \log n)$ Algorithms.

	Average Number of Operations Needed to Sort a List		
n	$O(n^2)$	$O(n^{3/2})$	$O(n \log_2 n)$
10	100	32	40
100	10,000	1,000	700
1,000	1,000,000	32,000	10,000
100,000	10^{10}	3,200,000	1,700,000
500,000	2.5×10^{11}	3.5×10^8	10^7

sorting a list of 500,000 items, an $O(n \log n)$ algorithm performs better by more than 4 orders of magnitude than the simpler but slower class of $O(n^2)$ methods. These last examples comparing the performance capabilities of different classes of algorithms demonstrate a fundamental principle regarding the efficiency of computer programs:

> The single most important consideration in developing an efficient computer program is choosing an efficient algorithm of the lowest order possible.

Selecting a better technique typically results in an order of magnitude improvement in running time or space needs, as we just saw in our previous discussion on searching and sorting methods. This compares with the relatively smaller gains of about 10 to 50% that can be made by worrying about how to code that algorithm. When efficiency is critical and the size of the problem is large, finding the lowest-order algorithm must always be our first concern. A cleverer programmer or a faster computer cannot overcome the inherent efficiency problems of a poor selection. The simplest, most straightforward binary search program coded by a first-semester freshman will always be more efficient than a sequential search method coded by a team of crack programmers, even if it does not contain a single wasted microsecond.

To emphasize this latter point, assume that we were going to run one program from each of the two classes of sorting algorithm listed in Figure 17.6 [and a third "compromise" $O(n^{3/2})$ algorithm] on three quite different computers—a $1000 Apple IIe microcomputer, a $100,000 VAX-11/750 minicomputer, and a $10,000,000 CRAY-2 supercomputer. The CRAY will run the inefficient $O(n^2)$ method, the VAX will execute the $O(n^{3/2})$ algorithm, while the tiny Apple IIe will be assigned the efficient $O(n \log_2 n)$ technique. Furthermore, assume that we were able to measure the different performance capabilities of the three and develop exact formulas for the running times (in microseconds) of the algorithms on each machine. Assume these formulas are

$$t_1 = n^2 \text{ (for the CRAY-2)}$$
$$t_2 = 1,000 \, n^{3/2} \text{ (for the VAX-11/750)}$$
$$t_3 = 10,000 \, n \log_2 n \text{ (for the Apple IIe)}$$

FIGURE 17.7   Comparison of Running Times of Three
Algorithms on Three Different Computers.

		Approximate Running Time	
n	CRAY-2, $t = n^2$	VAX-11/750, $t = 1000\, n^{3/2}$	Apple IIe, $t = 10,000\, n \log_2 n$
100	0.01 sec	1 sec	7 sec
1,000	1 sec	33 sec	100 sec
10,000	100 sec	1,000 sec	1,300 sec
100,000	3 hr	9 hr	5 hr
1,000,000	12 days	12 days	3 days
10,000,000	3 years	10 months	24 days

Notice how much larger the constant of proportionality is for the VAX and Apple IIe to reflect the fact that they are 3 to 4 orders of magnitude slower than the CRAY-2. Figure 17.7 shows the hypothetical results of running the three different classes of sorting algorithm on the three machines. For small n (e.g., $n = 100$) the CRAY-2 supercomputer's immense speed would allow it to overcome the inherently inefficient method it is using, and it solves the problem 100 times faster than the VAX and 700 times faster than the Apple IIe. As the problem gets larger, this difference begins to disappear as the inherent inefficiencies in the methods themselves begin to overwhelm the abilities of the larger machine to keep up with the number of computations required. At $n = 100,000$, all three computers are taking about the same amount of time to solve the problem—on the order of a few hours. At $n = 10,000,000$, the efficiency of the $O(n \log_2 n)$ algorithm has become the dominant factor, and the Apple IIe is completing the sorting task 40 times quicker than the CRAY, a machine that costs 10,000 times more money and runs thousands of times more quickly! Simply recoding the $O(n^2)$ algorithm or buying more memory for the CRAY may postpone the problem, but it will not make the problem disappear. It is simply part of the definition of the concept of a lower-order algorithm that there will exist a point (about $n = 100,000$ in our example) at which the lower-order algorithm will always take less time to complete the task, regardless of the constants of proportionality.

As a final example, let us analyze the complexity of the well-known operation of matrix multiplication, $C = A \times B$, defined as follows:

$$C_{ij} = \sum_{k=1}^{n} A_{ik}B_{kj} \qquad i = 1, \ldots, n; j = 1, \ldots, n$$

If we assume that both A and B are $n \times n$ matrices (not a necessary requirement for matrix multiplication), then the above formula shows that the determination of each separate element of the product matrix C will require $2n - 1$ operations—n multiplications and $(n - 1)$ additions. These $2n - 1$ operations must be repeated for each of the

$n \times n$ positions in the resulting matrix C. Thus, the total number of operations required to obtain C is $n^2(2n - 1) = 2n^3 - n^2$, and we could say that the complexity of the matrix multiplication operation is $O(2n^3 - n^2)$. However, as we mentioned before, constant coefficients are generally not important in evaluating the behavior of algorithms. Similarly, lower-order terms of the complexity function can also be disregarded because, for large values of n, $n^3 >> n^2$ and all we are interested in is the general limiting, or *asymptotic behavior* of the function. The contributions of the n^2 (and lower) terms will be relatively insignificant. Thus, we would say that the complexity of matrix multiplication as given by the previous formula is $O(n^3)$. Improved matrix multiplication algorithms have been developed whose time complexity has been reduced to approximately $O(n^{2.81})$.

So far in our discussion, most of the complexities have been of the form $O(n)$, $O(n^{3/2})$, $O(n^2)$, and $O(n^3)$. Algorithms with these types of time complexities are called *polynomial time algorithms* because their time and space complexity functions are polynomial functions of relatively small degrees. The computational demands of these algorithms are usually manageable, even for large problems, because their time and space needs do not grow unreasonably fast. However, not all algorithms are of this type. A second fundamental class contains what are called *exponential time algorithms*. For these problems, no polynomial time algorithm has yet been discovered. The typical complexity displayed by the exponential class of algorithms is $O(2^n)$, $O(n^2 2^n)$, or $O(k^n)$. The time and space demands of these algorithms grow extremely fast and consume vast amounts of resources, even for small problems. In most cases it is not feasible to attempt to solve any realistically sized problem using an exponential algorithm, no matter how clever the programmer or how fast the computer.

This class of algorithms is not just of academic interest. They occur frequently in several areas of computer science, applied mathematics, and operations research. An important area of research has developed specifically to study this category of "computationally intractable" problems. An example of such an algorithm is the well-known *traveling salesman problem*. In this problem, certainly one of the most famous in computer science, we have a salesman who must travel to N other cities, visiting each one only once, and end up back home. This is called a *tour*. We want to know if it is possible to make such a tour within a given mileage allowance, k. That is, the sum of all the distances traveled by the salesman must be less than or equal to k. For example, given the following mileage chart, showing the distances between four cities—A, B, C, and D

	A	B	C	D
A	—	500	100	800
B	500	—	900	150
C	100	900	—	600
D	800	150	600	—

and a mileage allowance of 1500 miles, a legal tour is possible, starting at our home base A—namely, A → B → D → C → A (of length 1350 miles). If the mileage allowance were only 1000 miles, no legal tour is possible.

FIGURE 17.8 Listing of Some Common Computational
Complexities.

Complexity	Comments	Examples
O(1)	Solution time is independent of the problem size	Extracting the (i,j)th element from an $(n \times n)$ array. Table lookup using hashing (no collisions)
O($\log_2 n$)	Called "logarithmic time"	Binary search
O(n)	Called "linear algorithms"	Sequential search
O($n \log n$)	Theoretically optional sorting time	Quicksort, heapsort
O(n^2)	Called "quadratic algorithms"	Selection sort Matrix additions Simple pattern matching
O(n^3)	Called "cubic algorithms"	Matrix multiplication
O(k^n)	An exponential time complexity	The traveling salesman problem

No algorithm has yet been discovered that will allow us to solve this problem in a reasonable (i.e., polynomial) time. For example, an exhaustive search of all possible tours would say that we could select any one of the N cities as the starting locations. We could then select any one of the remaining $(N - 1)$ cities to visit next, then any of the remaining $(N - 2)$ cities, and so on. The total number of tours that we would need to examine would be

$$N \times (N - 1) \times (N - 2) \times \ldots \times 1 = N!$$

and the complexity of this *brute force*, exhaustive search solution to the traveling salesman problem is O($N!$), which can be shown mathematically to behave much like an exponential function of the form N^N. Better algorithms have been developed, but they all still display this characteristic explosive exponential growth, which makes this problem unsolvable in the general case for anything but tiny values of N.[4]

Figure 17.8 summarizes some of the most common complexity functions and lists some well known algorithms which display that behavior.

The examples presented here—searching, sorting, matrix multiplication, and the traveling salesman problem—have all analyzed the *time complexity* of an algorithm. However, as stated at the beginning of the chapter, memory space is also an important resource, and we can develop and analyze *space complexity* measures in a virtually identical fashion. In analyzing space complexity, we wish to develop a formula that relates n, the problem size, to the amount of memory space needed to solve the problem. For example, both the sequential and the binary search methods require a

---

[4] If a computer could evaluate 1 billion tours per second, it would take approximately one million centuries to enumerate all the tours when $N = 25$.

table large enough to hold all n items and are therefore $O(n)$ in terms of space complexity.

Memory space and computer time are usually inversely related; we can frequently reduce space requirements by increasing processing time or, conversely, reduce processing time by making more memory available. This is called the *space-time trade-off*.

For example, in storing the elements of an $n \times n$ matrix using the following array declaration:

var
    matrix = **array** [1 .. n, 1 .. n] **of** integer;

we obviously are using n^2 memory locations, and the space complexity of an algorithm utilizing this declaration would be $O(n^2)$. However, what if most of the cells in this array are zero, as in

$$\begin{bmatrix} 0 & 0 & 0 & 0 & 0 & 0 \\ 0 & 0 & 36 & 0 & 0 & 0 \\ 0 & 0 & 0 & 0 & 0 & 0 \\ 0 & 0 & 0 & 0 & 0 & 17 \\ 0 & 0 & 0 & 0 & 0 & 0 \\ -1 & 0 & 0 & 0 & 0 & 0 \end{bmatrix}$$

This type of structure is called a *sparse matrix,* and there are much more efficient ways to store values from a sparse matrix. For example, we could create a $3 \times k$ data structure, which stores only the row and column indices of the k nonzero elements. We could create this data structure using the following declaration:

var
    sparse = array [1 .. k] **of**   { k is a symbolic constant }
        record
            row : 1 .. n;
            column : 1 .. n;
            value : integer
        end;

Now, our previous sparse matrix, which contained only three nonzero values, would be stored as follows:

Row	Column	Value
2	3	36
4	6	17
6	1	−1

The space needs of this alternative representation are linear with respect to the number of nonzero values—that is, $O(3k)$, where k is the number of nonzero entries. This represents a significant improvement in space efficiency. With the previous $O(n^2)$ technique, a sparse matrix that grew in size from 10×10 to 100×100 would require an additional 9900 memory cells to store the additional values, even if they were all, or mostly all, zeroes. The modified sparse matrix representation would require only three additional cells for each nonzero entry. If both the 10×10 and 100×100 matrices contained the same number of nonzero elements, their space needs would be exactly the same, since the space complexity of the sparse representation is not dependent on the value of n, the array dimensions.

In exchange for that reduction in space, we will generally have to spend additional time processing data in this reduced representation. For example, printing the contents of a two-dimensional $n \times n$ matrix in the normal square format is a simple $O(n^2)$ operation, if the matrix has been stored as a traditional two-dimensional array:

```
for i := 1 to n do
    begin
        for j := 1 to n do
            write (A[i,j]);
        writeln
    end
```

When the data have been stored in the reduced representation, it is not quite so easy. For each $[i,j]$ position we will print, we must first look up the row and column indices in the data structure to see whether that element is there or not. The algorithm will look something like the following:

```
for i := 1 to n do
    begin
    for j := 1 to n do
        begin
        value := find (A,i,j); { see if the [i,j]th entry of A is in the reduced representa-
                                  tion. If yes, find returns its value, if not find returns a 0. }
        write (value)
        end
    writeln
    end
```

If the find function searches the reduced data structure sequentially, then it will take about $O(k)$ operations to determine if the $[i,j]$th entry is there, where k is the number of nonzero elements in the table. Since this operation will be done n^2 times, the overall printing operation now becomes a $O(kn^2)$ algorithm, rather than its previous $O(n^2)$ performance characteristic. We have saved space at the expense of increasing the computational time needed to carry out operations on that data.

Similarly, inserting a nonzero value into the $[i,j]$th position of the array, which used to be a simple $O(1)$ operation:

```
A[i,j] := x;
```

is now a complex operation in which we must search the data structure to determine if the entry is already there and, if not, add it in the proper place. The algorithm and its analysis is left as an exercise to the reader.

This has been a brief discussion of a critically important topic—the complexity analysis of algorithms. Future course work in computer science will address this issue in much greater detail. The important point to remember now is the fundamental and central importance of algorithmic behavior to the overall efficiency of the final solution.

17.4
Coding Efficiency

We arrive finally at the topic of coding efficiency and hope that the discussion leading up to this section has helped to put it in its proper perspective. Our concern for writing very fast, tight code should come *last,* not first (except for the special cases discussed earlier). We should always try to select the most efficient method available and then develop a straightforward, clear, readable (and correct!) implementation of that method. Then, if we can improve the code to make it run faster without impairing the clarity, *and* if we are willing to spend the time, *and* if we (or someone else) are willing to pay the salaries involved, *and* if it will result in a net savings, we might consider using the techniques we will be discussing in this section. Remember, however, the typical gains to be made will be nothing like the order of magnitude improvements we discussed earlier. If we are lucky, the reductions in space (or time) to be gained by code manipulations will be on the order of 10 to 50% (unless the program was horrendously inefficient to begin with).

Before embarking on optimizing a running program, it is also important to remember that our goal is not necessarily to create the fastest program possible, but only a program that meets the requirements laid out in the problem specification document described in Chapter 10. If we are constructing a program whose average response time t must meet a design goal of $t < 2$ seconds, and the current program has an average response time of $t = 0.8$ seconds, then code optimization is unnecessary. It would be a waste of time (and money) to spend a great deal of programmer effort trying to make minor reductions in running time. However, if $t = 2.3$ seconds, then this effort *is* important and 10 to 50% efficiency gains may be crucial to the success of the project. Finally, if $t = 10.0$ seconds, code efficiency improvements alone may not be enough, and we will likely have to rethink our choice of algorithms and data representations.[5]

As an example of code optimization, consider the bubble sort algorithm in Figure 12.3 (ignoring the side effect in the first **for** loop). We can improve the implementation of that algorithm by noting that, after pass i, the last i items in the list are in their proper place and do not need to be checked. The algorithm could be recoded to eliminate these unnecessary comparisons, and the results are shown in Figure 17.9. The changes in

---

[5] This situation should happen rarely, though, if we do some rough "ball-park estimates" before we begin implementation. These running time estimates, though very crude, should be able to tell us if we are coming close to the design goal or whether we are 200, 300, or 400% off the mark.

FIGURE 17.9   Improved Bubble Sort Algorithm.

```
j := n; { top of the already sorted portion of the list }
repeat
      sorted := true;
      j := j - 1;
      for i := 1 to j do
           if (list[i] > list[i + 1]) then
                 begin
                 sorted := false;
                 { exchange the items that are out of place }
                 temp := list[i];
                 list[i] := list[i + 1];
                 list[i + 1] := temp
                 end { of if statement }
until sorted
```

Figure 17.9 can improve the running time of the bubble sort up to 50%, depending on the size and initial contents of the list.

However, before you begin to modify a program, you should be aware of a fundamental characteristic of computer programs called the *80/20 rule,* which states that approximately 80% of the execution time of a program will be spent in only 20% of the program modules. In all programs there will be some modules that are executed only a few times while others will be executed thousands of times. For example, referring to the simulation program in Chapter 15, the procedure initialize will be executed once per run. The procedure arrivalevent will be executed once for each new student who enters the terminal room. For the data in Figure 15.9 this is about 375 arrivals per simulation run. It makes sense to concentrate our limited efforts on only those frequently used routines where the payoff is greatest. We can get the needed information through a programming technique called *profiling* the code. This is simply a count of how many times, for a typical data set, each module of a program was entered. After the program is completed, this information is printed out in an *execution profile* (Figure 17.10). Referring to the profile of Figure 17.10, we should obviously attempt to optimize only the statements within modules C and E and leave the others as is.

The execution profile of a program is sometimes available directly as a service of the computer system (much like the trace or debug features described in Chapter 16).

```
program main
      .
      .
      .
begin
      profile(true); { turn counter on to measure module execution }
```

FIGURE 17.10   Execution Profile of a Program.

Unit	*Times Executed*
A	*
B	**
C	***************************
D	***
E	***************
Main	*

However, even if this service is not automatic, we can still get this important information ourselves by *instrumenting* our program. We define the following global data structures:

```
type
    modulenames = (name1,name2, . . . ,name N);
var
    tally: array [modulesnames] of integer;
```

where name1, name2, . . . , name*N* are related to the names of all the subprograms used in our program. (Using the exact same name is illegal.) Now, as the first line of each subprogram used, we simply write

```
procedure modulename1;
    .
    .
    .
begin
    if measuring then
        tally[name1] := tally[name1] + 1
```

(We assume that at the beginning of the program or in an initialize routine we will clear all entries in tally to zero.) Now we can turn on our profiling instrument by the inclusion of one line at the beginning of our program.

```
measuring := true
```

We can turn off our instrument when it is not needed by rewriting that initialization so that it reads

```
measuring := false
```

However, we should leave these profiling statements in our program in case they are needed again in the future.

Just as we measure the usage of modules within a program, we should also analyze the frequency of execution of statements *within* a module. As before, we will see that there is enormous variation in the number of times different statements are executed. For example, the following code fragment multiplies two matrices: a, which is $p \times m$, and b, which is $m \times n$. We produce a result matrix c, which is $p \times n$, as well as a p-element vector, row, that contains the sum of the elements in each row of the new matrix c.

Line		Times Executed
1	**for** i := 1 **to** p **do**	
2	**begin**	
3	rowtotal := 0;	p
4	**for** j := 1 **to** n **do**	
5	**begin**	
6	sum := 0;	pn
7	**for** k := 1 **to** m **do**	
8	sum := sum + (a[i,k] * b[k,j]);	pnm
9	c[i,j] := sum;	pn
10	rowtotal := rowtotal + c[i,j]	pn
11	**end**; { of loop on j }	
12	row[i] := rowtotal	p
13	**end** { of loop on i }	

For values of $p = m = n = 25$, the assignment statements on lines 3 and 12 will be executed 25 times, the assignment on lines 6, 9, and 10 will be done 625 times, and the assignment on line 8 will be done 15,625 times. Again, it is obvious where we should apply our efforts. Always try to concentrate on the most frequently executed portions of a program unit—usually the innermost loops in a nested set and the condition clause (**then** or **else**) with the greatest chance of being entered.

A partial list of suggestions to help increase coding efficiency and reduce program running time would include the following operations:

1. Avoid the unnecessary computation of repeated subexpressions. Sequences such as

```
a := a + sqrt(sqr(sin(x)) − sqr(cos(x)));
b := b + sqrt(sqr(sin(x)) − sqr(cos(x)));
c := c + sqrt(sqr(sin(x)) − sqr(cos(x)))
```

can be rewritten as

```
diff := sqrt(sqr(sin(x)) − sqr(cos(x)));
a := a + diff;
b := b + diff;
c := c + diff
```

This has reduced the number of operations that must be carried out from 24 to 13.

2. Avoid unnecessary use of the real data type. Statements such as

```
counter := 0.0; { we will count from 0 to 50 by ones }
  .
  .
  .
counter := counter + 1.0;
  .
  .
  .
if counter > 50.0 then . . .
```

will run at about a factor of 3 to 10 times slower than their integer counterparts.

3. Reduce the *strength* of an operation. This means replace one operation with another that does the same thing but faster. On most machines $+$ and $-$ are executed faster than $*$, which in turn is faster than $/$, which is faster than a procedure call. For example, on the PDP-11/23 computer manufactured by the Digital Equipment Corporation, the following are the instruction times for various arithmetic operations ($\mu = 10^{-6}$ second).

add, sub	.85 μsec
floating point add	2.40 μsec
mul	3.84 μsec
div	7.44 μsec
procedure call and return	8.50 μsec

Thus, in most cases, we would gain by rewriting the following assignments as shown:

Slower	*Faster*
a := b * 2	a := b + b
a := b / 2.0	a := b * 0.5
a := succ(b)	a := b + 1
a := sqr(b)	a := b * b

4. Reduce the number of repetitive subscript evaluations. Subscript evaluations are very time-consuming, and duplications should be eliminated. Instead of

```
sum := a[i,j,k−1] + a[i,j,k+1];
diff := a[i,j,k−1] − a[i,j,k+1]
```

we could reduce the number of subscripts evaluated from four to two by writing

```
left := a[i,j,k−1];
right := a[i,j,k+1];
sum := left + right;
diff := left − right
```

5. Remove constant operations from inside loops. The computation of $\sum_{i=1}^{N} ax_i$ could be written as

```
sum := 0;
for i := 1 to n do
    sum := sum + a * x[i]
```

but we have unnecessarily included an extra multiplication within the loop. It would have been better to write the loop as

```
sum := 0;
for i := 1 to n do
    sum := sum + x[i];
sum := a * sum
```

6. Take fullest advantage of the capabilities of the programming language you are using. For example, in Pascal it is more efficient to replace

if (x = a) **or** (x = b) **or** (x = c) **or** . . .

with

if x **in** [a,b,c, . . .]

Similarly, Pascal provides the pack and unpack operations to reduce the space needs of arrays.

7. Structure your conditional tests so that the least likely predicate is evaluated by itself, eliminating the need to evaluate any remaining predicates. For example, if P_1 is a predicate that is false 99% of the time, then the statement

if P$_1$ **and** P$_2$ **and** P$_3$ **then** S;

would be better written as

if P$_1$ **then**
　　if P$_2$ **and** P$_3$ **then** S;

In the former, P_2 and P_3 will always be evaluated even if P_1 is false. In the latter, P_2 and P_3 will be evaluated only 1 time in 100. If P_2 and P_3 are time-consuming operations, this can result in some significant savings.

This has been a partial listing of coding techniques to improve the execution-time efficiency of programs. There are more, but many will depend on an analysis of timing characteristics of a particular computer to determine whether they will actually result in a net savings. However, be aware that the gains to be made are usually not enormous.

If the program fragments in the fifth suggestion were run on a PDP-11/23, then by removing one fixed-point multiply from inside the loop, we have saved 3.84 microseconds per cycle. If $n = 10,000$ (a reasonably large value), we would have 9999 fewer multiplications and would save

$$9999 \times (3.84 \times 10^{-6}) \text{ seconds} = 0.038 \text{ second}$$

Not very impressive!

There is one final comment to be made about code optimization of the type just described; it is frequently done for you by the compiler itself. An *optimizing compiler* is a language translator that attempts to produce fast, efficient machine-language code. It usually accomplishes this at the expense of increased compile time and numerous passes over the source program. This type of compiler will attempt to do what we have just discussed—reduce the strength of operations, remove constants from loops, and the like. Most students do not have access to such a compiler because their needs are quite different—fast compilations and helpful error messages. However, optimizing compilers are used frequently in production programming environments, especially for the final translation of routines that will be used often. Thus, when available, they further strengthen our statement that programmers should not spend much of their valuable time modifying code to achieve minor gains in space or time. Work on selecting a good method, analyzing it to see if it will generally meet your needs, and if so, writing a readable and reliable program to implement your algorithm. If coding efficiency is still of concern, translate your program into machine language using the best optimizing compiler available. We cannot stress too emphatically the futility of "diddling around" with a working program trying to shorten the code by a few statements or trying to get it to execute a few milliseconds quicker. Unless the program was highly inefficient to start with or the change is obvious, these efforts are rarely cost-effective. They can actually *increase* costs over the life of the program because of the increased programmer time needed to implement future changes.

This does not imply that working programs should never be reviewed and, possibly, improved. It simply means that any changes to increase performance should address *gross* inefficiencies that can produce a real cost savings, and the change should not significantly reduce the program's clarity, readability, and good structure. The "efficiency game" is generally won or lost when the algorithms are selected and sketched out, not when the program is written.

Exercises for Chapter 17

1. The most common computing times for algorithms are

$O(1)$	$O(n^2)$
$O(\log_2 n)$	$O(n^3)$
$O(n)$	$O(2^n)$
$O(n \log_2 n)$	

Graph these time complexities in the range $1 \leq n \leq 128$ and compare their rates of growth. (Assume the coefficients in all cases are 1 and that all lower-order terms are disregarded.) What is the difference between $O(n^2)$ and $O(2^n)$ for $n = 4, 8, 64$? What is the point $n*$ where the above time complexities are ordered in this sequence? That is, for any $n > n*$, $O(1) < O(\log_2 n) < O(n) < O(n \log_2 n) < O(n^2) < O(n^3) < O(2^n)$.

2. In reality, time complexities have coefficients other than 1 and have lower-order terms that are not considered. For example, the actual time or space complexity of an $O(n^3)$ algorithm might be

$$(1/2)n^3 + 500n^2 - 1$$

However, this does not change the fact that if $f(n)$ is of a lower order than $g(n)$, there will always be a point $n*$ such that, for all $n > n*$, $O[f(n)] < O[g(n)]$. Find the point $n*$ where the first complexity function is always less than the second.

    a. $(1/2)n^2 + (1/2)n - 1$ $(1/8)n^3$
    b. $\log_2 n$ $10,000n$
    c. $3n^3 + 50$ $(1/50)2^{n/2}$
    d. 5×10^6 $(1/10,000)n$

3. The functions pack and unpack are standard Pascal functions that can be useful in reducing the total space needed to store large arrays. If the following declarations have been made:

A : **array** [a .. b] **of** T;
B : **packed array** [x .. y] **of** T;

and if $(b - a) \geq (y - x)$, the call

pack(A,a,B)

means pack elements $A[a]$ through $A[y - x + a]$ into $B[x]$ through $B[y]$. The statement

unpack(B,A,a)

means unpack elements $B[x]$ through $B[y]$ into $A[a]$ through $A[y - x + a]$.

Write the procedures pack and unpack as described. If a single element of a packed array can hold k elements of type T while an element of an unpacked array holds 1, what are the space gains to be made by performing:

pack(A,a,B)

if A and B are as defined above?

   *4.   What is the time complexity of the integration procedure shown in Figure 14.3?

Your answer should be given as a function of N, the number of trapezoids used in the approximation.

*5. What is the time complexity of the generalized pattern matching program shown in Figure 14.5? Your answer should be given as a function of n, the length of the text, and m, the length of the pattern being matched. Check to see what happens to your time complexity under the two special cases $m = 1$ and $m = n$.

6. The function e^x can be approximated by using the formula

$$e^x = 1 + x + \frac{x^2}{2!} + \frac{x^3}{3!} + \ldots + \frac{x^k}{k!}$$

What is the complexity of this evaluation as a function of k, the number of terms in the expansion?

7. a. A polynomial

$$P = a_n x^n + a_{n-1} x^{n-1} + \ldots + a_1 x + a_0$$

can be evaluated in many different ways. The straightforward way is

$$P = a_n * \underbrace{x * x * \ldots x}_{n \text{ times}} + a_{n-1} * \underbrace{x * \ldots * x}_{n - 1 \text{ times}} + \ldots + a_0$$

Write a procedure to evaluate a polynomial with coefficients $a_0, \ldots, a_n$ at the point x. Determine how many multiplications, additions, and assignments are required as a function of the degree, n, of the polynomial.

b. An alternative way to evaluate P is to *factor* the polynomial in the following manner (called *Horner's rule*):

$$P = (\ldots ((a_n x + a_{n-1})x + a_{n-2})x + \ldots + a_1)x + a_0$$

Write a procedure to evaluate a polynomial with coefficients $a_0 \ldots a_n$ at point x using Horner's rule. How many multiplications, additions, and assignments are required as a function of the degree, n?

c. Using the PDP-11 timing statistics in Section 17.4 (assume an assignment is 0.85 millisecond and that polynomials use integer add and multiply), approximately how much time is saved in evaluating a polynomial of degree $n = 5$ by Horner's rule? If $n = 25$?

8. In Exercise 13 in Chapter 13 you were asked to determine if, for a given set of nodes and links, there is a *path* between any two arbitrary nodes, i and j. You were given a matrix $M[i,j]$ that describes the physical connections between nodes:

$M[i,j] = 1$ if there is a link from node i to node j.
$M[i,j] = 0$ if there is no link from node i to node j.

For example, if our connections are

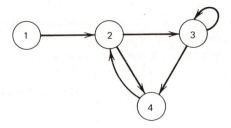

M would look like

$$
\begin{bmatrix}
0 & 1 & 0 & 0 \\
0 & 0 & 1 & 1 \\
0 & 0 & 1 & 1 \\
0 & 1 & 0 & 0
\end{bmatrix}
$$

There is a path from node 1 to node 3 $(1 \rightarrow 2 \rightarrow 3)$, but no path from 4 to 1 or from 3 to 2. If you have not done so already, develop a Pascal procedure that, given *M* and some specific *i* and *j*, determines if there is a path from node *i* to node *j*. Determine the time complexity of your algorithm as a function of the number of nodes. Is your complexity polynomial or exponential?

9.   In our example of running three different sorting algorithms on three different computers, the time complexity of the algorithm running on the CRAY-2 was $t = n^2$. If we changed that to $t = 0.00001n^2$ would that change our conclusion? At what point (if any) would the Apple IIe and CRAY perform identically?

*10.   Assume that we analyzed algorithm *P* and found that its time complexity was $O(\log_2(\log_2 n))$. Where would that complexity function fit with the ordered list of functions shown in Figure 17.8.

11.   Try to write the most efficient program to solve the following problem: You will be given an array *A* of length *N*. The elements of *A* are signed integers. Your program should find the subscript values *i* and *j* such that the sum of the contiguous values $A[i] + A[i + 1] + \ldots + A[j]$ is the largest possible quantity. For example, given the following seven-element array

A	10	−18	−2	40	21	−5	16
	1	2	3	4	5	6	7

your program would output the two values, (4,7), since the largest sum of values is contained in $A[4]$ through $A[7]$ (the sum is 72). After writing the program, evaluate it for efficiency in terms of the following:

    a.   Its time complexity (as a function of *N*).
    b.   Its space complexity.
    c.   The time it takes to execute a standard benchmark data set.

Be careful with this problem, as there are many different ways to solve it with complexities running all the way from $O(n^3)$ down to $O(n)$.

12.   Write a procedure called insert to add a new value X to position $A[i,j]$, when A is stored in the sparse matrix representation shown in Section 17.3. The calling sequence is

insert (A,i,j,X)

Your procedure should look up the row and column indices (i,j) in the reduced representation of array A. If it is there, the procedure should change the value field to X. If it is not there, the procedure should add it so that the table is still sorted by row and column index. What is the time complexity of the insert procedure?

*13.   Take a look at the program in Figure 14.1 for changing dates from calendar form to Julian dates. Can you see a way to improve the running time of that program significantly? (*Hint:* Would you want to store different values in the days array?) If we assume that an arithmetic operation takes about 1 millisecond, about how much time did your enhancement save?

*14.   Assume that we were writing an interactive program that prompted the user for a flight number, looked up that flight number in a flight information disk file, and, when it found the number, displayed the information about that flight on a screen. Would it be okay to use a simple sequential search of the records on the disk if the problem specifications required us to provide an average response time of less than 3 seconds? Here are some other values:

> Number of flight records in the file: 1300.
> Average disk access time to one record: 38 milliseconds.

Would we be able to use sequential search if the average disk access became 18 milliseconds? If the number of flight records was 85?

15.   Try to think of techniques for improving coding efficiency in addition to the seven suggested in Section 17.4. Using timing data for the computer available to you, determine exactly what savings there will be in computing time (or memory space) for typical cases.

16.   If we wanted to store the complete contents of a CRT screen with 80 columns and 24 rows, a straightforward approach would be to use the following structure.

var screen : **array** [1 . . 24, 1 . . 80] **of** char;

This will require saving 1920 characters. Design a data structure that saves the contents of a screen using less memory space. (*Hint:* What if most of the spaces are blanks?) Using your data structure, write a Pascal procedure to display, on an 24 × 80 screen, the information that was saved. The characters should be placed in their proper position on the screen. What is the space complexity of your new representation?

17.   A matrix of the type M from Exercise 11 is also called a *directed graph*. An interesting problem with directed graphs is to find out if one can *tour* the graph.

(Formally, this is called finding a *Hamiltonian cycle*.) Touring means visiting every node exactly once and ending back at the original starting point. For example,

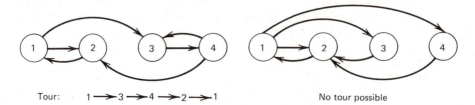

Tour: $1 \longrightarrow 3 \longrightarrow 4 \longrightarrow 2 \longrightarrow 1$ No tour possible

Write a procedure that takes an *n*-by-*n* directed graph and a starting point *i* and determines if there is a tour of the graph beginning at node *i*. The best-known algorithm has an exponential time complexity of $O(n^2 2^n)$. This value grows unbelievably fast, so the problem is effectively unsolvable for large graphs. Try out your procedure with *n* = 4, 8, 16, and 32 and see what happens to computing time.

18. The following procedure computes the value *X* defined as follows:

$$X = \sum_{i=1}^{k} Pi^2 + \sum_{i=1}^{k} Pi^3$$

```
procedure inefficient (P : real; k : real; var X : real);
var
     i, sum2, sum3 : real;
begin
     i := 1.0;
     sum2 := 0.0;
     while i <= k do
          begin
          sum2 := sum2 + P * sqr(i);
          i := i + 1.0
          end;
     i := 1.0;
     sum3 := 0.0;
     while i <= k do
          begin
          sum3 := sum3 + P * i * i * i;
          i := i + 1.0
          end;
     X := sum2 + sum3
end;
```

It is highly inefficient and violates many of the guidelines on coding efficiency given in Section 17.4. Rewrite it so that it is a time- and space-efficient program. Benchmark both the original inefficient program and your efficient variation with the test case *k* = 25 to see how much time was actually gained.

CHAPTER 18

DOCUMENTATION, MAINTENANCE, AND PROGRAMMING SUPPORT ENVIRONMENTS

18.1
Introduction

Just because this is the last chapter of the book, one should not develop the mistaken impression that documentation is performed only after all other programming steps have been completed. Documentation is developed *continually* during program design and implementation. Each step in the development process contributes textual material that will eventually become part of the overall program documentation package. Figure 18.1 lists some programming steps and the corresponding documentation usually developed during that phase.

Documentation is usually presented as the final phase of program development *only* because at the completion of our project we take all existing documentation of the type listed in Figure 18.1 and produce a more finished and elegant product. This includes rewriting, condensing, editing, typesetting, and binding—whatever it takes to produce usable and readable finished copy.

Documentation materials fall into two distinct classes—*user documentation* and *technical documentation*. The next two sections will discuss each of these classes separately.

18.2
User Documentation

18.2.1 What it Contains

User documentation is intended solely for *end-users*. These people may or may not be familiar with computers, with Pascal, or even with the program they are trying to run. They simply want to provide some data to the program and get back the correct results.

FIGURE 18.1   When Documentation Is Developed.

Program Development Phase	Typical Documentation
1. Problem definition	1. Written specification documents Feasibility studies User needs statements User manuals
2. Outlining and structuring the solution	2. Macro-level (system) flowcharts Structure charts High-level program and data structure descriptions Cost estimates for software development
3. Selecting solution methods	3. Time and space complexity analysis Micro-level flowcharts Pseudocode Abstract data type descriptions
4. Coding	4. Listings Program comments Lower-level procedure and data structure descriptions
5. Debugging and testing	5. Sample outputs Error logs Formal verification documents Listings of all changes and modifications Timings and benchmarks

The inner workings of the program are immaterial to their needs. Therefore, user documentation concentrates almost exclusively on the *input/output characteristics* of the program and presents a general overview of what it does. Lower-level implementation details about specific procedures, parameters, or data structures are usually inappropriate.

The major piece of user documentation is a separately bound book, manual, or write-up called the *user's guide* or *user's manual.* It includes, in nontechnical language, all the information a user needs to employ the program properly. The exact format and contents are a matter of personal writing style, but certain information should always be included.

Not technical

1. The program *name*.

2. A brief, nontechnical *description* of what the program does. This should include an explanation of the results that are produced and, if appropriate, the algorithm or method used. Important assumptions made in solving the problem should also be described.

3. The *input data* required by the program. This should include what values are required, what limits are placed on the values, where and how they should be entered (the input format), the order in which they must be entered, and from what input device they may be entered. This is especially critical with a very general-

ized program (see Section 14.4) in which users may have to provide a great deal of data to customize the program to their personal needs. Also, if default input values are assumed, they should be specified here.

4. The *normal output* of the program when presented with valid data. This should probably include an actual output listing from the program along with explanatory notes for each value describing what it is, how it is to be interpreted, and in what units it is being presented.

5. The *exception reports*. These are the error messages, warnings, or other abnormal output the program produces when it encounters invalid or suspicious data. For each error message, the manual should explain what causes that error and how users can repair it. Between points 4 and 5, every message, normal or abnormal, that could be produced by the program should be listed and explained.

6. *Program limitations*. These are bounds or constraints inherent in the program itself that cannot be exceeded by users. Examples might include limits on accuracy (because of the physical characteristics of the computer), or maximum amounts of input (because of fixed **array** declarations).

7. The *command sequence* needed to execute the program on a specific computer system. This will usually be in the form of a listing of a complete input file ready for submission, or a sample terminal session.

8. The name, address, and telephone number of the person responsible for providing assistance.

The manual should provide everything users need to prepare the necessary data, run the program, and interpret the results.

Section 18.2.2 is an example of the user documentation for the simulation case study developed in Chapter 15. The write-up, which assumes that the program is currently stored in a program library called lib, describes how to use the program on the VAX-11/782 at the Macalester College Computer Center. Naturally, this location-dependent information will be different for user's guides at different installations.

Most people would assume that a user's guide of the type shown in Section 18.2.2 would be written *after* the program has been coded and tested. Actually, it is frequently written *before* the coding is even begun, as we mentioned in Chapter 10. The user's guide is a specification document that describes exactly what the program will provide to users. If we write this before we code, users will know exactly what we plan to do. If it is not what is wanted, we can easily change the specifications. Once the program has been written, these changes are more time-consuming and expensive.

For example, if users found that the simulator as coded in Chapter 15 was not exactly what was needed, it would require costly and time-consuming software modification. However, if we wrote the user's guide in Section 18.2.2 *before* we coded that program, we could let users know exactly what we were going to do before we invested time in coding and testing. A change at this point would affect only a specification document, not a working program. Writing the user's manual during program design is common practice among programmers and systems analysts.

18.2.2 Example of User Documentation
(For the Simulation Program in Chapter 15)

1. *Program name*. SIMULATOR.

2. *Description*. This program is a discrete event simulation model of a computer terminal room. The model assumes that users enter the terminal room and wait in a queue to use one of *nterms* identical computer terminals. When a terminal becomes available, the next person in line is assigned to it. After completing the terminal session, the person may either leave the room or wait in a queue for assistance from a single consultant. After being helped, the person goes back to the end of the terminal queue. The overall organization of the terminal room is summarized by the following diagram.

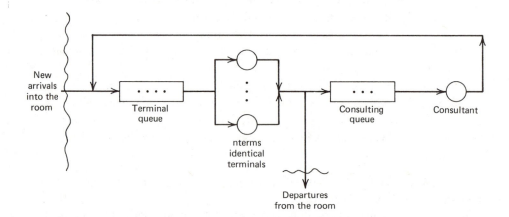

The simulation model runs for a simulated time period specified by the user. Upon completion of the simulation, the program outputs a number of statistics related to the behavior of the system. Users may then study the output and decide whether to rerun the simulation with different parameters or to terminate the program. The main purpose of the program is to allow the user to determine the optimal number of terminals to place in the room to minimize both student waiting time and equipment costs.

3. *Assumptions made by the program*. The simulation program makes certain fixed assumptions about four key model parameters.
    a. Average arrival rates into the terminal room.
    b. Average length of a terminal session.
    c. Average length of a consultation session.
    d. Percentage of students who utilize the consultant after a terminal session.

The assumptions are that these four parameters will follow the statistical distributions in Figure 15.9. If these statistical assumptions are unacceptable, the program code must be modified. Contact the person responsible for program maintenance for exact instructions on changing the program (see Section 8 of this document).

4. *Input*. The two input parameters are
   a. *Nterms*. The number of terminals in the terminal room—(integer) nterms $\geq$ 1. There is no upper bound on the value of nterms.
   b. *Maxtime*. The simulation time in minutes—(real) maxtime > 0.0. (*Caution:* Large values of maxtime can produce excessive machine costs. Using values of maxtime > 5000.0 should be carefully considered in terms of available funds.)

When the program begins, it will produce the following messages: (A "?" is a prompt by the computer to indicate that it is waiting for input).

Welcome to the terminal room simulation program, version 3.1
Please enter values for the number of terminals and the total simulation time
in minutes:
?

At this point you should enter the two values, in the format described above, with at least one blank separating the two quantities. The line is terminated by hitting RETURN. For example, to simulate the behavior of a room with three terminals for 10 minutes, you would enter the following:

3   10.0 (CR)   ((CR) represents hitting the RETURN key)

immediately after the "?".

After getting the results of a single simulation run, the program will ask the following question:

Do you wish to run the simulation program again?
Type yes or no
?

Users simply type "yes" or "no" (or just the first letter "y" or "n") followed by a carriage return. If a "yes" is entered, users will be allowed to enter new values for nterms and maxtime and rerun the model. If the user types "no," the program will produce a good-bye message and terminate.

5. *Output*. In addition to echo printing the input data, the program produces seven results at the conclusion of each simulation run:
   a. The total number of students who entered the room during the simulation. This counts *all* students regardless of whether they exited the terminal room by the end of the simulation run.
   b. The total number of students who exited the terminal room during the simulation run.
   c. The average overall time per student (in minutes) spent in the terminal room, including waiting time, terminal sessions, and consultation. This average

includes only those students who exited the room during the simulation. It does *not* include those still within the room when the simulation ended.

d. The average waiting time per student (in minutes) in the terminal queue. This is the average waiting time *per terminal session.* A student who uses the terminal five times will encounter this delay each time.

e. The average waiting time per student (in minutes) in the consulting queue. Again, this is the average for *each* consulting session.

f. The percentage of time (0 to 100%) the "nterms" terminals are busy. This is the percentage of busy time averaged over *all* terminals. That is, if there are two terminals, one of which was used 50% of the time and another that was used 25% of the time, the value printed by the program would be 37.5%.

g. The percentage of time (0–100%) that the consultant was busy helping a student.

6. *Error conditions.* The following error messages may be produced by the program:

a. *** You made an error in the input. ***
Cause: The value of either nterms or maxtime was entered improperly. They must be entered as shown.

nterms : integer value, nterms > 0
    must be the *first* value entered
    must not contain a decimal point
    must be followed by at least one blank

maxtime : real value, maxtime > 0.0
    must be the *second* value entered on the same or the following line

b. *** Fatal Error—We encountered an empty calendar. Dump followed by a system halt. ***
Cause: This is a major program malfunction that should never occur. If it does, there is nothing users can do personally to recover. Contact the individual responsible for program maintenance for advice on how to proceed (see Section 8 of this document).

7. *Command sequence.* The program simulator is currently stored in a translated version on the public file called lib on the VAX-11/782 system at Macalester College. To run the program, users must type the following commands. (The symbol "c" denotes any alphanumeric character. Symbols in *italics* are messages from the computer.)

>*Macalester College VAX-11/782 System*
>*User Name:* ccccccc   (This is your one- to seven-character log in name)
>*Password:* ccccccc   (This is your one- to seven-character password. It will not
                                   be printed on the screen.)
>get simulator/fn = lib
ready
>run simulator

Welcome to the terminal room simulation program, version 3.1

.

.

.

If there are any problems accessing the program on the Macalester College computer facilities, users should contact the Computer Center, User Services HELPline at (xxx)xxx-xxxx. They are open 8 A.M. to 4 P.M., Monday to Saturday.

8. *Program maintenance.* For more information about this program or how to modify the code, contact

Dr. G. Michael Schneider
Department of Computer Science
Macalester College
1600 Grand Ave
St. Paul, Minnesota 55105
     Effective Date: January 1, 1987
     Revision No.: 1.2

18.2.3   On-Line Documentation

In addition to the user's manual discussed in the previous two sections, there is one other important piece of user-oriented documentation, and that is *on-line assistance,* also called *help mode.* This is helpful, user-oriented information that is kept on-line and can be accessed and displayed on the terminal either automatically or under user control.

The user's manual and on-line assistance are intended to complement, not replace, each other as sources of information. Although the user's manual can be thorough, even encyclopedic in its description of a program, on-line information generally describes the highlights and key features of a program in units of about 25 lines (one screen of text). The user's manual is appropriate for browsing and learning about the program in general, but the on-line assistance is more useful for providing the user with a specific fact or piece of information, quickly and efficiently.

Once a rarity, on-line assistance is now quite a common part of most medium- and large-scale interactive programs. Just as we developed tools to help us prepare a program (editors), correct it (on-line debugging tools), test it, and store it (file systems), we now have a tool to help us learn about the program as well.

Since on-line assistance is part of the program itself, we cannot leave its design until the end of the project, and then retrofit the code into the finished program. This will produce a help mode that looks and behaves as if it were an afterthought of the designer, which it was. We should include the concerns of on-line assistance into our plans from the very earliest stages of program design and implementation.

Questions about on-line assistance that should be asked and answered during program design include the following:

1. What subset of information from the user's manual should be kept on-line?

2. What data structures/file organization should we use to store this on-line textual information?

3. How shall we allow the user to browse through and select information from these on-line help files?

4. When should we transfer between program execution mode and help mode? Only under user control? Automatically?

5. How can we present the information to the user in a way that is more easily understood? How do we best exploit the graphical/sound capabilities of our terminal?

There are many different answers to these questions and many different approaches to the design of on-line assistance packages.

One powerful, but quite simple, approach is to use a *hierarchical keyword* system. When the user initially enters help mode (typically by entering a keyword such as "help") he or she is presented with a top-level *menu* of alternatives, from which one can be selected. For example,

```
?help
     Please select the command you want explained by typing the first letter of the
     command name, followed by return.
          (S)ave
          (R)estore
          (D)elete
          (C)opy
Type Q to quit help mode and return to program execution.
```

When the user selects an option he or she may be presented with yet another menu, which begins to focus in on the specific information that the user needs:

```
?S
     Please select the information you desire about the save command.
          (G)eneral description of the command and what it does
          (O)ptions available on this command
          (E)rror messages and their causes
Type Q to quit and return to the previous menu.
```

Eventually the specific information requested will be presented to the user as a unit (termed a *frame*), which is geared to the physical characteristics of the user's terminal (e.g., 25 lines × 80 characters). Thus, the accessing of information is done in a rigidly hierarchical fashion as the user moves up and down the branches of an information tree, which produces a menu at the nonterminal nodes and one or more distinct frames of information when we reach a terminal node.

This type of highly structured search is quite different from what is possible with written materials such as a user's manual in which you can browse and jump about at will. That is why these two distinct types of assistance are both important and why they should both be part of the user documentation package.

One reason that a hierarchical keyword system is so popular is that it is quite easy to implement. The top level of our hypothetical help mode can be sketched out as follows:

```
repeat
    done := false;
    repeat
        TopLevelMenu;          { Print out the menu }
        GetResponse (R);       { Get response from the user }
        Validate (R,ok)        { If response valid, set ok to true, else false }
    until ok;
    case R of
        'S' : SaveMenu;
        'R' : ReplaceMenu;
        'D' : DeleteMenu;
        'C' : CopyMenu;
        'Q' : done := true
    end
until done
```

The routines SaveMenu, ReplaceMenu, and so on would be quite similar in structure to the code just shown—putting up a menu, soliciting a response, validating that it is legal, and activating another lower-level routine. Eventually, when a terminal node is reached, we will not activate another menu routine, but instead print one (or more) frames of information:

```
PrintFrame(i)     { Print one chunk of text, then stop }
```

where i is a sector address in some text file that contains the desired frame of information.

Although the proposed design works, it lacks generality and is somewhat inefficient. If we want to change any of the menus (e.g., by adding some additional option) we must change the code and recompile the program. Some exercises at the end of the chapter propose possible changes to the help mode design we have introduced here to make it more general and flexible.

The important points to keep in mind are that on-line assistance is an important part of the overall package of user documentation, and planning for it must begin during the earliest stages of program design.

18.3
Technical Documentation

Technical documentation is the material the *maintenance programmer* needs to change, correct, or understand the program. This material is not intended for end-users but for technical specialists. The *structure* of the program (not simply its input/output characteristics) is of primary importance to these people.

Technical documentation must describe two distinct aspects of a program—*low-level coding details* and *high-level program structure*.

The low-level detail is totally contained in the *program listing*. The listing is actually one of the most important pieces of technical documentation available to programmers. This is why the rules on programming style in Chapters 13 and 14 are so important. They result in a simple, readable program listing that greatly facilitates maintenance. In addition, the modularity rules presented in Chapters 11 and 12 also enhance the clarity of the listing by dividing the program into independent, logically coherent pieces that can be treated as separate units. Writing programs with the following points in mind will greatly facilitate extracting middle- and low-level details from the program listing:

1. Good descriptive commentary.

2. Clear mnemonic names.

3. Helpful indentation.

4. Clear, understandable control structures.

However, except for relatively short programs, a listing alone may be insufficient. For large programs with thousands of lines of code, it takes too long to study a listing of dozens or even hundreds of pages. What we need is separate technical documentation that gives an overview of the *high-level* or *global* structure of the program. However, we already have such a document. It is the program design document first introduced in Chapter 11. The three components of the design document—the structure chart, module specifications, and data dictionary—provide exactly the global overview needed by a technical specialist. By using the design document, we will know where to look in the listing for additional information. This document is both a "technical summary" and a program "table of contents," since it contains both high-level descriptive material and numerous pointers to lower-level detail.

Again, the exact format of a program design document is a matter of personal taste and company policy. However, the following types of information are almost always included:

1. *Program name and purpose.* This will be similar to what we included in the user's guide, points 1 and 2. It is simply a few paragraphs describing what the program does.

2. *The historical development of the program and its current status.* This includes the names and addresses of the original authors and anyone who had responsibility for program maintenance. It includes the completion and acceptance date of the original work as well as dates and descriptions of listings showing changes, the testing of these changes, and the date of final acceptance.

3. *The overall program structure.* This will probably be displayed as a structure chart, similar to the one shown in Figure 11.5, or some other pictorial representa-

tion. This shows how the individual modules and data structures are related to each other.

4. *Description of each module.* Every module contained in the structure chart of part 3 should be individually described in terms of its high-level structure. This should include the following:
    a. Module name and type.
    b. Author and date of completion.
    c. Calling sequence.
    d. Purpose.
    e. Entry and exit conditions.
    f. Assertions about program behavior.
    g. Where it is called from.
    h. What other routines it activates.
    i. What data items are modified by this module.
    j. Reference to the location of this module in the listing (i.e., line number).
    k. History of changes/modifications to the original program.

    Figure 18.2 shows how the module enqueue from the simulator program of Chapter 15 might typically be documented in a program design document.

5. *Description of key data structures.* All important files and data structures should be individually described. This should include the following:
    a. Data structure name.
    b. Purpose.
    c. Operations on this data structure.
    d. Underlying implementation.
    e. Which modules access or modify this structure.
    f. Reference to where in the listing this data structure is originally declared and initialized.

    Figure 18.3 shows the description of the data structure called calendar, also from the simulator.

6. *Built-in maintenance aids.* If the program includes any debugging and testing aids or efficiency instruments for timing or profiling the code, the design document should include a guide to their use. This would include such aids as

    if debugging **then** . . .
    if testing **then** . . .
    if profiling **then** . . .

    which were introduced and discussed in Chapters 16 and 17.

7. *Testing/acceptance criteria.* The technical documentation should contain a list of test cases to be used during testing of the individual modules and during system integration.

The user's manual, on-line assistance, program design document, and the most current program listing are the four major items in the set of program documents.

FIGURE 18.2   Technical Description of Module
Enqueue.

1. *Name.* enqueue

2. *Author.* Written by G. M. Schneider, January 1, 1987.

3. *Calling Sequence.* **procedure** enqueue(p : studentptr; **var** q : queue);

   where p is a pointer to a student record and
         q is the head of a queue of student records.

4. *Purpose.* This procedure will add the student record pointed at by p to the *end* of the queue pointed at by the head node of q. q may be either the terminal queue or the consultant queue.

5. *Entry Conditions*

   p : points to student being placed in line
   q : points to the queue of 0 or more students

   Exit Conditions

   p : the next field of the record pointed to by p is set to **nil**
   q : has had student p placed at the end of the line

6. *Where Called from*

arrivalevent	line 16	(to add a newly arriving student to a terminal queue)
termevent	line 19	(to add a student to a consulting queue)
consultevent	line 11	(to add an existing student to a terminal queue)

7. *Other Procedures Called*

   None

8. *Major Data Items Accessed(A) or Modified(M)*

   (A) p -- pointer to student record
   (M) p ↑ .next -- next field of student record is set to **nil**
   (M) termqueue, consultqueue

9. *Location in Listing.* lines *mmmm* − *nnnn*

10. *Error Conditions That May Occur*

    None

11. *Current Version*

    The current version is 1.2. No major changes have been made to the original version.

FIGURE 18.3   Technical Documentation of Calendar Data Structure.

1. *Data Structure Name.* calendar

2. *Type.* A pointer to the head of a linked list of event records. The calendar itself is contained as a field within the record structure called staterec.

```
type staterec = record
    calendar : eventptr;
        .
        .
        .
            end;
    eventptr = ↑ event;
    event   = record
        eventtype : eventclass;
        eventtime : real;
        studptr     : studentptr;
        link        : eventptr
            end;
```

3. *Purpose.* Calendar is used to hold the list of events that must be processed by the simulation program. The events are stored on the calendar sorted by increasing time in the eventtime field. The calendar should never be empty.

4. *Operations That Access or Modify Calendar.*

    getnextevent: removes the first item on the calendar and resets the head pointer accordingly.

    schedule: adds a new event to the calendar. It is added in the proper location so that calendar is sorted by increasing time in the eventtime field.

5. *Declaration*
    Module main, line 40

    Initialization
    Module initialize, lines 6–7

18.4
Program Maintenance

Program maintenance is the process by which programs are corrected and updated to reflect changes in the problem specification. Unlike student programs, which have a short life (usually one successful run), most large production programs are used for a long time; 3 to 5 years is common and 10 to 15 years is not unheard of. Events that cause changes to the original program include

1. *Newly discovered bugs.* Errors that were not detected during the original testing phase may be discovered during actual program operation. (Hopefully, the testing and verification methods discussed in Chapter 16 will keep this problem to a minimum.)

2. *Program improvements.* User's may not be happy with the way the program currently operates. (Perhaps it is too complex or too confusing to use.) The program needs to be improved to rectify user complaints.

3. *Specification changes.* The original problem changes because of new laws, new discoveries, different users, or changing consumer demand. The program must be modified to reflect this change.

4. *Specification expansion.* The original program must be expanded to provide additional capabilities that had not been anticipated and included in the original program.

5. *New equipment.* The program must be rewritten to take advantage of a newer computer or compiler.

The time and costs involved with program maintenance are usually grossly underestimated by most programmers. Too often they think only of the one-time costs associated with the original design and implementation. However, as we mentioned at the beginning of this chapter, software products have a very long life, typically 5, 10, or 15 years. Therefore, a better judge of costs associated with software design and development is *life-cycle costs*—the total costs involved with both the original development and the ongoing maintenance of a software product over its entire useful life. Most studies have shown that the ratio of these maintenance costs to the original development costs are on the order of about 2:1 to 3:1. For poorly designed and poorly written programs, this figure can go much higher. Other studies have shown that typical programmers will spend only about 40% of their time on designing and implementing new software, while the other 60% of their time is spent on maintaining or enhancing existing software products.

It is only quite recently that programming project managers have begun to appreciate the magnitude of these maintenance costs. This has led to a demand for techniques that reduce maintenance costs, speed up changes, and minimize the risk of introducing errors. Most of the programming techniques, styles, methods, and approaches we have presented in this text have been designed for precisely that purpose. In reviewing these techniques, we can now appreciate why they are so critical.

1. *Clarity and readability.* The program listing is the primary piece of technical documentation. The clarity of that listing significantly affects the time it takes to implement a program change.
2. *Portability and generality.* Software tends to last longer than hardware. Therefore, a program written with portability in mind will create much less havoc when the inevitable new computer arrives. Likewise, when user needs change, a truly general program will require less programmer time to adapt to the new specifications.
3. *Structured code.* The most common maintenance operation is tracking down bugs that went unnoticed during the testing phase. A program implemented as a series of single entry–single exit blocks will facilitate debugging and testing.
4. *Robustness.* A robust program will not ''bomb out'' without any helpful error message. Instead, it will terminate gracefully with useful information that will help the maintenance programmer (or the user) locate and correct the problem.
5. *Logical coherence and independence.* When a change can be localized to a single module, it makes maintenance much easier. We do not need to worry about the effects of that change rippling throughout other modules in the system.
6. *Debugging and testing.* A formalized debugging and testing scheme reduces the likelihood of undetected bugs getting into the finished program, thus reducing the maintenance required on that program.
7. *Documentation.* The technical documentation of a program is necessary because many other programmers will be working with and maintaining that program over its life span.

The needs of programmers during the maintenance phase is a common thread running throughout our discussion and motivating much of what we have presented. The stylistic guidelines and implementation methods we have stressed make the most sense when you remember these key points:

1. Programs change often. They are not static entities.
2. Programs tend to be used for long periods of time, typically 5, 10, even 15 years. The people that developed the original program may not be available to explain or clarify the design.
3. A program will be maintained by many different programmers over its lifetime, and most of them will be initially unfamiliar with its contents or structure.
4. The most expensive component of any computer system is *personnel costs*.

Together these points indicate how important it is to develop programs that are easy for *people* to use, as well as for computers.

18.5
Programming Support Environments

Because of the soaring costs of personnel, programmer productivity is a critically important issue when designing new software as well as maintaining existing packages. One way to enhance productivity was mentioned in the last section—to follow the design and implementation guidelines laid out in the earlier chapters of this text. Well-designed, well-structured, legible code is easier to work with, understand, and change. There is also another way, and that is the technique used to enhance the productivity of any worker, whether it be a dishwasher, steel worker, or computer programmer—to provide that individual with a better and more powerful collection of *tools* with which to work.

Computers are used to solve problems, but executing a program to produce output is certainly not the only problem we encounter during the many stages involved in the programming process. More and more powerful tools are being developed to assist the programmer with problems that occur during *all* phases of programming.

The earliest support tools available to programmers were *language processors*— assemblers and compilers—which eliminated the need for coding directly in machine language. These language tools were developed in the early 1950s right along with the first commercial computers. Not much later came *editors,* to help us prepare source code, *linkers,* to support independent compilation units, and *file systems,* to help store and retrieve the source and object files. These tools have been around for more than 20 years. However, for many programmers this is the extent of the support environment in which they create and work. While hardware features and capabilities have exploded in the last 5 to 10 years, the software environment in which many programmers work, as shown in Figure 18.4, is not a great deal different from that of 5, 10, or even 20 years ago.

The majority of the support tools available and pictured in Figure 18.4, suffer from at least three major problems:

1. They are not extensive enough. Looking at the tools listed in Figure 18.4, we can see they are almost all directed at helping us during the coding phase. There is little to help the programmer with specification, design, testing, formal verification, or maintenance. As we have mentioned many times, coding occupies only about 15 to 25% of the overall time of a software project. Tools that helped us during the other 75 to 85% could produce significant savings.

2. The tools are not always *integrated.* Typically, each of the routines listed in Figure 18.4 is developed as a stand-alone package, separate from the other facilities on the system. Integrated software is designed and written as a single, complete package and is intended to work together as a unit. For example, the following scenario is quite typical of a debugging session using nonintegrated software:

   Run the compiler. Get a syntax error.
   Mark down on which line the error occurred.

FIGURE 18.4   Typical Programming Support Tools.

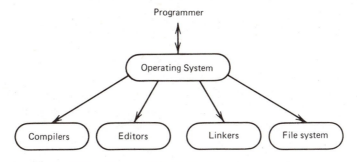

Exit the compiler and return to the operating system.
Enter the editor, typically on line 1.
Ask the editor to search for the line containing the error.
Move the cursor to the character in error.
Correct the syntax error.
Exit the editor and return to the operating system.
Ask the filer to save the new version of the program.
Ask the filer to delete the old version of the program.
Enter the compiler and recompile the program.

This process can be quite slow and would need to be repeated for each run with syntax errors. In an integrated system, when the compiler located a syntax error, it could automatically enter the editor with the cursor positioned on the correct line and directly over the erroneous character. When the change was made, the system could automatically save it and initiate recompilation. This eliminates the jumping in and out of programs so typical of nonintegrated software.

3.   The tools are not *standardized*. The Pascal language has been standardized and, except for local extensions, is virtually identical on all computer systems. However, the tools of Figure 18.4 have often not been standardized, and screen editors running on a VAX-11/782, IBM-4300, or an AT&T 3B might all be quite different. Worse still, different packages on the same system may not even operate in a similar fashion. (On one well-known system, you exit from one software package by entering LO, another with EXIT, a third with BYE, and a fourth with CNTL-Z.)

In the last few years there has been extensive work on the development of more powerful, more extensive, and more useful programming tools that can help with many different aspects of software development. These tools offer great promise in enhancing programmer productivity. It is becoming much less common to work in the type of minimalist environment diagrammed in Figure 18.4. More and more programmers are

FIGURE 18.5   Example of a Powerful Program Support
Environment.

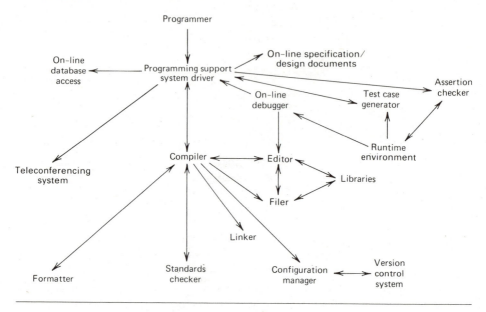

working within what are called *programming support environments*. This is a software
development system that contains the following:

1.   Powerful new fourth-generation programming languages, such as LISP, PRO-
     LOG, or SmallTalk.

2.   An extensive set of tools that address all phases of the programming process from
     specification to maintenance.

3.   An additional set of support tools that enhance oral and written communications
     between programmers, including networking, teleconferencing, and on-line data-
     base access to both technical information and experts in the field.

4.   Yet an additional set of tools that support the management aspects of program
     development, including scheduling, budgeting, source code management, and
     personnel.

5.   The tools are integrated to support, easily and efficiently, the transfer of both
     information and control between programs.

6.   The tools are standardized and present a common interface to the programmer.

A programming support environment can be viewed as its own self-contained operating system for the special purpose of designing and implementing correct software in
the most cost-efficient manner. A more realistic and up-to-date pictorial representation
of the environment in which programmers might operate is shown in Figure 18.5.

The list of tools in Figure 18.5, though certainly not exhaustive, includes tools that are typical of those being developed to enhance programmer productivity. In the following pages we will introduce some of the more interesting and widely used packages. These or similar tools may be available at your installation, and if they are you should learn how to make use of them.

1. *New programming languages.* Newer procedural languages such as Ada and Modula-2 are providing additional capabilities not available from older languages such as BASIC, FORTRAN, COBOL, or even Pascal. These features include

   Data abstraction mechanisms
   Exception handling capabilities
   Multitasking and parallelism
   More powerful scope rules
   More powerful procedural abstraction facilities

   In addition to new procedural languages there is also research work going on in the development of *specification languages,* also called *nonprocedural languages.* These are languages in which we need only write out in our program the input and desired output, not the technique for solving the problem. Examples include database query languages and PROLOG.

   In a traditional procedural language, to determine if an element occurs in a table, we must write out the explicit algorithm to carry out this task.

   ```
   i := 0; found := false;
   while (i < N) and not found do
       begin
       i := i + 1;
       if key = table[i] then found := true
       end
   ```

   In a nonprocedural language, we would simply say something like "find key in table." For example, in the language called PROLOG, this same table lookup problem might be expressed as follows:

   ```
   is (X : equal (X,key) and member(X,table))
   ```

   which asks if there exists any object, X, which is equal to the key and which is also contained in the table. This expression is called a *query,* and the answer will be yes or no. We do not care at all how the computer answers our query, and we are totally ignorant of whether it uses sequential search, binary search, or some totally different algorithm.

   Comparing these two approaches to programming, we see quite clearly that nonprocedural languages offer an enormous opportunity to increase programmer productivity by eliminating some of the work that the programmer must now do in designing and coding algorithms.

2. *Standards checker*. A standards checker is a tool (which may or may not be part of the compiler) that identifies syntactic components which are not part of the officially published language standard:

```
case i of
     1 : p1;
     2 : p2;
     3 : p3;
else p4
*** Warning : else clause in case statement is a nonstandard language
     feature ***
end
```

As mentioned in Chapter 14, adhering to the standard syntax of the language is important for ensuring portability. Using a standards checker can guarantee that we do not unintentionally use any nonstandard features.

3. *Formatter*. As mentioned in Chapter 13, there are many different indentation schemes for formatting your program. Although it is not too important which one you use, it is helpful if all programmers on a single project adhere to the same indentation standard. A formatter takes a source program as input and produces a new source program as output, which has been indented according to a fixed set of rules. For example,

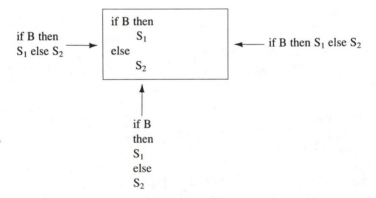

4. *On-line debugging tools (ODT)*. We first mentioned ODTs in Chapter 16. They are packages that allow you to execute your program in a special operating environment called *debug mode*. In this mode you can stop your program whenever you desire, observe program behavior, trace variables, and change the contents of any of the data objects at will. Having an ODT eliminates much of the need for the programmer to insert his or her own debugging tools (i.e., write statements) into the program. It also gives the programmer capabilities he or she would not otherwise have, such as the ability to set a *breakpoint*—a program interrupt placed in the code that, when executed, temporarily suspends program execution.

The following quite simple program to average a set of input values contains a bug:

Line number	Statement
1	**program** Aver (input, output);
2	**var**
3	i, sum, num, average : integer;
4	**begin**
5	i := 1;
6	sum := 0;
7	readln(num);
8	**while** (num <> −1) **do**
9	**begin**
10	sum := sum + num;
11	i := i + 1;
12	readln(num)
13	**end**;
14	average := sum **div** i;
15	writeln('average =',average)
16	**end**

A typical execution scenario for this program using an ODT might go like this: (The ''>'' is the prompt from the debugger. Information in italics is output from the debugger).

```
>set breakpoint = 6      (Put in a breakpoint after line 6 of the program)
>run                     (Begin execution of the program)
breakpoint reached after line 6 (Program is suspended after executing line 6)
>examine i               (Asking for the current value of i)
i = 1
>examine sum             (Asking for the value of sum)
sum = 0
>examine average
average is undefined
>change breakpoint = 11 (Move breakpoint from line 6 to line 11)
>run                     (Start up program execution from where it was
                          suspended)
?10                      (This is the normal input operation in Pascal)
breakpoint reached after line 11 (Program is suspended after line 11)
>examine i
i = 2
>examine sum
sum = 10
```

At this point we will probably notice the bug in our program (i is too large by 1; it should be initialized to 0). If not, we could continue in this type of environment—running the program in small pieces and then closely examining its behavior.

A real ODT will have a great many additional services not mentioned here and not shown in the previous example. An ODT is a powerful system that can provide a great deal of assistance in helping to locate and correct bugs.

5. *Test case generators.* A test case generator (TCG) is a software tool that examines the source code of a program and attempts to determine the test cases needed to test every statement in that program. Given the following code fragment:

```
If (a > 5) then
      S₁
else
      if (b = 8) then
            S₂
      else
            S₃
```

a TCG could determine that we would initially need two classes of test data—one in which the initial boolean expression is true, to enter the true clause, and one in which it is false, to execute the else clause:

Case 1: $(a > 5)$
Case 2: **not** $(a > 5)$, that is $(a \leq 5)$

In the second case, it could determine that we again need two cases to fully test the else clause.

Case 2a: $(a \leq 5)$ **and** $(b = 8)$
Case 2b: $(a \leq 5)$ **and not** $(b = 8)$, that is $(a \leq 5)$ and $(b <> 8)$

The output of the TCG would be a list of test cases needed to execute each control path in the program, in this case:

Case 1: $(a > 5)$
Case 2: $(a \leq 5)$ **and** $(b = 8)$
Case 3: $(a \leq 5)$ **and** $(b <> 8)$

However, the problem is not quite as simple as it seems. It is not always possible for a TCG to determine, strictly from an examination of the source code, exactly what input data will force execution of every statement and every control path. That is, although a TCG can tell you that you need one test case in which $(a < 5)$, it may not be able to tell you how to set your input values to achieve this condition. For example, given the following fragment:

```
read (a,b,c);
if (b <> c) then
    begin
        d := a + b;
        e := c - b;
        if (d = e) then
```

A TCG will be able to say that we will need test cases in which $(b <> c)$, $(b = c)$, $(d = e)$, and $(d <> e)$. But it will probably *not* be able to tell you how to generate a condition like $(d = e)$ directly from the input variables a, b, c. (An examination of the code shows that $d = e$ when the first and the third input variables differ by a quantity that is twice the second input parameter.) This is a much more complex problem that is unsolvable for arbitrary programs. Therefore, a TCG should be viewed more as a "helper" and a "double checker" when carrying out empirical testing rather than a replacement for the manual procedures described in Chapter 16.

6. *Assertion checker*. In Section 16.5 we introduced the concept of an *assertion*—a boolean predicate describing the state of the computation at a point in the program and which we assert to be true. Using these assertions we can prove certain characteristics about program behavior. We also indicated that it is a good idea to include your assertions as comments within the program. An *assertion checker* is a software tool that, at execution time, can check the truth of those assertions included within the source code. If it evaluates an assertion and comes up with a value of false, it will typically halt with what is called an *assertion violation*. This would correspond directly to an error in your proof of program correctness, since assertions are always supposed to be true.

For example, if we use the notation {{ }} to indicate these special assertion comments, then the following line in a source program:

{{{(x > y) and (i <> 0)}}}

asserts that, at this point in the program's execution, it will always be the case that x, y, and i will be defined, x will be strictly greater than y, and i will be nonzero. If this condition is violated, the assertion checker will let us know immediately. Assertion checkers appear to offer a significant help in making formal verification a practical and useful tool.

7. *Comparator*. One of the most common problems encountered during maintenance is determining exactly where two versions of the same program differ. That is, what change did we make in program P_1 to reach program P_2. A program will typically have dozens of changes made in it during debugging, testing, and maintenance. It is all too easy to forget which change was made to which version. A *comparator* is a tool that takes as input two source programs, compares them character by character, and prints out exactly where the two programs differ, thus letting you know exactly what modifications have been made. For example, look-

ing back at the bug in the averaging program in Section 4, if we fixed the bug, and then ran the old and new programs through our comparator, we would get something like

	Program 1	*Program 2*
line 5:	$i := 1;$	$i := 0;$

This would immediately identify P_2 as the version in which the bug has been corrected, and P_1 as the old one.

8. *Configuration management system.* Related to the problem mentioned in the previous paragraph is the larger problem of managing the development of a software project composed of hundreds or thousands of modules, each being debugged, tested, enhanced, updated, and changed and existing in possibly a dozen different versions, varieties, and variations. Keeping track of the state of all of these modules, ensuring that all have passed the required acceptance tests, and guaranteeing that you are including the correct version into the completed system is a very complex management problem. A *configuration management system* (CMS) is a tool that helps the programming team leader track the individual components of the program and manage their integration into the overall system. A CMS includes a database that lists, for every module in the system, the following types of information:

a. How many different versions of this module exist?
b. How is each version uniquely identified?
c. Exactly how do these versions differ?
d. Who made the version?
e. What was the date of the change?
f. When did the version pass acceptance testing, or, if it did not, what state is it currently in?
g. Are there any known problems or bugs with this version?

In addition to maintaining this database, a CMS may allow us to build a complete system by collecting any desired version of each module. For example, a program may be composed of 50 modules, $P_1, \ldots, P_{50}$. Module P_{50}, the output module, may exist in three varieties: one for a color graphics terminal, one for an alphanumeric CRT, and one for a hard-copy printer. A CMS might allow us to equate symbolic names with a collection of modules and say

>build color-graphic-system, place in f.

The CMS would now collect the latest source code version of modules $P_1, \ldots,$ P_{49}, together with the latest version of the color graphics variety of module P_{50}, which it can locate in its CMS database), compute and link them, and store the finished object code on a file called f.

A configuration management system is an important management, rather than technical, tool to ensure the development of correct and reliable software.

This discussion has introduced you to only a small number of powerful program support tools that are or will be widely available. Other tools, not mentioned here, but also quite important include

> Program specification and design tools.
> Advanced screen editors.
> Cross-reference table generators.
> Library managers.
> Source code complexity analyzers.
> Profilers, code analyzers.
> Documentation support systems (page layout, typesetting, font design).
> On-line education and information systems (CAI).
> Teleconferencing systems/local networks.
> On-line database access systems.

The important point for a programmer to realize is that one's productivity is a function of the tools one has to work with, and on a typical computer system there will usually be a wealth of tools available in addition to the compiler with which you are so familiar. Learn to be knowledgeable of and comfortable with these tools, and use them to help you through all stages of the programming process.

Future courses in software engineering and computer science will introduce you further to many of the programming support products mentioned in this section.

18.6
Conclusion

Programming is a complex operation with a number of important phases, each with its own techniques and guidelines. Programmers must be familiar not only with the syntax of a particular programming language, but also with project management techniques, algorithmic analysis, advanced data structures, human factors engineering, testing and verification methods, and technical writing. The difference between coding and programming is like the difference between grammar and creative writing. A knowledge of the former will allow you to write correctly, but a knowledge of both will allow you to write elegantly. If you have mastered the techniques and guidelines in this text, you are on your way to becoming a *programmer* in the fullest sense of the word.

Exercises for Chapter 18

1.   Write a complete user's manual for the Idiot's Delight program in Chapter 2. When writing the manual, you should assume the following of users:

    a.   They do not know Pascal.

    b.   They will not have access to the program listing.

    c.   They are naive about computers but do know how to log on and use a terminal.

Your user's manual should contain everything users need to use the program at your installation correctly.

   2.   Write the necessary technical documentation for the "wcwreverse" program in Section 2.2.4. First, study the listing (comments, style, structure) and state whether or not you feel it is acceptable as written. If not, suggest changes that would make the listing a more useful technical document. Next, write the technical documentation for "wcwreverse." Follow the general guidelines in Section 18.3, but feel free to add other information that you feel is critical.

   3.   Exchange your technical documentation from Exercise 3 with someone else in the class and, using that documentation, make the following modification to "wcwreverse." Change the program so it will accept an *arbitrary* number of characters, c, between the strings w and w'. That is, the program will recognize strings of the form:

$$\underbrace{wccc.\ .\ .\ .\ .\ .ccc}_{\text{1 or more}}w'$$

   4.   Develop and write the technical documentation for a program that others in the class may not have seen or studied recently (a homework assignment, a program from another Pascal textbook, or a program from one of the earlier chapters). Now exchange programs and documentation and have them perform some modification to that program. Keep track of how helpful the technical documentation and the listing were in making the modification. Make suggestions to the original author on how and where the documentation could have been more helpful, complete, and detailed. Perform the following modification operations. For each modification discuss how the program's structure, modularization, and coding style did or did not facilitate making this change.

   5.   The users of procedure trapezoidrule (Figure 14.3) are worried about integrating over a function that is undefined somewhere within the interval.

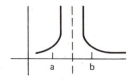

They want you to modify the program so that if the value of $f(x)$ at some point x_0 exceeds a preset maximum:

$$|f(x_0)| > \text{max}$$

where | | means absolute value, then the program will print out the following message:

*** Warning, integral not defined over this interval ***

6.   The users of the grade analysis program "statistic" (Figure 13.9) are unhappy with one aspect of the output: the histogram is too long. If, for example, the scores were 0 to 200, the histogram would be 201 lines long (about four pages!). Rewrite the program so that users can provide a value for a quantity called range, which specifies the *width* of the intervals to be used when printing the histogram. As a result, the histogram will specify the number of values that fall in this range. If, for example, our scores were 0 to 200 and range was 45, the histogram would look like this:

180–200	**
135–179	*********
90–134	*******
45–89	****
0–44	*

The range, r, need not be an even multiple of the possible scores. The last interval will simply include all remaining scores (as in the range 180 to 200). Naturally r must be greater than 0 and less than the total possible values. If it is not, produce an appropriate error message.

7.   Have half the class modify the merge code fragment of Figure 13.7 and the other half modify the fragment in Figure 13.8 so that in addition to merging the two lists the code also eliminates any duplicate items that occur in both alist and blist. For example,

1	2	1
2	3	2
3	4	3
8	6	4
11	8	6
		8
		11
alist	blist	clist

Keep track of the following:
   a.   The total time it takes to make this change.
   b.   The number of runs it takes to get the code working properly.

Now compare the time and effort of the two groups in making the change. What does this say about the effect of program style and structure on program maintenance?

8.   The users of the code for the merge operation (Figure 13.8) are worried that if the original lists alist and blist are not properly sorted, the merged result (clist) will be incorrect. Modify the fragment so that if alist or blist is not properly sorted, the following error message is printed:

** Warning — list xxx not properly sorted into ascending order. The value out of sequence is xxx. The merge operation is terminated **

9. Talk to a professional programmer and find out the following information:
    a. What percentage of his or her time is spent in maintaining existing software packages versus writing totally new programs.
    b. What is the most common cause of this necessary change—bugs, new features, new hardware.
    c. How old the software being maintained is. What the current version number is.
    d. What programming tools are commonly available at this installation to assist the programmer in the maintenance operation.

10. Discuss whether or not the tools that are available to you at your installation and that you used in the courses called Computer Programming I and Computer Programming II were well integrated with the compiler. Did they allow easy switching between programs? Did they allow for easy sharing of files between programs? How could these tools have been improved?

11. What additional features would you like to see in future versions of Pascal that would be directed specifically at easing the problems of program maintenance? List the specific features and discuss in what ways it would help the programmer.

12. Find out whether or not your installation has any of the following programming tools:
    a. ODT
    b. Test case generator
    c. Program formatter
    d. Standards checker
    e. Assertion checker
    f. Configuration manager
    g. Source code comparator

If it does, learn how to use any one of them and prepare a report for the class describing how it operates, what features it contains, and how it can help to increase programmer productivity.

Bibliography for Part Three

Aho, A., J. Hopcroft, and J. Ullman. *The Design and Analysis of Computer Algorithms*. Reading, MA: Addison-Wesley, 1984.

Brooks, F. *The Mythical Man-Month*. Reading, Mass.: Addison-Wesley, 1975.

Brown, A. R., and W. A. Sampson. *Program Debugging*. New York: American Elsevier Publishing Co., 1973.

Cassel, Don. *The Structured Alternative: Program Design Style and Debugging*. Reston Publication Co., 1983.

Dijkstra, E. *A Discipline of Programming.* Englewood Cliffs, N.J.: Prentice-Hall, 1976.

Goodman, S. E., and S. T. Hedetniemi. *Introduction to the Design and Analysis of Algorithms.* New York: McGraw-Hill, 1977.

Gries, David. *The Science of Programming.* New York: Springer-Verlag, 1981.

Hetzel, W. C., ed. *Program Test Methods.* Englewood Cliffs, N.J.: Prentice-Hall, 1973.

Horowitz, E., and S. Sahni. *Fundamentals of Computer Algorithms.* Potomac, MD: Computer Science Press, 1978.

Kernighan, B., and P. Plauger. *Software Tools in Pascal.* Reading, Mass.: Addison-Wesley, 1981.

London, K. R. *Documentation Standards,* Petrocelli/Charter, 1974.

Poole, P. C. "Debugging and Testing," in *Advanced Course in Software Engineering.* New York: Springer-Verlag, 1973.

Van Tassel, D. *Program Style, Design, Efficiency, Debugging, and Testing,* 2nd ed. Englewood Cliffs, N.J.: Prentice-Hall, 1978.

Yeh, R. T. *Current Trends in Programming Methodology, Vol. II: Program Testing and Validation.* Englewood Cliffs, N.J.: Prentice-Hall, 1977.

The following journals contain articles related to the material covered in this section:

Software: Practice and Experience
IEEE Transactions on Software Engineering
The monthly newsletters of the following special interest groups (SIG) of the ACM: SIGSOFT (software engineering), SIGDOC (documentation), and SIGMETRICS (performance evaluation).

APPENDICES

APPENDIX A

SYNTAX OF THE
Pascal LANGUAGE[1]

Represents Pascal reserved words or syntacic
entities that are not defined further (e.g., a letter
or a digit)

Represents a Pascal operator

Represents a syntactic entity that is
defined by another flow diagram.

Program

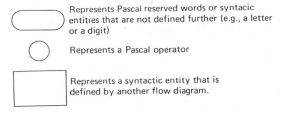

[1]This appendix is taken from Appendix D, pp. 116–118, of Jensen and Wirth, *PASCAL Users Manual and Report,* Springer-Verlag, 1974, with their permission.

Block

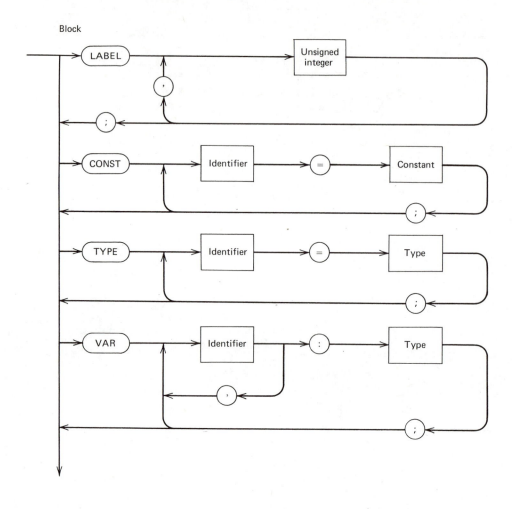

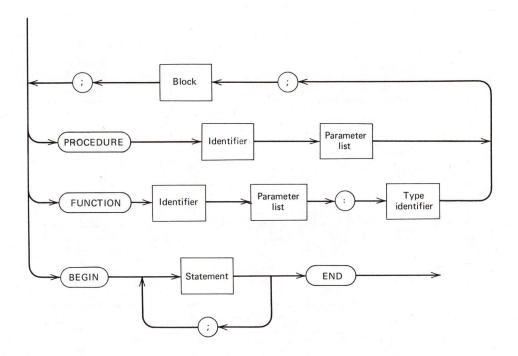

Statement

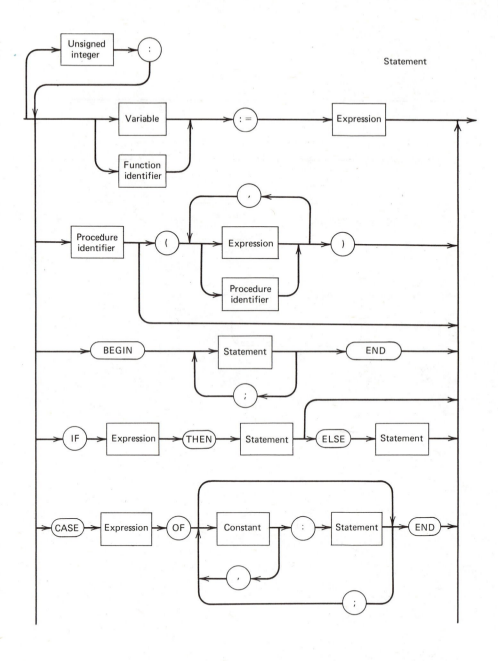

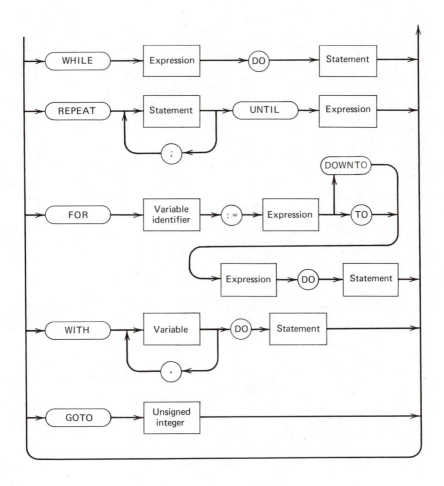

Type

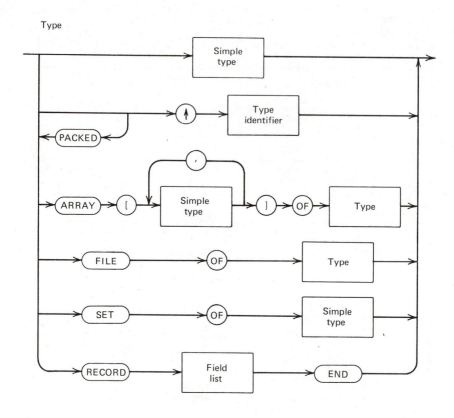

Simple type

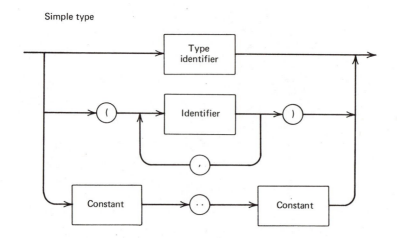

Parameter list

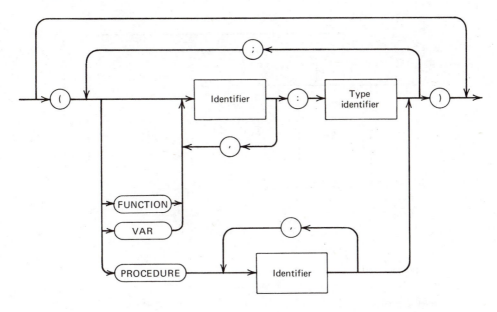

Field list

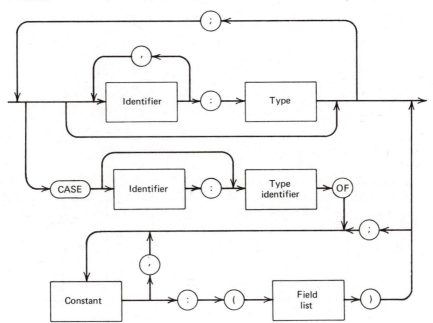

Expression

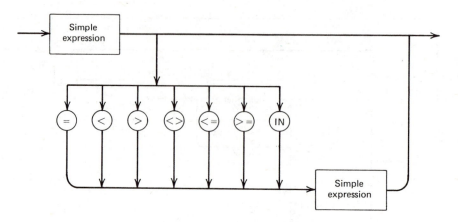

Simple expression

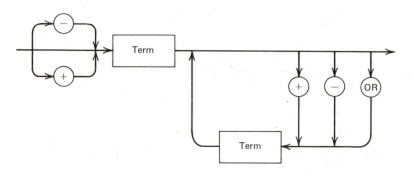

Term

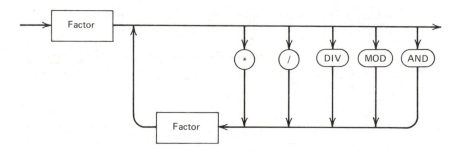

Factor

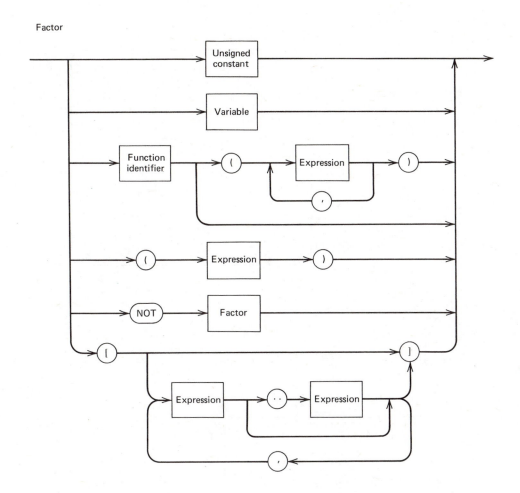

Variable

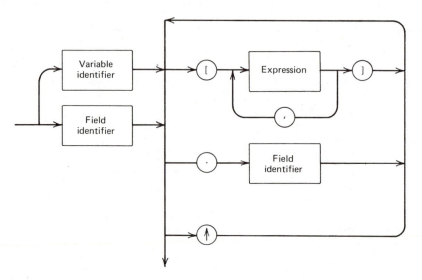

Unsigned constant

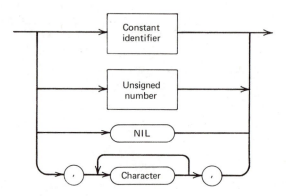

Constant

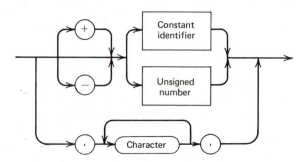

Identifier

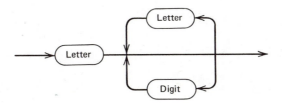

Unsigned integer

Unsigned number

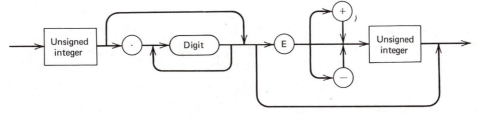

STANDARDIZED
Pascal IDENTIFIERS

B.1
Reserved Words

and	end	nil	set
array	file	not	then
begin	for	of	to
case	function	or	type
const	goto	packed	until
div	if	procedure	var
do	in	program	while
downto	label	record	with
else	mod	repeat	

B.2
Standard Identifiers

Constants

false   true   maxint

Types

integer   boolean   real   char   text

Files

input   output

Functions

Name	Types Parameter	Result	Description
abs(x)	integer or real	Same as parameter	Absolute value
arctan(x)	integer or real	real	Inverse tangent
chr(x)	integer	char	Character whose ordinal number is x
cos(x)	integer or real	real	Cosine
eof(f)	file	boolean	End-of-file indicator
eoln(f)	file	boolean	End-of-line indicator
exp(x)	real or integer	real	e^x
ln(x)	real or integer	real	Natural logarithm
odd(x)	integer	boolean	True if x is odd False otherwise
ord(x)	User-defined scalar, char, boolean	integer	Ordinal number of x in the scalar data type of which x is a member
pred(x)	Scalar, but not real	Same as parameter	Predecessor of x
round(x)	real	integer	x rounded
sin(x)	real or integer	real	Sine
sqr(x)	real or integer	Same as parameter	Square of x
sqrt(x)	real or integer	real	Square root
succ(x)	Scalar, but not real	Same as parameter	Successor of x
trunc(x)	real	integer	x truncated

Procedures

Name (parameters)	Description
dispose(p)	Returns the dynamic variable referenced by pointer p to the available space list
get(f)	Advances file f to the next component and places the value of the component in f ↑
new(p)	Allocates a new variable that is accessed through pointer p
pack(a,i,z)	Takes the elements beginning at subscript position i of array a and copies them into packed array z beginning at the first subscript position
page(f)	Causes the printer to skip to the top of a new page before printing the next line of text file f
read(. . .) readln(. . .)	Reads information from text files.
reset(f)	Positions file f at its beginning for reading
rewrite(f)	Empties file f and allows it to be written into
unpack(z,a,i)	Takes the elements beginning at the first subscript position of packed array z and copies them into array a beginning at subscript position i
write(. . .) writeln(. . .)	Writes information to text files.

B.3
Summary of Operators

Operator	Description	Types Operand(s)	Result
:=	Assignment	Any, except file	—
+	Addition	Integer or real	Integer or real
	Set union	Any set type	Same as operand
−	Subtraction	Integer or real	Integer or real
	Set difference	Any set type	Same as operand
*	Multiplication	Integer or real	Integer or real
	Set intersection	Any set type	Same as operand
div	Integer division	Integer	Integer
/	Real division	Integer or real	Real
mod	Modulus	Integer	Integer
not	Logical negation	Boolean	Boolean
or	Disjunction	Boolean	Boolean
and	Conjunction	Boolean	Boolean
<=	Implication	Boolean	Boolean
	Set inclusion	Any set type	Boolean
	Less than or equal	Any scalar type	Boolean
=	Equivalence	Boolean	Boolean
	Equality	Scalar, set, or pointer	Boolean
<>	Exclusive **or**	Boolean	Boolean
	Inequality	Scalar, set, or pointer	Boolean
>=	Set inclusion	Any set type	Boolean
	Greater than or equal	Any scalar type	Boolean
<	Less than	Any scalar type	Boolean
>	Greater than	Any scalar type	Boolean
in	Set membership	Left operand: scalar	Boolean
		Right operand: set with base type the type of the left operand	

APPENDIX C

CHARACTER SETS

The charts in this appendix depict the ordering for several commonly used character sets. Numbers are base 10 and only printable characters are shown.

Many other character sets and collating sequences not included here are in current use.

C.1
CDC Scientific, with 64 Characters

Left Digit	Right Digit									
	0	1	2	3	4	5	6	7	8	9
0	:	A	B	C	D	E	F	G	H	I
1	J	K	L	M	N	O	P	Q	R	S
2	T	U	V	W	X	Y	Z	0	1	2
3	3	4	5	6	7	8	9	+	−	*
4	/	(	)	$	=		,	.	≡	[
5	]	%	≠	↱	∨	∧	↑	↓	<	>
6	≤	≥	¬	;						

591

C.2
ASCII (American Standard Code for Information Interchange)

Left Digit(s)	0	1	2	3	4	5	6	7	8	9
							Right Digit			
3		blank	!	''	#	$	%	&	'	
4	(	)	*	+	,	−	.	/	0	1
5	2	3	4	5	6	7	8	9	:	;
6	<	=	>	?	@	A	B	C	D	E
7	F	G	H	I	J	K	L	M	N	O
8	P	Q	R	S	T	U	V	W	X	Y
9	Z	[	\	]	∧	—	`	a	b	c
10	d	e	f	g	h	i	j	k	l	m
11	n	o	p	q	r	s	t	u	v	w
12	x	y	z	{	|	}	~			

Codes 00 to 31 and 127 (decimal) represent special control characters that are not printable.

C.3
EBCDIC (Extended Binary Coded Decimal Interchange Code)

Left Digit(s)	0	1	2	3	4	5	6	7	8	9
					Right Digit					
6					blank					
7					¢	.	<	(	+	|
8	&									
9	!	$	*	)	;	¬	−	/		
10							|	,	%	—
11	>	?								
12		`	:	#	@	'	=	''		a
13	b	c	d	e	f	g	h	i		
14						j	k	l	m	n
15	o	p	q	r						
16		~	s	t	u	v	w	x	y	z
17				[						
18										]
19			{	A	B	C	D	E	F	G
20	H	I							}	J
21	K	L	M	N	O	P	Q	R		
22					\		S	T	U	V
23	W	X	Y	Z						
24	0	1	2	3	4	5	6	7	8	9

Codes 00 to 63 and 250 to 255 represent nonprintable control characters.

ANSWERS TO
SELECTED EXERCISES

Chapter 2

1. $\text{loc}(a[i,j]) = \text{loc}(a[l_1,l_2]) + (i - l_1) + (u_1 - l_1 + 1)(j - l_2)$

2. $\text{loc}(a[i,j]) = \text{loc}(a[l_1,l_2]) + (j - l_2) + (u_2 - l_2 + 1)(i - l_1)$

5. **type**
      person   =
          record
               name   : alfa;
               height   :
                  record
                     feet   : integer;
                     inches   : integer
                  end;
               eyecolor   : (blue,green,brown,black,hazel, . . .);
               age   : 0 .. 200;
               sex   : (male,female);
               weight   : integer
          end { of **record** person }

8. $ab*cd + e\char94 *fg - h\char94 *i - jk*/l-$

9. **function** ackermann(m : integer; n : integer) : integer;
    begin
        if m = 0 **then** ackermann := n+1
        else
        if n = 0 **then** ackermann := ackermann(m−1,1)
        else ackermann := ackermann(m−1,ackermann(m,n−1))
    end { of **function** ackermann }

    $A(3,2) = 29$

Try running the following program with the debug write statements inserted:

```
program ackermann(input,output);

function ackermann(m : integer; n : integer) : integer;
begin
    if m = 0 then
    begin
        writeln('A(0,',n:1,')=',n+1);
        ackermann := n+1
    end
    else
    if n = 0 then
    begin
        writeln('A(',m:1,',0)=A(',m-1:1,',1)');
        ackermann := ackermann(m-1,1)
    end
    else
    begin
        writeln('A(',m:1,',',n:1,')=A(',m-1:1,',A(',m:1,',',n-1:1,'))');
        ackermann := ackermann(m-1,ackermann(m,n-1))
    end
end; { of function ackermann }

begin
    writeln('A(3,2)=',ackermann(3,2))
end.
```

10.
```
function binomialcoefficient(n : integer; m : integer) : integer;
begin
    if n >= m then
    begin
        if m < 0 then binomialcoefficient := 0
        else
        if m = 0 then binomialcoefficient := 1
        else
        if m = 1 then binomialcoefficient := n
        else
        binomialcoefficient := binomialcoefficient(n-1,m) +
                binomialcoefficient(n-1,m-1)
    end
    else binomialcoefficient := 0
end { of function binomialcoefficient }
```

Chapter 3

1. **procedure** dequeue(**var** item : char; **var** rear : queuepointer;
     var successful : boolean);
   var
        node   : queuepointer;
   begin
        if rear <> **nil then**   { nonempty queue }
        begin
             item := rear^.next^.data;   { return item at head of queue }
             node := rear^.next;   { save pointer to head of queue }
             dispose(node);   { return node to available space }
             if node = rear **then** rear := nil;
             successful := true   { dequeue operation successful }
        end
        else successful := false   { indicate queue underflow }
   end { of **procedure** dequeue }

2. **function** numberofnodes(ptr : nodepointer) : integer;
   var
        count   : integer;
        firstnode   : nodepointer;
   begin
        { initialize }
        count := 0;
        firstnode := ptr;

        { walk through list }
        while ptr <> **nil do**
        begin
             { we have seen one more node in list }
             count := count + 1;

             { if we are dealing with circular list and we are about to go back to
               head node, set ptr to nil so that we can terminate while loop;
               otherwise advance ptr down the list }
             if ptr^.next = firstnode
             then ptr := **nil**
             else ptr := ptr^.next
        end;

        { return number of nodes }
        numberofnodes := count
   end { of **function** numberofnodes }

4.
```pascal
procedure reverse(var ptr : nodepointer);
var
    p      : nodepointer;
    q      : nodepointer;
    r      : nodepointer;
begin
    { initialize }
    p := ptr;
    q := nil;

    { traverse list reversing links as we go }
    while p <> nil do
    begin
        r  := q;
        q := p;
        p := p^.next;
        q^.next := r
    end;

    { reset head of list }
    ptr := q
end { of procedure reverse }
```

6.
```pascal
type
    queuepointer        = ^queueelement;
    queueelement        =
        record
            data    : char;
            next    : queuepointer
        end;
    headpointer         = ^headelement;
    headelement         =
        record
            front   : queuepointer;
            rear    : queuepointer
        end;

procedure enqueue(item : char; var head : headpointer);
var
    node    : queuepointer;
begin
    { create new queue element and initialize its fields }
    new(node);
    with node^ do
    begin
        data := item;
        next := nil
    end;
```

```
                    { add new node to rear of queue }
                    with head^ do
                    begin
                        if front = nil then              { queue is empty }
                        begin
                            front := node;               { front and rear will point }
                            rear := node                 { to the only element in the queue }
                        end
                        else
                        begin
                            rear^.next := node;          { add new node to rear of queue }
                            rear := node                 { establish a new rear of queue }
                        end
                    end
                end; { of procedure enqueue }


            procedure dequeue(var item : char; var head : headpointer;
                    var successful : boolean);
            var
                node      : queuepointer;
            begin
                with head^ do
                begin
                    if front <> nil then                 { nonempty queue }
                    begin
                        item := front^.data;             { return item at head of queue }
                        node := front;                   { save pointer to head of queue }
                        front := front^.next;            { update front pointer }
                        dispose(node);                   { return node to available space }
                        successful := true               { dequeue operation successful }
                    end
                    else successful := false             { indicate queue underflow }
                end
            end; { of procedure dequeue }
```

8. If the elements being enqueued and dequeued were records, then it would proba-
    bly be better to return a pointer to the element.

10.
```
    procedure readdata(var ptr : nodepointer);
    begin
        { establish a new node to put values read in }
        new(ptr);
        { read in data }
        with ptr^ do
        begin
            { input data }
            read(index1,index2,value)
        end
    end; { of procedure readdata }
```

Chapter 5

1. **procedure** Reverse Print (p : ptr);
   begin
       if p <> **nil then**
       begin
           Reverse Print (p ↑ .next);
           writeln (p ↑ .data)
       end
   end { of procedure Reverse Print }

4. See Chapter 2, No. 9.

Chapter 6

1. Terminals: H,I,C,L
   Nonterminals: A,B,D,K

4. Do any of the three traversal methods and when you ''visit the root'' check whether you have empty left and right subtrees; we will use a postorder traversal.

   procedure countleafnodes(root : nodepointer; **var** count : integer);
   begin
       if root <> **nil then**
       begin
           { visit the left subtree }
           postorder(root^.leftsubtree);

           { visit the right subtree }
           postorder(root^.rightsubtree);

           { visit the root - count the number of leaf nodes }
           if (root^.leftsubtree = **nil**) **and**
            (root^.rightsubtree = **nil**) **then**
             count := count + 1
       end
   end; { of **procedure** countleafnodes }

   begin
       count := 0;
       countleafnodes(rootoftree,count)
   end

5. **function** equal(rootoftree1 : nodepointer; rootoftree2 : nodepointer)
        : boolean;
    begin
        if (rootoftree1 = **nil**) **and** (rootoftree2 = **nil**) **then** equal := true
        else
        if rootoftree1^.data = rootoftree2^.data **then**
        begin
            if equal(rootoftree1^.leftsubtree,rootoftree2^.rightsubtree)
            then equal := equal(rootoftree1^.rightsubtree,rootoftree2^.rightsubtree)
            else equal := false
        end
        else equal := false
    end { of **function** equal }

6. **function** inordersuccessor(node : nodepointer) : nodepointer;
    var
        tempnode   : nodepointer;
    begin
        tempnode := node^.rightsubtree;
        if node^.rightthread **then**
            while tempnode^.leftthread **do**
                tempnode := tempnode^.leftsubtree;
        inordersuccessor := tempnode
    end { of **function** inordersuccessor }

7. **procedure** traversethreadedtree(treenode : nodepointer);
    var
        headoftree   : nodepointer;
    begin
        headoftree := treenode;
        repeat
            treenode := inordersuccessor(treenode);
            if treenode <> headoftree **then** visit(treenode)
        until treenode = headoftree
    end { of **procedure** traversethreadedtree }

Chapter 8

3. reset(f);
    count := 0;
    while not eof(f) **do**
    begin
        get(f);
        count := count + 1
    end

4. f : | 10 |

Chapter 9

6. When giving a problem to a person to solve, you can assume a measure of "common sense." Therefore, you can frequently omit the specifications of how to handle exceptional or unusual conditions. For example, when giving someone instructions on how to put together a bicycle, you do not specify what to do if the individual does not own a wrench. You assume sufficient intelligence that they will go out and buy one! In a specification document for a computer solution you cannot assume this level of common sense. The detail of handling all cases, no matter how unusual, exceptional, or silly, must be included in the specification document.

7. Because you are using the technique of divide and conquer, you are breaking up a large task into a series of simpler subtasks. In addition, you are specifying the relationship between these subtasks.

10. The error is in step 5. It should read

    5   go to step 10

    The logic is very disconnected and hard to follow. A much better solution would be

    If x > y **then**
        If x > z **then**
            set biggest to x
        else
            set biggest to z
    else
        if y > z **then**
            set biggest to y
        else
            set biggest to z

Chapter 10

3. a. Any of the values a, b, and c are not numeric.
    b. The values of a and b are both 0. This is an illegal equation.
    c. The value of $a = 0$. This is a legal linear equation, but it is not a valid quadratic equation. We cannot use the quadratic equation because of division by 0.
    d. $\sqrt{b^2 - 4ac} < 0$. This is a quadratic equation, but the roots are complex and cannot be solved using only real arithmetic.
    e. The user provides only one or two pieces of data, rather than the required three.

5. a. You are to read in, from the terminal, a single integer value $N \geq 1$ but $\leq$ 5000. If N is nonnumeric, $N < 1$, or $N > 5000$, then print the following error message:

List length was illegal. It must be an integer value greater than 0 and less than or equal to 5000. Please reenter

and let the user reenter the value. When you have a legal value for N, proceed to read in exactly N integers from the terminal. There will be one value per line and all values will be in the range $[-\text{maxint} .. +\text{maxint}]$. When you have read all the values, sort them into descending order, and then produce the following output:

Values Sorted into Descending Order:

XX

XX

.

.

.

XX

Total Number of Values = XX

After you have produced this output, terminate the program.

7. a. Much too vague. Personal computers vary greatly in size and capability.
    b. Still too vague. The IBM-PC can have anywhere from 128K to 640K of memory and may or may not have a hard disk.
    c. The word "most" is too vague. Does it mean 80%, 95%, 99%?
    d. Fine. No ambiguity in this statement.
    e. Fine.
    f. Fine.
    g. Fine.
    h. What is the "longest" name? We should be told exactly how many characters are in this largest name.
    i. Fine.
    j. This would be difficult for answers like 2, which will never have three significant digits. Must allow for this possibility.
    k. What does "available" mean. This is a vague term. What if the program is OK, but the hardware is down?

8. The table does not specify what to do if both the condition $x > 0$ is false and the condition $y > 0$ is false. As it stands, the table is incomplete. We must add a column (or columns) to describe this input condition.

13. Final state: S_3
    Actions: A_1, A_3, A_2, A_1, A_2, A_1, A_2, A_3

14.

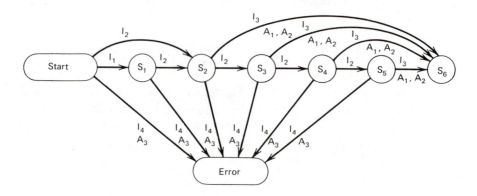

Input	Actions
I_1 : $+$, $-$	A_1 : Print "Valid number"
I_2 : digits '0', . . . , '9'	A_2 : Convert to a number
I_3 : blank, CR	A_3 : Print "Invalid number"
I_4 : Anything else	

Chapter 11

·3.

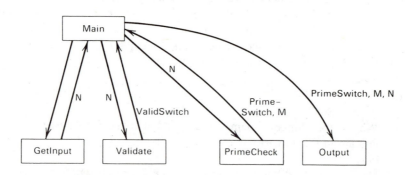

Module Specifications

procedure GetInput (**var** N : integer);
  { It is the job of GetInput to prompt the user for input and to input a
  single integer value. The value entered is returned to the calling
  program. }

procedure Validate (N : integer; **var** ValidSwitch : boolean);
  { Procedure validate is given an integer value, N, and validates that is in
  the range $1 < N \leq$ maxint. If it is ValidSwitch is set to true, otherwise it is
  set to false. }

procedure PrimeCheck (N : integer; **var** PrimeSwitch : boolean;
                     var M : integer);
   { Procedure PrimeCheck is given a value N, N > 1, and it determines if N
   is or is not a prime number. If it is prime, PrimeSwitch is set to true, and
   M is undefined. If it is not prime, PrimeSwitch is set to false and M is set
   to the value of any factor of N, other than 1 or itself. }

procedure Output (PrimeSwitch : boolean; N,M : integer);
   { Output is given a boolean switch. If it is true, it prints out the phrase
      "N" is prime.
   If it is false it prints out the phrase
      "N" is not prime, "M" is a factor.
   where "N" and "M" are replaced by the value of the parameters N
   and M, respectively. }

5. The use of the words "first" and "and then calls" connotes the idea of a temporal ordering of calls. However, there is no ordering information contained in a structure chart. It is possible that M_3 will be called before M_2. It is also possible that M_2 or M_3 or both will never be invoked.

6. a. In a top-down implementation, we would likely specify the module in the following order:

$$\text{Main, } M_1, M_2, M_3, M_4, M_5, M_6, M_7, M_8, M_9, M_{10}$$

   b. In a mixed implementation we would start implementing both the highest and lowest level routines first. The highest level routines could be implemented in either a breadth-first or depth-first order.

   Breadth-first: Main, $M_1, M_2, M_3, M_4, M_5, M_6, M_7, M_8$
   Depth-first: Main, $M_1, M_4, M_5, M_2, M_6, M_3, M_7, M_8$

   at the same time we would likely start the implement of the two lower-level utility routines M_9 and M_{10}.

   c. The "spheres of influence," or set of related routines, might be

   (M_1, M_4, M_5)
   (M_2, M_6)
   (M_3, M_7, M_8)
   (M_9, M_{10}) {The two utilities used by many other modules}

8. **procedure** LookUp (PartNum : PNtype; InvFile : IFileType;
                     var success : boolean; **var** InvRecord : IRType);
   { Procedure LookUp is given a unique PartNum, which is the key field
   for locating records in the inventory file called InvFile. It is the job
   of LookUp to search the entire inventory file to locate the unique
   inventory record with the given part number. If the record is found in
   the file, then the entire record is returned in the parameter called
   InvRecord, success is set to true, and the file pointer is positioned at the

given record. If the desired record is not found, then success is set to false, the value of InvRecord is undefined, and the position of the file pointer is unspecified. In addition, if the record is not found, LookUp will activate a module called ErrorHandler, and pass it the value of PartNum. }

11. A **for** loop cannot be named. (A label does not name the loop but just identifies a single statement.) It cannot be compiled separate from the rest of the program and stored in a library. Declarations cannot be made within a **for** loop.

13. The description contains a statement about what algorithm is to be used. In most cases, this is not part of the high-level design of a module. We may, at some future time wish to keep the specifications of the module the same but change the algorithm we will use. We should be able to do this without changing the design document.

Chapter 12

3. See page 605 for solution.

5. a. No. The computation of hours worked is an operation dealing with time/date calculations. The computation of pay rates is an operation dealing with payment computations, overtime rules, and company policies. They are not at all related and should be placed in separate modules.

   b. Possibly not. Although they are both time/date calculations, it is quite possible that we may want to carry out one operation but not the other. For example, to see if one person starts work after another, we may want to convert their two starting times to decimal but then only compare the two values, not actually determine the exact interval between them. By placing these two operations in separate modules, such as the following:

   ConvertToDecimal (a : clocktime; **var** b : decimaltime);
   DetermineInterval (a,b : decimaltime; **var** interval : decimaltime);

   we can use one feature without having to use the other.

6. The procedure is quite simple, but it has been made more confusing by the inclusion of details of random number generation. It would have been far superior to put those details into two lower-level routines called InitRandom and random(low, high). Then the program would be

```
InitRandom;
for i := 1 to 52 do
    begin
    R := random (1, 52);
    switch (D, R, i)     { interchange D[R], D[i] }
    end
```

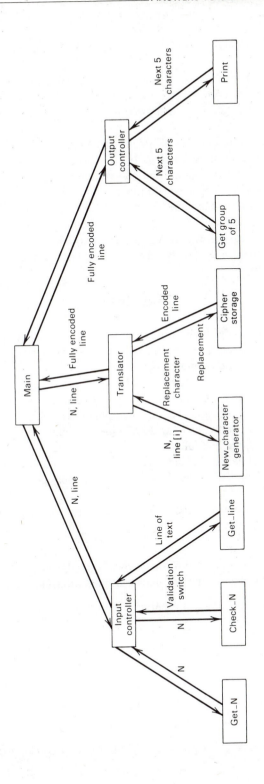

7. a.   It refers to listsize as a global variable. It should be passed as a call-by-value parameter.

    b.   It assumes that the calling program will initialize count to 0.

    c.   It intermixes computation and output in a single procedure. It would be better to separate them and place them in different modules.

9. Not true. The procedure is still taking advantage of its special knowledge that the valid range of numbers is 0 to 10. If, at some point in the future, we made a change to the specifications and allowed numbers in the range 0 . . 20, our program would no longer work properly. It would be far better to make no a priori assumptions about the upper bound of legal values when coding this program. (Or, alternatively, have the upper bound passed in as a parameter UB, and then temporarily set the -1s to the value $UB + 1$.) We want to develop programs that do *not* need to have massive change every time specifications change slightly.

Chapter 13

1. a.   The name of the program (ex) is not very descriptive at all. A name like EToThePowerX or something similar would be much more helpful in determining what the program does.

    b.   There are no comments at all in the program. It would be greatly helped by an introductory comment (a prologue) explaining who wrote the program, what its purpose is, and what approximation technique is used. Also, comments on the individual **var** declarations explaining the role of each variable would be quite helpful.

    c.   There is a total lack of indentation. Everything is entered flush with the left-hand margin. This hides the scope of the various control constructs, such as loops.

    d.   The variable names chosen are very poor and totally unhelpful. Better ones might be

        sum instead of s
        denominator instead of d (or maybe factorial)
        numerator instead of n (or maybe EtothePowerN)

    e.   The statement $[n/d > (-0.01)]$ and $[n/d < (0.01)]$ would be clearer if it were written as

$$abs \ (n/d) < 0.01$$

    f.   The constant 0.01, which appears to be used as a limit of accuracy, should be given a descriptive name using a **const** declaration

        const
            desiredAccuracy = 0.01; { level of accuracy desired }

The same is true for the maximum number of terms summed before we stop (10 in this example).

MaximumTermCount = 10;

program eToThePowerX (input, output);
{
    a program to compute an approximation to e^x using Cramer's Rule. It will either produce an answer accurate to ±0.01 or it will stop after 10 terms of the series
    }

const
    AccuracyDesired   = 0.01;   { This level of accuracy will terminate the program }
    MaximumTermCount = 10;   { or summing this many terms will stop the program }

var
    factorial   : real;   { will hold the denominator 2!, 3!, 4!, ... }
    i   : integer;   { loop index }
    numerator   : real;   { will hold the numerator x^2, x^3, ... }
    sum   : real;   { will accumulate the sum of the terms }
    x   : real;   { the point at which we want to evaluate e^x }

begin
    readln (x);

    { initialization section }
    sum := 0;
    numerator := 1;
    factorial := 1;
    i := 0;

    { evaluate Cramers Rule until accuracy reached or we have summed the maximum number of terms }
    repeat
        sum := sum + (numerator/factorial);
        numerator := numerator * x;
        i := i + 1;
        factorial := factorial * i
    until (abs (numerator/factorial) < AccuracyDesired) **or** (i > MaximumTermCount);
    writeln ('Approximation of E to the power', x, ' is ', sum)
end.

2. a. The introductory prologue comment is quite good, explaining in fairly clear style what the procedure does and what each of the parameters represents.

    b. The comments on the individual variables in the **var** declaration are quite helpful, especially because some of the names in the program (e.g., fq, tq . . .) are not especially descriptive.

c. The comments on the **end** lines identifying their matching **begin** can be very helpful. Even though, in this case, the fragment is small and the begin and end can be easily located, these types of comments can be among the most useful, especially during program maintenance.

d. The comments that simply ''parrot back'' the obvious intent of a Pascal statement are quite useless. For example,

```
{ set switch to false }
fail := false

{ set switch to true }
fail := true
```

They serve no useful purpose and clutter up the listing. When a program becomes 50, 75, to 90 percent comments, it can be more difficult to work with because you have to search through these comments to find the desired code.

e. The second comment in the body of the program is *wrong*. It does not match the operation it is describing. As written the sort routine must sort into descending order.

11.
```
x := 0;
overflow := false;

repeat
    value := f(x); { assume function f is defined }
    if value > limit then
        overflow := true
    else
        begin
        table[x] := value;
        x := x + 1
        end
until (x > 500) or overflow;

if overflow then
    writeln ('Value of function overflowed at point', x)
```

Chapter 14

1. a. It is possible that *every* examination score will be outside the legal range low . . high. This could happen, for example, if the user misunderstood the input format or what values were to be entered. If this were the case, then the assignment statement on line 14 of the program

```
average := sum / (scorecount − bad)
```

would terminate abnormally with a "division-by-zero" error. To prevent this from happening, you could check this condition prior to execution of the statement:

```
if scorecount = bad then
    writeln ('**Warning, no legal scores')
else
    average := sum / (scorecount – bad)
```

b.   It is possible that salaryclass will not be one of the three values specified by the case label list. We should check for this before we execute the case statement:

```
if salaryclass in [salaried, hourly, piecework] then
    case salaryclass of
        .
        .
        .
    end { of case }
else
    writeln ('**Warning, illegal value for salary class')
```

This problem could also be handled by a case statement that allowed for a "default" match. (Typically, this is called an *otherwise clause*.) Many Pascal compilers support this facility, but since it is not standard, we have chosen not to use it.

e.   If *p* is the *last* item in the user-defined type then succ(*p*) is not defined. You should check this condition before invoking the succ function. For example,

```
type colors = (red, . . . , blue);
    .
    .
    .
if not (p = blue) then p := succ (p);
```

3.   **procedure** validate (M : arraytype; n : integer; **var** errorflag : errortype);
```
{
    entry conditions : M, a real n × n matrix
                       n, the dimensions of the matrix, n ≥ 1
    exit conditions : errorflag specifies the following error conditions
            negative, one of the elements in M is negative
            diagonal, $M_{ii}$ = 0 for all i
            triangular, all elements above the diagonal are zero.
}
```

```
var
    i, j           : integer;      { for loop indices }
    diag, tri      : boolean;      { used to check for error conditions }
begin
    diag := true; tri := true;
    errorflag := [ ]; { initially assume no errors }
    for i := 1 to n do
        for j := 1 to n do
            begin
            if M[i,j] < 0 then errorflag := errorflag + [negative];
            if i = j then
                if M[i,j] <> 0 then diag := false
            else
                if j > i then
                    if M[i,j] <> 0 then tri := false;
            end; { for loops }
    if diag then errorflag := errorflag + [diagonal];
    if tri then errorflag := errorflag + [triangular];
end; { procedure validate }
```

6. | 5 | 30 | 15 |
    |----|----|----|
    | 15 | 30 | 5 |
    | 5 | 10 | 30 |

9.  ```
    function power (a, b : real) : real;
    {
        entry conditions : a, b are real values
        exit condition : power will have the value a^b
        special conditions : 0^x = 0 for any value of x
                             x^0 = 1 for any non-zero x
    }
    begin
        if a = 0.0 then power := 0.0
        else
            if b = 0.0 then power := 1.0
            else
                if b < 0.0 then power := 1.0/exp (b * ln (abs(a)))
                            else power := exp (b * ln (a))
    end; { function power }
    ```

10. The one area where the program shows a lack of generality is that the age breakdowns 0, 17, 29, 39, 49 are fixed and are part of the code. A more general program would allow the user to specify two additional pieces of data:

    1. The number of age classifications that are desired.
    2. The low and high limits of each age classification.

    This would make it usable for a much wider segment of problems.
    ```

11. As it now stands, the procedure would "blow up" in the function *f,* which was passed to it as a parameter. This would happen in the third line of the for loop. That function does not make allowances for undefined values, either by use of a special error flag or a special function return value such as maxint. To solve this problem we have to ensure that we will always return from the function *f* with a notification of the discontinuity of the function. For example,

.

.

.

```
x := x + delta;
value := f(x);
if value <> maxint then
      sum := sum + value
else
      errorprocedure;
```

Chapter 15

2. **Terminal Queue** (TQ)
   a. *Description*   A linear structure containing student records. All entries are made at one end while all removals are made at the other end. It represents a waiting line for students waiting to use a terminal.
   b. *Information fields*   Each entry in the terminal queue is a student record containing the time this student entered the system and the time he or she entered the terminal queue.
   c. *Operations*

   ```
   enqueue (S, TQ); Place student S at the end of the TQ
   dequeue (S, TQ); Remove first student from the TQ and place in S
   empty (TQ); True if TQ empty, false otherwise
   ```

   d. Where referenced (R) or changed (C):

Initialize (C)	Empty (R)
Enqueue (C)	Arrival Event (R)
Dequeue (C)	Consult Event (R)
Everybodyout (C)	Terminal Event (R)

4. The greatest disadvantage would be that we must pick a constant value for maxsize, and this bounds the size of the calendar. With a linked list, there is no fixed upper bound (except for the amount of physical or virtual memory).

Chapter 16

1. a. Incorrect. The two boolean clauses must be enclosed in parentheses.
    b. Correct.
    c. Correct.
    d. Incorrect. A read statement must contain a read list.
    e. Correct. The then clause contains only the null statement.

2. a. **if** (i >= 2) **and** (j <= 9) **then**
            x[i,j] := x[i−1, j+1] + 1;
    b. readln (num);
        if (num >= 1) **and** (num <= 10) **then**
            y := num;
    c. **if** y **in** [1 .. 9] **then**
                case y **of** . . .
    d. **if** (b + 1.5) >= 0 **then**
                a := sqrt (b + 1.5);
    e. **if** periods <> 0 **then**
            principle := (1 + i*N)/periods;

6. *Regular cases*
    1. A list of length n > 1, which is out of order.
    2. A list of length n > 1, which is already in order (no interchanges needed).

    Extremal cases
    3. A list of length n = 1
    4. A list of length n = 0

    Illegal cases
    5. Firstelement < lowerbound
    6. Lastelement > upperbound
    7. Firstelement > lastelement
    8. Lowerlimit > upperlimit

9. No, it is incorrect for two reasons: (1) We should not go through all *n* values, because we will switch the values twice, restoring them to their original condition. (2) The interchange is not being done correctly. For example, if we started with

$$\begin{bmatrix} 1 & 2 \\ 3 & 4 \end{bmatrix}$$

    We would end up with

$$\begin{bmatrix} 1 & 2 \\ 2 & 4 \end{bmatrix}$$

The correct code would be

```
for i := 1 to n do
    for j := 1 to i do
        begin
            Temp := a[i,j];
            a[i,j] := a[j,i];
            a[j,i] := Temp
        end
```

10.   It would take at least eight distinct cases. The eight flow paths are

$$
\begin{array}{lll}
S_1 & S_5 & \\
S_1 & S_5 & S_6 \\
S_2 & S_5 & \\
S_2 & S_5 & S_6 \\
S_4 & S_5 & \\
S_4 & S_5 & S_6 \\
S_3 & S_4 & S_5 \\
S_3 & S_4 & S_5 & S_6
\end{array}
$$

12.   You should carefully check the following cases during extremal and boundary checking:
a. $i = 1$ and $i = 100$. These are the limits of the legal values of i.
b. $i = 50$. The boundary of the cutoff in the second if. ($i = 49, i = 51$ would also be good test selections).
c. $i = 90$. The upper limit on the repeat loop ($i = 89, 91$ would also be good choices).

Chapter 17

4. $O(N)$

5.   It is an $O(m)$ operation to check the pattern against the text one time. There are $(n - m + 1)$ places where the match could possibly take place. Therefore the overall operation is

$$O(m * [n - m + 1]) = O(mn - m^2 + m)$$

$$
\begin{array}{ll}
\text{If } m = 1 & O(n) \\
\text{If } m = n & O(n)
\end{array}
$$

10. $O(\log \log N)$ is a lower order than $O(\log N)$ but a higher order than $O(1)$.

13. Instead of storing in days [*i*] the number of days in month *i*, store the *sum* of days in all months 1, . . . , *i* − 1. That is,

```
days [1] := 0;
days [2] := 31;    { The 31 days in January }
days [3] := 59;    { plus 28 days in February }
days [4] := 90;    { plus 31 days in March }
```

Now to find the Julian date for calendar date *i*/*j*, we just compute (days [*i*] + *j*). The for loop is no longer necessary (although we must still check for leap year).

14. The sequential search would not work. A simple, "ball-park" computation shows that the average response time would be about

$$\frac{1300 * 0.038}{2} \approx 25 \text{ seconds}$$

With an 18-millisecond response time, we still cannot meet specifications

$$\frac{1300 * 0.018}{2} \approx 12 \text{ seconds}$$

But if there were only 85 flight records, it would not be a problem at all:

$$\frac{85 \times 0.038}{2} \approx 1\frac{1}{2} \text{ seconds}$$

INDEX